# SUPPLY CHAIN MANAGEMENT

## SECOND EDITION

## A GLOBAL PERSPECTIVE

**Nada R. Sanders, Ph.D.**
*D'Amore-McKim School of Business*
*Northeastern University*

# WILEY

| | |
|---|---|
| EDITORIAL DIRECTOR | Veronica Visentin |
| EXECUTIVE EDITOR | Darren Lalonde |
| SPONSORING EDITOR | Jennifer Manias |
| EDITORIAL MANAGER | Gladys Soto |
| CONTENT MANAGEMENT DIRECTOR | Lisa Wojcik |
| CONTENT MANAGER | Nichole Urban |
| SENIOR CONTENT SPECIALIST | Nicole Repasky |
| PRODUCTION EDITOR | Linda Christina E |
| COVER PHOTO CREDIT | © joyfull/Shutterstock |

This book was set in 10/12 TimesLTStd by SPi Global and printed and bound by Lightning Source, Inc.

Founded in 1807, John Wiley & Sons, Inc. has been a valued source of knowledge and understanding for more than 200 years, helping people around the world meet their needs and fulfill their aspirations. Our company is built on a foundation of principles that include responsibility to the communities we serve and where we live and work. In 2008, we launched a Corporate Citizenship Initiative, a global effort to address the environmental, social, economic, and ethical challenges we face in our business. Among the issues we are addressing are carbon impact, paper specifications and procurement, ethical conduct within our business and among our vendors, and community and charitable support. For more information, please visit our website: www.wiley.com/go/citizenship.

Copyright © 2018, 2012 John Wiley & Sons, Inc. All rights reserved. No part of this publication may be reproduced, stored in a retrieval system, or transmitted in any form or by any means, electronic, mechanical, photocopying, recording, scanning or otherwise, except as permitted under Sections 107 or 108 of the 1976 United States Copyright Act, without either the prior written permission of the Publisher, or authorization through payment of the appropriate per-copy fee to the Copyright Clearance Center, Inc., 222 Rosewood Drive, Danvers, MA 01923 (Web site: www.copyright.com). Requests to the Publisher for permission should be addressed to the Permissions Department, John Wiley & Sons, Inc., 111 River Street, Hoboken, NJ 07030-5774, (201) 748-6011, fax (201) 748-6008, or online at: www.wiley.com/go/permissions.

Evaluation copies are provided to qualified academics and professionals for review purposes only, for use in their courses during the next academic year. These copies are licensed and may not be sold or transferred to a third party. Upon completion of the review period, please return the evaluation copy to Wiley. Return instructions and a free of charge return shipping label are available at: www.wiley.com/go/returnlabel. If you have chosen to adopt this textbook for use in your course, please accept this book as your complimentary desk copy. Outside of the United States, please contact your local sales representative.

ISBN: 9781119392194 (PBK)
ISBN: 9781119392248 (EVALC)

*Library of Congress Cataloging in Publication Data:*
Names: Sanders, Nada R., author.
Title: Supply chainmanagement : a global perspective / by Nada R. Sanders,
   Ph.D., D'Amore-McKim School of Business, Northeastern University.
Description: Second Edition. | Hoboken : Wiley, [2017] | Revised edition of
   the author's Supply chain management, c2012. | Includes bibliographical
   references and index. |
Identifiers: LCCN 2017028808 (print) | LCCN 2017030985 (ebook) | ISBN
   9781119392323 (epub) | ISBN 9781119392309 (pdf) | ISBN 9781119392194
   (pbk.) | ISBN 9781119392248 (EVALC)
Subjects: LCSH: Business logistics.
Classification: LCC HD38.5 (ebook) | LCC HD38.5 .S26 2017 (print) | DDC
   658.7—dc23
LC record available at https://lccn.loc.gov/2017028808

The inside back cover will contain printing identification and country of origin if omitted from this page. In addition, if the ISBN on the back cover differs from the ISBN on this page, the one on the back cover is correct.

# Contents

Preface     IX

## 1 Introduction to Supply Chain Management     1

What Is Supply Chain Management (SCM)?,     3
    *Supply Chain Leader's Box: Amazon.com*,     9
The Boundary-Spanning Nature of SCM,     9
The Rise of SCM,     12
    *Supply Chain Leader's Box: Dell Computer Corporation*,     13
Characteristics of a Competitive Supply Chain,     14
    *Global Insights Box: Zara*,     15
Trends in SCM,     16
    *Supply Chain Leader's Box: Wal-Mart*,     16
    *Big Data Analytics Box: Tesco*,     18
    *Managerial Insights Box—Outsourcing Innovation: Goldcorp Inc.*,     22
Careers in SCM and Professional Organizations,     23
Chapter Highlights,     23
Key Terms,     24
Discussion Questions,     24
    *Case Study: McNulty's Muscular Materials (MMM)*,     24
    *Case Questions*,     24
References,     25

## 2 Supply Chain Strategy     26

What Is Supply Chain Strategy?,     28
Achieving a Competitive Advantage,     29
    *Supply Chain Leader's Box: Wal-Mart*,     30
    *Global Insights Box: Toyota Motor Corporation*,     32
Building Blocks of Supply Chain Strategy,     32
    *Managerial Insights Box—Outsourcing Alliances: Li & Fung Ltd.*,     38
Supply Chain Strategic Design,     39
    *Supply Chain Leader's Box: Barlean's Organic Oils*,     42
Strategic Considerations,     43
    *Big Data Analytics Box: Amazon*,     44
Productivity as a Measure of Competitiveness,     44
Chapter Highlights,     46
Key Terms,     47
Discussion Questions,     47

Problems, 47
   *Case Study: Surplus Styles*, 47
   *Case Questions*, 48
References, 48

## 3   NETWORK AND SYSTEM DESIGN   49

The Supply Chain System, 51
   *Supply Chain Leader's Box—Moving to Process Thinking: LG Electronics*, 54
Understanding Processes: Theory of Constraints (TOC), 54
Integration of Supply Chain Processes, 58
Designing Supply Chain Networks, 60
   *Managerial Insights Box: Coca-Cola*, 61
   *Big Data Analytics Box: Segmentation in Retail*, 64
Enterprise Resource Planning (ERP), 64
Chapter Highlights, 67
Key Terms, 67
Discussion Questions, 67
Problems, 67
   *Case Study: Boca Electronics, LLC*, 68
   *Case Questions*, 68
References, 69

## 4   MARKETING   70

What Is Marketing?, 72
   *Supply Chain Leader's Box: Gap Inc.*, 73
   *Supply Chain Leader's Box—Accommodating Changing Customer Preferences: PepsiCo*, 75
Customer-Driven Supply Chains, 76
   *Managerial Insight's Box—Understanding the Customer: Target*, 78
Delivering Value to Customers, 80
   *Global Insights Box—Global Customer Service: Coca-Cola Japan*, 84
Channels of Distribution, 85
   *Managerial Insights Box—Changing the Distribution Channel: Steinway Pianos*, 87
   *Big Data Analytics Box: Oasis*, 90
Chapter Highlights, 90
Key Terms, 91
Discussion Questions, 91
   *Case Study: Gizmo*, 91
   *Case Questions*, 91
References, 92

## 5   OPERATIONS MANAGEMENT   93

What Is Operations Management (OM)?, 95
   *Supply Chain Leader's Box: Wal-Mart*, 98

Product Design, 99
   *Big Data Analytics Box: Honda,* 100
   *Global Insights Box: Ryanair,* 102
Process Design, 105
   *Managerial Insights Box—A New Manufacturing Process: Rapid Manufacturing,* 108
Facility Layout, 108
   *Managerial Insights Box: Mazzi's versus Totino's Pizza,* 110
Line Balancing in Product Layouts, 111
Process Automation, 114
   *Global Insights Box: KUKA Robotics Corp.,* 115
Chapter Highlights, 116
Key Terms, 116
Discussion Questions, 116
Problems, 116
References, 117

# 6 Sourcing 118

What Is Sourcing?, 120
   *Supply Chain Leader's Box—Co-Creation: The Auto Industry,* 123
The Sourcing Function, 123
Sourcing and SCM, 125
   *Global Insights Box - Outsourcing Analytics: Accenture,* 126
   *Supply Chain Leader's Box—Risk Management: IBM,* 127
   *Managerial Insights Box—Outsourcing Alliances: Roots,* 130
   *Big Data Analytics Box: FedEx,* 132
Measuring Sourcing Performance, 132
Chapter Highlights, 133
Key Terms, 134
Discussion Questions, 134
Problems, 134
Class Exercise: Toyota, 135
   *Case Study: Snedeker Global Cruises,* 135
   *Case Questions,* 136
References, 136

# 7 Logistics 137

What Is Logistics?, 139
   *Supply Chain Leader's Box: United Parcel Service (UPS),* 140
Logistics Tasks, 145
   *Big Data Analytics Box—Driverless Cars: Uber,* 145
Transportation, 147
   *Supply Chain Leader's Box: Sysco,* 148
   *Global Insights Box—Rail Service Between China and Europe: "Northeast Passage",* 150

Warehousing, 150
Third-Party Logistics (3PL) Providers, 153
Chapter Highlights, 153
Key Terms, 154
Discussion Questions, 154
Problems, 154
    Case Study: Strategic Solutions Inc., 154
    Case Questions, 156
References, 156

## 8  Forecasting and Demand Planning   157

What Is Forecasting?, 159
    Managerial Insights Box: Forecasting beyond Widgets, 160
    Global Insights Box—Matching Supply and Demand: World Health Organization (WHO), 162
The Forecasting Process, 163
    Managerial Insights Box: Predictive Analytics, 165
Types of Forecasting Methods, 166
    Big Data Analytics Box—Improving Weather Forecasting: NOAA, 168
Time Series Forecasting Models, 169
Causal Models, 175
Measuring Forecast Accuracy, 178
Collaborative Forecasting and Demand Planning, 180
    Supply Chain Leader's Box—Using Collaborative Technology: Li & Fung, 181
Chapter Highlights, 183
Key Terms, 183
Discussion Questions, 183
Problems, 184
    Case Study: Speedy Automotive, 185
    Case Questions, 187
References, 187

## 9  Inventory Management   188

Basics of Inventory Management, 190
    Managerial Insights Box—Service Inventory: Zoots, 191
    Supply Chain Leader's Box: John Deere & Company, 195
Inventory Systems, 195
Fixed-Order Quantity Systems, 198
    Big Data Analytics Box—Analytics Driven Inventory: Dell, 205
Fixed-Time Period Systems, 205
Independent versus Dependent Demand, 207
    Global Insights Box: Intel Corporation, 208
Managing Supply Chain Inventory, 208

Chapter Highlights, 212
Key Terms, 212
Discussion Questions, 212
Problems, 213
References, 213

## 10   LEAN SYSTEMS AND SIX-SIGMA QUALITY    214

What Is Lean?, 216
   *Big Data Analytics Box: General Electric*, 218
   *Supply Chain Leader's Box: U.S. Army*, 219
Lean Production, 220
   *Global Insights Box: UPS*, 221
Respect for People, 223
Total Quality Management (TQM), 224
   *Managerial Insights Box: Lean Tools in the Popular Press*, 227
Statistical Quality Control (SQC), 228
   *Supply Chain Leader's Box: Intel Corporation*, 229
Six Sigma Quality, 236
The Lean Six Sigma Supply Chain, 237
Chapter Highlights, 240
Key Terms, 240
Discussion Questions, 240
Problems, 241
   *Case Study: Buckeye Technologies*, 242
   *Case Questions*, 242
References, 243

## 11   SUPPLY CHAIN RELATIONSHIP MANAGEMENT    244

Supply Chain Relationships, 246
   *Big Data Analytics Box—The Network Effect: Amazon*, 249
   *Supply Chain Leaders' Box—Open Innovation: Proctor & Gamble*, 251
The Role of Trust, 252
   *Global Insights Box—Growth Through Partnership: Coca-Cola in Africa*, 256
Managing Conflict and Dispute Resolution, 256
   *Managerial Insights Box: Commodity Swapping*, 260
Negotiation Concepts, Styles, and Tactics, 260
Relationship Management in Practice, 265
Chapter Highlights, 267
Key Terms, 267
Discussion Questions, 267
   *Case Study: Lucid v. Black Box*, 268
   *Case Questions*, 268
References, 268

## 12 Global Supply Chain Management  270

Global Supply Chain Management,  272
  Supply Chain Leader's Box—Challenges of Global Culture: Wal-Mart,  273
Global Market Challenges,  276
  Managerial Insights Box: Coca-Cola's China Branding Challenge,  278
Global Infrastructure Design,  280
  Big Data Analytics Box—Supplier Risk: Cisco,  281
Cost Considerations,  282
  Managerial Insights Box—Beyond Cost: BMW,  283
Political and Economic Factors,  284
Chapter Highlights,  286
Key Terms,  286
Discussion Questions,  287
  Case Study: Wú's Brew Works,  287
  Case Questions,  291
References,  292

## 13 Sustainable Supply Chain Management  293

What Is Sustainability?,  295
  Global Insights Box: The Great Pacific Garbage Patch,  296
  Supply Chain Leaders Box: Fibria Celulose,  298
Evaluating Sustainability in SCM,  302
  Big Data Analytics Box: Coca-Cola,  310
Sustainability in Practice,  312
  Managerial Insights Box: Carbon Fiber Auto Parts,  313
Chapter Highlights,  316
Key Terms,  316
Discussion Questions,  317
  Case Study: Haitian Oil,  317
  Case Questions,  318
References,  318

**Appendix**  319

**Glossary**  321

**Index**  329

# PREFACE

Supply chain management (SCM) is the fastest-growing area of business today and is at the core of success of most leading companies. Knowledge of SCM is necessary to participate in this growing and exciting career field. However, SCM is challenging in scope and complexity. Even today there is a misunderstanding of SCM. Most people assume that SCM is part of logistics and distribution, or purchasing, or perhaps marketing. They do not understand the intricacies and broad reach of this rapidly evolving area of business. This book is designed to provide students with a comprehensive understanding of SCM, key issues involved, and the very latest business thinking. This book is different from other SCM textbooks. It is specifically written as a comprehensive SCM text providing an integrated global and technology focused perspective.

Recent trends have made the study of SCM especially challenging. Today's business environment has forced companies to compete in very different ways than just a few years ago. The following is true of today's organizations:

- In addition to competing on traditional dimensions such as quality, time, cost, and customization, companies must be rapid innovators. They must stay abreast of quickly changing customer demands and have responsive supply chains in place.

- Technological advancements—including big data analytics, autonomous vehicles, 3-D printing, Internet of Things (IoT), and next generation RFID—have transformed supply chains. The "intelligent supply chain" that is technologically driven is becoming the norm for companies.

- Today's organizations operate in a global environment and are affected by global trade. Many companies serve multiple global markets, with products sourced and produced across many continents. They must plan, design, and manage a complex supply chain network.

- Focus on "green" and sustainability has become prominent. Issues of environmental and social responsibility are becoming critical elements of SCM, spanning concerns such as sourcing, packaging, manufacturing, and distribution.

- Unprecedented threats to security are forcing companies to invest in systems to protect products and information throughout every step of the supply chain. Addressing issues of security in supply chain design is a critical aspect of SCM.

- A global recession has created tremendous financial pressures on companies and their supply chains. Companies are being forced to remain competitive and innovative while cutting, or maintaining, costs.

This text addresses SCM within this realistic global and technologically driven business environment, in a complete and comprehensive manner. It is written in an accessible manner enabling students to easily grasp the material, then extend and elevate discussion in the classroom. Each chapter ends with a business case to reinforce the concepts learned. The textbook is intended to provide the foundational concepts for undergraduate and graduate-level classes in SCM, as well as related areas such as operations management and purchasing. In addition, the book is an excellent resource for executive education and training seminars.

## Goals of the Book

**1. Provide a Comprehensive Foundation of SCM.** This text is written to provide a comprehensive foundation of SCM, from its broad meaning and strategic implications, to operational concepts and techniques. While there are some excellent textbooks that provide foundational concepts of SCM, few present these concepts in a comprehensive and integrated manner that is the hallmark of SCM.

The text begins with an introduction to the holistic and integrated nature of SCM. Supply chain strategy is discussed next, as the driver of SCM, followed by the design of the supply chain network. Participation of organizational functions—including marketing, operations, sourcing, and logistics—are discussed, as well as their linkages to SCM. Next, planning and controlling the supply chain is discussed, from forecasting and materials management, to lean and Six Sigma. Attention is devoted to topics that are of specific interest to SCM, including collaborative forecasting methods such as CPFR and S&OP. Finally, the text looks at issues of managing the supply chain. This includes managing supply chain relationships, from developing alliances to negotiation strategies. Entire chapters are devoted to the most cutting-edge issues in business today: global business, a technologically driven environment, and sustainable supply chain management.

**2. Provide Cross-Functional and Integrative Coverage of SCM.** This text is written to present SCM with an equal and balanced coverage of key business functions, their interactions, and their integration. SCM is truly boundary spanning and is intertwined with all organizational functions. Also, SCM is cross-functional in its decision-making requirements and needs to be presented as such, rather than as an offshoot of another business function. This text has equal coverage of the relevant business functions, their integration, and their impact on the functionality of SCM.

**3. Provide Understanding of Business Issues.** SCM is intertwined with best business practices. It is at the core of success of leading companies such as Apple, BMW, Wal-Mart, P&G, Amazon, Zara, Starbucks, Tesla motor company and others. These companies have achieved world-class status in large part due to a strong focus on SCM. This text is rich in business examples that illustrate SCM best practices and showcase the complexity of SCM business decisions. These examples show SCM to be an exciting area of study, on the cutting edge of business.

## Features

**1. Cross-Functional Coverage.** SCM is presented as a cross-functional area of business study with equal coverage of functions such as marketing, operations, sourcing, and logistics, and their integration.

**2. Global Focus.** Today's supply chains traverse the globe. This creates numerous challenges, such as designing a global supply network, dealing with international tariffs and foreign government regulation, differences in transportation and technology, managing cross-cultural work teams, and addressing customer issues that arise from cultural expectations. Each chapter has at least one box labeled "*Global Insights*," which provides a summary of a global issue that pertains to the topic at hand and an associated business example.

**3. Managerial Focus.** The text is rich with cutting edge SCM business examples. Each chapter has at least one box labeled '*Supply Chain Leaders Box*' that illustrates the latest business practices of the topic addressed. Each chapter begins with a current business example. In addition, each chapter ends with a unique case written to address key managerial issues and a strong emphasis on managerial decision making.

**4. Strategic Focus.** SCM is a strategic function. As a result, the text has a strong strategic focus. Each chapter has at least one box labeled "*Managerial Insights Box*," which illustrates current business thought, using established and recognized sources (*HBR, Business Week, The Wall Street Journal, Supply Chain Management Review*, etc.).

**5. Strong Pedagogy.** The text is written in a readable and accessible manner. Each chapter ends with discussion questions, a case with questions designed to promote managerial thinking, and, where appropriate, homework problems and exercises. Icons throughout chapters show focus on cross-functional coverage, global coverage, sustainability, technology, and the service supply chain. Further, the chapters in the text are linked to the overall topic rather than being presented as an assembled compilation of material.

## Changes to This Edition

A number of changes have been made to this edition to make the text as current, user-friendly, and relevant as possible. All the chapters have been upated to incorporate the latest available information, with increased emphasis on technology, digitization, and analytics. The business examples have been updated, and a large number of class exercises have been added. The following features have been added to this edition:

**Big Data Analytics:** All chapters have been updated to include state-of-the-art impact of big data analytics on supply chains. Each chapter now has one '*Big Data Analytics Box*' that showcases an example of how big data analytics is impacting the topic covered in the chapter. This ranges from how retailers such as Target capture customer preferences, to how UPS uses its state-of-the-art navigation system.

**Technology Focus:** Advancements in technology are changing supply chains. These include 3-D printing, driverless vehicles, next-generation RFID, Internet of Things (IoT), cloud computing, machine learning, and many others. These technologies have enabled the "intelligent supply chain" and are discussed in every chapter.

**Classroom Exercises:** Each chapter now includes class exercises designed to foster classroom discussion. These exercises are classroom tested and include instructor details on how to conduct the exercise and provide a series of questions with suggested solutions to guide the discussion.

**Updated Examples:** Throughout the chapters all examples and data have been updated. The focus of the update was to make the revision rich in examples of both large supply chains, as well as those of small and medium firms to highlight key concepts.

## Instructor Resources

The instructor's website offers several resources designed to assist professors in preparing lectures and assignments, including:

*Instructor's Manual* Includes a suggested course outline, teaching tips and strategies, answers to all end-of-chapter material, additional in-class exercises, and more.

*Test Bank* A comprehensive Test Bank comprised of true/false, multiple-choice, short answer, and essay questions is available on the instructor site. The questions are also available as a Computerized Test Bank.

*PowerPoint Slides* Full color slides highlight key figures from the text as well as many additional lecture outlines, concepts, and diagrams. These provide a versatile opportunity to add high-quality visual support to lectures.

## Acknowledgments

The development of this second edition of *Supply Chain Management* benefited greatly from the comments and suggestions of colleagues. I'd like to acknowledge the contributions made by the following individuals:

Anthony J. Avallone, *Berkeley College*
Ming-Ling Chuang, *Western Connecticut State University*
Verda Blythe, *University of Wisconsin*
Thomas W. Buchner, *University of Minnesota*
Robert R. Bugge, *Temple University*
John F. Kros, *East Carolina University*
Simon Croom, *University of San Diego*
Donald B. Fisher, *Dixie State College*
John D. Hanson, *University of San Diego*
Roger Dean Iles, *University of Memphis*
Sham Kekre, *Tepper School of Business, Carnegie Mellon University*
Dale Franklin Kehr, *University of Memphis*
Rhonda Lummus, *Indiana University*
Mary J. Meixell, *Quinnipiac University*
Michael J Racer, *University of Memphis*
Young Ro, *University of Michigan*
Jeffrey Schaller, *Eastern Connecticut State University*
Sridhar Seshadri, *University of Texas*
Theodore Stank, *University of Tennessee-Knoxville*
Srinivas Talluri, *Michigan State University*
Tina Wakolbinger, *University of Memphis*

## Special Thanks

I would also like to offer special acknowledgment to the publishing team at Wiley for their creativity, talent, and hard work. Thank you also to John Wood for his help with research on sustainability and supply chain relationships, as well as to countless students with their assistance on case development and end-of-chapter problems.

# Introduction to Supply Chain Management

## 1

**LEARNING OBJECTIVES**

*After completing this chapter, you should be able to:*

- Define "supply chain management," and explain the activities involved.
- Identify the flows through a supply chain, and explain the bullwhip effect.
- Describe the rise of supply chain management and its global implications.
- Describe characteristics of a competitive supply chain.
- Identify and explain key trends that drive today's supply chains.

**CHAPTER OUTLINE**

- **What Is Supply Chain Management (SCM)?**
  *SCM Activities*
  *Managing Flows Through the Supply Chain*
  *The Bullwhip Effect*
  *Customer Focus*
  *The Service Supply Chain*

- **The Boundary-Spanning Nature of SCM**
  *Intraorganizational Integration*
  *Cross-Enterprise Integration*
  *SCM Versus Logistics*

- **The Rise of SCM**

- **Characteristics of a Competitive Supply Chain**
  *Responsiveness*
  *Reliability*
  *Relationship Management*

- **Trends in SCM**
  *Globalization*
  *Outsourcing*
  *Information Technology*
  *Big Data Analytics*

*3-D Printing, Additive Manufaturing, and Robotics*
*Postponement*
*The Lean Supply Chain*
*Managing Supply Chain Disruptions*
*Supply Chain Security*
*Sustainability and the "Green" Supply Chain*
*Innovation*
*The Financial Supply Chain*

- **Careers in SCM and Professional Organizations**
- **Chapter Highlights**
- **Key Terms**
- **Discussion Questions**
- **Case Study: McNulty's Muscular Materials (MMM)**

---

Most of us have had the experience of sitting at a Starbucks coffee shop enjoying a cup of coffee, a frappuccino, or perhaps a pumpkin spice latte. We have enjoyed the "Starbucks experience," sipping a beverage, lounging in one of the many chairs, and perhaps reading a newspaper or a good book. We may have briefly noticed that Starbucks' coffee beans come from all across the globe, including Guatemala, Sumatra, Brazil, Kenya, Mexico, and Ethiopia. However, we have probably not given much thought to the complexity of decisions and coordination required to make sure that we, the customers, receive the beverages we are enjoying as we sit in the café.

In fact, for Starbucks to be able to deliver such a high-quality, consistent, and broad product offering to more than 23,000 store locations worldwide, it must manage an extensive global network of trading partners, from coffee growers to roasting plants to coffee distributors. It must manage relationships, ensure the highest quality, and guarantee product availability at each store location, all the while maintaining efficiency and keeping costs as low as possible. So while we, the customers, sit in the dimly lit and hip café enjoying the "Starbucks experience," behind the scenes is a company that is managing one of the biggest global supply chains in the world.

Supply chain management (SCM) is the fastest-growing area of business today. In fact, it is at the core of the success of such companies as Amazon, Nike, Toyota, Wal-Mart, P&G, Zara, PepsiCo, BMW, L'Oréal, and McDonalds, as well as Starbucks, and countless others. These companies have achieved world-class status in large part due to a strong focus on SCM.

Most people assume that they have some idea of what SCM is about. They usually think it is part of logistics and distribution, or purchasing, or perhaps marketing. It is likely, however, that you do not yet know the full complexity and broad reach of this rapidly evolving business concept. At a recent conference Paul Mathews, Executive VP of Supply Chain for the Limited, joked that people still think of SCM as "kicking boxes and licking labels." He wanted to highlight the misunderstanding of SCM many people still have.

The purpose of this book is to help you develop a comprehensive understanding of SCM. This includes understanding the key issues involved and becoming familiar with the very latest business thinking. This will prepare for you for a successful career in a new and exciting business field.

Today's business environment has forced companies to compete in very different ways from just a few years ago. In addition to competing on traditional dimensions such as quality, time, cost, and customization, companies must be rapid innovators. They must stay abreast of quickly changing customer demands and increasing global competition. Advances in technology, the Internet, big data analytics, and unprecedented threats to security are forcing companies to be flexible and responsive. At the same time, a down economy has created tremendous financial pressures. SCM is the business concept through which companies can achieve this level of competitiveness while maintaining costs, and it is intertwined with today's best business practices. Companies understand that they cannot achieve the needed level of competitiveness in the current global economy without SCM.

Knowledge of SCM will give you the skills needed to help your organization gain a competitive advantage in the marketplace. It will also help you move into one of the fastest-growing career fields today.

## What Is Supply Chain Management (SCM)?

**Supply chain management (SCM)** is the design and management of flows of products, information, and funds throughout the supply chain. It involves the coordination and management of all the activities of a supply chain. As such, SCM may appear deceptively simple. In fact, it is a complex business concept that is far reaching in the nature and type of decisions involved. Before we can begin to look at the full complexity of SCM, it is important to first understand the meaning of the term *supply chain*.

A **supply chain** is the network of all entities involved in producing and delivering a finished product to the final customer. This includes sourcing raw materials and parts; manufacturing, producing, and assembling the products; storing goods in warehouses; order entry and tracking; distribution; and delivery to the final customer. A simple supply chain is illustrated in Figure 1.1.

The flows through the supply chain begin with suppliers who supply and transport raw materials and components to producers or manufacturers. Manufacturers transform these

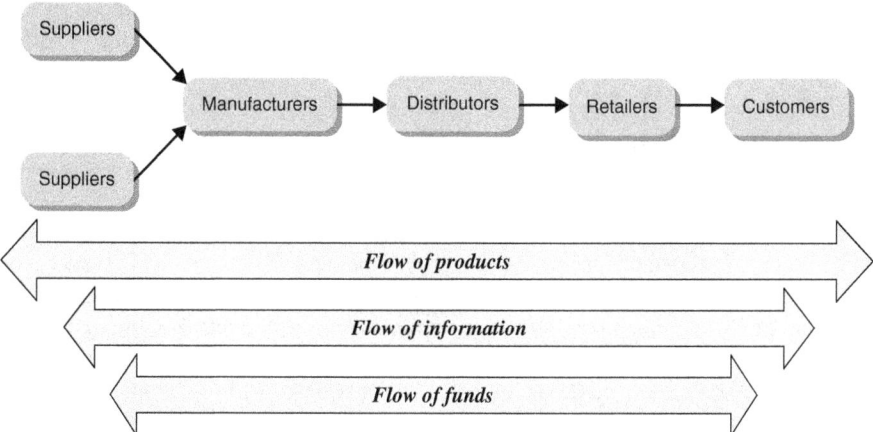

**FIGURE 1.1** A simple supply chain.

materials into finished products that are then shipped either to the manufacturers' own distribution centers or to wholesalers. Next, the products are shipped to retailers who sell the product to final customers. Consider the Starbucks supply chain we just discussed. At the beginning of the supply chain are coffee farmers at various locations across the globe that grow the coffee beans. The coffee beans are picked, packaged in burlap bags, and transported to coffee roasters, entities that roast the beans. The roasted beans are then sent to coffee distributors, who then sort, package, and move the beans to retailer outlets such as Starbucks cafés, to be purchased by the consumer.

A typical supply chain may involve many different trading partners, called stages. These supply chain stages may include the following:

- Suppliers
- Producers
- Wholesalers/Distributors
- Retailers
- Customers

Note that every supply chain is different and that these stages are a generic representation of a supply chain. In fact, each stage may not be present in every supply chain. The number of stages that are part of a supply chain and its appropriate design will depend on both the customer's needs, the roles of the stages involved, and the value each stage provides.

Supply chains are under increasing financial pressure, and stages that do not add value to the supply chain are quickly bypassed or eliminated. For this reason, a supply chain is often called a **value chain** or a **value network**. Today's concept of the supply chain comes from the concept of a "value chain" that was introduced by a Harvard Business School professor, Michael Porter, in the l980s. Michael Porter explained that a company's competitive advantage cannot be understood by looking at a firm as a whole. Rather, its competitive advantage comes from the many discrete activities that a firm performs and that each of these activities contributes to the firm's total cost position. This concept of each activity contributing to the total value has now been extended to the entire supply chain. In fact, it has been often said that it is not companies that compete. Rather, it is their supply chains that compete.

As we look at a supply chain it is important to point out some common terminology used to describe the relationships of supply chain stages to one another. Each company in a supply chain has its suppliers and customers. The stages of the supply chain that comprise the inbound direction toward the company, or the "focal firm," are called the "upstream" part of the supply chain.

The stages of the supply chain away from the "focal firm" are termed "downstream." This is shown in Figure 1.2. For example, if the focal firm was a manufacturer, all inbound suppliers would be considered "upstream," whereas distributors/wholesalers and retailers/customers would comprise the "downstream" part of the supply chain. Being able to refer to parts of the supply chain as either "upstream" or "downstream" provides a convenient point of reference. Similarly, suppliers that directly supply goods or services to a company are termed "first-tier suppliers." Suppliers that supply to a company's "first-tier suppliers" are termed "second-tier suppliers," and so on moving up the chain. This provides a common terminology for companies to understand which suppliers are being referenced.

The term *supply chain* implies a linear chain of participants from suppliers to final customers. A true supply chain is actually more like a complex network, as shown in Figure 1.3. A producer may receive materials from multiple suppliers. Many distributors and wholesalers receive inventory from many manufacturers, and most retailers receive products from many different distributors. For this reason a supply chain is often referred to as a supply chain network or supply web, to more accurately describe the nature of these relationships. In fact, many companies are part of multiple supply chains.

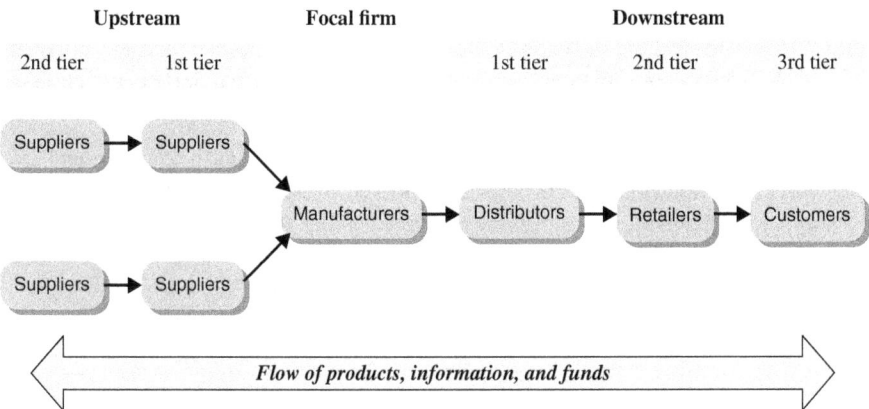

**FIGURE 1.2** Stages of the supply chain.

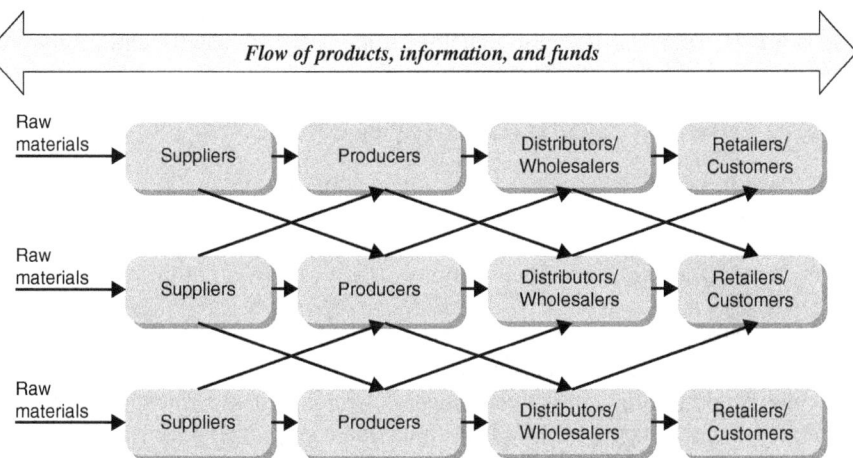

**FIGURE 1.3** The supply chain network.

The supply chain network can actually take on many different shapes. Some are linear, as shown in Figure 1.3. Others take on the form of hub-and-spoke or a web. Often the type of network can be related to the number of suppliers, their locations, and the type of product being produced. For example, Dell Computer Corporation became famous for mandating that all its first-tier suppliers must be within a 15-minute radius anywhere around its Austin, Texas, manufacturing facility. This is an example of a hub-and-spoke supply network, with the focal firm in the center of the design, and a model that has been followed by many other manufacturers.

## SCM Activities

Now that we understand what constitutes a supply chain or supply network, we can look at the issues involved in managing it. Recall that SCM involves the coordination and management of *all* the activities of a supply chain. It is responsible for managing the system of flows between the different entities of a supply chain to satisfy the final customer and maximize total supply chain profitability. SCM is a dynamic and ever-changing process that requires coordinating all activities among members of the supply chain.

SCM activities include the following:

- **Coordination:** SCM involves coordinating the movement of goods and services through the supply chain, from suppliers to manufacturers to distributors to final customers; it also includes movement of goods back up the supply chain, as products may be returned. Coordination also involves the movement of funds through the supply chain as products are purchased and sold. This includes various financial arrangements and terms of purchase between buyers and suppliers.

- **Information Sharing:** SCM requires sharing relevant information among members of the supply chain. This includes sharing demand and sales forecasts, point-of-sale data, promotional campaigns planned, and inventory levels. Consider that a manufacturer must know if a retailer is planning an advertising campaign to ensure that enough of the product is being produced. Otherwise, the retailer may run out of stock. Similarly, the manufacturer's suppliers must be aware of increased production plans to provide sufficient component parts. Sharing this information enables the entire chain to work in unison.

- **Collaboration:** SCM requires collaboration between supply chain members so that they jointly plan, operate, and execute business decisions as one entity. This is important for decisions that range from product design and process improvement to implementing business initiatives or following a particular business strategy. For example, this may include collaborating on ways to cut costs or improve quality standards throughout the entire supply chain.

## Managing Flows Through the Supply Chain

Recall that many flows move through a supply chain network. The first is the flow of **products** through the supply chain, from the beginning of the chain through various stages of production, to the final customer. However, goods also flow back through the chain. This is in the form of returned products that are unacceptable to customers for a variety of reasons, such as damaged or obsolete goods. This is an area of SCM called *reverse logistics* because the direction of product flow is reversed. The increased focus on customer accommodation has resulted in an increase in the amount of goods returned from customers.

The second important flow through the supply chain is that of **information** that is shared between members of the supply chain. Many simplified supply chains view the product flowing from suppliers to customers and information flowing in the opposite direction, from point-of-sale back to suppliers. In this simplified case, the primary information is demand or sales data, which is used to trigger replenishment and serves as the basis for forecasting. In a more realistic case, sales information is shared on a real-time basis, which leads to less uncertainty and less safety stock. The sharing of real-time information serves to compress or shorten the supply chain from a time standpoint. The result of this more timely and accurate information is a reduction in the amount of inventory carried throughout the supply chain.

The third important flow through the supply chain is that of **funds**. In a simplified supply chain, financial flow is often viewed as one directional, flowing backward in the supply chain as payment for products and services received. However, as products flow in both directions so does the transfer of funds. A major impact on fund transfer and the financials of companies has been supply chain compression. A shorter order cycle time means that customers receive their orders faster. It means that they are billed sooner and that companies receive payment sooner. This speeding up of the money collection process has had a huge impact on the profitability of certain firms. Consider Dell Computer Corporation, a company that has gained much from the compressed supply chain. Dell turns over its inventory roughly every four days. However, they often receive payment a week in advance, well before Dell pays its suppliers, providing a large financial benefit to Dell.

The key to successful SCM is the management of these flows through the chain. SCM is a dynamic process and provides many opportunities to reduce the cost of doing business and improve customer service. At the same time, the challenges of SCM are often underestimated. In fact the reason for the failure of many online businesses is due to their inability to manage supply chain flows effectively. Many have excellent business concepts and marketing strategies, but are unable to make products available to customers in a cost-effective manner. For example, Webvan, an online grocery delivery company, was unable to bring the cost of grocery picking and delivery to a competitive level and went out of business. The success of Internet retailers such as Amazon.com has been primarily driven by the improvements in their supply chains.

## The Bullwhip Effect

A supply chain is composed of many different companies, or stages, each with their own objectives. For a supply chain to be highly competitive, it is critical that its members engage in the activities of coordination, information sharing, and collaboration. Otherwise, each stage of the supply chain will have differing and possibly conflicting objectives and may focus on simply maximizing their own profits. Similarly, if information is not shared between stages, but is delayed or distorted, each stage may have a distorted view of final customer demand. As a result, they will likely not produce the right quantities of items needed, resulting in either shortages or excess inventory. Both situations result in lowered profitability of the entire supply chain.

It has been observed that fluctuation and distortion of information increases as it moves up the supply chain, from retailers, to manufacturers, and to suppliers. This is called the **bullwhip effect**, as inaccurate and distorted information travels up the chain like a bullwhip uncoiling. In response, each stage of the chain carries progressively more inventory to compensate for the lack of information. The bullwhip effect has been well documented in many industries and is costly for all supply chain members.

One of the best-known examples of the bullwhip effect was observed by Proctor & Gamble (P&G) in the supply chain of its Pampers diapers. The company discovered that even when demand for diapers was stable at the retail store level, orders for diapers from P&G fluctuated significantly. Even greater fluctuation was observed in orders for raw materials from suppliers over time. Although consumption of the final product was stable, orders for raw materials were highly variable.

A similar example was observed at Hewlett Packard (HP). HP observed that fluctuations of orders increased significantly as they moved from the resellers up the supply chain to the printer division to the integrated circuit division. Like P&G, HP observed that although final product demand was fairly stable, orders placed at every stage up the supply chain significantly increased in variability. Both P&G and HP found that the result of the bullwhip effect was an increase in cost and difficulty in filling orders on time.

The longer the supply chain, the greater the opportunity for the bullwhip effect, as manufacturers and suppliers are further away from final customer demand. If there is no coordination or sharing of information, these stages do not know final customer demand or when a replenishment order might arrive. As a result of this higher uncertainty, they stockpile inventory. The way to combat the bullwhip effect is to share point-of-sale information, available from most cash registers, with all members of the supply chain. This allows all stages of the supply chain to make replenishment decisions from the same information source. In addition to information sharing, coordination and collaboration will enable stages of the supply chain to work toward the same goals.

## Customer Focus

The final customer is the driving force of the supply chain. In fact, the primary purpose for the existence of a supply chain is to respond to customer demands and generate profits for companies that are members of the chain. Therefore, meeting customer demands is the primary objective. The process is driven by a customer having a particular product need. The retailer tries to satisfy the customer by ensuring that the product is available. As customers continue to purchase

# INTRODUCTION TO SUPPLY CHAIN MANAGEMENT

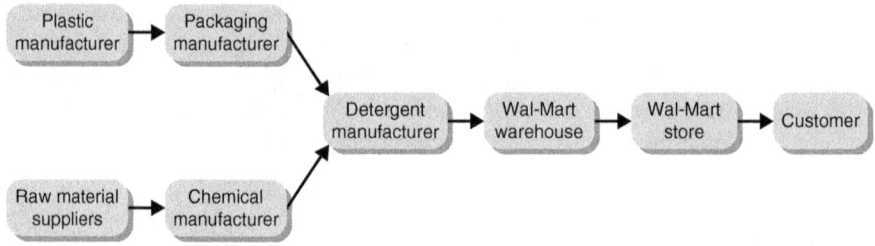

**FIGURE 1.4** Products are "pulled" through the supply chain.

products, the retailer requests additional products from its suppliers to replenish those sold. These suppliers then purchase materials from their suppliers, and the process "pulls" raw materials through the rest of the chain needed to produce more quantities of the product.

Consider a customer walking into a Wal-Mart store to buy laundry detergent, as shown in Figure 1.4. The process that drives the supply chain starts with the need of the customer to buy detergent. The customer visiting Wal-Mart takes detergent off the shelf that Wal-Mart stocked from inventory supplied from its finished-goods warehouse or by a distributor. Sales of the detergent trigger the warehouse or distribution center to replenish the sold items. The items "pulled" out of the warehouse or distribution center trigger the manufacturer, such as Proctor & Gamble (P&G), to produce more and fill the warehouse with more items. To produce more items, in turn, P&G has to request more raw materials from their suppliers, such as those that supply packaging and chemical components. As P&G requests more raw materials from their suppliers, their first-tier suppliers request more material from lower-tier suppliers. In this manner products are moved through the supply chain.

SCM is a dynamic process and involves the constant flow of information, products, and funds between different entities of the supply chain. To see how this works, once again consider the example of Wal-Mart. Wal-Mart provided the product (detergent in this case) to the customer, and the customer transferred their funds to Wal-Mart. Using point-of-sales data, Wal-Mart then conveyed the need to replenish orders to the warehouse or distributor, who transferred the replenishment order via trucks back to the store. After the replenishment was made, Wal-Mart transferred funds to the distributor. Wal-Mart, the distributor, and the manufacturer shared pricing information, delivery schedules, and forecasts of future sales. This type of flow of information, products, and funds takes place across the entire supply chain.

This example illustrates that to provide timely product availability, all the participants in the chain need to coordinate their plans and respond to the same information. Also, notice that there are many flows moving through the supply chain. The process is driven by a customer order and ends when a customer has paid for their purchase. SCM is the coordination and orchestration of all the activities necessary for this process to occur in the most efficient, cost-effective, and timely manner.

## The Service Supply Chain

SCM is just as relevant to companies in the service industry, ranging from healthcare to real estate to banking, as it is to manufacturing companies that produce tangible products. However, service supply chains differ from manufacturing in the role of the customer and the direction of flow of the delivery process. Unlike manufacturing supply chains that focus on the production and delivery of a tangible product, service supply chains tend to focus more on the interaction between the customer and provider. For this reason, the role of the customer is even greater in driving the service supply chain than it is in manufacturing. In service organizations the customer is also a supplier of inputs and information, which can change the service delivery. Consider the legal environment, where the course of legal action greatly depends on information provided by the client to the attorney. Similarly, a university student may have the option to conduct an independent study under the supervision of a faculty member, changing the set course of study.

Service supply chains tend to be considerably shorter than manufacturing supply chains. The provider typically interacts directly with customers, without the buffer of retailers and distributors, enabling easier sharing of information. Service supply chains also tend to look more like hubs than chains. One of the disadvantages is that they do not have the buffers of inventory as seen in manufacturing. This means that they need to have other organizational mechanisms that give them flexibility when handling the variation of customer-supplied inputs and demands. This also makes information sharing with customers much more critical.

Even service companies that provide pure content to customers, such as those in the entertainment industry, rely heavily on their supply chains to deliver customer value and remain competitive. This includes industries such as film, computer games, and sports and includes companies such as Disney, Warner Bros., and Ticketmaster. These companies are increasingly relying on SCM process and technology improvements to ensure coordination of information and maintain competitiveness.

## Supply Chain Leader's Box

### AMAZON.COM

The largest Internet-based retailer in the world, Amazon.com, has sought to make itself a customer-centric company from its beginning in July 1995. Amazon.com is a service company that is a leading merchandiser of everything from gourmet food to apparel to electronics, in addition to books and music. From the very beginning, Amazon understood that its focus must be on satisfying the customer by providing the highest levels of service. Rather than focusing on marketing or advertising, Amazon placed its focus on having a superior supply chain that provides uncompromised delivery to customers. In addition, Amazon conducts business on an international scale, shipping to more than 200 countries. Coordinating and orchestrating this range of product offerings to so many global locations with perfect deliveries is a daunting task. To achieve this, Amazon has built an impressive logistics network that includes its own fleet of jets, automated warehouses, robots, drones, and a digitally driven supply chain. For Amazon, logistics, shipping, and a super SCM have combined to give the company its stellar reputation.

Part of Amazon's supply chain proficiency is based on its strict operations philosophy, which focuses on lean systems, quality, and efficiency. It is more reminiscent of industrial manufacturing than traditional retail practices. For instance, Amazon takes a Six Sigma[1] approach to its distribution operations and applies lean manufacturing and total quality management (TQM) methodologies to its processes. Amazon's online proficiency is such that many brick-and-mortar retailers such as Target and Toys "R" Us use the Amazon website for their e-commerce efforts.

Adapted from: Leonard, David, "Will Amazon Kill FedEx?" *Bloomberg Business Week*, August 31, 2016.

## The Boundary-Spanning Nature of SCM

To orchestrate and optimize all flows from source to consumption, SCM must take a total systems viewpoint. SCM must ensure that the needs of final customers are satisfied through the coordination of materials and information flows that extend from the marketplace, through the firm and its operations to all its suppliers.

---

[1] Six Sigma performance is characterized by 3.4 defects per million, or 99.99966% perfect. We will discuss this in detail later in the text.

SCM is unique, as it is truly boundary spanning. First, it spans and integrates functions and processes within the enterprise, called *intra*organizational coordination. Second, it spans and integrates functions and processes between enterprises of the supply chain, called *cross-enterprise* coordination. In essence, a supply chain needs to function as an extended enterprise. To achieve this, supply chain management has to cross over the boundaries of individual firms and integrate business functions and processes across enterprises.

## Intraorganizational Integration

SCM requires participation and coordination of activities between different organizational functions. The relationship between the functions of marketing, operations, sourcing, and logistics is particularly important. For an organization to be effectively integrated with other members of its supply chain, it must have internal coordination. This means that the various functions must share information and conduct coordinated activities. The relationship between the various functions is shown in Figure 1.5.

**Marketing** is the function responsible for linking the organization to its customers and identifying what customers want in products and services. It is the function that interfaces with the customer. **Operations** ensures that the exact products customers want are produced efficiently and in a cost-effective manner. It is the function whose job is to organize the transformation of raw materials into finished products. **Sourcing** is the function responsible for linking the organization to its suppliers and ensuring an efficient supply of materials. **Logistics** is responsible for moving and positioning inventory throughout the supply chain and ensuring that the right products are delivered to the right place at the right time. SCM would not be possible without the support of these functions.

To support SCM, each individual function must also have a systems viewpoint. This type of effort requires company-wide integration and a way of organizational thinking that is different from the traditional "silo" mentality, where each organizational function operates independently. Creating systems thinking can be a big challenge for many companies.

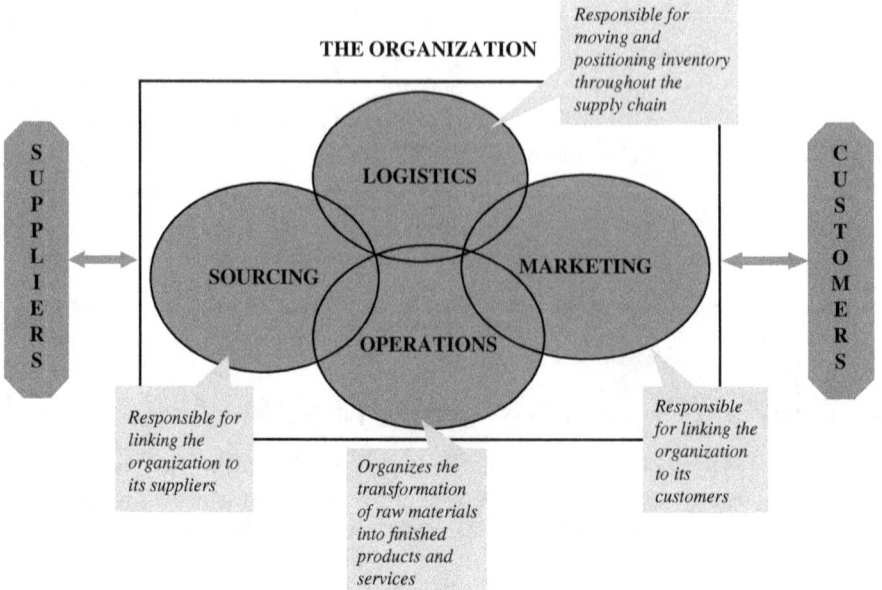

**FIGURE 1.5** Organizational integration of enterprise functions.

The classic illustration of the "silo" mentality can be seen between the marketing and operations functions of an organization. Historically, the operations function was focused on improving the efficiency of the operating system, through proper scheduling, minimization of setup times, and achieving product standardization. The lexicon of the operations manager, as a result, had focused on operating measures of performance such as productivity measures, units produced, and number of defects. On the other hand, marketing focused on achieving a competitive advantage through expanding market share, creating new market opportunities, offering product variety, and responding to market changes. The lexicon of the marketing manager, by contrast, has focused on sales, profitability, and market share. As a result, often operations and marketing managers were not able to communicate and had different goals.

Today's highly competitive business environment is not forgiving to this type of segmented approach between organizational functions. The need to understand and meet customer requirements is a prerequisite for supply chain competitiveness and survival and is the responsibility of marketing. At the same time, economic competitiveness has placed great pressure on cost competition, improvements in quality, and response time, placing the operations function in the limelight. SCM is dependent on operations and marketing working together, sharing information, and making joint decisions.

Another organizational function that has gained increasing appreciation for its critical role in SCM is procurement or purchasing, also known as sourcing. Historically, procurement was concerned with purchasing issues of a primarily transactional nature. Today, leading-edge companies place great focus on the supply side of the chain, which is the domain of purchasing. Not only is the cost of purchased materials and supplies a large part of the total cost of most companies, but also purchasing creates an opportunity to integrate the capabilities of the supplier with producers. Therefore, whereas marketing focuses on the customer side of the organization, procurement focuses on the supply side.

Finally, the function of logistics coordinates the materials and information flows that extend from the marketplace, through the firm and its operations and beyond that of the suppliers to ensure that goods are delivered to the right place. Therefore, like SCM, logistics is an integrative function that has a systems-wide view of the organization, from the customer or market side, to the supply side. It has a critical responsibility to ensure that the demands of the marketplace are passed on from marketing to manufacturing and then are linked to purchasing and distribution.

## Cross-Enterprise Integration

The management of a supply chain as an extended enterprise involves coordinating two-way flows of goods and services, information, and funds. The integration across the boundaries of several organizations means that the supply chain should function like one organization in satisfying the final customer. In fact, the ultimate goal of a supply chain is to operate as a single entity. Information technology is the key enabler of this capability, without which cross-enterprise integration would not be possible.

This integration can be difficult, as real-world supply chains are usually complex and have many supply chain participants. Achieving integration and coordination of activities in the supply chain is predicated on relationship management. Concepts such as partnerships and alliances have become a part of the SCM vocabulary. Traditional adversarial relationships with suppliers have given way to long-term partnering. However, supply chain relationships need to incorporate more than shared information and a focus on total supply chain cost. Supply chains need to achieve a level of integration that involves collaboration among partners in developing strategic plans and joint setting of long-term goals. An important factor to achieving this level of integration is for companies to have an internal, cross-functional team that engages in ongoing external efforts with suppliers, transportation carriers, and distributors. Toyota is a good example of successful supplier collaboration. Toyota engages in collaboration with suppliers from the earliest stages of product design—a system called "early supplier involvement." This has led to a significant cost reduction in producing its cars.

In addition to collaborative planning, achieving full cross-enterprise integration requires the sharing of risks and rewards. Most organizations still function in a way that minimizes their own risk and maximizes their own rewards. This strategy may mean that outcomes they achieve are at the expense of other companies. The cooperative and collaborative approach of SCM is predicated on the win–win outcome. Although adversarial relationships can provide financial gain, the win–win strategy has shown to be the best strategy over the long run.

## SCM Versus Logistics

Many people confuse SCM with logistics. Therefore, it is important to clarify their different roles in developing a competitive advantage. SCM is about the collaboration between supply chain partners in a strategic effort to achieve superior competitiveness. Therefore, SCM requires managing different aspects of the coordination process, such as information, technology, distribution, products, raw materials, finances, and most of all, relationships. The relationships involved in SCM are complex and require coordinating managerial processes within firms (intraorganizational) and between firms (cross-enterprise).

Logistics, in contrast to SCM, consists of the tasks involved in moving and positioning inventory throughout the supply chain, as shown in Figure 1.6. Logistics is a function that supports SCM on par with marketing, operations, and sourcing. SCM, on the other hand, is a strategic and managerial concept. The function of logistics involves order processing and tracking, inventory management, transportation, warehousing, material handling, and packaging. These activities need to be coordinated and integrated throughout all entities of the chain. Without logistics there would be inventory stock-outs at some locations and too much inventory at others. Consequently, logistics is a function that supports SCM.

Notice that SCM is about managing and coordinating many flows, including inventory. Logistics, on the other hand, is the part of SCM that is concerned with managing the flow of inventory.

Logistics is vital to SCM as it is a key supporting function. Logistics must plan and coordinate all material flow from source to users as one integrated system, rather than a series of independent activities as has been done in the past. Logistics is the function that is basically responsible for linking the marketplace with the manufacturing process, sourcing activities, and the distribution network to provide high customer service at lower costs. In essence, logistics is the link between the marketplace and the operating activities of the business. The scope of logistics spans from management of raw materials through the delivery of the final product.

## The Rise of SCM

To fully appreciate SCM, it is important to look at its rapid rise as a critical business concept. SCM evolved in the 1990s and ushered in a new era of business competition. This was a direct result of great economic changes of the time for the global economy and an increasingly uncertain business

**FIGURE 1.6** The logistics function.

environment. Leading-edge companies, such as Amazon, demonstrated that reduction in order fulfillment time coupled with customization can be a competitive advantage that the supply chain can provide. In fact, SCM enables companies to significantly reduce the time required to design, process, and deliver products to customers, at a lower cost. This allows for greater responsiveness and has evolved into a major strategic tool for companies.

Interest in SCM has rapidly grown over the years, as it has proven to be a necessary ingredient for successful global competition. A number of forces have contributed to this trend. First, in recent years many companies have discovered the large magnitude of savings that can be achieved by planning and managing their supply chain more effectively. Second, advances in information technologies have provided access to comprehensive data from all components of the supply chain. Finally, improvement in transportation methods has led to a reduction in transportation costs, while significantly increasing speed of delivery to multiple locations. One of the most striking examples of this is Wal-Mart's success, which is primarily attributed to mastery of its supply chain. Wal-Mart is highly successful in collaborating with their suppliers, using the latest available technology for data gathering and transfer, and implementing the latest transportation techniques.

Prior to the SCM revolution, order processing was a long process and prone to errors. In the 1980s and 1990s, for example, the average time to process and deliver an order to a customer ranged from weeks to months. There were many steps in the order-to-delivery cycle that had to be completed for the customer to receive the order. Also, many of the steps were performed inefficiently. The customer initiated the order process through telephone, fax, or mail. This order was then processed either manually or using a computer system. The process involved credit authorization, order placement to a warehouse or distribution center, and the arrangement of product delivery by shipper. Often mistakes were made in this process, such as inventories being out-of-stock. This resulted in expediting orders at extra cost when goods finally arrived. Shipments were often sent to the wrong location, and mistakes were made in the manual processing of forms. To help guard against these problems, companies began to stock large amounts of inventories in warehouses to ensure that they had stock available. Duplicate inventories were often held in different warehouses. The result was a higher cost that was ultimately passed on to the customer. The larger amounts of inventories, however, still did not guarantee no stock-outs, and many firms found themselves having too much of the "wrong" inventory and not enough of what the customer wanted. All this made companies less competitive.

This changed in the 1990s when leading-edge companies such as Dell Computer Corporation began offering highly customized products with a significantly reduced customer response time. Suddenly, other companies had to follow suit or risk going out of business. The result was that historical management of order fulfillment suddenly became obsolete. Companies found that they had to go beyond their own organizations and design competitive supply chains.

## Supply Chain Leader's Box

### ■ DELL COMPUTER CORPORATION

Dell Computer Corporation made its reputation as an icon of how a company can design and manage their supply chain to reduce customer response time, while still offering product customization at a price lower than competitors. This provided Dell with a clear competitive advantage and a model that others tried to emulate. A customized Dell computer could be en route to the customer within 36 hours of order placement. Such a quick response enabled Dell to reduce its inventory levels compared to the industry standard. Dell has been able to achieve success due to its agile, adaptable, and short supply chain, requiring suppliers to be within a 15-minute radius of their assembly plant, permitting just-in-time delivery. The system has been set up so that suppliers automatically restock warehouses as needed, and Dell is billed for items only after they are shipped. The result is better value for the customer and less cost for Dell.

Dell's supply chain model was the industry norm for many years. However, as other companies began to emulate this model it was no longer an industry differentiator. To remain competitive Dell has used the strength of its supply chain to shift focus on different industry segments, providing technology to healthcare, education, and the military. The iconic supply chain has enabled the company to be limber and easily adapt to changing markets.

Adapted from: Phillips, Erica E. "Dell's EMC Purchase Marks Shift from Consumer Supply Chain." *The Wall Street Journal*, October 15, 2015.

One factor driving the growth of SCM has been the massive change in the capability and availability of information technology. The economy of the 1990s was forever changed by information availability through the Internet and computerization. These technologies provided rapidly accessible information to all parties. They created the foundation for rapid and economical methods of doing business, such as business-to-business (B2B) and business-to-consumer (B2C), from which the new economy quickly emerged.

Another significant factor was greater customer affluence and sophistication, resulting in greater customer demand for a wide choice of quality goods and services. The Internet and other information technologies accelerated this change by empowering consumers. Customers suddenly shifted from being passive and powerless participants to drivers of the new economy. Customers today demand customized products with high quality delivered at record speed.

Advances in information technology, transportation methods, and greater customer empowerment created a rise in SCM. The 1990s witnessed SCM becoming a part of the standard vocabulary of corporate presidents and CEOs. SCM has become a new order of business and a tool for companies to survive and thrive. Managers are now focusing on improving all aspects of the process from product design to product delivery, focusing on improving customization, speed of delivery, and a commitment to a concept of zero defects called Six Sigma performance.

## Characteristics of a Competitive Supply Chain

There are three key characteristics of a competitive supply chain: responsiveness, reliability, and relationship management. We discuss these here.

### Responsiveness

The ability to respond to customers' requirements in ever-shorter time frames has become critical. Today customers want shorter lead times, greater flexibility, and greater product choice. This means that the supplier and manufacturer have to be able to meet the precise demands of the customer in a shorter amount of time than ever before. The ability for a supply chain to have this level of responsiveness is often described as "agility," which is the ability to move quickly to meet customer demands. In fact, in rapidly changing environments, agility is more important than long-term strategy, as there is no "long term." Agility will come from short supply chains that are much more demand driven—responding to what the customer "demands"—rather than forecast driven.

### Reliability

Uncertainty is a fact of life for most businesses, such as uncertainty about future demands, uncertainty about a supplier's ability to meet deadlines, or uncertainty about the quality of component materials. In fact, uncertainty is the main reason why companies carry safety stock inventories—to guard against this uncertainty—which then results in higher costs. The best way to reduce uncertainty is by increasing reliability through the redesign of processes that impact performance.

One factor that greatly improves reliability in supply chains is improved visibility. Typically, the further one goes up the supply chain, the more limited the "visibility" of downstream activities. Organizations that are further up the chain have typically relied on demand from their immediate customer in the chain to forecast demand. This lack of coordination has resulted in the classic "bullwhip" effect. Supply chain coordination and sharing of real-time data and information through information technology has permitted visibility to all entities in the chain. This results in greatly improved visibility and, consequently, supply chain reliability.

## Relationship Management

An important characteristic of competitive supply chains is their focus on relationship building and collaboration, rather than the arm's-length adversarial relationships that had been dominant in the past. In many industries, for example, the practice of "single-sourcing" is widespread. It has been documented that such practices improve quality, product innovation, and design while reducing costs and improving overall responsiveness. Underlying this idea is that the buyer–supplier relationship should be based on a partnership of trust, commitment, and fairness. There are numerous advantages to such relationships that can be long term and mutually beneficial. The competitive advantage of companies such as Toyota and Honda over their competitors in the auto industry comes from the collaborative relationships they have developed with their suppliers. As we have seen thus far, SCM is primarily about the management of relationships across complex networks of companies. Successful supply chains will be those that are governed by a constant search for win–win relationships based on reciprocity of trust.

## Global Insights Box

### ZARA

The Spanish retailer Zara exemplifies that to operate a successful global operation a company may have to defy most of the current conventional wisdom about how supply chains should be run. Zara has adapted numerous best practices to create its own brand of global SCM that may seem unorthodox to some. For example, Zara has been known to send a half-empty truck across Europe, pay to airfreight coats to Japan twice a week, or move unsold items out of its retail stores after only two weeks. For most observers, this would be no way to run a supply chain. Of course, none of these tactics are especially effective by themselves. Rather, they stem from a holistic approach to SCM that optimizes the entire chain instead of focusing on individual parts.

In today's economy, where most companies have rushed to outsource, Zara keeps almost half of its production in-house. Rather than pushing its factories to maximize output, the company focuses capital on building extra capacity to give it flexibility. Also, Zara manufactures and distributes products in small batches, rather than chasing economies of scale. To ensure top performance, the company manages all design, warehousing, distribution, and logistics functions itself. The result is a super-responsive supply chain uniquely tailored to fully support Zara's business model. Zara can design, produce, and deliver a new garment to its 2,100-plus stores worldwide in just a few days. However, Zara keeps a limited amount of inventory. In a Zara shop, customers can always find new products but they know that supply is limited. This creates a sense of urgency for the customer to purchase rather than waiting for a markdown, translating into high profit margins and a consistent yearly growth. More recently Zara has noticed growth in online sales and is shifting more inventory to be available online, using the same supply chain strategy. Zara offers a model where profits are gained through controlling the entire end-to-end supply chain.

Adapted from: "Zara Looks to Online Growth and Cuts Store Sales Forecasts." *Fortune*, March 2016.

## Trends in SCM

Today's organizations face a number of trends that impact the way supply chains are designed and managed. These trends are a result of a fast-changing global and technologically connected economy that creates unique challenges companies must address. We look at these here.

## Globalization

In the eyes of the economist Thomas Friedman, globalization has replaced the so-called Cold War of the post–World War II era as the dominant driving force of world economics.[2] The concept of the "global marketplace" has changed the meaning of how and where business is conducted, for all enterprises and for individual customers. Changes in information technology, transportation, and government policies have made the concept of the global economy a fact of life. A number of countries have aggressively pursued opening up international trade. This has served to open new markets and sources of supply for most companies, both large and small. Further, these opportunities have been made possible through information technology, which has helped break the distance barrier. Companies have benefited from a larger choice of product sources. Consumers have also benefited due to greater product choice, higher quality, and lower cost.

Managing global supply chains, however, has a number of challenges. The distance factor can become a significant barrier when shipments move thousands of miles from suppliers to customers. In an environment of reduced cycle times, expected higher levels of reliability, and emphasis on efficiency, the distance factor presents special challenges to supply chain managers.

## Outsourcing

**Outsourcing** is hiring a third party to perform a set of tasks for a fee. Companies have historically and routinely outsourced certain activities, such as janitorial services, records management, or uniform cleaning. The difference today is that companies are outsourcing almost all activities and on a much larger scale.

Increased competitive pressure has forced companies to recognize that they compete through their **core competencies** (sometimes termed "distinctive competencies"). This means that an organization creates superior value for customers by managing their core competencies better than competitors. To be able to focus on core competencies, many companies outsource other activities to those that can do them better. Outsourcing can involve hiring out one aspect of the operation, such as shipping, to outsourcing an entire part of the manufacturing process. The practice has rapidly grown in recent years and has helped companies be more efficient by focusing on what they do best.

## Supply Chain Leader's Box

### ■ WAL-MART

Even some of the most successful companies have encountered difficulties in managing their global supply chains. For example, Wal-Mart encountered large problems when entering the Brazilian market. Wal-Mart quickly found that they needed to adapt product offerings to local tastes, such as replacing footballs with soccer balls and offering deli counter items that included sushi. Changing product lines, however, was the easy part. There were other aspects of Wal-Mart operations that caused greater problems. The logistical aspects of operating in the South American markets have

---

[2]Thomas L. Friedman, *The Lexus and the Olive Tree* (New York: Farrar, Straus and Giroux, 1999), 1–25.

been especially challenging. For example, rapid order fulfillment time is not nearly as easy to accomplish in Brazil as in the United States, where Wal-Mart has easy access to suppliers and transportation companies.

São Paulo is characterized by bumper-to-bumper traffic, which impedes timely delivery and smooth replenishment for Wal-Mart stores. Further, there are occasional mysterious "disappearances" of shipments that create significant delivery problems. Finally, large stores in Brazil have difficulty achieving the economies of scale of their U.S. counterparts. Still, Wal-Mart feels that there is tremendous potential for growth and expansion, and it is confident that it can adjust to be successful.

Adapted from: Friedman, Thomas L. *The Lexus and the Olive Tree.* New York: Farrar, Straus and Giroux, May 1999.

---

The convergence of technologies at the turn of this century has taken the concept of outsourcing to a new level. Massive investments in technology, such as worldwide broadband connectivity, the increasing availability of lower-cost computers, and the development of software such as e-mail, search engines, and other software have allowed individuals to work together in real time from anywhere in the world. The result has been the outsourcing of virtually any job imaginable. Manufacturers have outsourced software development and product design to engineers in India, accounting firms have outsourced tax preparation to India, and even some hospitals have outsourced the reading of CAT scans to doctors in India and Australia.

## Information Technology

An important driver of supply chain management is technology. Technological advances have enabled companies to produce products faster, with better quality, at a lower cost, and this trend will continue. Many processes that were not imaginable only a few years ago have been made possible through the use of information technology.

Advancements in **information technology** have in particular had the greatest impact on SCM. Information technology is technology that enables storage, processing, and communication within and between firms. In fact, information technology can be viewed as an enabler of SCM, as without it coordination between supply chain members would not be possible. The most popular type of information technology, and most familiar to all, is the Internet, which has had the greatest impact on the way companies conduct business. The Internet has linked trading partners—customers, buyers, and suppliers—and has enabled electronic commerce and the virtual marketplace. This is one of the greatest forces that has made information sharing along the supply chain possible.

Another powerful information technology is enterprise software, such as **enterprise resource planning (ERP)**. These are large software programs used for planning and coordinating all resources throughout the entire enterprise. They allow data sharing and communication within and outside the firm, enabling collaborative decision making.

Other examples of information technologies that have impacted the supply chain include **wireless communication technologies**. We are all familiar with cellular phones and pagers from everyday life. However, these technologies can also significantly improve business operations. For example, wireless homing devices and wearable computers are being used in warehouses to quickly guide workers to the locations of goods. This serves to significantly improve warehouse operations and logistics. Wireless technologies, enhanced by satellite transmission, can rapidly transmit information from one source to another. For example, Wal-Mart uses company-owned satellites to automatically transmit point-of-sale data to computers at its warehouses for replenishment.

**Global positioning systems (GPS)** are another type of wireless technology that uses satellite transmissions to communicate exact locations and have dramatically improved logistics transportation. GPS has numerous logistics applications such as in distribution, where trucking companies use GPS technology to identify the exact location of their vehicles.

**Radio frequency identification (RFID)** is yet another wireless technology that is dramatically changing supply chain operations. RFID uses memory chips equipped with tiny radio antennas that can be attached to objects to transmit streams of data about the object. For example, RFID can be used to identify any product movement, reveal a missing product's location, or have a shipment of products "announce" their arrival. Empty store shelves can signal that it is time for replenishment using RFID, or low inventories can signal the vendor that it is time to order more products. In fact, RFID has the potential to become the backbone of logistics, as it can identify and track billions of individual objects all over the world, in real time.

These information technologies collectively provide access to data never before available. This information has changed how products are bought and sold and has changed the modus operandi of the marketplace. Buyers no longer have to go to the seller's place of business to view and buy products. Rather, consumers can complete purchases seven days a week, 24 hours a day. IT has changed how buyers and sellers interact in the marketplace, both **business-to-business (B2B)** and **business-to-consumer (B2C)**.

## Big Data Analytics

**Big data analytics** has had one of the biggest impacts on supply chain management. **Big data** refers to large datasets whose size is so large that the quantity can no longer fit into the memory that computers use for processing. Businesses are awash in data captured from every source imaginable, which can be structured or unstructured. This data includes point-of-sale (POS), radio-frequency identification (RFID), or global positioning systems (GPS) data, or it can be in the form of Twitter feeds, Facebook, call center data, or consumer blogs. This data can be captured, stored, communicated, aggregated, and analyzed. **Analytics** is applying math and statistics to these large datasets. Many of these statistical tools, such as correlation and regression analysis, have been around for decades. What is different is the combination of big data with statistical algorithms—or analytics—fueled by today's computing power. This combination creates the ability to extract meaningful insights and turn information into intelligence. Further, advancements in machine learning and artificial intelligence (AI) have created significant new opportunities to use big data and develop new and more powerful algorithms.

Few areas of business have been transformed by big data analytics as much as supply chain management. Technology has enabled physical objects to be embedded with electronics, such as sensors and software, enabling these objects to collect and exchange data. These objects can be buildings, vehicles, machines, and all other entities that make up the supply chain. The connectivity of these physical objects with electronic devices is called the **Internet of Things (IoT)**. As consumers, we are all accustomed to same-day retail deliveries and the ability to quickly find and purchase items online. However, achieving such high responsiveness requires a data-driven, end-to-end, supply chain system.

## Big Data Analytics Box

### ■ TESCO

Consider the supply chain of Tesco, the British multinational grocery and general merchandise retailer. The company uses its loyalty program to create big data by tracking all sales and linking them to customer information. The data is then mined to inform a variety of decisions, such as best ways to microsegment its customer base, targeting promotions, optimizing product mix, and pricing. Based on data analysis, the company then aligns organizational efforts toward each segment, such as tailoring store formats to particular locations, ranging from convenience stores to online stores. As a result, Tesco can determine exactly what types of customers buy from each store format, determine what products they buy, and ensure availability. These insights are digitally linked to sourcing, transportation, distribution, and all areas of the supply chain. This ensures the supply chain is responding to customer availability of these products when and where customers want them. This is a strategy used by almost all major retailers, from Amazon to Wal-Mart to CVS. This is the **digital supply chain**.

## 3-D Printing, Additive Manufaturing, and Robotics

Research conducted by IBM has identified three emerging and transformative manufacturing technologies: three-dimensional (3-D) printing, a new generation of intelligent assembly robots, and the rise of open-source hardware. Each of these trends taken alone is transformative. However, their power is multiplied when they are combined together with big data analytics.

The first of these trends is **3-D printing** or **additive manufacturing**, a technology that is changing the way manufacturing is being conducted. This technology is similar to ink-jet and laser-jet printers we are familiar with, except that these are three-dimensional printers. These printers work by depositing thick layers of materials one on top of the other, such as layers of plastics and metals. The layering of these materials gradually builds up until the object is produced. The final creation is a solid object from a software design. This process has enabled desktop manufacturing of one object at a time and does not require economies of scale. Additive manufacturing is just an industrial version of 3-D printing. This technology is already being used to make items such as medical implants, and to produce plastic prototypes for engineers and designers. A number of manufacturers, such as General Electric, are already developing plans to implement 3-D printing on a broader scale.

The second of these trends is a new generation of **intelligent assembly robots**. These robots have greater capabilities than in the past, while the cost and installation requirements of these technologies have made them broadly accessible. Unlike past robotic systems that required large complex installations and typically started at around $250,000 per assembly station, the new generation costs a fraction of that price, and can be installed in a day. These advancements have made state-of-the-art automation within reach of even small manufacturing companies.

The third of these trends is **open-source hardware**. In the past, design information for electronic or computer hardware was copyrighted or licensed. Often companies engaged in reverse engineering to learn how the product was made. The new trend in open-source hardware allows electronic and computer hardware design to be made available for use at no charge. This allows sharing of all the information needed to build the product—such as documentation, schematic diagrams, construction details, parts lists, and logic designs. This will significantly accelerate design and creation of new products.

Collectively these trends and technologies are removing the physical constraints historically associated with manufacturing, such as building molds, ordering parts, and reconfiguring assembly machinery. The manufacturing process can now be run through software. Driven by big data analytics, it drives the digital supply chain.

## Postponement

Companies are continually struggling to reach global markets, while providing local customization. Even in a geographically compact area like Europe there are still significant needs for local customization. For example, consider differences in preferences for washing machines in different European countries. The French, for example, prefer top-loading machines, whereas the

British prefer front-loaders. The Germans prefer high-speed spins, but the Italians prefer a lower speed. Similar differences occur with other products, such as soft drinks, requiring the Coca-Cola Corporation to offer many different soft-drink flavors to cater to the unique local tastes. These differences significantly affect SCM.

The challenge for a global company is to achieve the cost advantage of standardization while still catering to local taste. This is essentially mass customization coupled with rapid delivery. One way a company can achieve this is to seek standardized parts, components, and modules, and then, through flexible manufacturing and logistics, provide specific product demands to each market. This is sometimes called **postponement**, where completion of the final product is postponed to the last possible moment until local demands are known with greater certainly. Hewlett-Packard (HP) was known for this in the production and distribution of their printers in the European market. The company completed the manufacture of the product, storing it in a central location, then waited to finalize packaging and specific country/language labeling until local demand was known. Postponement is an important strategy for companies to reach diverse geographic areas while still providing customization.

## The Lean Supply Chain

The lean philosophy has been of great importance in business as it has focused on the elimination of waste and has helped numerous companies become more competitive. The importance of lean thinking has now been extended to the supply chain. It has been recognized that although individual firms can become lean by themselves, waste anywhere in the supply chain is passed on to the customer, and ultimately everyone in the supply chain pays for it. For example, shifting inventories to suppliers is ultimately passed on to the customer in the form of higher cost and makes the entire supply chain less competitive.

The lean supply chain can be defined as the set of all organizations directly linked by upstream and downstream flows of products, services, finances, and information that collaboratively work to reduce cost and waste. As such, a lean supply chain requires all supply chain organizations to work together. It requires a coordinated effort among partners to eliminate waste across the entire supply chain by analyzing processes and identifying areas for improvement.

## Managing Supply Chain Disruptions

SCM and global sourcing have lowered purchase prices and expanded market access. This wide reach, however, has increased the level of supply chain risk. There is an increased risk of product and service flow disruptions and in the magnitude of these disruptions. Supply chain disruptions are a significant corporate crisis and can be very costly. Imagine, for example, a producer of an influenza vaccine suddenly not being able to receive its key ingredients from a supplier during peak flu season. Production may be halted, the company's survival may be of serious concern, and the welfare of customers might be jeopardized.

Managing supply chain risks is challenging because disruptions can occur for a wide variety of reasons. This can include transportation delays; industrial plant fires; work slowdowns or stoppages; natural disasters, such as earthquakes or hurricanes; and man-made disasters, such as the 9/11 terrorist attacks. As companies have increasingly focused on lean operations, they no longer have the inventory or excess capacity to make up for production losses caused by such disruptions. As a result, they are highly vulnerable to even a short material-flow problem. Companies are continuing to look for ways to guard their supply chains against disruptions. Some strategies include having access to backup suppliers, building excess capacity into the system, screening and monitoring suppliers for supply chain risks, requiring suppliers of critical items to develop detailed disruption plans, and including the expected costs of disruptions in the total cost of sourcing.

## Supply Chain Security

Related to supply chain disruption is the study of supply chain security and maintaining product integrity as goods are moved across the globe between borders. Today's strict security initiatives make supply chain relationships much more complex, and the study of ways to protect security while maintaining efficiency is now a key issue. This is particularly critical when dealing with international freight movement. Tighter security and inspection at ports can significantly increase transit time and increase costs. Government regulations aimed at preventing terrorist threats, such as Customs-Trade Partnership Against Terrorism (C-TPAT) and the Container Security Initiative (CSI), require companies to engage in high levels of compliance. Although these measures are necessary, companies are working to find ways to comply while still engaging in outsourcing, offshoring, and global sourcing on a cost-efficient scale.

Other concerns are theft and product tampering. This is especially true for high-valued goods and pharmaceuticals, although anything that has intrinsic value can potentially be stolen. Supply chain security looks at different ways to protect the product, from using electronic seals to prevent tampering, to using RFID and GPS technologies to track product location.

## Sustainability and the "Green" Supply Chain

Environmental concerns, including climate change, energy use, environmental contamination, and resource depletion, are here to stay. Consider that the economies of India and China are growing at double-digit rates, and the population of the world continues to grow, creating shortages of many resources that we used to take for granted. Corporations are increasingly aware that they must design their supply chains for sustainability. This means designing processes to use environmentally friendly inputs and creating outputs that can be recycled and that do not contaminate the environment.

Sources of supply and movement of goods are huge factors in ensuring sustainability. Consider that Starbucks selects and manages their growers to ensure integrity of their environment. Starbucks mandates harvesting practices of their growers that do not damage rainforests.

Other aspects of the supply chain are also important to sustainability, such as packaging and transportation to reduce environmental impacts. Changes such as reducing the amount of cardboard or filler by designing "smart packages" can save companies money. McDonald's has recently introduced new packaging with a pledge to source 100% of all fiber-based packaging from recycled or certified sources by 2020. Coca-Cola has been producing a partially bio-based PlantBottle and is working toward a 100% bio-based PlantBottle, whereas PepsiCo is experimenting with edible packaging. In transportation companies are working to optimize delivery strategies that reduce the carbon footprint. For example, 3M has developed an innovative system to install adjustable decks in trucks, allowing placement of pallets on two levels, thus reducing the number of daily truckloads. Companies are also realizing that these types of measures are not only important to compliance with environmental regulation and consumer demand, but they are also good business practices. Starbucks, for example, realized that by working with growers to protect the environment, they are assured of a consistent and reliable source of supply.

## Innovation

Innovation is increasingly becoming a critical capability for companies across the globe. This can include designing new products that satisfy customer demands, designing new cost-cutting production processes, or coming up with more efficient product delivery mechanisms. For example, consider a pharmaceutical company recently involved in developing the flu vaccine for the recent outbreak of H1N1. Innovation involves identifying the vaccine components and doing clinical trials, as well as production, packaging, and distribution. This must be done efficiently, ensuring the highest security, all the while doing it as expediently as possible to reach the market quickly.

Companies that compete on innovation realize that their entire supply chain must be designed to support their efforts and are designing them accordingly. These chains are typically shorter to reduce time to market. Also, innovative products need greater protection from copying and tampering, and security issues become critical. The role of suppliers is especially important in these supply chains. Suppliers need to be involved early in the product design process to shorten the design time. Also, suppliers are an excellent source of product ideas and process improvements. As competitive pressures increase, continuing to find ways to manage supply chains for innovations will remain an important issue. This means coming up with new ideas and being able to produce and deliver products faster than competitors.

## Managerial Insights Box—Outsourcing Innovation

### ■ GOLDCORP INC.

Goldcorp Inc., one of the world's top gold producers, was facing a big problem a few years ago. Some of its mines were consistently performing below standard, and the mining engineers were at a loss on how to increase production. Finally, Robert McEwen, the CEO of Goldcorp at the time, decided to try an unusual strategy. He decided to offer $575,000 in prize money, with a top award of $105,000, to the person or company that would find a way for Goldcorp to mine more gold.

The challenge, which was broadcast via the Internet, paid off for Goldcorp. Two Australian companies collaborated to come up with a three-dimensional (3-D) depiction of Red Lake mine, which was especially problematic. The 3-D graphical depiction produced a surprise breakthrough in terms of how to approach and mine more gold at the Red Lake facility. With the new process, the mine produced 504,000 ounces at a production cost of $59 an ounce, compared to 53,000 ounces at a production cost of $360 an ounce.

Goldcorp showed that the traditional procurement activity can be used in many different ways, even for innovation. The company had effectively outsourced part of its engineering activity to a supplier. More significantly, this was not one of its preferred or even regular suppliers, but one that they had not known previously. Rather than being found and evaluated by Goldcorp's procurement group in the context of predetermined supplier criteria, the supplier had offered their services in innovation through competitive motivation. Goldcorp had moved beyond seeking innovation from its own staff and even its own "local" suppliers and has shown that sources of innovation can be found anywhere in the supply chain.

Adapted from: Weiss, Madeline and Drewry, June. "Outsourcing in the 21st Century Ambient Organization." *CIO Magazine*, June 14, 2016.

## The Financial Supply Chain

The financial supply chain is intimately tied to SCM, and managing the flow of funds is an essential ingredient for its success. In today's downturned global economy, companies are under greater financial pressures than ever before to cut costs. The result has been a push to redesign entire supply chains and search for less-costly sources of supply. This includes strategies such as global sourcing and production outsourcing, trying to achieve labor cost advantages by pushing operations offshore, and outsourcing noncore activities. As companies send operations offshore, however, there are significant financial implications. These include masked hidden costs, such as managing more expensive plants and equipment in emerging countries. Pushing inventory downstream to suppliers often means higher inventory costs, as these suppliers typically have a higher cost of capital. Also, global operations can wreak havoc on the financial supply chain, as the longer chain has a higher amount tied up in working capital.

Another area of interest for management is the "**cash-to-cash cycle**," which is the time it takes to convert an order into cash. Although management has long recognized the competitive impact of shorter order cycles, it has recently seen the impact the total order process has on working capital. This is another financial supply chain issue that companies are trying to closely manage.

As the supply chain provides a significant cost-cutting opportunity, the trend of managing finances and identifying the risks and challenges of the financial supply chain will continue to be a significant trend in the future.

## Careers in SCM and Professional Organizations

SCM has become an essential competency for corporate executives and managers. According to the Council of Supply Chain Management Professionals (www.cscmp.org), corporate spending on SCM is growing faster than the overall economy, creating tremendous job opportunities for business professionals. As SCM is boundary spanning, it enables business professionals to touch and see every aspect of the product and provides exceptional upward mobility.

There are many routes to success in SCM. The career path can take an individual to many types of organizations, require them to conduct a variety of tasks, and take them to virtually any location in the world, if they so desire. Potential employers range from traditional manufacturers and retailers to service organizations that are increasingly relying on SCM. They also include specialty organizations such as consulting firms and transportation service providers.

Entry-level management positions in SCM can include titles such as Demand Planner, Vendor Management Inventory (VMI) Analyst, or Consultant. Duties may include conducting product evaluation, product planning, generating forecast reports, managing product investment targets, and performing online replenishment. Middle-level management positions include titles such as Sourcing Management, Director of SCM, or Director of Operations. They are responsible for all aspects of product flow and accurate and timely product movement throughout the facility and supply chain. Finally, senior executive positions include VP of SCM or VP of Global Logistics. These are prominent organizational positions that command top salaries. Duties here include managing and optimizing the global supply chain network with multiple distribution centers. The individual is responsible for documenting and executing a global and comprehensive SCM plan that optimizes customer services and profitability.

Careers in SCM abound, offering individuals opportunities in a great variety of positions and providing the chance to have a high impact on the business as a whole.

### CHAPTER HIGHLIGHTS

1. SCM is the design and management of flows of products, information, and funds throughout the supply chain. A supply chain is the network of all entities involved in producing and delivering a finished product to the final customer.

2. The bullwhip effect is the fluctuation and distortion of information as it moves up the supply chain, from retailer, to manufacturer, and to supplier.

3. SCM activities involve coordination, information sharing, and collaboration.

4. Intraorganizational integration is participation and coordination of activities between different organizational functions within the organization.

5. Cross-enterprise integration is the participation and coordination of activities between different organizations that comprise the supply chain.

6. Logistics, in contrast to SCM, consists of the tasks involved in moving and positioning inventory throughout the supply chain.

7. Competitive supply chains are responsive, are reliable, and engage in relationship management with members of the supply chain.

8. Trends that impact today's supply chain include globalization, outsourcing, information technology, big data analytics, 3-D printing, additive manufacturing, robotics, postponement, lean supply chain, supply chain disruptions, security, sustainability or "green" supply chain, innovation, and the financial supply chain.

## KEY TERMS

- Supply chain management (SCM)
- Supply chain
- Value chain
- Value network
- Products
- Information
- Funds
- Bullwhip effect
- Marketing
- Operations
- Sourcing
- Logistics
- Outsourcing
- Core competencies
- Information technology
- Enterprise resource planning (ERP)
- Wireless communication technologies
- Global positioning systems (GPS)
- Radio frequency identification (RFID)
- Business-to-business (B2B)
- Business-to-consumer (B2C)
- Big data analytics
- Big data
- Analytics
- Internet of Things (IoT)
- Digital supply chain
- 3-D printing
- Additive manufacturing
- Intelligent assembly robots
- Open-source hardware
- Postponement
- Cash-to-cash cycle

## DISCUSSION QUESTIONS

1. Identify the primary ways in which SCM has improved the order fulfilment process. What other benefits has SCM provided to businesses?

2. Explain the relationship between SCM and logistics. Identify the differences and similarities. Is one a part of the other? How does one support the other?

3. Identify two competing enterprises and their supply chains (e.g., Dell Computer versus Apple; Amazon versus Wal-Mart; Toyota versus GM; UPS versus FedEx). Identify the elements of each chain from source of supply to final customer, and explain how the two chains are meeting (or not meeting) business objectives. Which supply chain appears longer? Does the structure of one appear simpler than the other?

4. Identify the primary flows in a supply chain. Explain why there is flow in both directions, and provide examples of each.

5. Identify key activities of SCM. Identify other drivers not mentioned in the text.

6. Identify at least three trends that impact SCM. Identify other trends not discussed in the text.

## Case Study: McNulty's Muscular Materials (MMM)

Clayton McNulty, owner of McNulty's Muscular Materials (MMM), is sitting in his dim office located at the top of an old brown brick building, in an industrial area of South Boston. Clayton had just gotten off the phone with Sarah Holden, his longtime friend and sole supplier of his most popular fabric, when his telephone rings again. This call is from John Masterson, his number-one client.

"Clay Buddy," John says. "Just got off the phone with the owner of Southside Sluggers. Guess who got the New Jersey contract? That's right, pal, and I want you to get 'em to me. That'll be 10,000 jerseys, and I need them by the end of the month. How much do you love me, Clay baby? I'll get you the designs by Monday. Ciao."

Clayton hangs up the phone, stares out of his small, double-paned office window and watches the rain slide down the glass. Sure, Clayton was excited about the large bid, but how was he to produce the baseball jerseys in time? The season was to start in three months. The one-month deadline was deadlocked, and there was no room for negotiation. The fans will want the new merchandise before the season gets under way.

MMM was a small sports attire manufacturer that primarily focused on making jerseys for local sports teams. Luckily, the factory had been set up for expansion and was capable of handling a production of this magnitude. But where would he get the needed fabric to produce such a large volume? The most he had ever had to produce was one-tenth of the size that John had just ordered. A big order like this means big publicity, and more orders were sure to start rolling in over the next few months.

A call to Sarah confirms his suspicions. She can't produce that much fabric in such a short amount of time. He needs another supplier, and he needs one fast. It's a rainy day in South Boston, and Clayton McNulty has some tough decisions to make.

*Case Questions*

1. What potential options does Clayton have to procure the needed volume of fabrics to meet the deadline?
2. What are the trade-offs for each of these potential options?
3. What should Clayton do?
4. What lessons can be learned from Clayton's situation?

# REFERENCES

Brody, Paul. "Get Ready for the Software-Defined Supply Chain," *CSCMP's Supply Chain Quarterly*, 4 (2013): 27–30.

Chopra, Sunil, and Peter Meindl. *Supply Chain Management*, 6th edition. Boston: Pearson Education, 2016.

Court, David. "Getting Big Impact from Big Data." *McKinsey Quarterly*, January 2015.

Fisher, Marshall. "What Is the Right Supply Chain for Your Product?" *Harvard Business Review*, March–April 1997: 83–93.

Lee, Hau L. "The Triple-A Supply Chain." *Harvard Business Review*, October 2004: 102–114.

Liker, Jeffrey, and Thomas Choi. "Building Deep Supplier Relationships." *Harvard Business Review*, December 2004: 104–113.

Sinchi-Levi, David. "Finding the Weak Link in Your Supply Chain." *Harvard Business Review*, June 9, 2015.

"The New Software-Defined Supply Chain—Preparing for the Disruptive Transformation of Electronics Design and Manufacturing," *IBM Institute for Business Value*, 2013 (www-935.ibm.com/services/us/gbs/thoughtleadership/software-defined-supply-chain/).

# 2 Supply Chain Strategy

**LEARNING OBJECTIVES**

*After completing this chapter, you should be able to:*

- Define supply chain strategy, and explain how it supports the business strategy.
- Explain how the right supply chain design can create a competitive advantage.
- Identify and explain the building blocks of a supply chain strategy.
- Explain differences in supply chain design based on organizational competitive priorities.
- Explain how productivity can be used to measure competitiveness.

**CHAPTER OUTLINE**

- **What Is Supply Chain Strategy?**
  *Strategic Alignment*
- **Achieving a Competitive Advantage**
  *Cost–Productivity Advantage*
  *Value Advantage*
  *SCM as a Source of Value*
- **Building Blocks of Supply Chain Strategy**
  *Operations Strategy*
  *Distribution Strategy*
  *Sourcing Strategy*
  *Customer Service Strategy*
- **Supply Chain Strategic Design**
  *Competing on Cost*
  *Competing on Time*
  *Competing on Innovation*
  *Competing on Quality*
  *Competing on Service*
  *Why Not Compete on All Dimensions?*

- **Strategic Considerations**
  *Small versus Large Firms*
  *Supply Chain Adaptability*
- **Productivity as a Measure of Competitiveness**
  *Measuring Productivity*
  *Interpreting Productivity*
- **Chapter Highlights**
- **Key Terms**
- **Discussion Questions**
- **Problems**
- **Case Study: Surplus Styles**

---

Walk into a Zara clothing store, whether in New York, Miami, Atlanta, or London, and you experience the feel of high fashion. The ambiance is contemporary, with dim lighting and the beat of modern music pulsating in the background. The clothing styles on the racks capture the latest fashion for men and women, and there is a wide array of choices. Surprisingly, however, the price point is reasonable and much lower than found at any comparable retailer or boutique. This is what makes Zara unique.

Zara is the highly successful Spanish retailer with over 2,000 stores worldwide that launches around 12,000 new fashion designs each year. It is known for its quick design and delivery, and it needs just two weeks to develop a new product and get it to stores, compared with a six-month industry average. Zara has been called a fashion imitator. It focuses on copying the latest fashion items customers want and delivering them at a considerably lower price. Unlike other retailers, it does not advertise and does not promote the season's trends to influence shoppers. To achieve this level of success Zara has a most unusual strategy, and its secret lies in supply chain management (SCM).

Zara is a vertically integrated retailer and controls most of its supply chain, including sourcing, design, production, and distribution. This is highly unusual in an industry that overwhelmingly tends to outsource fashion production to low-cost countries. In fact, whereas most competitors outsource all production to Asia, Zara makes over half of its merchandise at a dozen company-owned factories in Spain and Portugal, where labor is cheaper than in Western Europe. Only items with a longer shelf life, such as basic T-shirts, are outsourced to low-cost suppliers in Asia and Turkey. A large part of this is to support its strategy of offering high-fashion items. To accomplish this, Zara designers are located on the floor of its manufacturing facility to shorten production time, and they have weekly talks with store managers across the globe to find out what customers want.

Borrowing best practices from the Toyota Motor Corporation, Zara has a very efficient and lean production process. Zara carries little inventory of expensive items. However, to give itself flexibility and offer a wide product assortment, Zara carries excess inventories of inexpensive items. This includes buttons and zippers, which Zara's designers can use to create differences in clothing items. As a result, Zara can offer considerably greater product variety than its competitors. Also, Zara has an extremely quick design turnover compared to competitors. New designs are developed daily—sometimes three to four a day—and quickly put into production. This short production cycle means greater success in meeting consumer preferences. If a design doesn't sell well within a week, it is withdrawn from shops, further orders are canceled, and a new design is pursued. No design stays on the shop floor for more than four weeks, which encourages Zara's shoppers to make repeat visits. Customers know that end-of-season markdowns, so common in the retail industry, do not occur at Zara, so they feel a greater need to buy the item they have in hand.

Zara uses its supply chain strategy as a competitive weapon. For Zara, this has proved to be a very successful decision.

Adapted from: Loeb, Walter. "Zara Leads in Fast Fashion." *Forbes*, March 30, 2015.

## What Is Supply Chain Strategy?

A company must have a long-range business strategy if it is going to maintain a competitive position in the marketplace. A **business strategy** is a plan for the company that clearly defines the company's long-term goals, how it plans to achieve these goals, and the way the company plans to differentiate itself from its competitors. A business strategy should leverage the company's core competencies, or strengths, and carefully consider the characteristics of the marketplace.

**Supply chain strategy** is a long-range plan for the design and ongoing management of all supply chain decisions that support the business strategy. Consider that the design of a supply chain should differ based on how the company intends to compete in the marketplace. To maintain competitiveness, companies must design their supply chains to be aligned with their business strategy, to satisfy the needs of the customers, take advantage of the company's strengths, and remain adaptive. This relationship between the business strategy and the supply chain strategy is shown in Figure 2.1.

Consider the case of Zara, discussed in the chapter opener. Zara's business strategy is to produce and deliver look-alikes of the latest fashion trends to customers at an affordable price. Zara understands that the key to accomplishing this is through a well-thought-out supply chain strategy designed to support its goals. For this reason the company chooses to be vertically integrated, giving it speed, flexibility, and control of product design and delivery. Also, the company chooses not to outsource most of its production, as doing so would hurt Zara's ability to quickly adapt to fashion trends. As we can see, Zara's supply chain strategy is designed to enable the company to achieve the goals set by its business strategy.

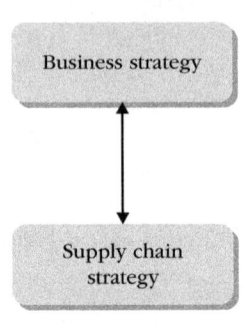

**FIGURE 2.1** Supply chain and business strategies are aligned.

## Strategic Alignment

It is important to remember that there must be strategic alignment between the business strategy and supply chain strategy. A company's supply chain strategy should be developed to drive and support its business strategy. Consider an electronics company that has formulated a business strategy to compete on delivery excellence, such as order-fulfillment time. As a result, the supply chain strategy may be designed for speed of delivery, although perhaps at a higher cost. Now imagine that the company decides to change its business strategy to compete on cost rather than delivery, considering current market competition and customer perceptions of value. If this change in business strategy is not communicated to SCM, the supply chain will continues to focus on delivery rather than cost. The company will continue to excel at delivery, while incurring a higher cost, and not meeting the business goals set for the company.

The supply chain should not be designed to merely mimic its competitors or solely focus on cost-cutting efforts. The supply chain should be designed and positioned to support the strategic direction of the firm, giving it a competitive advantage in the marketplace. As we will see later in this chapter, supply chains can have a very different design based on their competitive focus. Today's most successful companies, as illustrated by Zara, have achieved world-class status in large part due to a skillfully designed supply chain strategy that is manifested in the design of its supply chain. Companies all over the globe understand that they cannot achieve the competitiveness needed to survive and thrive in the current global economy without strategically thinking about their supply chains.

In addition to SCM, all organizational functions should be designed to support the business strategy. This includes marketing, operations, distribution, purchasing, and even finance. In addition, the organizational functions should support each other. This functional support is especially important for SCM given its boundary-spanning nature and high dependence on logistics, marketing, and operations. This functional unity and support of the business strategy will enable the organization to function in a synchronized manner.

# Achieving a Competitive Advantage

Given the highly competitive environment of today's marketplace, seeking a sustainable competitive advantage has become a top business concern. Unlike in the past, where creative marketing initiatives were sufficient to promote products, today's marketplace requires a higher level of strategic positioning. In this section we will look at how a well-designed supply chain can provide companies with needed competitive advantage.

To understand supply chain competitiveness, let us look at the concept of competitive advantage. At the most basic level, corporate success in the marketplace can result from two aspects. The first is a **cost or productivity advantage**; the second is a **value advantage**. In the first case, advantage comes from offering the lowest-cost product or service. In the second case, the advantage comes from providing a product with the greatest perceived differential value compared with its competitors. In the ideal situation a company would have both a cost and a value advantage. These two basic advantages provide a basis of strategy and competitive positioning. We now look at these strategic dimensions in more detail.

## Cost–Productivity Advantage

Every marketplace typically has one competitor who is the low-cost producer and who has the greatest sales volume in the particular market. Consider Wal-Mart, which competes on cost and, as a result, is a leader in sales volume in the retail market. In fact, there is much evidence to suggest that a large volume can contribute greatly to a cost advantage. One factor contributing to this are economies of scale that enable the company to spread its fixed costs over a greater volume.

Another factor contributing to this is the impact of the **experience curve**—derived from the traditional concept of the learning curve. The learning curve tells us that with experience workers become more skilled in processes and tasks and do them more efficiently. The same is true of organizations. Organizational costs are reduced due to experience and learning effects that result from processing a higher volume. This is the experience curve, which describes the relationship between unit costs and cumulative volume, where the cost per unit of a product decreases with increased volume.

Based on the experience curve, it has been assumed that the only way to gain cost reductions, and compete on a cost–productivity advantage, is to increase sales volume. Although this is one way to achieve a cost advantage, another way is through an efficient supply chain network. The reason is that an efficient supply chain network can increase efficiency and improve productivity, thereby reducing overall cost per unit.

## Value Advantage

Consider that customers do not buy products but rather the benefits or value provided by those products. Therefore, there may be multiple products that provide customer value. Also, it is not just the stand-alone product that is the ultimate customer's desire, but many intangible benefits a product offers. For example, customers will often buy a product for its image and reputation rather than pure functionality. On the other hand, a product may be purchased due to performance value that it offers over its competitors and rivals.

### Supply Chain Leader's Box

#### ■ WAL-MART

Sam Walton was a strategic supply chain visionary who developed the low-cost responsive retail strategy. This was supported by a supply chain strategy of not buying from distributors, but rather directly from manufacturers of a broad range of merchandise. In fact, Wal-Mart's legendary partnership with Procter & Gamble (P&G), where replenishment of inventories is done automatically, illustrated to other companies the power of integrating with key suppliers. Wal-Mart extended this type of relationship to other suppliers, letting suppliers manage their own inventories at Wal-Mart's warehouses, a system called **Vendor Managed Inventory (VMI)**. These supply chain actions were designed to help Wal-Mart meet its overall competitive strategy, which is to provide its customers with a wide product offering at a low price.

Wal-Mart has continued this strategy by using technology, such as RFID, to cut inventory costs and maintain its cost position. Today the company continues to invest in emerging technologies, having created an end-to-end digital supply chain. It is for these reasons that Wal-Mart has held a place among Gartner's top 25 supply chains for half a decade.

An important competitive advantage for companies is to distinguish their products or services in some way from their competitors. Otherwise, their products will be seen as a commodity. When a product is viewed as a commodity, it is typically bought on the spot market for the lowest price. Therefore, it is important for companies to add value to the products and services they offer that differentiate them from their competitors.

## Achieving a Competitive Advantage

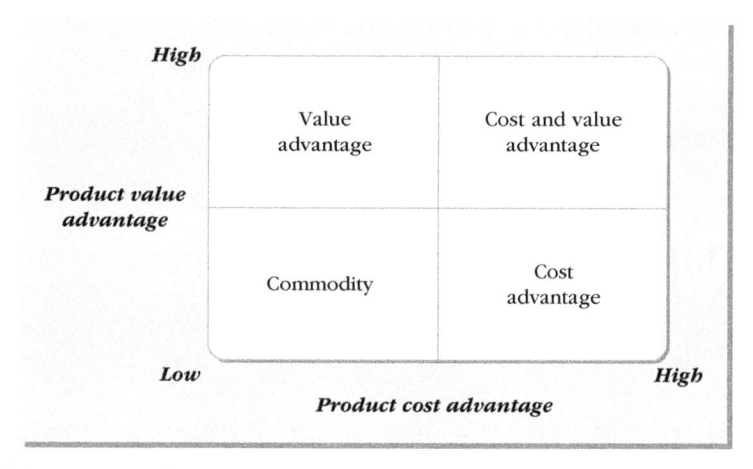

**FIGURE 2.2** Competitive advantage matrix.

Let's look at some of the ways by which companies can gain a value advantage. One way is by segmenting the market and identifying "**value segments**" in the marketplace. This means that different customer groups place value on different product benefits. This analysis permits the company to see which market segments place value on what product features. It may then be possible to create a differential appeal tailored to different segments. For example, auto manufacturers create different versions of the same vehicle to compete in different market segments, such as a basic two-door model versus the four-door, high-performance model. These options enable the manufacturer to satisfy the value of different market segments.

In addition to the product itself, companies are increasingly focusing on service as a way to add value. In fact, competition based on technology and product alone is becoming increasingly difficult. One reason for this is that technology and best production practices are becoming more of a commodity. Service is one dimension that is more difficult to replicate. This is creating a new way for companies to seek differentiation and a competitive advantage. Service addresses issues such as developing relationships with customers, delivery, after-sales support, financial packages, technical support, maintenance, and other similar services.

Companies can gain competitiveness either through a cost–productivity advantage or a value advantage. In practice, however, some of the most successful companies are those that position themselves based on both. This is shown in Figure 2.2. Let's now discuss the options provided to companies by this matrix.

The least desirable place for a company to be on the matrix shown in Figure 2.2 is in the "commodity" section, namely the bottom left-hand corner. The reason is that here the company has not differentiated its product from that of its competitors. The result is having to sell the product at the lowest possible price. For companies to remain competitive, they usually try to move to a more desirable competitive position. One option is to move to a position of cost leadership. Another is to move toward value leadership. The ideal position, however, is at the top right-hand corner, where a company has competitive positioning along both cost and value dimensions.

## SCM as a Source of Value

SCM provides a powerful way for companies to achieve a cost–value advantage over their competitors. For example, improvements in the supply chain can dramatically reduce inventory, distribution, and coordination costs. This is a highly effective way to move up the quadrant to a position of cost–value leadership. In later chapters of this text, we will look at specific ways that companies can achieve this, such as developing a lean supply chain and implementing Six Sigma quality.

## Global Insights Box

### ■ TOYOTA MOTOR CORPORATION

The Toyota Motor Corporation is a leader in the auto industry and a model of strategic supply chain design. The company has experienced unparalleled growth over the last two decades. Toyota understands that it must have an effective global supply chain strategy to continue this level of success. This has involved building superior strategic alliances with its suppliers, designing an agile global distribution network, and positioning production facilities strategically. To have a highly responsive supply chain, Toyota's strategy has been to open factories in every market it serves. An important element of this decision was the production capability at each plant. Prior to 1996, Toyota used a supply chain strategy where every plant was specialized and capable of supplying only local production. Since the early 2000s, however, Toyota redesigned its network for plants to be more flexible and to supply multiple markets, enabling it to easily shift production from one market to another as needed. This strategy has continued, relying on analytics to optimize these decisions, and has enabled Toyota to remain agile.

---

Another way that firms can move to a cost-leadership position is to develop strategic differentiation based on service excellence. Therefore, the "good" itself remains a commodity, but the total product package is now differentiated from other customers. This is a good strategy, as today's customers demand greater responsiveness and reliability from their suppliers. Customers want shorter lead times, just-in-time deliveries, and services that help them do a better job of serving their own customers. SCM can provide this type of advantage.

Yet another option is through the introduction of new supply chain technologies. Such technologies can provide an opportunity for a company to lower its cost over competitors. Such has been the case with Wal-Mart, as we discussed earlier. However, this option is typically available to competitors as well, particularly in today's marketplace, where information travels rapidly. Still, this strategy may preempt competition if the company uses the technology in a way that provides greater customer value.

## Building Blocks of Supply Chain Strategy

Strategic SCM involves designing a supply chain that is uniquely configured to meet the company's overall business strategy. This is especially challenging given the boundary-spanning nature of SCM. Consequently, the development of a supply chain strategy involves consideration of each of the traditional business functions and their impact on the supply chain. These are the building blocks of a supply chain strategy and include the following:

- Operations strategy
- Distribution strategy
- Sourcing strategy
- Customer service strategy

Historically, companies tended to either make decisions regarding each of the preceding functions informally or make decisions about them in isolation from each other. As we mentioned

Building Blocks of Supply Chain Strategy

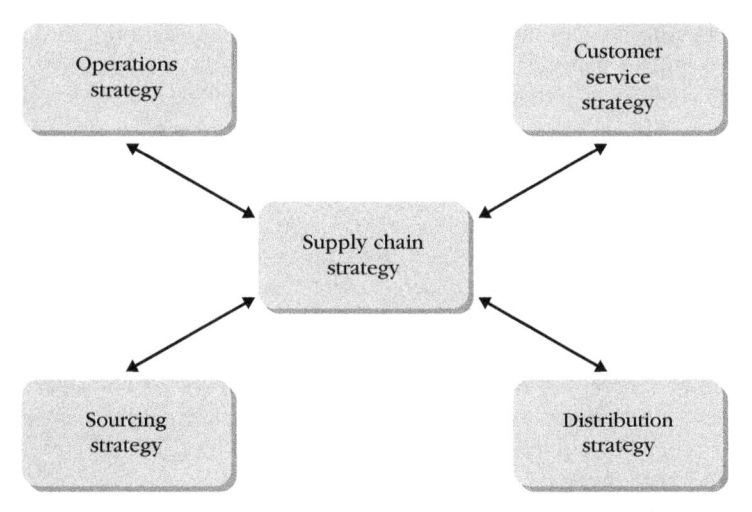

**FIGURE 2.3** The building blocks of supply chain strategy.

earlier, successful companies understand that organizational functions are interdependent. For example, marketing cannot sell products that operations cannot make and vice versa. Supply chain strategy is directly impacted by the decisions of the four building blocks and how they are used to support the business. This is shown in the diagram in Figure 2.3. Let's now look at these individual building blocks and how they impact the development of the supply chain strategy.

## Operations Strategy

The **operations strategy** of a company involves decisions about how it will produce goods and services. The operations strategy determines the design and management of a company's manufacturing process, the design of internal processes, use of equipment and information technology, as well as the types of employee skills needed.

One of the most important aspects of operations strategy is the degree of product customization it offers, called the **product positioning strategy**. This decision directly relates to the form in which the company stores its finished products and the length of delivery lead time it can provide to its customers. There are three options in this area:

- Make-to-stock
- Assemble-to-order
- Make-to-order

**Make-to-stock** is a strategy that produces finished products for immediate sale or delivery, in anticipation of demand. Companies using this strategy produce a standardized product in large volumes. Typically this strategy is seen in assembly line type operations. Delivery lead time is shortest with this strategy, but the customer has no involvement in product design. This is the best strategy for standardized products that sell in high volume. The production system is set up to produce large production batches that keep manufacturing costs down, and having finished products in inventory means that customer demand can be met quickly. Examples include off-the-shelf retail clothing, soft drinks, standard automotive parts, or airline flights. A hamburger patty at a fast-food restaurant such as McDonald's is made-to-stock. Customers gain speed of delivery with this strategy, but lose the ability to customize the product.

**Assemble-to-order** strategy, also known as built-to-order, is where the product is partially completed and kept in a generic form, then finished when an order is received. The inventory that the company holds is that of standard components that can be combined to customer specifications. Delivery time is longer than in the make-to-stock strategy, but allows for some customization. This is the preferred strategy when there are many variations of the end product and the company wants to achieve low finished-goods inventory and shorter customer lead times than make-to-order can deliver. Examples include computer systems, prefabricated furniture with choices of fabric colors, or vacation packages with standard options.

**Make-to-order** is a strategy for customized products or products with infrequent demand. It is used to produce products to customer specifications after an order has been received. The delivery system is longest with this strategy, and product volumes are low. Examples are custom-made clothing, custom-built homes, and customized professional services. Companies following this strategy produce a final product only when a firm order has been received. This keeps inventory levels low while allowing for a wide range of product options. The differences in the three strategies are illustrated in Figure 2.4.

Changing the company's operations strategy from one type to another can be a source of competitive advantage. It may not be possible, however, to move from one extreme position to another, such as from make-to-order to make-to-stock. In that case a company would be completely changing its product offering. One option might be to occupy a position of middle ground, such as in an assemble-to-order strategy.

For example, moving from make-to-stock to assemble-to-order can serve to improve customer service while reducing inventory. The reason is that in a make-to-stock strategy inventories of all finished goods are carried in stock. This may result in there being too much of one type of inventory and not enough of another. An assemble-to-stock strategy can result in storage of considerably lower amounts of inventory, primarily held in a generic form. The final assembly can then take place when demand for specific products is known with greater certainty.

**I. Make-to-stock strategy**

Processing → Assembly → Inventory stock → Shipping

*Delivery lead time* (from Inventory stock to Shipping)

**II. Assemble-to-order strategy**

Processing → Inventory stock → Assembly → Shipping

*Delivery lead time* (from Inventory stock to Shipping)

**III. Make-to-order strategy**

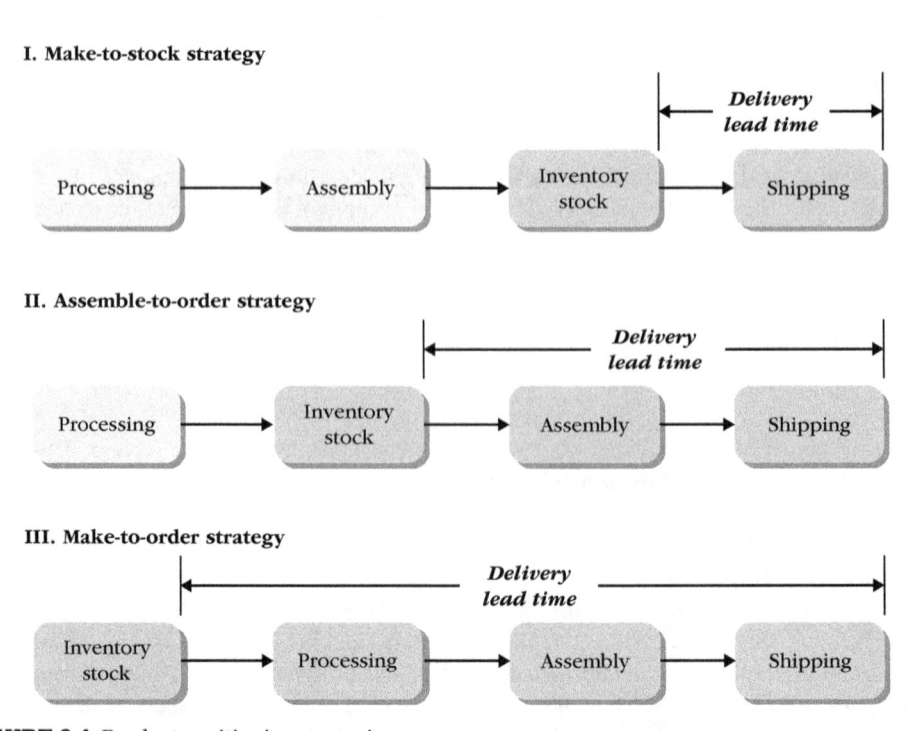

Inventory stock → Processing → Assembly → Shipping

*Delivery lead time* (from Inventory stock to Shipping)

**FIGURE 2.4** Product positioning strategies.

In some industries, however, it may be difficult to pursue any strategy other than make-to-stock, given high manufacturing costs. For example, automobile manufacturers have historically used a make-to-stock strategy, though some have moved to assemble-to-order, particularly in the high-end European market. The problem with an assemble-to-order strategy in this market is that there are potentially a countless number of end-product configurations. Trying to satisfy the many different product variations makes it difficult to maintain a competitive lead time. One way to accomplish this is to have suppliers fully integrated into the production process. In addition, it is highly expensive to incur the cost of changing the manufacturing process (called "setup") so that unique characteristics can be produced. The easiest alternative is to have limited product options, as has been done by most automakers. Otherwise, manufacturing costs become prohibitive.

Operations strategy, like any strategy, is a dynamic process rather than a static one-time decision. It is also highly related to the product life cycle. In the early stages of a product life cycle, demand for a product is uncertain, and companies are better off with a make-to-order strategy as key product attributes are still unknown. As the product moves through its life cycle, companies often move from a make-to-order to an assemble-to-order to reduce inventories while making sure that there is product availability at a competitive price. Products in the mature stage of their life cycles tend to be produced by manufacturing processes that are designed for make-to-stock. The reason is that in the mature stage of its life cycle a product's market is predictable in both its demand and volume. Consequently, the operations strategy needs to change with the product as the product moves through the different life-cycle changes.

## Distribution Strategy

A company's **distribution strategy** is about how it plans to get its products and services to customers. An important decision here is whether the company is going to sell directly to customers, such as using the Internet or a direct sales force, or indirectly through distributors or retailers (channel intermediaries). This type of direct-to-customer strategy is the model historically used by Dell. However, in 2009, Michael Dell announced that Dell Computer Corporation would be changing its distribution strategy to sell through retailers such as Best Buy. This change in Dell's distribution strategy was in response to changing markets and shows the importance of this strategy for competitiveness.

The selection and development of a distribution strategy requires doing market segmentation, analyzing the perceived value of each segment, as well as the competition and profitability of each segment. The best distribution strategy varies depending on which market segment the company is trying to reach. Consequently, it is best to use a mix of distribution strategies that vary by market segment and target a particular market. Market segmentation is also valuable to determine which segments should be first to receive the product in situations of product shortages. In Chapter 4 we will discuss market segmentation and implications on SCM in more detail.

A good example of how market segmentation can be used to select different types of distribution strategies is illustrated by the bottled water industry. Most companies in the industry have two markets. One is spring water and the other is distilled water. Spring water is collected and bottled on-site, whereas distilled water can be bottled at any one of many water sources using any local bottling company. Companies in this industry use two different distribution methods to serve their customer segments. The first strategy is using traditional retail distributors who serve the retail customers, and the second is direct to customer, where the water is replenished on-site at either the customer's home or office. Further, the two distribution channels have different versions depending on which market segment they serve. To satisfy each segment, the supply chain uses different processes and assets and has different relationships.

A new entrant in the bottled water industry would have to make some important decisions. First, the company might have to decide whether it wants to sell to distributors who probably have a good relationship with the retailers, or sell directly to the retailers. If a company chooses to use distributors, it will have to make decisions such as whether to purchase an integrated order management system such as that of the distributor. Also, it may have to decide which distributors will be the company's strategic partners and for which the company may be willing to carry extra inventory. These decisions should not be made in isolation, but in concert with the overall business strategy, as they could have a profound impact on profitability and efficiency of the supply chain.

## Sourcing Strategy

**Sourcing strategy** relates to which of a company's business it is going to outsource versus the ones it will retain internally. This includes decisions regarding supplies and component parts, as some companies choose to make these themselves. This decision has great bearing on supply chain strategy, as it directly imposes a particular aspect of the supply chain structure—relationships with outside entities.

The process of developing a sourcing strategy typically begins with a company analyzing its existing supply chain skills and expertise. The company has to identify what areas it is really good at and what areas of its expertise have the potential to become strategic differentiators. These activities have to be kept in-house and made even better. On the other hand, activities with low strategic importance that can be performed by another company are good options for outsourcing.

Outsourcing means that a company has hired a third party or a vendor to perform certain tasks or activities for a fee. This could range from the mundane, such as outsourcing proofing of legal documents or outsourcing the management of unimportant inventory items, to the outsourcing of the entire manufacturing process of even the entire management of the supply chain.

Outsourcing enables companies to quickly respond to changes in demand and enables them to quickly build new products or gain a competitive position in the marketplace. Through outsourcing, a company can leverage another company's capacity and its expertise. This provides a tremendous amount of flexibility that is necessary in today's marketplace, which demands high specialization, despite the fact that no company can do everything well. In fact, that is a very important realization for companies—the fact that they cannot effectively do all tasks well and may need to turn to vendors for help. Outsourcing something like communication network management to a company that is a leader in that area can provide an advantage. Outsourcing, most important, allows a company to focus on their core competencies. The famed management guru Tom Peters was known for saying: "Do what you do best, and outsource the rest!"

Outsourcing used to be considered by managers as a simple make or buy decision, where they considered the cheapest alternative. Today, however, managers understand that sourcing is a strategic decision. It may be more expensive to purchase the expertise of an outside vendor, but it may prove to be more time-saving and lucrative in the long run. Before making the final decision, however, companies need to fully consider the risks associated with outsourcing. Whenever control over a task is placed in the hands of a third party there is a risk of loss of control. The more important the outsourced task, or the more strategic in nature it is, the greater the risk. The introduction of new products and ensuring that the configuration of the supply chain supports the competitive lead times are activities that typically should not be delegated to a third party.

Other considerations related to outsourcing are whether the skills or activities that are being outsourced are going to continue to be maintained internally. This is an important decision as, on the one hand, a company may not want to duplicate what is already being outsourced. On the other hand, a company may choose not to eliminate the activity internally as it may completely lose the capability, and it may find that it is completely dependent on the vendor. Some years ago a divestiture of an outsourcing agreement occurred between AT&T and Bank One. AT&T

was responsible for all of the bank's information technology needs. However, Bank One decided that even though IT was not its core competency, it was a highly important capability, given that it directly supports the bank's core competency. Consequently, it brought the function back in-house.

Outsourcing tasks or functions to third parties can provide a significant competitive advantage. The first advantage is cost, as a third party may be able to offer products or services at a lower price. The reason is that they have reached economies of scale in their production systems for producing this type of product or service. Another advantage is that it enables a company to expand its offering into new markets or geographic areas through outsourcing partners that have reach in those areas. For many companies this type of access might not be possible if it were not for outsourcing. Finally, outsourcing may help companies achieve state-of-the art technological capability virtually overnight, which would not be possible otherwise. In fact, for many companies it requires a significant financial investment to develop these capabilities internally, and they simply may not have the resources to keep up. Outsourcing enables a company to take advantage of this expertise from another firm.

All outsourcing engagements, however, entail certain risks that companies need to consider when making the outsourcing decision. In general, more sophisticated sourcing engagements bring greater benefits, but also involve significantly higher risks. A number of risk factors need to be considered before a firm passes responsibility to external vendors.

One risk to consider is the risk of **loss of control**. As the scope of the task passed to the vendor increases, the ability to retain control of the task or function decreases. The purpose of outsourcing is to tap into the talent and unique capability of the vendor. However, unless very specific outcome expectations are set up, the final outcome may not meet expectations. Identifying key performance metrics and their values is a challenge, particularly for service types of tasks, where the final "product" is intangible and often difficult to quantify. For small firms this can be particularly damaging as internal processes are less insulated from disruption.

Another risk to consider is **dependency risk**. As a firm engages in more sophisticated sourcing engagements, it often tailors and adapts its operations to match those of its vendor. By doing so, the firm may benefit by taking advantage of the vendor's economies of scale. This is particularly true in cases that require specialized technology and equipment and specialized training of staff. However, these arrangements create a risk that the firm will become overly dependent on the vendor. This can have short-term problems, such as lack of performance on the part of the vendor that disrupts operations. It can also have strategic consequences, as the firm's future direction is tied to that of the vendor. The decision of whether to outsource should be based on the interdependence of the outsourced function with other internal processes. Companies should not outsource such highly integrated functions, particularly when high adaptation with the vendor or supplier is required.

As you can see, outsourcing isn't always the right decision. Before turning to outside vendors, a company should always be clear on its source of competitive advantage and not outsource that aspect of its operation. Interestingly, for a number of companies, manufacturing is not seen as a strategic function, and they choose to outsource it. Examples of this are provided by Cisco in the electronics industry and Nike in footwear. These companies outsource all aspects of manufacturing. Almost all industries, however, use third-party logistics providers for delivery, transportation, warehousing, and other logistics services. In fact, the role of third-party logistics providers has been increasing to include activities such as final packaging, software loading, and even final assembly.

## Customer Service Strategy

Customer service is extremely important, as it is about bringing value to the customer. Consequently, the mechanism by which this is achieved is a key building block of SCM strategy. The customer service strategy of a company should be based first on the overall volume and

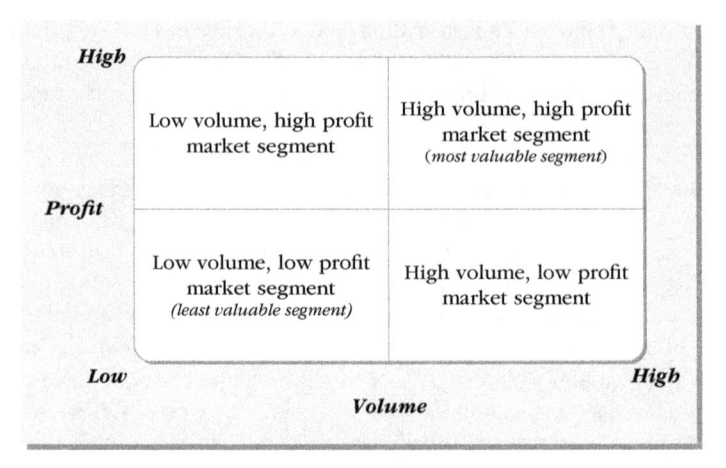

**FIGURE 2.5** Market segmentation based on volume and profitability.

profitability of market segments. The company then must understand what the customers in each segment want and make a decision on how the company is going to meet the demands of its customers. Typically this requires dividing the market by volume and profitability. This is shown in Figure 2.5.

## Managerial Insights Box—Outsourcing Alliances

### ■ LI & FUNG LTD.

Strategic alliances are not static but evolve over time as the company's strategy changes. In early 2010, Wal-Mart announced that they were forming a strategic alliance with Li & Fung Ltd., a supply chain giant based out of Hong Kong. Li & Fung is known as an intermediary between retailers and manufacturers, especially those wishing to do business in China. Founded in southern China a century ago, Li & Fung does not own any factories or equipment but orchestrates a network of 12,000 suppliers in 40 countries. It sources goods for numerous retailers including The Limited, Walt Disney, Kate Spade, and Target Corporation. In 2008, Li & Fung had a turnover of $14 billion, indicating the sheer volume of their business. So, what benefit could Wal-Mart gain from the alliance?

The alliance provided benefits to both companies, each taking advantage of the other's strength. Wal-Mart benefited by consolidating a part of its multibillion-dollar sourcing portfolio that supplies the goods it sells in stores. In addition, Wal-Mart had access to all of Li & Fung's global connections and was able to leverage its huge purchasing power. In turn, Li & Fung was able to expand beyond its core sourcing operations and move into higher-margin businesses such as retailing and brand licensing. In addition, the alliance with the retail giant significantly contributed to its financial position.

In 2015, however, Wal-Mart decided to bring back 'in-house' some of the product sourcing that had been handled by Li & Fung. With the changing business environment Wal-Mart was under financial pressure to squeeze out costs from its supply chain, and outsourcing costs needed to be reduced. Wal-Mart decided to modify its relationship with Li & Fung by choosing to handle some product sourcing internally while keeping Li & Fung to handle purchases for its Sam's Club stores.

Entering into such an alliance demonstrates that Wal-Mart understands its sourcing strategy and that using an "expert" to source on a large global scale can make good business sense when needed. This not only is an excellent example of advantages that outsourcing alliances can provide but also shows that these relationships change with a company's strategy.

Adapted from: "Wal-Mart to Bring In-House Some Sourcing Handled by Li & Fung." May 22, 2015. www.reuters.com.

Some market segments will be small in volume and low in profit, and pursuing them may not be worthwhile. At the other extreme are market segments that are high in volume and profitability, which are highly desirable. The other two segments, low volume, high profit and high profit, low volume, are segments the company needs to closely evaluate and make a decision that prioritizes resources giving priority to the top right-hand quadrant.

In developing a customer service strategy, companies need to make decisions such as whether all customers need to get same-day delivery or whether different service levels should be designed depending on the importance of the customer. A related decision is whether all products should be equally available to all customers. A company may decide that some customers should have quicker access than others. For example, Delta Airlines, as most airlines, has two separate customer service lines: one for regular customers and one for "platinum" customers. Although the transactions received are the same on both lines, customers that call on the "platinum" line absolutely never have to wait for a customer service representative and receive more prompt service overall.

It is important to keep in mind that not all customers need, or even want, the same level of service. Therefore, it is critical for a company to know exactly which customers want which type of service and identify the high-value customers. For example, in the computer industry many commercial customers may not care as much about price as they do about customer service help support that provides rapid problem resolution. In the personal computer market, however, customers care more about price. A good strategy here is to segment the market and provide different service help support for the different market segments. High customer service is costly, and it should not be wasted on market segments that do not place value on it.

This means that companies need to segment the market carefully and consider how to effectively meet demands of those segments. The implications for supply chain management strategy is that there may be different supply chains for different market segments.

## Supply Chain Strategic Design

Companies often do not give much thought to the design of their supply chains. They often focus on cost reduction through low-cost purchasing, manufacturing, or logistics. This can translate into supply chains that do not necessarily support the overall business strategy. In the previous section we discussed the building blocks of supply chain strategy. We now address the strategic design of the supply chain and the overriding criteria that must drive its development.

The way a company competes in the marketplace is called a **competitive priority**. Supply chain strategy and supply chain design greatly depend on a company's competitive priorities. The companies that follow this process—companies like Amazon, Wal-Mart, Toyota, Nike, McDonald's, and IBM—have been very successful. Unfortunately, too many companies just mimic others in their industry and create supply chains that look just like that of their competitors. This does not lead to a strong competitive advantage—it simply leads to being a follower in one's industry.

There are five primary competitive priorities:

1. Cost
2. Time
3. Innovation
4. Quality
5. Service

Let's look at each of these competitive priorities and show how each results in differing strategic supply chain designs.

## Competing on Cost

If the company's business strategy is to compete on cost, then the supply chain strategy must be designed to support this. Companies that compete on cost offer products at the lowest price possible. These companies are either maintaining market share in a commodity market, or they are offering low prices to attract cost-sensitive buyers. Once a company's business strategy has determined that the company will compete on cost, the other functional strategies—including the supply chain strategy—should be designed to support this.

For example, competing on cost requires highly efficient, integrated operations that have cut costs out of the system. The supply chain plays a critical role in keeping both product and supply chain costs down. It may also require going to the least-expensive suppliers rather than focusing on high-quality components. The low-cost supply chain focuses on meeting efficiency-based metrics such as asset utilization, inventory days of supply, product costs, and total supply chain costs. The operation strategy is designed for product and process standardization, as are operations of the suppliers. Notice that the supply chain design would be different had the chosen business strategy focused on something else, such as competing on customization. In that case, cost would be less of an issue as would be the ability to provide a wide range of customized products.

Although Dell Computer Corporation has been a model of supply chain excellence, Dell does not compete on cost. In fact, Dell does not claim to offer the least expensive computers, but merely customized computers in record time. That is the major difference. Dell's computer prices are within the industry range. This is unlike Wal-Mart, which promises the lowest prices but not special customized products. The important thing is that each company's supply chain is designed to support the chosen business strategy.

Although efficiency and low cost are hallmarks of excellence, they cannot be achieved at the expense of service, innovation, or quality, if one of these is an element of the business strategy. An example of this is the apparel industry, where manufacturers typically outsource production to Southeast Asia. The manufacturers insist on fixed production schedules to keep their costs low. This, however, impacts their flexibility and can hurt retailers when demands unexpectedly shift, such as when there is an unexpected surge of demand. This limits retailers in their ability to respond to demand. For many retailers, being out of stock on a regular basis can play havoc with customers and erode market share. Focusing on price alone, without considering other aspects of the business strategy, may result in a poor supply chain strategy.

## Competing on Time

Time is one of the most important ways companies compete today. Companies in all industries are competing to deliver high-quality products in as short a time as possible. Amazon, FedEx, LensCrafters, and United Parcel Service (UPS) are all examples of companies that compete on time. Customers today are increasingly demanding short lead times and are not willing to wait for products and services. Companies that can meet needs of customers who want fast service are becoming leaders in their respective industries.

Making time a competitive priority means competing based on all time-related dimensions, such as rapid delivery and on-time delivery. Rapid delivery refers to how quickly an order is received; on-time delivery refers to the number of times deliveries are made on time. When time is a competitive priority, the job of the operations function is to critically analyze the system and combine or eliminate processes to save time. Companies can use technology to speed up processes or they can rely on flexible workforce to meet peak demand periods and eliminate unnecessary steps in the production process.

FedEx is an example of a company that has chosen to compete on time. The company's slogan is that it will "absolutely, positively" deliver packages on time. To support this business strategy, the entire supply chain has been set up to support this criteria. Bar code technology is used to speed up processing and handling, and the company has discovered that it can provide faster service by using its own fleet of airplanes. This technology has enabled FedEx to compete on time, but it is costly. Consequently, FedEx neither competes on cost nor does it make any claims regarding its prices. Its business strategy is to compete on time, and all the other functions are aligned to support this strategy.

## Competing on Innovation

Companies whose primary strategy is innovation focus on developing products that the customers perceive as "must-haves" and thereby pull the product through the supply chain with significant demand. Examples of such companies include Sony and Nike—companies that deliver innovative products customers want. Due to the "must-have" nature of these products, these companies can typically command a premium price, which is to their advantage because competing on innovation requires a sizable financial commitment. In addition to the supply chain capability, the real ability to compete on this dimension lies in superior marketing and product development, which is directly related to the supply chain.

Companies that compete on innovation typically have a very short window of opportunity before the imitators enter the market and begin to steal market share. Companies competing on innovation are aware that they must enter the market early with an innovative design. The supply chains of these companies typically focus on two features: speed and product design. This requires a carefully integrated supply chain that enables collaboration on product design between suppliers and manufacturers. Manufacturers with this type of supply chain have to have both internal integration between functions and integration externally with suppliers.

Another challenge for innovative supply chains is the ability to quickly raise production volumes should demand suddenly increase. An innovative product doesn't accomplish much if the company cannot quickly deliver a large volume of the product to the market to meet demand. Often this cannot be accomplished by one company's manufacturing process alone, and the ability to access production capacity when needed provides a significant competitive advantage. That is why most of these companies, such as Nike, are "virtual companies." This means that marketing and product design are their strength, yet they outsource all the other aspects of their supply chain and manufacturing processes, albeit through a tightly controlled system.

## Competing on Quality

Competing on quality means that a company's products and services are known for their premium nature. Two important elements of this competitive priority are consistency and reliability. Examples of companies known for competing on quality are Mercedes, General Electric, and Motorola. Many aspects of the supply chain are altered when companies compete on quality versus another dimension, such as cost. This includes sourcing of components, as well as the implementation of concepts such as total quality management (TQM) and Six Sigma throughout the entire supply chain. This means embedding quality in all aspects of transportation, delivery, and packaging. This is particularly challenging when items are perishable, fragile, or of high value, such as luxury goods.

As supply chain management is a boundary-spanning activity, an important attribute of competing on quality is **product traceability**. This means that the supply chain has the ability to easily trace a product from point of origin in the supply chain, through to the customer, and back down the supply chain in the case of returns. This feature is increasingly becoming important with greater emphasis on security and sustainability. Radio frequency identification (RFID) tags have provided excellent product traceability. Consider industries where this might be of particular importance, such as the pharmaceutical industry, where safety is critical. Another industry is the area of luxury goods, where counterfeiting is a problem, and traceability is very important in the identification of goods.

## Supply Chain Leader's Box

### ■ BARLEAN'S ORGANIC OILS

Barlean's Organic Oils provides an example of a company that competes on quality and has designed a supply chain to support this strategy. Barlean's is a company that sells health supplements, but it is most known for its flaxseed oil. In fact, Barlean's is a sales leader in the market for flaxseed oil. The business strategy of Barlean's is to focus on quality and freshness. The company maintains a four-month expiration date where competing products may be five months old even before they get to the retail shelf. It is the manufacturing and distribution processes that give Barlean's its edge. Typical competitors have manufacturing processes that expose the flaxseeds to heat, light, air, and overprocessing, all of which reduce the potency of the flaxseeds. In contrast, Barlean's starts with organic flaxseeds and has a system where the seeds are protected from the elements. The seeds are not pressed until an order has already come in from the retailer. Barlean's uses an express mail system for shipping orders to expedite arrival at the retailer. Although this is a more expensive alternative, it is one that supports the company's commitment to quality.

Adapted from: Cohen, Shoshanah and Joseph Roussel. *Strategic Supply Chain Management*. New York: McGraw-Hill Company, 2005, 25–26.

## Competing on Service

Competing on service means that a company understands the dimensions that its target customers define as high service and has chosen to tailor their products to meet those specific needs. An important aspect of this strategy is that these companies typically build customer loyalty, which can often guarantee continued sales. These companies typically have exceptional order fulfillment systems, with fast invoicing that enables them to be consistent and reliable. These companies typically do not compete on cost and cannot offer the lowest-priced product. However, their target market is one that wants high-quality service and is willing to pay the extra cost.

From an operational viewpoint, companies with superior customer service often avoid unnecessary costs related to expediting orders or the costs of product returns, often faced by other companies. These companies also have a strong ability to segment their customer based on perceived value. This way they can offer services of one type to one market and a modified version to another. For these firms, the relationship between product cost and profitability is well defined. Consequently, highly customized services that are costly to deliver are only offered for customers who meet strict business criteria and tend to be in the high-value segment.

## Why Not Compete on All Dimensions?

Successful companies understand that they cannot effectively compete on all dimensions, as they cannot be all things to all people. This is a very important and difficult point for most companies, as they typically want to be good at everything. The companies that succeed are those that understand which dimensions to excel on and are able to focus their energies on those dimensions. This does not mean that a company will have poor performance on the other dimensions. In fact, companies have to continually trade off one competitive dimension for another. However, this means that a company should have merely satisfactory performance, or stay within the norms of the industry, on those strategically less important dimensions.

Two important concepts that companies need to monitor are **order winners** and **order qualifiers**. Order winners are those characteristics that win the company orders in the marketplace. Order qualifiers are those characteristics that will qualify the company to be a participant in a particular market. This means that a company just needs to stay within the industry standard on its order qualifiers to ensure that it is on par with competitors. However, when it comes to order winners—that is where it should excel.

Recall that a supply chain must be designed to support the business strategy, so alignment between the two should be a top priority. It should be remembered, however, that strategy is a dynamic rather than a static process. As such, strategies change over time, and supply chains must adapt accordingly.

# Strategic Considerations

## Small versus Large Firms

When developing a supply chain strategy, it is important to understand the company's strengths and weaknesses to realistically determine what it can and cannot accomplish. The company must play to its strengths.

For many supply chain companies, a large source of power comes from their sheer size. Companies like Amazon, Wal-Mart, Toyota, and Home Depot are large firms with equally large market clout. These companies are sometimes called "**supply chain masters**" and have the ability to "strong-arm" their suppliers into compliance. However, not all companies have this advantage.

When designing its supply chain strategy, a company needs to understand how much influence or power it has in the marketplace. Large companies have the advantage of being able to buy larger quantities of goods and command lower prices due to quantity discounts. Due to their size, these companies can impose their own processes and rules on suppliers and customers.

Large companies can also impose the supply chain structure they want. They can impose their own process rules on suppliers and maintain a high degree of control over the entire supply chain. In the auto industry, for example, manufacturers stipulate that if a supplier's delay in delivery shuts down the production line, the supplier can be subject to a substantial penalty due to revenue lost while the line is down. Not every company can make this kind of demand.

Smaller companies have, however, developed their own supply chain strategies. For example, when developing their supply chain strategies, smaller companies should consider that size is relative. Few companies are large on a broad, global scale. When the scope narrows to a particular market segment or region, companies can find that they are really not that small. In that case, they can find select suppliers within that market segment with whom to work and develop strategies to compete within that market. Also, smaller suppliers can create cooperatives to aggregate their power.

## Supply Chain Adaptability

Successful companies understand that change is a natural part of the business environment and adapt their supply chains in anticipation. As market and environmental conditions shift, new products emerge, and new technology is developed, business strategies need to change. A company's supply chain strategy must quickly adapt to stay in sync with the business strategy. Consequently, the supply chain strategy must be adaptive.

The rate of change and the need for responsiveness, however, vary by industry. Some industries experience frequent and constant change, as seen in the personal computer industry. In this industry, companies need to change constantly such as selling through the Internet, exploring new distribution channels, or moving to an assemble-to-order strategy. In other industries, however, change can take much longer. One example of this is the aerospace industry, where changes in the supply chain typically occur after many years.

Numerous factors can require significant adaptability on the part of a company's supply chain. One of these is the development of a new technology that can change a business and its industry. The Internet is a good example, which created a direct link between businesses and customers. Companies such as Amazon, Dell, and many others could now sell directly to customers and cut out distributors. The Internet completely changed the "rules of the game" for the business community and required companies to quickly adapt their supply chains.

Another factor that requires supply chain adaptability is a change in the scope of a company's business. Any time a company offers new products or services, targets new markets, or expands geographically, it needs to completely rethink its supply chain strategy. The reason is that the company may likely need to expand its manufacturing capacity, add new distribution capabilities, develop new channels, or find new suppliers. Any time the scope of the business changes, the supply chain needs to adapt.

Although these events require adaptability, creating and implementing a supply chain strategy is a dynamic process that should be done on a continual basis. It is not an annual or biannual event. Any change in a company's competitive position—a new competitor entering the market, a shift in the market or competitive strategy—should automatically result in a reassessment of the company's supply chain strategy.

## Big Data Analytics Box

### ■ AMAZON

Amazon is a company that uses analytics to be adaptable and promote its customer-centric strategy. More recently it has been working on a plan that would ship products to customers before purchases are even made. The company recently gained a patent for "anticipatory shipping," a system that would allow Amazon to send items to shipping hubs in areas where it believes these items will sell. Amazon is able to develop this intelligence from the big data it has developed by storing customer data. This includes previous searches and purchases, wish lists, and also how long the customer's cursor hovers over an item online.

Using advanced analytical algorithms Amazon wants to engage in "predictive purchasing" that determines where products will go. Amazon can then preemptively ship products they expect customers to buy. The company may even load products onto trucks and have them sent to shipping hubs in areas where the company believes the purchases will take place. The importance of this idea is to use analytics to cut down delivery times. This would also keep the online retailer ahead of others in the industry. Although the scenario may lead to unwanted deliveries and even returns, the company believes these will be relatively small, given the increased sales and delivery benefits.

Adapted from: Opam, Kwame. "Amazon Plans to Ship Your Package Before You Even Buy Them." *The Verge*, January 18, 2014.

## Productivity as a Measure of Competitiveness

The purpose of supply chain strategy is to provide higher competitiveness to firms. Being able to measure competitiveness provides a scorecard for companies to evaluate how they are doing. One of the most common measures of competitiveness is productivity. We now look at its computation and interpretation.

| | | |
|---|---|---|
| Total productivity measure (output to all inputs) | $\dfrac{\text{Total output produced}}{\text{All inputs used}}$ | *Example:* Productivity of an entire warehouse |
| Partial productivity measure (output to only one input) | $\dfrac{\text{Output}}{\text{Labor}}$ or $\dfrac{\text{Output}}{\text{Machines}}$ or $\dfrac{\text{Output}}{\text{Materials}}$ or $\dfrac{\text{Output}}{\text{Capital}}$ | *Example:* Productivity of sorting machines |
| Multifactor productivity measure (output to several inputs) | $\dfrac{\text{Output}}{(\text{Labor} + \text{Machines})}$ or $\dfrac{\text{Output}}{(\text{Labor} + \text{Materials})}$ or $\dfrac{\text{Output}}{(\text{Labor} + \text{Capital} + \text{Energy})}$ | *Example:* Productivity of truck fleet and drivers |

**FIGURE 2.6** Productivity Measures.

## Measuring Productivity

Productivity is a measure of how well a company uses its resources. It is computed as a ratio of outputs to inputs, where the inputs can be labor or materials and outputs can be goods and services.

$$\text{Productivity} = \frac{\text{Output}}{\text{Input}}$$

The productivity measure can be used to measure performance of an individual resource, such as workers or machines. It can also be used to measure performance of the entire organization such as a warehouse, an entire supply chain, or even a nation. This is shown in Figure 2.6.

Total productivity is used when we want to measure utilization of all resources combined, such as labor, machines, and capital. Let's say that a dry-cleaning company has a monthly dollar value of outputs worth $18,000. This includes all items dry-cleaned for customers. Let's also say that the value of its inputs, such as labor, materials, and capital, is $9,000. The company's total monthly productivity would be computed as follows:

$$\text{Total Productivity} = \frac{\text{Output}}{\text{Input}} = \frac{\$18,000}{\$9,000} = 2.00$$

If the company wanted to compute the productivity of its machines, it would use a partial productivity measure. Say that its machines can clean 32 garments in eight hours, their productivity would be computed as follows:

$$\text{Machine productivity} = \frac{\text{Number of garments}}{\text{cleaning time}}$$

$$\text{Machine productivity} = \frac{32 \text{ garments}}{8 \text{ hours}} = 4 \frac{\text{garments}}{\text{hour}}.$$

## Interpreting Productivity

The more efficiently a company uses its resources, the more productive it is and, therefore, the higher the productivity ratio. However, interpreting productivity is more complicated than it may appear.

Consider the numbers we just computed, such as a machine productivity of four garments per hour. Does that number mean anything to you? The answer is no. The reason is that to interpret the meaning of a productivity measure, it must be compared against a baseline. For example, if we know that a competing dry-cleaner has a machine productivity of six garments per hour, then the productivity number we just computed—four garments per hour—tells us that our productivity is low. For our competitor, however, this is good news, as their productivity is higher and suggests that they are more competitive.

In addition to benchmarking productivity measures against others, productivity should be measured over time to observe changes. Let's say that our dry-cleaner chose to track machine productivity on a monthly basis and had chosen to purchase new machines in the third month. Perhaps the following is observed:

| Month | 1 | 2 | 3 | 4 | 5 |
|---|---|---|---|---|---|
| Productivity (in garments per hour) | 3.8 | 4.0 | 5.3 | 6.4 | 6.9 |

Now we can see that productivity had gone up after the purchase of the new machines. However, productivity continued to grow perhaps as the workers adjust to using the new equipment. Looking at productivity over time provides a very different level of understanding than looking at just one number. The best alternative is to track productivity over time and benchmark against industry standards.

When computing productivity, it is important to consider the units used in its computation, as they provide different meanings. Consider a restaurant that measures productivity as either a ratio of customer serviced to labor-hour versus customer serviced to square footage. The first measure looks at utilization of labor, whereas the second measure looks at utilization of space. One consideration is how a company competes in the marketplace. For example, a company that competes on speed would probably measure productivity in units produced over time. However, a company that competes on cost might measure productivity in terms of costs of inputs such as labor, materials, and overhead. Well-chosen units can make productivity a useful metric for evaluating competitiveness over time.

## CHAPTER HIGHLIGHTS

1. Supply chain strategy is a long-range plan for the design and ongoing management of the supply chain to support the business strategy.

2. Strategic alignment needs to exist between the business strategy and the functional strategies. A company's supply chain strategy should be developed to support the company's business strategy.

3. Companies can gain a competitive advantage through either a cost–productivity advantage or a value advantage. A company with a cost–productivity advantage maintains competitiveness by offering the lowest-cost product or service. A company with a value advantage maintains competiveness by providing a product with the greatest perceived differential value compared with its competitors.

4. The experience curve describes the relationship between unit costs and cumulative volume, where organizational costs are reduced due to experience and learning effects that result from processing a higher volume.

5. The four building blocks of supply chain strategy are operations strategy, sourcing strategy, distribution strategy, and customer service strategy.

6. The way a company competes in the marketplace is called a competitive priority. The supply chain strategy and supply chain design will be different based on a company's competitive priorities.

7. Competitiveness can be measured by productivity, which is a measure of how a company utilizes its resources.

## KEY TERMS

Business strategy
Supply chain strategy
Cost–productivity advantage
Value advantage
Experience curve
Vendor-Managed Inventory (VMI)
Value segments
Operations strategy
Product positioning strategy
Make-to-stock
Assemble-to-order
Make-to-order
Distribution strategy
Sourcing strategy
Loss of control
Dependency risk
Competitive priority
Product traceability
Order winners
Order qualifiers
Supply chain masters

## DISCUSSION QUESTIONS

1. Find an example of a company whose product you like. Identify its business strategy and its supply chain strategy. Explain whether or not the supply chain strategy supports the business strategy.

2. Identify ways a company can move from a "commodity" position to one of a cost and/or value advantage. Is a commodity position always bad, and how can companies differentiate themselves in this position?

3. Explain the differences between vertical integration and outsourcing. Identify the strategic advantages of each, and explain how each position can be used to help supply chain strategy.

4. Provide business examples of the three operations strategies: make-to-stock, assemble-to-order, and make-to-order. Explain what it would take for a company to move from a make-to-stock strategy to make-to-order, and vice versa. What are the advantages and disadvantages of each strategy?

5. Provide business examples of companies that compete on each one of the identified competitive priorities. Explain how their supply chain strategies are different based on their specific competitive priority. Select one of the business examples you provided, and explain how the company would need to change its supply chain strategy if it shifted its competitive priority.

## PROBLEMS

1. Mario's Pizzeria is a local pizza shop. Mario is trying to evaluate the productivity of his operation. One worker can make approximately three pizzas in 30 minutes, whereas another four pizzas in 20 minutes. Which worker is more productive?

2. An automated packaging machine used in warehousing can sort and pack six large boxes in 15 minutes. A new machine that is being considered can sort and pack four boxes in 8 minutes. How much more productive is the new machine?

3. The diagnostic department at Saints Memorial Hospital provides medical tests and evaluations for patients, ranging from analyzing blood samples to performing magnetic resonance imaging (MRI). Average cost to patients is $60 per patient. Labor costs average $15 per patient, materials costs are $20 per patient, and overhead costs are averaged at $20 per patient.

   **a.** What is the multifactor productivity ratio for the diagnostic department? What does this finding mean?

   **b.** If the average lab worker spends three hours for each patient, what is the labor productivity ratio?

## Case Study | Surplus Styles

Surplus Styles is a manufacturer of hair care products, including shampoos, conditioners, and hair gels. The company, located in Southern California, bottles the shampoos and other various hair products in their manufacturing plant, but sources the content from a number of chemical suppliers. The company has historically competed on cost and has used competitive bidding to select suppliers and award yearlong contracts. The Director of Sourcing, Derick M. Frizzle, has managed the competitive bid process for the past 10 years, having moved up the ranks from purchasing. He was particularly proud that the company was cost-competitive in its market segment.

One recent day the president of the company, Frederick Davenport, called for a meeting with Mr. Frizzle. Derick could tell from the tone of Davenport's message that the meeting would be accompanied by less-than-stellar news. As Derick took the infamous ride up the wood-paneled elevator with green marble floors to the top of their office building, he contemplated what he could have possibly done wrong. He had followed the same type of supplier bidding process for years, and the company was doing well financially. He was anxious to hear what Davenport had to say.

Derick entered Davenport's vast office, a room highlighted by ceiling-to-floor windows. He could see Mr. Davenport sitting at the end of the long, dark wooden table, with his two aides accompanying him on each side. The man on the right was Bo Jenson, and the woman on the left was Gertrude Masterson; neither were taken lightly within the company. Derick could always tell when it was going to be a bad day.

"Darn hippies," Davenport rumbled. "Bo and Gertrude have some troubling news. This swing toward animal rights and 'quality goods' is about to cost me a lot of money," Davenport continued, making mocking "bunny ears" with his bulbous index and middle fingers. "Apparently market trends are changing again and not for the better." Davenport continued to explain that there was going to be a change in the competitive strategy of the firm. The competition in the hair care market had become fierce, and there was greater focus on quality. Specifically, the recent trend in animal rights and natural, organic products meant ensuring that the shampoo content did not go through animal testing and that it was ensured to be hypoallergenic. The current products were produced to compete for price and did not agree with the new demands. Davenport wanted to see products on the retail shelf with this quality standard as soon as possible. "Do it," Davenport continued and sat back down.

This concluded the meeting. Luckily Mr. Frizzle had an easy exit, as he had only gotten one foot in the door before his task was demanded.

Derick M. Frizzle was rather pleased with his new detail, as he cared greatly for nature and had always refrained from purchasing his own company's products due to their lack of consideration for both the individual and the environment. However, Derick was now confronted with a problem. His current suppliers offered the lowest cost in the business and would likely not be able to provide the needed quality assurances. His expertise had been in procuring the least-expensive ingredients available, and he did not know where to begin changing his sourcing practices.

*Case Questions*

1. Identify the steps that Derick should take to solve his problem.
2. Should Derick ask for the required changes from the current suppliers? If they do not comply, should he solicit new suppliers? How might he do this?
3. Should Derick go through a competitive bid in the future? If so, should he do it for all purchased products or just some products?
4. What are the differences when looking for suppliers to meet cost standards versus quality standards?

## REFERENCES

Capelli, Peter, and Anna Tavis. "The Performance Management Revolution." *Harvard Business Review*, October 2016: 58–67.

Cohen, Shoshanah, and Joseph Roussel. *Strategic Supply Chain Management*. New York: McGraw-Hill Company, 2005.

"Gartner Announces Rankings of the 2016 Supply Chain Top 25." May 19, 2016 (www.gartner.com).

Lambert, Douglas M., and A. Michael Knemeyer. "We're in This Together." *Harvard Business Review*, December 2004: 114–122.

Sinchi-Levi, David. "Finding the Weak Link in Your Supply Chain." *Harvard Business Review*, June 9, 2015.

# Network and System Design

## 3

### LEARNING OBJECTIVES

*After completing this chapter, you should be able to:*

- Describe the supply chain as a system of processes.
- Understand how to manage processes across the supply chain.
- Explain system constraints and variation in managing a supply chain network.
- Describe the stages of supply chain integration.
- Describe key factors in designing a supply chain structure.
- Explain enterprise resource planning (ERP) as a system integration technology.

### CHAPTER OUTLINE

- **The Supply Chain System**
  *Processes across the Supply Chain*
  *What Is a Business Process?*
  *Managing Supply Chain Processes*

- **Understanding Processes: Theory of Constraints (TOC)**
  *System Constraints*
  *System Variation*
  *Capacity Implications*

- **Integration of Supply Chain Processes**
  *Stages of Integration*
  *Vertical Integration versus Coordination*

- **Designing Supply Chain Networks**
  *Supply Chain Structure and Management*
  *Designing Segmented Structures*

- **Enterprise Resource Planning (ERP)**
  *IT as an Enabler of SCM*
  *What Is ERP?*

*ERP Configuration*

*ERP Implementation*

- **Chapter Highlights**
- **Key Terms**
- **Discussion Questions**
- **Problems**
- **Case Study: Boca Electronics, LLC**

In 1949, Mr. Kihachiro Onitsuka began making basketball shoes out of his living room in Kobe, Japan. He chose to make sports shoes, as he thought this to be the best way to encourage the young to play sports. He wanted his shoes to be the best in footwear and chose to call his company ASICS, an acronym for the Latin phrase *anima sana in corpore sano*, meaning "a sound mind in a sound body."

After years of hard work ASICS had become a leading maker of athletic footwear, sports apparel, and accessories. Today ASICS' worldwide sales total around $2.4 billion. Although its great success was welcome, ASICS found it to be both a blessing and a curse.

In 2008 ASICS America found itself growing 21% annually, and the company found it difficult to keep ahead of demand. ASICS had only one distribution center in the United States, which had reached capacity. This single distribution center (DC), located in Southaven, Mississippi, was able to handle a maximum of 50,000 units per day. However, the growth in demand resulted in 70,000 units per day being shipped to the DC. This capacity constraint was not only slowing down order fulfillment, but also was now preventing the company from serving new customers and markets. The DC had become a "bottleneck" in the supply chain design network causing service slowdowns. The company understood that the supply chain network had to be changed if they were going to support this new level of demand.

The company's U.S. network was fairly straightforward. It used contract manufacturers in China, Vietnam, and Indonesia to make its shoes and clothing. Those items were shipped in ocean containers to the ports of Los Angeles and Long Beach. It then used a third-party logistics provider—APL Logistics (APLL)—to unload ASICS' ocean containers. The merchandise was then reloaded onto 53-foot trailers for shipment to the 350,000-square-foot DC in Southaven. That facility then shipped orders to the company's 3,000 retail customers in the United States.

ASICS understood that this current network had to be restructured. It turned to Fortna Inc., a consulting company, for help. After analyzing the network and current demands, Fortna recommended shifting some distribution operations to the West Coast to provide relief for the current distribution center and then constructing a second distribution center close to the original site. Fortna's analysis indicated that establishing a West Coast operation to break down imported containers and build mixed loads for shipment to customers in the western United States could save the company time and money.

The company immediately began to divert a portion of its orders directly to customers and bypass its current distribution center, using its third-party logistics (3PL) provider.

These were typically full container loads of products already destined for customers on the West Coast. Its problems had been solved. In 2011 the company constructed a second distribution center in Byhalia, Mississippi, about 20 miles from the current distribution center. The new 520,000-square-foot facility uses state-of-the-art technology. The company completely transformed the way it processes orders. It uses technology to efficiently manage all assets and shipping operations, such as using mobile equipment to keep real-time checks of inventory. The company has positioned itself for continued growth and has learned that a good distribution network requires more than buildings and facilities. Mr. Onitsuka would be proud.

Adapted from: Napolitano, Maida. "ASICS Finds the Perfect Fit." *Logistics Management*, February, 2013.

# The Supply Chain System

## Processes across the Supply Chain

A supply chain can be viewed as a system of processes that cuts across organizations and delivers customer value, rather than as a series of separate organizations and functions. In this case, the focus is not just to manage each process within the organization, but to manage processes across the entire supply chain. One example might be the order management process, which includes managing the customer order from placement to product receipt through the entire chain. This requires process thinking and requires managers to view the collection of processes as a system designed to satisfy customer needs.

Let's consider the situation of ASICS, from the chapter opener. Their distribution process required managing the entire network as a system. Their only distribution center—which was the hub of the network—had a maximum capacity of 50,000 units per day. When the rest of the network began processing 70,000 units per day, the distribution center could not accommodate this volume. The result was a "bottleneck," or constraint, in the network that limited how much the system could process. It was not enough to grow sales and improve each individual facility in the supply chain. The supply chain network needed to be improved as a system.

Supply chain strategy provides the long-range plan for this entire system, which we discussed in Chapter 2. Two key elements support this strategy. The first is the **supply chain network design**, which includes the physical structure and business processes included in the system. The second is the **information technology (IT) design**, which enables data sharing, communication, and process synchronization. IT is the backbone of supply chain management (SCM) that enables managing processes. Without IT, communication, coordination, and decision making across the supply chain could not take place. Together the supply chain network design and IT system design support the supply chain strategy, as shown in Figure 3.1. These elements have to be aligned and work in unison as one system.

## What Is a Business Process?

Given that supply chains can be viewed as a collection of processes, we need to see what makes a process. A **business process** is a structured set of activities or steps with specified outcomes. Consider the "process" involved in enrolling in a class at your university. There are application forms to be reviewed by the admissions office, financial forms to complete at the bursar's

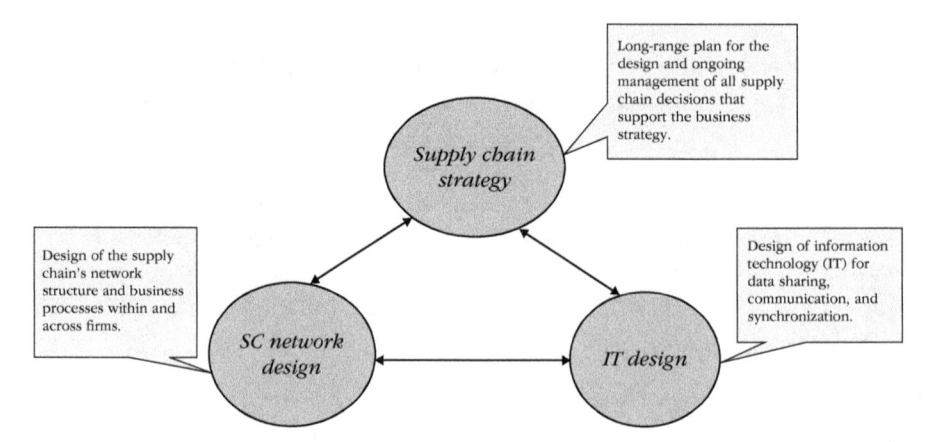

**FIGURE 3.1** Network and IT design support supply chain strategy.

office, and class registration to be completed at the registrar's office. The sequence of steps required, their timing and coordination, the simplicity of forms, and their ease of submission are all part of the enrollment "process." The sequence of process steps goes beyond the organization and cuts across a supply chain network, as in the case of ASICS. ASICS' distribution process required unloading shipments from Asia at California ports, loading them onto trailers for shipments to the distribution center in Mississippi, and then sending shipments to individual retail customers.

Organizations, and entire supply chains, can be viewed as a collection of processes, rather than just a collection of departments or functions.[1] For example, there is the customer service process that involves a series of activities designed to enhance the level of customer satisfaction by meeting or exceeding their expectations. This may involve a series of well-coordinated activities, such as billing and invoicing, handling product returns, providing real-time information on promised shipping dates, and product availability. Another example is the order fulfillment process, which involves ensuring that customer orders are filled. It may involve activities such as receiving and processing the order, ensuring movement of product and delivery, and customer follow-up. Other examples of processes include the manufacturing process, which involves ensuring production of products; the demand management process, which balances demand requirements with operational and supply chain capabilities; and the distribution process, which involves distributing and delivering products to specified locations.

Organizations have many other processes, with each having a series of activities designed to create a particular output for the customer, whether it be a service or a tangible product. The output is a result of the process that produces it. If we want to improve the output, we must improve the process. Process improvement involves making changes and enhancements to the process. In the example of course registration, this may involve reducing the time it takes to register for a class by reducing the number of forms needed, simplifying each form, or shortening the time it takes to review them.

Every process has structural and resource constraints that limit its amount of output. Because processes are a series of activities, the constraints of each activity are important as well as how the activities are linked. For example, if the university's bursar's office is slow in processing payments, there may be a delay in course registration as the registrar's office waits to get financial approval. In the example of ASICS, the slow processing at the distribution center prevented goods from moving through the system.

---

[1] Douglas M. Lambert, *SCM: Process, Partnership, Performance*, 4th ed. (Sarasota, FL: Supply Chain Management Institute, 2014).

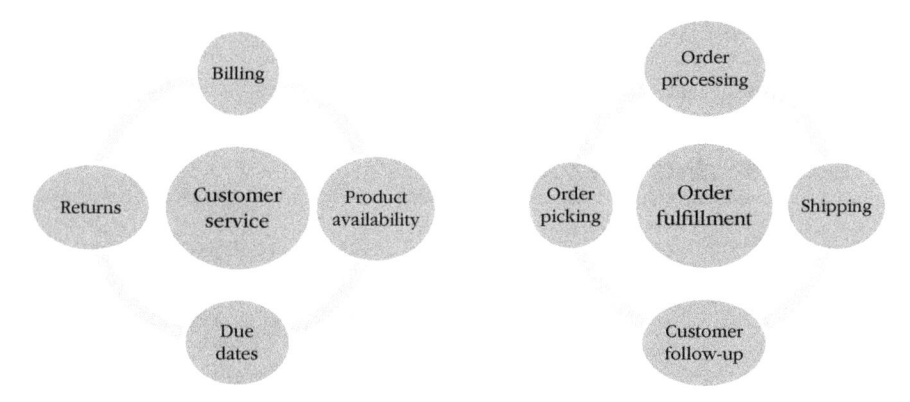

**FIGURE 3.2** Organizational processes cut across many functions.

Notice that processes involve many organizational functions as shown in Figure 3.2. For example, the customer service process cuts across a number of different functions. It must involve marketing that interfaces with the customer, logistics that ensures product delivery and movement, and operations that may deal with repairs. Similarly, order fulfillment requires operations to ensure order availability and processing, logistics to arrange for order picking and shipping, and marketing for customer follow-up. For processes to be effective and efficient, organizational functions must work together and be well coordinated. In addition, these processes require coordinating with suppliers and customers. As such, they cut across not only organizational functions but also the entire supply chain. Let's look at this next.

## Managing Supply Chain Processes

Just as organizations need to coordinate internal functions for processes to run efficiently, they must do so across the supply chain. As the entire supply chain is a collection of processes, rather than separate organizations and functions, the focus is to manage them across the entire supply chain. This requires process thinking and requires managers to view the process as a system designed to satisfy customer needs.

There are two differing views on how to manage processes across the supply chain. The first is the **transactional view** that focuses on making supply chain processes more efficient and effective based on quantitative metrics. This can be achieved through supply chain network redesign to promote speed and eliminate redundancy, by standardizing transactions to improve efficiency, and by implementing better information technology to improve transfer of information and improve accuracy.

The second, the **relationship view**, is focused on managing relationships across the supply chain. This involves managing relationships between people and organizations and linking-up processes across organizations of the supply chain. For example, this might mean managing the order fulfillment process throughout the entire chain coordinating with suppliers and measuring performance along the chain. This also means that managers from each organization who are part of the process coordinate activities, work toward common goals, and have a common language.

Each approach to managing processes across the supply chain has its advantages. With the first, the focus is to make supply chain transactions more efficient and effective based on measurable metrics. With the second, the objective is to structure interfirm relationships in the supply chain for the long-term benefit of all the supply chain members. This requires a joint vision and partnering. Ultimately the best way to manage processes across the supply chain is to use both approaches—focus on efficiency of transactions and create long-term interfirm relationships.

Once again consider ASICS. It focused on both approaches. It first brought efficiency to the distribution network by balancing flows through the network. It also relied on its relationship with its 3PL provider to take over some duties and handle the "overflow" of goods.

## Supply Chain Leader's Box—Moving to Process Thinking

### ■ LG ELECTRONICS

A few years ago LG Electronics made a large organizational shift. Specifically, the company moved from functional thinking to a more process-oriented systems thinking. This change was part of a large effort by then Chief Executive Nam Yong to shake up a siloed company where managers seldom shared their ideas.

Procurement is an excellent example of this change. Prior to the change, the procurement process of the company was completely decentralized. Each division manager made their own deals with suppliers such as TSMC, a Taiwan-based chipmaker. That meant a procurement manager at the handset unit in Seoul didn't know how much his counterpart at a flat-screen TV factory in Mexico paid for chips from the same foundry. This lack of coordination and systems thinking was costly, and the company decided to coordinate the entire process.

Since the change, however, no one at LG has been able to issue a purchase order without clearance from the office of "procurement engineering." This innovation generated huge savings. For example, by centralizing purchases, LG was able to cut more than $2 billion from its annual $30 billion shopping bill.

Prior to the change, LG had a mishmash of processes developed over the years for 115 factories and subsidiaries around the world. Part of the change involved merging these processes into a single 50-page procurement manual. This resulted in other savings such as enabling a direct comparison of material prices. For example, the company was able to uncover that by buying aluminum instead of high-priced copper for home appliances, they could save $25 million. This change of moving to process thinking resulted in significant cost-cutting and more efficient functionality for LG. It also helped LG get through a global downturn better than many of its competitors.

Adapted from: Raymond Tsang, Amit Sinha, and Gerry Mattio. "*Winning with Procurement in Asia.*" Bain Briefs, December 2013 (Bain & Company).

## Understanding Processes: Theory of Constraints (TOC)

To manage the supply chain as a system we need to understand the basic principles that govern how processes interact. This is offered by a management philosophy called **theory of constraints (TOC)**, which was introduced by Dr. Eliyahu M. Goldratt in his book, *The Goal*.

The premise behind TOC is that every system has one or more limiting factor that is preventing it from further achieving its goal. This is analogous to the weakest link of a chain. For a system to attain significant improvement that weakest link—or a constraint—must be identified. The whole system must be managed with this constraint in mind, and there is always at least one constraint. The TOC process seeks to identify the constraint and restructure the rest of the organization around it to eliminate its impact. The principles offered by TOC apply to managing any system of processes, whether in an organization or the entire supply chain. Let's look at the basic principles of TOC.

### System Constraints

The basic principle of TOC is that every system has at least one constraint. A constraint is anything that prevents the system from being able to achieve its goal and is sometimes called the

## Understanding Processes: Theory of Constraints (TOC)

"bottleneck." A constraint can be equipment, which may be limited by how much it can produce. It can be people, who may lack skills or simply processing capability. It can also be facilities, such as their size, which may limit how much can be stored. The focus of TOC is to uncover the constraint and manage it.

The system cannot produce any more than the output of its bottleneck or constraining activity. Also, how much a process can produce is related to the structure of the process and the way the activities in the process are linked. Activities in a process can be linked serially, which is in sequence one right after the other. They can also be linked in parallel, where some activities take place simultaneously. Let's look at examples of each.

Recall ASICS' distribution network prior to restructuring. It had a serial network structure, which is simply a series of processes as shown in Figure 3.3. The first process, Process A, was unloading cargo from ships in California ports. Let's assume that this activity had a rate of 95,000 units per day. The next step in the process, Process B, was to load trailers for shipment to the DC, assuming a rate of 80,000 units per day. The goods are then processed at the DC, Process C, which likely involved breaking bulk, sorting, and packing, at a rate of 50,000 units per day. Finally, there was Process D, which involved shipping trailers of goods to retail customers at a rate of 80,000 units per day.

Look carefully at Figure 3.3. What is the maximum number of units that this system can process in a day? It is 50,000 units per day, or the bottleneck activity. The reason is that even though Processes A and B can handle more units than Process C, no more than 50,000 units can go through the bottleneck. The extra units will simply accumulate in front of it, as they cannot be processed any faster. This is the constraint.

It is critical to manage the constraints or bottlenecks in the system. The constraint must always be busy, as time lost there is time lost in the entire system. Notice that if ASICS' DC loses an hour of production, the entire system loses an hour of production. However, if the activity of unloading cargo loses an hour it has no impact on the final output of the system, as it is already constrained by the bottleneck of 50,000 units per day. If we want to increase output, we need to find ways of increasing the capacity of the bottleneck or constraint. In the case of ASICS, it involves increasing output at the DC. Finding ways to increase output of the other activities is a waste of resources, as it doesn't do anything for the overall output.

Imagine if the company spent money to increase the number of units that could be loaded and shipped onto the trailers going to the DC from 80,000 units per day to, say, 100,000 units per day. What would this accomplish? Nothing. The only thing that would happen is more units would accumulate in front of the DC, which can only process 50,000 units. Understanding how constraints in the system work is an important example of systems thinking.

As part of restructuring their supply chain network, ASICS diverted a part of the unloaded cargo to their 3PL to ship directly to clients. The amount was approximately 20% of 70,000 units per day, which was the average number of daily units needing to be processed. This was approximately 14,000 units per day. The result is shown in Figure 3.4. Notice what happens to the output. While the DC is still processing 50,000 units per day, 14,000 units are being sent directly to customers. This is happening in parallel and is enabling a total of 64,000 to pass through the system. The maximum output of the system is the new bottleneck, which is 64,000 units per day.

| | A | B | C | D |
|---|---|---|---|---|
| | Unload cargo from ships in California | Load trailers for shipment to DC | Process goods at DC | Trailers ship goods to retail customers |
| Output | 95,000 units per day | 80,000 units per day | 50,000 units per day | 80,000 units per day |

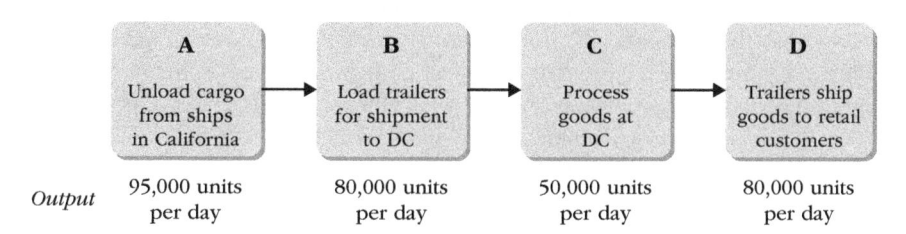

**FIGURE 3.3** A serial process: ASICS' original distribution network.

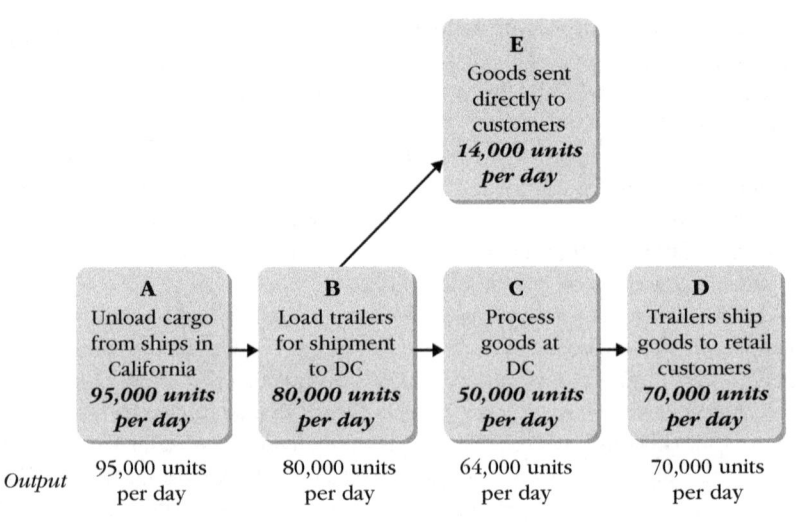

```
                                    E
                                 Goods sent
                                 directly to
                                 customers
                                 14,000 units
                                   per day

         A              B              C              D
    Unload cargo    Load trailers    Process      Trailers ship
    from ships in   for shipment    goods at     goods to retail
     California        to DC           DC          customers
    95,000 units    80,000 units   50,000 units   70,000 units
      per day         per day        per day        per day

Output  95,000 units    80,000 units   64,000 units   70,000 units
          per day         per day        per day        per day
```

**FIGURE 3.4** A parallel process: ASICS' redesigned distribution network.

Notice that now there is a new constraint—64,000 units per day. Remember that in a system there is always at least one constraint. TOC teaches us to manage the constraint using the following steps:

1. **Identify the constraint.** In the ASICS example it was the DC's processing capability.

2. **Exploit the constraint.** Decisions must be made on how best use the constraint and ensure that the constraint's time is not wasted doing things that it should not do.

3. **Subordinate all other processes to the above decision.** This means align the whole system around the constraint.

4. **Elevate the constraint.** If possible, increase capacity of the constraint. ASICS bought more capacity by "bypassing" the DC.

5. **When the constraint changes, return to Step 1.** This means identify the new constraint.

6. **Engage in continuous improvement.** Continue these steps, as this is a never-ending process.

## System Variation

Every system or process has variation. Variation is simply variability in the amount of output that is produced or processed. The activities of a process also exhibit variation. Think about your own performance and how sometimes you are very productive and other times, no matter how hard you try, you are not. The same is true of workers in a factory, warehouse, restaurant, office environment, or medical facility. There is also variation in equipment and facilities. Sometimes processes run smoothly, whereas other times there are breakdowns requiring unexpected repairs.

Variation is a problem as it consumes resources. This can be time—sometimes it takes more time to do an activity; space—such as needing extra storage; or labor—such as tasks having to be repeated. Variation also adds complexity and uncertainty. Consider the variation that occurs in consumer demand at a retail store, such as The Gap. The Gap makes forecasts of average demand for a given week or day, but rarely is the forecast exactly equal to actual sales. Sometimes there are unexpected surges in demand, and other times there are slumps. These variations then propagate throughout the supply chain, as retailers either have to rush in more inventory or end up having to find storage for unsold goods. These variations in demand create variations in production schedules of manufacturers and suppliers, which create coordination problems. Also, different activities may become constraints at different times adding to the complexity. The result may be not having enough inventory at certain times, missing component parts at the manufacturing facility, or simply carrying too much inventory.

Process variation needs to be managed as it can create significant problems for a system. There are three ways this can be accomplished. First, attempts should be made to reduce or eliminate as much variation as possible. This requires identifying the source of variability in the system, such as workers or equipment, and correcting the problem. Quality control methods that are discussed later in this text are good tools to use for this purpose.

Second, it may be possible to create buffers to deal with the variation. Buffers, in the form of excess inventories, can be placed before and after highly variable activities. They can be placed before the constraint, ensuring that the constraint is never "starved." They can also be placed behind the constraint to prevent downstream failure to block the constraint's output. Buffers used in this way protect the constraint from variations in the rest of the system. Third, managers can deal with variation by designing more flexibility into the process to respond to the variation. This may be in the form of flexible technology or cross-training workers.

## Capacity Implications

Capacity refers to the maximum amount of output that can be achieved by a process over a specified period of time. Different businesses measure capacity in different ways, all trying to assess a measure of processing capability. For example, a healthcare clinic measures capacity in terms of patients seen per day, restaurants in terms of customers served, a delivery company in terms of the number of packages delivered, and an insurance company in terms of the number of claims processed. Capacity can also be measured in terms of size or storage limit. For example, a hospital may also measure capacity in terms of the number of hospital beds available, a restaurant in terms of the number of seats available, and a warehouse in terms of its square footage.

In supply chain network design it is important to remember that different supply chain members have different levels of capacity. As we link organizations in the chain we need to make sure that levels of capacity match. Otherwise, we will have bottlenecks or constraints, as not every organization can produce at the same level as the others. To understand the capacity of a facility, we need two types of information. The first is the amount of available capacity, which specifies exactly how much capacity a facility has. The second is effectiveness of capacity use, which specifies how effectively available capacity is actually being used.

Consider a bakery. Suppose that on the average the bakery can make 200 cupcakes per day. However, during peak periods—such as holidays—it can make 300 cupcakes per day. This is the maximum but cannot be sustained for any long period of time. Stating that the bakery has a capacity of 300 cupcakes per day would be misleading. On the other hand, saying that 200 cupcakes per day is the capacity does not indicate that the production can be increased to 300 per day. This example illustrates that different measures of capacity are useful, as they provide different kinds of information. Following are two of the most common measures of capacity.

**Design capacity** is the maximum output rate that can be achieved by a facility. A company achieves this output rate by using temporary measures, such as overtime, overstaffing, using equipment at the maximum rate, and subcontracting.

**Effective capacity** is the maximum output rate that can be sustained under normal conditions. These conditions include realistic work schedules and breaks, regular staff levels, scheduled machine maintenance, and none of the temporary measures that are used to achieve design capacity.

Regardless of how much capacity a company has, it needs to measure how well it is utilizing it. Capacity utilization is a metric that indicates how much of capacity is actually being used and is computed as follows:

$$\text{Utilization} = \left[\frac{\text{Actual output rate}}{\text{Capacity}}\right](100\%)$$

However, because there are two unique capacity measures, utilization should be measured relative to each of them:

$$\text{Utilization}_{\text{effective}} = \left[\frac{\text{Actual output}}{\text{Effective Capacity}}\right](100\%)$$

$$\text{Utilization}_{\text{design}} = \left[\frac{\text{Actual output}}{\text{Design Capacity}}\right](100\%)$$

### Example 1   Computing Capacity Utilization

Assume that a retail warehouse can process 100,000 orders in a single day, under maximum conditions, using overtime labor. However, the facility was designed to process 70,000 orders per day under normal conditions. During the month of June the facility was processing 80,000 orders per day. What is the warehouse's capacity utilization for both design and effective capacity?

**SOLUTION:**

$$\text{Utilization}_{\text{effective}} = \left[\frac{\text{Actual output}}{\text{Effective capacity}}\right](100\%)$$

$$= \left[\frac{80{,}000}{70{,}000}\right](100\%) = 114.3\%$$

$$\text{Utilization}_{\text{design}} = \left[\frac{\text{Actual output}}{\text{Design capacity}}\right](100\%)$$

$$= \left[\frac{80{,}000}{100{,}000}\right](100\%) = 80\%$$

The utilization rates show that the current output of the warehouse is higher than effective capacity. It can likely operate at this level for only a short period of time.

# Integration of Supply Chain Processes

## Stages of Integration

Traditionally organizations have viewed themselves as independent entities that exist separately from other firms with which they compete. They have a "survival of the fittest" mentality, rather than one of cooperation. However, as companies evolve in their supply chain strategy, they typically move through a set of integration stages—from little or no integration to complete integration of supply chain processes. First, this involves internal integration where organizational

**1. Organizational functions are independent.**

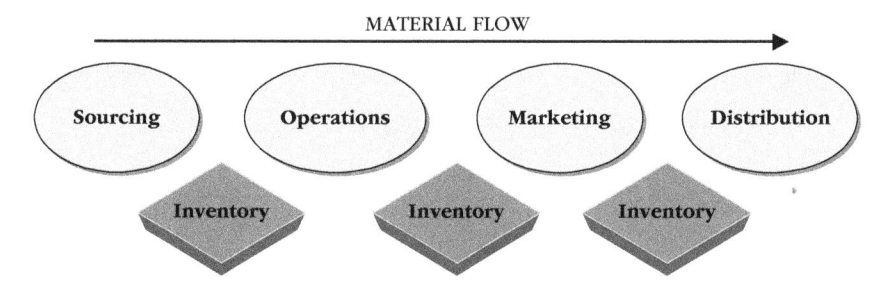

*Figure: Material flow through Sourcing → Operations → Marketing → Distribution, with separate Inventory buffers.*

**2. Functions are integrated within the organization.**

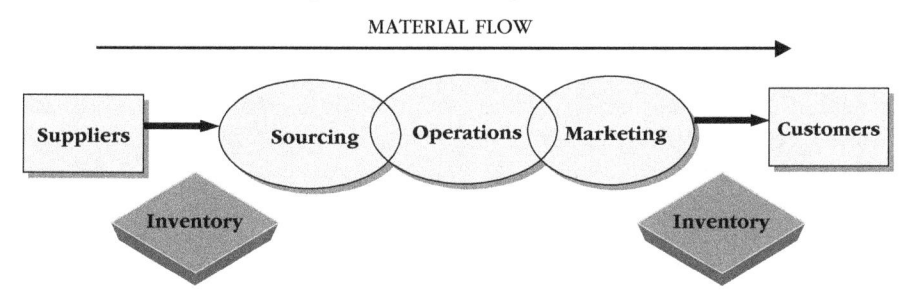

*Figure: Suppliers → Sourcing/Operations/Marketing (overlapping) → Customers, with Inventory at each end.*

**3. Functions are integrated across the supply chain.**

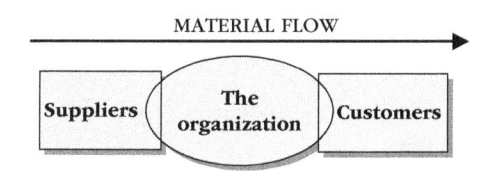

*Figure: Suppliers → The organization → Customers.*

**FIGURE 3.5** Stages of supply chain integration.

functions, such as operations, marketing, and purchasing, work in unison. Next, integration involves progressively more cohesion with other members of the supply chain. This evolution of integration is illustrated in Figure 3.5.

There are three stages of integration. Stage 1 represents complete functional independence, whereas Stage 3 represents complete process integration. In Stage 1, the functions in the company operate in complete isolation of one another, sometimes called the "silo" mentality. Here operations, for example, may focus on maximizing production of products being produced without regard to sales or the buildup of finished goods inventories or the impact on working capital. Similarly, marketing may promote products without consideration of whether operations can reasonably produce them. Large amounts of inventory are carried to compensate for lack of coordination and communication.

Companies that are in Stage 2 have internal functional cooperation and coordination, but not across the supply chain. Stage 3 companies, however, represent true supply chain integration. Here the concept of linkages and coordination extends beyond the boundaries of the firm to supply chain partners.

As companies evolve they move from one stage to the next, progressively becoming more integrated with other members of the supply chain and carrying less inventory. However, companies often do not go through this evolution willingly, as it requires significant organizational change and restructuring. Rather, they typically evolve in response to competitive pressures and threats.

## Vertical Integration versus Coordination

Each organization in the supply chain network is dependent on the other. Consider a shirt retailer who depends on the shirt manufacturer who depends on the weavers of fabrics, who all depend on the web of various distributors and warehouses. It may seem that coordination between supply chain members may be easiest through **vertical integration**, which involves ownership of upstream suppliers and downstream customers. This was once thought to be a desirable competitive strategy, which some companies still use. For example, the Dole Corporation owns pineapple farms in Hawaii as well as all the production facilities. Increasingly, however, organizations have focused on "core competencies," namely the activities that are essential to their business. By focusing on core competencies a company can learn to do these activities exceptionally well and is not encumbered by activities considered less important. These less important activities are increasingly being outsourced.

Recall that **outsourcing** is hiring an outside company to do certain tasks for a fee. Common examples of activities that are often outsourced include data network management, human resources, records archiving, and management of maintenance, repair, and operating (MRP) inventory items. However, many companies outsource manufacturing, such as Nike in footwear and sportswear. The trend is even toward "virtual" companies, where everything is outsourced, including product design and R&D. This trend has significant implications for strategic issues of supply chain management. The decision of whether to outsource has a great deal to do with identifying core competencies or what a company is good at, deciding what to outsource, who to partner with, how to manage suppliers, how to coordinate the flow of materials, and what items to treat as a commodity. These are important strategic decisions. They also require coordinating processes between multiple entities.

Historically, the relationships companies had with their suppliers and downstream customers (such as distributors and retailers) were adversarial rather than cooperative. Today, there are still a number of companies that try to achieve cost reductions at the expense of their suppliers. These companies, however, do not realize that transferring costs upstream or downstream does not make them any more competitive. All it does is merely shift the cost from one "column" to another, as these costs will ultimately make their way to the final marketplace in the form of the price paid by the end user. More efficient supply chains, by contrast, will deliver the same product at a lower price.

## Designing Supply Chain Networks

### Supply Chain Structure and Management

All firms belong to one or more supply chains that begin with the source of raw materials and end with consumption. There are two aspects of the supply chain network that are important. First is the actual physical structure of the network itself. Second is the management of the network. These two aspects are completely intertwined, as not all aspects of the physical structure need to be managed equally. Let's look at the physical structure first.

## Managerial Insights Box

### ■ COCA-COLA

Coca-Cola provides an example of an aligned and analytics-driven end-to-end supply chain. The cola giant has an algorithm to engineer the taste of its orange juice. The company has developed a computer model that directs everything from picking schedules to the blend of ingredients needed to maintain a consistent taste. Coke has spent $114 million to expand its technology-driven U.S. juice bottling plant and claims to be the world's largest. It is at this plant that the company uses an algorithm it calls Black Book. Black Book uses big data from more than 600 flavors that make up the "taste" of what customers perceive as an orange. The data are matched to a chemical profile that specifies acidity, sweetness, and other attributes of each batch of raw juice. The algorithm then tells Coke how to blend batches to replicate a consistent taste, including the amount of pulp that should be added. However, the use of analytics does not end at the plant, but is used to connect to the entire supply chain. The algorithm is linked to satellite imaging of fruit groves to ensure fruit is picked at the optimal time. Every aspect of the supply chain is optimized and includes external factors such as crop yield, current prices, and weather patterns. The mathematical model can be quickly updated with new information to create new plans—in a matter of 5 or 10 minutes. The entire supply chain network has been standardized and optimized. According to Jim Horrisberger, Director of Procurement: "You take Mother Nature and standardize it."

Adapted From: "Coke Has a Secret Formula for Orange Juice, Too." *Bloomberg Businessweek*, February 4–10, 2013, pp. 19–21.

---

Each supply chain network structure is defined by three elements:

1. **The number of companies that are part of the supply chain.** Some supply chains are complex and have many members; others have few.

2. **The structural dimensions of the network.** This is the number of tiers in the supply chain and how many members are in each tier. A supply chain can have many tiers but few members in each tier, or it can have few tiers but many members in each.

3. **The number of process links across the supply chain.** The more process links that must be managed across the supply chain, the more complex the management of the chain. Examples include any one of the processes discussed earlier, such as customer relationship management, demand management, order fulfillment, or manufacturing flow management.

There are countless network structure types, and the structure itself evolves based on many factors. One factor is product type and its characteristics. Perishable products, for example, typically have a shorter and more streamlined supply chain. Items requiring intricate work from many specialty suppliers result in a more complex network. Innovative products that must have quick access to production facilities may have a network with few tiers but many members in each tier to provide quick production options—such as Nike or Sony. Other factors that affect the structure are the number of available suppliers and availability of raw materials, as well as ease of access to customers.

Some firms are at the beginning, whereas others at the very end of the network structure, such as Wal-Mart. Others are in the middle of the supply chain, such as Proctor & Gamble (P&G), Hewlett Packard, or Intel. Each firm considers themselves to be the focal firm, and the supply chain structure will look different if you are at the beginning, middle, or end of the network.

Most companies belong to more than one supply chain network, and the network itself may have many branches. Not all of the supply chain branches and links need to be managed equally.

Management needs to decide on the type of relationship that is appropriate for each particular supply chain link. For example, sourcing a standard component part that is a commodity with many suppliers does not require relationship building. This link in the network can be managed in a contractual way. By contrast, alliances and partnerships need to be managed differently. It is especially important to identify and manage key process links across the chain and recognize that processes need to be managed across the entire supply chain. Managing these process links requires a change from managing individual functions to integrating activities into supply chain management processes. As we discussed earlier in this chapter, thinking of the organization and supply chain in functional terms impedes process thinking.

## Designing Segmented Structures

Designing supply chain networks that provide a competitive advantage has become increasingly difficult. The reason is that most companies operate in global markets with rapidly changing consumer expectations. Over the past decade companies have seen complexity increase in every link of their supply chains, from consumers to retail channels to manufacturers to suppliers. One factor driving this complexity is an increase in demand by consumers for customized products, which has fueled the growth of mass customization. Numerous companies like Timbuk2, Reebok, and Nike permit customers to design their own products online.

The supply chain implications of such a large product proliferation are vast. First, this high level of product diversity makes forecasting demand more difficult and inevitably results in either excess inventory or stock-outs. At the same time, however, supply chains have reduced their buffer stocks of inventories due to financial pressures. Retailers have also contributed to the complexity. To be responsive to customers they have increased their service expectations. Today major retailers demand in-stock levels in excess of 98%, placing higher delivery expectations on their suppliers. Adding to the complexity is that many companies have increased the number of routes, with many now offering both conventional and online channels. If we add to this transportation cost issues and environmental concerns, we can see how complex these decisions can become.

Traditional "one-size-fits-all" supply chain structures cannot accommodate these variations. For example, a company can work hard to build an effective supply chain structure designed to deliver high-volume items and minimize overall supply chain costs. This supply chain structure, however, will not permit the company to respond to peaks in demand from customers that want slower moving items. If the company takes steps to avoid stock-outs in this case, it will likely incur additional costs, such as transportation. In one such example, an apparel manufacturer found itself making extensive use of courier deliveries from factory to retailer to meet unpredicted demand. At one point the company found that they were moving one-third of their shipments this way, at a 30% increase in transportation cost.

To effectively meet these challenges, an increasing number of companies are abandoning a "one-size-fits-all" supply chain structure for one that relies on a segmented network. The best way to structure supply chains to meet varying customer requirements and keep the network manageable is to create segmented supply chains. Segmentation offers an effective way to bring under control this growing complexity. It requires understanding which elements of a network matter most to certain customer segments and designing differentiated supply chain structures for those segments.

A good example of simple segmentation is offered by a mid-sized U.S.-based pharmaceutical company. To address problems of stock-outs and waste, the company created a few simple segments. One segment was for high-volume, low-volatility items, which it stocks in inventory using the make-to-stock approach. Another segment was for low-volume, high-volatility items, which it offers in a make-to-order approach to eliminate unnecessary inventory. These simple segments resulted in better performance for the company, shorter lead times, and less waste.

A three-step approach can be used to successfully segment a company's supply chain network:

1. **Identify key drivers of operational complexity.** This means identifying what matters most to a particular customer group or channel. For example, volume flexibility and supply chain responsiveness are much more important to outlets that attract customer traffic with large, temporary price cuts than they are to "everyday low price" outlets. Similarly, quick time-to-market matters much more to fashion-oriented, short-life-cycle merchandise than to long-lasting, core products. Also, not all customers need the same level of customer service. Traditional supply chains attempt to continuously deliver high service levels across the board, to where it is and is not needed. The result is that they often fall short due to profitability pressures. A segmented supply chain forces the company to identify where investment in customer service results in the largest gain.

2. **Design differentiated supply chain segments tailored to address these unique complexities.** Once key drivers of each customer group are identified a supply chain segment must be created to operationalize each one of those characteristics. This will likely require designing multiple supply chain segments to meet the identified requirements. The number of segments, however, should not be too large and should remain reasonable to manage, such as five or six.

3. **Create a customized end-to-end operational blueprint and performance metrics for each supply chain segment.** Once the segments have been created, details of putting them into operation must be established, including aligning processes and metrics across the supply chain.

There are numerous ways that segmentation can be conducted. Figure 3.6 shows some examples that can be used to segment supply chains. Notice that each segment will result in a different supply chain structure. For example, high-volume, low-variability demand will likely require a cost-efficient supply chain structure, with dedicated production facilities to drive the lowest cost. High-volume, high-variability demand, on the other hand, is less predictable. The segment may be further differentiated based on customer priority. High-priority customers may be offered a responsive service, whereas less-profitable segments are offered more limited options, helping to reduce variability in that segment. Low-volume, low-variability products may be shipped to high-priority customers using responsive inventory systems, while limiting choices for lower-priority customers.

By segmenting its supply chain, a company can offer increased responsiveness for fast-growing channels and product lines while providing better cost control in mature, stable segments.

---

- Fast-moving versus slow-moving products
- Fast-growth versus slow-growth products
- Traditional versus innovation versus online channel
- High-priority customers versus low-priority customers
- Low-volume/low-variability versus low-volume/high-variability
- High-volume/low-variability versus high-volume/high-variability

---

**FIGURE 3.6** Ways to segment supply chains.

**Big Data Analytics Box**

■ SEGMENTATION IN RETAIL

Technology has enabled retailers to identify and track customers through their loyalty programs and credit card data. This big data is then analyzed to track customers, create segments, and personalize offerings. The personalized offerings may be based on simply extrapolating existing customer behavior patterns such as buying and returning products. As a result retailers have been delivering targeted promotions through e-mail, Web pages, and in-store kiosks. Drugstore chain CVS tracks customer purchases through its ExtraCare card. Tesco, the UK-based retailer, tracks all sales through its ClubCard. Similarly, Hallmark uses its Gold Crown card to segment customers, to customize direct-mail offers, and to assess customer reactions to promotions. Virtually every retailer today has some type of loyalty program. These loyalty programs have proven invaluable in gathering customer data and using big data analytics to create segments of customers, which are then linked to supply chains.

# Enterprise Resource Planning (ERP)

## IT as an Enabler of SCM

For a supply chain to function as a system all chain members must have access to the same information. Information technology (IT) enables communication, storage, and processing of data within and between firms. It is also used to organize information to help managers with decision making. IT is considered as an enabler of supply chain management (SCM), as SCM depends on the sharing of information that makes possible the planning, coordination, and execution of all processes. IT enables the linking of processes across the supply chain and provides visibility into supply chain activities occurring at other points across the network, often far removed from the final customer. This information is then used to help managers throughout the network make effective decisions and appropriately respond to situations, rather than reacting blindly based on educated guesses.

Consider a giant retailer such as Wal-Mart that operates over 11,000 stores worldwide, has more than two million employees, and handles over 200 million customer transactions each week. The sheer scale of the data in Wal-Mart's system is daunting. To manage its inventory Wal-Mart uses an IT system called Retail Link, which enables suppliers to see the exact number of their products on every shelf of every store at that precise moment. The system shows the rate of sales by the hour, by the day, and over the past year. Retail Link gives suppliers a complete overview of when and how their products are selling and even provides information on other products consumers have placed in their shopping cart. This lets suppliers make better decisions, better managing their inventory and deliveries. For this reason, companies such as Wal-Mart are prepared to spend large amounts of money to develop and continually update their IT systems.

A wide variety of information is needed for a supply chain to perform as a coordinated system. This requires information that supports both long-range and day-to-day decision making. It includes information such as customer demand, customer orders, inventory levels, delivery status, and production plans. This information must also effectively flow within the organization and between members of the supply chain to ensure the timely flow of materials and funds in the system.

In Chapter 1, we discussed the many types of information technologies that enable SCM. They range from the Internet, which we are all familiar with, to radio frequency identification (RFID) to global positioning systems (GPS). One of the most significant information technologies has been **enterprise resource planning (ERP)**, which has enabled sharing of information and data across the enterprise for better decision making. Let's look at ERP systems next.

# What Is ERP?

Enterprise Resource Planning (ERP) systems are a fully integrated computer-based technology used by organizations to manage resources throughout the supply chain. The purpose of ERP is to facilitate the flow of information between all business functions inside the boundaries of the organization and manage the connections to other members of the supply chain. These systems integrate all functions of an enterprise and are used to manage materials, financial resources, and human resources and interface with customers and suppliers. ERP systems consolidate all business operations into an enterprise-wide system that operates in real time and uses a centralized database that is accessed by all applications. Through the use of a single database, ERP serves as a business support system across functions and processes.

ERP systems typically tie together all business processes, such as sales, production, inventory management, warehousing, delivery, accounting, billing, and human resource management. ERP systems are cross-functional and enterprise-wide, connecting functions such as marketing, operations, sourcing, and logistics. An ERP system uses a central database that allows every department within a business, or even supply chain, to store and retrieve information in real time. The system is designed to have the data inputted in a standardized format, increasing reliability. The software is developed in components, or modules, specific to each function or process. Components of these modules are shown in Figure 3.7. This allows a business to select desired components for use, mix and match components from multiple vendors, or install a fully encompassing suite from a single vendor.

# ERP Configuration

ERP systems can be configured in a number of ways. One option is for the configuration to be fully customized software. Another, and a very different option, is the use of standardized

**Manufacturing**
- Bills of material
- Scheduling
- Capacity
- Workflow
- Quality control
- Cost management
- Manufacturing process

**Finance**
- General ledger
- Cash management
- Accounts payable
- Accounts receivable
- Fixed assets

**Human Resources (HR)**
- Payroll
- Training
- Hourly involvement
- Employee tracking
- Benefits

**Supply Chain Management**
- Inventory
- Order entry
- Purchasing
- Supply chain planning
- Supplier scheduling
- Product inspection

**Project Management**
- Costing
- Billing
- Time expense
- Activity management

**Customer Relationship Management (CRM)**
- Sales and Marketing
- Commissions
- Service
- Customer contact
- Customer information
- Call Center support

**FIGURE 3.7** Enterprise Resource Planning modules.

"off-the-shelf" software modules. Finally, ERP can be configured as a mix of these two options, where modules are mixed and customized.

Fully customizing an ERP package can be very expensive and complicated. It is also time consuming and can significantly delay implementation of an integrated system. However, customized systems have the advantage of being designed around organizational processes currently in place, capturing the way the organization works. On the other hand, applying standardized modules may force changes in the processes of the organization to accommodate the modules themselves.

The advantage of modular design is flexibility, as it permits implementation of some functions but not others. Different companies select different configurations based on their needs and resources. For example, modules such as finance and accounting are needed by almost all companies; other modules—such as human resource management—may not be needed by everyone; a service company will likely not acquire a manufacturing module. Sometimes companies will not adopt a module because they already have their own proprietary system in place. Similarly, a company with a well-established IT department, but limited funds for enterprise resource planning (ERP) implementation, may select to mix and match different components to satisfy their most pressing business needs. In this case "middleware" can be developed to connect existing applications with standard modules.

The advantage of ERP is that its modules can exist as a system or can be utilized in an ad hoc fashion, enabling businesses to create a configuration best suited for their needs. To further accommodate this, ERP vendors have made changes to the software to help businesses in the implementation process. One improvement in standardized software has been the creation of built-in "configuration" tools to help customers change how the "out-of-the-box" system works and adapt them more easily to their business. Another is the incorporation of "best practices" into most ERP software packages. This provides the organization with the option to modify their processes to line up with the "best practice" function delivered in the "out-of-the-box" version of the software.

## ERP Implementation

ERP software systems are complex and usually impose significant changes in organizational processes. Implementing ERP software is typically too complex for in-house developers, who lack the required skills, and it is better to hire outside consultants who are knowledgeable in implementing these systems. Implementation time can be significant and depends on the size of the business, the number of modules being implemented, the degree of customization, and the scope of the changes. It is also affected by the flexibility of the organization to adapt to the change required. The advantage of ERP systems is that they are modular, so they don't all need to be implemented at once. Implementation can then be divided into various stages, which begin with consultation and end with ongoing support following implementation.

Although ERP vendors have designed their software modules around standard business processes, including best practices, these modules are all of a standardized nature. This means that implementation of a noncustomized ERP system requires the organization to adapt their processes to the existing ERP package. This can be very trying for the organization, and planning prior to implementation can greatly help. Four general steps should be followed. First, develop a map of current business processes, conducting a thorough business process analysis. Second, evaluate ERP vendors, identifying which vendor's ERP modules most closely match the mapped organization's processes. Third, identify steps to unify the ERP modules with organizational processes in the most efficient manner possible. Fourth, plan during implementation to further refine the unity between these two.

ERP implementation is considerably more difficult than organizations anticipate and often requires outside consultants and change management professionals. The benefits of an ERP

## CHAPTER HIGHLIGHTS

1. A supply chain can be viewed as a system of processes. SCM involves managing these processes.
2. A business process is a structured set of activities or steps with specified outcomes.
3. The transactional view of supply chains focuses on the efficiency and effectiveness of managing supply chain processes.
4. The relationship view of supply chains focuses on managing relationships across the supply chain.
5. TOC explains how to manage a system. According to TOC, every system has at least one constraint. A constraint is anything that prevents the system from being able to achieve its goal and is sometimes called the "bottleneck." A system should be improved by managing the constraint.
6. Design capacity is the maximum output rate that can be achieved by a facility. Effective capacity is the maximum output rate that can be sustained under normal conditions.
7. ERP systems are a fully integrated computer-based technology used by organizations to manage resources throughout the supply chain.

## KEY TERMS

Supply chain network design
Information technology (IT) design
Business process
Transactional view
Relationship view
Theory of constraints (TOC)
Design capacity
Effective capacity
Vertical integration
Outsourcing
Enterprise Resource Planning (ERP)

## DISCUSSION QUESTIONS

1. Explain what a process is and how activities in a process function as a system. Find an example of a process, and identify the different activities involved. How would you improve this process? What would that involve?
2. Find an example of a business, and identify the processes needed to deliver the product to the final customer. What do you think is the bottleneck in this process? How would you suggest it be managed?
3. Explain how constraints in a system work. Find an example of a constraint you have encountered recently in your everyday life—whether at work or shopping. How did the constraint affect you? What would happen if the constraint was removed?
4. Explain vertical integration and how it is different from SCM. In what cases would it make sense for a company to vertically integrate?

## PROBLEMS

1. Shex Hotel can accommodate 300 guests in a single day under maximum conditions. However, under normal conditions this hotel is designed to accommodate 200 guests per day. In September, the hotel accommodated 150 guests in one day. What is the hotel's capacity utilization?

2. Leopard Transportation Company is designed to process 80 orders per day but can process as many as 100 orders per day under extreme conditions. For the past month, it has processed 90 orders per day. What is the company's capacity utilization? What comments can you make regarding its processing rates? Can the company maintain this rate?

3. Papi Toys can produce 500 toys in a single day under maximum conditions. However, it is designed to produce 400 units per day under normal conditions. In February, it produced 480 units per day. What was Papi Toys' capacity utilization for both design and effective capacity? What do these numbers tell you?

## Case Study: Boca Electronics, LLC

Boca Electronics, a manufacturer of semiconductor components, was established in Houston, Texas, in 2002 after spinning off from its parent company. Originally a branch of Vissay Inc., Boca Electronics had a solid customer base and strong sales with some major firms such as IBM, Compaq, and Motorola. Semiconductors included a wide array of products that were broken down according to their application and material. Some of their main products include microprocessors, light-emitting diodes (LEDs), rectifiers, and suppressors. Boca Electronics operated on a mainframe system that it inherited from its parent company and used additional stand-alone systems to perform many of its other business functions. For the last four years the company had performed well financially, so little concern had been given to the business operations. However, recent slowdowns in the economy and an increase in competition in the semiconductor industry had forced Boca Electronics to take another look at the way it operated its business.

Ron Butler, the purchasing manager at Boca Electronics, was responsible for ordering raw materials and ensuring that their delivery was on time and met production requirements. Ron used his own forecasting software to determine purchasing needs based on past sales. Although this worked most of the time, Ron often found himself scrambling to meet large customer orders at the last minute and was forced to expedite a lot of orders to meet the production needs. Ron felt this was due largely to the lack of communication between his department and the sales force. Although he received production forecasts and projected sales from the sales department, it occurred on an irregular basis, and the forecasts would often change by the time he had placed orders to the suppliers. In addition, Ron had a difficult time synchronizing with suppliers and determining factors such as lead times and product prices. He had previously recommended a new software system that would integrate with suppliers of key components but the proposal was turned down by senior management due to a "current lack of need for such an investment."

Boca Electronics also faced issues regarding its cash flows. It took several weeks for the accounting department to process invoices and usually had to e-mail back and forth with the sales manager to make multiple corrections. Because both departments used different systems to manage customer accounts, some of the data was redundant and inaccurate (customer accounts would be updated in the sales department, but not in accounting). Although this issue went largely unnoticed during thriving periods, the recent slowdown in the economy revealed potential repercussions of the current business operations, as Boca Electronics began to run short on its cash flows.

In the last month, one of Boca Electronics' largest customers began requiring all its suppliers to integrate their manufacturing operations to improve the sharing of information and further improve its supply chain. This company had recently implemented an ERP system from a major provider and was encouraging its suppliers to do the same. Suppliers had the option of implementing middleware software to integrate operations. Whether suppliers chose to keep their current systems and implement middleware, or implement an ERP system that would integrate with the company, they had one year to make the changes to continue doing business with this customer.

Paul Andrews, the CIO at Boca Electronics, was well aware of the issues facing the company. He knew that something had to be done to improve communication and information sharing within the company, and the current mainframe system was outdated and inefficient. He was also aware of the constraints that Ron was facing in Purchasing and how much it was costing the company. With the new request from one of its largest customers for further integration, the idea of implementing an ERP system for Boca Electronics seemed like a viable solution to Paul. However, recent economic downturns and a limited amount of capital made such a large capital outlay a risky investment for the company.

### Case Questions

1. Determine the trade-offs of implementing an ERP system in the company versus buying best-of-breed software and using middleware to integrate.
2. What are the potential impacts of such an implementation on the company's suppliers and customers?
3. If the company chose to stay with the system it currently has, what are some potential consequences that can occur in the future?
4. Based on the business nature of the company, the industry, and the current environment, what would you recommend doing?

# REFERENCES

Hayes, R. H., G. Pisano, D. Upton, and S. C. Wheelwright. *Operations Strategy and Technology: Pursuing the Competitive Edge*. New York: John Wiley & Sons, 2005.

Hayes, R. H., and S. C. Wheelwright. "Link Manufacturing Process and Product Life Cycles." *Harvard Business Review*, 57 (January–February 1979): 133–140.

Hayes, R. H., and S. C. Wheelwright. *Restoring Our Competitive Edge: Competing Through Manufacturing*. New York: John Wiley & Sons, 1984.

Lambert, Douglas M. *SCM: Process, Partnership, Performance*, 4th ed. Sarasota, FL: Supply Chain Management Institute, 2014.

LaMonica, Martin. "GE, the World's Largest Manufacturer, Is on the Verge of Using 3-D Printing to Make Jet Parts." *MIT Technology Review* (2016).

# 4 Marketing

## LEARNING OBJECTIVES

*After completing this chapter, you should be able to:*

- Define marketing and explain its role in supply chain management.
- Describe how market segmentation impacts supply chain design.
- Describe the tools of customer relationship management (CRM).
- Explain the voice of the customer (VOC) and quality function deployment (QFD).
- Explain channels of distribution and their role in supply chain management.
- Explain the impact of e-commerce on channels of distribution and the supply chain.

## CHAPTER OUTLINE

■ **What Is Marketing?**
  *The Marketing Function*
  *Evolution of Marketing*
  *Impact on the Organization*
  *Impact on the Supply Chain*

■ **Customer-Driven Supply Chains**
  *Who Is the Customer?*
  *Types of Customer Relationships*
  *Managing Customers Using CRM*

■ **Delivering Value to Customers**
  *Voice of the Customer (VOC)*
  *What Is Customer Service?*
  *Impact on the Supply Chain*
  *Measuring Customer Service*
  *Global Customer Service Issues*

■ **Channels of Distribution**
  *What Are Channels of Distribution?*
  *Designing a Distribution Channel*

*Distribution versus Logistics Channel*
*The Impact of E-Commerce*
*The Omni-Channel*

- **Chapter Highlights**
- **Key Terms**
- **Discussion Questions**
- **Case Study: Gizmo**

---

Marketing experts say that consumers do follow their noses. This began with real estate agents using the tactic of encouraging owners to fill their home with the scent of freshly baked bread or coffee in advance of property viewings, creating a "homey" feel for potential buyers. Today technology is using scent to dramatically increase sales in all consumer areas. This includes gel cartridges that emit smells from the TV while watching a cooking program, to iPhone scent cartridges that release scents when certain apps are switched on, to gyms that are scented to increase performance. Welcome to the new age of marketing—a form of sensory branding known as "ambient scenting" or "scent marketing."

Even before you enter an Abercrombie & Fitch store, you can smell the characteristic woodsy aroma that is associated with the brand. A combination of citrus, fir-tree resin, and Brazilian rosewood extract, "Fierce" creates a sense of excitement and pleasure. Since its rollout in stores across the country a few years ago, Abercrombie's cologne, which also pervades sidewalks outside the clothier's stores, has become an integral part of the shopping experience. A part of the ambience, the scent is designed to enhance the feel of being at the store, create brand association, and ultimately promote sales. Popular demand compelled the company to produce the trademark scent in bottle form. The brand association with the trademark scent has since become so strong that some customers even complain when store-bought T-shirts lose the smell after multiple washes.

No longer confined to lingerie and candy stores, ambient scenting is custom designed to create brand association and a particular outcome. For example, Westin Hotel & Resorts disperses white tea to provide the "zen-retreat" experience. The Mandarin Oriental in Miami sprays "meeting scent" in conference rooms in an effort to enhance "productivity." Omni Hotels uses the scent of sugar cookies in its coffee shops.

Scent branding is becoming just as prevalent in retail, as researchers show that ambient scenting allows consumers to make a deeper brand connection. Just recently Samsung had a scent designed for its stores with the intention to create an association between the brand and concepts of innovation and excellence. The creators even claim that customers—under the subtle influence of the scent—spend an average of 20% to 30% more time mingling among the electronics.

This new approach to reach customers has also created a new supply chain. A growing industry of companies worldwide specializing in ambient scent-marketing and dispersion technology has emerged. These enterprises typically pair with fragrance companies to design customized fragrances for businesses. There is also scenting equipment and technology for dispersion that must be designed, as well as equipment maintenance that can vary depending on the size of the space to be scented. Distributors, dealers, and agents are added to the network.

As marketing develops novel alternatives to reach customers, improve brand recognition, and enhance sales, supporting supply chains evolve. Marketing drives the development of the supply chain to meet what the customer wants.

Adapted from: "Etc. Branding." *Bloomberg Businessweek*, June 21, 2010.

# What Is Marketing?

## The Marketing Function

Marketing is the function responsible for linking the organization to its customers and is concerned with the "downstream" part of the supply chain. This is highlighted in Figure 4.1. The task for marketing is to identify what customers need and want, create demand for a company's current and new products, and continue to identify market opportunities. Marketing plays a critical role, as providing value to customers drives all actions of the organization and the supply chain.

For an organization and its supply chain to be competitive, they must be better than competitors at meeting customer needs. Marketing is the function responsible for identifying what these needs are, determining how to create value for customers, and building strong customer relationships.

Marketing is a far more complex function than it may appear, as customers are driven by much more than their basic needs for products and services. The key is to understand and develop the combination of products and services that precisely meet the expectations for a particular set of customers. For example, if most customers of athletic shoes only care for three different color choices, offering the product in five colors makes little sense. There would be little benefit, and the supply chain implications—extra sourcing, manufacturing, distribution, and inventory—would be significant. It is critical to understand exactly what satisfies customers and to precisely match product and service offerings to their psychological needs or conscious preferences.

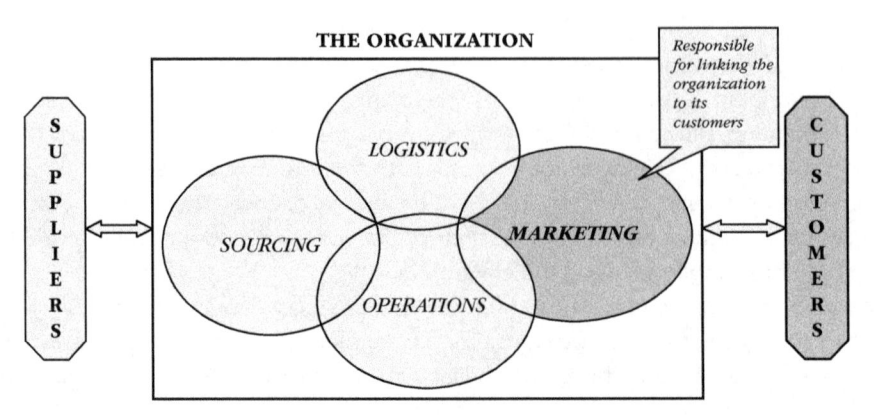

**FIGURE 4.1** The marketing function.

```
        1930s           1970s          Present
          |               |
The production concept  The selling concept   The marketing concept

    Transactional marketing    |    Relational marketing
```

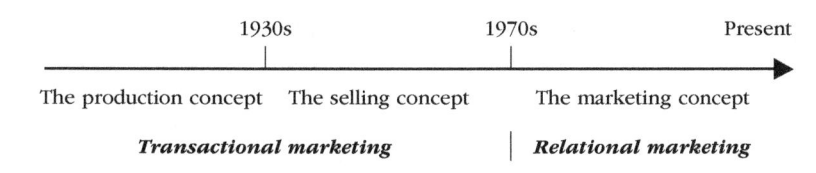

**FIGURE 4.2** The evolution of marketing.

Marketing is further complicated by the fact that there is no single market for any given product or service. All markets can be broken down into multiple segments, each of which has somewhat different requirements. A critical challenge is to distinguish markets—called **market segmentation**—in a meaningful and effective way. At one end of the spectrum is **mass marketing**, which refers to treating the entire market as a homogenous group and offering the same marketing mix to all customers. Mass marketing reduces costs through economies of scale but may miss large segments of the market with an offering that is too general. Segments that are too broad (e.g., all women in the world over the age of 30) do not permit the company to target a narrow enough group. On the other hand, segments that are too narrow (e.g., high school students who work part-time in Lima, Ohio) may not be cost-effective. **Target marketing** recognizes the diversity of customers and does not try to please all of them with the same product offering. The challenge for marketing is to identify the most effective market segments and their needs. As we will see shortly, this must also take into account the supply chain requirements needed to service each segment.

## Evolution of Marketing

The function of marketing has changed and evolved over time corresponding to changes in the general business environment. Three major perspectives dominated marketing over its history—the production concept, the selling concept, and the marketing concept, as shown in Figure 4.2. This most recent perspective also ushered in an era that focused on creating relationships with customers, called relational marketing, which is different from merely focusing on making individual sales transactions. We now look at this in more detail.

### Supply Chain Leader's Box

#### ■ GAP INC.

Consider that Gap Inc., one of the largest specialty retailers, owns three popular brands: Banana Republic, Gap, and Old Navy. Although all three carry fashion apparel, their target markets are very different. Old Navy carries "great fashion at great prices" and is focused on offering a low price point for a target market that includes families and children. Gap offers a classic style at a slightly higher price point targeting college-age students. Finally, Banana Republic focuses on offering "accessible luxury," has the highest price points, and targets fashion-conscious individuals.

The three different brands have three different supply chains to support the different target markets. Old Navy has the lowest price point and primarily sources from China, which is driven by a focus on cost. Gap sources from South America with slightly higher quality goods but also higher prices. Finally, Banana Republic primarily sources from Europe. It offers the highest-quality fashion of the three brands, but at a higher price. The three different supply chains are specifically geared to support each target market. This strategy also gives Gap Inc. supply chain flexibility. When there are problems with any one supply chain the company can easily switch to one of the other chains to support its brands.

The early part of the 20th century witnessed a large unfulfilled demand for products that met basic needs and gave rise to the production concept in marketing. At that time virtually anything that could be produced was easily sold, and the primary challenge was to sell products at a price that exceeded the cost of production. Firms focused on products that could be made most efficiently, as offering low-cost products in the marketplace automatically created demand.

The 1930s, however, witnessed greater market competition and ushered in an era that now focused on selling. Mass production had become commonplace, competition had increased, and there was less unfulfilled demand. Unlike the time of the production concept, where mere product availability created demand, this new era required marketing to persuade customers to buy their products through tools such as advertising and personal selling. Marketing was a function that was performed after the product was developed and produced. The sales concept paid little attention to what the customer actually needed, and the goal was to simply beat competitors at the sale. As a result, marketing often involved hard selling, something that is still associated with marketing.

The 1970s witnessed a proliferation of product variety and greater selectiveness on the part of customers. Hard selling no longer could be relied on to generate sales. Customers now had increased discretionary income and would buy only those products that precisely met their needs. In addition, in an increasingly global environment, their needs began changing rapidly and were not immediately obvious. The marketing concept developed in response, focusing on identifying what customers want and how to keep customers satisfied. Companies changed their focus to identify customer needs before developing the product and aligning all functions of the company to meet those needs.

The marketing perspectives prior to the 1970s were part of an era termed "**transactional marketing**," which focused on obtaining successful exchanges, or transactions, with customers. Companies focused on maximizing short-term transactions with their customers, as opposed to building long-term relationships. The focus was primarily on selling existing products and using promotional techniques to maximize sales, rather than developing insights into the future needs of customers. Then in the 1970s firms moved from a "selling" orientation to a "marketing" orientation. Here marketing research techniques are used to understand customer psychology and then to make decisions that satisfy customers better than the competition.

The growth of supply chain management created a shift in philosophy regarding the nature of marketing strategy, termed "**relational marketing**." Relational marketing focused on developing long-term relationships with key supply chain participants—customers and suppliers. The emphasis is to understand their long-term preferences, provide them with high customer service, and therefore engender loyalty. Relational marketing is based on the understanding that it is more cost-effective to retain current customers than to work to attract new ones.

The focus on customers has further been magnified with the turn of the century. Today's business environment is characterized by an empowered customer that is the driving force of the supply chain. The single greatest factor that contributed to this shift was the Internet, a technological development that armed consumers with a wealth of information and provided them with bargaining power unseen before. Consumers today have the ability to gain information on the latest product choices, product characteristics, costs, and consumer reviews, and they perform global searches of companies and industries. This has enabled them to become knowledgeable buyers who can realistically demand choices in products and services. Trying to accommodate this new breed of customers has resulted in a major shift in business philosophy and has changed virtually every aspect of supply chain management.

## Impact on the Organization

The knowledge and information that marketing provides has critical importance for the entire organization as it is used to guide the actions of all other functions within the firm. We can see this from the PepsiCo example, in the Supply Chain Leader's Box, where the entire organization is changing to accommodate new customer preferences. For marketing to be successful, it must be supported by the entire organization, and the products customers want must be made available.

As we have seen, it is common for marketing research techniques to determine that consumers desire a new type of product. Marketing then needs to work with operations to ensure production of the product with the exact characteristics needed; sourcing needs to ensure that supplies are available in a timely and cost-effective manner; logistics needs to ensure deliveries of exactly what is needed throughout the supply chain; also, finance needs to be involved in securing appropriate funding. All this coordination needs to happen simultaneously, while marketing is promoting and advertising the new product.

## Supply Chain Leader's Box—Accommodating Changing Customer Preferences

### ■ PEPSICO

PepsiCo is a great example of a company making product changes to align with customer preferences. Initially their products were carbonated beverages and snacks. Consider that back in February 2007, when Derek Yach, a former executive director of the World Health Organization and an expert on nutrition, took a new job with PepsiCo, his mother worried. "You are aware they sell soda and chips, and these things cause you to get unhealthy and fat?" she asked him. Yach's former colleagues in public health had similar concerns. However, Yach said he knew what Pepsi made, but he wanted to help guide the snack food multinational toward a healthier product menu.

The company that made its reputation on junk food has changed its direction, under the leadership of Chief Executive Nooyi. Nooyi says she has no choice but to move toward healthier fare, as consumers become more health conscious. For over a decade, consumers have gradually defected from the carbonated soft drinks that once comprised 90% of Pepsi's beverage business. Many have switched to bottled water and other healthier beverages. In addition, criticism grew steadily over Pepsi's largest business, Frito-Lay snacks, which are laden with oil and salt. In response to changing consumer demands, the company has decided to emphasize research to create truly healthy fare.

"Society, people, and lifestyles have changed," Nooyi says. "The R&D needs for this new world are also different." As a result, she has increased the R&D budget 38% over three years with the goal of expanding healthy products to $30 billion in sales, twice the company's overall historical average. To do this, Pepsi hired a dozen physicians and PhDs, many of whom built their reputations at the Mayo Clinic, WHO, and like-minded institutions. Some researched diabetes and heart disease, the sort of ailments that can result in part from eating too much of what Pepsi sells. The goal is to continue creating healthy options while making the bad stuff less bad.

The researchers hunt for healthier ingredients that can go into multiple products. For example, technological improvements to an all-natural zero-calorie sweetener derived from a plant called "stevia" allowed Pepsi to devise several new fast-growing brands. This included healthier beverages such as Pomegranate Blueberry, Pineapple Mango, and Trop50, a variation on its Tropicana orange juice. PepsiCo has also launched an organic Gatorade.

PepsiCo's strategy to follow customer preferences is proving profitable. As preferences have changed PepsiCo has worked hard to respond to them.

Adapted from: Berry, Donna. "Beverage Trends 2016." www.foodbusinessnews.net. January 2016; and "Pepsi Brings in the Health Police." *Bloomberg Businessweek*, January 12, 2010.

Notice that marketing brings the voice, the mind, and the heart of the customer into the decision-making process of the company. Collectively the organization then translates customer desires into viable and profitable products. None of this organizational functioning could take place without marketing to drive it.

## Impact on the Supply Chain

Just as marketing drives the decisions of the organization to produce and deliver exactly what customers want, it also drives supply chain decisions. Marketing decisions generally fall into four distinct categories known as the marketing mix or the 4Ps. These decisions are product, price, place (distribution), and promotion. Although they are the domain of marketing, these decisions directly involve supply chain management.

**Product** involves decisions that encompass the bundle of product characteristics that satisfies customer needs. They relate to brand name and functionality. They also address decisions of quality and packaging, which are directly supported by supplier standards and logistics packaging decisions. **Price** refers to the pricing strategy developed for the product. This includes volume and sales prices, seasonal pricing, as well as price flexibility. Although they are the domain of marketing, pricing strategies and price flexibility are directly tied to supply chain costs. **Place** deals with having the product where it is needed and when it is needed. These decisions include selection of distribution channel and market coverage. They also include traditional logistics, sourcing, and operations decisions such as inventory management, order processing, transportation, and reverse logistics. Finally, **promotion** deals with advertising and sales techniques to increase product visibility and desirability. Decisions involve promotional strategies and advertising, sales promotions, and public relations.

In the past companies primarily focused on meeting the demands of the average customer. These companies basically supplied products to customers without trying to determine or satisfy the unique needs of each individual customer. Today, consumers are knowledgeable; they demand what they want at the highest quality, low price, delivered at record speed. Also, today's customers expect a world-class organization to provide high levels of customer service. To compete in this new economy, companies are putting forth a great deal of effort and money to precisely understand their customers, to provide unprecedented levels of customer service, and to provide one-on-one customization. This has resulted in large changes in SCM of companies and the relationships between supply chain members who aim to deliver what consumers want. We now look at key issues in designing customer-driven supply chains.

## Customer-Driven Supply Chains

### Who Is the Customer?

Today's economy is characterized by a shift in power from companies to customers, where the customers are the dominant force. Customers now expect to receive the products they want, when they want them at a low price. As a result, companies are focused on capturing the individual customer, which requires a shift in focus from merely supplying goods and services to customers to actually capturing loyalty. The competition for customers has resulted in a proliferation of product choices and alternatives, which has had huge supply chain implications.

The focus on the customer has required supply chain companies to work together to provide customers with more value than competing supply chains. As a result companies are making large changes in their organizational structure and their supply chain relationships.

A company's supply chain contributes to its success because it provides more value to the customer than a competing supply chain. This may mean that it provides superior delivery and greater product availability. For supply chains to meet customer demands, they need to know exactly *who* the customer is. This also requires an understanding of the term "customer." Most people assume that the term refers to the final customer or consumer. However, supply chain management as a concept requires a careful understanding of the term "customer."

The "customer" can have many different meanings. Typically there are two types of end users. The first is the **end consumer**, which could be an individual or a household that purchases

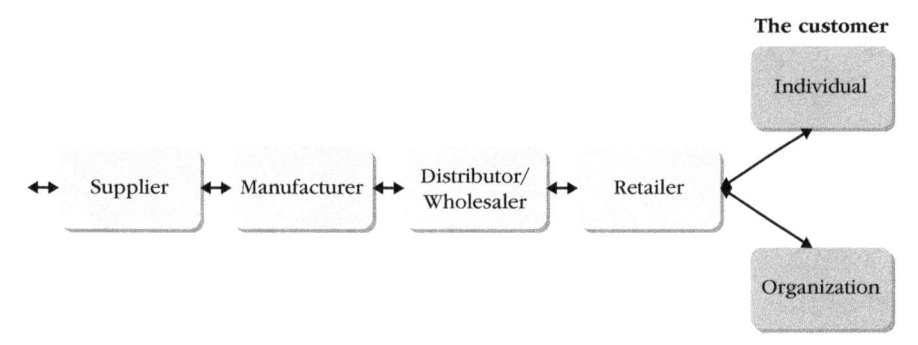

**FIGURE 4.3** Traditional view of the "customer."

products and services to satisfy personal needs. The second type of customer is an **organizational end user**. In this second case, purchases are made by an organization or institution for employees to perform their jobs in the organization. An SCM perspective requires that all firms in the supply chain focus on meeting the needs and requirements of customers, whether they are individual consumers or organizational end users. This is shown in Figure 4.3.

From an SCM perspective, a customer is at any delivery location, not necessarily the last location in the supply chain. This includes a range of possible locations from consumers' homes, to retail and wholesale businesses, to the receiving docks of manufacturing plants and distribution centers. Often the customer is a different organization or individual than the one who is taking ownership of the product or service being delivered. Sometimes the customer is a different facility of the same firm or a business partner at some other location in the supply chain. For example, the logistics manager of a Wal-Mart warehouse would think of the Wal-Mart retail location as its customer. They may be part of the same overall organization, but one serves the other as its customer.

Within the supply chain context there is a broad perspective of the term *customer*. The total supply chain looks at the end user of the product or service as the primary customer whose needs or requirements must be accommodated. The supply chain perspective, however, recognizes that the supply chain is made up of intermediate organizations, from raw material suppliers at the beginning of the chain to final consumers at the end of the chain. Each organization in the chain is dependent on the organization that immediately precedes it in the chain and serves as its supplier. Therefore, all organizations in the supply chain are both suppliers and customers to other members of the chain. For example, Wal-Mart may sell Tide laundry detergent to the final customer in the supply chain. Proctor & Gamble (P&G) provides Tide laundry detergent to Wal-Mart and is therefore its supplier. However, P&G is a "customer" to their suppliers from which it receives supplies such as chemicals and plastics. Therefore, Proctor and Gamble is a "customer" of its suppliers and a "supplier" to retailers such as Wal-Mart. Although each entity in the chain serves their immediate customer, they are ultimately driven by the demands of the final customer in the chain. This is shown in Figure 4.4.

## Types of Customer Relationships

The traditional marketing approach has been to pursue a strategy of increasing the number of customer transactions to increase revenues and profits. This is transactional marketing as it focuses primarily on increasing the number of customer transactions. This type of relationship does not consider the long-term impact that comes from building alliances. Rather, it is only a short-term view of the supplier–customer relationship. Often this strategy is used together with the marketing

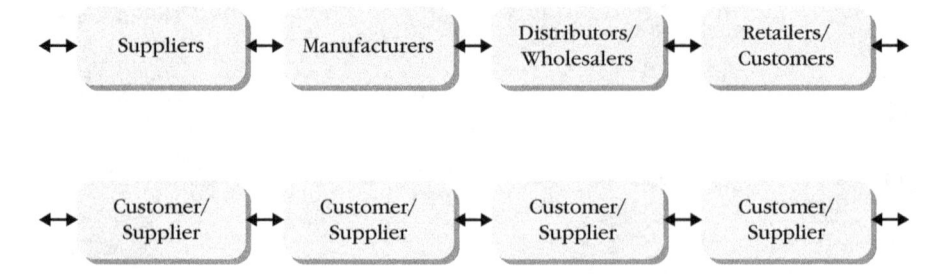

**FIGURE 4.4** Every supply chain member is both a supplier and customer.

practice of developing target markets, such as grouping customers based on demographics or buying patterns. Usually these groupings are very large, and specific customer needs are neglected. Three of the most common strategies used to satisfy customers in various target markets are the following: standardized strategy, customized strategy, and niche strategy.

## Managerial Insight's Box—Understanding the Customer

### ■ TARGET

Target uses sophisticated computer systems to understand its customers. The company tracks customer purchases, collects big data, and applies advanced analytics to the data set. The algorithm is even able to determine that a female shopper is pregnant based on a purchase assortment of 25 items that a woman buys. Some of the purchased items include vitamins, zinc, cocoa butter, and large clothing. Throw in a rocking chair, and the computer model says the purchaser is pregnant. Based on this assortment the algorithm even determines the timing of the pregnancy, identifying the purchaser as being in the second trimester. The algorithm has established that if it can lure mothers-to-be in their second trimester, they will maintain the highest customer loyalty rates.

The way this works is that Target assigns every customer an ID number that is tied to their name, e-mail address, and credit card number. The company then uses this information to track purchases and send coupons based on customer preferences.

Unfortunately in the case of Target, an irate father scolded a Target manager because his teenage daughter received baby coupons in the mail. As it turned out, his daughter was indeed pregnant. The algorithm was correct.

Adapted from: Kashmir Hill, "How Target Figured Out a Teen Girl Was Pregnant Before Her Father Did," *Forbes*, February 12, 2012.

In the **standardized strategy** all customers are viewed in the same way. It provides a minimal amount of product customization. When market segmentation is used, it ultimately averages out the needs of all the customers in the group. The company then develops products to satisfy the needs of the average of the customers in the group, rather than satisfying individual customer needs. This has large cost advantages in that all processes from manufacturing, logistics, and marketing are streamlined and predictable. The advantage is that the customer receives a product at the lowest cost possible.

However, many customers may not be satisfied under this strategy, as they are unable to receive the products that meet their specific needs. There are many examples of "one-size-fits-all" products. For example, the pain reliever acetaminophen, sold under the brand name of Tylenol, was historically available only as a standard pain reliever. However, it is now available in many versions, including sinus-relief Tylenol, Tylenol PM, and Tylenol tablets versus gel-caps. This has provided greater options, but has also increased supply chain costs.

**Customized strategy** is a differentiated strategy that capitalizes on information that comes from market segmentation and target markets. The strategy enables the company to develop different versions of a product based on specific market needs. This results in higher-priced products due to the complexities involved in producing and coordinating multiple products being sent to multiple locations. Differences occur in the manufacturing process, distribution channel, logistics, and marketing. For example, Coca-Cola is an agile company that changes features of its product to meet different markets. Product sizes are smaller in the Asian and European markets. Also, the company has moved to producing various juice drink alternatives and teas, particularly popular in the Asian market, as opposed to colas.

The **niche strategy** is a strategy that targets only one segment of the overall market by offering very precise products that specifically meet customer needs. It is the opposite of the undifferentiated strategy. This is typically a strategy exploited by small firms or new companies. For example, there are many specialty retail stores that target niche markets, such as maternity clothes, or suits for tall men, or petite women. These companies are smaller and offer products at higher prices to compensate for the greater customer focus of their offering.

The ultimate in customer relationship management is to focus on each individual customer and to design a product to meet their individual needs. This approach is called **micro-marketing** or **one-to-one marketing**, and recognizes that each individual customer may have their own unique requirements. This could be an end customer such as an individual, or an intermediary customer such as a manufacturer or retailer. For example, large suppliers to Wal-Mart are required to develop information systems that directly match those of Wal-Mart to provide seamless information transfer.

One-on-one relationships may not be feasible with every customer. Also, many customers may not care for a customized relationship and may prefer a standardized product at a lower cost. However, one-to-one relationships can significantly reduce transaction costs between supply chain intermediaries by making transactions routine and ultimately lowering costs for the end customer. One-to-one relationships with the end customer can also be a significant factor in building brand loyalty.

Today, a high degree of one-to-one customization has been made possible with the development of **customer relationship management (CRM)** software that focuses on the interface between the firm and its customer. These systems collect customer-specific data, which allow the firm to provide customer-specific solutions. We look at these systems in more detail next.

## Managing Customers Using CRM

CRM involves managing long-term relationships between the company and its customers to improve profitability. It is a concept that has gained great popularity over the past few years given the advances in technology and the tremendous benefits it provides to the company and the supply chain.

To keep customers coming back, firms must offer distinct capabilities that provide value to customers. We know that in general terms customers perceive value through reliable, on-time delivery of high-quality products and services at competitive pricing. The problem, however, is that today's customers demand a greater amount of customization than ever before. Companies have to work hard to identify very precise needs of each customer group.

The ability to capture detailed customer information has become a reality with today's sophisticated technology. CRM uses automated customer transactions to gather data and customize communication. This data is captured through suites of software modules that are part of larger enterprise resource planning (ERP) systems. They collect information through automated transactions to create large databases that, in turn, can be mined to design customer-specific solutions. For example, American Airlines uses CRM applications to precisely identify their most profitable customers. This information is then used to build strong customer relationships. One example of this might be sending a personalized text message to a highly valued customer that their planned flight is going to be delayed.

The advantage of CRM is that it provides information that aids market segmentation as we can better create clusters of customers based on profitability and other factors. It also helps to predict customer behavior and create customized customer communication. Therefore, CRM plays a critical role in SCM.

## Delivering Value to Customers

### Voice of the Customer (VOC)

The central focus of supply chain management is to create value for the customer. However, how can we create value if we don't know exactly what the customer wants? The key issue is to understand exactly what it is the customer perceives as value. This is the responsibility of marketing and is not as easy as it sounds.

Understanding what the customer wants and perceives as value is a complex process. Most customers have a difficult time defining value, but they know it when they see it. For example, although you probably have an opinion on which cell phone provider provides the highest value, it may be difficult for you to define the specific standard of value in precise terms. Also, your friends may prefer a different cell phone provider, as they have a different opinion regarding what constitutes value.

**Voice of the customer (VOC)** is the process of capturing customer needs and preferences. Customer needs can be broken into three levels: basic needs, performance needs, and excitement needs. Basic needs are minimum customer expectations that are understood. If these needs are not met, the customer would be extremely dissatisfied. For example, brand-new rain boots that leak in wet weather would be considered unacceptable. Performance needs differentiate one product from another relative to the prices. An example here may be finding two pairs of rain boots at a comparative price, but one has a skid-proof sole. Excitement needs are normally not known by the customer in advance, but they elicit delight over the product. An example here may be purchasing the boots and finding that there is a free 10-year replacement guarantee for any dissatisfaction. Understanding different types of needs is critical information in designing products and services and their associated supply chains.

The definition of value depends on the point of view of the customers defining it. In the rain boots example, the definition of value would be different if the customer was a parent buying rain boots for their child versus a firefighter buying waterproof boots for work. For this reason, VOC begins by dividing customers into their market segments. As we discussed earlier, we can segment customers by their demographic features or how, where, and when they use the product. This marketing information can help focus our attention on critical customer requirements in each market segment. After market segmentation, market research is used to gather information from customers in each segment using a variety of tools, such as interviews and focus groups. This enables marketing to identify key drivers of value in each market segment. Finally, the last step in translating the VOC is to use a tool called **quality function deployment (QFD)** to translate general customer requirements into specific product characteristics. These steps are shown in Figure 4.5.

QFD is a tool for translating the voice of the customer into specific technical requirements. Customers often speak in everyday language. For example, a product can be described as "attractive," "strong," or "safe." To produce a product the customers actually want, these vague expressions need to be translated into specific technical requirements. This is the role of QFD.

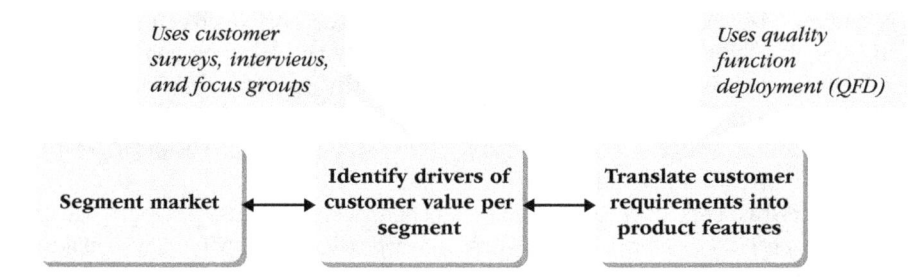

**FIGURE 4.5** Translating the voice of the customer.

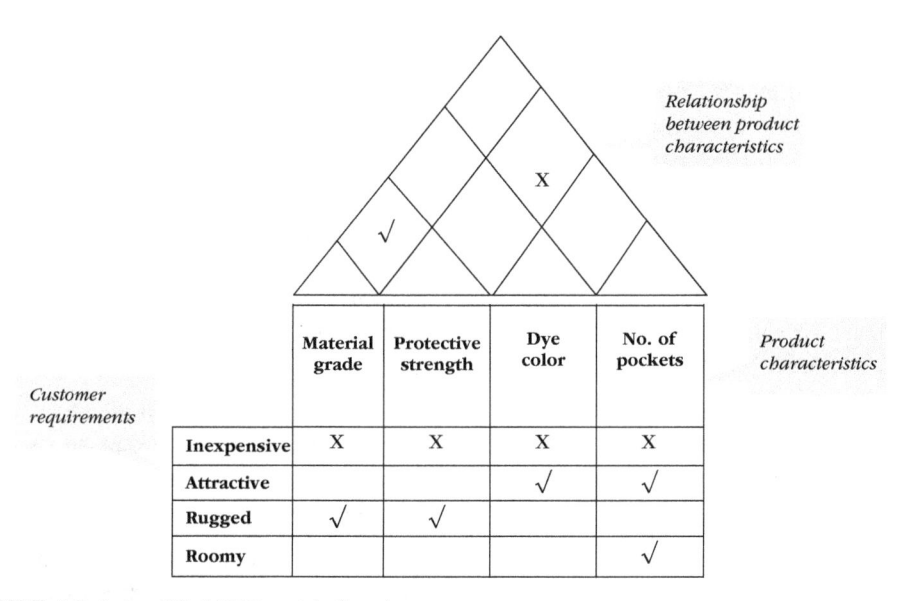

**FIGURE 4.6** A simplified QFD matrix for a laptop case.

QFD is also used to enhance communication between different functions, such as marketing, operations, and engineering.

Figure 4.6 shows a simplified example of a QFD matrix for a laptop computer bag. This matrix is sometimes called the "house of quality," as it resembles a picture of a house. The left side of the matrix lists general customer requirements that marketing gathers from customers using tools such as interviews or focus groups. The customers may say they want the computer bag to be inexpensive, attractive, rugged, and roomy. Along the top of the matrix is a list of specific product characteristics. The main body of the matrix shows how each product characteristic supports the specific customer requirements. For example, "rugged" is supported by material strength and grade. Finally, the "roof" of the matrix shows the relationship between some of the features. Strength of material and grade go together, whereas more compartments may take away from the bag's protective strength. The QFD matrix moves the organization from these general customer requirements to specific product characteristics. It can also show where conflict may exist between some of the features and where trade-offs may have to be made.

# What Is Customer Service?

Today's customers are very different from those just a few years ago. They demand higher performance standards than ever before, and brand loyalty is not necessarily something that they routinely support. They expect high-quality and low-cost products delivered at their convenience. The problem is that these competitive dimensions can easily be copied by competitors. Excellence on these dimensions is expected but does not necessarily provide a competitive advantage. The one competitive dimension, however, that is difficult to copy and can provide a competitive advantage is customer service. As a result, many companies have made customer service their focal point and the driving force of their supply chains.

**Customer service** can be defined as a process of enhancing the level of customer satisfaction by meeting or exceeding customer expectations. It can provide a competitive advantage to the firm and the supply chain by maximizing the total value to the final customer. Within an organization customer service can be viewed in three distinct ways, each requiring progressively more commitment. They are

- **An Activity.** This first view looks at customer service as an activity that a firm must do to satisfy customers. This includes activities such as billing and invoicing, product returns, and handling claims. Companies with this view believe they are meeting their obligations by having a customer service department responsible for handling customer problems and complaints.

- **A Set of Performance Measures.** This second view looks at customer service in terms of specific performance measures that must be met. Examples would be percentage of orders delivered on time or the number of orders processed within acceptable time limits. A company with this view would consider it has met its customer service requirements if the performance measures were being met.

- **A Philosophy.** This last view looks at customer service as a firm-wide commitment to customers through superior customer service. It is a philosophy that permeates all decisions throughout the company. This view of customer service is consistent with the emphasis on today's quality management, which we discuss in Chapter 10.

The first view of customer service looks at it as a mere activity and requires the least amount of involvement on the part of the company. From this perspective, customer service activities are at the transactional level. For example, the activity of accepting product returns from customers in a retail store adds no value to a product. The activity is merely a transaction to please customers. Companies with this view of customer service have only a limited opportunity to add value to the customer.

The second view of customer service provides an objective way of measuring customer service performance and can serve as a benchmark to gauge improvement. However, it is not sufficient to create customer service excellence. Customer service needs to be an organizational philosophy to provide a competitive advantage.

## Impact on the Supply Chain

Customer service excellence can provide a competitive advantage. However, it requires commitment of the entire supply chain and can be costly to implement. Supply chain managers have to balance the benefits attained from increased customer service levels against the cost of providing that service. Consider, for example, a retail customer that can lower their inventories if their supplier uses air rather than truck transport. The customer can lower inventory costs as a result of shorter transit time. However, higher transportation costs are going to be incurred, as air transport is costlier than transport via truck. Supply chain managers have to find the optimum balance of these costs.

Customer service impacts the supply chain on four dimensions: time, dependability, communications, and convenience. Let's look at these in a little more detail.

1. **Time.** Time is concerned with the speed at which the company responds to its customers. From a supply chain perspective this refers to the time to complete an order and deliver it to the customer, called the order cycle time. Competition based on time has been primarily enabled by the function of logistics, which today has the ability to guarantee a given level of order cycle time. Successful logistics operations have a high degree of time control over the elements of moving goods through the chain, such as order processing, order preparation, and order shipment. By effectively managing these activities, companies have ensured that order cycles will be responsive and of short duration.

2. **Dependability.** Dependability refers to consistently meeting promises made to customers, including order cycle time and level of quality. In fact, for some customers dependability can be more important than delivery time or other dimensions. For example, some customers might prefer a longer lead time, knowing with certainty the exact time of delivery. This allows customer firms to minimize their inventory levels if lead time is consistent. A company that knows with certainty that lead time is going to be 10 days can make better plans than being promised a shorter lead time with the possibility of fluctuation. This level of dependability translates into carrying less inventory as safety stock and results in lower costs.

3. **Communication.** Communication is an aspect of customer service that involves providing real-time order status to all supply chain customers. Communication with customers is vital to monitoring customer service levels relating to dependability. It involves integrated information technology (IT) across the supply chain that tracks the order filling process and is enabled by communication tools such as electronic data interchange (EDI) or the Internet. In addition to providing status update, these communication tools can reduce errors in transferring order information as the order moves through the chain. The simplification of product identification is one strategy companies use to make this process more efficient. One example of this is using product codes to reduce order picker errors.

4. **Convenience.** Companies are offering more customer conveniences as they move toward providing a greater amount of customization to their customers. In turn, this requires that the supply chain be more flexible to accommodate a range of requirements. The simplest option is to have one or a few standard service levels that apply to all customers. However, this is only possible when the requirements are the same for all customers. For example, one customer may require the supplier to place all products on pallets and ship everything by rail. Another customer may require truck delivery only, using no pallets. Some customers may require special delivery times that must be met. This all places large demands on the supply chain and especially the logistics function. It also impacts decisions regarding packaging, mode of transportation, and routing.

One strategy to deal with this problem is to group customer requirements by factors such as customer size, market area, and the product line the customer is purchasing. This grouping, or market segmentation, makes it easier to meet customer expectations economically.

## Measuring Customer Service

Developing and measuring standards of customer service performance is essential, as it allows a company to monitor how it is doing in meeting set objectives. The company can also benchmark its performance against others in its industry.

Historically, companies used measures that viewed performance from the perspective of the supplier, solely focusing on customer service dimensions prior to shipping. This did not permit the supplier to know whether the customer was satisfied and if there were any problems with

| Supplier-Oriented Standards | Customer-Oriented Standards |
|---|---|
| • Order shipped on time | • Orders received on time |
| • Orders shipped complete | • Orders received complete |
| • Orders shipped damage free | • Orders received damage free |
| • Order preparation time | • Orders filled accurately |

**FIGURE 4.7** Supplier-oriented versus customer-oriented standards.

the delivery. Also, these measures did not enable the seller to identify whether there were any problems and whether its improvement efforts were successful.

Effective performance measures focus on customer service from the viewpoint of the customer rather than the supplier, as shown in Figure 4.7. These measures provide the data to make an evaluation of how successful the product delivery system is. They can also serve as an early warning system of potential problems as they develop. For example, monitoring customer service delivery may show that on-time delivery has slipped from 99% to 95%, triggering the company to evaluate the system for potential problems. In fact, the on-time delivery measure is particularly important in supply chain management, as it has become common practice for buying companies to give specific delivery appointment times for deliveries. The move to lean supply chain systems, which we discuss in Chapter 10, requires a very narrow delivery time "window" for suppliers and has made achieving on-time deliveries much more difficult than in the past.

Most companies, however, do not rely on one, but multiple measures of customer service performance. Using multiple measures enables a company to address potential problems on many customer service dimensions. Having multiple performance measures, however, can make it even more difficult to achieve high levels of customer service.

## Global Customer Service Issues

Companies that take a global view of customer service find that it adds even more complexities. Rather than dividing world markets into separate entities with very different product needs, as might be expected, a better approach is searching for common market demands worldwide. Different parts of the world have different service needs that are related to issues such as information availability, order completeness, and expected lead times. Other factors that contribute to differences in customer service are the availability of a supporting infrastructure, such as roads, power, communication network, the local congestion, and time differences. These factors may make it impossible to achieve the same levels of customer service globally.

Global customer service levels should be designed to match local customer needs and expectations to the greatest degree possible. A strong argument can be made for the implementation of a centrally coordinated global supply chain strategy. However, the one activity that should be conducted locally is setting the customer service standard.

## Global Insights Box—Global Customer Service

### ■ COCA-COLA JAPAN

Most global companies typically provide different levels of customer service based on location. An example is Coca-Cola, which provides very different types of service in Japan than in the United States or Europe. For example, in Japan the company provides a much higher level of service to its retail customers and merchants, but it meets local standards. The drivers of Coca-Cola delivery trucks are responsible for providing merchandising in supermarkets, helping in processing bills in small mom-and-pop operations, and responding to signals from communication systems in vending machines so that time is not wasted delivering to full machines. The Coca-Cola vending machines are equipped with efficient electronic money sensors and are stocked with product choices that include a variety of Japanese tea brands catering to local taste and focusing on healthy options. Developing the service to match the needs of the country creates the most efficient and effective customer service policy, rather than simply implementing the same strategy worldwide.

# Channels of Distribution

## What Are Channels of Distribution?

A **channel of distribution** is the way products and services are passed from the manufacturer to the final consumer. It is made up of the entities involved in getting products and services to final customers and can involve a variety of intermediary firms, including wholesalers, distributors, or retailers. Decisions regarding the distribution channel are critical to a company's success, as they are directly related to the ability for the organization to access the final customer.

Channels of distribution can be classified as either **direct** or **indirect**. A direct channel structure is one where the transaction is directly from the producer to end user or final consumer. An example might be a farmer that sells directly to the final consumer, as at a farmers market. Another example is the sale of jet aircraft that are custom designed and sold directly to the airline. This channel usually gives the company greatest control on how the product is being designed for the final customer. However, distribution costs incurred by the manufacturer are higher, making it necessary for the firm to have substantial sales volume, market concentration, or higher product cost.

Indirect channels are those that use intermediaries, such as wholesalers and retailers, to sell to final consumers. In this case the external institutions or agencies (e.g., carriers, warehouses, wholesalers, retailers) assume much of the cost, burden, and risk. The manufacturer receives less revenue per unit than with the direct channel, but it also carries lower risk.

There is no "best" distribution structure. Rather the best distribution channel structure varies by the nature of the product and the market. The structure design depends on numerous factors, such as buying patterns of end customers, competitors, and market saturation. Characteristics of the product itself are another important factor. Complex products, for example, may require a demonstration, which implies that they may need to be sold directly to the consumer. An example is the Kirby vacuum cleaner, which is sold by distributors directly to consumers with in-home demonstrations. Difficult-to-move products may be sold through an intermediary, such as automobiles that are shipped directly to dealers. Many products are shipped through wholesalers who may be better equipped to efficiently combine products from many different suppliers. Sometimes agents may be involved that negotiate between manufacturers, distributors, and retailers.

Most companies want to identify a "best" channel structure, but there is no "best" channel structure for all firms producing similar products. Management must determine the channel structure that is appropriate given the firm's corporate and marketing objectives. For example, if the firm has targeted multiple market segments, then management may have to develop multiple channels to service these markets efficiently. The distribution channel selected has important policy implications for the organization. Consider that direct-to-customer strategy is the model historically used by Dell. However, recently Michael Dell announced that Dell Computer Corporation would be changing its distribution channel to sell through retailers such as Best Buy. This change in Dell's distribution strategy is in response to changing markets and shows the importance of changing distribution channels based on the business environment.

## Designing a Distribution Channel

The theory of channel structure was first developed by Louis P. Bucklin, who explained that the purpose of the distribution channel is to provide consumers with the desired products and services at minimal cost. The best channel structure forms when no other channel generates more profits or provides greater consumer satisfaction per dollar of product cost. According to Bucklin, to achieve the optimal channel structure, functions over time shift from one channel member to another to improve delivery and cost. As a result, channel structure is not static but is constantly changing to meet customer demands. Given a desired product and service combination by the consumer, channel members arrange their functional tasks in a way that minimizes total channel costs. As specific functions shift along the channel, there may addition or deletion of channel members. Although organizations design channel structures taking into account many factors, it is consumers who ultimately determine the channel structure through their purchasing patterns.

Three factors influence the structure of the distribution channel. These are market coverage objectives, product characteristics, and customer service objectives. The first of these, market coverage objectives, involves decisions regarding the size of specific market areas and the intensity of coverage of specific geographic regions. For example, this could be measured by the number of retail outlets in a particular region relative to the concentration of customers.

Three basic market coverage alternatives exist. The first alternative is **intensive distribution**. This involves the placement of a product in as many outlets or locations as possible. An example of this would be a product, such as Tide laundry detergent, that is available at almost all supermarket locations. The second market alternative is **selective distribution**. This involves the placement of a product or brand in a more limited number of outlets within a specific geographic area. Last is **exclusive distribution**, which involves placement of a brand in only one outlet in each geographic area. Exclusive distribution is an alternative that should be related to the types of customers the company wants to serve.

Product characteristics are another significant factor in the design of the distribution channel. For example, one important characteristic is the value of the product. High-value products typically require a shorter supply chain to minimize cost, whereas low-value products should have intensive distribution to maximize sales. Highly technical products usually require product demonstration and are better suited for a direct channel. Highly perishable products need to be delivered to markets fast due to their short life cycle.

Customer service objectives are another consideration in designing a channel structure. Customer service is used to differentiate the product or influence the market price, provided that customers are willing to pay more for better service. In addition, the supply chain structure determines the costs of providing a specified level of customer service. This means that customer service levels and the design of the appropriate distribution channel should carefully balance customer needs and costs.

## Distribution versus Logistics Channel

The distribution channel is different from the logistics channel. However, the logistics channel and the distribution channel are interrelated and are both part of the supply chain. These channels are illustrated and compared in Figure 4.8.

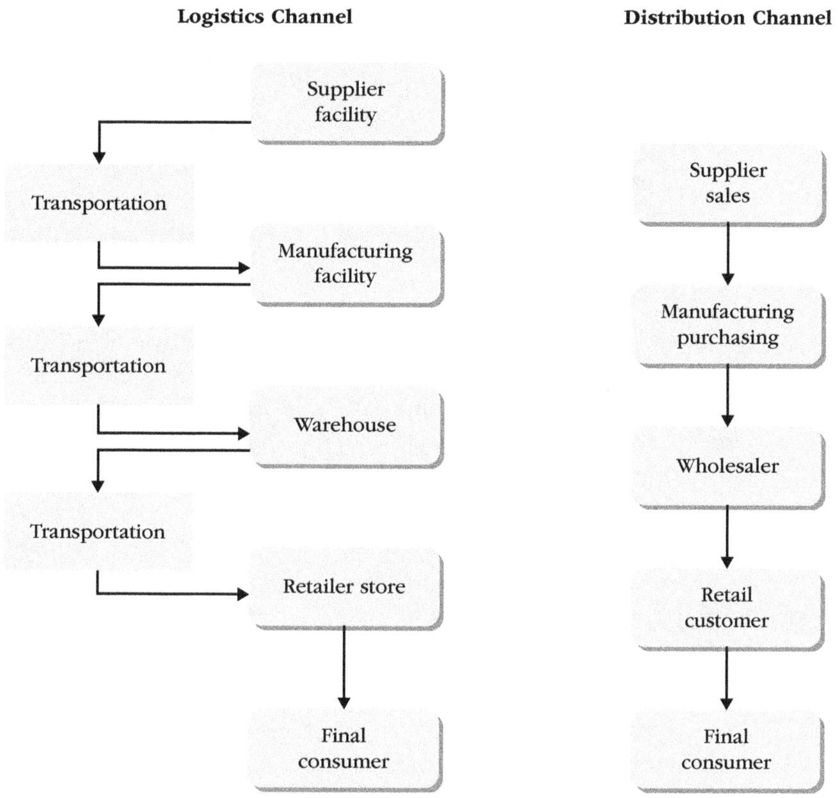

## Logistics Channel

```
Supplier facility
    ↓
Transportation → Manufacturing facility
    ↓
Transportation → Warehouse
    ↓
Transportation → Retailer store
                    ↓
                 Final consumer
```

## Distribution Channel

```
Supplier sales
    ↓
Manufacturing purchasing
    ↓
Wholesaler
    ↓
Retail customer
    ↓
Final consumer
```

**FIGURE 4.8** Logistics versus marketing distribution channel.

# Managerial Insights Box—Changing the Distribution Channel

## ■ STEINWAY PIANOS

When Bruce Stevens joined Steinway & Sons as CEO in 1985, the maker of legendary hand-crafted pianos found itself in the middle a slowdown crisis. Sales had slowed dramatically, and excess inventory was clogging the sales channel. In fact, the company had over four months' worth of finished goods inventory—over 900 unsold pianos—just sitting in inventory. Its 150 authorized dealers were complaining about low profit margins and the costs associated with supplying concert pianos for Steinway Artist performers. The company was clearly in trouble.

The dealers were critical to Steinway's success. They were the ones that represented the company through trained salespeople, beautiful showrooms, and good displays. To understand their concerns, Stevens spent six months visiting the discontented dealers across the country and listening to their concerns. Based on what he heard, Stevens developed a relationship plan with dealers called the "Steinway Working Partnership." At the core of this program was an offer to provide expanded and exclusive territories to dealers, as well as profit opportunities in exchange for their stepped-up commitment to display and promote Steinway products. Many dealers were reluctant to make the required investment. It required upgrading showrooms, increasing inventory, and adding salespeople, while sales were running at 20% below average.

The dealer network was slowly trimmed. The dealers that remained saw Steinway making good on its promises of expanding territories, and they signed on to the program. By 2009, only 63 dealers remained in Steinway's U.S. dealer network, less than half of the mid-1980s level. However, those remaining dealers were far more profitable. It took the company almost six years to gain the trust needed to fully implement the program, but it was a big success for Steinway and the dealers that remained. As a result, sales rebounded, and more dealers were selectively added on.

For Steinway, downsizing the distribution channel was the best way to increase dealer profitability and sales for the company. Rather than waiting and reactively managing its distribution channel, Steinway proactively pruned the channel to make it stronger.

Adapted from: Johnson, M.E., and R.J. Batt. "Channel Management: Breaking the Destructive Growth Cycle." *Supply Chain Management Review*, 13 (5), July 2009: 26.

---

The logistics channel refers to the physical movement of products from where they are available to where they are needed. The distribution channel, on the other hand, refers to the transactional entities involved, such as dealers, distributors, and wholesalers. Consider that a "warehouse" is part of the logistics channel, whereas a "wholesaler" is part of the distribution channel. The wholesaler may not even hold the actual product in the warehouse but may simply serve as an agent between the manufacturer and retailer. Successful supply chain management requires proper management and integration of both types of channels.

## The Impact of E-Commerce

The Internet has provided unprecedented ability for companies to access massive numbers of customers across the globe. However, this broad reach must be coupled with a suitable distribution network to fulfill orders that are placed over the Internet. E-commerce can provide success to a firm only if the firm can integrate the Internet with existing channels of distribution in a way that uses the strengths of each appropriately. There are numerous examples of companies that have created an online presence but subsequently failed due to the inability to integrate it with the physical channels. One example was Kozmo.com, a web-based home delivery company founded in 1997. Kozmo's mission was to deliver products to customers—everything from the latest video to ice cream—in less than an hour. Kozmo was technology enabled and rapidly became a huge success. However, the initial success gave rise to overly fast expansion. The company found it difficult to coordinate the physical distribution channel with the promises made on its website. The consequences were too much inventory, poor deliveries, and losses in profits, and they had to close their doors in April 2001.

The coupling of the virtual network with the physical network has been referred to as "clicks and mortar." The success of an e-business is closely linked to the distribution capabilities of the existing supply chain. Separating them typically adds to inefficiencies.

A company needs to find ways to use its physical assets to satisfy both online orders and customers who want to shop through traditional routes for the most effective way to integrate e-business within its supply chain network.

E-commerce has created other challenges for companies. For example, shipping small bundles of products to many different customers is very different than shipping in bulk to one location, such as a retailer warehouse. Often companies underestimate and do not adequately calculate shipping costs. For example, it is not a good option for companies to charge standard shipping fees without consideration of size, weight, and destination. Otherwise they will incur losses. Many e-businesses have incurred financial losses due to incomplete consideration of shipping costs. Companies must have an accurate assessment of the costs incurred to fulfill an order and reflect this cost in the prices they charge.

The e-commerce distribution system should also be modified to accommodate shipping of small bundles. E-business has required a change in distribution from shipping large quantities to retail locations to shipping small packages to individual customers. For example, "bricks-and-mortar" bookstores, such as Barnes & Noble, send all their merchandise in large quantities to replenish their stores. In contrast, online booksellers must send small packages to individual customers that may contain only one or two books. This can prove to be very expensive from a distribution point of view. Therefore, it becomes critical for companies to exploit every possible opportunity to consolidate shipments to lower costs. This may involve partnering with other firms to consolidate shipments. To increase consolidation and reduce transportation costs, e-businesses must try to bundle an entire customer order into a single package.

Recall that handling returns is a critical part of the supply chain. As a result, the distribution channel should be designed to efficiently handle returns. Customers purchasing products online are likely to have a higher rate of return than customers purchasing from a physical store due to their inability to physically handle the product beforehand. Regardless of how good a website is, it cannot match the customer experience of touching and seeing the product at a retail store, and the product purchased online is often different from the customer's expectation. Handling returns is a big challenge for e-businesses and can have a strong impact on customer satisfaction. Customers are more likely to shop from e-businesses that make returns easy.

A strategy that has worked well for successful e-businesses is to have the retail locations handle the returns by allowing customers to return unwanted merchandise at a store. Pure e-businesses that do not have a "bricks-and-mortar" location, however, have no other choice but to allow customers to mail back the unwanted merchandise. The easier the return process for customers, such as providing preprinted return labels, the higher the supply chain cost to the company. On the other hand, the more difficult the process, the less satisfied the customer will be and the more reluctant to purchase online in the future.

## The Omni-Channel

The **omni-channel** is an approach to sales that seeks to provide the customer with a seamless shopping experience across multiple channels. This is regardless of whether the customer is shopping online from a desktop or mobile device, by telephone, or in a bricks-and-mortar store. It is essentially a seamless experience in real time across channels.

With a traditional multichannel the customer can use alternative shopping channels, such as a physical shopping environment or an online one. However, as technological capability evolves it has become more integrated in the lives of consumers. This means that the lines between what customers purchase online and in real life is blurring. Customers no longer think of a "desktop experience" separated from a "bricks-and-mortar experience," which is separated from a "mobile experience." Rather, they want a shopping experience that is holistic and integrated. That is the omni-channel.

In an omni-channel the customer experiences true integration between the different channels on the "back end." All the information and history is completely transparent across channels. In an omni-channel environment the customer can go online to the company's website to check inventory by store, purchase the item later on with a smartphone if they choose, and pick up the product at the customer's chosen location. At the retail location this means that a customer service representative is able to immediately reference the customer's previous purchases—whether online or in store—and preferences just as easily as the customer service representative on the phone or online. The key is that all channels are integrated. It is technology that has enabled this to happen.

The omni-channel is rapidly becoming the norm in many industries such as retail, as customers demand seamless interface among their various shopping experiences. It has also helped the supply chain better coordinate inventory across the different channels.

## Big Data Analytics Box

### ■ OASIS

Oasis is a UK fashion retailer that has embraced the omni-channel and, with state-of-the art-technology, has connected all shopping channels. This includes their e-commerce site, mobile app, and the bricks-and-mortar stores. They have also fused these channels into a consistent presentation with matching displayed images across their site and social channels. They cover all popular social media channels, with image-led accounts on platforms including Pinterest, Instagram, and Facebook, and they have made them easy to navigate.

At their store locations all shop floor assistants are equipped with an iPad. They have the most up-to-date stock information and can check stock levels on all products for customers. If the item is not in stock, they order it direct to the customer's house. The iPad also acts as a cash register, making it easy for associates to ring you up from anywhere in the store.

Oasis goes even further to connect the in-store and online experience. The technology enables the customer to book a personal shopping slot with their stylists, available at 15 of their stores across the UK. They break down the different personal shopping occasion slots for events, such as "birthday," "sun seeker", and "wardrobe overhaul," and they even allow the customer to read a bit about the personal stylist with whom they will be meeting.

This type of seamless experience across channels is increasingly becoming a customer expectation. Technology is making it a reality.

Adapted from: Jackson, Helen. "What Can You Learn from Oasis' Omni-Channel Strategy?" *Retail News, Fashion News, Omni-Channel*, November 6, 2015.

## CHAPTER HIGHLIGHTS

1. Marketing is the function responsible for linking the organization to its customers and is concerned with the "downstream" part of the supply chain. It is responsible for identifying customer needs, determining how to create value for customers, and building strong customer relationships.

2. Marketing decisions drive all actions of the organization and the supply chain. These decisions fall into four distinct categories known as the marketing mix or the 4Ps. They are product, price, place (distribution), and promotion.

3. The traditional marketing approach has been to pursue a strategy of increasing the number of customer transactions to increase revenues and profits—transactional marketing. Today's approach to marketing is to develop long-term relationships with customers—relational marketing.

4. CRM is sophisticated technology that gathers data and customizes communication from automated customer transactions. This data is captured through suites of software modules that are part of larger enterprise resource planning systems (ERPs).

5. Customer service is the process of enhancing the level of customer satisfaction by meeting or exceeding customer expectations. It can be viewed in three distinct ways: an activity, a set of performance measures, and an overarching philosophy.

6. A channel of distribution is the way products and services are passed from the manufacturer to the final consumer. It is made up of the entities involved in getting products and services to final customers and can involve a variety of intermediary firms, including wholesalers, distributors, or retailers.

7. Channels of distribution can be direct or indirect and are part of the overall supply chain.

8. E-commerce requires changes in the channel of distribution through changes in pricing structure, shipping small bundles, and handling returns.

## KEY TERMS

| | | | | |
|---|---|---|---|---|
| Market segmentation | Price | Customized strategy | Voice of the customer | Direct |
| Mass marketing | Place | Niche strategy | (VOC) | Indirect |
| Target marketing | Promotion | Micro-marketing | Quality function | Intensive distribution |
| Transactional marketing | End consumer | One-to-one marketing | deployment (QFD) | Selective distribution |
| Relational marketing | Organizational end user | Customer relationship | Customer service | Exclusive distribution |
| Product | Standardized strategy | management (CRM) | Channel of distribution | Omni-channel |

## DISCUSSION QUESTIONS

1. Describe the differences between transactional and relational marketing. Provide an example from your own life where you have encountered them. How did each make you feel as a customer?

2. Find an example of a product where you felt there were too many product choices. Explain the implications for the company and their supply chain.

3. Identify a product market that is currently experiencing changes in customer preferences. How are the companies in that industry responding to the changing preferences? What are the supply chain implications?

4. Identify a product currently marketed for household use. Imagine you were asked to market the product for commercial use. How might the product characteristics change, and what would be the impact on the supply chain?

5. We all encounter CRM in our everyday lives—from our purchases at the grocery store to our online searches. Provide examples from your everyday life in which companies were able to gather information about your consumer preferences.

## Case Study | Gizmo

Orange Company was based out of Southern California and was doing remarkably well considering that only 10 years earlier the company had been merely a hobby for Sam Wilkerson. Sam was fascinated by taking apart computers, adding memory, then putting them back together. He never expected that his weekend hobby would turn into one of the highest-earning computer companies in the world. The company's relaxed atmosphere encouraged creativity and product innovation. The developers were never afraid to try something new. In fact, it was one of these highly experimental projects that led to their newest product: a smart phone that can do it all—simultaneously surf the Internet, text message, do voice recognition note taking, and play music and movies, while still maintaining superior functioning for making telephone calls. With no buttons to get in the way, only a touch screen, it was unlike anything seen on the market.

Although the management at Orange felt that their new smart phone—named Gizmo—would be well received by consumers as innovative and cutting edge, they had concerns. They were not sure about their target market, the marketing strategy, and the resulting supply chain implications. These decisions were directly tied to their pricing strategy and had capacity and delivery implications. Who would be their target market, and how would they price the product given its abundant features? Should the product be targeted to business professionals or students or the public in general? If the Gizmo did significantly better than expected, could their supply chain handle the added demand?

Orange was considering partnering with the largest mobile service provider in the industry, Random Wireless, for exclusive distribution. This would mean that they could utilize an already established distribution channel for their first smart phone release. Orange believed that this would mean significant distribution savings and the ability to reach a wider market. They would also be able to provide service support at many locations. However, there were also disadvantages to going through one exclusive distributor.

Orange knew that they had a wonderful product, but the key to success would be good marketing, an excellent distribution network, and a reliable supply chain. They had some decisions to make.

*Case Questions*

1. Identify at least two different possible target markets for the Gizmo. How would the marketing strategy differ for each target market? How would the pricing strategy and the

volume sold change? Identify the supply chain implications for each target market.

2. If Orange decided to go after multiple market segments, identify the supply chain requirements. Should they have multiple supply chains?

3. Discuss the advantages and disadvantages to going with one exclusive distributor. How would this decision be affected by the selection of target market? What would be the implications on the supply chain? What would you do if you were Orange?

## REFERENCES

Armstrong, Gary, and Philip Kotler. *Marketing: An Introduction*, 13th ed. New York: Pearson, 2016.

Holt, Doug. "Branding in the Age of Social Media." *Harvard Business Review*, March 2016: 40–48, 50.

Lambert, Douglas M. *SCM: Process, Partnership, Performance*, 4th ed. Sarasota, FL: Supply Chain Management Institute, 2014.

Palmatier, Robert, Louis Stern, Adel El-Ansary, and Erin Anderson. *Marketing Channel Strategy*, 8th ed. New York: Routledge, 2016.

Stock, James, and Douglas M. Lambert. "Becoming a 'World Class' Company with Logistics Service Quality." *The International Journal of Logistics Management*, 3(1), 1992: 73.

# Operations Management

# 5

## LEARNING OBJECTIVES

*After completing this chapter, you should be able to:*

- Define operations management (OM), and explain its role in the supply chain.
- Describe operations decisions, and explain how they impact supply chain management (SCM).
- Explain product and process design and their impact on supply chain operations.
- Describe categories of facility layouts and their link to process design and the supply chain.
- Describe the process of line balancing in designing product layouts.
- Explain the role of process automation in layout design.

## CHAPTER OUTLINE

■ **What Is Operations Management (OM)?**
  *The OM Function*
  *OM Decisions*
  *Manufacturing versus Service Operations*
  *Evolution of the Operations Function*
  *Impact on the Organization*
  *Impact on SCM*

■ **Product Design**
  *What Is Product Design?*
  *Design of Services*
  *The Product Design Process*
  *Break-Even Analysis*
  *Factors Impacting Product Design Decisions*

■ **Process Design**
  *What Is Process Design?*
  *Intermittent Processes*

*Repetitive Processes*

*The Continuum of Process Types*

■ **Facility Layout**

*Facility Layout Planning*

*Types of Facility Layouts*

■ **Line Balancing in Product Layouts**

*Step 1. Identify Task Times and Precedence Relationships*

*Step 2. Determine Cycle Time*

*Step 3: Determine the Theoretical Minimum Number of Workstations*

*Step 4: Assign Tasks to Workstations*

*Step 5. Compute Efficiency*

■ **Process Automation**

*Advantages and Disadvantages*

*Automation in Services*

■ **Chapter Highlights**

■ **Key Terms**

■ **Discussion Questions**

■ **Problems**

---

There's a mystique about Tesla Motors, the electric automotive and energy storage company. Tesla's CEO, Elon Musk, is one of the most dynamic figures in the world of science, technology, and innovation, and the company has developed an almost a cult-like following. People believe that Tesla's vehicles are different from other cars. Just consider that its Model S can go from zero to 155 miles per hour in 10.9 seconds—what Tesla terms "Ludicrous Mode." The company is indeed different, and one of the differences is Tesla's supply chain. Tesla has made unique operations decisions that are aligned with their goals and vision, and are supported by a vertically integrated digital supply chain. Let's look at this more closely.

The foundation of Tesla vehicles—the Model S sport sedan, the Model X crossover, and the Model 3 family sedan—is that these vehicles are designed and engineered to be electric vehicles from the start. Other automakers have moved into the electric car arena and have had to retrofit their facilities to produce these new products. Tesla, however, did not have to make these compromises. Rather, Tesla's entire system has been developed to focus precisely and solely on electric vehicles. Tesla has designed the vehicles from the ground up as a hybrid of mechanical and digital technology. It has also designed the facilities specifically to produce these products.

Unlike conventional wisdom to move manufacturing to low-cost labor locations, Tesla produces its cars in California. In fact, Tesla's plant in Palo Alto sits on some of the most expensive real estate in the world with a cost of living to match. However, Tesla's plant is also less than 18 miles away from company headquarters in an area with some of the best technical talent in the world the company can tap into. The company has selected its location to focus on proximity to innovative talent and corporate leadership rather than cost.

Tesla has invested an extraordinary amount in advanced robotics. These technological advancements in robotics are enabling Tesla to have state-of-the-art manufacturing. Tesla relies heavily on KUKA robots, the leading producer of industrial robots in the world. These robots are designed for flexibility and also interaction with thousands of workers on the shop floor. Tesla is also heavily vertically integrated. Their manufacturing facility is full-service with a plan for a supplier park in the immediate vicinity to focus on large parts. Also significant is the integration with its giant lithium-ion battery factory, called the Gigafactory, in nearby Nevada, which serves as its supplier. When fully completed this plant will be the world's second-largest building by usable space. The Gigafactory is expected to significantly reduce production cost of batteries and directly supply manufacturing.

Tesla is also continuing to invest in a network of supercharger stations around the country, in order to have a complete end-to-end supply chain. This will ensure that customers have a viable alternative to gas stations as they fuel their electric cars. Lastly, the Tesla supply chain is digitally controlled with end-to-end coordination using algorithms that automatically update over the cloud. Tesla clearly understands the importance of coordinating its supply chain and all its operations in order to produce the products it wants.

# What Is Operations Management (OM)?
## The OM Function

Operations management (OM)—or "operations"—is the business function responsible for producing a company's goods and services in an efficient and cost-effective way. It is the function responsible for transforming a company's inputs, obtained by the sourcing function, into finished goods and services, which marketing sells to final customers. Without operations, there would be no products to sell, whether tangible goods or services. The functional position of operations in the organization is highlighted in Figure 5.1.

OM is responsible for planning, organizing, and managing all the resources needed to produce a company's goods and services. This includes people, equipment, technology, materials, and information. It is a core function of every company, whether large or small, service or manufacturing, profit or nonprofit. Consider Gap Inc., one of the largest specialty retailers, discussed in Chapter 4. Gap's marketing function identifies characteristics of products desired by customers for each of its three brands, Banana Republic, Gap, and Old Navy. However, it is OM that must design and produce the merchandise, from T-shirts to jeans. It must also ensure that the right products—in terms of variety, colors, and styles—are available in the right quantities at various retail locations across the globe.

OM serves a **transformation role** in the organization by converting a company's inputs into finished goods and services, shown in Figure 5.2. These inputs include human resources, such as workers, staff, and managers; facilities and processes, such as buildings and equipment; it also includes materials, technology, and information. Outputs are the goods and services a company produces. At a manufacturing plant the transformation is the physical change of raw materials

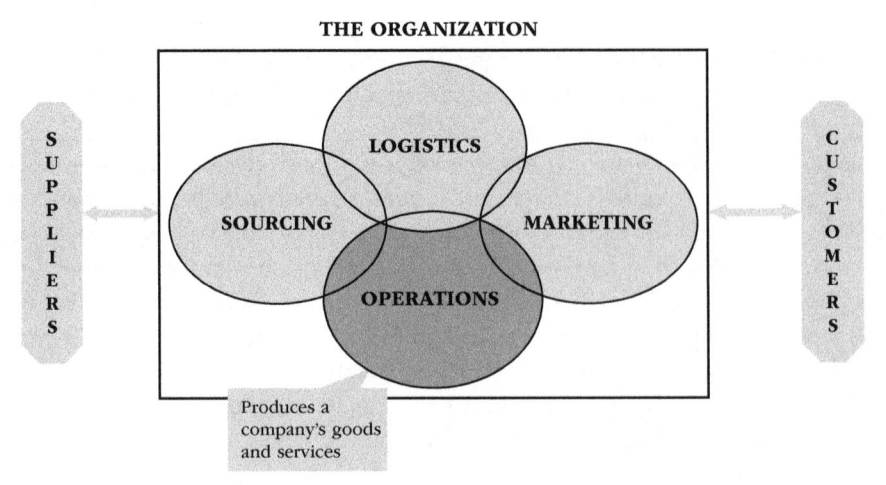

**FIGURE 5.1** The operations function.

**FIGURE 5.2** The transformation role of OM.

into products, such as transforming leather and rubber into sneakers, denim into jeans, or plastic into toys. At a hospital it is organizing resources, such as doctors, medical equipment, and medications, to transform sick patients into healthy people. Consider the example of Ryanair in the Global Insights box later in the chapter. Like traditional airlines, Ryanair transports passengers and their luggage from one location to another. However, the transformation process at Ryanair is organized very differently from traditional airlines, by involving the customer in aspects of the transformation process itself.

## OM Decisions

OM is complex, as many different types of decisions are involved in transforming inputs into finished products. Some of these are listed in Figure 5.3. For operations to be able to design and produce the products customers want, customer preferences—such as likes and dislikes—have to be translated into tangible product characteristics. It is then up to operations to decide on the exact type of process needed to produce the desired product. This includes equipment, level of technology, automation, skill levels, job requirements of workers, and capacity of facilities.

Consider your university and the transformation role it performs in educating students. Think about the location of the university, size and proximity of classrooms; consider the course offerings, capabilities of faculty and staff, and schedules provided; think about the resources—from cafeterias and conference rooms to computers and athletic facilities. These are all examples of OM decisions designed to create a transformation process.

| OM Decision | What it means |
| --- | --- |
| Product design | Designing unique product features |
| Process design | Creating the production process to produce the designed products |
| Quality management | Establishing and implementing quality standards |
| Inventory management | Decisions on amounts of inventory to carry and when to order |
| Facility layout | Deciding the physical layout of the production facility |
| Facility location | Deciding on the best location for facilities |
| Scheduling | Creating schedules for workers, machines, and facilities |

**FIGURE 5.3** OM decisions.

## Manufacturing versus Service Operations

Manufacturing and service organizations each pose unique challenges for the operations function. There are two primary distinctions between them. First, manufacturing organizations produce physical, tangible, goods that can be stored in inventory before they are needed. By contrast, service organizations produce intangible products that cannot be produced ahead of time. Second, in manufacturing organizations most customers have no direct contact with the operation. For example, a customer buying a bottle of Pepsi never sees the bottling factory. However, in service organizations the customer is typically present during the creation of the service, such as at hospitals, colleges, theaters, and barber shops.

The differences between manufacturing and service organizations are not as clear-cut as they might appear, and there is much overlap between them. Most manufacturers provide services as part of their business, and many service firms manufacture physical goods they use during service delivery. For example, a manufacturer of furniture may also provide shipment of goods and assembly of furniture. A barber shop may sell its own line of hair care products. Even in pure service companies some segments of the operation may have high customer contact, whereas others have low customer contact. The latter can be thought of as "backroom" or "behind the scenes" segments. Examples would include the kitchen segment at a fast-food restaurant, such as Wendy's, or the laboratory for specimen analysis at a hospital.

## Evolution of the Operations Function

OM has significantly evolved and changed over time, as shown in Figure 5.4. As a result of global business trends and changes in competitive requirements, operations has evolved from being a "backroom" production function to taking on a strategic role and becoming a tool for competitive advantage. This is also reflected in the change of its name, which was formerly "production management," indicating that it was just about "producing." The term then evolved into "production & operations management" reflecting a broader organizational focus. The function was ultimately coined "operations management," reflecting a broad and strategic organizational reach.

1950s — *Production management*
1980s — *Production & Operations management*
Present — *Operations management*

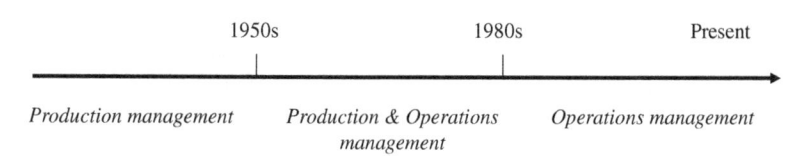

**FIGURE 5.4** The evolution of OM.

Prior to the 1950s, OM served merely a production role in the organization. The key opportunities at the time were in marketing, to develop markets for new products, and in finance, to support this growth. Operations was seen more as a "backroom" function that simply "made things."

Although operations began taking on a broader organizational role in the 1950s and 1960s, its role changed abruptly in the 1980s. U.S. companies experienced large declines in productivity growth, and international competition began to challenge many U.S. markets, especially in the auto industry. While U.S. firms had neglected their operations processes, foreign firms from countries such as Germany and Japan were rebuilding their facilities and designing new production methods. Suddenly, many U.S. firms found themselves turning to operations to regain their competitiveness.

Today's global competition and focus on SCM have placed even greater importance on operations. Organizations within the supply chain network must operate at the highest level of efficiency and utilize the most current operations methods. In fact, many inroads that are made in competitive markets come from innovations in operations, such as Tata Motors producing less-expensive vehicles due to new production techniques.

## Impact on the Organization

Operations play a critical role in the organization, as without OM there would be no product to sell. However, operations cannot work in isolation from other business functions. For example, operations must work with marketing to understand and design the exact products customers want and to create the production processes that efficiently produce these products. Marketing, on the other hand, must understand operations' capabilities, such as the types of products it can, and cannot, produce. Otherwise, the company may find itself marketing products the company isn't able to deliver. Consider a furniture manufacturer in North Carolina, where marketing pushed for the selling of laminated versus customized furniture, only to find that the operations requirements were completely different for one versus the other. Operations must also work with sourcing to understand material availability, such as sources of supply, quality standards, and availability of materials. Sourcing, in turn, must understand operational production requirements to develop and manage an appropriate supply base.

## Supply Chain Leader's Box

### ■ WAL-MART

Companies often learn the hard way that operations decisions must be tied to customer expectations. Just consider what happened at Wal-Mart a few years ago. When the CEO of Wal-Mart, Mike Duke, stepped into his position in 2009, he was faced with having to address a large operational change in the company that had already been under way. The company was in the process of implementing an overhaul of its U.S. retail stores called Project Impact. The goal was to make the stores more "Targety," putting in more space and making the stores look cleaner and less cluttered.

Duke immediately understood not only the marketing needs but also the operational challenges. Larger aisles and cleaner stores meant a significantly lower number of inventory items and stock-keeping units (SKUs). This was in direct contrast to the vision of Sam Walton, who favored a cluttered presentation; "Stack 'em high and let 'em fly!" was his philosophy. For decades the layout of the stores had included the so-called Action Alley, which is the long aisle shoppers face when entering the store. Action Alley was designed to be cluttered and display the deep discounted items. Under Project Impact, store managers were ordered to clear the Action Alleys completely. In addition, Wal-Mart had to cut thousands of items that it carried in each store, deciding that it would be more efficient to focus on fewer brands. So, for example, a very popular laundry detergent—Wisk—was eliminated among the thousands of other SKUs.

The problem with Project Impact, however, was that customers were now buying less. Wal-Mart found that fewer products meant less clutter, but it also meant lower sales. Customers came to Wal-Mart for the product variety and low prices and not having the variety meant customers were leaving. Duke quickly began to remedy the problem. By March of 2010 he started to bring back many of the products that had been dropped, including Wisk laundry detergent. He understood that facility layout, inventory management, and all the other operations decisions were the lifeblood of ensuring the company met customer expectations.

Adapted from: "Meet the CEO of the Biggest Company on Earth." *Fortune*, September 27, 2010: 80–94.

## Impact on SCM

It is not enough for a company to manage its own operations function. Each company depends on other members of its supply chain to be able to deliver the right products to its customers in a timely and cost-effective manner. Recall that in Chapter 3 we learned how processes operate as a system and that every system has a constraint that must be managed as it creates a bottleneck. In the upstream part of its supply chain, a company depends on its suppliers for the delivery of raw materials and components in time to meet production needs. If deliveries of these materials are late or are of poor quality, production will be delayed, regardless of how efficient a company's operations process is. On the downstream side, a company depends on its distributors and retailers for the delivery of the product to the final customer. If these are not delivered on time, are damaged in the transportation process, or are poorly displayed at the retail location, sales will suffer. Also, if the operations function of other members of the supply chain is not managed properly, excess costs will result, which will be passed down to other members of the supply chain in the form of higher prices.

The companies that comprise a supply chain need to coordinate and link their operations functions so that the entire chain is operating in a seamless and efficient manner. Just consider the fact that most of the components Dell uses are warehoused within a 15-minute radius of its assembly plant and Dell is in constant communications with its suppliers. Dell considers this essential to its ability to produce and deliver components quickly.

# Product Design

## What Is Product Design?

Product design is the process of specifying the exact features and characteristics of a company's product. Features of every product—from a Starbuck's café latte to Ikea's kitchen chairs to HP's DeskJet printer—were determined during product design. This is also true for the design of services, ranging from in-room dining offerings at Marriott Hotels to shipping options at FedEx. All of a product's features are determined by product design. Ideas for which features to include are usually driven by marketing, which understands what customers want. Marketing understands that consumers respond to a product's appearance, color, texture, and performance. Marketing then works with operations to create a product that meets these consumer preferences.

Product design decisions are one of the most important in OM as they drive many other decisions. One of these is process design, which is the design of the production process needed to produce the desired product. Product design defines a product's characteristics and then translates them into measurable dimensions the process can use to produce the product.

Product and process design affect product quality, product cost, and customer satisfaction. Consider Apple's iPhone 4 manufactured in 2010. The product design specified white to be one of the color options. However, after white iPhones were produced, consumers found the white casing to "leak" too much light into the phone unit, washing out pictures and creating other problems. If the product is not well designed, or if the production process is not capable of producing the exact product design features, the quality of the product will suffer. Therefore, for a product to succeed in the marketplace it must have a good design *and* a good production process.

## Design of Services

Product design in the service industry has an added complication as the product is intangible and there is a high degree of customer interaction. Service design requires the design of the entire service concept. As with a tangible product, the service concept is based on satisfying customer needs. However, there are aesthetic and psychological benefits that the service provides that must be considered. Services are "experienced" by the customer, and details that enhance this experience are all part of the service concept. Recall that in Chapter 4 we discussed the use of scents to enhance the service experience, such as Abercrombie & Fitch's use of their signature fragrance as part of the retail ambience, or Omni hotels scenting their coffee shop with the smell of sugar cookies. These are all attempts at enhancing the "service experience," to improve customer satisfaction and promote sales.

The service concept has three elements, each of which must be designed. The first is the **physical element of the service**. This may be a haircut at the barber shop, an investment made by the financial planner, or the filling your dentist just put in your tooth. The second are the **psychological benefits** of the service, which are elements such as promptness and friendliness. Finally, there are **sensual elements** of the service, which are part of the experience, such as ambiance, image, and "feel good" elements of the service. Part of the service design is to specify all the elements of the service concept and to make sure that they work together. Consider the differences in service design between Hyatt Hotels, which provide upscale accommodations for travelers, and Hyatt Place, which provides lower-priced accommodations but ample amenities for the business traveler.

## Big Data Analytics Box

### ■ HONDA

Honda is an excellent example of how companies can use big data to impact quality and customer service. The company has developed software to provide an "early warning system" that identifies major quality problems with their vehicles before they become catastrophic. The goal is to use analytics to make customers happy and save lives. The company uses analytical software to mine three sources of data—warranty service records categorizing quality problems (e.g., "brake system," "headlamps"), free text notes from mechanics, and transcripts of phone calls from customers to call centers—to identify trends or emerging problems. These are then forwarded to human analysts to make risk management judgment calls. This type of system illustrates how big data analytics can enhance and improve human decision making. It also shows how current analytics capability can incorporate unstructured data such as text notes. These types of quality improvements have been adopted by other automakers, all with the goal of using big data to improve quality.

Adapted from: Davenport, Thomas H., and Jeanne G. Harris. *Competing on Analytics: The New Science of Winning*. Cambridge, MA: Harvard Business School Publishing Corporation, 2007.

# The Product Design Process

A significant challenge for today's companies is the need to regularly bring out new product designs. Some industries have a predictable cycle of new product development, such as new car models every year or new retail fashions every season. Some products come out seasonally, such as Starbuck's specialty drinks during the holiday season, or Bath and Body Works floral scented soaps available in the spring.

The product design process follows a predictable set of steps:

1. **Idea development.** Product ideas can come from many sources, such as marketing, which tries to determine what customers want, a company's R&D, engineering, or suppliers. Often suppliers participate in a program called **early supplier involvement (ESI)** and get involved in the early stages of product design. Ideas can also come from competitors, by observing their products and success rate. Companies can also buy a competitor's product then analyze its parts and features. This is a process called **reverse engineering** and was used by Ford in the design of its Ford Taurus.

2. **Product Screening.** All product ideas go through a screening stage, where they are evaluated to determine their likelihood of success. Product screening considers the viability of the product based on the needs of each of the business functions. Each function has its own concerns, which are shown in Figure 5.5. Deciding which ideas should pass the screening stage involves managerial skill and experience. Roughly 80% of ideas not making it past the screening stage are due to the concerns illustrated in Figure 5.5. One decision-making tool that can be especially helpful at this stage is break-even analysis, and we will look at its use later in this chapter.

3. **Preliminary Design and Testing.** Following the screening stage a product idea moves into preliminary design and testing. This is the stage where design engineers translate vague and general performance specifications (e.g., "pretty blue color" or "strong material") into specific technical specifications. Prototypes are built and tested, and changes are made. In service organizations this stage may entail pretesting the product on small groups of customers and then refining the service concept accordingly.

| Function | Product screening concerns |
|---|---|
| **Marketing** | What is the potential size of the market for the proposed product? |
| | How long will it take to capture the market? |
| | What is the long-term product potential? |
| **Operations** | What are the production process needs of the proposed product? |
| | Do we have the facilities, equipment, and labor skills needed? |
| | How easy would it be to acquire the needed production skills? |
| | Is there enough capacity to produce the new product? |
| **Sourcing** | What is the availability of sources of supply? |
| | What is the cost of materials for production? |
| | How easy is it to obtain available materials? |
| **Finance** | What are the financial requirements of the new product? |
| | What are the cost and the expected return on investment (ROI)? |

**FIGURE 5.5** Functional concerns at the product screening stage.

4. **Final Design.** Product testing results in the specification of the final product design. At this stage specifications are translated into specific instructions used to manufacture the product, such as materials, equipment, and quality standards.

## Global Insights Box

### ■ RYANAIR

Ryanair became famous for pioneering the rock-bottom budget airline. Just consider a situation that occurred in July 2002 when passengers in England were boarding a Ryanair flight bound for Dublin. The pilot announced that the baggage handlers loading the plane were short staffed. A major delay was imminent, the pilot said, unless people volunteered to move luggage. Soon after, a handful of passengers stepped out on to the tarmac to load bags onto the plane.

This is Ryanair—the largest low-cost airline in Europe, based in Dublin, Ireland. Michael O'Leary, chief executive officer, says that someday he would like to see what happened in England happen on all Ryanair flights. "Airports are ludicrously complicated places only because we have this utterly useless transaction of taking your bag from you upon departure, just so we can give it back to you at arrival," he says. "Get rid of all that crap. You take your own bag with you. You bring it down. You put it on." In fact, O'Leary wants to completely change the operation of the airline industry. His dream is that someday all passengers will fly for free on Ryanair and that all of the company's income will come from ancillary revenue, such as baggage fees, in-flight sales, and commissions on travel insurance, hotels, and car rentals sold through the carrier's website.

O'Leary has a very different operation in mind from the way airlines currently run. "In exchange for cheap fares," he says, "passengers will put up with just about anything." On Ryanair, that can include high luggage fees, sales pitches for smokeless cigarettes, and scratch-off lottery games. Ryanair boasts of its minimal customer service, expensive food, and cramped seats. Eventually, O'Leary would like to eliminate two of the three toilets on all short flights, which would allow Ryanair to pack in more passengers at lower fares. He would charge passengers one euro to use the remaining toilet. Recently he announced that he was planning to replace the last 10 rows of seats on his aircraft with 15 rows of upright "standing seats"—vertical benches with shoulder harnesses and arm rests, which would allow him to pack 30 more passengers into each plane. "The European consumer would crawl naked over broken glass for cheap fares," O'Leary says.

This would all seem comical if Ryanair had not grown from a tiny regional airline into a legitimate powerhouse and has become the second-largest European airline by passenger flights. "If you don't approach air travel with a radical point of view, then you get in the same bloody mindset as all the other morons in this industry," O'Leary says.

Ryanair has organized their operation to increasingly involve the customer. Although this approach has been used in other industries, its success remains to be seen in the airline industry.

Adapted from: "The Duke of Discomfort." *Bloomberg Businessweek*, September 6, 2010.

## Break-Even Analysis

Break-even analysis is a tool that can be used to evaluate the success of a new product at the product screening stage. It is used to compute the product quantity that needs to be sold for a company to cover their costs, called the "break-even point." Products with a high break-even point may be a risky choice, as the company must sell a large quantity before it can cover costs.

At the break-even point, total cost equals revenue, which is money made from sales. Total cost of producing a product or service is the sum of its fixed and variable costs. Fixed costs are those that do not vary with the quantity produced. They include overhead, taxes, and insurance and are incurred regardless of how much is produced. Variable costs, on the other hand, are costs that vary

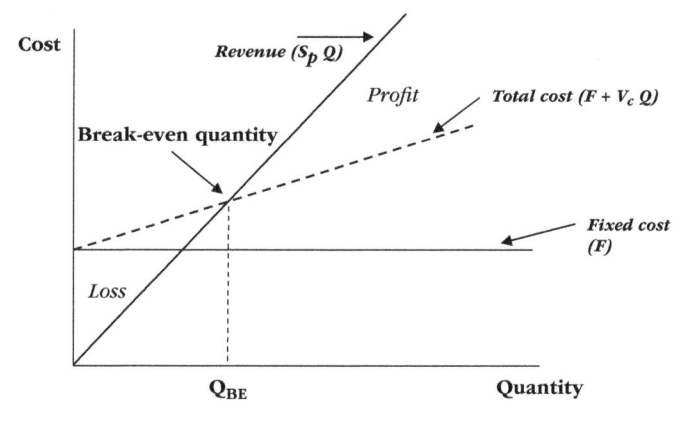

**FIGURE 5.6** Graphical representation of the break-even quantity.

directly with the amount produced and include items such as direct materials and labor. Together, fixed and variable costs add up to total cost:

$$\text{Total Cost} = F + V_C Q$$

where

$F$ = fixed cost

$V_C$ = variable cost per unit

$Q$ = number of units sold

Figure 5.6 shows a graphical representation of these costs and the break-even quantity. When $Q = 0$, total cost and fixed cost are equal. However, as $Q$ increases, so do variable cost and total cost. Revenue from sales is computed as:

$$\text{Revenue} = S_P Q, \text{ where}$$
$$S_P = \text{selling price per unit}$$

When $Q = 0$, revenue is zero, as there are no sales. As sales increase so does revenue, until the break-even point is reached when all costs are covered. Sales beyond the break-even point result in a profit for the company. At the break-even point total cost is equal to revenue:

$$\text{Total Cost} = \text{Revenue}$$
$$F + V_C Q = S_P Q$$

Solving for Q at the break-even point—$Q_{BE}$—we get the following equation:

$$Q_{BE} = \frac{F}{S_P - V_C}$$

$Q_{BE}$ computes the break-even quantity, or the quantity needed to be sold for the company to break even. We could also find the break-even point by graphing total cost and revenue.

Break-even analysis can also be useful for conducting a sensitivity analysis to evaluate how changes in product price affect the break-even quantity. In addition, it can be used to make other product and process decisions, such as evaluating cost and benefits of different processes or deciding whether the company should make or buy a product.

### Example 1   Computing the Break-Even Quantity

Shu Chen plans to produce a new line of children's scarves and is considering the scarves' processing needs and market potential. She estimates that the variable cost for each product is $25 and the fixed cost per year is $15,000. If Shu offers each scarf at a selling price of $30, how many scarves must she sell to break even? If Shu sells 4,000 scarves at the $30 price, what will be the contribution to profit?

**SOLUTION:** To compute the break-even quantity:

$$Q_{BE} = \frac{F}{S_P - V_C}$$

$$Q_{BE} = \frac{\$15,000}{\$30 - \$25} = 3,000 \text{ scarves}$$

This means Shu needs to sell 3,000 scarves to cover her costs. To compute the contribution to profit with sales of 4,000 scarves, we look at the relationship between cost and revenue:

$$\text{Profit} = \text{Total Revenue} - \text{Total Cost}$$
$$= (S_P)Q - [F + (V_C)Q]$$
$$\text{Profit} = \$30(4,000) - [\$15,000 + \$25(4,000)]$$
$$\text{Profit} = \$5,000$$

The contribution to profit is $5,000 if Shu can sell 4,000 scarves from her new line.

## Factors Impacting Product Design Decisions

Some additional factors need to be considered during the product design process:

1. **Design for manufacture (DFM).** DFM is a series of guidelines that should be followed to produce a product easily and profitably. Consider that product design processes are typically driven by the desire to create the exact product the customer wants. However, it is also important to consider how easy it is to manufacture. Otherwise, a product that is either difficult or too costly to manufacture may be created. DFM guidelines focus on two issues: design simplification and design standardization. Design simplification means reducing the number of parts and features of the product whenever possible.

    A simpler product is easier to make, fewer mistakes are made, and it is less costly to produce. Design standardization, on the other hand, refers to the use of common and interchangeable parts. By using interchangeable parts, a greater variety of products can be made with less inventory, significantly lower cost, and greater flexibility. DFM includes rules such as minimize parts, design common parts for different products, use modular design, avoid tools, and simplify operations.

2. **Product life cycle.** Another factor to consider is the stage of the product life cycle. Most products go through a series of stages of changing product demand called the **product life cycle**. There are typically four stages: introduction, growth, maturity and decline. In the

introductory stage, neither the product nor the market are well defined, and all the "bugs" have not been worked out. In the growth stage the product is more established, although both product and market continue to be refined. In the maturity stage, the product and market become fairly stable and predictable. Finally, in the decline stage the product experiences declining demand due to competing product designs or market saturation. In the first two stages of the product life cycle—called the early stages–the product and market are still being refined. Here product design involves product improvement and refinement based on market response. In the last two stages—called the later stages—the product and market are stable. The product, however, is approaching the end of the life cycle, and product design may involve major changes or reinventions to either revitalize an old product or create a new one for the market.

3. **Concurrent engineering.** Historically, product design was made sequentially, where an idea was developed and then passed on to each function for evaluation. This was a time-consuming and inefficient process. Today, companies engage in concurrent engineering that requires all the functions to work together simultaneously to design and evaluate the product.

4. **Remanufacturing.** Remanufacturing uses components of old products in the production of new ones. It has enormous environmental and cost benefits, as the remanufactured products can be a fraction of the price of their new counterparts. Remanufacturing is especially popular in the electronics industry, such as the production of computers and televisions.

# Process Design

## What Is Process Design?

Process design involves developing a production process that can create the exact product that has been designed. Look at different products around you and consider the processes used to create them—from a box of chocolates to the software on your computer. Some processes produce standardized "off the shelf" products, like Totino's Pizza Rolls in your freezer, and some work with customers to customize their product, like pizzas made to order at a local pizza shop.

Although there seem to be large differences between processes of companies, many have certain characteristics in common. Based on common characteristics processes can be grouped into two broad categories: **intermittent** and **repetitive processes**. These two categories differ in almost every way. The most common difference, however, is along two dimensions: **product volume** and **degree of product standardization**. Product volume is the quantity produced and can range from making few one-of-a-kind customized products to producing large quantities of products in batches. Product standardization is the amount of product variety. Examples of standardized products are white undershirts, sugar, and postal service. Process requirements—including equipment and labor—are quite different for producing standardized versus customized products.

Characteristics of both intermittent and repetitive processes are shown in Figure 5.7. Understanding these differences can help us match processes across the supply chain network, understand their strengths and weaknesses, and ensure optimal flow.

## Intermittent Processes

Intermittent processes are used to produce a large variety of products with different processing requirements in lower volumes. Examples are an auto body shop, a tool and die shop, or a healthcare facility. As different products have different processing needs, there is no standard route that

| Decision | Intermittent processes | Repetitive processes |
|---|---|---|
| Product variety | Large | Small |
| Product standardization | Low | High |
| Product life cycle | Early stage | Later stage |
| Resources | Grouped by function | Line flow |
| Critical resources | Labor-intensive | Capital-intensive |
| Type of equipment | General-purpose | Specialized |
| Throughput time | Longer | Shorter |
| Work-in-process inventory | High | Low |

**FIGURE 5.7** Differences between intermittent and repetitive processes.

all products take through the facility. Instead, resources are grouped by function, and the product is routed to each resource as needed. Think about a healthcare facility. Each patient is routed to different departments as needed. One patient may need to get an x-ray, go to the lab for blood work, and then go to the examining room. Another patient may need to go to the examining room and then to physical therapy.

Intermittent processes tend to produce products in the early stages of the product life cycle, where the product is still not well defined. They tend to be labor intensive, rather than capital intensive, to remain flexible. Workers need to be able to perform a variety of tasks, depending on the products' processing needs. These processes rely on highly skilled workers and give them discretion to perform their jobs. Equipment is more general-purpose to satisfy different processing requirements. Automation is less common because automation tends to be product specific, and it is not cost efficient to invest in automation for only one product type.

## Repetitive Processes

Repetitive processes are used to produce one, or a few, standardized products in high volume. Examples include an automobile assembly line, a cafeteria, and an automatic car wash. Resources, such as machines and workers, are organized in a line flow to efficiently accommodate production of the product.

Repetitive processes tend to produce products in the later stages of the life cycle, and the larger volumes are justified by a well-established market. To produce a large volume of one type of product, these processes tend to be more capital, rather than labor intensive. An example is "mass-production," where companies usually have much invested in their facilities and equipment to provide a high degree of product consistency. Often these facilities rely on automation and technology, rather than on labor skill, to improve efficiency and increase output. The volume produced is usually based on a forecast of future demands rather than on direct customer orders.

## The Continuum of Process Types

The two process categories—intermittent and repetitive—can be further divided to provide greater detail. Intermittent processes can be divided into **project processes** and **batch processes**. Repetitive processes can be divided into **line processes** and **continuous processes**. This provides a continuum of process types as shown in Figure 5.8.

Process Design

```
Low │  1. Project process
    │     (customer job shop;
    │     construction)        ⎫
    │                          ⎬ Intermittent
    │     2. Batch process     ⎪ processes
    │        (education classes;⎭
Product │     bakery; printing shop)
standardization
    │        3. Line process
    │           (assembly lines;
    │           cafeteria)      ⎫
    │                           ⎬ Repetitive
    │        4. Continuous processes ⎪ processes
    │           (oil refinery;       ⎭
    │           water treatment plant)
    ▼
High         Product volume
      Low                        High
```

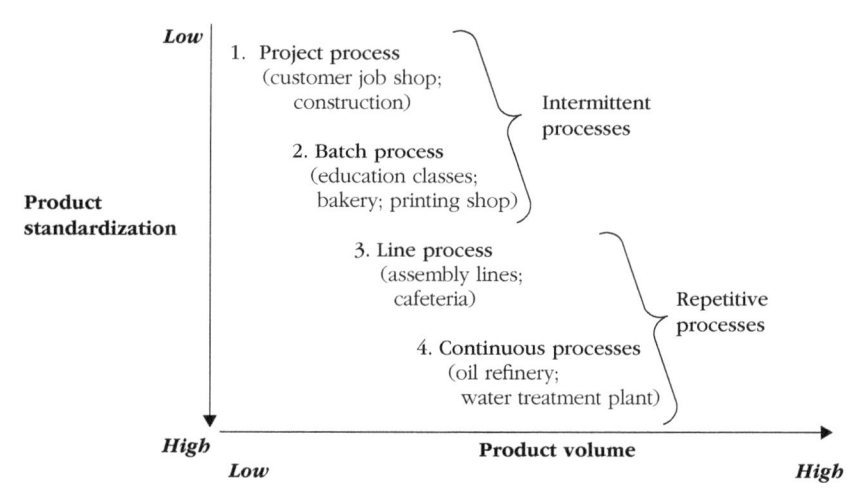

**FIGURE 5.8** Continuum of process types.[1]

1. **Project processes** are used to make one-of-a-kind products exactly to customer specifications. These processes are used where there is high customization and low product volume, as each product is different. Examples include construction, shipbuilding, medical procedures, custom tailoring, and interior design.

2. **Batch processes** are used to produce small quantities of products in groups or batches based on customer orders or product specifications. They are also known as job shops. The volumes of each product produced are still small, and there can still be customization. Examples can be seen in bakeries, education, and printing shops. The classes you take at the university use a batch process.

3. **Line processes** are designed to produce a large volume of a standardized product for mass production. They are also known as flow shops, flow lines, or assembly lines. With line processes the product that is produced is made in high volume with little or no customization. Think of typical assembly lines that produce everything from cars, computers, television sets, and shoes to candy bars, and even food items.

4. **Continuous processes** operate continually to produce a very high volume of a fully standardized product. Examples include oil refineries, water treatment plants, and certain paint facilities. The products produced by continuous processes are usually in continual rather than discrete units such as liquid or gas. They usually have a single input and a limited number of outputs. Also, these facilities are usually highly capital intensive and automated.

Note that both project and batch processes have low product volumes and offer customization. The difference is in the volume and degree of customization. Project processes are more extreme cases of intermittent processes, compared to batch processes. Also, note that both line and continuous processes primarily produce large volumes of standardized products. Similarly, continuous processes are more extreme cases of high volume and product standardization than are line processes.

Figure 5.8 positions these four process types along the diagonal to show the best process strategies relative to product volume and product customization. Companies whose process strategies do not fall along this diagonal may not have made the best process decisions. Keep in mind, however, that not all processes fit into only one of these categories: a company may use both batch and

---

[1] Robert H. Hayes and Stephen C. Wheelwright, "Link Manufacturing Process and Product Life Cycles." *Harvard Business Review*, January–February 1979: 133–140.

project processing to good advantage. For example, a bakery that produces breads, cakes, and pastries in batches may also bake and decorate cakes to order. Also, today's advances in technologies have created greater processing options. For example, many companies are moving toward mass customization, which provides increased variety while still getting the advantages of repetitive processes. Consider companies such as Dell that allows customers to design their own computer online, or Nike their own footwear. Here customers can "design" a product by choosing from a range of options. Mass customization uses advanced technologies to customize products quickly and at a low cost. These companies store inventory in standard modules that are then configured to the exact product specification desired by the customer.

## Managerial Insights Box—A New Manufacturing Process

### ■ RAPID MANUFACTURING

Rapid manufacturing (RM) is a state-of-the-art process that is changing the way products are made. It is a technique used to quickly manufacture a prototype model from a CAD (computer-aided-design) file and uses 3-D printing or additive manufacturing (AM). RM uses technology to make products to order when needed, exactly where they are needed, and is considered to be one of the most important potential influences on the future of manufacturing. Rapid manufacturing is in fact an application of 3-D printing or AM, which we discussed in Chapter 1.

RM involves the economic manufacture of low-volume products, or prototypes, on demand at multiple locations near the point of consumption. It relies on new developments in three-dimensional (3-D) printing technologies or additive manufacturing (AM). AM consists of three basic steps. First, a 3-D computer representation is fed into a specially designed layer manufacturing machine, which can come from a variety of sources including computer-aided-design (CAD). Next, the image is digitally sliced up into hundreds of two-dimensional layers, each representing a profile of the part to be manufactured. Finally, the layers are rebuilt inside the AM machine one at a time, from the bottom up, until the part is complete.

There has been a rapid rise in the number of companies using RM. Companies such as Boeing, Airbus, BAE Systems, Renault, and Honda are all using RM for a variety of applications. Healthcare has many applications as well. For example, RM is being used to manufacture bone-replacement material for reconstructive surgeries and for creating customized prosthetics. RM is also used to design disposable surgical cutting guides, which are personalized to the individual patient. Dentistry is one of the best-known applications for RM; doctors are using the technology to manufacture customized dental caps, bridges, and crowns. Also, it is used in the production of personalized in-the-ear hearing aids, which are manufactured to fit exactly into each patient's ear. Another example is the manufacture of invisible dental braces. Invisalign Inc. is a company that uses RM to manufacture forming tools over which disposable, transparent dental braces are individually formed in sets for each patient.

# Facility Layout

## Facility Layout Planning

Product and process design directly impact the organization of resources needed to produce the product. One aspect of the operation that is especially impacted is facility layout, which is the physical arrangement of all resources within a facility. These resources include everything that is part of the operation: a work center, a machine, an entire office, or just the location of a desk. Facility layout planning is made any time there is a change in the arrangement of resources. This could be redesign of the operation to produce a new product. It can also be the change in resources being used, such as a new worker being added, a machine being moved, or a change in the process. Facility layout has a significant impact on performance, especially production cost, time and flexibility. Most people are surprised to learn that poor facility layouts are one of the most significant contributors to inefficiency and increased production cost. For this reason managers spend a great deal of effort ensuring that facility layouts are efficient and enhance work flow.

## Types of Facility Layouts

There are four distinct layout types: **fixed position**, **process**, **product**, and **cellular**. The type of process design selected influences the physical layout of the operation, including arrangement of the equipment, employees, inventory, and aisles for movement. Different layouts lend themselves to producing different types of products, and it is important to match product designs with appropriate layouts.

1. **Fixed Position Layout.** A fixed-position layout is used when a product cannot be moved during production, usually due to size. They are typically used for producing large products such as homes, buildings, bridges, large ships, airplanes, and spacecraft. The greatest supply chain challenge here is for all of the resources to come together at the product's location in the right sequence at the right time. Consider the process of construction where different tasks must be performed in sequence, such as installing electrical wiring and plumbing, putting up drywall, and installing flooring. Each has different timing and sequence requirements. Due to the fixed nature of the product, the layout problem becomes a scheduling problem requiring timing and sequencing of different tasks.

2. **Process Layout.** Process layouts are best suited when producing many different types of products in low volume, as seen in intermittent processes. Here products have different processing needs, and it would be almost impossible to create a sequence of departments to accommodate each one. As a result resources are grouped by process—hence the term "process" layout. Here the product is moved between groupings based on need. Consider a hospital where functional groupings are created, such as maternity, pharmacy, laboratory, and X-ray. The patient—the product in this case—is moved between departments based on their need. A grocery store is another example, where food items are grouped based on their use, with sections for dairy, meat, bakery, canned goods, and produce. Retailers also use process layouts, with departments for shoes, children's clothing, cosmetics, and jewelry. Figure 5.9 shows a process layout for a small clinic.

    In process layouts, each product or customer takes a different route through the operation. This results in a number of disadvantages. First, material handling costs are high as products have to be moved from one department to another. Second, processing times and work in process inventory tend to be high as products or customers wait to be processed in different departments. Finally, there is also time lost to switching equipment from working on one product to another.

    Process layouts provide the ability to produce a large variety of products. However, scheduling, planning, and control of the operation are difficult. It is very easy for these layouts to become inefficient if they are not designed properly. When designing process

| Waiting room | Examining room | Surgical room |
|---|---|---|
| Office | Laboratory | Recovery |

**FIGURE 5.9** Process layout.

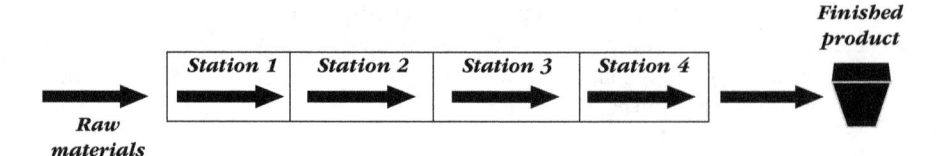

**FIGURE 5.10** Product layout.

layouts, the objective is to arrange the departments so that the time and cost of moving materials and people are minimized.

3. **Product Layout.** A product layout arranges resources in sequence to enable efficient production of the product. It is a layout most suited for producing a high volume of one, or a few similar, products. An automotive assembly line, an automatic car wash, or a buffet table are perfect examples. Every product going through the line is almost exactly the same. Product layouts minimize processing times, and planning, scheduling, and control are simplified. An example of flow through a product layout is shown in Figure 5.10.

   Product layouts are highly efficient and minimize cost of producing high-volume products. However, they also have a number of disadvantages. First, they lack flexibility found with process layouts and are unable to produce variations of products. Second, because workstations are highly dependent on one another, a stoppage at a single workstation can cause the entire line to stop producing. Similarly, quality problems or delays in shipments from suppliers can have the same effect as product layout design extends to the supply chain.

4. **Cellular Layouts.** Cellular layouts attempt to combine the efficiency and repetition of product layouts with the flexibility of process layouts. Cellular layouts group items based on similar processing characteristics and arrange workstations to form a number of small assembly lines called work cells. Then workstations within each individual work cell are arranged using product layout principles. The first step in designing a cellular layout is to use group technology to identify products that have similar processing requirements, called product families. These product families may have similar shapes, sizes, process flows, or demand. Then each work cell can be dedicated to make a product family.

## Managerial Insights Box

### ■ MAZZI'S VERSUS TOTINO'S PIZZA

Consider two companies that both make the same type of product—pizza—but in a very different operations setting. One uses a process layout; the other a product layout. Totino's makes frozen pizza that you can purchase in your local grocer's freezer. The pizzas are made in an assembly line format en masse with strict ingredients and predictable quality standards. The production output is set, and the sequence of operations is repetitive and predictable. It uses a make-to-stock strategy, with defined versions of the product, limiting product variety. It also sources large quantities of ingredients from its standard suppliers.

By contrast, Mazzi's—a family-owned Italian restaurant—makes everything from scratch. It uses a process layout format and custom makes many of its entrees and pizzas to order. The bread and dough are baked on premises in the bakery. The produce is obtained locally. It has its own farm and also sources locally from a variety of independent farmers. As a result, the menu might change depending on availability of fresh vegetables and what is in season. This offers greater product variety and more customization.

The layouts of both facilities are tied to each company's business strategy and their target markets. Each layout enables the company to achieve its set goals and meet the expectations of its respective customers.

# Line Balancing in Product Layouts

Product layouts arrange resources in sequence so the product can be made as efficiently as possible. This type of layout is used when producing a large volume of one standardized product and there is repetition of the process. In product layouts the material moves continuously and uniformly through a sequence of operations until the work is completed.

Look at Figure 5.10 and notice that there is simultaneous work going on at each workstation. This is different from having one person do all the work beginning to end. This type of process allows a large volume to be produced. When designing product layouts, the objective is to decide on the sequence of tasks to be performed by each workstation. To accomplish this we need to consider the logical order of the tasks to be performed and the time required to perform each task. Also, we need to consider the speed of the production process, which specifies how much time each workstation has to perform the assigned tasks. This entire process is called **line balancing**. Below are the steps that must be followed in designing product layouts:

## Step 1. Identify Task Times and Precedence Relationships

The first step in line balancing is to identify the tasks that must be performed in order to produce the product, their duration and the sequence in which they need to be performed. This is called a precedence relationship.

Figure 5.11 illustrates tasks, task times, and the immediately preceding task for a pizza assembly. Notice that some tasks cannot be performed until other tasks are completed. For example, the dough must be rolled before the sauce can be added. However, sausage, pepperoni, or mushrooms are added only after the cheese. This precedence relationship is shown in diagrammatic form in Figure 5.12.

## Step 2. Determine Cycle Time

Recall that the product being produced on the assembly line moves in a continuous fashion. This means that each workstation has exactly the same amount of time to complete their assigned tasks. The maximum amount of time each station on the assembly line has to complete its assigned tasks is called **cycle time** or **takt time**. The actual work time assigned to each station cannot exceed the

| Task | Description | Task time (sec) | Preceding task |
|------|-------------|-----------------|----------------|
| A | Roll dough | 60 | – |
| B | Add pizza sauce | 40 | A |
| C | Sprinkle cheese | 35 | B |
| D | Add sausage | 25 | C |
| E | Add pepperoni | 35 | C |
| F | Add mushrooms | 25 | C |
| G | Shrinkwrap pizza | 15 | D,E,F |
| H | Add label | 10 | G |
| Total time | | 245 sec | |

**FIGURE 5.11** Precedence relationships for pizza assembly.

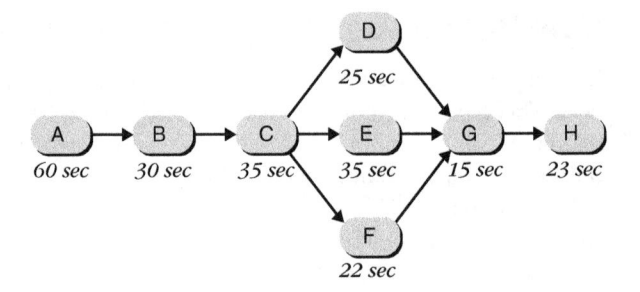

**FIGURE 5.12** Precedence diagram of pizza assembly.

assigned time, or cycle time. Otherwise, there would not be enough time to complete the work. This is also the frequency with which each unit is produced. Therefore, cycle time is directly related to the number of units produced.

The total task time to produce one pizza is 245 seconds, if a single person singlehandedly carries out all the tasks from beginning to end without a break. In such a case, the maximum output in one hour would be:

$$\text{Maximum output} = \frac{3{,}600 \text{ seconds/hour}}{245 \text{ seconds/hour}} = 14.7 \text{ pizzas/hour}$$

However, if we want to produce more pizzas than that, we will have to divide the work among a number of people working simultaneously at workstations to achieve the desired output rate. The first thing to compute is the cycle time:

$$\text{Cycle time} = \text{Amount of time allowed to complete work at each station}$$

$$\text{Cycle time} = \frac{\text{Available production time per day}}{\text{Desired number of units per day}}$$

Notice that the time periods given to compute cycle time are per day, but they can also be given per hour or another time period, as long as the time periods are consistent. Remember that operations run continuously for eight hours per day. This means that the numerator—available production time per day—can be assumed to be 480 minutes per day or 28,800 seconds per day.

The denominator—the desired number of units—is the amount we wish to produce in a certain time period. Let's say we want to produce 300 pizzas per day. We can then compute the cycle time needed.

$$\text{Cycle time} = \frac{28{,}800 \text{ seconds per day}}{300 \text{ pizzas per day}} = 96 \text{ seconds per workstation}$$

## Step 3: Determine the Theoretical Minimum Number of Workstations

The goal in line balancing is to assign tasks to workstations to achieve the best efficiency. It is usually helpful to have a baseline of what is theoretically the minimum possible number of stations we will need, although the balanced line may have more stations. The theoretical minimum number of stations computes the number of stations needed if we were 100% efficient. Remember

# Line Balancing in Product Layouts

that when determining the number of stations, round up to the next whole number, as you can never have a partial station.

$$\text{Theoretical minimum no. of stations (N)} = \frac{\text{Sum of the task times}}{\text{Cycle time}}$$

The numerator—sum of the task times—is the total task time if one person was doing all the tasks. In our case it is 245 seconds. The denominator is the cycle time we wish to produce at. In our case it is 96 seconds per workstation.

$$N = \frac{245 \text{ seconds}}{96 \text{ seconds per station}} = 2.55 \text{ stations} = 3 \text{ stations}$$

## Step 4: Assign Tasks to Workstations

We can now proceed to assign tasks to workstations. Notice that we have to follow our precedence relationships to ensure the right sequence. For example, this means that you cannot put the cheese on before adding the sauce.

As we assign tasks to workstations, following the precedence, we have to make sure that the sum of the task times at any station does not exceed the cycle time. Otherwise, the person working at that station will not have time to complete his or her task. Also, sometimes we have a choice of tasks to assign to a station. For example, we can decide whether to put either pepperoni or mushrooms or sausage next in the sequence. There are two rules we can follow here to make it easier:

- Select the task with the longest tasks time (**Longest Task Time Rule**).
- Select the task with the most number of followers (**Number of Followers Rule**).

These are just rules of thumb, or what we call "heuristics." They will not necessarily result in the optimal solution, but will give us a good solution. In our examples we will use the longest task time rule. However, when assigning tasks in large and complex processes, multiple rules are used to balance the line, all with the goal of providing the highest efficiency.

Figure 5.13 shows the assignment of tasks to workstations using the longest task time rule. Notice that the line is not balanced very well, as the last station has much idle time—73 seconds—compared to the other stations. Once we have made these initial assignments

| Station | Eligible task | Assigned task | Time | Cumulative time | Idle time |
|---------|---------------|---------------|------|-----------------|-----------|
| 1       | A             | A             | 60   | 60              | 36        |
|         | B             | B             | 30   | 90              | **6**     |
| 2       | C             | C             | 35   | 35              | 61        |
|         | D, E, F       | E             | 35   | 96              | **0**     |
| 3       | D, F          | D             | 25   | 25              | 71        |
|         | F             | F             | 22   | 47              | 24        |
|         | G             | G             | 15   | 62              | **9**     |
| 4       | H             | H             | 23   | 23              | 73        |

There isn't enough time remaining to add more tasks to this station. Start another station.

Selection of tasks is made using the longest task time rule.

**FIGURE 5.13** Assigning tasks to workstations. *Note: Cycle time is 96 seconds/station.*

we can go back and modify the tasks or the sequence to balance out the workload at each station. There are many strategies that can be used. For example, the last task, placing the label, may be modified and simplified to cut down on the time. Another option might be to give additional tasks to that station that were not originally included, such as doing a quality check.

### Step 5. Compute Efficiency

Once we have assigned tasks to workstations on the line we need to compute our efficiency:

$$\text{Efficiency} = \frac{\text{Sum of task times}}{\text{Number of workstations} \times \text{Cycle time}}$$

$$= \frac{245 \text{ seconds}}{4 \text{ stations} \times 96 \text{ seconds}/\text{station}} = 63.8\%$$

Our efficiency could be improved with better utilization of the line. One option may be to split tasks into smaller work elements or change technology to reduce the time required. More workers also can be assigned to the bottleneck tasks, which is task A in our case. This could reduce the time it takes and allow us to balance the line more efficiently.

## Process Automation

An important operations design decision concerns the use of automation in operations processes. Technological advancements have significantly changed and enhanced the ways in which we can produce products. We are able to use technology to do much of the work for us, such as using robotics. This enhances processing speed through mechanization, provides greater accuracy, and enables handling of dangerous and difficult tasks. Automation also reduces the need for human involvement and decision making. Consider UPS, which sorts millions of packages per day for various destinations. UPS does this through a completely automated process that uses bar codes and readers to sort packages efficiently and accurately. Repetitive assembly line processes, such as the types we just discussed, rely heavily on automation. Automation enables repetition to occur without worker fatigue, such as for tasks that need repetition of picking and sorting. It improves consistency and accuracy of processes. Automation also enables the use of robots for hazardous tasks, such as welding.

### Advantages and Disadvantages

As we can see from the KUKA example, automation has transformed today's operations. However, there are both advantages and disadvantages to using automation. One of the main advantages of automation is the replacement of human workers with automated processes for tasks that are physically dangerous, such as involving jobs in dangerous environments, such as extreme heat, fire, or nuclear facilities. Automation can take workers out of physically difficult jobs or monotonous jobs, which can result in higher error rates due to fatigue when using human workers. It also enables handling of jobs that are beyond human capabilities, such as carrying heavy loads, working with substances that are either too hot or cold for human contact, or at speeds that exceed human capability.

Other advantages of automation relate to economic improvements. Automation enables production to continue without stoppage around the clock, literally 24 hours a day, seven days a week. Automation brings product consistency and improved quality, due to a much lower error rate. Finally, automation improves security, as many of these jobs are risky for humans.

## Global Insights Box

### ■ KUKA ROBOTICS CORP.

The German company KUKA Robotics Corp. is a leading producer of industrial robots for a variety of industries, from automotive and fabrication, to food processing. Their industrial robots are used in production processes by companies in the auto industry (e.g., General Motors, Chrysler, Ford, Audi, and Volkswagen), aircraft production (Boeing), electronics (Siemens), furniture (IKEA), jewelry (Swarovski), retail (Wal-Mart), food processing (Budweiser, Coca-Cola), and numerous other industrial applications. These industrial robots are used in material handling, loading and unloading of machines, palletizing, and welding. They cut steel, carry glass, and repetitively sort items without ever having to worry about danger or fatigue. They are used to cut stone kitchen counters to precision, cut steel in the manufacture of steel bridges, or weld metal parts together with heat that humans could not survive.

To design their robots, KUKA works closely with client companies to develop specific robots and control technologies for what is needed. For example, KUKA has designed robots for assembly lines where several robots work together to machine the same parts at the same time, reducing cycle times. They can also be designed to jointly handle heavy parts to share the weight or "payload." KUKA is also working on new concepts focusing to improve the cooperation between robots and human operators with overlapping workspaces to achieve an optimal degree of automation. This would enable maximizing the advantages of both human and robot, and enable cooperative work.

For most of us, robots are part of science fiction. In fact, KUKA robots have been seen in many Hollywood movies, from James Bond to Harry Potter. However, we may not realize their use in everyday life, which is in almost all of today's large-scale production processes.

Adapted from: www.kuka-robots.com.

---

There are, however, disadvantages to automation. First, the initial cost of automation can be very high for companies. For this reason automation makes more sense for mature products that have an established demand and are produced in high volume. This enables the recouping of the initial financial investment, which can be very high. Second, there are limits to technology, and there are many tasks that simply cannot be automated. This can be a problem when designing assembly lines and adding automation to one part of the process, as the automated tasks may have considerably faster processing speeds than the tasks performed by humans. The human processing may create a bottleneck and not enable taking full advantage of the processing capability of the automation. Enabling the two to work in unison in the right balance is a major challenge and is precisely what KUKA is currently working on.

## Automation in Services

Automation goes well beyond manufacturing. Service organizations do not have the buffering mechanisms of inventory typically found in manufacturing. Therefore, managing operations is much more difficult. To address this issue, services have turned to technology. Consider that telephone operators of yesteryear were replaced by a completely automated process. Other service processes, such as banking and much of purchasing, have become automated and online. Also, today, many medical screens, such as screening of genes or tissue samples, are automated.

The decision for service organizations to automate must be strategic, in addition to considering costs. Automation in services provides consistency and requires fewer employees, lowering labor cost. However, automation of service processes can impact the customer's perception of service quality. It must also relate to the target market. For example, a number of banks have extensive online banking services with bricks-and-mortar facilities staffed with only a skeleton crew. However, in geographic markets with an older and wealthier clientele that expects traditional levels of customer service, banks have placed larger and well-staffed facilities. Therefore, automation in services needs to also be tied to the target market and their expectations.

## CHAPTER HIGHLIGHTS

1. Operations Management (OM), or "operations," is the business function responsible for producing a company's goods and services, in an efficient and cost-effective way. It is the function responsible for transforming a company's inputs, obtained by the sourcing function, into the finished goods or services, which marketing sells to final customers.

2. The operations function performs the transformational role of the organization. It has evolved from being a strictly production function to having a strategic organizational role.

3. OM involves making many varied decisions. These include product and process design, quality management, inventory management, facility layout and location, and scheduling. Competitive bidding and negotiation are two different methods used to reach agreement and develop contracts with potential suppliers.

4. Product design is the process of deciding on the specific characteristics and features of each of the company's products. Process design is developing the process needed to produce the exact product designed.

5. Layout planning is deciding on the best physical arrangement of centers of economic activity. There are four types of layouts: fixed position, process, product, and cellular.

6. Line balancing is the process of designing product layouts. It involves assigning tasks to workstations considering their precedence relationships, cycle time, and tasktimes.

## KEY TERMS

Transformation role
Physical element of the service
Psychological benefits
Sensual elements
Early supplier involvement (ESI)
Reverse engineering
Product life cycle
Intermittent process
Repetitive process
Product volume
Degree of product standardization
Project processes
Batch processes
Line processes
Continuous processes
Fixed position
Process
Product
Cellular
Line balancing
Cycle time
Takt time

## DISCUSSION QUESTIONS

1. Identify major differences between a service and manufacturing operation. Find an example of a service and manufacturing company you are familiar with, and compare them.

2. Find a company you are familiar with, and explain how it uses operations. How is its operations function tied to its supply chain? Do you have any suggestions for their improvement?

3. Find an example of a process layout of a local business. Draw a diagram, and try to find a way to improve it.

4. Explain the concept of cycle time, and explain how it affects layout. How does it affect suppliers?

## PROBLEMS

1. Green Go Monitors is ready to release their new intelligent monitors. The variable cost for each product is $2,000. Fixed cost per year is estimated to be $100,000. If the company sells each product at a price of $2,500, how many products must be sold to break even? If the company sells 1,000 products at the price of $2,500, what will be the contribution to profit?

2. James Pens has designed a new lawn care product called the mini-mower and is now considering its processing needs. The variable cost for each mini-mower manufactured is $30. Fixed cost per year is estimated to be $20,000. James is planning to sell each mini-mower at a price of $40. How many products must be sold to break even? If James sells 5,000 products at the price of $40, what will be the contribution to profit?

3. A company's break-even quantity for a product is 1,000. What is the selling price for each product assuming $10,000 fixed cost per year and $20 variable cost per product? If the company sells 2,000 products at the selling price, what will be the contribution to profit?

4. Given the following manufacturing precedence relationships, compute the cycle time per day and the minimum number of workstations assuming eight working hours a day and 400 products need to be produced per day.

| Task | Description | Task Time | Preceding Task |
|---|---|---|---|
| A | Punching | 30 seconds | |
| B | Bending | 20 seconds | A |
| C | Combining | 30 seconds | B |
| D | Painting | 40 seconds | C |
| E | Polishing | 60 seconds | D |

5. Lewis Noodles has the following cooking procedures. You will need to compute the cycle time per day and the minimum number of workstations assuming eight working hours a day and 500 units need to be made per day.

| Task | Description | Task Time | Preceding Task |
|---|---|---|---|
| A | Cook vegetables | 2 minutes | |
| B | Cut noodles | 1 minute | A |
| C | Cook noodles | 5 minutes | B |
| D | Cook meat | 3 minutes | C |
| E | Mix ingredients | 1 minute | D |

# REFERENCES

Ghosh, Carlos. "Making the Car a Mobile, Connected Workspace." *Harvard Business Review*, October 2016: 100–106.

Hamel, G., and C. K. Prahalad. *Competing for the Future*. Boston: Harvard Business School Press, 1996.

Iansiti, Marco. "The History and Future of Operations." *Harvard Business Review*, May 2016.

Lee, H. L. "Aligning Supply Chain Strategies with Product Uncertainties." *California Management Review*, 44(3), Spring 2002: 105–191.

Reeves, Phil. "How Rapid Manufacturing could Transform Supply Chains." CSCMP's *Supply Chain Quarterly*, Quarter 4, 2008.

Skinner, W. *Manufacturing in the Corporate Strategy*. New York: John Wiley & Sons, 1978.

# 6 Sourcing

## LEARNING OBJECTIVES

*After completing this chapter, you should be able to:*

- Define sourcing, and explain the differences between purchasing, strategic sourcing, and supply management.
- Explain the impact of the sourcing function on the organization and the supply chain.
- Describe the sourcing process.
- Explain characteristics of different types of sourcing engagements.
- Explain how to measure sourcing performance.

## CHAPTER OUTLINE

- **What Is Sourcing?**
  *Purchasing, Sourcing, and Supply Management*
  *Evolution of the Sourcing Function*
  *Commercial versus Consumer Sourcing*
  *Impact on the Organization and the Supply Chain*
- **The Sourcing Function**
  *The Sourcing Process*
  *Cost versus Price*
  *Bidding or Negotiation?*
- **Sourcing and SCM**
  *Functional versus Innovative Products*
  *Single versus Multiple Sourcing*
  *Domestic versus Global Sourcing*
  *Outsourcing*
  *Electronic Auctions (E-Auctions)*
- **Measuring Sourcing Performance**
- **Chapter Highlights**

- ■ **Key Terms**
- ■ **Discussion Questions**
- ■ **Problems**
- ■ **Class Exercise: Toyota**
- ■ **Case Study: Snedeker Global Cruises**

In early 2010 all major headlines clamored over the news that Toyota was recalling more than eight million vehicles in the United States, Europe, and China for problems with sticking accelerator pedals. Production in the United States had been suspended for eight car models, including the Camry, America's top-selling car, and sales at most Toyota dealers had come to a screeching halt. For a company known for zero defects, this was devastating. Toyota Motor Corporation had been the icon of the quality movement and considered a leader in the automotive industry. Toyota placed blame on one of its suppliers, a company that manufactures accelerator pedals. Given the close relationship Toyota has with its suppliers, how could such a major fault get past them?

Supplying to Toyota is highly coveted among car-parts suppliers, and Toyota is known for making it difficult for suppliers to get contracts. Suppliers that are selected are typically monitored very carefully and are rewarded with loyalty. Toyota is known for playing a large role in engineering the parts made by outside firms. Suppliers make parts to Toyota's exact specifications, but are often not involved in product testing. Between the years of 2000 and 2008 Toyota doubled its sales, and the ability to maintain quality during such rapid growth was challenging. To keep up with costs the company demanded that suppliers make parts more cheaply. An executive at a major U.S. supplier said that Toyota had insisted his firm make each generation of parts 10% cheaper. Rapid growth in such a competitive industry may have shown up in the quality of Toyota's cars.

The close relationship between supplier and buyer, as seen between Toyota and its suppliers, makes it difficult to identify the true source of quality problem when they occur. The fault could be with the supplier in manufacturing the part, or with the component parts the supplier sources from their own supplier. The latter situation occurred a few years earlier when the toy manufacturer Mattel had to recall toys due to the use of lead paint by its supplier's supplier in China. Another source of the quality problem could be the specifications defined by the manufacturer. Yet another could be the treatment that supplier parts may go through after receipt by the manufacturer.

Although the close relationship between supplier and buyer is necessary to achieve rapid response in today's competitive marketplace, it illustrates the importance and complexity of the sourcing function. Purchasing parts is not merely about the lowest price. It is about building lasting long-term relationships and helping each other through challenging times.

# What Is Sourcing?

## Purchasing, Sourcing, and Supply Management

**Sourcing** is the business function responsible for all activities and processes required to purchase goods and services from suppliers. Every organization has customers and suppliers. The sourcing function has primary responsibility for the supply side of the organization, whereas marketing has primary responsibility for the customer side of the organization. We can also say that sourcing addresses the "upstream" part of the supply chain. Figure 6.1 highlights the functional position of sourcing within the organizational framework.

The sourcing function is often referred to by a number of different terms, and there is some confusion regarding its name. These names include "purchasing," "procurement," "sourcing," "strategic sourcing," and "supply management." Although they are often used interchangeably they do not necessarily mean the same thing. In this text we use the term "sourcing" to refer to the overall management of the supplier base, encompassing all the terms and the range of activities, from tactical to strategic. However, let us clarify the differences in these terms.

**Purchasing** is a term that defines the process of buying goods and services. It is a narrow functional activity with duties that include supplier identification and selection, buying, negotiating contracts, and measuring supplier performance. The term *purchasing* is also frequently used as the title of the business function within organizations.

Over the years the purchasing function has evolved to include a much broader and more strategic responsibility, which is termed "strategic sourcing" or "supply management." Strategic sourcing is not the same as purchasing and involves a much more progressive approach to the sourcing function. **Strategic sourcing** goes beyond focusing on just the price of goods to looking at the sourcing function from a strategic and future-oriented perspective. It considers sourcing opportunities that will solve greater problems for the buying firm and give it a competitive advantage. This requires expanding the role of sourcing from mere buying, to building close and longer-term working relationships with specially selected suppliers and partners. Therefore, it is important to remember that purchasing and strategic sourcing are not the same, as illustrated in Figure 6.2.

## Evolution of the Sourcing Function

Historically sourcing, or purchasing, was regarded primarily as a clerical activity. This involved managing the buying transactions and filling out required forms. However, during the mid-1900s, particularly during World War II, the ability to acquire raw materials when needed became critical. Scarcity of many materials resulted in price increases, and finding affordable sources of supply

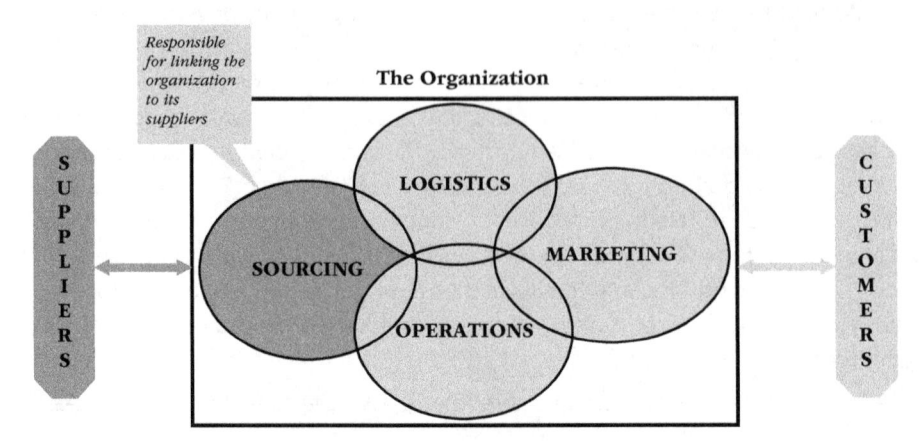

**FIGURE 6.1** The sourcing function.

*MORE STRATEGIC*

**STRATEGIC SOURCING**

*MORE TACTICAL*

**PURCHASING**

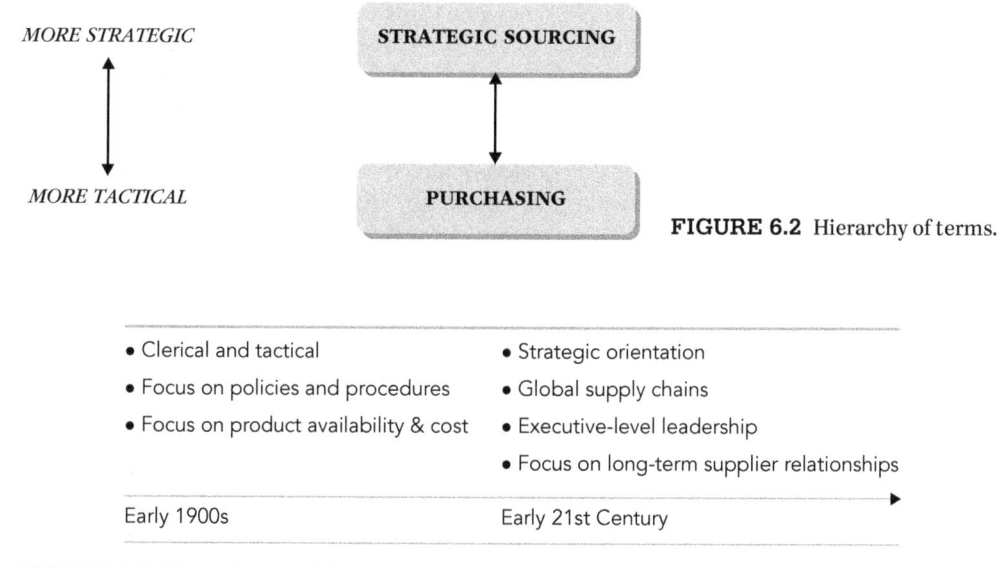

**FIGURE 6.2** Hierarchy of terms.

- Clerical and tactical
- Focus on policies and procedures
- Focus on product availability & cost

- Strategic orientation
- Global supply chains
- Executive-level leadership
- Focus on long-term supplier relationships

Early 1900s                    Early 21st Century

**FIGURE 6.3** The evolution of the sourcing function.

became a managerial challenge. As a result, sourcing slowly moved from being a mere buying function to one responsible for cultivating suppliers and ensuring a large and continuous supply base.

The importance of sourcing has continued as companies now compete globally for sources of supply. In the late 1900s, supply chain competition became the norm, and companies found that they were increasingly dependent on the performance of their suppliers. Further, technological developments in the early part of the 21st century created high expectations for supply chain integration, lower transaction costs, and faster response times. The Internet and B2B (business-to-business) e-commerce changed the way sourcing of goods was conducted. As a result, the role of the sourcing function within the organization had become elevated, moving to the highest ranks of the organization, such as vice president of purchasing and vice president of supply. This evolution of the sourcing function is shown in Figure 6.3.

## Commercial versus Consumer Sourcing

Most people assume that they understand and have an expertise in sourcing as they are familiar with personal buying. However, commercial sourcing is very different from personal buying, or consumer buying. One difference relates to the number of buyers versus suppliers. In consumer buying there are many suppliers of common items, and the buyers are typically final consumers of the items they purchase. Also, each individual buyer comprises a relatively small portion of the supplier's total business and has little ability to negotiate purchase price. Just consider the large number of shoppers at Home Depot purchasing everything from lightbulbs to refrigerators. Compare the number of these transactions to those that take place between Home Depot and, say, the lightbulb manufacturer, which is much smaller in comparison.

In commercial buying the volumes purchased are on a much larger scale, and organizations typically have very specialized purchasing needs. Unlike in personal buying, where there tend to be many choices of suppliers, in commercial buying the number of potential suppliers may be limited. Given the large volumes that are typically purchased, buyers in commercial sourcing spend large sums of money, and suppliers may have a large stake in the individual customer. The stakes are high, sums of money are very large, and often there is an imbalance in power based on the size of the buyer versus supplier. As a result companies may go to great lengths to secure the buying contracts. For example, many retail suppliers compete for a contract with a retailer such as Wal-Mart or Target, where they can get a wide reach to the market.

The primary function of commercial buying is acquiring the right materials and services, and making sure they are available to all parts of the organization in the right quantities, at the right price, at the right time. Remember that many different items are sourced that fulfill the needs of all parts of the organization, everything from materials directly used in manufacturing, to support services and office supplies. Sourcing must also make sure that it follows all legal and ethical procedures and abides by environmental and security regulations. As a result commercial buying is much more complex than that of personal buying.

## Impact on the Organization and the Supply Chain

The sourcing function provides a number of critical roles for the organization and the supply chain. The first is **operational impact**. The operational performance of an organization and its supply chain is dependent on an efficient and effective sourcing function. It is sourcing that ensures that the right materials are available throughout the organization and supply chain, in the right quantities, and at the right places exactly when needed. Sourcing must also do this while striking an optimal balance between having enough inventory and not too much. Shortages of materials can stop an organization from functioning. Too much inventory, on the other hand, can mean tied-up capital and financial losses. Finding the right balance is an enormous task.

Sourcing also has a critical **financial impact** on the organization. Companies spend large sums of money on sourcing goods from their suppliers, and the savings that can result from proper management of this function can have a huge impact on the organization. Consider that in most manufacturing organizations the sourcing function represents the largest single category of spend for the company, ranging from 50% to 90% of revenue. In fact, almost 80% of the cost of an automobile is purchased cost, where the manufacturing facility merely assembles purchased items. The large financial impact of sourcing is precisely the reason this function has been elevated to such a prominent role in the organization.

Sourcing also has a significant *strategic impact* on the organization. Recall from Chapter 2 that all organizational decisions need to support the business strategy of the organization. This means that sourcing must find suppliers that support the company's competitive priorities. For example, companies that compete on cost will have different criteria for supplier selection than those competing on quality or other dimensions. Poor supplier quality may result in higher levels of scrap or returned items that slow down manufacturing. On the other hand, poor supplier management may result in paying significantly more for supplies than competitors. It is up to the sourcing function to ensure that the source of supply supports the strategic direction of the organization.

Another impact on the organization is **risk mitigation**, by minimizing risks of supply disruptions and erosion of image that can result from improper sourcing selection. Consider that sourcing is not a one-time event but occurs on a continual basis. As such, it is important to ensure a continuous source of supply rather than taking risks that may cause supply disruptions. This means evaluating suppliers not only on a one-time purchase basis, but as a longer-term source of supply. Also, sourcing must ensure that suppliers meet a range of performance standards, including legal and ethical. Sourcing from unethical suppliers, regardless of how low the cost, will erode a company's image.

Sourcing also has an **information impact** on the organization. Sourcing is continually gathering information on availability of suppliers and goods, and prices, as well as new products and technology. It brings new knowledge to the organization and its supply chain. This helps companies in many ways, from having clear product cost expectations to understanding available technologies that can be used in product design.

## Supply Chain Leader's Box—Co-Creation

### ■ THE AUTO INDUSTRY

According to recent estimates companies such as Toyota, Fiat, and Nissan have all cut new-model development time by close to 50% as they engage in co-creation with their suppliers. **Co-creation** is a process of product development in which manufacturers and suppliers work together to create the product. Current technological capability enables integrating and sharing sets of big data, applications and platforms that allow manufacturers and suppliers to work together in "co-creation." Just consider industries such as automotive and aerospace, where a new product is often assembled with hundreds of thousands of components supplied by hundreds of suppliers from around the world. Designers and manufacturing engineers can share data, and quickly and cheaply create simulations to test different designs, select choice of parts and suppliers, and compute associated manufacturing costs. This is co-creation, and it significantly speeds up development time. It also creates cost savings as decisions made in the design stage typically drive 80% of manufacturing costs. In fact, Toyota claims to have eliminated 80% of defects prior to building the first physical prototype through this process. This is all due to co-creation.

Adapted from: Manyika, James, Michael Chui, Brad Brown, Jacques Bughin, Richard Dobbs, Charles Roxbargh, and Angela Hung Byers. *Big Data: The Next Frontier for Innovation, Competition, and Productivity.* Chicago: McKinsey Global Institute, June 2012.

# The Sourcing Function

## The Sourcing Process

The sourcing function is responsible for every aspect of acquiring goods and services, ranging from identifying potential suppliers to negotiating and awarding contracts and ensuring contract standards are met. The purchasing process begins when a purchase need within the organization is identified and clearly specified. The job of the sourcing function is to select appropriate suppliers, negotiate contracts, and manage the process of acquisition. Sourcing must first decide if the need can be met with existing suppliers or whether new suppliers must be identified. Sourcing typically maintains an acceptable list of suppliers for ongoing purchases, but also evaluates suppliers for new needs that occur on an ongoing basis.

Supplier selection is an important part of the sourcing function and involves identifying potential suppliers and soliciting business from them either in the form of a **request for quotation (RFQ)**, a **request for proposal (RFP)**, or a **request or invitation for bid (RFB)**.

It is important for the sourcing function to be in charge of the supplier base and that supplier management and selection is directed through the sourcing function. "Maverick buying," a practice where internal users attempt to buy directly from suppliers and bypass the sourcing function, often occurs in companies. It is acceptable for such practices to occur occasionally, such as a restaurant employee running out to buy bread or an office worker buying paper. However, this should not be done on a routine basis as it bypasses sourcing and erodes all the benefits sourcing brings to the organization, such as economies of scale when dealing with a large supply base.

The sourcing function must act as the primary contact with suppliers, but other functions should also be able to interact with suppliers as needed. Involving members from multiple functions improves the communication process with suppliers, especially when identifying needs and evaluating supplier capabilities. This may involve the function of engineering, to assess tolerance specification requirements for purchased items; operations, in deciding which sourcing choice is better given the current production process; or even marketing, to decide if product changes influenced by sourcing selection will impact sales. Companies often have sourcing teams and must consider inputs from all other organizational functions.

Sourcing personnel are responsible for understanding a range of material requirements and whether they can meet organizational needs. For example, it is the responsibility of sourcing to review material specifications and question whether a supplier's lower-cost material can meet the performance standards that may have been set by operations or engineering. Sourcing also needs to be able to review a number of different requisitions and identify whether different users require the same material, allowing it to combine purchase requirements and lower costs.

## Cost versus Price

Sourcing managers are responsible for buying goods and services and determining fair price. For that reason they must understand the relationship between cost and price, remembering that cost and price are not the same. They must also understand what constitutes fair price under a range of circumstances.

Cost is the sum of all costs incurred to produce the product. The total cost of producing a product, or service is the sum of its fixed and variable costs. Recall from Chapter 5 that fixed costs are those the company incurs regardless of how much it produces, such as overhead, taxes, and insurance. For example, a company must pay for overhead and real estate taxes regardless of whether it produces 1 unit or 1,000 units. Variable costs, on the other hand, are costs that vary directly with the amount of units that are produced. They include items such as direct materials and direct labor. Together, fixed and variable costs add up to total cost:

$$\text{Total Cost} = F + V_C Q$$

where

$F$ = fixed cost

$V_C$ = variable cost per unit

$Q$ = number of units sold

The price of an item is the amount at which it is being sold in the marketplace. Buyers understand that a supplier must cover total cost, including overhead, and make a profit to stay in business. The profit also needs to reflect the risks the supplier is taking. The goal in developing purchasing contracts and negotiation is to find a **fair price**, which is the lowest price that can be paid while ensuring a continuous supply of quality goods. This is illustrated in the following example:

| | |
|---|---|
| *Variable cost* | |
| Materials | $ 5,000 |
| Labor | $ 2,000 |
| + | |
| *Fixed cost* | |
| Facility overhead | $ 3,500 |
| **Total cost** | $10,500 |
| + | |
| **Profit** | $ 1,000 |
| **Selling price** | $11,500 |

A better way to evaluate price in purchasing is to estimate the **total cost of ownership (TCO)** before selecting a supplier. The reason is that there may be additional costs that are incurred when

**COMPETITIVE BIDDING**

- Performance criteria and specifications can be clearly defined
- Volume purchased is high
- Products being purchased are standardized
- Many qualified suppliers exist in the marketplace
- Time is available for bid evaluation

**NEGOTIATION**

- Performance criteria and specifications cannot be clearly defined
- Many criteria exist for supplier selection (e.g., cost, quality, delivery, and service)
- Product being purchased is new or technically complex
- Few qualified suppliers exist in the marketplace
- Suppliers customize the product to buyer

**FIGURE 6.4** Criteria for using competitive bidding versus negotiation.

acquiring the item in addition to the selling price. Total cost of ownership is the purchase price plus *all* other costs associated with acquiring the item. This includes transportation, administrative costs, follow-up, expediting, storage, inspection and testing, warranty, customer service, and handling returns. In the preceding example these additional costs need to be added to the selling price to get a more accurate assessment.

## Bidding or Negotiation?

Another important role of the sourcing function is determining how to award buying contracts. Once suppliers have been identified, competitive bidding and negotiation are two different methods used to reach agreement and develop contracts with potential suppliers. Competitive bidding has the objective of awarding the business to the most qualified bidder, once specific criteria have been identified, and can pit suppliers against one another. Negotiation, on the other hand, is a communication process between two parties that attempts to reach a mutual agreement.

Both bidding and negotiation achieve the goal of reaching agreement and awarding a contract to a supplier; however, they do so under different circumstances. A significant factor to consider is the type of relationship needed between buyers and suppliers. For purchasing standard items that are a commodity and that have standard specifications, such as stationary or cement, competitive bidding is the most efficient and effective method. However, when there are many factors to consider in awarding a contract, and when it is important to work with suppliers in product development, it is best to rely on cooperative negotiation. Consider Figure 6.4.

# Sourcing and SCM

## Functional versus Innovative Products

Supply chains have uncertainty on both the demand and supply side. Demand uncertainty occurs when product demand is unstable and difficult to predict. Supply uncertainty occurs when there is uncertainty regarding sources of supply and their capabilities. Demand and supply uncertainties are related to the type of product and their supply chains. Understanding these uncertainties makes it easier to manage the supply chain.

## Global Insights Box - Outsourcing Analytics

### ACCENTURE

Companies outsource many activities that are not their core competency. Analytics is such an activity as it is not part of the core competency of most companies. To tap into the full potential of analytics, firms need to somehow acquire this skill. The most common way is by **outsourcing analytics**. Like third-party logistics (3PL) firms that have specialized skills in logistics, analytics firms have specialized skills in data and software and are on the technology frontier. Their expertise on key data sources and analytical techniques makes them uniquely qualified to help with analytics. Further, many external providers specialize in certain industry segments and can bridge the gap between industry and technical knowledge.

There are numerous examples of such outsourcing arrangements. Accenture provides consulting and outsourcing services to many companies, including Best Buy. Accenture helps companies with analytical strategy, selection of appropriate applications, and manages the major components of a firm's IT function. Software firm Teradata works closely with Hudson's Bay Company to implement an approach to reducing fraud in the merchandise returns process. Alliance Data works with retailers, such as Limited Brands and Pottery Barn, to establish and manage their loyalty programs. Mu Sigma provides analytical services to Wal-Mart and other retailers. Given the deep knowledge analytics requires, even leading analytics companies outsource at least some aspect of their analytics capability.

Adapted from: Davenport, Thomas H. "Realizing the Potential of Retail Analytics: Plenty of Food for Those with the Appetite." Working Knowledge Research Report, Babson Executive Education White Paper, 2009, 1–42.

---

Two broad categories of products result in very different supply chains and have differing levels of demand uncertainty. Products can be classified as either primarily **functional** or primarily **innovative**.[1] Depending on their classification, they will be sourced differently and will require different types of supply chains. Functional products are those that satisfy basic functions or needs. They include items such as food purchased in grocery stores, gas and oil for transportation and heating, and household items from batteries to lightbulbs. In contrast, innovative products are purchased for other reasons, such as innovation or status, and include high-fashion items or technology products, such as those seen in the computer industry.

Functional products typically have stable and predictable demand and long life cycles. It is easier to source for functional products due to this stability. Their supply chains are easier to manage; however, they typically have low profit margins. Innovative products, on the other hand, have highly unpredictable demand and short life cycles. New and innovative products are introduced quickly, and their demand is difficult to forecast. Although they have higher profit margins, their supply chains are much more difficult to manage.

Just as there are uncertainties on the demand side, there are also uncertainties on the sourcing side. The supply side of the supply chain can be classified as either a **stable** or an **evolving supply process**. A stable supply process is where sources of supply are well established, manufacturing processes used are mature, and the underlying technology is stable. Consider sourcing apples, lumber, or undershirts. In contrast, an evolving supply process is where sources of supply are rapidly changing, the manufacturing process is in an early stage, and the underlying technology is quickly evolving. Examples would include alternative energy sources, certain organic food items, or high-end computer technology. It is challenging to manage supply chains with either demand or supply uncertainty. It is especially challenging to manage supply chains with both uncertainties as shown in Figure 6.5.

Efficiency-focused supply chains have both low demand and supply uncertainty and are easiest to manage. These supply chains typically don't have high profit margins. However, their

---

[1] H. L. Lee, "Aligning Supply Chain Strategies with Product Uncertainties," *California Management Review*, 44(3), Spring 2002: 105–119.

|  | *Demand uncertainty* | |
|---|---|---|
| *Supply uncertainty* | Low (functional products) | High (innovative products) |
| Low (stable process) | Efficiency-focused SC *Least challenging* | Responsive SC |
| High (evolving process) | Risk-hedging SC | Agile SC *Most challenging* |

**FIGURE 6.5** Demand versus supply uncertainty.

operations are highly predictable, and the gains in these supply chains come from efficiency and elimination of waste.

Responsive supply chains are used for innovative products that have a stable supply base. The primary challenge here is to ensuring being able to quickly respond to customer demands. Mass-customization strategies such as **postponement**, where the supply chain is designed to delay product differentiation as late in the supply chain as possible, are effective here. A good example is the case of HP printers that are kept in generic form as long as possible. They are differentiated with country and language-specific labels that are added at the last point in the system.

Risk-hedging supply chains are those with high uncertainty on the supply side. These supply chains must do everything possible to minimize risks of supply disruptions and inventory shortages. These supply chains typically rely on higher inventory safety stocks and engage in a practice where resources are pooled and shared between different companies.

## Supply Chain Leader's Box—Risk Management

### IBM

A decade ago IBM used analytics to move from a regional procurement process that was globally dispersed to a single integrated global supply chain. Today the tech giant continues to use analytics to manage every aspect of their supply chain, especially the supplier network. The company relies on analytics to manage cost containment and risk, and uses software to model the impact of potential scenarios of suppliers.

Analytics helped IBM respond in a timely and effective manner when a natural disaster threatened to disrupt the company's supply chain. In April of 2010 a volcano in Iceland halted flights throughout most of Europe. IBM relied on its algorithm to identify what to do. The software algorithm told IBM to focus on Asia rather than Europe, indicating that the critical link in IBM's supply chain was Hong Kong. To management this did not make sense at first. Then the reason became clear.

The algorithm predicted that if IBM did not take steps to secure sufficient air capacity once the volcanic eruption stopped and flights resumed, it would encounter a bottleneck in Hong Kong. This would occur as a result of the company having to quickly move a backlog of products from Asian manufacturers to European customers. IBM followed the recommendation of the algorithm. The company booked space on commercial and charter aircraft from Hong Kong to Europe in plenty of time. "We didn't sit and watch what was going on with the disaster," said Timothy E. Carroll vice president of supply chain operations. "We prepared ourselves for what to do once the disaster lifted." This turned out to be the best decision. Now, a dedicated team within IBM regularly reviews various scenarios to prepare a response to any disaster or crisis anywhere in the world.

Adapted from: James Cook, "From Many, One: IBM's Unified Supply Chain," *CSCMP Supply Chain Quarterly*, Quarter 4, 2012.

Agile supply chains are used in cases of both high demand and supply uncertainty. They are the most difficult to manage as they simultaneously must be responsive to an uncertain demand while using strategies to hedge risks to ensure there are no supply disruptions. These supply chains use mass customization strategies on the demand side, while carrying higher safety stock and engaging in resource pooling on the supply side.

## Single versus Multiple Sourcing

Traditionally companies held the view that multiple sources of supply were best to increase cost competition and ensure supply security. This view has been challenged for quite some time, and the notion of single sourcing is becoming the acceptable norm. Single sourcing focuses on building closer supplier relationships and cooperation between buyers and suppliers and moves away from arm's-length relationships. It focuses on moving away from competitive bidding, using cooperative negotiation, and building long-term relationships.

Single sourcing has a number of benefits. Splitting the order among multiple suppliers can be costly as it doesn't permit consolidating purchase power. Splitting the order also has an impact on quality as there will be natural variations between different sources, even if minimal. Single sourcing also lowers freight costs, it enables easier scheduling of deliveries, and the supplier may be more cooperative in addressing special needs knowing they are the only source.

In some cases there may not be a choice but to go with a single source. This may occur, for example, when a supplier is the only source of a particular material. They may be the only one that has the needed process or they are the sole owner of the patent for the product. Having a single source of supply, however, is risky in practice. When a supplier is small the buyer's business may utilize most of the supplier's capacity. This makes the supplier highly vulnerable if there is a discontinuity of purchase from the buyer. At the same time the buyer may not wish to be tied to a source that is so highly dependent on them. Similarly, by relying on one supplier, the buyer is vulnerable if there is a disruption in the supplier's production process, such as a fire at a plant, a labor strike, or a work stoppage, as the supplier's supplier has a problem.

One strategy companies should consider is to use a "portfolio" of a small number of multiple suppliers. Similar to a financial portfolio, these suppliers can be selected to create a balance of requirements. Some can be local for rapid deliveries; others may be global but less expensive. This strategy can help balance the risks of relying on a single supplier in case of supply chain disruptions. Another rule to consider is that one buyer should not make up more than 20% or 30% of the total supplier's business, otherwise making the supplier highly vulnerable.

## Domestic versus Global Sourcing

Another challenge to consider is whether to use domestic or global sourcing, also called "**off-shoring**." Global sourcing has been on the rise as companies have been attracted to cheaper labor costs in other parts of the world. It has been most prominent for sourcing products with easily defined standards, such as in the retail industry. It is also used heavily in the service industry, such as running call centers, processing claim forms, or in software development. Even in medicine the reading of diagnostic tests, such as x-rays, is often off-shored. However, with a rise in fuel prices the labor savings are often negated, or even outweighed, by high transportation costs. This is called "**re-shoring**." Therefore, a number of companies are turning toward domestic sources to reduce transportation costs, monitor quality more closely, and have closer buyer–supplier relationships. Also, with an emphasis on sustainability and "green" there has been a push toward sourcing local versus global goods.

Companies that engage in global sourcing need to possess a certain amount of multinational experience. This can be especially problematic for small- to medium-sized firms that are more likely to lack this expertise. Global sourcing, by definition, requires work groups of individuals from different companies, and different cultures and languages to work together effectively. This concept, known as *virtual teaming*, poses special challenges due to the significant potential for culture clashes and misunderstandings. These differences in culture and business practice can put offshore source initiatives at risk, particularly for enterprises with limited international experience.

## Outsourcing

An important sourcing decision is whether to "outsource" certain aspects of the sourcing function. Recall that outsourcing involves choosing a third party, such as an outside supplier or vendor, to perform a task, function, or process to incur business benefits. Companies may choose to outsource activities or tasks for many reasons, rather than performing them internally. These include lower costs, access to technical skills, and the ability to free themselves of doing noncore activities.

Outsourcing has become a mega trend in many industries and is continuing to grow, as companies focus on their core competencies and shed tasks perceived as noncore. A good example has been the growth in outsourcing of transportation of goods to 3PL providers, such as UPS and FedEx. Transportation and movement of goods requires investment of specialized resources, such as fleets of trucks, aircraft, and state-of-the-art information system for product tracking. Outsourcing this activity to specialty companies is a much more cost-effective decision for most firms. Good outsourcing decisions can result in lowered costs and a competitive advantage, whereas poorly made decisions can increase costs, disrupt service, and even lead to business failure. Although financial aspects of outsourcing are important, outsourcing has increasingly taken on a broader strategic organizational focus.

Two key dimensions that help define outsourcing are the **scope** and **criticality** of the outsourced task. Scope is the degree of responsibility assigned to the supplier. Criticality, on the hand, is the importance of the outsourced activities or tasks to the organization. The greater the scope of the outsourced task, the larger the relinquishing of control by the buyer. Similarly, the greater the criticality of the outsourced task the greater the consequences of poor performance to the buying firm and greater the requirement for supplier management. It is important to understand these dimensions when considering outsourcing. Companies should be especially careful when outsourcing activities with large scope and criticality and should especially monitor such outsourcing engagement to ensure a successful outcome, as illustrated in Figure 6.6. We discuss the importance of scope and criticality in more detail in Chapter 13.

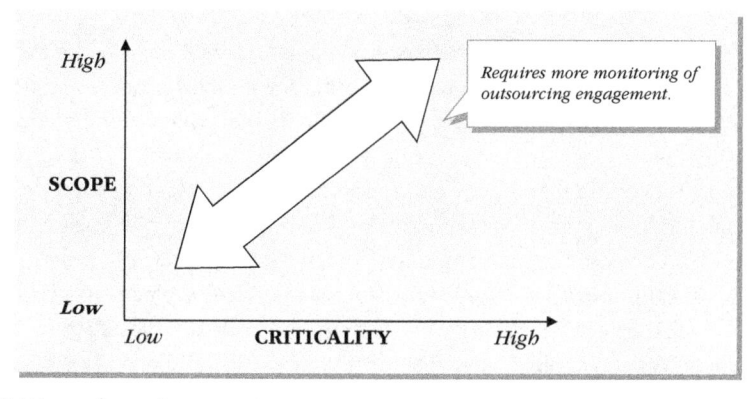

**FIGURE 6.6** Dimensions of outsourcing.

## Electronic Auctions (E-Auctions)

E-auctions are the use of Internet technology to conduct auctions as a means of selecting suppliers and determining aspects of the purchase contract. This includes determination of price, product quality, volume allocation to different suppliers, as well as supplier delivery schedules. Auctions have been used throughout history as a means of providing competition between suppliers. It is Internet technology, however, that has given sourcing managers an important tool for supplier selection to conduct this process online in an efficient and effective manner. E-auctions have enabled increasing the pool of potential suppliers for any one item and to more efficiently and accurately compare sources of supply.

There are many benefits to using e-auctions. They include market transparency, decreased error rate, and simplified comparison of sources of supply. They also include increased buying reach, as companies can tap into a much broader source of supply through the use of the Internet. There is also a reduction in ordering cycle time as the process is automated and more efficient than the traditional method of sourcing, such as issuing an RFP or RFQ.

There are, however, potential problems with e-auctions that must be considered. One problem is that suppliers can bid unrealistically low prices during the e-auction process, with the idea of renegotiating after the contract has been awarded. As a result, potentially better and more realistic sources of supply may be eliminated. Another problem is the inclusion of suppliers in the e-auction who do not actually plan on participating, but merely want to gather market intelligence. There are also risks to interrupting a good supplier relationship. Putting products on an e-auction sends a signal to current suppliers that the company is considering switching to a new source of supply and that price may be the determining factor in source selection. This may potentially damage good supplier relationships and may not be the best strategy when building long-term relationships.

## Managerial Insights Box—Outsourcing Alliances

### ROOTS

The Canadian apparel manufacturer and retailer, Roots, is an example of a company that succeeded as a result of shifting its sourcing strategy to involve collaboration with its supplier and demonstrates the benefits that can be attained from supplier collaboration. Roots, a company with a stellar reputation, was given the task of handling licensed USA logo Olympic wear during the 2002 Winter Games in Salt Lake City. The forecast called for 100 calls per day into the Roots customer service center, which was well below the actual 1,500 per day peak. However, the 2002 Winter Games experienced a surge of patriotism, following the September 11 attacks. The result was an unexpected flood of demand that Roots was initially unable to meet. Roots found itself unable to handle the 50,000 orders per month for USA Olympic gear from its Canadian operation. At the last minute, the company was forced to revamp its entire distribution strategy, opening a separate Web-based ordering channel. With the help of a third-party call center and fulfillment provider, it added two U.S.-based call centers, moved distribution to Memphis, and changed delivery carriers. The company did this almost overnight while orders were still flooding in.

The company's forecast of expected demand was based on two of the prior Olympic events. Based on this forecast of demand, raw materials were ordered, production was scheduled, and a third-party relationship for a call center and fulfillment operation was set up. However, the surge in demand in the post 9-11 climate was not anticipated. Further, Roots manufactures locally in Canada, so it has a short supply chain for finished products resulting in lower inventory levels. Roots quickly realized that it could not succeed alone and needed a partner. Roots turned to its 3PL provider. Together they quickly set up a system that involved reporting, check points, and audits throughout the fulfillment chain. The systems were scalable and well planned, rules and procedures were in place, and it was clear who had what authority regarding issues such as customer service, manufacturing, or distribution. The system turned out to be a success, allowing Roots to meet its orders. Building a close relationship with its 3PL has helped Roots showcase its brand and serve the market as a first-class retailer.

This level of responsiveness helped Roots establish itself. The company continues its success and was the provider of team uniforms for the Canadian team for the Olympic Games in Rio 2016.

See: www.roots.com.

---

There are many types of e-auctions that are classified based on the way competition between sellers or buyers is conducted. For example, in an **open auction**, suppliers can select the items they want to place offers on, see the most competitive offers from other suppliers, and enter as many offers as they want until a specified closing time. In a **sealed bid auction**, sellers have a certain amount of time to submit one best and final bid, with bidders never having knowledge of what the other sellers are bidding. With forward auctions, bids increase in value, whereas in reverse auctions they decrease in value.

The most common type of e-auction is the **reverse auction**, which involves one buyer with many sellers. Sellers place decreasing bids on a set of goods or services and follow a specified set of rules that governs the auction. A reverse auction is an online, real-time declining price auction involving one buyer and a number of prequalified suppliers. The bidding process is dynamic. Suppliers compete for the business by bidding against each other online using specialized software. Suppliers are given information concerning the status of their bids in real time, and the supplier with the lowest bid is usually awarded the business.

E-auctions are one of many methods for sourcing goods and services. To use e-auctions for sourcing a few criteria need to be in place. First, the specification for goods or services needs to be well defined. Buyer expectations must be clear, including product characteristics, quality standards, and technological requirements, as well as delivery expectations. Second, there must be a competitive market in place and a sufficient number of qualified suppliers. Too few suppliers may not provide enough competition, whereas too many may create confusion. A rule of thumb suggests that the number of suppliers participating in an e-auction should be between three and six. Third, there must be a clear understanding of market standards to set appropriate expectations. Fourth, the buyer believes the cost of the e-auction is justified by the savings in price. This item is often overlooked, as running an e-auction, including software and training, can prove to be more expensive than most companies anticipate. Fifth, clear rules for running the e-auction are specified, such as extending the auction and selection criteria.

The e-auction process involves three stages: preparation, the auction event, and follow-up. In fact, preparation is often the determining factor of an e-auction's success or failure. In the preparation stage, the buyer must identify and prequalify suppliers who will participate. The buyer must also set the product requirements—such as quality, quantity, delivery, service, and the length of contract. In addition, they must train everyone involved in the technology that will be used to run the auction and pretest the auction technology to ensure functionality. They must also specify how the auction will be conducted. For example, suppliers must understand how long the auction will run and the rules if the targeted closing time will be extended. Some e-auctions have a "hard" closing time, which permits no extension of time, whereas other auctions permit time extension. Typically an e-auction will experience a surge of activity in the last few minutes of the auction, and it is important for suppliers to understand these types of rules governing the auction to adjust their behavior accordingly.

Today's technology allows the buyer a variety of alternative approaches in terms of conducting auctions. For example, price visibility can be viewed in many ways, such as a rank order, by percentages, or by proportional differences. The technology also allows the ranks to be adjusted for nonprice factors, such as differences in transportation costs, quality, or delivery time. Most auction software allows suppliers and the buyer to communicate with each other during the auction, and the software options can specify whether messages may be visible to other suppliers participating in the auction. In addition, technical assistance must be made available during the auction in case problems arise.

Conducting e-auctions is much more complicated, and often more expensive, than companies realize. It also automates the buyer–supplier relationship, diminishing the potential of building a long-term relationship. Although e-auctions can provide large benefits in sourcing, companies should be selective when using this sourcing approach.

## Big Data Analytics Box

### FEDEX

Security is essential for companies such as FedEx. The company handles nine million shipments a day and manages all the data required to coordinate these activities. Recently the company decided to harness the power of its large stores of data to address security needs. To do this FedEx decided to link its stores of big data to physical items. It created a next-generation, first-of-its-kind information service called SenseAware that combines a GPS sensor device and a Web-based collaboration platform. This technology was originally used by the healthcare and life sciences industries to track high-value or extremely time-sensitive shipments, but is now available to all industries. SenseAware attaches digital information to packages, providing information such as precise temperature readings, information about a shipment's exact location, and notification when a shipment is opened or if the contents have been exposed to light. It then shares real-time alerts and analytics between authorized parties regarding the shipment. The device is equipped with a radio that constantly broadcasts this information back to FedEx. This results in an enormous amount of data being generated that must be acted on in real time. This has provided top-level security and efficiency for FedEx, while generating even more data for large-scale analysis.

Adapted from: Larry Dignan, "FedEx Launches SenseAware: Collaboration Meets GPS Meets Sensory Data," *Smartplanet*, November 16, 2009.

## Measuring Sourcing Performance

As we can see, the sourcing function has a large responsibility over supply chain inventory. Sourcing must ensure that there are enough inventory items needed at the right locations, but not too much inventory given large inventory costs. There are two common performance measures that can be used to measure the performance of the sourcing function relative to its utilization of inventory. These are **inventory turnover** and **weeks-of-supply**.

Inventory turnover measures how quickly inventory moves. It is computed as:

$$\text{Inventory turnover} = \frac{\text{Cost of goods sold}}{\text{Average inventory value}}$$

### Example 1  Inventory Turnover

Jenco Incorporated is a producer of children's dolls for the toy industry. It has high inventory costs and is concerned that its inventory is selling at an appropriate rate. It has an annual cost of goods sold of $8,000,000 and an average inventory in dollars is $2,000,000. What is the annual inventory turnover?

**SOLUTION:**

$$\text{Inventory turnover} = \frac{\$8,000,000}{\$2,000,000} = 4 \text{ inventory turns per year}$$

In general, the higher the inventory turnover rate the better the company utilizes its inventory. However, there is no one number that is considered correct. Some companies need to turn their inventories over faster than others. For example, perishable items such as food or medicine need to turn over faster than machinery or commodity items. Also, certain industries have much higher inventory turns than others. For example, innovative products with short life cycles need to turn over very quickly or they may become obsolete. To get good guidelines on acceptable inventory turns it is important for companies to consider their industry standards as a benchmark of performance.

The second performance measure, weeks of supply, provides the length of time demand can be met with on-hand inventory. It is computed as follows:

$$\text{Weeks of supply} = \frac{\text{Average on-hand inventory}}{\text{Average weekly usage}}$$

### Example 2  Weeks of Supply

Jenco Inc. is concerned about having enough inventory in stock and wants to compute its weeks of supply. Recall that we already know that Jenco has an $8,000,000 annual cost of goods sold.

**SOLUTION:** Weekly cost of goods sold can be computed by dividing the annual cost of goods sold by 52 weeks per year. Weeks of supply can then be computed as follows:

$$\text{Weeks of supply} = \frac{2,000,000}{\$8,000,000/52}$$

$$\text{Weeks of supply} = \frac{2,000,000}{\$153,846.15}$$

$$\text{Weeks of supply} = 13 \text{ weeks of supply}$$

Weeks of a supply tells the manager how long the current on hand inventory will last based on current demand. A large "weeks of supply" value means too much inventory is being held, whereas a value that is too low increases the chances of a stock-out or lost sales. Notice that the value of this metric depends on demand. Given that product demand often changes due to factors such as seasonality, managers need to consider that the best value of this metric will likely change throughout the year. As with inventory turnover, companies should benchmark this metric against industry best practices.

## CHAPTER HIGHLIGHTS

1. Sourcing is the business function responsible for all activities and processes required to purchase goods and services from suppliers.

2. Terms such as "purchasing," "procurement," "sourcing," "strategic sourcing," and "supply management" are used interchangeably but are not the same. Purchasing defines the process of buying goods and services, whereas strategic sourcing, or supply management, involves looking at sourcing from a strategic and future-oriented perspective.

3. The sourcing function provides a number of critical roles for the organization. These are operational impact, financial impact, strategic impact, risk mitigation impact, and information impact.

4. The sourcing process involves every aspect of acquiring goods and services, ranging from identifying potential suppliers to negotiating and awarding contracts, and ensuring contract standards are met.

5. Competitive bidding and negotiation are two different methods used to reach agreement and develop contracts with potential suppliers.

6. Products can be classified as either primarily functional or primarily innovative. Depending on their classification, they will be sourced differently and will require different types of supply chains.

7. Outsourcing engagements can be classified based on scope and criticality of outsourced tasks.

8. E-auctions are the use of Internet technology to conduct auctions as a means of selecting suppliers and determining aspects of the purchase contract.

9. Inventory turnover and weeks of supply are two metrics that can be used to measure performance of the sourcing function.

## KEY TERMS

Sourcing
Purchasing
Strategic sourcing
Operational impact
Financial impact
Risk mitigation
Information impact

Co-creation
Request for Quotation (RFQ)
Request for proposal (RFP)
Request or invitation for bid (RFB)

Fair price
Total cost of ownership (TCO)
Outsourcing analytics
Functional
Innovative
Stable

Evolving supply process
Postponement
Off-shoring
Re-shoring
Scope
Criticality
Open auction

Sealed bid auction
Reverse auction
Inventory turnover
Weeks-of-supply

## DISCUSSION QUESTIONS

1. Identify the primary ways in which the sourcing function impacts supply chain management (SCM). Find an industry example where sourcing has significantly benefited the firm and where it has significantly hurt the firm.

2. Think of a recent purchase you made in your everyday life. Explain how this purchasing process would be different if you were buying the same product for a firm on a regular basis versus purchasing it for yourself.

3. Find at least one business example of outsourcing. Explain the risks and benefits.

4. There has been in a push in many communities to source locally. Identify the risks and benefits of sourcing globally versus locally.

5. Explain the differences between sourcing manufactured products versus services. Identify some key challenges that would occur in defining service specifications versus manufacturing specifications. Provide an example of each.

## PROBLEMS

1. Jerry's Auto Repair is concerned about the effective use of parts inventory. His average inventory in dollars is $300,000, and cost of goods sold is $1,500,000.

   a. What is the inventory turnover for Jerry's Auto Repair?

   b. Assuming 52 weeks per year, what is the weeks of supply?

   c. What do these numbers tell you about Jerry's inventory utilization?

2. Urbanite Hip is a clothing store catering to college students and young professionals. It carries fashion merchandise and wants to ensure that it is using inventory effectively. Cost of goods sold is $5,000,000, and average inventory in dollars is $250,000.

   a. What is their inventory turnover?

   b. What is the weeks of supply, assuming 52 weeks per year?

   c. Urbanite Hip is expecting to increase sales by 10% next year while maintaining the same level of average inventory. How will their inventory turnover and weeks of supply change?

3. Phoenix & Chow is a family-owned restaurant with an annual cost of goods sold of $520,000 and an average inventory of $50,000. What is the value of weeks of supply assuming 52 weeks per year?

4. H & H store is a retailer of stationary and paper products. It has an annual cost of goods sold of $100,000 and an average inventory of $50,000. What is the annual inventory turnover? If the industry average is three turns per year, how does H & H compare?

5. Climb and Fly Sports has annual cost of goods sold of $1 million. What is the average inventory assuming 52 weeks per year and weeks of supply equal to 5?

## CLASS EXERCISE: TOYOTA

You are Manager of Strategic Sourcing at Toyota Motor Corporation and have just been called in by the VP of Global Sourcing, to whom you report. There has been a problem with at least eight vehicles exhibiting sticking accelerator pedals, and your boss is very upset. Strong evidence points to a problem with CTS, an electronics supplier, which has been recognized for high-quality standards by Toyota. You have been asked to provide your boss with the following:

1. Identify the exact sequence of steps—a "project plan"—on how to handle this problem, from dealing with customers to identifying causes. Explain what should be done and why.

2. What should be said to your customers? How should you explain the problem?

3. What information do you want to collect and from whom to identify causes?

4. What should you say to your supplier? How should you say it (e.g., in public or private; in a meeting or in writing)? What action do you expect them to take?

5. Do you continue long-term contracting with this supplier? Do you penalize this supplier?

6. What are the risk trade-offs in your decision (e.g., placing blame versus accumulating evidence; dropping a supplier versus standing by a supplier)?

## Case Study | Snedeker Global Cruises

It was August 7th, and Brandt Womack had just been given his first assignment by his purchasing manager at Miami-based Snedeker Global Cruises Inc. It was the "E-Auction Development Program" (EDP). The purpose of EDP was to identify potential products that could be purchased through e-auctions, determine the necessary steps to conduct a successful e-auction, and assess the impact of e-auctions on supplier relationships. As a newly hired supply chain manager, Brandt wondered how to proceed.

Snedeker Global Cruises incorporated in 1986 and is a cruise company with 35 cruise ships and over 70,000 berths. Snedeker Global serves the contemporary and premium segments of the cruise vacation industry and offers a variety of itineraries to destinations worldwide, including Alaska, Asia, Australia, the Caribbean, Europe, Hawaii, Latin America, and New Zealand.

In 2005, Snedeker incurred its highest-ever procurement costs in sourcing the products and services needed for cruise ship operations and wanted to combat this trend. To that end Snedeker had been working on changing its buying practices. In the past, each individual cruise ship made all its own purchases for the upcoming season. Purchasing was decentralized, with each ship making purchasing decisions based on its needs alone. The company began moving away from this practice and put into place a centralized purchasing department in charge of making purchases for the entire cruise line. The centralized purchasing strategy provided many cost-saving opportunities for the company and greatly reduced the overall order costs of the company. The company wanted to continue to pursue ways in which the centralized purchasing practice could reduce costs, and e-auctions became a viable option. However, senior management at Snedeker was concerned about the impact on quality and the effect e-auctions might have on suppliers.

At Snedeker, the purchasing cycle began with a master forecast for the upcoming year with orders being placed 8 to 10 months prior to need. This master forecast included everything from replacement engine parts to chocolate mints placed on pillows in cabins. When the forecast was generated it was given to the Senior Purchasing Manager, Kasey Davis. Kasey scheduled a meeting with Brandt to discuss the E-Auction Development Program, giving Brandt the master list of all the products needing to be purchased for the next year. Kasey instructed Brandt to determine which products would be best to purchase through e-auctions and wanted to know how the e-auction process would work. In addition, Kasey wanted Brandt to determine the effect that e-auctions would have on relationships with current suppliers.

Brandt walked out of Kasey's office overwhelmed. It was his first assignment, and he did not know where to begin the E-Auction Development Program (EDP).

*Case Questions*

1. Suggest steps Brandt should follow to begin the EDP process.
2. Identify differences between traditional purchasing and use of e-auctions. How can Brandt use these differences to make his selection? What types of items would be best suited for purchase through e-auctions?
3. Assume Brandt has identified products to purchase through e-auctions. What steps does he need to take to conduct a successful e-auction?
4. What negative impact can e-auctions have on supplier relationships, and how can Brandt ensure that they do not occur?

# REFERENCES

Coase, R. H. "The Nature of the Firm." *Economica*, 4(1), 1937: 386–405.

Ellram, L. "Purchasing: The Cornerstone of the Total Cost of Ownership Concept." *Journal of Business Logistics*, 14(1), 1993: 161–183.

Ellram, L. "A Taxonomy of Total Cost of Ownership Models." *Journal of Business Logistics*, 15(1), 1994: 171–191.

Fisher, M. L. "What Is the Right Supply Chain for Your Product?" *Harvard Business Review*, March–April 1997: 105–116.

Fogarty, David and Peter C. Bell. "Should You Outsource Analytics?" *MIT Sloan Management Review*, Winter 2014.

Hamel, G., and C. K. Prahalad. "The Core Competence of the Corporation." *Harvard Business Review*, 68(3), 1990: 243–244.

Hamel, G. and C. K. Prahalad. *Competing for the Future*. Boston: Harvard Business School Press, 1996.

Lee, H. L. "Aligning Supply Chain Strategies with Product Uncertainties." *California Management Review*, 44(3), Spring 2002: 105–119.

Nowosel, Kai, Abigail Terrill, and Kris Timmermans. *Procurement's Next Frontier*. Accenture Strategy, June 2015, 1–43. (www.accenture.com)

# Logistics

# 7

## LEARNING OBJECTIVES

*After completing this chapter, you should be able to:*

- Define logistics and explain its impact on supply chain management.
- Identify and describe key logistics tasks.
- Explain reverse logistics and its challenges.
- Explain differences between modes of transportation.
- Explain the role of warehousing on logistics and describe cross-docking.
- Explain the role of third-party-logistics (3PL) providers.

## CHAPTER OUTLINE

- **What Is Logistics?**
  *The Logistics Function*
  *Evolution of Logistics*
  *Impact on the Organization*
  *Impact on the Supply Chain*
  *Reverse Logistics*
- **Logistics Tasks**
  *Transportation*
  *Storage*
  *Material Handling*
  *Packaging*
  *Inventory Control*
  *Order Fulfillment*
  *Facility Location*
- **Transportation**
  *Truck*
  *Water*
  *Air*

  *Rail*
  *Pipeline*
  *Multimode*
- **Warehousing**
  *Role of Warehouses in the Supply Chain*
  *Cross-Docking*
  *Facility Location*
- **Third-Party Logistics (3PL) Providers**
- **Chapter Highlights**
- **Key Terms**
- **Discussion Questions**
- **Problems**
- **Case Study: Strategic Solutions Inc.**

---

The arrival of *Harry Potter and the Deathly Hollows* was full of heightened anticipation for fans of the Harry Potter series of books. The 12 million copies of books were scheduled to hit the shelves of thousands of retail stores all over the United States in synchronized fashion on July 21st 2007, and be available through online bookstores. This was a record first printing in publishing. Strict security had to be implemented at all stages to minimize the risk of someone leaking the book's ending. Marketing was pushing a big publicity launch, and the mystery of the ending added to the excitement. For the executives at Scholastic, however, this was a major headache. Achieving synchronized deliveries of millions of books at thousands of different locations and meeting deadlines all depended on logistics.

  Accomplishing the goal required everyone in the supply chain to work in tight coordination. This included executives from Scholastic's manufacturing and logistics divisions, printers, distributors, and trucking companies, all working to make sure the deliveries, tight schedules, and turnarounds were met. The author, J. K. Rowling, delivered the manuscript just in time to the publisher, who then sent it to printers R. R. Donnelley & Sons and Quebecor World, which worked around the clock to guarantee books would be ready by the release date. In order to reduce time, Scholastic bypassed its own warehouses, using hired trucks to ship from six printing sites directly to large retailers like Barnes & Noble and Amazon.com, as well as numerous distributors of independent booksellers. To expedite loading and unloading, trucking companies such as Yellow Transportation and J. B. Hunt Transport Services used same-size trailers and pallets. To ensure security, every trailer shipping the Potter books had a GPS transponder that would alert Scholastic if the driver of the trailer veered off designated routes.

  The timing was especially tricky for e-tailers, which had to ship in advance for the books to hit customer doorsteps precisely on July 21. Barnes&Noble.com even developed special algorithms that enabled its shipping team to figure out when to release books to the U.S. Postal Service or UPS to ensure a simultaneous arrival around the country on that day. Who could have imagined that printing and delivering books could be such a logistical nightmare?

Adapted from: "Harry Potter and the Logistical Nightmare." *Business Week*, August 6, 2007: 9.

# What Is Logistics?

## The Logistics Function

**Logistics** is the business function responsible for transporting and delivering products to the right place at the right time throughout the supply chain. In essence, it is about movement and storage of product inventories throughout the chain. Logistics has a critical responsibility for the functioning of both the organization and the supply chain, as without it materials would not arrive when and where they are needed. To achieve its goals, logistics must plan and coordinate all material flows from source of supply to all users in the chain. As we can see by the logistics requirements to deliver Harry Potter books, this task is more complicated than it appears.

Unlike marketing, which focuses on the "downstream" part of the supply chain, and sourcing, which focuses on the "upstream" part, logistics connects the organization to both its customers and suppliers. Logistics works with sourcing to link the organization to its external suppliers and to ensure that materials are delivered inbound to the organization when needed. This is critical for the operations function, which is responsible for transforming sourced materials into finished products. Logistics also works with marketing to connect the organization to the final customer by ensuring distribution and delivery of outbound products to external customers. This is shown in Figure 7.1.

The function of logistics is complex and requires a great deal of coordination. As we will see in this chapter, many important decisions have to work together to enable proper logistics functioning. This includes organizing and managing the entire distribution network, including location of warehouses, distribution centers, and plants, and coordinating the modes of transportation between them. It also includes design and management of operations throughout the network for efficient storage and quick movement of goods. Recall that in the Harry Potter example, pallets of

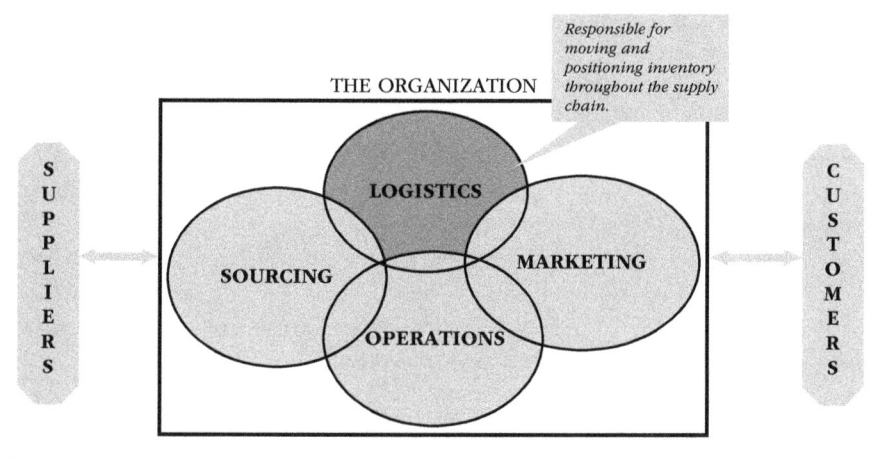

**FIGURE 7.1** The logistics function.

the same size were used to expedite movement, and even seemingly small decisions were found to be significant, such as the size of trailers used.

Logistics must also have access to information in real time to be able to track product movement and plan exact timing and location of deliveries. It must ensure security of goods from theft or tampering while the products are moved. For example, in the case of Harry Potter, all trailers that carried the books had GPS transponders to enable the company to monitor product location at all times. Adding to the challenge is that all of this must be accomplished while meeting exact customer delivery dates and at the lowest cost possible. It is a challenge of high magnitude.

Logistics is a function that requires large investments in infrastructure, such as transportation vehicles, material handling equipment, and information technology. For this reason, many companies outsource this function to outside firms. Companies such as United Parcel Service (UPS), Federal Express (FedEx), and DHL have made it their business to provide logistics services to their clients. These companies have invested in the needed infrastructure, such as their own fleet of airplanes and trucks, and the latest technology to track packages from point of origin to destination using bar code technology and scanners. In addition to moving products, these companies can be contracted to perform a range of logistics functions, including designing an entire distribution network for their clients. They can also provide services such as management of inventory, warehouse management, and even customer interface.

## Supply Chain Leader's Box

### ■ UNITED PARCEL SERVICE (UPS)

UPS is the world's largest package delivery company, both in terms of revenue and volume, and a global leader in supply chain solutions. It is known as a third-party-logistics (3PL) provider, as it provides logistics services to companies. Although the primary business of UPS is the time-definite delivery of packages and documents, they have extended their capabilities in recent years to encompass the broader spectrum of services known as supply chain solutions. This includes designing a distribution network, freight forwarding, customs brokerage, fulfillment, returns, financial transaction, and even repairs.

UPS also maintains the highest quality and efficiency standards, implementing just-in-time (JIT) and lean systems throughout its facilities. It uses state-of-the-art technology for tracking packages, and shipments, as well as real-time location identification of any of its carriers using GPS technology.

One can discern the full logistics capability of UPS just from its sheer size. UPS services more than 220 countries and territories and operates 1,801 facilities. It has a delivery fleet of 96,105 package cars, vans, tractors, and motorcycles. It even has its own UPS aircraft fleet and is considered the ninth-largest airline in the word. This enables UPS to design optimal multimodal transportation for quick speed and lowest cost, delivering more than 15 million packages per day to almost 8 million customers.

UPS relies on technology and is an analytically driven company, optimizing every aspect of its logistics network. It uses GPS-enabled big data telematics and route optimization for maximum efficiency in transportation. Transport analytics can improve productivity by optimizing fuel efficiency, preventive maintenance, driver behavior, and vehicle routing. Tracking of weather and other disruptive events can continually optimize routes. UPS, for example, started gathering data more than 20 years ago. Today, the company uses a "data-drenched" tool called ORION (on-Road Integrated Optimization and Navigation) to help drivers find the most efficient path through their delivery areas.

The immense infrastructure and capability offered by UPS is the reason why companies use them for their logistics and supply chain solutions. Logistics is a highly capital-intensive industry, and the coordination is complex. In addition, most companies do not consider transportation and logistics to be their core competency and do not have the resources to perform this function. For this reason there has been a high growth in 3PL providers such as UPS and an increased demand for their services.

Check out: http://www.youtube.com/watch?v=mRAHa_Po0Kg.

# Evolution of Logistics

Today's business logistics is actually rooted in military logistics. Logistics has always been a critical part of national defense. Consider all the issues involved in moving military troops and convoys, planning optimal locations of depots, and delivery of supply items such as food, fuel, and spare parts. Logistics in the military is the function responsible for these activities. In addition, logistics in the military is also responsible for all issues related to equipment maintenance, reliability, and parts sourcing.

In the business arena logistics was introduced under the name of "**physical distribution**" in the 1960s and was primarily focused on shipping goods on the outbound side of the organization. The initial interest was on getting the product from the manufacturer to the final customer using the best arrangement of warehouses and distribution centers, and optimal modes of transportation. As a result, logistics developed a strong tie with the marketing function and focused on the "downstream" part of the supply chain (Figure 7.2).

In the 1970s and 1980s the use of logistics concepts was extended to the "upstream" part of the supply chain. There was an increased focus on strengthening manufacturing and a greater awareness of the need to deliver materials to manufacturing facilities in an accurate and timely fashion. This was termed *materials management*, which now looked at logistics for serving the inbound side of the organization in addition to the outbound.

The 1990s witnessed the growth of supply chain management (SCM) and the holistic understanding of the importance of managing the entire supply chain. As a result, logistics in the business sector was extended to include movement of goods through the entire supply chain, both upstream and downstream, serving both the inbound and outbound side of the organization.

Today there are three different types of logistics. The first is **business logistics**, which is focused on the movement and storage of goods throughout the entire supply chain. The second is **military logistics**, which is focused on supporting military needs. Finally, there is **event logistics**, which involves organizing and deploying resources in preparation for an event. Examples of this would be logistics involved in setting up the Olympic Games or deploying resources to provide disaster relief anywhere across the globe when needed.

# Impact on the Organization

Logistics has a significant impact on the organization by the mere fact that its role is to support all organizational functions by ensuring timely availability of products. On the inbound side of the organization, logistics works with sourcing to ensure that materials needed for operations are delivered when required. On the outbound side logistics works with marketing to ensure that products are delivered to various customers when needed. Let's look at this process a bit more closely.

1. **Impact on Operations.** Logistics interfaces closely with operations through the planning of the amounts of inventory that must be received at various points throughout the supply

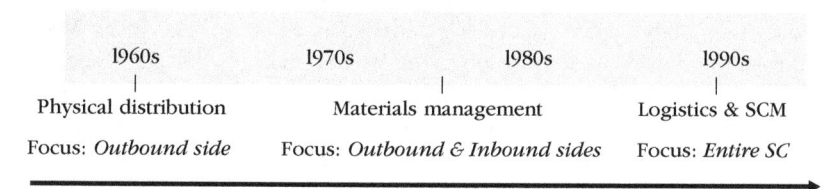

| 1960s | 1970s | 1980s | 1990s |
|---|---|---|---|
| Physical distribution | Materials management | | Logistics & SCM |
| Focus: *Outbound side* | Focus: *Outbound & Inbound sides* | | Focus: *Entire SC* |

**FIGURE 7.2** Evolution of the logistics function.

chain and the timing of those receipts. Logistics must understand exact delivery schedule requirements. It must also decide on the best balance between bringing extra inventory and arranging for storage, or risking not having enough inventory. This is directly related to operations scheduling and production run time, which is the amount of time required for a batch of goods to be produced before a "setup" or changeover is incurred. Historically companies used long production runs to incur economies of scale and stored the excess goods in inventory. The production process was then stopped to "set up" or change equipment for production of another product. This practice required logistics to deliver large amounts of inventory less frequently.

As more manufacturers have switched to just-in-time (JIT) or lean manufacturing, production run times have become significantly shorter. JIT or Lean, which we discuss in detail in Chapter 10, is known as a "pull" system, where demand "pulls" the product through the supply chain. This is different from traditional systems that "push" the product through the supply chain in anticipation of demand. JIT systems are characterized by short production runs to respond to demand. They require frequent deliveries of smaller quantities of inventories and carry little excess inventory as safety stock. As a result, precise timing of deliveries of inbound materials is essential.

It is up to logistics to work with operations to arrange for the precise timing of deliveries of the exact materials that are needed based on production schedules. If too much inventory is delivered too soon, inventory costs become high, and storage becomes an issue. If too little inventory is delivered, manufacturing processes will not be able to operate without the needed materials. Therefore, it is critical that logistics understands production schedules and strikes a balance between inventory holding cost and shortages.

This is especially difficult if we consider that demand patterns and production schedules are not necessarily fixed. Consider holiday demand or seasonal demand, such as sales of ice cream in the summer or shovels in the winter. In these cases most companies produce larger quantities of products in advance of production. It is up to logistics to ensure that these products are stored at the optimal location for quick delivery and that they work with operations to ensure that just the right amount of inventory is available.

The logistics function has an impact on all operations, whether they are manufacturing or service. Consider a large restaurant that specializes in seafood. It is up to logistics to ensure that the right quantities of fresh seafood are delivered at the right time. Seafood is highly perishable, so transportation time should be minimal. Also, logistics must ensure that the right packaging, handling, and temperature controls are correct at all times. It must also ensure that the seafood is delivered at just the right time in the right quantities. If seafood deliveries are late the chefs may not have enough time to prepare the planned menu. If the delivered quantities are low the restaurant may not have enough to serve its customers. In both cases customer service suffers. Similarly, if the seafood arrives too early, it must be stored, losing its freshness and risking loss due to its perishable nature. This can result in high inventory costs for the restaurant.

2. **Impact on Marketing.** On the outbound side logistics provides key support for marketing and order fulfillment. Logistics must work with marketing to understand customer requirements, as well as storage and delivery needs. A key element in sales is ensuring that the product is available when needed. Consider sales of orange and black M&Ms during the Halloween season. Marketing arranges for the color designs that are in keeping with the event to promote sales. However, if enough colored M&Ms are not on the retail shelves at the right time, sales will not occur. It is up to logistics to ensure the right timing of the shipment of M&Ms. If the shipment arrives too late or if quantities delivered as small, sales and marketing will suffer. On the other hand, if too much inventory arrives, the company will incur losses through markdowns of the colored M&Ms after Halloween passes.

3. **Impact on Packaging.** Another logistics decision is packaging of goods as they are being transported. This has a significant impact on the ability to move and handle the material. This decision also protects the items from damage and affects both operations and marketing. Consider the seafood restaurant example mentioned earlier. If logistics does not make proper decisions on packaging, including insulation and temperature monitoring, the product will lose its freshness. In the example of M&Ms, if proper packaging is not used, the candy can get crushed, broken, or damaged. In both cases, it is up to logistics to arrange for proper packaging that ensures product integrity.

4. **Impact on Finance.** Logistics has an especially important impact on the financial picture of the organization, as it is responsible for large capital expenditures, such as transportation, warehousing, and inventory. Its performance can be seen directly on financial measures such as return on assets (ROA) and return on investment (ROI).

   Consider that ROA is computed as follows:

$$ROA = \frac{(Revenue - Expenses)}{Assets}$$

$$ROA = \frac{Gross\ revenue}{Assets}$$

Notice in the equation that we can increase ROA in three ways. One is by increasing revenue, another by reducing expenses, and another by reducing assets. All three are directly impacted by logistics. First, inventory is considered an asset on the balance sheet and an expense on the income statement. This means that by reducing inventory, both expenses and assets are reduced, and ROA is affected positively. In addition, investments in transportation and warehousing are also considered assets. By reducing these assets ROA is significantly affected. This is also another reason why some companies choose to outsource logistics. It is an asset-heavy function, and by using a third party these assets can be eliminated. Finally, notice that ROA increases with an increase in revenue. Revenue can be increased through customer service and, as we already explained, logistics can play a key role in ensuring deliveries of the right quantities of goods to the right customers.

## Impact on the Supply Chain

We discussed in Chapter 1 that logistics, in contrast to supply chain management (SCM), consists of the tasks involved in moving and positioning inventory throughout the supply chain. Logistics is a function that supports SCM by being responsible for one of the flows in SCM, namely moving of goods or inventory. Logistics manages the movement of goods both downstream and upstream and is responsible for making all the decisions that enable this to happen efficiently and effectively. This includes order processing and tracking, inventory management, transportation, warehousing, material handling, and packaging. SCM could not function without logistics as there would be inventory stock-outs at some locations and too much inventory at others.

It can be said that logistics provides SCM with three utilities: place, quantity, and time, shown in Figure 7.3. Logistics provides place utility by ensuring that goods arrive at the right place in the supply chain. It is the function that extends the geographic region by effectively utilizing transportation. It is because of logistics that SCM has a broad place utility and can reach a wide geographic region. Similarly, logistics provides quantity utility by ensuring that the correct quantities are delivered at the right location. Once again, the trade-off here is between delivering too many goods and incurring inventory holding cost or not delivering enough and having shortages. Finally, logistics provides time utility by delivering the goods at precisely the right time needed. Recall that this is especially critical for JIT inventory systems and promotional items.

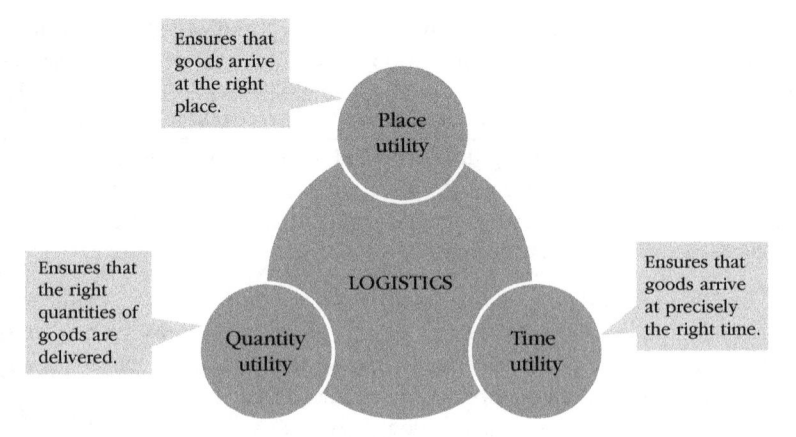

**FIGURE 7.3** Impact of logistics on SCM.

## Reverse Logistics

**Reverse logistics** is the process of moving products upstream from the customer back toward manufacturers and suppliers. This is the reverse direction from the way materials typically flow in a supply chain. This occurs for a variety of reasons, such as returns of damaged products or items the customer did not want. As with products that flow downstream, to move products upstream logistics has to organize transporting, storage, receiving, inspecting, sorting, and all other activities, to ensure efficient flow. Sometimes the items are returned directly to the manufacturer from the customer, as shown in Figure 7.4. Other times a 3PL provider may be used to handle returned items and arrange for repairs bypassing the manufacturer as shown in Figure 7.5.

Reverse logistics is especially challenging to design as this flow does not directly add value. Consider that many different types of items are being returned to many different locations. For example, the returned item may be a damaged product being returned for repairs, an overstock item that can be sold elsewhere, or an item that has been recalled or has failed and needs to be disposed of in an environmentally safe manner. If we think about the different types of items returned, we can see that there are many different paths returned items can take, and it is up to logistics to arrange for this in a cost-effective manner.

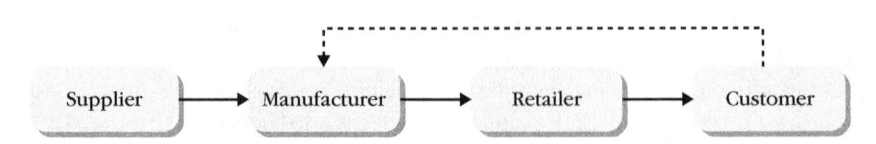

**FIGURE 7.4** Reverse logistics with returns to the manufacturer.

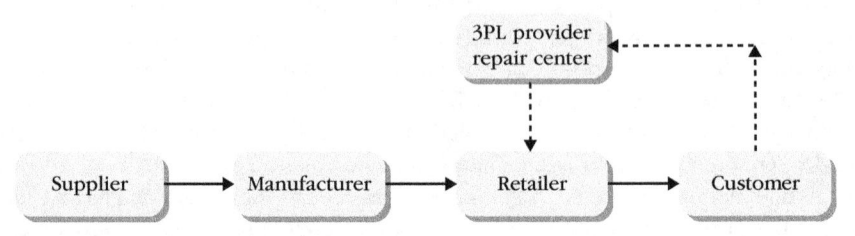

**FIGURE 7.5** Reverse logistics with returns to a 3PL provider for repairs.

Other issues add complexity to reverse logistics. One is handling the financials and the cash flows once items are returned. Another is arranging for warehouse and storage space in the reverse order that does not confuse or take away from flow of the usual downstream process. Another consideration is abiding by "green laws" in countries that have them that may require returning packaging materials for proper disposal.

As we can see, reverse logistics is complex and is especially challenging, as it does not directly add value. Further, the role of reverse logistics has become especially important in recent years. The reason is that companies are under increasing pressure to improve customer service and have made it ever easier for customers to return goods. This is especially prevalent in retail and Internet sales, where ease of returns is a major selling feature. The ability to easily return goods is becoming an "order qualifier" in much of retail, and it is up to logistics to continue to design ways for a cost-efficient process. For example, the success of the online retailer Zappos is in large part attributed to making returns convenient for customers.

# Logistics Tasks

As we already discussed, there are many tasks that logistics must do to perform the needed coordination for accurate and timely product deliveries. Here we describe the requirements of some of these tasks.

## Transportation

**Transportation** is probably the most important task logistics performs as it moves products throughout the supply chain. It is also an especially costly task given the high cost of transportation and distribution network design. Consider that some modes of transportation are less expensive than others, such as rail, but others are faster, such as air. The decision of which mode of transportation to use is directly tied to the consideration of the distance a product has to be moved. This is dependent on the span and complexity of the company's supply chain network. There are also other factors to consider, such as product characteristics. Perishable products, such as bananas, may need climate-controlled transportation. Highly innovative products, such as Apple's iPad, may need rapid delivery to areas with high demand. Products of very high value, such as diamonds, may need high security.

### Big Data Analytics Box—Driverless Cars

#### UBER

Driverless cars are vehicles capable of sensing their environment and navigating without human input. They are also referred to as autonomous vehicles, self-driving vehicles, or robotic cars. Regardless of the name, this is a disruptive technology that will change transportation. These cars use technology, sensors, GPS, radar, computer vision, and analytics to detect surroundings. Advanced control systems interpret sensory information to identify appropriate navigation paths and relevant signage. They also have control systems that are capable of analyzing sensory data to distinguish between obstacles, such as different cars on the road.

Although driverless cars were part of science fiction just a few years ago, Merrill Lynch predicted in a 2015 report that driverless taxis like Uber will make up 43% of new car sales by 2040. Similarly, the Boston Consulting Group wrote in a 2015 report that driverless taxi sales are going to rapidly rise and that 23% of global new car sales will come from driverless taxis by 2040.

Recently Uber, the company with the largest ride-share in the world, released its self-driving car to the public for the first time. As part of its pilot program, select Uber users in Pittsburgh are able to hail and ride in a driverless car. Initially the trips will be for free but eventually there will be charges. A number of other companies are following. Ford, for example, plans to roll out its first fully autonomous cars for purposes of ride-sharing by 2021. Google is doing the same and targeting 2020. Tesla is planning to make its vehicles part of a car-sharing network once its cars are fully autonomous. Although driverless vehicles have advantages and some disadvantages, they are rapidly changing transportation.

Adapted from: Muoio, Danielle. "Uber Is Winning the Driverless Race, Even Though It Isn't Using Its Own Cars—Here's Why." *Business Insider*. September 14, 2016.

## Storage

Directly related to transportation is the **storage** of goods. This involves deciding where goods will be stored, such as the number of warehouses and distribution centers, and the amounts of inventory that will be held at each center. We can see that the greater the number of storage areas and the wider their distribution, the lower transportation costs. The key is finding an optimal balance that minimizes costs but maximizes responsiveness to customers. This decision is directly related to warehouse management, inventory management, and material handling. It is also related to how the products will be handled in the storage area, from order picking, to order tracking, to degree of automation.

## Material Handling

**Material handling** is concerned with the physical handling of the product. This includes loading and unloading of goods from vehicles, placement and order picking of goods in the warehouse, and movement throughout facility, such as warehouse staging and dock areas. Efficient material handling saves cost, cuts down on time, and minimizes product damage in the process of movement. On the other hand, poor material handling can result in damaged products and excess processing costs.

Other issues of concern are the degree of automation used versus manual labor. There is a wide range of material handling equipment, from conveyors, forklift trucks, overhead cranes, and **automated storage and retrieval systems (ASRS)**. Unlike years ago where material handling was performed using manual labor, today many warehouses are completely automated and use very sophisticated ASRS.

## Packaging

**Packaging** of products is an important issue that directly relates to material handling. In addition to protecting the product during transportation and storage, packaging must be compatible with material handling equipment and material handling requirements of the warehouse. Packaging is also directly related to modes of transportation being used. Some modes of transportation require additional packaging, such as rail or water to prevent water damage. Other modes, such as air, typically require less packaging. Although one mode of transportation may cost less than another, cost of packaging needs to be factored into the decision as well. For example, water transport is much cheaper than air, but requires packaging that may prevent water damage.

## Inventory Control

All the logistics tasks we discussed so far are directly tied to **inventory control**. This involves maintaining needed amounts of inventory, arranging for timely replenishments, and maintaining accurate counts of all inventories.

Logistics is the function responsible for managing the quantities of inventory in warehouses and storage areas. This includes using inventory control systems to maintain an adequate level of inventory and replenishing the stock once shipments are made. Managing inventory is directly tied to transportation as arrangements must be made for timely inbound shipments of materials once stock is depleted. Logistics must also ensure accuracy of the inventory amounts. Inventory is typically monitored using electronic tracking systems. However, a process called "cycle counting" is used periodically where inventory is physically counted and any discrepancies with the electronic system reconciled. This is all done to ensure high levels of inventory control.

## Order Fulfillment

Logistics is often responsible for **order fulfillment**, which is completing, shipping, and delivering a customer order. Order fulfillment typically occurs from a warehouse or distribution center location, where orders are directly placed from retailers or manufacturers. Logistics must ensure that the specified lead time, the time from when the order is placed until it is received, is not exceeded. This means picking and packing the order, arranging for proper transportation, and shipping it out. This is an important role for logistics, as it involves directly dealing with the customer.

## Facility Location

Logistics is also involved in determining best location of warehouses, distribution centers, and other storage areas in relation to manufacturing facilities, customers, and suppliers. Decisions on **facility location** have a direct impact on the movement of products, distances traveled, cost of transportation, the ability to quickly respond to markets, and ultimately customer satisfaction. Optimal locations of distribution centers, for example, can have a dramatic impact on how quickly deliveries can be received at retail locations. Location decisions also have a huge impact on transportation costs and inventory levels. It is up to logistics to determine the best locations of these facilities, considering modes of transportation to move goods between them and to the final customer.

## Transportation

Transportation is one of the most important logistics tasks as it enables logistics to provide **place utility**. For this reason we want to look at this task more closely. Transportation deals with moving products and arranging for optimal modes of transportation. As we discussed earlier, transportation decisions are related to the span and complexity of the company's supply chain network. In developing optimal schedules, transportation must deal with both **economies of scale** (the larger the amount shipped at one time the lower the per unit cost) and **economies of distance** (the longer the distance moved at one time the lower the per unit cost). Let's look at these in a bit more detail.

Economies of scale is a term used to describe the fact that the larger the size of a shipment, the smaller the per unit cost of freight moved. It is because of this that shipping a partly filled vehicle, such as a partly filled truck, is very costly. This is called a less-than-truck-load (LTL) shipment, and companies try to avoid it whenever possible. The reason for this is that certain fixed costs have to be incurred regardless of how much is shipped. This includes equipment, labor, fuel, scheduling, and administrative costs. The larger the load over which these costs can be spread, the lower the per unit cost, and this is true of all modes of transportation.

Economies of distance is a term used to describe the fact that the longer the distance shipped at one time, the smaller the per unit cost of freight moved. Consider that sending one shipment 500 miles is cheaper than sending two shipments 250 miles each. Similarly, in your everyday life, consider that taking a taxi 10 miles is cheaper than taking two taxis 5 miles each. The reason is that the longer distance allows fixed cost to be spread over the larger number of miles.

The challenge for logistics managers is to find an optimal balance between the economies of scale and distance, while maintaining customer service levels. The decision becomes one of selecting the right mode of transportation or combination of modes, considering all the costs and benefits.

## Supply Chain Leader's Box

### SYSCO

Sysco is a Houston-based food distributor, which each year ships 21.5 million tons of produce, meats, prepared meals, and other food-related products to U.S. restaurants and cafeterias. To accomplish the significant task of getting such a large volume of food safely to the right place at the right time, Sysco manages a complex logistics system. It manages its own fleet of trucks and relies on state-of-the-art technology to keep everything moving efficiently.

In 2000, Sysco revamped its logistics operations to ensure it was being as efficient as possible. The redesign created a centralized supply-chain group in Houston, with the help of the software firm Manhattan Associates, to direct shipments from suppliers to one of two new redistribution centers. Once shipments are received at the redistribution centers, Sysco workers consolidate and pack large quantities of products onto trucks. They are then sent out to appropriate operating companies where they are assembled on pallets and sent out for delivery. In addition to redesigning the logistics network, Sysco also revamped its truck routes. To determine the most efficient routes for its trucks, Sysco uses Roadnet, a software program developed by UPS. The company felt this was necessary to address the problem of increasing fuel prices.

The result of the redesign of Sysco's logistics system has been fewer trucks on the road and each one fuller. The redesign has resulted in improvements on key performance metrics such as efficiency and cost of fuel usage. This example illustrates the kinds of savings that can be achieved through efficient logistics design.

Adapted from: "Veggie Tales." *Fortune*, June 8, 2009: 25–30.

Let's now look at common modes of transportation and their characteristics.

## Truck

Trucks are the most flexible mode of transportation given today's expansive highway system, and they pose few restrictions on weight or content. Also, trucks can go on a variety of roads typically maintained by the government, resulting in a relatively small fixed investment in vehicles. Given their easy access, they are utilized to some extent in almost all logistics movements. One challenge for this mode of transportation is stringent driver safety regulations, which can make labor requirements high. This has created a capacity constraint for some transportation companies who simply cannot find enough qualified drivers.

## Water

Water transportation has an advantage in its ability to transport very large and heavy shipments. It is the mode of choice for moving large bulk items, such as oil or coal. It is also a very affordable mode of transport. The disadvantage, however, is that it is an extremely slow mode of shipment and is obviously restricted to water access.

## Air

In contrast to water transportation, air is the fastest mode of transportation. However, it is also most expensive given high fixed and variable costs. Not only are aircraft and fuel expensive, but also air transport requires an airport location. Given the high cost, it is most appropriate for lighter, smaller, and higher priority items.

## Rail

Rail is the mode of transportation designed for moving heavy loads very long distances. The advantages are the same as with water: ability to handle large and heavy items at a low cost. The disadvantage is long transit time. Also, rail is restricted to a particular infrastructure, such as railroad tracks. For this reason rail typically has to be combined with another mode of transportation for final delivery to customers.

## Pipeline

Pipeline transportation is limited to liquids and gases, such as petroleum and natural gas. It is a highly specialized mode and requires a specific infrastructure, such as a pipeline.

## Multimode

Multimode is the combined use of multiple modes of transportation for product delivery. Given the constraints of each mode of transportation, as shown in Figure 7.6, it is almost impossible to exclusively rely on one mode. Often, a combination of a few modes provides optimal cost and customer service. However, the coordination effort can be a challenge for companies. This is one of the reasons many use a third-party-logistics (3PL) provider to handle shipments. Most 3PL providers, such as UPS, use multimode solutions to provide services to customers.

|  | **FIXED COST** | **VARIABLE COST** |
| --- | --- | --- |
| RAIL | High | Low |
|  | (e.g., equipment, terminals, tracks) | (e.g., can transport large tonnage) |
| TRUCK | Low | Medium |
|  | (e.g., highways publicly supported) | (e.g., fuel, maintenance, labor) |
| WATER | Medium | Low |
|  | (e.g., ships & equipment) | (e.g., can transport large tonnage) |
| PIPELINE | High | Low |
|  | (e.g., right-of-way, construction) | (e.g., no labor cost) |
| AIR | High | High |
|  | (e.g., aircraft, handling, cargo) | (e.g., fuel, labor, maintenance) |

**FIGURE 7.6** Cost structure by mode of transportation.

## Global Insights Box—Rail Service Between China and Europe

### ■ "NORTHEAST PASSAGE"

In today's jet-setting world we forget that challenges still exist with moving large and heavy cargo across the globe. For that reason there has been much excitement over the new rail freight service that is now running between China and Europe. In 2008, Germany launched an experimental service between China and Germany by way of Russia. Since then, the International Union of Railways (UIC) and rail infrastructure providers in Finland and Sweden have started promoting the so-called "Northern East-West Freight Corridor" for intermodal container service from the Far East to Scandinavia.

The new rail service promises to dramatically reduce transit times of containers being shipped from the Far East to Europe. Currently these shipments take well over six weeks by sea. With the new rail service the time should be just two weeks. This is a dramatic reduction in time and significantly improves access to markets. In addition, there may be benefits for regions beyond Europe, as some of the containers could then be moved across the Atlantic Ocean. The new rail service expands logistics possibilities for importers and connects the rapid-growing Far East to other parts of the globe.

As with any new transportation service, there are still challenges that have to be worked out. Recall that rail service is dependent on the tracks it runs on, and in this case the rail equipment will have to navigate tracks with different gauges across two continents. Some trains in Europe are equipped with changeable gauges so they can cross different tracks. However, many freight cars do not have this capability. In addition, trains currently run on an irregular basis and often do not depart until the operator has accumulated enough freight to justify the cost of the trip.

These snags will quickly be ironed out as demand for the new service increases. A rail service from China's interior to Europe is a significant option for inland manufacturers, for which transportation using water is time consuming and expensive. China's booming industry is rapidly shifting from the coast to inland, and this type of rail service offers a logistics opportunity to move Chinese goods to Western markets.

Adapted from: "New Rail Service Opens Up a 'Northeast Passage.'" CSCMP's Supply Chain Quarterly, Quarter 4, 2009: 68–69.

# Warehousing

## Role of Warehouses in the Supply Chain

Traditionally the role of warehouses has been to provide storage space for goods, as well as inbound and outbound transport. Goods that arrived at the warehouse via truck or rail were unloaded and then placed in storage bins in the warehouse. When customer orders arrived, goods were picked from their storage location, known as "order picking," then staged for transport, loaded on to trucks or rail, and shipped.

In addition to providing storage, contemporary warehouses are increasingly places for mixing inventory assortments to meet customer needs. They are driven by enhancing and expediting movement rather than lengthy storage. In fact, lengthy storage is discouraged, as it does not add value and just contributes to cost and obsolescence. Warehouses provide a centralized location that stores and organizes inventories of products before they get distributed to customers. For that reason they are often called distribution centers.

Warehouses or distribution centers play a critical role in the supply chain enabling efficient movement of goods on both the inbound and outbound side of the organization. For example, in JIT and lean manufacturing warehouses can be located close to the manufacturing facility enabling frequent deliveries of materials on a just-in-time basis. At the same time, warehouses can be utilized to create product assortments for customer shipments For example, a strategically located centralized warehouse can take advantage of consolidated shipments. The products can then be sorted and arranged for a particular customer and then shipped. In addition to these benefits many warehouses are increasingly performing tasks traditionally done at a manufacturing or retail sites. This may include repairs of items, putting garments on hangers and sequencing them to be rolled straight on to the retail floor, and adding labels and price tags.

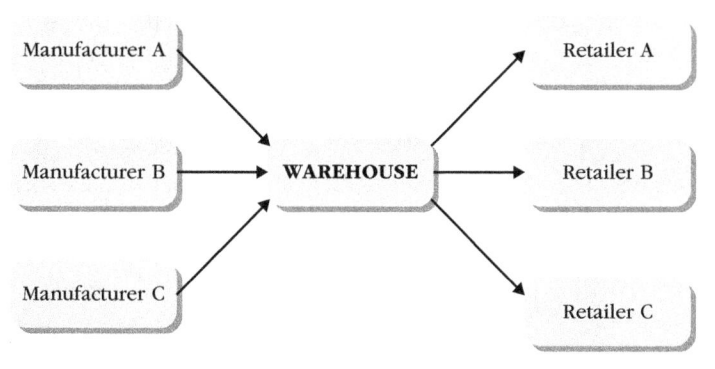

**FIGURE 7.7** Cross-docking.

## Cross-Docking

Warehouses perform a number of functions that essentially reconfigure flows from origin to destination in the supply chain to improve speed and accuracy of delivery. Two basic functions performed are breaking up of larger shipments on the inbound side, which results in lower transportation cost, and consolidation of orders for customers on the outbound side. The first is called a "**break-bulk**" operation, where a large shipment is received and then needs to be broken into smaller quantities for deliveries at multiple locations. The function of the warehouse in this case is to split the single order into multiple orders and arrange for deliveries.

Sorting of goods is yet another function performed by warehouses, enabling consolidation and mixing of orders to take place. One type of sorting that has gained popularity is called **cross-docking**. Cross-docking is an approach used to reconfigure bundles of product where, rather than making larger shipments, larger shipments are broken down into small shipments for local delivery in an area. This is shown in Figure 7.7. Cross-docking is often done in a highly coordinated manner so that the products are never stored in inventory. The term implies that the products literally "cross the dock" to be loaded on to the truck for final destination and are never stored.

Cross-docking requires precision in timing and coordination and uses state-of-the-art information technology to track inventories. Inventory must be received at precisely the right time from each manufacturer, unloaded at the warehouse, and sorted by customer and destination. Computerized systems track the exact quantities of goods requested by each customer at each location, and this is factored into the sorting process. Products are then moved across the dock and loaded onto trucks that are dedicated for a particular destination. This method is very effective for replenishing fast-moving inventory items at the store level. For this reason cross-docking is especially used in the retail industry, where shipments are sorted at distribution centers or centralized warehouses and then directly shipped to individual stores.

## Facility Location

Location of warehouses and distribution centers are important decisions logistics has to make. An optimal location will ease distribution of goods in a timely manner, whereas a poor location will make distribution more difficult. A number of factors must be considered.

The first factor to consider is proximity to customers or manufacturing facilities. It is important that the location be selected to be able to serve the largest geographic market size on the same or next day basis. Directly related to this is the availability of infrastructure and access to transportation. This includes convenient access to highway or rail, presence of a major airport, and proximity to inland or ocean port facilities. Ease of access and use of transportation coupled with customer proximity are key factors that must work together.

For labor-intensive operations, as is the case with most warehouses and distribution centers, the cost and availability of labor is another important factor. This includes considering levels of unemployment in the area, labor skills levels, productivity, work ethic, and degree of unionization. These are all important factors that must be considered carefully. Other considerations are business and personal taxes, as they have a significant impact on the cost of doing business. Also important is the overall business climate and whether it is welcoming to new business.

A number of techniques can be used to help determine where to locate warehouses and distribution centers. Some of these use quantitative models that compute distances between locations and try to find the optimal balance between costs and geographic coverage. Other methods are qualitative in nature and help the decision maker evaluate the benefits of each location. One of the more popular techniques is called **Factor Rating** and involves evaluating multiple alternatives based on a number of selected factors. It is a helpful procedure, as it can give structure to a seemingly chaotic process when many location factors need to be considered simultaneously. Next we look at how Factor Rating can be used to make a location decision.

**STEPS IN FACTOR RATING:**

Step 1: Identify key decision factors (e.g., proximity to customers, transportation, infrastructure, taxes).

Step 2: Assign weights to each factor based on its importance; factor weights must add to 100.

Step 3: Establish a scale for evaluating each location relative to each factor. The most common is scale is a five-point scale, with 1 being poor and 5 excellent.

Step 4: Evaluate each location based on the factors selected, using the scale setup in Step 3.

Step 5: Compute a score for each location by multiplying the weight of the factor by the score for that factor and summing the results of each alternative.

Step 6: Select location with the highest score.

**Example 1    Factor Rating**

Urban Apparel is deciding on where to locate its distribution center to serve its northeast retail stores. It has identified six factors it considers most important and has decided to use Factor Rating to evaluate the two location alternatives based on a five-point scale, with 1 being poor and 5 excellent. The weights assigned to each factor for each location are shown in Figure 7.8, as well as the factor score for each site. We can see that location 2 has a higher total score than location 1 and, therefore, appears to be a better location based on the set factors.

| Factor | Factor weight | Factor score at each location Location 1 | Location 2 | Weight score for each location (Factor weight × Factor score) Location 1 | Location 2 |
|---|---|---|---|---|---|
| Proximity to stores | 30 | 2 | 5 | 60 | 150 |
| Access to highway | 30 | 5 | 3 | 150 | 90 |
| Labor availability | 20 | 4 | 3 | 80 | 60 |
| Taxes | 10 | 4 | 3 | 40 | 30 |
| Building cost | 10 | 3 | 4 | 30 | 40 |
| Total | 100 | | | 360 | 370 |

**FIGURE 7.8** Factor rating for urban apparel's two DC location alternatives.

# Third-Party Logistics (3PL) Providers

Third-party logistics providers, or 3PLs, are companies that provide logistics and transportation services to other firms. They have had an increasingly important and prominent role in the supply chain as numerous companies have outsourced their logistics function. Traditional logistics management activities, such as transportation, warehousing, order processing, and related information technology support, are deemed as noncore activities for many firms. In addition, as we discussed earlier, logistics activities have significant asset requirements, making logistics a primary candidate for outsourcing. Finally, outsourcing logistics can offer the potential for large cost savings given its impact on ROA.

In the 1980s services offered by 3PL providers were relatively limited in scope. At that time 3PL providers provided traditional logistics services, such as transportation and warehouse management. However, as outsourcing logistics services grew in the 1990s, the role of the 3PL provider within the supply chain began changing accordingly. The role changed from initially offering transportation services, to offering a broad array of bundled services that also include warehousing, inventory management, packaging, cross-docking and technology management. More recently, however, the 3PL provider has taken on a more comprehensive strategic role as supply chain activities become more critical to the business.

Today, 3PL providers are engaged in strategic coordination of their customers' supply chain activities. Consider that United Parcel Service (UPS) evolved from a provider of simple delivery services to offering complete distribution management and network design. UPS claims that for their customers they will "act as eyes and ears around the world" (www.ups.com).

As entities that connect members of the supply chain, 3PL providers serve a critical role responsible for achieving effective logistics integration by which inter- and intrafirm activities are integrated to enhance customer satisfaction and provide a competitive advantage. As a result, 3PL providers have gained a prominent role in the coordination of the supply chain.

## CHAPTER HIGHLIGHTS

1. Logistics is the business function responsible for transporting and delivering products to the right place at the right time throughout the supply chain.

2. There are three different types of logistics: business logistics, which is focused on the movement and storage of goods throughout the entire supply chain; military logistics, which is focused on supporting military needs; and event logistics, which involves organizing and deploying resources in preparation for an event.

3. Logistics impacts the organization on both the inbound and outbound side. On the inbound side it ensures that materials needed for operations are delivered when required. On the outbound side it ensures delivery of products to various customers when needed.

4. Logistics is a function that supports supply chain management by being responsible for the flow of products. It provides SCM with three utilities: place, quantity, and time.

5. Logistics tasks include: transportation, storage, material handling, packaging, inventory control, order fulfillment, and facility layout.

6. Reverse logistics is the process of moving products upstream from the customer back toward manufacturers and suppliers.

7. Transportation is the primary function of logistics that enables logistics to provide place utility. There are five primary modes of transportation: truck, water, air, rail, and pipeline.

8. Cross-docking is a warehouse sorting approach used to reconfigure bundles of product, where, rather than making larger shipments, larger shipments are broken down into small shipments for local delivery in an area.

9. Factor Rating is one tool that can be used to make location decisions.

## KEY TERMS

- Logistics
- Physical distribution
- Business logistics
- Military logistics
- Event logistics
- Reverse logistics
- Automated storage and retrieval systems (ASRS)
- Place utility
- Economies of scale
- Economies of distance
- Transportation
- Storage
- Material handling
- Packaging
- Inventory control
- Order fulfillment
- Facility location
- Break-bulk
- Cross-docking
- Factor Rating

## DISCUSSION QUESTIONS

1. Find an example of a product you have recently purchased. Identify the logistics tasks that would have to take place for the product to be available for you to have the ability to purchase it.

2. Explain logistics tasks involved in one service supply chain, say, involving a hospital or restaurant. How different are these tasks versus those involved in a manufacturing supply chain?

3. Consider an event you are familiar with, such as a baseball game, a rock concert, or delivering aid to an underdeveloped country in need. Map out the logistics tasks needed and their sequence in organizing this particular event.

4. Consider an item you have recently returned. Identify the steps the company would have to go through to return the product back up the supply chain from where you have returned it. What costs do you think would be involved in this process? Is there a way the company can design this reverse logistics process in order to add value and make a profit?

## PROBLEMS

1. Quick Transport Logistics (QTL) is considering where to locate its warehouse to serve its northeast region. The search has been narrowed to two competing locations, and QTL has decided to use Factor Rating to make their decision. They have listed the factors they consider important and assigned a factor score to each location based on a five-point scale. The information is shown below. Use the procedure for Factor Rating to decide which location is better.

| Factor | Factor weight | Location 1 Factor score | Location 2 Factor score |
|---|---|---|---|
| Facility cost | 10 | 3 | 5 |
| Taxes | 15 | 2 | 4 |
| Proximity to airport | 30 | 4 | 1 |
| Labor source | 25 | 2 | 4 |
| Facility size | 20 | 3 | 3 |

2. DJ Bank is deciding on where to locate its new branch. It has identified three factors it considers most important and has decided to use Factor Rating to evaluate the two candidate locations based on a five-point scale, with 1 being poor and 5 excellent. The factors are population, average area salary, and cost of land, with weights 30%, 20%, and 50%, respectively. Location A has the following scores for the factors: 4, 3, and 3, whereas B has 3, 5, and 3. Please evaluate the two candidates based on Factor Rating.

3. An electronic company is deciding which of two new products should be put in production. It has identified three factors it considers most important and has decided to use Factor Rating to evaluate the two products based on a five-point scale, with 1 being poor and 5 excellent. The weights assigned to each factor are shown below in the table, as well as the factor score. Please evaluate the two products.

| Factor | Factor weight | Product 1 Factor score | Product 2 Factor score |
|---|---|---|---|
| Cost | 30 | 4 | 5 |
| Price | 30 | 4 | 2 |
| Demand | 40 | 3 | 4 |

## Case Study | Strategic Solutions Inc.

Strategic Solutions (SS) is a small 3PL provider that was started by Scott Crash in 1992. Scott began his career working in the logistics division of a large trucking company. He worked with fleet scheduling, customer support, and route scheduling before he saw the opportunity to start his own business offering similar services. Strategic Solutions provides

## Case Study: Strategic Solutions Inc.

logistics services to small businesses in Columbus, Ohio, and has recently acquired major accounts with two well-known grocery store chains. Their core competency is specializing in the movement of cold and frozen food products. Refrigerated trailers can be expensive, and if not transported using reliable equipment, it can prove to be very costly for all parties. Scott started his company by strategically combining LTL (less-than-truckload) shipments for small stores such as gas stations, pharmacies, and small grocery stores. He found his niche in climate-controlled trailer movements. Business has been growing since.

### The Business

Strategic Solutions operates by arranging customer shipments with the best for-hire transportation service they can find. Two of their main transporters are Frigid Movements and Problem Solved Shipments. Strategic Solutions has long-term contracts with most of its customers, but they also accept one-time shipments and business from random customers on a regular basis. Customers can either call or e-mail Strategic Solutions with the details, such as identifying the products that need to be shipped, the destination, and required time of delivery. Once Strategic Solutions has this information they can then arrange for the outbound shipments from the customer's distribution centers to the desired location. The customer base has increased substantially as a result of the company's success in the cold food movement area, and they have acquired new contracts with major grocery store chains.

### The Problem

Scott's company has begun to struggle with the business growth due to information technology constraints. Their current method of telephone and e-mail information exchange has become outdated, and customers have found it hard to communicate with Strategic Solutions. Customer satisfaction has dropped in the recent past, and Scott fears the loss of some of his top business clients. Something must be done so that Strategic Solution's reputation isn't damaged and no customers are lost.

### The Need for EDI or TMS

Scott understands that logistics depends on accurate real-time information, but isn't sure what type of system would be best suited for his operation and has decided to take a customer-oriented approach. He personally spoke with each of his customers to find out what would be the best system for them and how the two companies could best work together. He also spoke with his transportation providers to see what type of information exchange and transportation scheduling arrangements would best work for them. It seems that the ideal system would be a single point of contact for customer orders where information is updated in real time. It is inconvenient and time consuming for a customer to call and deal with busy phone lines and unanswered phone calls, or wait for an e-mail reply. There could also be clerical errors when transferring the information between different parties.

### The EDI versus TMS Expansion

Scott is not sure which system to implement and what would be the best investment. He assumes that electronic data interchange (EDI) can accomplish real-time information sharing with all of their customers as well as potential carriers. For customers, information can be available online with proper access codes so that scheduling arrangements involving shipments, equipment, and time schedules can be made with a single point of contact. The downside of an EDI system is the expense. Also, system failure could halt the business, potentially resulting in significant financial losses.

Another option is a transportation management system (TMS), which is a software system designed to manage transportation operations. TMS would enable Strategic Solutions to directly link to their transporters' systems to more efficiently identify and find potential routes. They wouldn't have to arrange shipments through telephone or e-mail, but could simply schedule them using the TMS. A downside to TMS is that it would leave out noncontracted carriers. If a certain time or route wasn't available through Frigid Movements or Problem Solved Shipments, Strategic Solutions would have to find other ways to schedule the transportation of their customers' goods.

Scott has estimated the following costs for both systems as well as customer preferences:

| Systems considered | Cost | Customer rank (1-3) |
| --- | --- | --- |
| **EDI** (for real-time information and single point of contact) | $15,000 | 3 |
| **TMS** (to link into transporters system and find routes and lanes) | $20,000 | 2 |
| Both systems | $35,000 | 3 |

*Case Questions*

1. Identify the characteristics of an ideal information system for this logistics environment. Gather information on both EDI and TMS, and compare their suitability for this environment.
2. Help Scott decide if he should invest in either EDI or TMS, or both. Is there another type of system that you would believe would be better? What kind of benefits, including performance and customer satisfaction, can Scott expect by making these proposed changes to the business process?
3. What are the key considerations for Scott when deciding on the best possible systems to implement?

REFERENCES

Ghosh, Carlos. "Making the Car a Mobile, Connected Workspace." *Harvard Business Review*, October 2016, 100–106.

Hamel, G., and C. K. Prahalad. "The Core Competence of the Corporation." *Harvard Business Review*, 68(3), 1990: 243–244.

Hamel, G., and C. K. Prahalad. *Competing for the Future*. Boston: Harvard Business School Press, 1996.

Lee, H. L. "Aligning Supply Chain Strategies with Product Uncertainties." *California Management Review*, 44(3), Spring 2002: 105–19.

"The 27th Annual State of Logistics Report." *CSCMP's Supply Chain Quarterly*, Volume 10, 2016.

# Forecasting and Demand Planning

# 8

## LEARNING OBJECTIVES

*After completing this chapter, you should be able to:*

- Explain the impact of forecasting on supply chain management.
- Describe the forecasting process.
- Identify key qualitative and quantitative forecasting models.
- Generate forecasts using quantitative models.
- Explain how to measure forecast accuracy.
- Describe methods of collaborative forecasting and demand planning.

## CHAPTER OUTLINE

■ **What Is Forecasting?**
*Forecasting versus Planning*
*Impact on the Organization*
*Impact on Supply Chain Management*

■ **The Forecasting Process**
*Principles of Forecasting*
*Steps in the Forecasting Process*
*Factors in Method Selection*

■ **Types of Forecasting Methods**
*Qualitative Forecasting Methods*
*Quantitative Forecasting Methods*

■ **Time Series Forecasting Models**
*The Mean*
*Moving Averages*
*Exponential Smoothing*
*Trend Adjusted Exponential Smoothing*
*Seasonality Adjustment*

- **Causal Models**
  *Linear Regression*
  *Multiple Regression*
- **Measuring Forecast Accuracy**
- **Collaborative Forecasting and Demand Planning**
  *Collaborative Planning, Forecasting and Replenishment (CPFR)*
  *Sales and Operations Planning (S & OP)*
- **Chapter Highlights**
- **Key Terms**
- **Discussion Questions**
- **Problems**
- **Case Study: Speedy Automotive**

Nike sells sportswear for men, women, and children, carrying everything from shoes and clothing, to gear and accessories. Have you ever walked into one of Nike's stores and considered the massive variety of products available on the retail shelves? There are numerous products in each category and an assortment of sizes and color variations. Imagine that you are looking for a men's athletic shoe and have your heart set on an Air Jordan in black and varsity red. You wear a size 11 and find they are out of stock. Chances are that you will go elsewhere and may select a competitor, say Reebok Zig Pulse in black and red, instead. Nike may have underestimated the demand for the Air Jordan in red but maybe overestimated the demand for the Nike Shox Turbo in red. The company may be surprised to find that the Shox Turbo in the color blue is the big seller and may have to discount the shoes in red as there are too many of them.

So how does Nike decide how much to have of each one of the different products? What should be the quantity of an Air Jordan in black and red versus an Air Jordan 1 Retro in high silver? How much should they order of Nike Air Maxim 1 in pink versus in blue? These decisions are based on a forecast of demand for each product and location. Now consider the range of product variety that must be stocked at various Nike locations around the globe, and you can understand the complexity of the forecasting task. Forecasting is extremely important to Nike. Forecasts drive the decisions regarding how much to carry of each individual product at each location, how much to produce, and what supplies to order for production, from leather to shoelaces. The entire supply chain is dependent on these forecasts.

In June 2000 Nike made headlines after going live with a highly touted i2 demand forecasting software intended to solve their forecasting challenges. Nine months later, its executives acknowledged that they would be taking a major inventory write-off because the forecasts from the automated system had been so inaccurate. In fact, the total cost to Nike was estimated at $400 million as the forecasts themselves were way off. Relying exclusively on the automated projections, Nike ended up ordering $90 million worth of shoes, such as the Air Garnett II, that turned out to be very poor sellers. The company also came up with an $80 million to $100 million shortfall on popular models, such as the Air Force One.

Nike has since bounced back as an innovation leader. The lessons learned, however, are the importance of forecasting, the cost of forecast errors, and the limitations of even the best demand forecasting software.

Adapted from: Koch, Christopher. "Nike Rebounds." *CIO Magazine.* July 12, 2004.

# What Is Forecasting?

## Forecasting versus Planning

**Forecasting** is the process of predicting future events. This can range from forecasting product demand, such as demand for purple-colored ketchup in October, to forecasting the passage of a healthcare bill in Congress. Any time we try to predict future events we are forecasting. **Planning**, on the other hand, is the process of selecting actions in anticipation of the forecast. The forecast drives the plan, and the plan is made in response to the forecast. This is shown in Figure 8.1.

Forecasting is one of the most important business activities because it drives all other business decisions. Decisions such as which markets to pursue, which products to produce, how much inventory to carry, and how many people to hire are all based on a forecast. Consider the example of Nike in the chapter opener. The company continuously makes forecasts of demand for its many products and, as a result, generates plans regarding which products to produce and how much inventory to carry. Nike's poor forecasting, as a result of overreliance on forecasting software, resulted in incorrect business decisions. A similar situation occurred with the Goodyear Tire & Rubber Company a few years earlier. After investing in a state-of-the-art forecasting software, the company did not achieve the anticipated forecast accuracy, resulting in high safety stock and too much inventory. As we can see, forecasting is a challenge. Also, poor forecasts result in poor planning and can leave the company unprepared to meet future demands. The consequences can be costly in terms of lost sales or excess inventory that cannot be sold.

Planning is the process of taking action to be prepared for the future. It requires organizing resources in anticipation of the forecast and being prepared for future events. As organizations attempt to decrease their vulnerability to chance, they need to forecast and plan their resources accordingly. Forecasting and planning have become especially important as the lag time between

**FORECASTING**
The process of predicting future events

**PLANNING**
The process of selecting actions in anticipation of the forecast

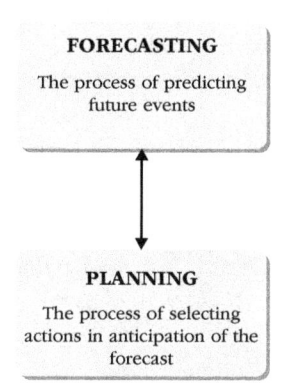

**FIGURE 8.1** Forecasting drives planning.

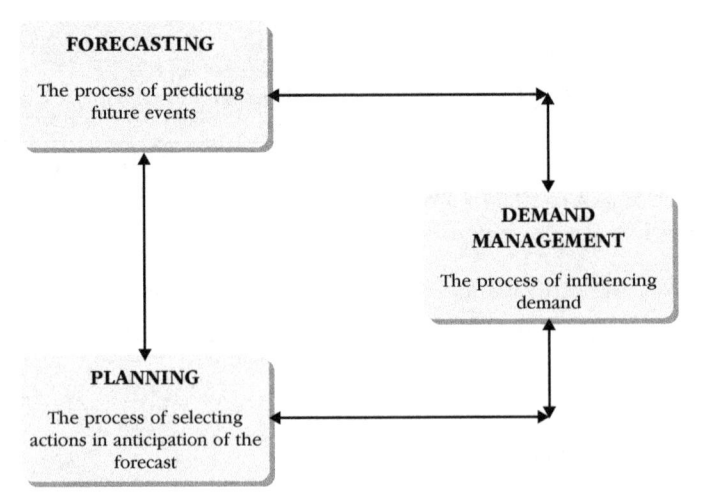

**FIGURE 8.2** Forecasting, planning, and demand management.

awareness of an impending event and the need to respond have become increasingly short. The shorter this lag time, the more critical forecasting and planning become.

Planning involves the following decisions:

1. **Scheduling existing resource.** For a business and its supply chain to be competitive, it must use its current resources in the most efficient way possible. This includes the production process, transportation, labor, facilities, and capital. An important aspect of planning is deciding how to best utilize existing resources.

2. **Determining future resource needs.** In addition to efficiently utilizing current resources, organizations must determine what resources are going to be needed in the future. These decisions depend on forecasts of emerging market opportunities, new technology, new products, and competition.

3. **Acquiring new resources.** It takes time for companies to acquire new facilities, new technologies, and new equipment or expand to new locations. Plans must be made well in advance, and procedures to acquire new resources and capabilities put in place well ahead of time.

Companies often confuse forecasting and planning. The reason is that companies have the ability to affect demand. This can be done through promotional campaigns and advertisements, offering incentives to sales staff and personnel, and cutting prices. This is called **demand management** and is the process of influencing demand.

Notice that demand management cannot occur without first having a forecast or a prediction of what future demand is going to be. Once a forecast and a resulting plan have been made, the organization may decide to influence demand to better utilize its resources, and the plan reconfigured accordingly. This is shown in Figure 8.2.

## Managerial Insights Box

### ■ FORECASTING BEYOND WIDGETS

Planning for any event requires a forecast of the future. Whether in business or in our own lives, we make forecasts of future events. Based on these forecasts we make plans and take action. As in the example of Nike, most of us think of forecasting in terms of estimating demand for tangible products and what it means for inventories and sourcing.

However, it is important to expand our concept of forecasting beyond that. Remember that all plans are based on a forecast. Let's look at some forecasting examples that go beyond the traditional and see how they impact planning.

1. **Crime Forecasting.** Crime forecasting is an area of forecasting that has gained quite a bit of interest. Consider that police departments must forecast different types of crimes by location and as a result schedule police officers and patrols, acquire resources, and provide training.

2. **Climate Change.** Numerous forecasting techniques are used to scientifically predict the effects of climate change. These forecasts impact the plans that are made by policymakers and how money and resources are allocated to mitigate catastrophic risk. These forecasts can have an enormous impact on preparedness in case these events materialize (see *PublicPolicyForecasting.com*).

3. **Health Forecasting.** Health and healthcare forecasting is important for policymakers and researchers. This involves projecting demographic changes, health resources needed, future impact of disease, health risk factor distributions, trends in population health, and healthcare spending. These forecasts are used to make decisions regarding allocating resources and planning for future resources, such as training of physicians and acquiring new capabilities.

4. **Political Forecasting.** You may not think that forecasting political elections has a huge impact on supply chain management, but it does. Consider all the resources required to run a political campaign and the resources that must be immediately in place once an election is won. Also, a political forecast has a significant impact on current business decisions, especially considering how favorable it is toward business (see *PoliticalForecasting.com*).

5. **Forecasting Decisions in Conflicts.** Forecasting decisions of parties in conflict is concerned with forecasting industrial disputes, corporate takeovers, intercommunal conflicts, political negotiations, diplomatic and military confrontations, and even counterterrorism. The planning that is done based on these forecasts requires training and mobilization of personnel, resources, and allocation of money. Just consider, for example, the operational and supply chain requirements that are involved when governments decide on increasing airport security or security at ports of entry (see *ConflictForecasting.com* and *TerrorismForecasting.com*).

6. **Tourism Forecasting.** This is a special area of forecasting concerned with forecasting trends and growth patterns in tourism. The large size of the hospitality industry—including hotels, cruises, and resorts—makes this is an important forecasting area. These forecasts translate into supply chain decisions such as whether Marriott Hotels will open a new facility in Cairo or how many cruise ships and staff size will be needed to travel the Adriatic Sea during May.

In addition to these examples, consider planning to mobilize resources to an area of need, such as an earthquake in Haiti, or supporting an event such as the Olympic Games. These plans are based on forecasts, and they require decisions regarding how best to manage resources in their respective supply chains (see *www.forecastingprinciples.com*).

## Impact on the Organization

Plans at all levels of the organization, from the strategic level, where long-range plans are made, to the tactical, where day-to-day scheduling is made, are based on forecasting. Also, forecasting drives the decisions of every organizational function. Marketing relies on forecasting to develop estimates of demand and future sales. Marketing also forecasts sizes of markets, new competition, future trends and emerging markets, and changes in consumer preferences. Finance, in turn, uses forecasting to assess financial performance and capital investment needs, predict stock prices and investment portfolio returns, and set budgets. Operations makes decisions regarding production and inventory levels, conducts capacity planning and scheduling, all based on a forecast.

Sourcing uses forecasts to make purchasing decisions and select suppliers. None of these organizational functions could do their job without a forecast of the future. Whether in business, industry, government, or other fields such as medicine, engineering, and science, proper planning for the future starts with a forecast.

## Impact on Supply Chain Management

The forecast of demand is critical not only to the organization but to the entire supply chain, as it affects all the plans made by each company in the chain. When members of the supply chain make their forecasts independent of one another, they are only looking at the demand of their immediate buyer not the final customer in the chain. The consequences are a mismatch between supply and demand because each member of the chain is working to fulfill a different level of demand.

Consider the forecasting and planning process of Dell and Intel, one of Dell's suppliers. Dell starts its planning process with a forecast of future demand that is used to determine order quantities. At the same time, Intel, who supplies Dell with microprocessors, needs to determine its production and inventory schedules. If Dell and Intel were to make their forecasts independent of one another, their forecasts would differ, and Intel would not be able to supply Dell with the exact quantities of microprocessors it needs. The best alternative is for Dell and Intel to collaborate. When there is collaboration between suppliers and manufacturers in generating the forecast, all entities are responding to the same level of demand.

Independent forecasting by members of the supply chain gives rise to the bullwhip effect, which we discussed in Chapter 1. The bullwhip effect refers to the increased volatility in orders as they propagate through the supply chain. The bullwhip effect occurs when each individual company in the supply chain forecasts its own demand, plans its stocking levels, and makes its replenishment decisions independent of other companies in the chain. This creates volatility in orders, which makes forecasting more difficult, leads to increases in inventory throughout the supply chain, has a higher stock-out risk, and results in inefficient use of working capital and production capacity.

As we can see, forecasting has an impact on all organizations in the supply chain. The answer to good forecasting, and mitigating the bullwhip effect, is the sharing of data with supply chain partners and jointly generating forecasts.

## Global Insights Box—Matching Supply and Demand

### ■ WORLD HEALTH ORGANIZATION (WHO)

On January 29, 2010, the World Health Organization (WHO) declared that even though the H1N1 virus was still spreading, the number of confirmed cases worldwide was finally on the decline. This was good news as the original forecast, which called for a viral outbreak that had the potential for a global catastrophe, was not met. In hindsight, however, the WHO and the Centers for Disease Control and Prevention (CDC) had learned two important lessons. First, predicting the viral outbreak was much more difficult than scientists originally thought. Second, the plans put in place as a response to the original forecast would have been utterly inadequate had the forecast been correct. Scientists at the WHO were trying to learn from this mistake. "Now a process has been established to help us learn," says Gregory Hartl, a spokesman for the WHO in Geneva.

Forecasting pandemics is difficult, yet forecasts must be made so that vaccine producers can decide how many units of vaccines to make. This also involves forecasting by demographic groups, such as the elderly, pregnant women, and individuals with other health risks. Adding to the complication is an estimate of the quantities needed by each group. For example, in the early stages of H1N1, there was a belief that two vaccines were needed for adults, a number that was later cut in half.

Directly related to the forecasting problem is the length of the vaccine production process. Flu vaccines are produced from viruses grown in eggs. This is a slow and labor-intensive process, which is a significant bottleneck. The first priority in matching supply and demand, many experts say, is to overhaul the vaccine production system. A shorter production time would enable quicker response to demand. The current technology, which involves growing flu vaccines in eggs, is so time consuming that drug makers have to start in February, the winter before, to ensure they'll have enough for the following fall.

Adding to the complication is that new virulent strains can emerge any time during the "production process," and flexibility in the supply chain is needed. H1N1 didn't emerge until April 2009, which forced both the CDC and drug companies to scramble in figuring out what to do. Their original plan was inadequate. There was too little of the vaccine when the virus was peaking and too much when it started tapering off. Now companies and universities are aggressively working to shorten the production process.

In addition to production lead time, another problem is the distribution network of getting the vaccines to the right locations. Initial orders for H1N1 came from individual states to the CDC and were then sent to the manufacturer, which arranged for shipment—a lengthy process. Also, packaging, security, and shipping times became an issue for ensuring speed and product safety.

The CDC is continuing to improve these processes as they prepare for another flu season. However, forecasting and matching supply with demand remain a challenge in this environment.

Adapted from: "Lessons from the Pandemic That Wasn't." *Business Week*, February 15, 2010.

# The Forecasting Process

## Principles of Forecasting

Some principles of forecasting hold true regardless of what is being forecast. Let's look at these briefly.

1. **Forecasts are rarely perfect.** A perfect forecast is rare as there are too many factors in the business environment that cannot be predicted with certainty. Forecasting the future involves uncertainty and forecasters know that they have to live with a certain amount of error, which is the difference between the forecast and what actually happened. It is easy then to wonder why we should bother with forecasting. Although we may not achieve a perfect forecast, we can maintain overall good forecast accuracy.

2. **Forecasts are more accurate for groups than for individual items.** When items are grouped together, such as in product groups or families of items, their individual high and low values cancel each other out. The data for a group of items can be stable even when individual items in the group are unstable. The result is that higher degrees of accuracy can be obtained when forecasting for a group rather than for individual items. Consider Frito-Lay, a division owned by PepsiCo Inc., which owns brands such as Lay's Potato Chips, Fritos, Doritos, Ruffles, Sun Chips, and other brands. Frito-Lay can expect to have much lower forecast accuracy when forecasting demand for one specific product line, such as Baked Lay's potato chips, versus forecasting demand for all chips combined.

3. **Forecasts are more accurate for shorter than longer time horizons.** The shorter the time horizon of the forecast, the lower the degree of uncertainty. Data do not change much in the short run. As the time horizon increases, however, there is a much greater likelihood that changes in established patterns and relationships will occur. For that reason long-range forecasting tends to be less accurate than short range. For example, it is more difficult to forecast the size of an emerging market in Europe two years from now, than the size of the mobile phone market in Europe next month.

## Steps in the Forecasting Process

Forecasts need to be credible to be accepted by others. To ensure credibility, some basic steps should be followed when making a forecast, regardless of what is being forecast or the model used. The steps are as follows:

1. **Decide what to forecast.** This step may seem overly simple but it actually requires a bit of thought. For example, do we want to forecast actual sales versus total demand? Remember that forecasts are made to help plan for the future. To do so, we have to decide what forecasts are actually needed to guide the plan.

2. **Analyze appropriate data.** This step involves analyzing available data and identifying patterns present. Some patterns can be observed in the data, although not every set of data has every pattern. It is important to identify which patterns are present and—in the next step—select the forecasting model most appropriate for that pattern. The most common data patterns are
   a. **Level or horizontal.** This is the simplest pattern and exists when data fluctuate around a constant mean. It is the easiest to predict and is common for commodity products in the mature stage of the life cycle, such as table salt or toothpaste.
   b. **Trend.** Trend is present when data exhibit an increasing or decreasing pattern over time. The simplest type of trend is a straight line, or linear trend. However, a trend can take other forms, such as an exponential trend.
   c. **Seasonality.** Seasonality is any pattern that regularly repeats itself. Most of us think of ice cream sales in the summer or snow shovels in the winter. However, any pattern that regularly repeats itself is a seasonal pattern, such as restaurant sales that peak on the weekend.
   d. **Cycles.** Cycles are patterns created by economic fluctuations. Examples include recessions, inflation, or even the life cycle of a product. The major distinction between seasonality and cycles is that cycles do not have a predictable or repeating length or magnitude. As a result they are most difficult to predict.

   In addition to these patterns, data contain random variation that cannot be predicted. The more random variation in the data, the harder it is to forecast. Forecasting focuses on the patterns in the data, knowing that the random variation will be present. This is shown below:

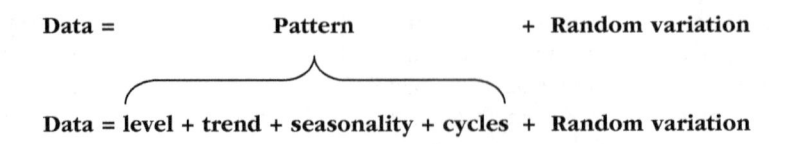

   Data = Pattern + Random variation

   Data = level + trend + seasonality + cycles + Random variation

3. **Select the forecasting model.** Once data patterns have been identified, the next step is to select an appropriate forecasting model. It is important to select the forecasting model best suited for the identified data pattern. Often we narrow the choice to two or three different forecasting models, then test them on historical data to see which one is most accurate. We will look at specific models later in this chapter.

4. **Generate the forecast.** Once a model has been selected, the forecast is generated.

5. **Monitor forecast accuracy.** After the forecast has been made and actual events occur, it is critical to evaluate forecast performance by measuring forecast error. This information should be used to improve the forecasting process. Remember that forecasting is an ongoing process that is always changing as new information and data become available.

## Factors in Method Selection

Someone new to forecasting might be overwhelmed by the choices in available forecasting methods. However, not all methods are appropriate for all forecasts. A few factors should be considered in method selection:

1. **Amount and type of available data.** Different forecasting methods require different types and quantities of data. Sophisticated quantitative models, for example, may require large amounts of data, whereas simpler methods may not. In some cases—such as when forecasting new products—no historical data may be available. This factor plays a key role in the forecasting method that can be selected.

2. **Degree of accuracy required.** Sophisticated quantitative models may generate good forecasts, but they may be costly to develop. The costs of the forecasting method need to justify the importance of the forecast. For example, forecasting paper clips or rubber washers doesn't justify a costly method of forecasting.

3. **Length of forecast horizon.** Some forecasting methods are better suited for short-term forecasts, whereas others are better suited for the long term. It is important to select the method most appropriate for the horizon being forecast. For example, forecasting emergency room visits at a hospital during the month of December is going to require a very different forecasting method than forecasting demand for natural gas over the next 10 years.

4. **Patterns in the data.** As we already mentioned, it is critical to select a forecasting model that is appropriate for the identified patterns in the data. Otherwise, we can be guaranteed a poor forecast. For example, trying to forecast a product with a known trend pattern using a forecasting method that cannot capture trend will ensure errors.

## Managerial Insights Box

### ■ PREDICTIVE ANALYTICS

One of the most significant aspects of big data analytics is the impact on forecasting. This is called **predictive analytics**. Predictive analytics uses a variety of techniques—such as statistics, modeling, and data mining—to analyze current and historical facts to make predictions about the future. It provides the ability to foresee events before they happen by sensing small changes over time. For example, IBM's Watson computer uses an algorithm to predict best medical treatments, and UPS uses analytics to predict vehicle breakdown. By placing sensors on machinery, motors, or infrastructure like bridges we can monitor the data patterns they give off, such as heat, vibration, stress, and sound. These sensors can detect changes that may indicate problems ahead, essentially forecasting a problem.

The reason these technologies are so beneficial in predicting "failure" is that things do not break down at once. There is a gradual wear and tear over time. The technology, sensors, and analytics used in the past were not sophisticated enough to detect these changes. The sensors of today, however, can identify small changes and specific patterns that typically emerge before something breaks. This may be the sound of a motor, excessive heat from an engine, or vibration from the bridge. In healthcare it may be changes in patient's vitals before the onset of disease. Google is famous for identifying location and propagation of the flu by simply tracking the volume and type of queries in its search engine.

Big data can also be used to uncover relationships, which improves prediction. Some years ago, Wal-Mart studied its huge database and noticed that right before a hurricane there was a run on flashlights and batteries, as might be expected. However, Wal-Mart also noticed a correlated surge of demand on Pop Tarts—in particular strawberry Pop Tarts. Initially this was a surprise. After consideration, however, it became clear that the snack would be a handy food in a blackout. Without big data the retailer would not have thought to stock up on Pop Tarts before a storm.

FORECASTING AND DEMAND PLANNING

Other examples abound. Best Buy discovered that 7% of its customers accounted for 43% of its sales, so it reorganized its stores to concentrate on those customers' needs. Airlines improved their yield management because analytical techniques uncovered that the best predictor that a passenger would actually catch a flight they had booked was ordering a vegetarian meal. Uncovering these relationships was almost impossible in the past. Now, access to information is changing the ability to mine data and is significantly improving forecast accuracy for companies.

Adapted from: "A Different Game: Information is Transforming Traditional Businesses." *The Economist*, February 28, 2010, pp. 6–7.

## Types of Forecasting Methods

Forecasting methods can be classified into two broad groups: qualitative and quantitative. They are shown in Figure 8.3.

**Qualitative forecasting methods**, often called judgmental methods, are methods based on subjective opinions and judgment of individuals, such as managers, sales staff, or customers. Asking customers whether they would buy a particular product, called "intention surveys," is a type of qualitative forecasting method. Another one is called "sales force composite" and occurs when the sales staff make a group forecast of upcoming sales. Qualitative methods are made by people and, as a result, are subject to human biases.

**Quantitative forecasting methods**, on the other hand, are based on mathematical modeling. These methods are objective and consistent, are capable of handling large amounts of data, and can uncover complex relationships. Provided that good data are available, these methods are generally more accurate than qualitative methods.

Both qualitative and quantitative forecasting methods have their strengths and weaknesses, as shown in Figure 8.4. Although quantitative methods are objective and consistent, they require data in quantifiable form to generate a forecast. Often, such data is not available, such as in new product forecasting or making long-range strategic forecasts. Also, quantitative methods are only as good as the data on which they are based. Qualitative methods, on the other hand, have the advantage of being able to incorporate last-minute "inside information." This may be last-minute notice of a competitor's advertising campaign, a snowstorm delaying a shipment, or a heat wave increasing ice cream sales. Each method has its role in the forecasting process, and a good forecaster learns to rely on both.

## Qualitative Forecasting Methods

There are numerous qualitative forecasting methods, ranging in degree of formality and structure. These methods are especially useful when identifying customer buying patterns and expectations and providing sales estimates of new products.

**Executive opinion** is a type of qualitative forecasting method where a group of managers, executives, or sales staff meet and collectively develop a forecast. This method is often used to

**FORECASTING METHODS**

QUALITATIVE
Judgmental, subjective, based on opinions

QUANTITATIVE
Objective, consistent, based on mathematical concepts

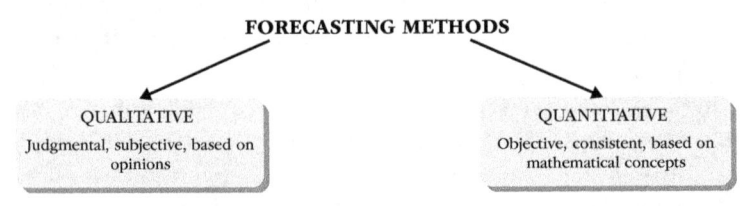

**FIGURE 8.3** Categories of forecasting methods.

### I. Qualitative forecasting methods

| STRENGTHS | WEAKNESSES |
| --- | --- |
| • Highly responsive to latest changes in environment. | • Cannot consider many variables. |
| • Can include "inside" and "soft" information difficult to quantify. | • Influenced by short-term memory. |
| • Can compensate for "one-time" or unusual events. | • Difficulty in understanding relationships. |
| • Provide user with a sense of "ownership." | • Biased (optimism, wishful thinking, political manipulation, lack of consistency). |

### II. Quantitative forecasting methods

| STRENGTHS | WEAKNESSES |
| --- | --- |
| • Can consider many variables and complex relationships. | • Only as good as the data and model. |
| • Objective. | • Slow to react to changing environments. |
| • Consistent. | • Costly and time consuming to model "soft" information. |
| • Can process large amounts of information. | • Requires technical understanding. |

**FIGURE 8.4** Qualitative versus quantitative forecasting methods.

forecast sales, market trends, make strategic forecasts, or forecast new products. Also, it can be used to modify existing forecasts to account for special events, such as slowed spending during a recession or a special promotional campaign.

The advantage of this method is the ability to include the latest information in the forecast. The disadvantage, however, is that it is subject to many human biases, such as optimism, inconsistency, and political manipulation. Also, because it is a group decision-making process, often the opinion of one member can dominate the forecast.

**Market research** uses surveys and interviews to determine customer likes, dislikes, and preferences and to identify new product ideas. Conducting market research requires understanding of how to conduct reliable surveys. Therefore, companies usually hire an outside marketing firm to conduct a market research study.

Market research can be a good determinant of customer preferences. However, it has a number of shortcomings. A common one is the potential inadequacy of the survey questionnaire design. For example, a market research firm may ask participants to identify a favorite hobby providing them with the following choices: gardening, fishing, cooking, or sports. The problem in this example is that the list is not exhaustive, as a participant may prefer music—an option not included. This questionnaire forces participants to select a category. As a result, the findings will incorrectly portray customer preferences and lead to misinterpretation of the market.

The **Delphi method** is designed to reach a consensus among a group of experts on a particular topic. Examples may include forecasting propagation of a disease, climate changes, or technological innovation. The process involves choosing experts in the field of inquiry, who maintain anonymity. Questionnaires are sent to the experts, the findings are summarized, and the process is repeated with updated questionnaires that incorporate the initial findings. This process continues until consensus between the experts is reached.

Delphi is based on the assumption that although experts in a field typically do not agree on many things, what they do agree on will likely happen. The researcher's job is to extract this information. Although it is time consuming, Delphi has been shown to be an excellent method

**FORECASTING METHODS**

- **QUALITATIVE** — Judgmental, subjective, based on opinions
- **QUANTITATIVE** — Objective, consistent, based on mathematical concepts
  - **Time Series Models** — Forecast based on analysis of patterns in the time series of data.
  - **Causal Models** — Forecast based on modeling relationships between variables.

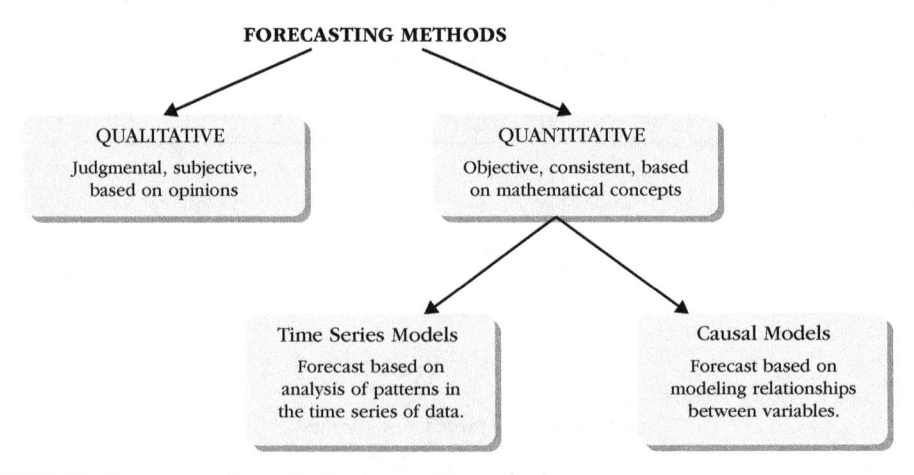

**FIGURE 8.5** Categories of quantitative forecasting methods.

for forecasting long-range product demand, technological change, and scientific advances in medicine.

## Quantitative Forecasting Methods

Unlike qualitative methods that are based on opinions, quantitative methods are based on mathematical concepts. Quantitative methods can be divided into two broad categories: time series and causal models, as shown in Figure 8.5. Although both are mathematical, the two categories differ in their assumptions and how the forecast is generated.

**Time series models** generate the forecast from an analysis of a "time series" of the data. A time series is simply a listing of data points of the variable being forecast over time taken at regular intervals. For example, data of student enrollment per semester at a university over the past five years is an example of a time series. Time series models assume that forecasts can be made by identifying and modeling the patterns present in the data.

**Causal models** assume that the variable being forecast is related to other variables in the environment. For example, university enrollment may be related to unemployment rates, recession levels, or salary levels. In this case the forecasting process involves identifying these relationships, expressing them in mathematical form, and using that information to generate a forecast.

Time series models are generally easier to use than causal models. They are also more readily available in forecasting software. Causal models, on the other hand, can be more complex, especially if relationships between multiple variables are being considered. However, time series models can often be just as accurate and have the advantage of simplicity. They are easy to use and can generate a forecast more quickly than causal models, which require model building. For this reason, time series models are used more frequently in environments where large numbers of items must be forecast on a regular basis, such as retail. Recall the many different products that must be forecast at Nike. Time series analysis would likely be best for that large variety of items.

## Big Data Analytics Box—Improving Weather Forecasting

### ■ NOAA

The current technological capabilities have not just improved business forecasting. They have affected every type of forecast—or prediction—generated. A great example is weather forecasting. Climate change is resulting in stronger and more frequent weather extremes being predicted, such as more intense downpours and stronger hurricane winds.

Improving weather prediction is critical to give communities more time to prepare for dangerous storms. These forecasts can save lives and minimize damage to property and infrastructure.

The key to better predicting the weather lies in the use of big data gathered by new radar technologies and satellites. Today, these new radar and satellite technologies combine with new computer models that run on more powerful supercomputers to allow forecasters to better "see" extreme weather. These technologies can process large amounts of data within minutes and create warnings of tornadoes, hurricanes, and other extreme weather events.

Weather forecasting models are based on physical laws governing atmospheric motion, chemical reactions, and other relationships. They need to be able to crunch millions of numbers that represent current weather and environmental conditions, such as temperature, pressure and wind, to predict the future state of the atmosphere. To accomplish this NOAA (National Oceanic and Atmospheric Administration) has invested in what is termed as "**brainware**." This is a combination of all these technologies that capture different types of data in huge amounts and make massive and quick computations.

With this new technology NOAA predicts that forecasters will not have to wait for a radar image to detect an actual storm before issuing a warning with 14 or 18 minutes of lead time. Instead they will be able to issue warnings well in advance. For example, highly accurate models can issue warnings for tornados, severe thunderstorms, and flash floods 30 to 60 minutes in advance, giving the public time to take safety precautions. These forecasting models based on big data will provide warnings well ahead of time so that people can prepare and respond.

# Time Series Forecasting Models

## The Mean

One of the simplest forecasting models is the mean, where the forecast is made by simply taking an average of all the data:

$$F_{t+1} = \frac{\sum D_t}{n}$$

$$F_{t+1} = \frac{[D_t + D_{t-1} + \cdots + D_{t-n}]}{n}$$

where

$F_{t+1}$ = forecast of demand for next period, $t+1$

$D_t$ = demand for current period, $t$

$n$ = number of data points

This method is only appropriate for a level data pattern. It is, however, a reasonable forecasting model to use for forecasting stable and mature products. One advantage of this method is that as more data is collected over time, and the average becomes based on a larger data set, the forecasts become more stable.

### Example 1   Forecasting with the Mean

Handy Power Tools is forecasting sales of its most popular drill. The company has been selling the drill for the past 15 years, and sales have been steady. The company uses a simple mean to forecast weekly sales. Sales over the past five weeks are available, and the company will use them to make a forecast for week six.

# FORECASTING AND DEMAND PLANNING

| Week | Drill Sales | Forecast |
|------|-------------|----------|
| 1 | 8 | |
| 2 | 10 | |
| 3 | 9 | |
| 4 | 12 | |
| 5 | 10 | |
| 6 | – | 10 |

The forecast is simply an average of the past five weeks:

$$F_6 = [8 + 10 + 9 + 12 + 10] = \frac{49}{5}$$

$$F_6 = 9.8 \approx 10 \text{ drills}$$

## Moving Averages

The **simple moving average** is a method that generates a forecast by averaging a specified number, $n$, of the most recent data rather than the entire data set. As new data become available, the oldest are dropped, and the number of observations used to compute the average is kept constant. In this manner, the simple moving average "moves" through time. Like the mean, this model is only appropriate for level data patterns. However, it does have the advantage of being responsive by averaging only the most recent observations.

The formula is as follows:

$$F_{t+1} = \frac{\sum D_t}{n}$$

$$F_{t+1} = \frac{[D_t + D_{t-1} + \cdots + D_{t-n}]}{n}$$

where

$F_{t+1}$ = forecast of demand for next period, $t + 1$

$D_t$ = demand for current period, $t$

$n$ = number of data points in the moving average.

Notice that $n$ is not the entire data set but only a subset of the data used in the average. For example, if $n = 3$ the average would include only the latest three data points. If $n = 5$ the average would include only the latest five data points, and so on. In general, the more data points that are used in the average, the more stable the forecast as more data is being averaged. On the other hand, the fewer the data points in the average, the more responsive the forecast.

### Example 2  Forecasting with the Simple Moving Average

La Petite Tableau forecasts sales of kitchen aprons using a three-period moving average. How many aprons should they expect to sell in April given the following sales figures for January, February, and March?

Time Series Forecasting Models

| Month | Actual sales |
|---|---|
| January | 38 |
| February | 27 |
| March | 42 |

To find the forecast for April we take an average of the last three observations:

$$F_{t+1} = \frac{\sum D_t}{n}$$

$$F_{April} = \frac{[D_{January} + D_{Feb} + D_{Mar}]}{3} = \frac{[38 + 27 + 42]}{3} = 35.7 \approx \sim 36 \text{ aprons}$$

If La Petite Tableau sells 42 aprons in April, let's make a forecast for May continuing to use a three-period moving average.

$$F_{May} = \frac{[D_{Feb} + D_{March} + D_{April}]}{3} = \frac{[27 + 42 + 42]}{3} = 37.$$

Notice that in a simple moving average all the data are weighed equally, that is $1/n$. Sometimes we may want to give more or less weight to certain data points, such as giving more weight to recent observations. This is called a **weighted moving average**. The computation is the same except that managers have the option of specifying the weights assigned to the data point.

## Exponential Smoothing

Exponential smoothing is a forecasting model that uses a special weighted average procedure to obtain a forecast. It is easy to use and understand and provides good forecast results. To make a forecast just three items are needed:

1. Current period's forecast
2. Current period's actual value
3. Value of a smoothing coefficient, $\alpha$, which varies between 0 and 1

**The equation for the forecast is**

$$F_{t+1} = \alpha D_t + (1 - \alpha) F_t$$

where

$F_{t+1}$ = forecast of demand for next period, $t + 1$

$D_t$ = actual value for current period, $t$

$F_t$ = forecast for current period $t$

$\alpha$ = smoothing coefficient

## Example 3  Forecasting with Exponential Smoothing

Cafe Nervosa uses exponential smoothing to forecast monthly usage of coffee cream. Its forecast for May was 24 gallons, but the actual usage turned out to be 28 gallons of coffee cream. The manager has chosen to use an alpha of 0.70. What is her forecast for June?

Using the exponential smoothing equation

$$F_{June} = \alpha D_{May} + (1 - \alpha) F_{May}$$
$$= (0.70)(28) + (0.30) 24$$
$$= 26.8 \text{ gallons}$$

---

The critical aspect of exponential smoothing is selecting a correct value for $\alpha$. High values of $\alpha$ place more weight on the current period's actual demand, whereas low values place more weight on the current period's forecast. Values of $\alpha$ that are low, say, 0.1 or 0.2, generate forecasts that are stable as more weight is placed in historical data and less on the current period's actual demand. However, these forecasts are less responsive to recent changes in demand. Values of $\alpha$ that are high, say, 0.7 or 0.8, place a large weight on the current period's actual demand. As a result, they generate forecasts that are responsive to the latest changes in demand, but can be less stable.

When using exponential smoothing for the first time, we may not have a forecast for the current period. The most common way to handle this is to use what is called "the naive method," which is using last period's actual value to generate an initial forecast. Another option is to average the last few periods—say the last three or four—just to get a starting point.

## Trend Adjusted Exponential Smoothing

The models discussed so far work only for a level pattern. If there is a trend in the data the models need to be modified, otherwise the forecasts will "lag" the trend. One of the more common ways to forecast trend is to use trend adjusted exponential smoothing. It is a simple modification of the exponential smoothing model we just discussed. The model takes the basic exponential smoothing equation and just adds a trend component to compensate for the additional pattern:

$$FIT_{t+1} = F_{t+1} + T_{t+1}$$

where

$FIT_{t+1}$ = forecast including trend for next period, t + 1
$F_{t+1}$ = unadjusted forecast for the next period = $\alpha D_t + (1 - \alpha)F_t$
$T_{t+1}$ = trend factor for next period = $\beta(F_{t+1} - F_t) + (1 - \beta)T_t$
$T_t$ = trend factor for the current period, t
$\beta$ = smoothing constant for the trend adjustment factor

*Notice that $F_t$ and $F_{t+1}$ feed into the trend equation*

To generate a forecast including trend, $FIT_{t+1}$, we need to follow these steps:

### Step 1  Generate an unadjusted forecast $F_{t+1}$

**Step 2** Generate trend $T_{t+1}$ (notice that $F_t$ feeds into the trend equation)

**Step 3** Add $F_{t+1}$ and $T_{t+1}$

### Example 4 — Forecasting with Trend Adjusted Exponential Smoothing

Looking at the following data, assume that we are at the end of January and want to forecast one period ahead using trend adjusted exponential smoothing. We have decided to use an α = 0.3 and a β = 0.4. Assume that we are rolling through time knowing the actual demand after we have made the forecast and using the information to forecast the subsequent period.

| Month | Demand | Unadjusted forecast $F_{t+1}$ | Trend $T_{t+1}$ | Adjusted forecast $FIT_{t+1}$ |
|---|---|---|---|---|
| January | 20 | 18 | 0 | |
| February | 21 | 18.6 | .24 | 18.84 |
| March | 24 | 19.32 | .43 | 19.75 |
| April | 25 | 20.72 | .82 | 21.54 |
| May | 26 | 22.00 | 1.00 | 23.00 |

How did we get the above numbers? Let's follow the steps to generate the forecast for February.

**Step 1** Generate an unadjusted forecast $F_{t+1}$

$$F_{FEB} = \alpha D_{JAN} + (1 - \alpha)F_{JAN}$$
$$F_{FEB} = F_{JAN} + \alpha (D_{JAN} - F_{JAN})$$
$$= 18 + (.3)(20 - 18)$$
$$= 18.6$$

**Step 2** Generate trend $T_{t+1}$ (notice once again that $F_t$ feeds into the trend equation)

$$T_{FEB} = \beta(F_{FEB} - F_{JAN}) + (1 - \beta)T_{JAN}$$
$$T_{FEB} = 0.4(18.6 - 18) + 0.6(0)$$
$$= 0.24$$

**Step 3** Add $F_{t+1}$ and $T_{t+1}$

$$FIT_{FEB} = F_{FEB} + T_{FEB}$$
$$FIT_{FEB} = 18.6 + 0.24 = 18.84$$

The other numbers in the table are obtained in the same manner. Notice the difference in the unadjusted versus adjusted forecast. How different do you think the adjusted values would be with a different value of β?

# FORECASTING AND DEMAND PLANNING

## Seasonality Adjustment

Seasonality is any regularly repeating pattern. Consider sales of ice cream in the summer or snow shovels in the winter, university enrollment in the fall, amusement park attendance in the summer, or sales of turkeys at Thanksgiving.

When seasonality is present we need to adjust our forecast to reflect the amount by which the particular "season" is above or below the average. This is estimated as a percentage, such as saying that amusement park attendance is 140% of the average during the month of June, whereas it is 70% of the average in March. This percentage is called the **seasonal index**. Adjusting for seasonality simply involves computing the seasonal index—or percentage—and using it to adjust the forecast. This is detailed in the following steps:

**Step 1 Compute average demand for each "season."** Total annual demand is divided by the number of "seasons" per year. For quarterly data the number of "seasons" would be 4, whereas for monthly data it would be 12.

**Step 2 Compute a seasonal index for each season.** A seasonal index is obtained by dividing the actual demand for each season by the average demand for each year. An average seasonal index is then obtained by averaging across the number of years available.

**Step 3 Adjust the average forecast for next year by the seasonal index.** Generate a forecast for next year using any of the methods we discussed, and calculate average demand per season. Use seasonal indexes to generate seasonally adjusted forecasts.

### Example 5 Generating Seasonally Adjusted Forecasts

Coco's Ice Cream Shop experiences high seasonality in customer sales. It sells ice cream throughout the year, with most sales occurring in the summer; it also sells hot chocolate, with most sales occurring in the winter. Coco has generated a forecast for next year to be 98,000 customers. Use the data below to create a seasonally adjusted forecast per quarter.

**SOLUTION:**

Number of customers (in thousands)

| Quarter | Year 1 | Year 2 |
|---------|--------|--------|
| Fall    | 14     | 15     |
| Winter  | 25     | 26     |
| Spring  | 20     | 20     |
| Summer  | 33     | 35     |
| Total   | 92     | 96     |

**Step 1 Compute average demand for each "season."**

$$\text{Year 1:} \frac{92}{4} = 23$$

$$\text{Year 2:} \frac{96}{4} = 24$$

## Step 2 Compute a seasonal index for each season.

### Seasonal indexes

| Quarter | Year 1 | Year 2 | Avg. seasonal index |
|---------|--------|--------|---------------------|
| Fall    | $\frac{14}{23} = 0.61$ | $\frac{15}{24} = 0.63$ | 0.620 |
| Winter  | $\frac{25}{23} = 1.09$ | $\frac{26}{24} = 1.08$ | 1.085 |
| Spring  | $\frac{20}{23} = 0.87$ | $\frac{20}{24} = 0.83$ | 0.850 |
| Summer  | $\frac{33}{23} = 1.43$ | $\frac{35}{24} = 1.445$ | 1.445 |

## Step 3 Seasonally adjust the average forecast for next year.

The forecast for next year is 98,000, so the average demand is 24,500.

### Number of Customers

| Quarter | Seasonally | Adjusted | Forecast |
|---------|-----------|----------|----------|
| Fall    | 24,500    | (0.620)  | = 15,190 |
| Winter  | 24,500    | (1.085)  | = 26,583 |
| Spring  | 24,500    | (0.850)  | = 20,825 |
| Summer  | 24,500    | (1.445)  | = 35,403 |

# Causal Models

## Linear Regression

**Linear regression** is a forecasting model that assumes a linear, or straight line, relationship between two variables. It assumes that the variable being forecast, called the dependent variable, is linearly related to another variable, called the independent variable. For example, if we assume that a person's weight and height are linearly related, we can create a linear regression model of this relationship. We can then use the model to forecast weight based on a person's height. It is also possible to use time as the independent variable if we want to see how a variable changes over time. In this case it could be used to forecast trend.

Linear regression is a method that fits a straight line through a set of data, as shown in Figure 8.6. You can see that the dependent variable is linearly related to the independent variable. The relationship between two variables is the equation of a straight line as follows:

$$Y = a + bX$$

where

$Y$ = dependent variable
$X$ = independent variable
$a$ = $Y$ intercept of the straight line
$b$ = slope of the straight line

**176**    FORECASTING AND DEMAND PLANNING

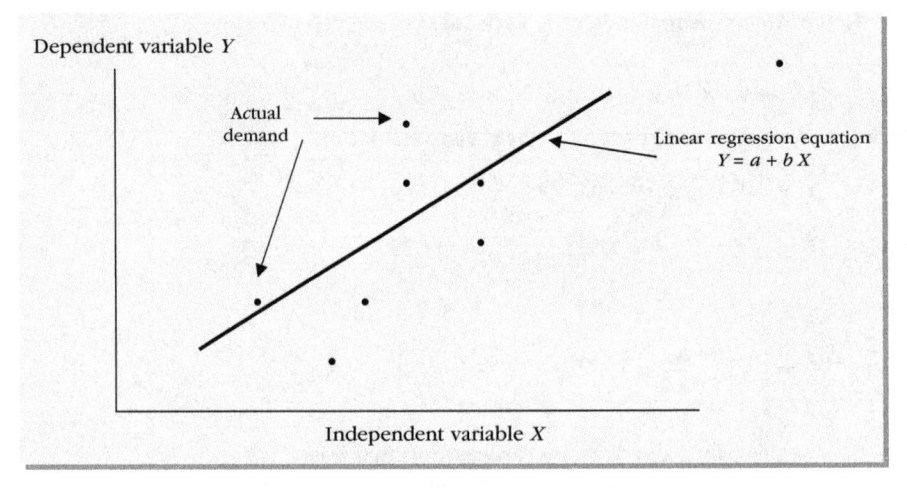

*[Figure: Linear regression scatter plot with dependent variable Y on vertical axis and independent variable X on horizontal axis. Data points shown with a linear regression line labeled Y = a + bX. "Actual demand" points indicated.]*

**FIGURE 8.6** Linear regression line.

Using linear regression requires first developing the linear regression equation. Then for any value of the independent variable, we can compute the value of the dependent variable, which is the variable being forecast. The steps involved are as follows:

**Step 1 Compute parameter *b*:**

$$b = \frac{[XY - n\overline{X}\,\overline{Y}]}{\left[\sum X^2 - n\overline{X}^2\right]}$$

where

$\overline{Y}$ = average of the Y values
$\overline{X}$ = independent variable
$n$ = number of data points

**Step 2 Compute parameter *a*:**

$$a = \overline{Y} - b\overline{X}$$

**Step 3 Substitute values for *a* and *b* in the equation:**

$$Y = a + bX$$

**Step 4 Generate a forecast for the dependent variable (*Y*).**
Substitute the appropriate value for the independent variable (*X*).

### Example 6    Forecasting with Linear Regression

Pizza Boy is trying to forecast the volume of pizza sold based on the amount of money it has put into advertising in the local newspaper. It has been tracking the relationship between pizza sales and advertising over the past four months. The results are as follows:

## Causal Models

| Pizza Sales | Advertising Dollars |
|---|---|
| 58 | 135 |
| 43 | 90 |
| 62 | 145 |
| 68 | 145 |

What would happen to pizza sales if Pizza Boy invested $150 in advertising for next month?
In this example pizza sales are the dependent variable (Y) and advertising dollars the independent variable (X). Following the outlined steps we formulate the following table:

| | Y | X | XY | $X^2$ | $Y^2$ |
|---|---|---|---|---|---|
| | 58 | 135 | 7,830 | 18,225 | 3,364 |
| | 43 | 90 | 3,870 | 8,100 | 1,849 |
| | 62 | 145 | 8,990 | 21,025 | 3,844 |
| | 68 | 145 | 9,860 | 21,025 | 4,624 |
| Total | 231 | 515 | 30,550 | 68,375 | 13,681 |

From the above we compute $\overline{X} = \frac{515}{4} = 128.75$ and $\overline{Y} = \frac{231}{4} = 57.75$

**Step 1  Compute parameter b:**

$$b = \frac{\sum XY - n\overline{XY}}{\sum X^2 - n\overline{X}^2}$$

$$b = \frac{30,550 - 4(128.75)(57.75)}{68,375 - 4(128.75)^2}$$

$$b = 0.391$$

**Step 2  Compute parameter a:**

$$a = \overline{Y} - b\overline{X}$$
$$a = 57.75 - (0.391)\,128.75 = 7.41$$

**Step 3  Substitute values for a and b in the equation:**

$$Y = a + bX$$
$$Y = 7.41 + 0.391\,X$$

**Step 4  Generate a forecast for the dependent variable (Y).** Substitute the appropriate value for the independent variable (X).

$$Y = 7.41 + 0.391(150) = 66 \text{ pizzas}$$

## Multiple Regression

**Multiple regression** extends linear regression by looking at a relationship between the independent variable and *multiple* dependent variables. The general formula for multiple regression is as follows:

$$Y = \beta_0 + \beta_1 X_1 + \beta_2 X_2 + \cdots + \beta_k X_k$$

where

$Y$ = dependent variable

$\beta_0$ = the $Y$ intercept

$\beta_1 \ldots \beta_k$ = coefficients that represent the influence of the independent variables on the dependent variable

$X_1 \ldots X_k$ = independent variables

For example, the dependent variable might be university student enrollment per semester, and the independent variables might be unemployment rate and per capita income. Other variables that can be included are seasonality and trend, as well as special events such as promotions that can be included as separate variables. Multiple regression is a powerful tool for forecasting. The drawback, however, is that it has increased computational and data requirements.

## Measuring Forecast Accuracy

Measuring forecast accuracy is a critical aspect of forecasting. This tells us how our forecasting methods are performing and enables us to improve performance over time. Data can change over time, and models that once provided good results may no longer be adequate. The model's accuracy can be assessed only if forecast performance is measured over time.

The first step in measuring forecast accuracy is to measure the forecast error. Forecast error is the difference between actual demand and the forecast for a given period:

$$e_t = D_t - F_t$$

where

$e_t$ = forecast error for period $t$

$D_t$ = actual demand for period $t$

$F_t$ = forecast for period $t$

However, computing error for one time period does not provide enough information. We need to measure forecast accuracy over time. Two of the most commonly used error measures are the mean absolute deviation (MAD) and the mean square error (MSE). MAD is the average of the sum of the absolute errors:

$$\text{MAD} = \frac{\sum |\text{Actual} - \text{Forecast}|}{n}$$

MSE is the average of the squared error:

$$\text{MSE} = \frac{\sum (\text{Actual} - \text{Forecast})^2}{n}$$

Both of these measures are useful and provide the forecaster with different information. An advantage of MAD is that it is based on absolute values. As a result, errors of opposite signs do not cancel each other out when they are added, providing a total sum of the average error. When comparing different forecasting methods we would select the method with the lowest MAD.

MSE has an additional advantage. Due to the squaring of the error term large errors are magnified, giving them greater penalty. This can be a useful error measure in environments where large errors are particularly destructive. As with MAD, when comparing the forecast performance of different methods we would select the method with the lowest MSE. Both error measures provide different information, and a good forecaster learns to rely on multiple measures.

### Example 7   Measuring Forecast Accuracy

Harry Thurber (HT) Apparel is comparing the accuracy of two methods that it has used to forecast monthly sales of its popular jeans. Forecasts of monthly sales from January through May for method A and method B are shown below against the actual sales. Which method provided better forecast accuracy?

|  |  | Method A |  |  |  | Method B |  |  |  |
|---|---|---|---|---|---|---|---|---|---|
| Month | Sales | Forecast | Error | \|Error\| | Error² | Forecast | Error | \|Error\| | Error² |
| Jan | 40 | 42 | −2 | 2 | 4 | 44 | −4 | 4 | 16 |
| Feb | 28 | 29 | 1 | 1 | 1 | 31 | −3 | 3 | 9 |
| Mar | 41 | 39 | 2 | 2 | 4 | 38 | 3 | 3 | 9 |
| Apr | 41 | 38 | 3 | 3 | 9 | 42 | −1 | 1 | 1 |
| May | 39 | 41 | −2 | 2 | 4 | 40 | −1 | 1 | 1 |
| Total |  |  | 2 | 10 | 22 |  | −6 | 12 | 36 |

Accuracy for method A:

$$\text{MAD} = \frac{\sum |\text{Actual} - \text{Forecast}|}{n}$$

$$\text{MAD} = \frac{\sum 10}{5}$$

$$\text{MAD} = 2$$

$$\text{MSE} = \frac{\sum (\text{Actual} - \text{Forecast})^2}{n}$$

$$\text{MSE} = \frac{22}{5}$$

$$\text{MSE} = 4.4$$

Accuracy for method B:

$$\text{MAD} = \frac{\sum |\text{Actual} - \text{Forecast}|}{n}$$

$$\text{MAD} = \frac{12}{5}$$

$$\text{MAD} = 2.4$$

$$MSE = \frac{\sum (\text{Actual} - \text{Forecast})^2}{n}$$

$$MSE = \frac{36}{5}$$

$$MSE = 7.2$$

Of the two methods, method A produced both a lower MAD and a lower MSE, which means that it provided better forecast accuracy.

## Collaborative Forecasting and Demand Planning

Forecasting is most effective when it is done in collaboration with supply chain partners. In this section we look at two of the most common processes for collaborative forecasting and demand planning.

## Collaborative Planning, Forecasting and Replenishment (CPFR)

**Collaborative Planning, Forecasting, and Replenishment (CPFR)** is a collaborative process of developing joint forecasts and plans with supply chain partners, rather than doing them independently. It is based on the premise that companies can be more successful if they work together to bring value to their customers, share risks of the marketplace, and improve their performance. CPFR was developed by the Voluntary Interindustry Commerce Standards (VICS) association, a nonprofit organization formed in 1986 to develop standards and guidelines for improving supply chain efficiency. CPFR is one such set of guidelines and provides a process to be followed in achieving coordination for both forecasting and inventory replenishment.

VICS membership includes major corporations such as Wal-Mart and P&G. These companies have demonstrated the benefits that can be achieved with CPFR. The organization has a specific "CPFR committee," which offers detailed guidelines on how supply chain members can collaborate to improve efficiency. The guidelines are based on standard technologies and are scalable, enabling ready implementation across different industries.

The distinguishing feature of CPFR is that members of the supply chain collaborate on business plans, and jointly execute the processes of forecasting and replenishment. Trading partners jointly set forecasts, plan production, replenish inventories, and evaluate their success in the marketplace.

The benefits of CPFR are impressive, and it has been implemented by many companies, including Wal-Mart, Target, Black & Decker, and Ace Hardware. In 2001 an AMR Research study found that by implementing CPFR retailers and suppliers jointly achieved higher sales, decreased inventory, and improved stock levels, while lowering their logistics cost. Similarly, Kurt Salmon Associates estimated the benefits from CPFR on the apparel industry as roughly being $8.3 billion annually (www.vics.org).

VICS offers a five-step process for adoption of CPFR:

**Step 1** **Create joint objectives.**

**Step 2** **Develop a business plan** (e.g., forecasting needs, production schedules, key performance metrics, or "KPIs").

**Step 3** **Create a joint forecast.**

**Step 4  Agree on replenishment strategies.**

**Step 5  Agree on a technology partner to bring CPFR to fruition.**

Although these steps seem simple, they can often be difficult to implement as they require companies to trust each other and be flexible and willing to work together. It should also be pointed out that CPFR is not a one-time event. Rather it is an ongoing process where the outlined steps are performed on a weekly or monthly basis, and the agreement between parties is evaluated annually.

## Sales and Operations Planning (S & OP)

In Chapter 2 we discussed that sometimes organizational functions—such as marketing and operations—operate independent of one another, resulting in overall poor performance. An organization can have several functional forecasts for the same products over the same time period, such as a financial forecast, an operations forecast, a marketing forecast, and a distribution forecast. As these functional forecasts are made independent of one another they typically do not agree. For example, marketing may forecast demand for products that neither manufacturing nor distribution can meet. For an organization to develop efficient and realistic plans for the future, it must generate forecasts that all functional areas agree on and can execute.

## Supply Chain Leader's Box—Using Collaborative Technology

### ■ LI & FUNG

Li & Fung is an example of a company that relies on collaborative technology and real-time information flows to forecast future trends and engage in collaborative planning. Li & Fung is one of the world's biggest supply chain operators, serving as an orchestrator of a network of 12,000 suppliers in 40 countries. Their clients include large retailers, such as Wal-Mart, Target, and Disney World. Serving as an intermediary between customers and suppliers, collaborative planning is critical for this company.

Li & Fung used to deal with clients mostly by phone and fax, with e-mail counting as high technology. However, the company has found the most important technology for collaborative planning to be videoconferencing. It allows buyers and manufacturers to jointly examine product details, such as the color of a material or the stitching on a garment. "Before, we weren't able to send a 500 MB image—we'd post a DVD. Now we can stream it to show vendors in our offices. With realtime images we can make changes quicker," says Manuel Fernandez, Li & Fung's chief technology officer. This enables quick product changes in response to the market.

The information system has also enabled Li & Fung to look across its operations to identify trends. For example, a shortage of workers and new legislation in southern China raised labor costs, so production moved north. "We saw that before it actually happened," says Mr. Fernandez. The company also got advance warning of the economic crisis from retailers' orders before these trends became apparent.

Adapted from: "A Different Game: Information is Transforming Traditional Businesses." *The Economist*, February 28, 2010: 6–7.

**Sales and Operations Planning (S & OP)** is an organizational process intended to match supply and demand through functional collaboration. S & OP requires teamwork among sales, distribution and logistics, operations, finance, and product development. This enables firms to provide better customer service, lower inventory, reduce customer lead times, and stabilize production schedules. The process is designed to coordinate activities between marketing and sales, with those of operations and sourcing, to ensure that supply meets demand requirements.

# FORECASTING AND DEMAND PLANNING

The S & OP process consists of a series of meetings with the goal of reaching an agreement between various departments on the course of action to achieve the optimal balance between supply and demand. It consists of a five-step process that needs to be followed to arrive at a consensus forecast:

**Step 1: Generate quantitative sales forecast.** This process is done using one or more of the forecasting techniques discussed in the previous section.

**Step 2: Marketing adjusts the forecast.** These adjustments include promotions of existing products, introduction of new products, or the elimination of products. This revised forecast is usually stated in terms of both units and dollars.

**Step 3: Operations checks forecast against existing capability.** This includes an evaluation of whether existing capacity is adequate to handle the forecasted volumes. Operations must analyze availability of resources, such as inventory, production capacity, scheduling, and labor, for meeting overall demand and "spike" demand. This may signal the need for extra resources to support special promotions.

**Step 4: Marketing, operations, and finance jointly review forecast and resource issues.** This is a joint meeting of the key business functions to review the forecast and any capacity issue that might have emerged during step 3. During this phase attempts are made to solve capacity issues and balance supply and demand. Alternative scenarios are usually developed and considered, identifying potential lost sales and costs associated with each scenario. At this stage the forecast is converted to dollars to assess whether the scenarios meet the financial plan of the organization.

**Step 5: Executives meet to finalize forecast and capacity decisions.** At this meeting executives from each functional area meet to make final decisions regarding sales forecasts and capacity issues. Executives reach agreement on the forecast and convert it into the operating plan for the organization.

This process is illustrated in Figure 8.7.

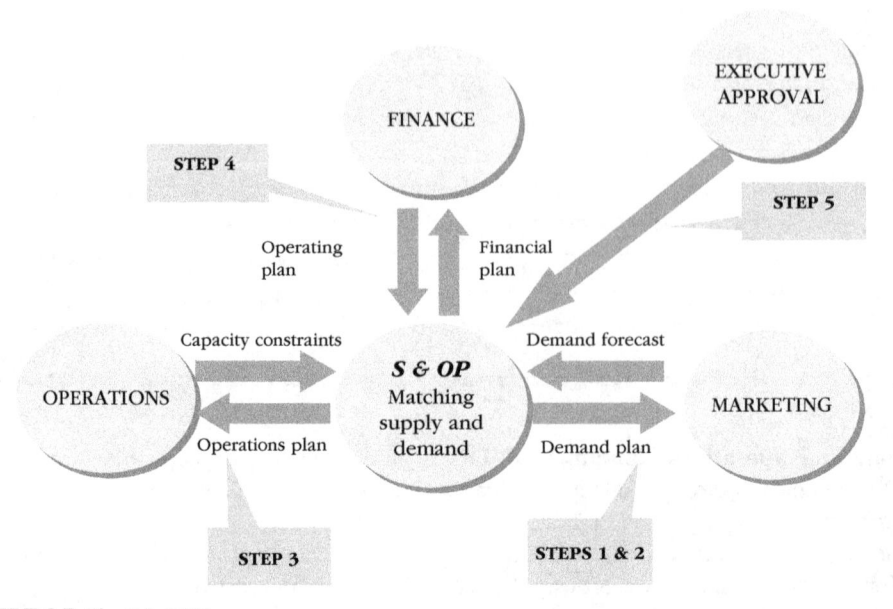

**FIGURE 8.7** The S & OP Process.

S & OP is an important process as it forces functional agreement and creates an understanding of revenue and cost trade-offs. It also forces the joint plan to measure functional performance in terms of metrics appropriate for each functional area, enabling it to support the overall business plan. For example, let's say that performance of the operations function is measured on "cost per unit." This metric encourages operations to keep costs low. A promotional campaign by marketing may mean higher per unit costs for operations, as it needs to extend its resources. These metrics for operations discourage it to support marketing. A better solution is to revise the metric for operations to something such as "compliance to schedule." This new metric would reward operations for making the planned quantities at the planned times. This is an example of what could be achieved through S & OP. S & OP encourages functions to jointly work together to achieve goals of the business plan.

## CHAPTER HIGHLIGHTS

1. Forecasting is the process of attempting to predict future events. Planning is the process of selecting actions with the hope that they will result in attainment of goals and objectives given the forecast.

2. There are three principles of forecasting: (a) forecasts are rarely perfect; (b) forecasts are more accurate for aggregated items than for individual items; and (c) forecasts are more accurate for shorter than longer time horizons.

3. Data are composed of pattern and randomness. Four of the most common patterns are level, trend, seasonality, and cycle.

4. Forecasting methods can be divided into qualitative and quantitative. Qualitative methods are subjective and based on opinions. Quantitative methods are mathematically based, objective, and consistent.

5. Quantitative forecasting methods can be divided into two categories: time series and causal models.

6. Time series models generate the forecast by identifying and analyzing patterns in a "time series" of the data. Causal models assume that the variable being forecast is related to other variables in the environment and develop a model identifying these relationships, expressing them in mathematical terms, and using that information to forecast the future.

7. CPFR is a collaborative process of developing joint forecasts and plans with supply chain partners, rather than doing them independently.

8. Sales and Operations Planning (S & OP) is an organizational process intended to match supply and demand through functional collaboration between marketing, operations, and finance, in order to ensure that supply can meet demand requirements.

## KEY TERMS

Forecasting
Planning
Demand management
Predictive analytics
Qualitative forecasting methods
Quantitative forecasting methods
Executive opinion
Market research
Delphi method
Time series models
Causal models
Brainware
Simple moving average
Weighted moving average
Seasonal index
Linear regression
Multiple regression
Collaborative Planning, Forecasting, and Replenishment (CPFR)
Sales and Operations Planning (S & OP)

## DISCUSSION QUESTIONS

1. Identify a nontraditional business event, such as forecasting demand for T-shirts following the Super Bowl, or the amount of relief aid needed following an earthquake. What do you think would be the best way to forecast such an event—qualitative or quantitative—and why? What are the implications of forecast error on supply chain management?

2. Think of a product you have recently purchased. How many different forecasts do you think the retailer had to make in order to decide how much product to stock? What are the consequences for that particular retailer if they had overforecast versus underforecast?

3. Imagine that you are starting a business. What type of forecasting model would you use to decide how many products you will be selling? Would you use the same forecasting model after you have been in business five years? Why or why not?

4. Identify an example where large errors would be extremely costly. Which forecast error metric would be best for this environment?

5. Identify the differences between the two methods of collaboration discussed in the chapter: CPFR and S & OP. How are they similar, and how are they different? Explain the differences in the organizational objectives they are trying to achieve.

## PROBLEMS

1. Beyond Tea Inc. wants to forecast sales of its menthol green tea. The company is considering either using a simple mean or a three-period moving average to forecast monthly sales. Given sales data for the past 10 months use both forecasting methods to forecast periods 7 to 10 and then evaluate each. Which method should they use? Use the selected method to make a forecast for month 11.

| Month | Sales (lbs) |
|-------|-------------|
| 1     | 5           |
| 2     | 8           |
| 3     | 15          |
| 4     | 18          |
| 5     | 20          |
| 6     | 19          |
| 7     | 17          |
| 8     | 18          |
| 9     | 19          |
| 10    | 21          |

2. Safe Spirit sells novelty hats in New York City. The company uses a simple mean to forecast monthly sales. The forecast of sales for month six was $5,000 obtained by averaging past five months' sales. Sales from months one to four were $6,000, $7,000, $4,000, and $5,000. However, the sales assistant accidently deleted the sale data for month five in the system. Now, the sales manager wants to determine sales for month five from the remaining data. How would she do that?

3. Mr. Zhou repairs computers. He had 45 customers for January, 50 customers for February, and 70 for March. He now wants to forecast his customers for April by using a two-period simple moving average. Compute the forecast.

4. Smile Cucumber Corp records its sales in a database system. The company wants to forecast monthly sales based on the record of the past three months. The value of the forecast is 10 million if the company uses the simple mean. What is the forecast if the company uses a three-period moving average? Explain.

5. Green Water Park uses exponential smoothing to forecast monthly visits of customers. Its forecast for June was 1 million, but the actual number of customers turned out to be 2 million. The forecaster decided to use an alpha of 0.8. What is the forecast for July?

6. Katherine is a forecast manager. She used exponential smoothing to forecast her sales of coffee cakes for next week, and this number is 200. Her forecast for this week was 180 but the actual number is 220. What is her choice for alpha?

7. The past two years sales at ACSR Inc. were 2 million and 4 million. Their forecast team used a two-period moving average to forecast its sales this year. But the actual sales for this year were 4 million. Now, the forecast team wants to forecast its sales for next year by using exponential smoothing with alpha equals 0.7. What is the forecast?

8. Gold Roof Hut is trying to forecast its number of customers based on the average price of food. It has been tracking the relationship between number of customers and food's average price over the past five weeks. The results are as follows:

| Number of customers (in thousands) | Average price (in dollars) |
|------------------------------------|----------------------------|
| 1                                  | 16                         |
| 1.2                                | 15                         |
| 1.4                                | 14                         |
| 1.8                                | 12                         |
| 1.8                                | 11                         |

What would be the number of customers if Gold Roof Hut set the average price to 10?

9. Alexandra is forecasting sales based on the salesperson's salary. She collected the following data and would like to forecast sales if salary is 6K:

| Sales (10 K) | Salary (K) |
|---|---|
| 1 | 2 |
| 1.5 | 3 |
| 2 | 3.5 |
| 3 | 4 |
| 3.2 | 5 |

10. Mixo Inc. is forecasting its product's quality on a scale of 0 to 100 based on how many hours are spent for each product. Data are in the following table:

| Quality | Hours spent |
|---|---|
| 50 | 10 |
| 60 | 15 |
| 70 | 20 |
| 80 | 24 |
| 90 | 30 |

How many hours should be spent if the company wants its product quality to be 95?

11. John Taylor Salons wants to forecast monthly customer demand from June through August using trend adjusted exponential smoothing. Given $\alpha = 0.2$, $\beta = 0.4$, $F_{MAY} = 45$, and a $T_{MAY} = 0$, forecast a FIT for months June through August.

| Month | Actual sales |
|---|---|
| May | 50 |
| June | 61 |
| July | 73 |
| August | 80 |

12. Henry Lo Manufacturing is comparing the accuracy of two methods that it has used to forecast monthly production. Forecasts of monthly productions from May through August are shown below against the actual productions. Which method provided better forecast accuracy?

| Month | Actual sales | Method A forecast | Method B forecast |
|---|---|---|---|
| May | 50 | 48 | 47 |
| June | 60 | 55 | 56 |
| July | 60 | 62 | 57 |
| August | 40 | 41 | 35 |

13. Samuel Bridge Company wants to compare the accuracy of two methods that it has used to forecast yearly profits. Forecasts of yearly profits from 2013 through 2017 are shown below against the actual productions. Comment on their forecast accuracy

| Year | Actual profits (million) | Method A forecasts (million) | Method B forecast (million) |
|---|---|---|---|
| 2013 | 10 | 12 | 11 |
| 2014 | 12 | 15 | 14 |
| 2015 | 6 | 16 | 18 |
| 2016 | 5 | 7 | 5 |
| 2017 | 8 | 10 | 7 |

14. Jay Sharp Guard wants to compare the accuracy of two methods that it has used to forecast monthly expenses. Forecasts of monthly expenses from September to November are shown below against the actual expenses. Which method provided best-forecast accuracy?

| Month | Expenses (million) | Method A forecasts (million) | Method B forecasts (million) |
|---|---|---|---|
| Sep | 3 | 3.5 | 3.1 |
| Oct | 4 | 4.1 | 3.8 |
| Nov | 5 | 5.3 | 5.1 |

## Case Study | Speedy Automotive

It is August 2017 and Speedy Automotive is one of four car dealerships located in rural Wyoming. The residents in the area replace their vehicles roughly every eight years. When they do replace their vehicles, they tend to visit the same dealership that sold them the first one, building a relationship with the dealership. This has kept sales relatively stable for all the dealerships in the area. Recently, however, customers have begun expanding their shopping options. Speedy Automotive believes this is due to the Internet and online shopping. Customers have begun coming to the dealership with an exact idea of what car they would like and have a price in mind. When Speedy Automotive does not have the model available or cannot meet the price, customers have started going to competitors.

This trend has the general manager of Speedy, Mike Leavy, worried. Mike runs the dealership like a small business and relies on repeat customers. Speedy is not a chain and has little access to outside capital, so cash flow is critical. If sales are low, Mike has to take out a loan to pay the manufacturer for the vehicles. If sales are high, Speedy loses potential customers due to lack of inventory. Mike has decided that he needs to be able to forecast this new variability to keep the business healthy.

Bill Goodson is the inventory manager at Speedy and has historically prepared the forecasts. Bill usually just takes the sales numbers from last year and adjusts them upward or downward based on his "gut feeling." This has worked well in the past, but Mike has told him to look into other forecasting methods. Bill is preparing the September 2017 sales forecast for Speedy and is not sure where to start. For the August forecast, Bill used the sales numbers from the same time of the previous year—August 2016. The August 2016 forecast was off by 10 cars and Bill hoped the 2017 version would fare better. Bill assumed the sales representatives would always work a little harder if sales were low and they could always take vacation time if they were above target.

Mike has told Bill to look into both time series and causal forecasting models, but Bill is not sure of the difference. Mike also wants Bill to determine the amount of profit being lost due to poor forecasting. Bill has access to sales and forecast data from the past 18 months and has already calculated various measures of error in Excel.

**Speedy Automotive Sales Forecast History**

| Month | Sales | Forecast | Error | Mean error | Mean absolute error | Sum of squared error | Absolute percentage error | Mean squared error |
|---|---|---|---|---|---|---|---|---|
| Mar-2016 | 100.00 | 103.00 | 3 | 3.00 | 3.00 | 9 | 3.00 | 9.00 |
| Apr-2016 | 119.00 | 120.00 | 1 | 2.00 | 2.00 | 10 | 0.84 | 5.00 |
| May-2016 | 478.00 | 441.00 | −37 | −11.00 | 13.67 | 1379 | 7.74 | 459.67 |
| Jun-2016 | 98.00 | 118.00 | 20 | −3.25 | 15.25 | 1779 | 20.41 | 444.75 |
| Jul-2016 | 110.00 | 104.00 | −6 | −3.80 | 13.40 | 1815 | 5.45 | 363.00 |
| Aug-2016 | 93.00 | 103.00 | 10 | −1.50 | 12.83 | 1915 | 10.75 | 319.17 |
| Sep-2016 | 104.00 | 105.00 | 1 | −1.14 | 11.14 | 1916 | 0.96 | 273.71 |
| Oct-2016 | 96.00 | 101.00 | 5 | −0.38 | 10.38 | 1941 | 5.21 | 242.63 |
| Nov-2016 | 96.00 | 98.00 | 2 | −0.11 | 9.44 | 1945 | 2.08 | 216.11 |
| Dec-2016 | 103.00 | 109.00 | 6 | 0.50 | 9.10 | 1981 | 5.83 | 198.10 |
| Jan-2017 | 94.00 | 99.00 | 5 | 0.91 | 8.73 | 2006 | 5.32 | 182.36 |
| Feb-2017 | 102.00 | 105.00 | 3 | 1.08 | 8.25 | 2015 | 2.94 | 167.92 |
| Mar-2017 | 98.00 | 101.00 | 3 | 1.23 | 7.85 | 2024 | 3.06 | 155.69 |
| Apr-2017 | 120.00 | 119.00 | −1 | 1.07 | 7.36 | 2025 | 0.83 | 144.64 |
| May-2017 | 469.00 | 453.00 | −16 | −0.07 | 7.93 | 2281 | 3.41 | 152.07 |
| Jun-2017 | 99.00 | 115.00 | 16 | 0.94 | 8.44 | 2537 | 16.16 | 158.56 |
| Jul-2017 | 99.00 | 106.00 | 7 | 1.29 | 8.35 | 2586 | 7.07 | 152.12 |

*Case Questions*

1. Is Speedy Automotive currently using a time series or causal forecasting? Explain the difference and how you can identify each.
2. Is this type of forecast appropriate, or would an alternative method produce more accurate results? Why or why not?
3. Which measure should Bill use to assess forecast error rates? Why?
4. If Bill's forecasts are consistently too high or consistently too low, which measure is most useful to remedy the situation? Why?
5. If the average sale price for one car is $20,000 and the average car costs $15,000 to acquire, how much profit is being lost each month as a result of poor forecasting? Note: For ease of calculation, assume all cars arrive on the 1st and all cars remaining on the 31st are disposed of with a 50% markdown.
6. What can Bill do to improve his forecasting based on your observations?

# REFERENCES

Armstrong, J. Scott. *Long-range Forecasting: From Crystal Ball to Computer*. New York: John Wiley & Sons, 1985.

Armstrong, J. Scott, and Fred Collopy. "Error Measures for Generalizing about Forecasting Methods: Empirical Comparisons." *International Journal of Forecasting*, 8, 1992: 69–80.

Collopy, F., and J. Scott Armstrong. "Rule-Based Forecasting: Development and Validation of an Expert Systems Approach to Combining Time Series Extrapolations." *Management Science*, 38(10), 1992: 1394–1414.

Kahneman, Daniel, Rosenfield, Andrew, Gandhi, Linnea, and Tom Blaser. "The Cost of Inconsistent Decision Making." *Harvard Business Review*, October, 2016: 38–46.

Lee, H., V. Padmanabhan, and S. Whang. "The Bullwhip Effect in Supply Chains." *Sloan Management Review*, 38(3), 1997: 93–102.

Makridakis, S., S. C. Wheelwright, and Rob J. Hyndman. *Forecasting: Methods and Applications*, 4th ed. New York: John Wiley & Sons, 2006.

# 9 Inventory Management

**LEARNING OBJECTIVES**

*After completing this chapter, you should be able to:*

- Describe different types of inventory, their uses, and their costs.
- Explain inventory systems and ordering policies.
- Understand how to compute order quantities, reorder points, and safety stock.
- Differentiate between independent and dependent demand.
- Understand practical issues of managing supply chain inventories.
- Explain ABC inventory classification and vendor managed inventory (VMI).

**CHAPTER OUTLINE**

- **Basics of Inventory Management**
  *What Is Inventory?*
  *Reasons for Carrying Inventory*
  *Types of Inventory*
  *Inventory Costs*

- **Inventory Systems**
  *Fixed-Order Quantity System*
  *Fixed-Time Period System*
  *Comparing Fixed-Order Quantity versus Fixed-Time Period Systems*

- **Fixed-Order Quantity Systems**
  *Economic Order Quantity (EOQ)*
  *Reorder Point (ROP)*
  *Safety Stock*
  *Economic Production Quantity (EPQ)*

- **Fixed-Time Period Systems**
  *Computing Target Inventory*

- **Independent versus Dependent Demand**

- ■ **Managing Supply Chain Inventory**
  - *ABC Inventory Classification*
  - *Practical Considerations of EOQ*
  - *Measuring Inventory Performance*
  - *Vendor Managed Inventory (VMI)*
- ■ **Chapter Highlights**
- ■ **Key Terms**
- ■ **Discussion Questions**
- ■ **Problems**

On an early July morning a crowd has gathered for the opening of Trader Joe's newest store location, in Manhattan's Chelsea neighborhood. As shoppers stand in line for the store's opening, they chat about their favorite Trader Joe's foods and discuss the benefits the store opening will bring to the area. Why the excitement? Trader Joe's is no ordinary grocery chain. It is offbeat and hip, having elevated food shopping to a cultural experience.

Trader Joe's has developed an almost cult following and is one of the hottest retailers in the United States, with 344 stores in 25 states and Washington, D.C. They see themselves as a national chain of neighborhood specialty stores, stocking shelves with a winning combination of low-cost, yuppie-friendly goods. This includes staples such as cage-free eggs and organic blue agave sweetener. They also carry the exotic, such as Belgian butter waffle cookies and Thai lime-and-chili cashews—items difficult to find anywhere else.

What is most remarkable about Trader Joe's is that they have found a unique way of addressing the problem that has traditionally plagued grocery stores: carrying large numbers of highly perishable food items in large varieties. A typical grocery store carries about 50,000 stock-keeping units (SKUs), while Trader Joe's carries about 4,000 SKUs. As a result, its stores sell an estimated $1,750 in merchandise per square foot, which is more than double that of Whole Foods. The company doesn't carry much inventory and has little backroom space for storage. However, the inventory that it does carry is carefully selected.

Trader Joe's pursues a limited-selection, high-turnover inventory model. One example is peanut butter. Trader Joe's sells 10 varieties, compared to most supermarkets that sell about 40. This has huge implications for inventory turnover. Imagine that a typical supermarket and a Trader Joe's both sell 40 jars of peanut butter a week. Trader Joe's would sell an average of four of each type, while the supermarket might sell only one. With the greater turnover on a smaller number of items, Trader Joe's can buy large quantities with deep discounts. It also has lower losses due to shelf life. This makes operations—from stocking shelves to checking out customers—much simpler.

Customers accept Trade Joe's limited variety trusting that the company will stock only the best. For example, there are only two kinds of pudding or one kind of polenta. As one former employee puts it, "If they're going to get behind only one jar of Greek olives, then they're sure as heck going to make sure it's the most fabulous jar of Greek olives they can find for the price."

Management has sought to minimize the number of hands that touch a product throughout the supply chain. Whenever possible, Trader Joe's buys directly from the manufacturer, which then ships the items straight to Trader Joe's distribution centers. For example, a U.S.-made cheese is sent to distribution centers nationwide, where it is cut and wrapped. At a traditional supermarket, that same cheese would typically go through a distributor first, adding another inventory cost to the supply chain. Trucks leave the distribution centers daily for the stores, which keep low inventory levels. Trader Joe's small stores don't have much of a back room, so ordering from the distribution centers has to be precise. All this has kept costs low, enabling Trader Joe's to be in an enviable financial position: having no debt and self-funding their growth.

Adapted from: "Inside Trader Joe's." *Fortune*, September 6, 2010: 86–96.

## Basics of Inventory Management

### What Is Inventory?

Simply put, inventory is quantities of goods in stock. This is true for any product, material, or good. Consider the books or CDs on your bookshelf. They comprise your inventory. They provide you with a certain value, such as enjoyment or the ability to share them with friends. They also have a certain financial cost. They cost money to purchase—money that cannot be used for something else. For Trader Joe's, inventory comprises all the items on their store shelves, in their distribution center, and even in transit. When we talk about inventory, we are simply talking about quantities of materials or "stuff" we have in storage. As we will see, this material serves many purposes, but it also ties up a great deal of funds. As a result, managing inventory throughout the entire supply chain is extremely important. The benefits, however, can be significant as demonstrated by Trader Joe's financial success.

Both manufacturing and service organizations carry inventory. A great deal of inventory must be carried to support basic processes of product creation. In manufacturing inventory can take a variety of forms, such as **raw materials** and **component parts**, which are delivered from suppliers. Once these items enter the production process they become **work-in-process (WIP)** inventory. Finally, when the production process is completed, inventory becomes classified as **finished goods**. Inventory also includes supplies and equipment.

As inventory moves through the supply chain it takes on different classifications. Consider the packaging supplier for Tide laundry detergent for Procter & Gamble. The supplier takes plastic material and creates the packaging. Their finished product then becomes a component part for the production of Tide at the P&G facility.

In services, inventory includes the tangible goods that support delivery of the service, such as medical tools in an operating room or soaps in a hotel chain. It also includes items that are sold as part of the service, such as hair products sold at a beauty salon. In addition, service personnel can be considered part of the inventory, as their skills define the type of services that can be offered. An example might be physicians on staff and their specialties—such as internal medicine or neurology, or attorneys on staff—such as specialty in tort law versus family law.

Services produce an intangible product, and finished services cannot be placed in inventory. However, this does not mean that some steps in the delivery process cannot be performed before the customer arrives. This stored work is also part of **service inventory**. Service inventory involves all activities that are carried out in advance of the customer's arrival. One strategy service organizations can use to improve their responsiveness is to create a service inventory of tasks they can do before customers arrive. As with physical inventories, service inventories allow firms to create a buffer against variability of demand, while providing customers with faster response times. Managing service inventory improves service response time and quality and reduces costs.

Inventory decisions relate to when to replenish stock and how large orders should be. This is called an **inventory policy** and addresses the basic questions of *when* and *how much* to order. Later in this chapter we will look at different types of inventory policies that help address these two questions. Let's first look at some reasons for carrying inventory.

## Managerial Insights Box—Service Inventory

### ZOOTS

A good example of how service inventories can be created is provided by Zoots, a dry cleaner that has transformed the task of dry cleaning into a highly efficient, streamlined workflow that results in a higher level of customer service. Consider that at many dry cleaners laundered shirts are stored separately from dry-cleaned items, and a customer must wait for both to be picked up from the back room. The retailer could save time if the work was performed before the customer arrived. Even more time would be saved if the customer's items were waiting at the front of the store. Zoots actually does this.

Zoots charges orders to the customer's credit card on file and then places the completed orders in lockers that are available 24 hours a day. Customers can simply arrive at the store at their convenience to pick up their clothes. They spend no time standing in line and waiting. Zoots has reduced the pickup time to a minimum by building up its service inventory.

The customers, however, are not the only ones to benefit. Zoots's employees can work at a more constant rate as opposed to responding to minute-by-minute fluctuations in demand. This enables Zoots to plan employee schedules more efficiently, improving productivity for the company and lowering production costs.

## Reasons for Carrying Inventory

We have all heard about problems of high inventory costs and the benefits of lean systems that minimize inventory levels. However, inventory is carried for many reasons, and all companies—even those that practice lean—carry inventory. In fact, organizations cannot function without a certain amount of inventory. There are different types of inventories that meet different organizational objectives.

1. **Protect Against Lead Time Demand.** One reason for carrying inventory is that goods cannot arrive immediately when we run out of stock. There is a certain amount of lead time that is needed for goods to be produced and delivered. There is also a normal amount of variation in this lead time. This may result from shipping delays, production problems at the supplier site, lost orders, defective materials, and numerous other problems. Even in lean systems, discussed in Chapter 10, where inventory is delivered in predicted intervals, there is still a certain amount of inventory that must be held in stock.

    Also, consider that sources of supply are rarely at the same location as demand, and we cannot locate a production facility everywhere there is demand. As a result, inventory has to be transported from one location to another, and sometimes held in a distribution center to be distributed when needed at the various locations.

2. **Maintain Independence of Operations.** Recall our discussion in Chapter 3 regarding how processes function and the challenge of balancing different processing capabilities. Inventory at different points in the system serves this purpose by evening out differences in processing capability and provides a cushion between operations. Extra stores of inventory can be placed at various points in the supply chain network, or at work centers within a facility, to give it flexibility.

   Consider the high interdependence of workstations on an assembly line, as discussed in Chapter 5. Inventory is typically placed between workstations to decrease their interdependence, so that a work stoppage at one station does not shut down the entire assembly line. In addition, there is natural variation in processing times between identical operations, and it is desirable to create a cushion of inventory so that output can occur at a constant rate.

3. **Balance Supply and Demand.** Demand is never known with certainty, and holding extra inventory enables an organization to meet unexpected surges in demand. Also, consider that demand occurs intermittently, rather than on a continuous basis. An example might be retail sales that are slower on weekday mornings but high over the weekends. Not having extra inventory may mean missed sales. Carrying inventory helps to address these natural variations in demand.

   Another important factor are seasonal demand patterns. This may result in high and low periods of demand, such as ice cream sales in the summer or demand for snow shovels in the winter. It would be very costly for production facilities to produce products in unison with the seasonality of demand. This might mean closed facilities and unemployed workers during low seasons and overtime production during high seasons. Switching production rates of large facilities can be extremely costly. A more common strategy is for companies, and their supply chains, to produce at a more uniform rate during the year. In this case extra products are stored in inventory and used during peak seasons. This is shown in Figure 9.1, where A represents inventory stored to be used up during segment B.

4. **Buffer Uncertainty.** Companies know that many unexpected events may occur that impact both supply and demand. This could be a batch of damaged goods being received, an unexpected delay due to weather, or a strike at a supplier's plant. Companies carry extra inventory in stock to protect themselves or "buffer" against these uncertainties. Think about yourself going to the movies with friends. The movie ticket might cost $8.00 but you will likely carry with you a bit more money. Why? Just in case something comes up. That is the same logic.

5. **Economic Purchase Orders.** Buying larger quantities means incurring a higher inventory holding cost. However, there are a number of reasons when this may be advantageous.

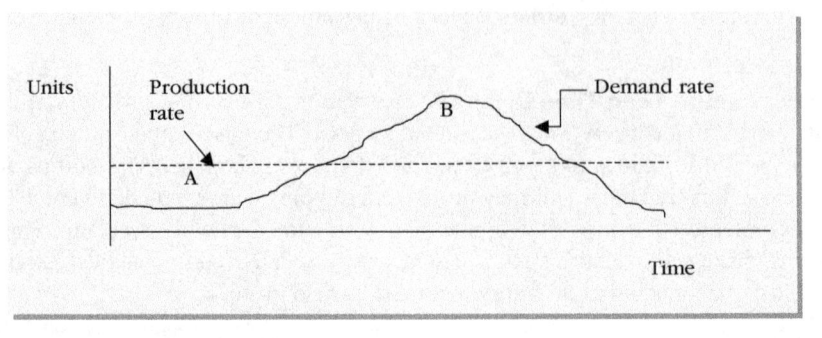

**FIGURE 9.1** Differences in production and demand rates.

For example, suppliers sometimes offer price discounts to encourage customers to purchase larger quantities at one time. Similarly, buying in large quantities may result in savings associated with transporting larger quantities at one time. Also, anticipating some type of price increase or disruption, which may lead to quantity shortages, leads companies to buy larger quantities. An example might be a drought in Africa, leading to an anticipated price increase of coffee.

## Types of Inventory

There are different types, or categories, of inventory designed to meet the different purposes for carrying inventory, and their quantities are computed differently. We look at these here.

1. **Cycle Stock.** These are also called lot size inventories. This is inventory for immediate use and is computed based on expected demand over a certain time period. It assumes demand is known with certainty and computes how much stock is needed over a set period of time. It also accounts for the fact that products are typically produced in batches. This is the quantity, or the size, of the batch that is produced during the production cycle. Therefore it is called "cycle stock."

2. **Safety Stock.** Safety stock, also called buffer stock, is the extra inventory we carry to serve as a cushion for uncertainties in supply and demand. It can be in the form of finished goods to cover unexpected demand. It can also be in the form of raw materials to guard against supply problems, or in the form of WIP inventories, to guard against production stoppages.

3. **Anticipation inventory.** As the name states, these inventories are carried in anticipation of certain events. Their one purpose is to compensate for differences in the timing of supply and demand and to smooth out the flow of products throughout the supply chain. They are also used when demand fluctuations are significant, but predictable, such as with seasonal variation. This is where companies carry extra inventory during a low season in anticipation of higher demands during the high season. For this reason they are sometimes called **seasonal inventory**. Finally, these are inventories that are carried in anticipation of a price increase or a shortage of products—sometimes called **hedge inventory**.

4. **Pipeline inventory.** Also called **transportation inventory**, this is inventory that is simply in transit. It exists because the points of demand and supply are not same. At any one time a global supply network has a large percentage of its inventory in transit—say on a barge, truck, or rail—being moved from one location to another, or waiting to be loaded or unloaded.

5. **Maintenance, Repair, and Operating Items (MRO).** In addition to inventories that directly support product creation, there are other inventories that are used indirectly. These are called maintenance, repair, and operating items (MRO). They include everything from office supplies and forms, to toilet paper and cleaning supplies, to tools and parts needed to repair machines. Collectively, MRO items make up a significant amount of inventory and need to be managed like all other inventories. Consider the abundance of printing paper in an office, paper cups at Starbucks, or latex gloves in a hospital.

## Inventory Costs

Two of the most important inventory costs are **holding cost** and **ordering cost**. These costs typically move in opposite directions, where reducing one means increasing the other. A third important cost is **shortage cost**. We look at these next.

1. **Holding Cost.** Holding cost, sometimes called **carrying cost**, includes all the costs that vary with the amount of inventory held in stock. This includes storage facilities, handling, insurance, pilferage, breakage, obsolescence, depreciation, taxes, and the opportunity cost of capital. Although we own the inventory, there are still costs associated with keeping it. Theft is not an uncommon occurrence; there are also damages that can occur; highly innovative or seasonal items can easily become obsolete if not sold on time.

   Inventory holding cost is typically described as a percentage of the value of the inventory that is held. It is generally denoted by H and is computed as follows:

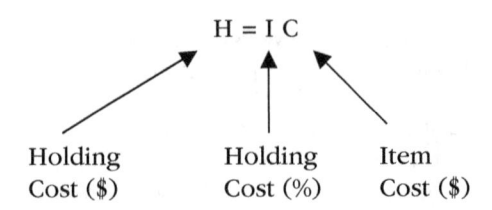

   $$H = I\,C$$

   Holding Cost ($)     Holding Cost (%)     Item Cost ($)

   H is the **dollar value** to hold one unit in inventory over some period of time. I is holding cost as a **percentage of item cost**, and C is cost of the item. Therefore, inventory holding cost can be provided as a percentage, say 30% of cost of goods annually. It can also be provided as a dollar value, such as $12 per unit per year. Notice that holding cost must be provided over some period of time, whether a day or month or year. The longer the time period the longer we are holding inventory in stock and the higher the inventory holding cost.

   Inventory holding cost is generally underestimated and can roughly vary from 15% of cost of goods per year to as much as 50% of cost of goods. Reducing holding costs means a reduction in inventory levels and results in frequent replenishment. This, however, then results in a higher ordering cost.

2. **Ordering Cost.** This cost includes all the costs involved in placing an order and procuring the item. It involves deciding on order quantities, clerical costs involved in placing the order, tracking the order, and receiving it. Ordering cost is sometimes called **setup cost** as it also includes the costs involved in preparing the production run, when the items are made in-house. If there were no costs, or loss of time, when changing from producing one product to another, companies would produce many small quantities. They would quickly switch from producing one product to another, reducing inventory levels. However, this is not the case, and there is cost associated with switching production from one product type to another.

   Notice that reducing ordering cost means ordering less frequently. This means that the quantities ordered have to be larger and will result in higher levels of inventory. This lower ordering cost, unfortunately, will result in a higher inventory cost as we then have to carry more in stock. Holding and ordering costs are the most common inventory costs, and the challenge is to find the right balance between them.

3. **Shortage costs.** Shortage costs occur when we run out of stock. This cost reflects the consequences of not having enough in inventory. Being out of stock means that the customer will have to wait for the item to arrive, or the order must be cancelled. Potentially there is a loss of sale. Also, there can be loss of goodwill and reputation with customers. There is a trade-off between carrying extra stock to ensure we can satisfy demand and the costs resulting from a stock-out. This balance is sometimes difficult to obtain, as it is hard to estimate true shortage cost and the impact of the shortage on customer behavior.

## Supply Chain Leader's Box

### ■ JOHN DEERE & COMPANY

Excess inventory can hurt financial performance. However, companies need to have enough products in showrooms to generate sales. The trick is to maintain the bare minimum yet have enough products available to support sales. John Deere & Company had to tackle this problem in its $4 billion worldwide Commercial and Consumer Equipment (C&CE) division. The company restructured that division's supply chain to reduce inventory and freight costs. The result was a major improvement in the company's financial performance.

A few years ago the company embarked on an effort to better manage their return on assets. A large part of the assets in the C&CE division was finished goods inventory, both in the factories and in dealers' hands. In an effort to free up capital John Deere began an inventory-reduction initiative. About 70% of the finished-goods inventory was at dealers' locations, which had to be reduced. However, the dealers were uncomfortable with this decision. The reason was that many of the products sold—such as lawn mowing equipment, utility vehicles, and golf course maintenance equipment—are things that customers like to sit on, touch, and try out before finalizing their purchase. This enhances sales. Also, the seasonal nature of the sales cycle complicated the inventory-reduction effort, as 65% of retail sales of lawn mowers occur between the months of March and July.

John Deere used advanced software to determine how to better align its production with demand to reduce inventory.

An analysis concluded that the division could reduce inventory by $1 billion if it held the right amount at the right location at each point throughout the year. Due to concerns of dealers, they chose to reduce inventory by $250 million each year over a four-year period in a process dubbed "stair-stepping." In addition, they decided to change their supply chain processes to ensure products were available to meet demand. They would react more swiftly to changes in demand as now there was less inventory to buffer demand swings. Processes had to be changed to become faster and more flexible to support a lower inventory level.

The division began by reducing target inventory levels, which required a change in the production schedule at its five factories throughout North America. In the past these inventory targets had been set high to compensate for the inability of factories to quickly respond to changes in demand. Now production schedules had to be changed to adjust to demand. In addition, the factories changed their assembly practices, producing at a more level rather than seasonal rate.

Through this process of restructuring the supply chain, John Deere cut inventory and reduced freight costs to better manage assets and enhance shareholder value. The company learned that operating a supply chain with less inventory means adjusting internal production and distribution processes. It also means significant financial rewards.

Adapted from: James A. Cook. "Running Inventory like a Deere." *Supply Chain Quarterly*, Issue 4, 2007.

# Inventory Systems

Every inventory system must answer the two basic questions: *when to order* and *how much to order*. There are two basic categories of inventory systems that accomplish this, and they work in slightly different ways. Let's look at these next.

## Fixed-Order Quantity System

The first inventory system is called a **fixed-order quantity system**. As the name suggests, the quantity that is ordered with this system is constant or fixed and is denoted by $Q$. An order is placed when the inventory position drops to a predetermined level, noted as the reorder point, or

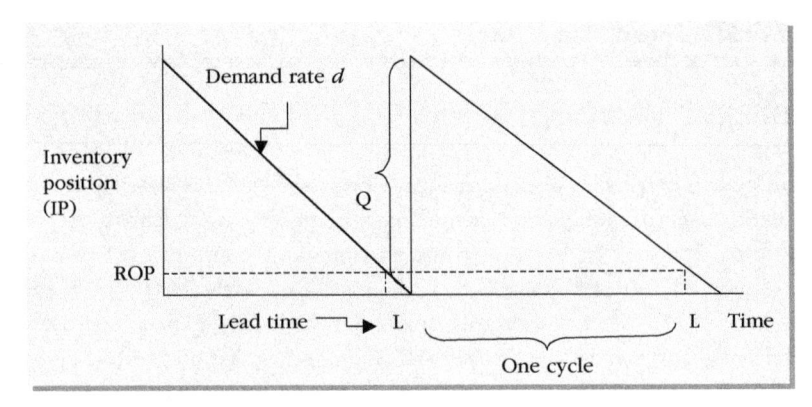

**FIGURE 9.2** Fixed-order quantity system.

ROP. Therefore, there are two variables that define this system and answer the two basic questions of when to order and how much: $Q$ and ROP. They specify when to place an order: *when inventory reaches the reorder point ROP*. They also specify how much to order: *the quantity Q*.

The fixed-order quantity model is shown in Figure 9.2. Notice that the system assumes a constant demand rate of $d$ by which the inventory position (IP) is reduced. When the IP reaches the reorder point (ROP), an order is placed for the quantity $Q$. When goods are received the inventory is replenished and the inventory position is increased by $Q$. However, inventory cannot arrive the moment an order is placed, as there is a certain amount of lead time, $L$, during which we have to wait for the order.

With this system inventory is checked on a continual basis, and the assumption is that we always know the current level of inventory. When inventory levels reach the reorder point ROP, an order of quantity $Q$ is placed. For example, let's assume that a hotel chain uses a fixed-order quantity system for its inventory of lavender bath soaps. Its policy is that it always orders 2,000 soaps, for which it gets a nice quantity discount, and the order is made when the number of soaps drops to 300. Therefore, the reorder point ROP = 300, and the order quantity $Q = 2,000$.

In the basic version of this system the order quantity $Q$ is computed as the economic order quantity (EOQ)—an economically optimal order quantity. For this reason this system is sometimes called the **EOQ model**. Other terms used to describe it are the **Q-model** as the quantity $Q$ is constant. Sometimes it is called a **continuous review system**, as the inventory levels are continuously monitored. The model has even been called a **sawtooth model**, as the graph of inventory looks like a sawtooth. All these terms refer to the same type of inventory system, describing different features of the system itself. Later in this chapter we will see how the EOQ value is computed.

## Fixed-Time Period System

The second inventory system is called a **fixed-time period system**, shown in Figure 9.3. Here inventory levels are checked in fixed time periods, $T$, and the quantity that is ordered varies. The system sets a target inventory level, $R$, to be maintained. Inventory is checked every $T$ intervals, say every week or every two weeks, and an order is placed to restore the inventory level back to $R$. Based on the inventory level at time period $T$, the amount of inventory that needs to be ordered will be some quantity $Q$ that varies from period to period. This quantity $Q$ is the difference between the target inventory $R$ and how much inventory is in stock, the inventory position ($IP$) at time $T$:

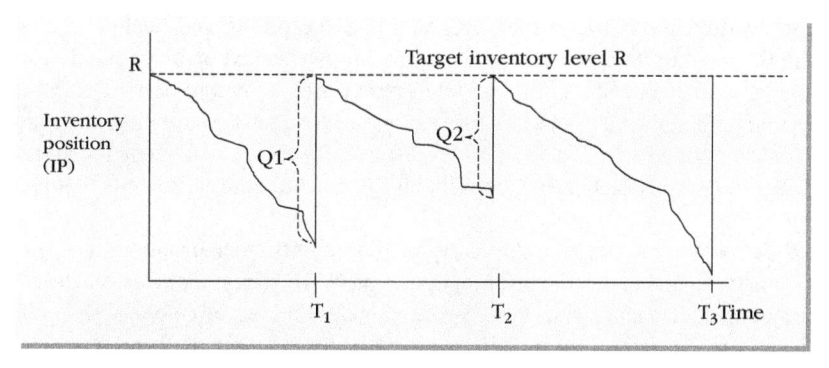

**FIGURE 9.3** Fixed-time period system.

$$Q = R - IP$$

where

$Q$ = order quantity

$R$ = target inventory level

$IP$ = inventory position

There are two variables that define this system and answer the two basic questions of when to order and how much are $T$ and $Q$. They specify when to place an order: *at time interval T*. They also specify how much to order: *quantity Q, computed as the difference between the target inventory, R, and the inventory position, IP*. Sometimes this system is called the **Periodic Review System** to indicate that the inventory level is checked periodically, rather than continuously.

Let's assume a hotel chain uses a fixed-time period model for its inventory of lavender bath soaps. Also, let's say its policy is to check inventory levels every two weeks, and that it has a target inventory level $R$ = 5,000 soaps. If after two weeks the company checks its inventory level and finds its inventory position $IP$ = 2,800 soaps, it would place an order for quantity $Q = R - IP$ = 5,000 − 2,800 = 2,200 soaps.

## Comparing Fixed-Order Quantity versus Fixed-Time Period Systems

Both inventory systems answer the question of when and how much to order, but they do it differently. Figure 9.4 shows a comparison of the two systems.

|  | Fixed-order quantity | Fixed-time period |
|---|---|---|
| How much to order? | Order quantity Q = EOQ | Order quantity Q = R − IP |
| When to order? | When inventory level drops to reorder point −ROP | When review period arrives—T |
| Order quantity | Fixed | Variable |
| Recordkeeping | Continual | Periodic—at review interval |
| Size of inventory | Lower | Higher |
| Time to maintain | Higher | Lower |
| Type of items | Higher valued items | Quantity discount options |

**FIGURE 9.4** Comparison of inventory systems.

The biggest difference between the two systems is the timing and quantities of the orders placed. With the fixed-order quantity system, inventory is checked on a continual basis, and the system is prepared to place orders multiple times per year on a random basis. This has an advantage of providing greater system responsiveness, but is also requires administrative processes to be in place on a continual basis. In addition, as different inventory items may reach their reorder points at different time periods, it may be difficult to obtain quantity discounts that are based on a bundled order.

The fixed-period order system requires carrying more safety stock inventory. The reason is that with this system we do not check the inventory position ($IP$) on a regular basis, and a sudden surge of demand could lead to a stock-out. This system, however, allows more organized purchasing as inventory levels are checked in set time intervals. Orders can be bundled and quantity discounts obtained easier. Imagine in our hotel example if the company used a fixed-order quantity model to place orders for various items, such as soaps, shampoos, lotions, and conditions. These different items may reach reorder points at different times generating many orders at random intervals. On the other hand, a fixed-period system could ensure that inventory levels are checked on a regular basis for all items, say every two weeks. Then the orders for all the items could be bundled.

In general, a fixed-order quantity system is more appropriate for high-value items as average inventory carried is lower. Also, it is more appropriate when stock-outs are less desirable, as inventory is monitored on a continual basis. However, this system is more costly to maintain as it requires technology to record all transactions and compute the inventory position in real time.

## Fixed-Order Quantity Systems

A fixed-order quantity system is one of the most important in inventory management. For that reason we need to look at how to compute the two variables that define it: the order quantity ($Q$) and the reorder point (ROP). Before we do that, however, we need look at the assumptions this system makes. Most important, the system assumes that all the variables occur at a constant rate and their values are known with certainty. For example, the system assumes that the demand, $d$, occurs at a constant rate and that there is no variability in demand. Also, the lead time $L$ is constant, the holding cost $H$ is known and fixed, as are stock-out cost $S$ and unit price $C$. Although these assumptions are not realistic, the model is highly robust and provides excellent results despite these assumptions.

### Economic Order Quantity (EOQ)

The first decision in the fixed-order quantity model is to select the order quantity $Q$. Recall that there are a number of inventory costs, most notably inventory holding cost and ordering cost. We want to select the "best" order quantity that minimizes these costs. This is called the economic order quantity or EOQ. This is computed by looking at the total annual inventory cost and finding the order quantity that minimizes it. Consider that the total annual cost comprises annual purchase cost, annual ordering cost, and annual holding cost and looks as follows:

$$\text{Total cost} = \text{Purchase cost} + \text{Ordering cost} + \text{Holding cost}$$

$$TC = DC + \left(\frac{D}{Q}\right)S + \left(\frac{Q}{2}\right)H$$

where

$TC$ = Total cost

$D$ = Annual demand

$C$ = Unit cost

$Q$ = Order quantity

$S$ = Ordering cost

$H$ = Holding cost

Let's look at these terms in a bit more detail:

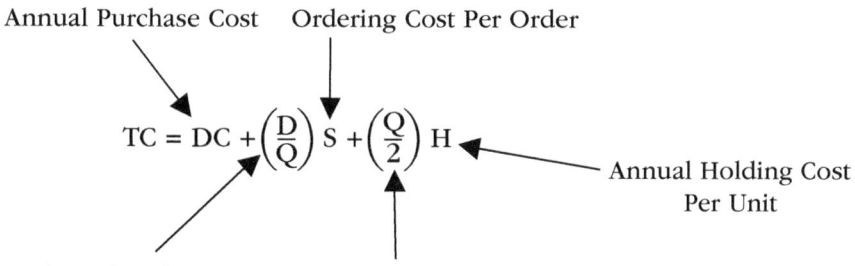

$$TC = DC + \left(\frac{D}{Q}\right)S + \left(\frac{Q}{2}\right)H$$

- Annual Purchase Cost: $DC$
- Ordering Cost Per Order: $S$
- Annual Holding Cost Per Unit: $H$
- Number of Orders Per Year: $\frac{D}{Q}$
- Average Annual Inventory: $\frac{Q}{2}$

The first term in the equation, $DC$ is the annual purchase cost for items. It comprises annual demand ($D$) times the unit cost of each item ($C$). The second term $\left(\frac{D}{Q}\right)S$ is the annual ordering cost. It is computed as the number of orders placed per year $\left(\frac{D}{Q}\right)$ times the cost of each order, $S$. Finally, the third term is annual holding cost where $\left(\frac{Q}{2}\right)$ is the average inventory held. Remember that our maximum inventory is $Q$ units when the order is received. When inventory is depleted we have zero. Therefore on average we have $\frac{Q}{2}$ units in inventory. $H$ is the annual holding cost per unit of inventory. Recall that H is a percentage computed as $H = IC$.

The behavior of the two costs is shown in Figure 9.5. Notice that inventory holding cost increases with the order quantity, $Q$. The reason is that higher order quantities mean holding more inventory. However, this also means that we are ordering less frequently, so ordering cost decreases. The opposite is true as the order quantity $Q$ is decreased. A smaller order quantity results in a lower holding cost, but a higher ordering cost, as we are ordering more frequently.

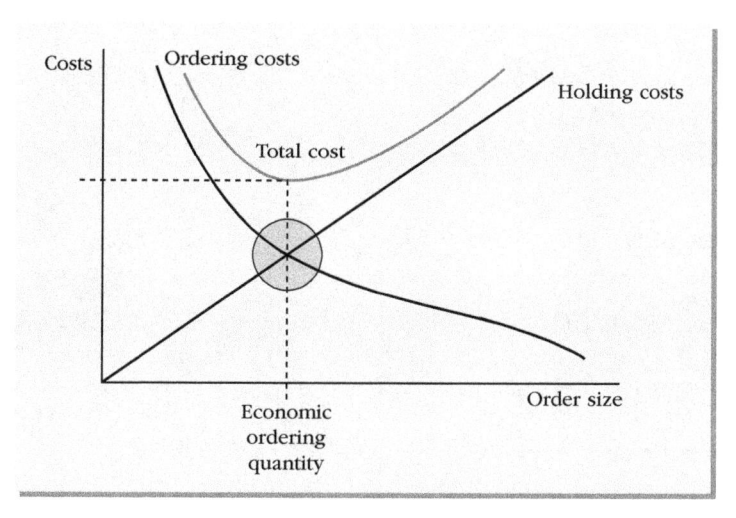

**FIGURE 9.5** Total cost curve.

## INVENTORY MANAGEMENT

The objective is to pick an order quantity that minimizes the sum of both the holding and ordering costs, which is the minimum point on the total cost curve. This is the "best" or optimal order quantity, $Q_{opt}$, also called the economic order quantity (EOQ). To find the minimum point on the total cost curve we use calculus. We take the derivative of total cost ($TC$) with respect to $Q$ and set this equal to zero. For the basic model considered here, the calculations are as follows.

1. Total cost equation:

$$TC = DC + \frac{D}{Q}S + \frac{Q}{2}H$$

2. First derivative of total cost equation:

$$\frac{TC}{dQ} = 0 + \frac{-DS}{Q^2} + \frac{H}{2} = 0$$

3. Solving the above equation for $Q$ we compute $Q_{opt}$, also called the EOQ:

$$Q_{opt} = EOQ = \sqrt{\frac{2DS}{H}}$$

This is the EOQ, or the "best" quantity to order in the fixed-order quantity system to minimize the sum of inventory cost and ordering cost.

### Example 1  Computing the EOQ at Georgia's Florists

You have taken over as inventory manager at Georgia's Florists. You would like to use EOQ to compute the best quantity of orchids to order. The previous manager at Georgia's ordered orchids once a month in quantities of 1,000 to simply match the monthly demand. Orchids are expensive to order with an ordering cost of $300 per order. Holding cost is estimated at 15% of product cost annually, with a product cost of $60 per unit.

What would be your order? What is the number of orders per year? What is the annual holding cost? Assuming four weeks/month and a lead time of one week, what is the reorder point?

**SOLUTION:** You were given the following information:

Annual demand (D) = 1,000 orchids per month × 12 months = 12,000 orchids
Holding cost (H) = (.15) 60 per unit
Ordering cost (S) = $300 per order

Computing the EOQ:

$$EOQ = \sqrt{\frac{2DS}{H}} = \sqrt{2\frac{(12{,}000 \text{ units})(\$300)}{(.15)\$60}} = 894.5 \approx 895$$

$$\text{Orders Per Year} = \frac{D}{Q} = \frac{12{,}000}{895} = 13.4$$

$$\text{Annual Holding Cost} = \left(\frac{Q}{2}\right)H = \left(\frac{895}{2}\right)\$9 = \$4{,}028$$

## Reorder Point (ROP)

The EOQ answers the question of how much to order, but we still need to determine when to order. Assume that the demand rate, $d$, and lead time ($L$) are constant and known with certainty. In that case the reorder point would simply be enough inventory to ensure that demand is covered during the length of the lead time. In this simple case, the reorder point would be computed as:

$$ROP = \text{demand during lead time}$$
$$ROP = d\,L$$

Let's go back to the Georgia Florists example. If lead time $L$ is one week and the demand, $d$, is 250 units per week, the ROP would be:

$$\text{Reorder Point} = ROP = d \times L = 1 \text{ week} \times 250 = 250 \text{ units}$$

The order policy for Georgia's Florists would be defined by the EOQ and ROP. This would mean ordering 895 orchids when inventory drops to 250 orchids.

## Safety Stock

Unfortunately, $d$ and $L$ are rarely fixed, and demand is often higher than expected. As a result we have to carry a bit more inventory to address this uncertainty. This is called **safety stock** or **buffer stock** and is inventory we carry in addition to the demand during lead time. Safety stock is added to the ROP calculation and is computed as follows:

$$ROP = \text{demand during lead time} + \text{safety stock}$$
$$ROP = d\,L + SS$$
$$ROP = d\,L + Z_k \sigma_L$$

We can see that $SS$ is equal to $Z_k \sigma_L$. Let's look at this second term in the equation to see what it means. $Z_k$ is the value of the standard normal variable for a particular service level $k$. The service level, $k$, is simply the probability that we will *not* run out of stock. This is set by the company based on the level of service they wish to provide for a particular product and customer base. Higher service levels mean higher levels of inventory. For example, a service level $k$ of 95% means a 95% probability of being in stock and a 5% probability (100% − 95%) of being out of stock. The value of $Z$ is obtained from the standard normal table in the back of the text for a particular value of $k$.

The service level, $k$, can be set in two ways:

1. Directly. This is a specified percentage, such as 95% service level.
2. Indirectly. This may be in terms of the number of stock-outs tolerated, such as five stock-outs per year. If we know the number of orders per year, we can then compute the value of $k$.

The second part of this term, $\sigma_L$, is standard deviation of demand over the lead time $L$. The higher the variability, the higher the standard deviation (computed as the square root of variance), the higher the safety stock.

### Example 2 Computing Safety Stock at Georgia's Florists

Earlier we computed an EOQ and ROP for Georgia's Florists, but assumed no safety stock. Let's now compute the amount of safety stock and the new ROP, assuming that you desire a 95% service level.

**SOLUTION:** We know the following:

$$\text{Demand (D)} = 1{,}000 \text{ orchids per month}$$
$$\text{Lead time (L)} = 1 \text{ week}$$
$$\sigma_L^2 = 64$$
$$k = 95\%$$

We then compute the ROP:

$$\text{ROP} = \text{demand during lead time} + \text{safety stock}$$
$$\text{ROP} = d\,L + SS$$
$$\text{ROP} = d\,L + Z_k \sigma_L$$
$$\text{ROP} = (250 \text{ units})(1 \text{ week}) + 1.645\sqrt{64} = 263.16 \approx 263 \text{ units}$$

Therefore, the new order policy would be to order 895 orchids when inventory drops to 263 orchids.

## Economic Production Quantity (EPQ)

The fixed-order quantity model assumes that the EOQ arrives in one lump sum after the order is placed. In the Georgia's Florists example, all the ordered orchids arrived in one shipment. This meant that the company had to have physical space for the entire EOQ quantity. Sometimes, however, the products ordered are made in-house or in close proximity. In that case the producing operation may not wait to produce all $Q$ units before passing them on to the operation that ordered them. This is called the **economics production quantity (EPQ)** and sometimes it is called the **production rate model**. The variables that define this model are still $Q$ and ROP, as these define how much to order and when. However, the computation of $Q$ is a little bit different.

Consider Samba Chocolate Co., which produces a variety of chocolates and makes their own packaging for their specialty chocolate: turtle truffles. The turtle truffle wrapping is made immediately next door to chocolate production. The chocolate production department orders the special wrapping from the packaging department. However, the packaging department does not wait to make all $Q$ units of wrapping before they get it to chocolate production. Rather, they begin passing the wrapping to chocolate production as it is being produced. If the wrapping is made at a rate of 80 units per day and chocolate production uses it at a rate of 60 units per day, the inventory will build up at a rate of 20 units per day. This is shown in Figure 9.6.

Figure 9.7 illustrates the way the EPQ system works. As with the basic fixed-order quantity model, a quantity $Q$ is ordered at the ROP. The production process starts at a rate of $p$. However, as the product is produced it is used at a rate of $d$, with $d \leq p$, and inventory builds up at rate of $p - d$. Production stops once the ordered quantity $Q$ has been made. This is one cycle. The cycle beings again when the ROP is reached.

## Fixed-Order Quantity Systems

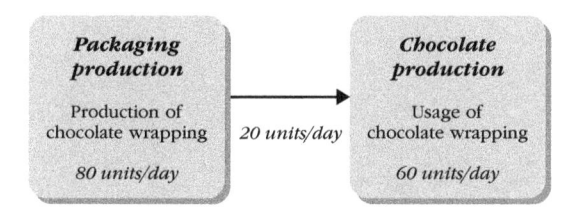

**FIGURE 9.6** Production and demand at Samba Chocolate Co.

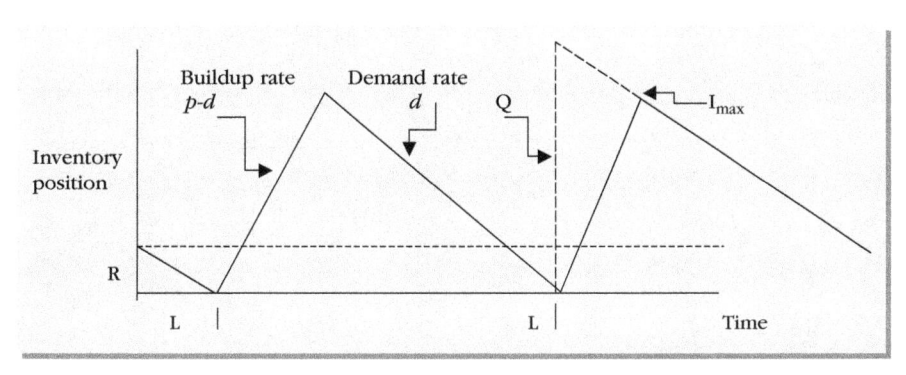

**Packaging production** — Production of chocolate wrapping — 80 units/day — 20 units/day — **Chocolate production** — Usage of chocolate wrapping — 60 units/day

**FIGURE 9.7** Economic production quantity system.

Notice that with this system we hold less inventory than with the basic EOQ system. The reason is that here we are using part of the inventory while it is being produced. The broken line in Figure 9.7 shows the amount of inventory $Q$ that we would hold if the inventory was received all at once. Instead, the maximum amount of inventory that we hold—$I_{max}$—is shown as the inventory peak.

The optimal quantity that should be ordered in this situation is different from the traditional EOQ as the inventory holding cost is lower. As before, to compute the optimal order quantity $Q_{opt}$ we begin with the total cost equation:

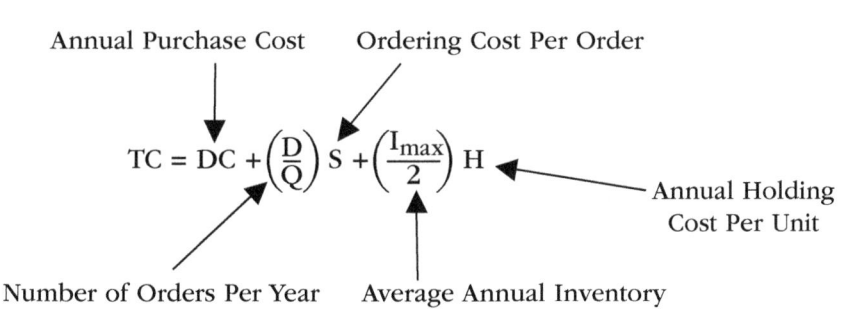

$$TC = DC + \left(\frac{D}{Q}\right)S + \left(\frac{I_{max}}{2}\right)H$$

- Annual Purchase Cost: $DC$
- Ordering Cost Per Order: $S$
- Number of Orders Per Year: $D/Q$
- Average Annual Inventory: $I_{max}/2$
- Annual Holding Cost Per Unit: $H$

Notice that in this equation the average annual inventory is computed as $\frac{I_{max}}{2}$ rather than $\frac{Q}{2}$ as in the basic EOQ derivation. The reason is that the maximum inventory we hold is no longer $Q$, but is $I_{max}$.

To compute the $Q_{opt}$ consider the following. Time to produce Q units is $\frac{Q}{p}$. During this time we lose to demand $d\left(\frac{Q}{p}\right)$ units. Therefore, the maximum held in inventory, $I_{max}$, computed as:

$$I_{max} = Q - d\frac{Q}{p}$$

$$I_{max} = Q\left(1 - \frac{d}{p}\right)$$

# INVENTORY MANAGEMENT

where

$d$ = daily demand rate

$p$ = daily production rate

Substituting this into the total cost equation we get the following:

$$TC = DC + \frac{D}{Q}S + \left(p - \frac{d}{2p}\right)QH$$

Using calculus we solve for $Q$ obtaining the equation for $Q_{opt}$:

$$Q_{opt} = \sqrt{\frac{2DS}{H}\frac{p}{(p-d)}} = \sqrt{\frac{2DS}{H\left(1-\frac{d}{p}\right)}}$$

### Example 3  Calculating EPQ and $I_{max}$

A bicycle manufacturer uses 50,000 wheels per year for its popular children's cycle. The firm makes its own wheels, which it can produce at a rate of 600 per day. The bicycles are assembled uniformly over the entire year. Carrying cost is $1 per wheel a year, and setup cost for a production run of wheels is $45. Considering that the plant operates 250 days per year, find the order quantity and $I_{max}$.

**SOLUTION:** The order quantity here is the EPQ. We just need to substitute values provided into the equation as follows.

$$Q_{opt} = \sqrt{\frac{2DS}{H}\frac{p}{(p-d)}} = \sqrt{\frac{2DS}{H\left(1-\frac{d}{p}\right)}}$$

Be careful when substituting to make sure that the units of time are the same in each denominator. Demand is given to be 50,000 wheels *per year*, which we use in the first denominator as holding cost $H$ is also given *per year*. However, the production rate $p$ is given *per day*, and we must convert demand to a daily rate here.

$$D = 50,000 \frac{\text{wheels}}{\text{year}}$$

$$d = \frac{50,000 \text{ wheels}}{250 \text{ days}} = 200 \frac{\text{wheels}}{\text{day}}$$

$$Q_{opt} = EPQ = \sqrt{\frac{2\left(50,000 \frac{\text{wheels}}{\text{year}}\right)\$45/\text{order}}{\$1 \text{ per wheel/year}} \frac{600 \text{ wheels/day}}{600 \text{ wheels/day} - 200 \text{ wheels/day}}}$$

$$Q_{OPT} = EPQ = 2,598.07 \text{ wheels} \approx 2,598 \text{ wheels}$$

$$I_{max} = Q\left(1 - \frac{d}{p}\right) = 2,598\left(1 - \frac{200}{600}\right) = 1,732 \text{ wheels}$$

Although the order is 2,598 wheels, there only needs to be space for 1,732 wheels.

## Big Data Analytics Box—Analytics Driven Inventory

### ■ DELL

Just a few years ago Dell customers could order customized computer configurations on the company's website using the company's configure-to-order model. Customers could design their computers choosing variations in models, software configurations, memory, screens, design, and numerous other features. These large options were great for customers. However, the combination of options created a huge challenge for Dell as this resulted in over seven septillion possible computer configurations—mathematically $10^{24}$ number of combinations. In practical terms this created an inventory mess.

The company then turned to an analytically driven system to optimize inventory decisions. The goal was to satisfy the diverse needs of a broad set of customers but also keep costs as low as possible. The analytics team decided to use historical order data to run cluster analysis to determine the most common configurations customers were choosing. Cluster analysis revealed that there was a lot of commonality in ordering. Going through the data, they were able to reduce the seven septillion options down to just a few million. They were then able to identify certain models so common that the company could stock them in preconfigured inventory just waiting to be shipped. These common configurations could then be built ahead of time with the lowest margins, kept in inventory and, if ordered today, the customer could have them tomorrow. The new analytically driven system increased customer service and reduced inventory cost, and resulted in an additional $40 million in revenue.

Adapted from: Hessman, Travis. "Putting Big Data to Work." *Industry Week*, April 2013, pp. 14–18.

## Fixed-Time Period Systems

In a fixed-time period system, inventory levels are checked in regularly set time intervals. The goal is to place an order to restore the inventory position to the target inventory level $R$. Therefore, the quantity that is ordered at time interval $T$ is

$$Q = R - IP$$

where

$Q$ = order quantity

$R$ = target inventory level

$IP$ = inventory position at time $T$

In this system the questions of *when to order* and *how much* are set as follows. Orders are placed at time interval $T$. This time interval is typically set for organizational convenience. For example, it may be every week, every two weeks, or once a month. The ordering process requires administrative responsibility, and the organization decides what is most convenient. Also, sometimes suppliers make routine visits to customers, and this timing may be considered when setting $T$. Finally $T$ can even be set as the time interval that would allow for a certain quantity $Q$ to be used up. This could be, for example, the optimal order quantity EOQ:

$$T = \frac{Q}{d}$$

$$T = \frac{EOQ}{d}$$

The quantity $Q$ that is ordered is the amount that will restore inventory levels back to $R$, the target inventory level. Therefore, the important decision is computing the target inventory level.

## Computing Target Inventory

The target inventory level needs to be large enough to cover three types of demand:

1. Demand during the length of the lead time $L$
2. Demand during the length of the review period $T$
3. Safety stock, $SS$, to guard against uncertainty

Therefore, the target inventory level can be computed as follows:

$$R = \text{demand during lead time} + \text{demand during review period} + \text{safety stock}$$
$$R = dL + dT + Z_k \sigma_{L+T}$$

As before, $Z_k$ is the standard normal variable for the desired service level. However, standard deviation of demand is now over both the length of the lead time $L$ and the review period $T$. Sometimes the standard deviation is provided over another time period $t$, other than the specified $L + T$. It is easy to make a mathematical conversation using the following equation:

$$R = DL + DT + Z_k \sigma_t \sqrt{\frac{L+T}{t}}$$

where

$t$ = interval over which standard deviation is given

$L$ = lead time

$T$ = review interval

Notice that the demand, lead time, and review period are over length of time, such as days, weeks, or years. Remember, however, that this length must be the same throughout the equation.

### Example 4 Computation of the Fixed-Time Period System

Gordon's Potato Chips reviews inventory every 14 days, with demand and lead time given below:

$$T = 14 \text{ days}$$
$$D = 30 \text{ units per days}$$
$$L = 7 \text{ days}$$
$$\sigma_{day} = 10 \text{ units}$$

If the company tolerates no more than two stock-outs per year, develop the ordering policy for a fixed-time period inventory system.

**SOLUTION:** Remember that an ordering policy specifies when to order and how much. Here we know that orders are placed every 14 days. To determine how much to order we must first compute the target inventory level R and substitute known values:

$$R = dL + dT + SS$$

$$R = 30 \text{ units/day (7 days)} + 30 \text{ units/day (14 days)} + Z_k(10)\sqrt{\frac{7+14}{1}}$$

Notice that we still have to compute $k$, the cycle service level. Let's look at what we know:

two stock-outs per year

an order placed every two weeks

52 weeks/year means 26 orders per year (52/2)

Therefore, the service level

$$k = \frac{26-2}{26} = .9231$$

$$Z_{92.3} = 1.426$$

$$R = 630 + 1.426(10)\sqrt{21} = 692 \text{ units}$$

Therefore, the ordering policy is to check inventory every two weeks and order the quantity that will restore inventory to 692 units.

# Independent versus Dependent Demand

One of the biggest differences in inventory is between dependent and independent demand. Understanding this difference is important, as the entire inventory policy for an item is based on this. **Independent demand** is demand for a finished product, such as a computer, a bicycle, or a pizza. **Dependent demand**, on the other hand, is demand for component parts or subassemblies. For example, this would be the microchips in the computer, the wheels on the bicycle, or the amount of cheese on the pizza.

The inventory systems we discussed thus far are for independent demand. Dependent demand is derived from its independent demand. We can forecast the amount of bicycles we expect to sell, then we can derive the quantities needed of wheels, tires, frame, and other component parts. For example, if a company plans to produce 200 bicycles in a day, it would need 400 wheels, 400 tires, and 200 frames. The number of wheels, tires, frames, and other component parts is dependent on the quantity of the independent demand item from which it is derived.

The relationship between independent and dependent demand is shown in a **bill of materials (BOM)**, which can be in the form of a table or a visual diagram. An example is shown in Figure 9.8. Item A is the independent demand item. All the other items are dependent demand. The quantities that go into the final item are shown in parentheses. Notice that two units of C are combined with one unit of B to make the final product. Similarly, two units of D and one unit of E are combined to make one unit of B.

Dependent demand order quantities are computed using a system called **material requirements planning (MRP)**, which considers not only the quantities of each of the component parts needed, but also the lead times needed to produce and receive the items. For example, 20 units of A means that 20 units of B are needed, as are 40 units of C. Similarly, 40 units of D and 20 units of E are needed. However, the system must also take into account differences in lead times, as

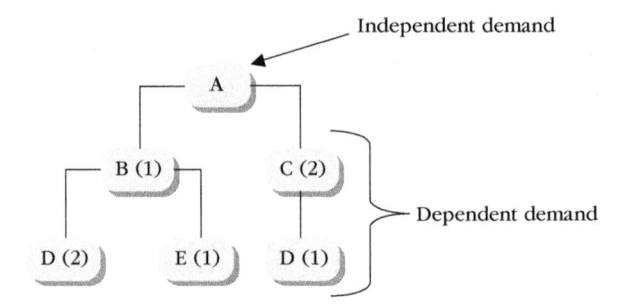

**FIGURE 9.8** A simple bill of materials (BOM).

receiving D may have a different lead time than receiving E. This means that the orders should be placed at different times. This system can also be tied to costs of goods and can link internal and external members of the supply chain. This is called **enterprise resource planning (ERP)**, discussed in Chapter 3.

## Global Insights Box

### ■ INTEL CORPORATION

Companies that make component parts are highly dependent on the success of the final product— their independent demand item. An example of this is Intel Corporation, which has become famous for their microprocessors, or chips, that run PCs. The problem for Intel has been the declining PC market, signaling a decline in demand for their chips and the famous "Intel inside" logo.

To leverage its dependent demand position, Intel has come up with a new strategy. The company understands that there is a limit to where their core business will take them. As a result they have pushed to be inside more than just PCs. They understand that their growth depends on sales of their independent demand items and are counting on other markets to break their dependence on the slowing PC market. The company is pushing to promote the fact that they are now inside a range of "Intel-powered devices," ranging from 3-D printers and robot assembly lines, to solar-powered cars and fitness trackers. Intel is also developing chips to power drones, sensors, and robot butlers, rather than just PCs. The company cannot change its dependent demand position but it can expand the range of independent demand items it supplies. Therefore, the strategy is to make Intel inside everything.

Adapted from: "Intel Wants to Be Inside Everything," *Bloomberg Businessweek*, September 6-12, 2010.

## Managing Supply Chain Inventory

The quantitative models we discussed help managers determine when and how much to order. However, managers should not just follow the models blindly. There are a number of practical implications to consider when managing supply chain inventories. We discuss these here.

### ABC Inventory Classification

All items in the supply chain are not of equal importance. Some are very important, such as specialized surgical equipment. Others are less important, such as latex gloves in a hospital. The first step in managing inventory is to classify inventory based on its degree of importance in order to manage it properly. The tool for this is ABC classification. Classifying inventory based on degree of importance allows us to give priority to important inventory items and manage those with care. It also prevents us from wasting precious resources on managing items that are of less importance.

Managing Supply Chain Inventory

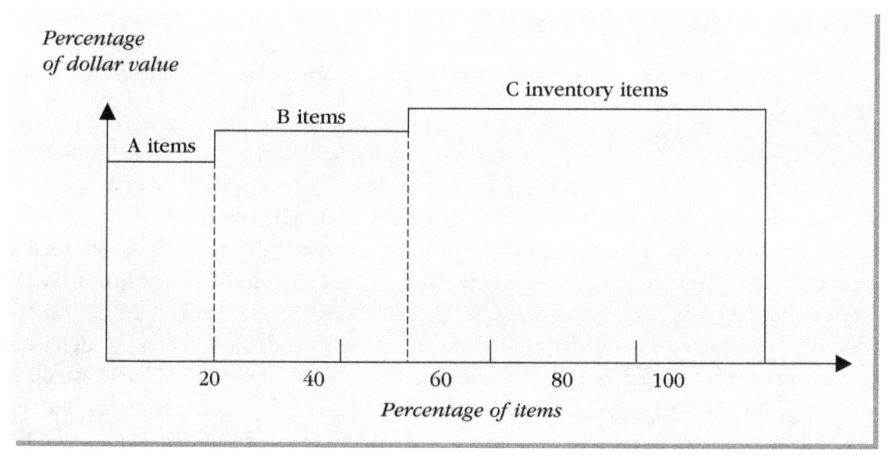

**FIGURE 9.9** ABC classification of inventory.

ABC classification is based on Pareto's law, which states that a small percentage of items account for a large percentage of value. This value can be sales, profits, or other measure of importance. Roughly 10% to 20% of inventory items account for 70% to 80% of inventory value. These highly valuable items are classified as A inventory items. Moderate value items account for approximately 30% of inventory items and contribute to roughly 35% of the total. They are called B items. Finally, approximately 50% of the items only contribute to roughly 10 percent of total inventory value. These are called C items and are of least importance. Figure 9.9 provides an example of ABC analysis.

Conducting an ABC classification of inventory is quite easy. The steps are as follows:

1. Determine annual usage or sales for each item.
2. Determine the percentage of the total usage or sales by item.
3. Rank the items from highest to lowest percentage.
4. Classify the items into groups.

After ranking the items from highest to lowest percentage, do not force groups to fit the preset percentages, as these are rough estimates. Rather, there are typically natural breaking points that will occur. The data will naturally group itself, and these are groupings that should be used.

ABC analysis is extremely important for determining order policies. The most sophisticated inventory systems should be used for A items. In fact, many managers personally oversee these. By contrast, C items are typically left for automated ordering systems as they do not warrant the cost of managerial involvement.

ABC analysis is also important in establishing safety stock levels. Remember that safety stock is extra inventory held to guard against uncertainty of demand and prevent stock-outs. All inventory items are not of equal importance, and the safety stock policy will be different based on ABC classification. The importance of not running out of stock of a particular item will enter the safety stock computation through the service level component, $k$. For example, a service level of 80% results in a significantly lower safety stock than a 98% service level. ABC classification is a critical part of the stocking decision given the costs of holding extra inventory, as well as the costs of stocking out.

## Practical Considerations of EOQ

A number of practical considerations must be taken into account when using the EOQ, rather than applying it blindly.

1. **Lumpy Demand (POQ).** EOQ assumes demand to be uniform. However, product demand can sometimes be "lumpy." This means that it occurs in a discontinuous or nonuniform fashion, with some periods exhibiting high demand and then other periods having zero demand. Using EOQ in this case results in carrying too much inventory over periods with no demand. A more practical option here is to use something called a **periodic order quantity (POQ)**.

   As with EOQ, the logic behind the POQ is to balance ordering and holding costs. The difference, however, is that ordering is done in whole periods of demand. To determine the number of periods to order, the first step is to compute the EOQ quantity. Next, we determine the average number of periods of demand covered by the EOQ, and then order that quantity rounding up. For example, let's say that weekly demand is 120 units with an EOQ of 350 units. This means the EOQ covers an average of 350/120 = 2.9 weeks of demand. This rounds to an "economic order period" of three weeks, meaning that we always order three weeks of demand at a time. This is the POQ.

2. **EOQ Adjustments.** Recall that the EOQ was computed as the minimum point on the total cost curve. However, this total cost curve is pretty flat around the minimum point. It is a soft curve rather than a sharp minimum point. This means that ordering slightly above or below the minimum point does not substantially change the total cost. This allows managers to increase or decrease the EOQ—within reason, of course—to accommodate container sizes, truck loads, and various types of discounts.

3. **Capacity Constraints.** When computing anticipation inventory we typically consider the balance between inventory holding cost and anticipated costs we are trying to avoid. One additional factor that needs to be considered is capacity or storage size. Ordering extra inventories to hedge against a price increase may result in unanticipated expenses if additional storage space needs to be leased.

## Measuring Inventory Performance

Inventory impacts the supply chain both in terms of customer service and cost. Given its importance, success of inventory policy must be measured and evaluated on a regular basis. The most common metrics to measure inventory are

1. Units
2. Dollars
3. Weeks of Supply
4. Inventory Turns

The first two measures directly address the number of units available and the dollars tied up in inventory. The last two measures were discussed in Chapter 7. Recall that "weeks of supply" is a measure of inventory quantity relative to usage, and "inventory turnover" gives us a sense of inventory movement. Their computations are as follows:

$$\text{Weeks of supply} = \frac{\text{Average on-hand inventory}}{\text{Average weekly usage}}$$

$$\text{Inventory turnover} = \frac{\text{Cost of goods sold}}{\text{Average inventory value}}$$

In Chapter 7 we were given average inventory value. Now that we know a bit about ordering policy we can compute it as follows:

$$\text{Average inventory value} = \left(\frac{Q}{2} + SS\right)C$$

The inventory turnover for an individual item is then computed as:

$$\text{Inventory turnover} = \frac{DC}{\left(\frac{Q}{2} + SS\right)C} = \frac{D}{\frac{Q}{2} + SS}$$

### Example 5  Average Inventory Calculation

Suppose that an item is being managed using a fixed-order quantity model with safety stock. The following information is given:

$$\text{Annual Demand } (D) = 1{,}000 \text{ units}$$
$$\text{Order quantity } (Q) = 250 \text{ units}$$
$$\text{Safety stock } (SS) = 50 \text{ units}$$

What are the average inventory and inventory turn for the item?

### SOLUTION:

$$\text{Average inventory} = \frac{Q}{2} + SS = \frac{250}{2} + 50 = 175 \text{ units}$$

$$\text{Inventory turnover} = \frac{D}{\left(\frac{Q}{2} + SS\right)} = \frac{1{,}000}{175} = 5.71 \text{ turns per year}$$

## Vendor Managed Inventory (VMI)

Historically companies owned and managed all of their inventories. They were responsible for the storing, controlling, replenishing, and overall management of the inventory. With supply chain management (SCM), most of this has changed. Today, many firms have implemented vendor managed inventory (VMI) arrangements. Here, the vendor is responsible for managing the inventory located at a customer's facility. The vendor stocks the inventory, places replenishment orders, and arranges its display. The vendor typically own the inventory until it is purchased by the customer.

VMI offers a number of important advantages to both the customer and the vendor. The vendor has greater control over their product. They are required to work much more closely with the customer, giving them better understanding of how to serve the market. The customer, in turn, has less responsibility and financial burden over the inventory items. VMI requires both the vendor and customer to work closely together. It represents one of the many partnership arrangements that have evolved in SCM.

## CHAPTER HIGHLIGHTS

1. There are many reasons for carrying inventory. They include protecting against lead time demand, maintaining independence of operations, balancing supply and demand, buffering against uncertainty, and achieving economic purchase orders.

2. There are different types of inventory intended for different purposes. Inventory types are *cycle stock, safety stock, anticipation inventory, pipeline inventory,* and *MRO*.

3. The three inventory costs are *holding cost, ordering cost,* and *shortage cost*. Inventory holding cost includes all the costs involved with holding inventory in stock. Ordering cost is the cost of placing an order. Shortage cost is the cost associated with being out of stock, such as loss of customer goodwill and possible lost sales.

4. Inventory systems answer two basic questions: *when to order* and *how much to order*. Two of the most common types of inventory systems are *fixed-order quantity system* and *fixed-time period system*.

5. In a fixed-order quantity system the order placed is constant or fixed. An order is placed when the inventory position drops to the reorder point, noted as ROP. In the basic fixed-order quantity system the order quantity is computed as an economic order quantity or EOQ. When production directly feeds demand, then it is computed as an economic production quantity or EPQ.

6. In a fixed-time period system orders are placed in regular time intervals denoted by $T$. The order that is placed varies and is the quantity that will return the IP to a target inventory level, denoted as $R$.

7. Independent demand is *demand for a finished product*, such as a computer, a bicycle, or a pizza. Dependent demand is *demand for component parts or subassemblies* that are a result of the independent demand item.

8. To manage inventory properly it must be classified based on its degree of importance. The tool for this is ABC classification. This allows us to give priority to important inventory items and manage those with care, while not wasting resources on items that are of less importance. A inventory items are of highest importance and must be monitored carefully. B items are classified as moderate importance, and C items are of least importance.

9. Inventory must be measured and evaluated on a regular basis given its impact on cost and customer service. The most common ways to measure inventory are in units, dollars, weeks of supply, and inventory turns.

10. Vendor managed inventory (VMI) is an arrangement where the vendor is responsible for managing the inventory located at a customer's facility. The vendor stocks the inventory, places replenishment orders, and arranges its display. The vendor typically own the inventory until it is purchased by the customer.

## KEY TERMS

| | | | | |
|---|---|---|---|---|
| Raw materials | Transportation inventory | Fixed-order quantity system | Periodic Review system | Material requirements planning (MRP) |
| Component parts | Holding cost | EOQ model | Safety stock | Enterprise resource planning (ERP) |
| Work-in-process | Ordering cost | Q-model | Buffer stock | Periodic order quantity (POQ) |
| Finished goods | Shortage cost | Continuous review system | Economics production quantity (EPQ) | |
| Service inventory | Carrying cost | Sawtooth model | Production rate model | |
| Inventory policy | Dollar value | Fixed-time period system | Independent demand | |
| Seasonal inventory | Percentage of item cost | | Dependent demand | |
| Hedge inventory | Setup cost | | Bill of materials (BOM) | |

## DISCUSSION QUESTIONS

1. Identify an example of inventory in your own life. Estimate how much it costs you to hold this inventory. Estimate the "ordering cost." How often do you replenish this inventory, and which of the inventory policies does this most closely resemble?

2. Think of a service you recently used. How might this service be restructured to create service inventory as in the example of Zoots? What would they have to do? What advantages would the company gain, and how would they better serve their customers?

3. Find at least one business example of a fixed-order quantity system versus a fixed-period quantity system. What are their differences? Which do you think is better, and why?

4. Provide an example of ABC classification in a business you are familiar with. What would be the A inventory items versus B and C? What ordering policies would you use for each of these?

5. Identify an example of VMI. Explain the benefits to both the vendor and retailer. Identify some of the risks for both parties.

## PROBLEMS

1. Ricky Orange's annual demand is 12,500 units. Ordering cost is $100 per order. Holding cost is estimated at 20% of product cost, which is $50 per unit. What is the number of orders per year using EOQ to compute the best quantity to order? What is the annual holding cost? What is the reorder point? Assume four weeks/month, lead time $L$ is one week, and demand rate is 250 units per week.

2. You are inventory manager of Diego Supplies Inc. You computed the EOQ to be 500 units. Annual demand for the company is 5,000 units, and holding cost is $4 per unit. What is the ordering cost?

3. G-Tech's monthly demand is 250 units. You are in charge of the inventory department. You know that the holding cost is $60 per unit and ordering cost is $100 per order. What is the EOQ? What is the number of orders per year? What is the annual holding cost? If lead time $L$ is one week and demand rate is 60 units per week, what is the ROP?

4. We know that Blue Pad Company's lead time $L$ is one week and demand rate is 100 units per week. Compute the amount of Safety Stock and new ROP, assuming that the company desires a 98% service level. Standard deviation of demand over lead time is eight.

5. Bright Light computed their new ROP to be 116.45. Assume that lead time $L$ is one week and demand rate is 100 units per week. What is the company's desired service level, assuming standard deviation of demand over lead time is 10?

6. Basic Code Tech desires a 95% service level to compute their safety stock. Variance of demand over lead time is 64. We computed its new ROP to be 14.16. What is the demand rate per week if we assume its lead time L is one week?

7. The Yacht Company builds personal yachts. Its annual demand is 10 yachts. This company can build at a rate of one yacht per month. Carrying cost is very expensive and is about $10,000 per year. The setup cost for a production run of yachts is $2,000. Find the order quantity and $I_{max}$.

8. Linden Jet's annual demand is 20. It can build at a rate of four jets per month. The setup cost for a production run of jets is $1,000. Find the order quantity and $I_{max}$, assuming carrying cost is $1,000 per year.

9. Lugini Watch's annual demand is 100. It can produce at a rate of 10 watches per month with a $100 setup cost for the production run. Find the order quantity and $I_{max}$, assuming carrying cost is $100 per unit.

10. Apple Cakes reviews inventory every two weeks with lead time of seven days, demand rate 40 units per day, and standard deviation five units per day. If the company tolerates no more than one stock-out per year, develop the ordering policy for a fixed-time period inventory system assuming 52 weeks per year.

11. Ice Ginger reviews inventory every two weeks. As the inventory manager of the company, you know that its lead time is seven days and its demand rate is 40 units per day. Given variance is 25 units per day, you calculated the target inventory level to be 881 units. Now, how many stock-outs per year are permitted by the company assuming 52 weeks per year? Show all calculations.

12. Pure Grapes reviews inventory every week. Lead time $L$ is seven days, and demand rate is 100 units per day. You know the company's standard deviation is 10 units per day and allows one stock-out per year. Develop the ordering policy for a fixed-time period inventory system assuming 52 weeks per year and 95% service level.

## REFERENCES

Callioni, Gianpaolo, Xavier de Montgros, Regine Slagmulder, Luk N. Van Wassenhove, and Linda Wright. "Inventory Driven Costs." *Harvard Business Review*, March 2005: 135–141.

Cohen, Morris A. "Inventory Management in the Age of Big Data." *Harvard Business Review*, June 24, 2015.

Council of Supply Chain Management Professionals, Matthew A. Waller, and Terry L. Esper. *The Definitive Guide to Inventory Management: Principles and Strategies for the Efficient Flow of Inventory across the Supply Chain*. Upper Saddle River, NJ: Pearson, 2014.

Lee, H. L. "Aligning Supply Chain Strategies with Product Uncertainties." *California Management Review*, 44(3), Spring 2002: 105–119.

Silver, Edward E., David F. Pyke, and Rein Peterson. *Inventory Management, Production Planning, and Scheduling*, 3rd ed. New York: John Wiley & Sons, 1998.

Timme, Stephen G., and Christine Williams-Timme. "The Real Cost of Holding." *Supply Chain Management Review*, July/August 2003: 30–37.

# 10 Lean Systems and Six-Sigma Quality

**LEARNING OBJECTIVES**

*After completing this chapter, you should be able to:*

- Describe Lean and Six Sigma, and explain the benefits of "Lean Six Sigma."
- Identify elements of the Lean philosophy.
- Explain Lean production.
- Explain Total Quality Management (TQM).
- Explain Statistical Process Control (SQC).
- Describe the Lean Six Sigma supply chain.

**CHAPTER OUTLINE**

■ **What Is Lean?**
  *Lean Six Sigma*
  *Lean Philosophy*
  *Elements of Lean*

■ **Lean Production**
  *The Pull System*
  *Visual Signals*
  *Small Lot Production*
  *Uniform Plant Loading*

■ **Respect for People**
  *Role of Workers*
  *Role of Management*
  *Role of Suppliers*

■ **Total Quality Management (TQM)**
  *Voice of the Customer*
  *Costs of Quality*
  *Quality Tools*
  *ISO 9000*

- **Statistical Quality Control (SQC)**
  *Sources of Variation*
  *Process Capability*
  *Process Control Charts*
  *Control Charts for Attributes*
- **Six Sigma Quality**
  *What Is Six Sigma?*
  *Six Sigma Methodology*
- **The Lean Six Sigma Supply Chain**
  *Developing a Lean Six Sigma Supply Chain*
  *Impact on Supply Chain Activities*
    Suppliers
    Operations
    Logistics
- **Chapter Highlights**
- **Key Terms**
- **Discussion Questions**
- **Problems**
- **Case Study: Buckeye Technologies**

---

Orthopedic surgeon Doug Woolley was frustrated. A bottleneck in the recovery room at the Community Medical Center in Missoula limited the total number of joint replacements he could do each week. The system limited him to four procedures, although he himself had time to do at least one more. He turned for help to Cindy Jimmerson, who worked with the hospital to implement a management system called Lean. They began by conducting observations of the system and quickly noticed some key problems. They observed nurses working hard and automatically going "around" barriers without even considering that the barriers could be removed.

They identified a few big things that could be improved immediately. One was posting a physician's or nurse's beeper number in an obvious place where it could be immediately seen. Although it seems simple, this prevented a common bottleneck—having to call somebody to find the number. These types of changes were made immediately, and the results were astounding. Patient time in the recovery room went from 90 minutes to 62 minutes, and as a result, the patient's bill went down. The hospital's productivity increased, and now Dr. Woolley is able to perform more procedures per week.

Similar benefits are occurring across the country as hospitals and medical centers implement Lean. At Goshen Health System on-time start in the hospital's operating department went from 15% to 80% in only eight weeks after implementing Lean. A team of employees examined the processes. They determined that the factor most responsible for the late start time was not having everything needed at the right place at the right time. This included supplies, staff, physicians, and the patient. As a result, the team developed process improvements so that everything was in its place and worked to educate physicians and staff on the impact of late arrivals. As a result of these efforts, the system reduced its average operating room turnover time from 30 minutes to 15 minutes.

As these examples illustrate, we are seeing organizations in all industries, including hospitals and healthcare clinics, improve their efficiency by implementing Lean systems. Although originally developed for manufacturing, the key goals of Lean—eliminating waste, simplifying the system, and continually improving—can be applied to all organizations.

Adapted from: Panchek, Patricia. "Lean Health Care? It Works!" at the AME Canadian Regional Conference, June 2007.

## What Is Lean?

### Lean Six Sigma

**Lean** is a management approach for creating value for the end customer through the most efficient utilization of resources possible. Lean is about eliminating waste of every type and involves numerous organizational efforts that work in unison. One of the most significant is the focus on quality and the use of a stringent methodology to identify and eliminate root causes of quality problems called **Six Sigma**. For this reason the two are often combined through the term **Lean Six Sigma**. Lean Six Sigma combines the benefits of both approaches, as shown in Figure 10.1, utilizing the tools from each. In this chapter we will look at each one and see how they work to create an efficient Lean Six Sigma supply chain.

### Lean Philosophy

Originally pioneered by Toyota in the 1970s, Lean has been widely adopted in numerous industries. Its implementation often results in large cost reductions, improved quality, and increased customer service. In fact, the benefits are so impressive that Lean has become a standard in many industries, such as auto, aerospace, and the computer industry. It is used by companies such as Honda, General Electric, Boeing, Lockheed Martin, Hewlett-Packard, and IBM. Companies in

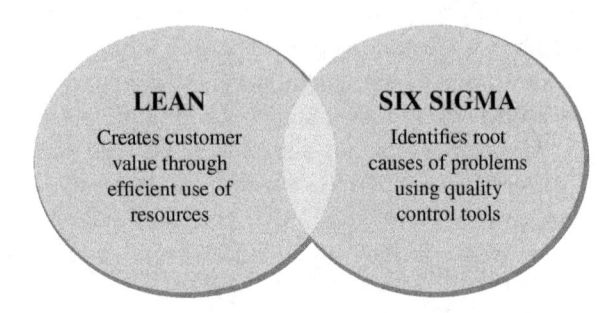

**LEAN**
Creates customer value through efficient use of resources

**SIX SIGMA**
Identifies root causes of problems using quality control tools

**FIGURE 10.1** Lean Six Sigma.

## What Is Lean?

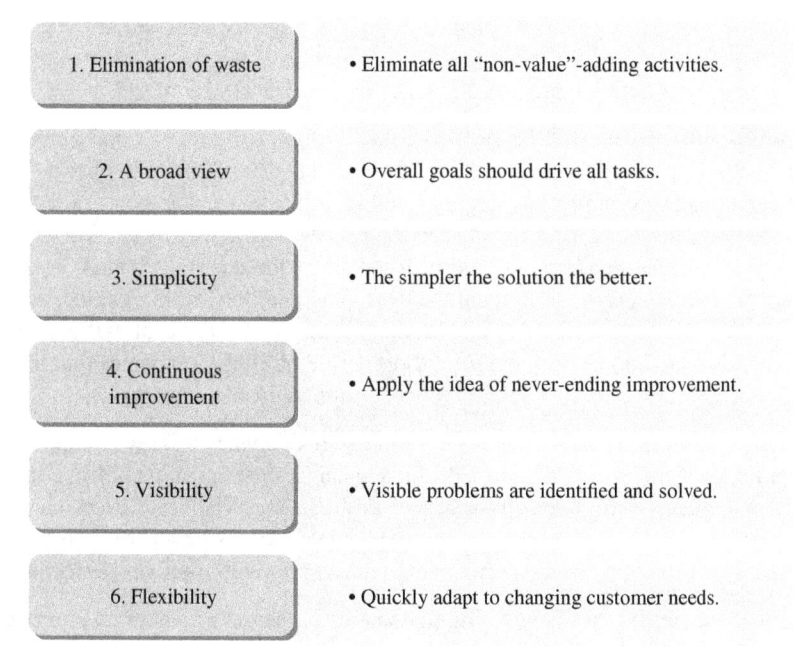

| | |
|---|---|
| 1. Elimination of waste | • Eliminate all "non-value"-adding activities. |
| 2. A broad view | • Overall goals should drive all tasks. |
| 3. Simplicity | • The simpler the solution the better. |
| 4. Continuous improvement | • Apply the idea of never-ending improvement. |
| 5. Visibility | • Visible problems are identified and solved. |
| 6. Flexibility | • Quickly adapt to changing customer needs. |

**FIGURE 10.2** Tenets of the Lean philosophy.

retail, such as Zara, Target, and Amazon, have also implemented Lean, and so have many hospitals and healthcare institutions, as we have seen in the chapter opener.

Lean is often thought of as just another type of production process, given its roots in manufacturing. However, Lean is an all-encompassing organizational philosophy founded on six tenets shown in Figure 10.2. The most significant of these is eliminating **waste**, where waste is defined as anything that does not add value. We look at these in more detail next.

1. **Elimination of Waste.** Waste is anything that does not add value to the system. This includes excess material, equipment, time, energy, space, or human activity that does not contribute to the value of the product or service being produced. The concept of waste, however, has an even broader meaning. Waste can be found in the production process itself through waiting and excess stock. It is seen in poor layout design of facilities that requires transporting goods from one part of the facility to another. Waste can exist in unneeded motion, such as searching for parts or supplies. Waste is poor quality resulting in scrap and rework, which is costly and adds no value.

    Consider the healthcare facility discussed in the chapter opener. Value-adding activities include registering, triaging, and examining the patient. On the other hand, sitting in the waiting room, filling out duplicate forms, or waiting in an examining room are non-value-adding. Eliminating this type of waste is the focus of Lean.

2. **A Broad View.** All tasks and processes should be driven by one goal—to serve the customer. It is easy for a company to think of its own needs and not that of the entire supply chain. Similarly, it is easy for employees to focus exclusively on their own jobs and view the organization solely from their assigned tasks. A broad view involves understanding that all supply chain partners, and their employees, are ultimately responsible for providing value to the final customer. Decisions should be made for the success of the entire chain rather than their individual success.

3. **Simplicity.** Lean emphasizes simple solutions to problems. It is easy to solve an organizational problem using complex and expensive methods. Finding a simple solution that

addresses the root cause of the problem is quite difficult. Just consider how, in the chapter opener, something as simple as posting a physician's beeper number where it could be immediately seen helped improve process efficiency in the recovery room.

4. **Continuous improvement.** Emphasis on quality and continuous improvement—called **kaizen**—is an important element of Lean. Continuous improvement applies to everything from reducing costs to improving quality to eliminating waste. The premise is that organizations are never perfect and can always be improved in some way. A number of companies utilize a continuous improvement approach called a "**kaizen blitz**." This is an improvement tool that utilizes cross-functional teams to plan and deliver improvements to specific processes during two- or three-day marathon sessions. The process allows a small team to intently concentrate on one problem for a short period of time. Companies find that a kaizen blitz can quickly deliver dramatic and low-cost improvements to processes.

5. **Visibility.** Lean tells us that waste can be eliminated only when it is seen and identified, and it cannot be identified if it is hidden. For this reason Lean stresses visibility. Lean facilities are open and clean, with ample floor space. Problems are visible to everyone. The Lean philosophy stresses that a cluttered environment creates confusion and disrespect toward the workplace. In contrast, a clean environment creates order and improves performance.

6. **Flexibility.** Flexibility means adapting to changes in the environment. A company can be flexible in many ways. Flexibility can mean rapidly changing production volumes as demand changes. Flexibility is also the ability to produce a wide variety of products. Lean systems are designed to easily switch from one product type to another, using flexible workers that perform many different tasks. Processes are designed to be highly efficient but flexible to accommodate changing customer demands.

One factor that enables flexibility is relying on general-purpose equipment capable of performing a variety of different functions. In manufacturing this might be a drilling machine able to drill holes in an engine block and also perform milling and threading operations. This is different from having specialized equipment that can perform only one task. Just consider the benefits of having an all-in-one printer, copier, fax, and scanner.

## Big Data Analytics Box

### ▪ GENERAL ELECTRIC

GE is the icon of best management practices and the management efficiency approach such as "Lean" and "Six Sigma." These were the hallmarks of GE under the leader of CEO Jack Welsh in the 1980s and 1990s. However, as other companies adopted these best practices they no longer provided a unique competitive advantage. For GE, Lean and Six Sigma continue to be the hallmarks of their culture. As the company has evolved, they have taken excellence in these practices as a foundation for other ventures. One such involves combining big data with lessons in Lean from entrepreneurship.

Big data and digitization are speeding up all processes in every industry sector. Companies are now competing more like the software industry, which is characterized by short product life cycles and rapid decision making. GE has responded to this changing environment and has worked to apply an approach called "Lean Startup." It is a Lean approach developed for entrepreneurs to develop new products with short cycles. It involves "sprints" (quick deliverables) and fast learning and applies Lean principles. GE has branded it "FastWorks" and believes that the rapid learning cycles with customers will reduce the risk of building products the customers don't want. GE has applied FastWorks to product development with excellent results. It has so far cut program cost and development speed in half.

Adapted from: Power, Brad. "How GE Applies Lean Startup Practices." *Harvard Business Review*, April 23, 2014.

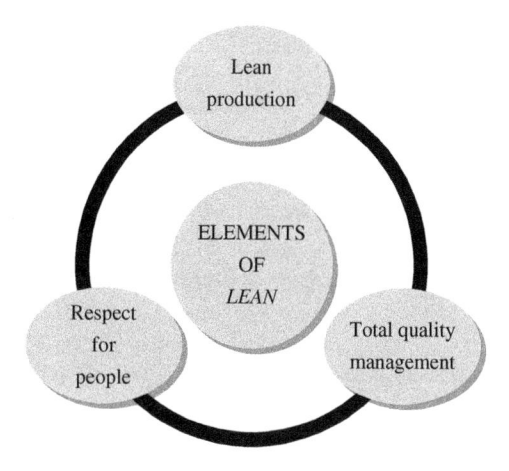

**FIGURE 10.3** Elements of Lean.

## Elements of Lean

Lean is composed of three elements that work in unison: **Lean Production**, **Total Quality Management (TQM)**, and **Respect for People**. They are shown in Figure 10.3. Note that Lean Production is just one element of Lean—a frequent misunderstanding. It is the three elements that work together to create a complete Lean system.

Lean Production focuses on the operations and delivery system. It involves developing an efficiently coordinated system that makes it possible to produce the exact products desired and deliver them in the right quantities to where they are needed just in time. For this reason it is often called **just-in-time (JIT)**. Lean Production is known as a **pull production** system that keeps minimal levels of inventory, relies on efficiencies gained by repetition, elimination of all unnecessary steps and motions, and use of visual signals.

The second element of Lean is the focus on quality through concepts such as Total Quality Management (TQM), which we discuss later in the chapter. TQM is integral to Lean as it identifies customer quality standards and serves to eliminate waste, such as defects, scrap, and rework. Quality is integrated into all functions and levels of the organization as the entire supply chain must be designed to provide the level of quality expected by the final customer. Consider that traditional quality control systems use the concept of acceptable quality level (AQL) to indicate the acceptable number of defective parts. In Lean there is no such measure—no level of defects other than zero is acceptable.

Respect for People is the third element of Lean. Lean considers people the most important resource, and their involvement is central to the Lean philosophy. The Lean philosophy believes in treating all employees with respect and offering significant rewards for well-performed tasks. Lean requires total organizational reform, which cannot occur without everyone's participation. Lean relies on workers to perform multiple tasks and to work in teams, including management, labor, staff, and suppliers. Respect for People extends to all members of the supply chain, where the focus is on developing long-term relationships.

## Supply Chain Leader's Box

### U.S. ARMY

In 2009 the Corpus Christie Army Depot (CCAD)—one of two U.S. Army Aviation depots—faced a dilemma. The Depot was receiving a steady flow of battle-damaged helicopters for refurbishment and overhaul from Iraq and Afghanistan. In addition, it was being asked to carry out two major helicopter upgrades, with no additional resources. The problem for the leadership: how to do more with less.

The Depot conducts repair and overhaul of aircraft for the U.S. Army. It has many production capabilities that include machining, fabrication, and computer-aided design and manufacturing. It is the largest single industrial employer in the region with a workforce of more than 4,000 employees plus 1,000 contractors and occupies approximately 50 buildings. Such an extensive operation decided to turn to Lean and Six Sigma for help. Lean had been successful in manufacturing, and it made sense to apply it to the military.

As soon as the Depot began incorporating Lean principles, improvements were seen. One of the helicopter lines increased production by 40%. The other lines reduced their average cycle time by 25%. In addition, inventory was reduced. "We met our one-aircraft-per-week goal. We now are capable of completing more Black Hawks per year than before the new procedures," says George Kunke III, the Depot's process optimization manager.

So how did they do this? The first step was to reduce work-in-process (WIP) inventory. The logic was to work on fewer aircraft at a time, devoting resources to only those aircraft. They admit that working on fewer aircraft simultaneously seemed "counterintuitive," but it provided focus, and the Depot saw immediate improvements in inventory. The second step was to instill broad or global thinking and break down the "silo" mentality. The Depot division chiefs were asked to work cooperatively as members of the core team and required to take a global view of the Depot's operations, rather than just concentrating on their own areas of responsibility.

Other changes were made, such as better management of bottlenecks. When a bottleneck was detected, an "issue resolution team" was immediately dispatched to direct all available resources to solve the problem. To enhance efficiency they also started using "full kitting," where a kit is an assembly of all items needed for a job. In this case, a kit is more than parts and manuals. Like in the healthcare example in the chapter opener, a kit includes *all* resources needed to complete an assembly on time—including personnel. This means that all the supporting entities are concentrated at the place where the task is being done. With the implementation of Lean and Six Sigma, the Depot has exceeded its expectation and expects even better results in the future.

Adapted from: "How CCAD Tackled A Growing Workload." *Rotor & Wing Magazine,* January 2010: 17–20.

# Lean Production

## The Pull System

Traditional organizations and supply chains work as "push" systems, where goods are produced based on a forecast then stored in anticipation of demand. Lean Production is based on a "pull," rather than a push system, to produce and move products. In the operation of an organization the process starts with the last workstation in the facility and works backward through the system. Each station requests the precise amount of products needed from the previous workstation. The pull system works in the same way throughout the entire supply chain. Each stage in the supply chain requests quantities needed from the previous stage in the chain. If products are not requested, they are not produced, and no excess inventory is generated.

A major aspect of Lean is how it views inventory. In traditional systems inventory is carried to cover up problems—such as poor deliveries, inefficiency, lack of coordination, and demand uncertainty. Lean views inventory as a cost that provides no value and should be eliminated. Inventory also hurts the organization, as it does not permit visibility of problems. Eliminating inventory permits problems to be seen and corrected, rather than wasting resources to compensate for them. An often-used analogy to describe inventory is that of a river, with the rocks being problems and the water being inventory. The water covers the rocks, and they cannot be seen. However, as water is reduced the rocks emerge. Similarly, as inventory is reduced, problems are seen and can then be solved.

## Global Insights Box

### ■ UPS

Virtually all transportation carriers today use Global Position System (GPS) based telematics devices in their vehicles. These devices provide a wide variety of data about driving behavior, speeds under various conditions, and traffic. These types of systems have other sensing and monitoring capabilities as well. For example, they can alert drivers to when vehicles need repairs or software updates. UPS has already employed telematics data to redesign its global logistical network.

UPS uses geo-location data for many aspects of its operation to be lean, be efficient, and eliminate waste. As a result it optimizes every aspect of the operation from routes to labor management. Its vehicles are fitted with sensors, wireless modules, and GPS, all gathering data. This data is then fed to headquarters, which uses algorithms for predictions such as engine trouble and to schedule maintenance. The system lets the company track routes in real time and knows the location of every vehicle. The company can monitor drivers and scrutinizes their scheduled deliveries to optimize routes. The system can also improve safety and efficiency, such as identifying routes with fewer turns that must cross traffic intersections.

## Visual Signals

For the pull system to work there must be communication between the work centers in a production facility and between supply chain partners. This communication is made possible by the use of a signaling system called a **kanban**, which means "signal" or "card" in Japanese. A kanban card typically contains information such as product name, part number, and the quantity that needs to be produced, and it is attached to a container. When workers need products from the station before them, they pass an empty container with an attached kanban to that station and take a full container. The kanban authorizes the worker at that station to produce the amount of goods specified on the kanban and fill the empty container. In effect, the kanban authorizes production. Production cannot take place unless a container is empty and a kanban card has authorized production. This is shown in Figure 10.4.

In many facilities the kanban system has been modified so that actual cards do not exist but some other signaling mechanism is used to pull the goods through the system. This may be as simple as a square drawn on the floor that identifies where the material should be stored. An empty square indicates that more goods are needed and is called a "kanban square." Another type of signal might be a flag that is raised to indicate it is time to produce the next container of goods,

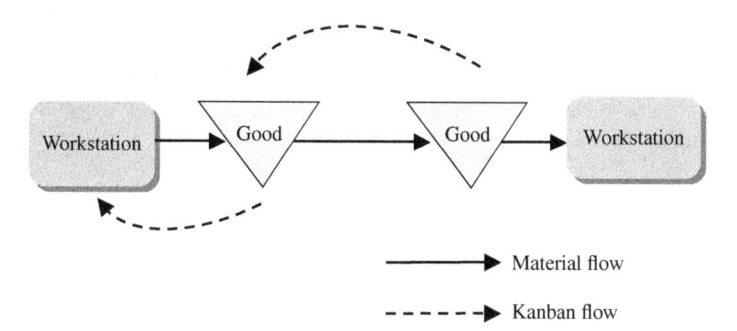

**FIGURE 10.4** Flow of kanban cards between workstations.

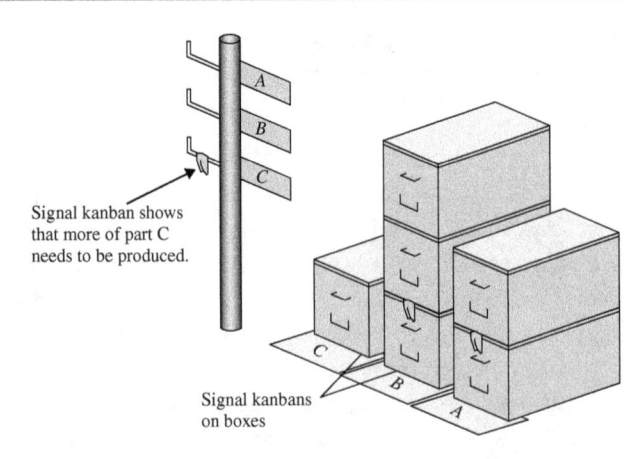

**FIGURE 10.5** Visual signals.

and is called a "signal kanban." When the inventory level is reduced to the point of reaching the signal, the signal is removed and placed on an order post, indicating that it is time for production. These visual signals are shown in Figure 10.5.

In the supply chain kanbans can be used to coordinate supplier deliveries and are called supplier kanbans. The suppliers bring the filled containers to the point of usage in the factory and at the same time pick up an empty container with a kanban to be filled later. Because a manufacturer may have multiple suppliers, "mailboxes" can be set up at a factory for each supplier. The suppliers can check their "mailboxes" to pick up their orders. Kanbans are usually made of plastic, or metal, but there are also bar-coded kanbans and electronic kanbans that further ease communication with suppliers.

## Small Lot Production

Small lot production means that the amount of products produced at any one time is small, say 10 versus 1,000. Producing in small lots is the primary way of eliminating inventory and excess processing while increasing flexibility. The manufacturer can produce many lots of different types of products. It also shortens the manufacturing lead time, the actual time it takes to produce a product, because it takes less time to produce 10 units than to produce 1,000.

Small lot production gives a company flexibility and allows it to respond to customer demands more quickly. However, to be able to achieve small lot production, companies have to reduce **setup time**. Recall from Chapter 9 that this is the time it takes to set up equipment for a production run. This includes cleaning and recalibrating equipment, changing blades and other tools, and all other activities necessary to switch production from one product to another.

To produce only the quantities needed, the setup time must be low so it is easy to switch from producing one type of product to another. This approach allows companies to respond quickly to changes in demand. Using Lean principles many large manufacturers have been able to reduce setup times from hours to only a few minutes, giving them tremendous flexibility. The ultimate goal of Lean is to be able to economically produce one item at a time as the customer wants it.

## Uniform Plant Loading

Demand for a product can exhibit sudden increases or decreases, which can mean disruptive changes in production schedules. These demand changes are typically magnified throughout the supply chain and contribute to inefficiency and waste. Lean reduces this problem by making adjustments as small as possible and setting a production plan that is frozen for the month. This is called uniform plant loading or "leveling" the production schedule. The term *leveling* comes from the fact that the schedule is uniform or "level" throughout the planning horizon. This helps suppliers better plan their own production and delivery schedules.

# Respect for People

According to Lean, respect for all people, including labor, management, and suppliers, must exist for an organization to be its best. It is up to company leadership to create such an organizational culture. Lean requires all supply chain members to work together in cross-functional teams to solve problems. Lean organizations have a hierarchy that is generally flatter compared to that of traditional organizations, and organizational layers are not strictly defined. Great responsibility and autonomy are given to ordinary workers, and their input is highly valued. In this section we look at some specific issues that relate to respect for people in the Lean environment.

## Role of Workers

In traditional organizations production workers often perform their jobs in an automatic fashion. In Lean organizations, however, they are actively engaged in pursuing the goals of the company. Lean relies on cross-functional worker skills, which is the ability of workers to perform many different tasks on many different machines. Part of worker duties is to be actively engaged in improving the production process, monitor quality, and correct quality problems. Lean considers those closest to the problem best suited to make improvements in their jobs. They are given autonomy, and their opinions are highly valued.

Production workers are responsible for quality and are required to continually check and monitor the quality of the production process. They are responsible for inspecting their own work as well as the materials received from previous operations to detect quality problems. An example of worker responsibility can be seen through **jidoka**, which is the authority of every worker to stop the production process and fix problems as they occur rather than pushing them down the line. Jidoka requires workers to take ownership of poor quality and have the confidence to take on the responsibility. Discovering quality problems is seen as a goal, not something that should be covered up or blamed on others.

Teams are an integral part of Lean. One of the most popular teams is the **quality circle**. Quality circles are groups of about 5 to 12 employees who come together to solve quality problems. Although participation is usually voluntary, meetings take place during regular work hours. Quality circles usually meet weekly and attempt to develop solutions to problems and share them with management.

## Role of Management

The role of management is to create the cultural change in the organization needed for Lean to succeed. This is a difficult task as it involves creating an organizational culture that provides an atmosphere of close cooperation and mutual trust. Recall that Lean relies on production workers to independently solve production problems and take on many additional tasks. To be able to do this, employees must be problem solvers and be empowered to take action based on their ideas. Workers must feel secure in their jobs and know that they will not be reprimanded or lose their jobs for being proactive. They must also feel comfortable enough to discuss their ideas openly. It is up to management to develop an incentive system that rewards and motivates this type of behavior.

## Role of Suppliers

Lean emphasizes building long-term supplier relationships. The traditional approach of competitive bidding and buying parts from the cheapest supplier runs counter to the Lean philosophy. Lean companies understand that they are in a partnership with their suppliers, who are viewed as the external factory. The number of suppliers is typically much smaller than in traditional systems, and the goal is to shift to single-source suppliers that provide an entire family of parts for one manufacturer. Together the supply chain partners focus on improving process quality. Having few suppliers makes it easier to develop stable and repetitive delivery schedules and eliminate paperwork.

With a long-term relationship, a supplier can act as a service provider rather than a one-time seller. An important part of such a relationship is information sharing. The manufacturer shares demand information and production schedules, allowing the supplier to "see" what is going to be ordered. The supplier, in turn, shares cost information and cost-cutting efforts with the manufacturer. Both parties help each other and together reap the benefits.

## Total Quality Management (TQM)

Total quality management (TQM) is an integrated organizational effort designed to improve quality at every level. Meeting quality expectations as defined by the customer and eliminating defects is an integral aspect of Lean. For this to succeed, every member of the supply chain must adopt the same quality standards. Poor quality anywhere in the supply chain will be passed down the chain, resulting in dissatisfied customers and higher cost for all members of the chain.

The meaning of quality has changed and evolved over time. In the early 20th century quality management meant inspecting products to ensure that they met specifications. Today it means meeting and exceeding customer expectations. A number of individuals have contributed to our knowledge and understanding of quality and have made TQM what it is today. They are showcased in Figure 10.6.

### Voice of the Customer

The overriding feature of TQM is the focus on customers. Therefore, quality is defined as meeting or exceeding customer expectations. This is called the **voice of the customer (VOC)**, as we discussed in Chapter 4. The goal is to first identify, and then meet, customer expectations. TQM recognizes that a perfectly produced product has little value if it is not what the customer wants. Therefore, the ultimate definition of quality is customer driven.

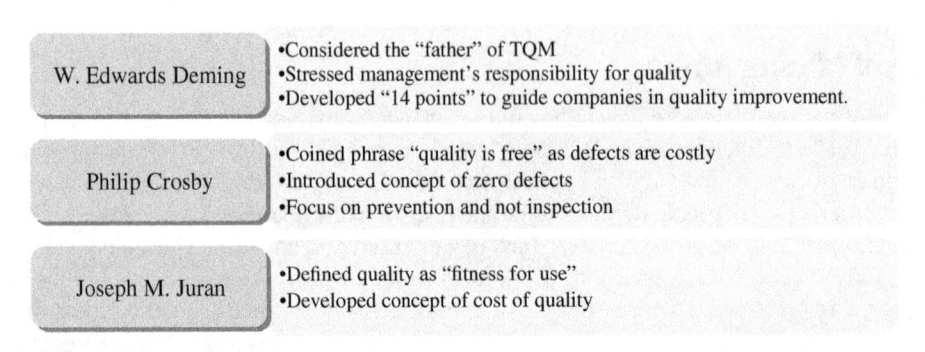

**W. Edwards Deming**
- Considered the "father" of TQM
- Stressed management's responsibility for quality
- Developed "14 points" to guide companies in quality improvement.

**Philip Crosby**
- Coined phrase "quality is free" as defects are costly
- Introduced concept of zero defects
- Focus on prevention and not inspection

**Joseph M. Juran**
- Defined quality as "fitness for use"
- Developed concept of cost of quality

**FIGURE 10.6** Quality gurus.

Total Quality Management (TQM) 225

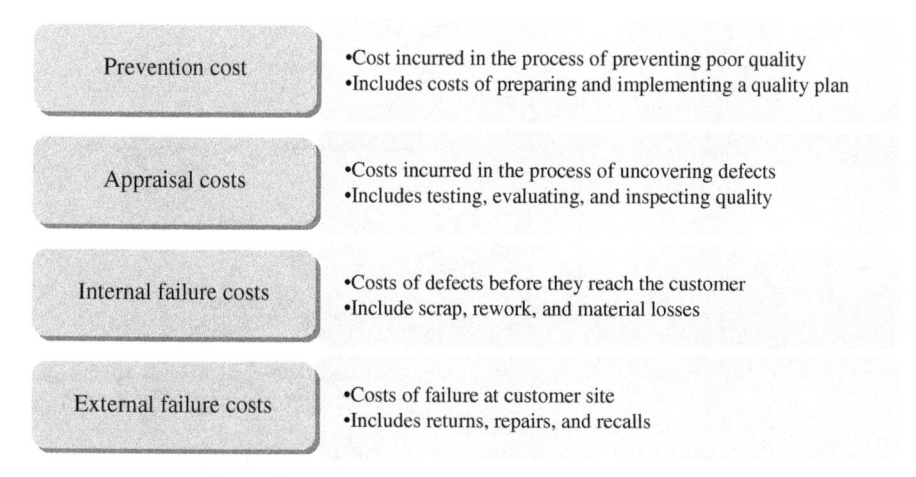

| Prevention cost | •Cost incurred in the process of preventing poor quality<br>•Includes costs of preparing and implementing a quality plan |
| --- | --- |
| Appraisal costs | •Costs incurred in the process of uncovering defects<br>•Includes testing, evaluating, and inspecting quality |
| Internal failure costs | •Costs of defects before they reach the customer<br>•Include scrap, rework, and material losses |
| External failure costs | •Costs of failure at customer site<br>•Includes returns, repairs, and recalls |

**FIGURE 10.7** Costs of quality.

Although this may sound simple, it is not always easy to determine what the customer wants, as consumer tastes and preferences are constantly changing. As we discussed in Chapter 4, customers often don't know or cannot articulate what they want. Consider the retail industry, where fashion trends and tastes change rapidly. Companies often conduct focus groups, market surveys, and customer interviews just to determine what customers want at any one time.

## Costs of Quality

Companies understand the high cost of poor quality. The most obvious consequence is when poor quality creates dissatisfied customers leading to loss of business. Costs of quality are shown in Figure 10.7. The first two costs—prevention and appraisal costs—are incurred with the hope of preventing the second two—internal and external failure.

## Quality Tools

Lean places great responsibility on all workers to identify and correct quality problems. To do this workers need proper training. They need to understand how to assess quality using a variety of quality control tools, interpret findings, and correct problems. In this section we look at seven quality tools often called the "seven tools of quality control," shown in Figure 10.8. Although simple, they are extremely useful in identifying and analyzing quality problems. Workers can use only one tool at a time, but often a combination of tools is most helpful. These are the seven tools of quality control:

**Cause-and-effect diagrams**—sometimes called "**fishbone diagrams**"—are tools used to identify causes of a particular quality problem. The causes may be a machine, workers, measurement, suppliers, materials, and other aspects of the production process. Each of these individual causes is caused by more specific factors. For example, a problem with a machine could be due to a need for adjustment, old equipment, or tooling problems. Similarly, a problem with workers could be related to lack of training, poor supervision, or fatigue.

**Flowcharts** are schematic diagrams of the sequence of steps involved in an operation or process. They provide a visual tool that is easy to use and understand, and develop a clear picture of where problems could arise.

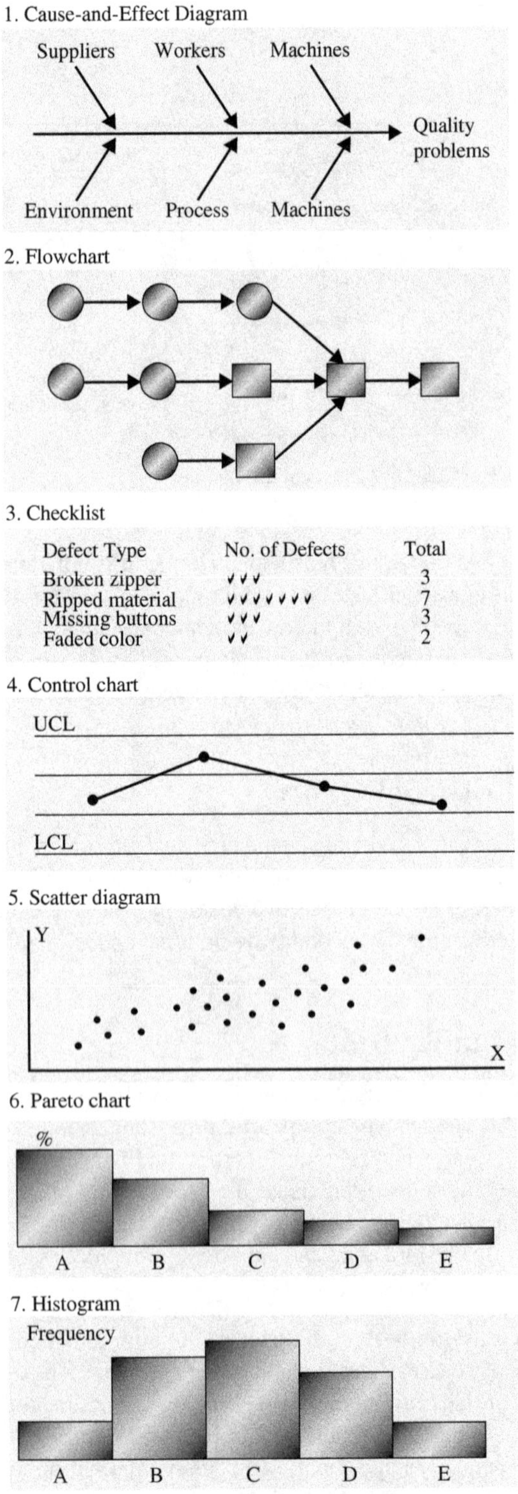

226 LEAN SYSTEMS AND SIX-SIGMA QUALITY

1. Cause-and-Effect Diagram

Suppliers   Workers   Machines
                                    → Quality problems
Environment  Process  Machines

2. Flowchart

3. Checklist

| Defect Type | No. of Defects | Total |
|---|---|---|
| Broken zipper | ✓✓✓ | 3 |
| Ripped material | ✓✓✓✓✓✓✓ | 7 |
| Missing buttons | ✓✓✓ | 3 |
| Faded color | ✓✓ | 2 |

4. Control chart

UCL

LCL

5. Scatter diagram

6. Pareto chart

A B C D E

7. Histogram

A B C D E

**FIGURE 10.8** The seven tools of quality.

**Checklists** are lists of common defects and the number of occurrences of the defect observed. Although simple, checklists are a highly effective tool at identifying defects.

**Control charts** are charts used to determine whether a process is operating within expectations for a dimension of interest. This could be product weight or volume, or the number of customer complaints in a given week.

**Scatter diagrams** are graphs that visually show how two variables are related to one another. They are particularly useful in detecting a relationship between two variables.

**Pareto analysis** is a technique used to identify quality problems based on their degree of importance. Pareto analysis tells us that there are a small number of causes that create the majority of quality problems.

**Histograms** are charts that show the frequency distribution of observed values of a variable. The plot shows the distribution a particular variable, such as whether it has a normal distribution and whether it is symmetrical.

## ISO 9000

Increased international trade during the 1980s created a need for universal standards of quality. As a result the International Organization for Standards (ISO) published its first set of standards for quality management, called ISO 9000, in 1987. These have become the internationally adopted standards of quality for all types of companies in a range of industries. Today many industries consider ISO certification a requirement for doing business.

ISO 9000 consists of a "family" of standards that address various aspects of the quality management process. For example, ISO 9001 provides a set of standards for management systems. Collectively these standards document what the company is doing to fulfill the customer's quality requirements and meet applicable regulatory requirements. Note that ISO 9000 are process standards, not product quality standards. They verify that a company is meeting standards of measuring and documenting their quality processes, but says nothing about the actual product.

ISO provides a certification process for companies to follow in order to become ISO certified. ISO 9000 certification demonstrates that a company has met the standards and has appropriate quality processes in place. To receive ISO certification, a company must provide extensive documentation of their quality processes, including methods used to monitor quality, frequency of worker training, job descriptions, inspection programs, and statistical process control tools used. Detailed documentation of all processes is critical. The company is then audited by an ISO inspector, who visits the facility and verifies all documentation.

## Managerial Insights Box

### ■ LEAN TOOLS IN THE POPULAR PRESS

Lean tools are so powerful they are even espoused in the popular press. An Amazon Best Book of the Month titled *The Checklist Manifesto: How to Get Things Right* focuses on the benefits of following simple checklists in the workplace—a hallmark of Lean.

The author explains how tragic errors can be dramatically reduced with just a piece of paper and a pencil. A range of disparate tasks is illustrated, from flying a plane to building a skyscraper, to show how checklists can improve outcomes. The logic behind checklists is that they help organize information rather than relying on the brain to reliably remember tasks. Using simple checklists has been shown to be a reliable guide in fields that range from healthcare to finance to government.

One example of checklist success occurred in healthcare when a critical care specialist at Johns Hopkins, Dr. Peter

Pronovost, devised an operating room checklist. On a plain sheet of paper he wrote out five steps doctors and nurses should follow in the operating room (OR). These were simple steps, such as washing hands with soap; sterilizing the patient's skin; putting sterile drapes over the entire patient; wearing a mask, gown, and gloves; and putting a sterile dressing over incisions. Within a year of implementing the checklist the rate of infections related to IV tubes at the hospital went from 11% to zero. Since then Michigan mandated the inclusion of these five steps in every hospital in the state. Within three months infections related to IV tube insertions dropped 66%. Although they seem simple, it is easy to see how the steps can be overlooked on a repetitive basis.

Another example is the famous US Airways Flight 1549, which safely landed on the Hudson River in January 2009 after hitting a flock of geese near New York. It turns out that the pilot, Captain Sullenberger III, known as "Sully," followed a detailed emergency checklist that multiplied their chances of success. He and his copilot had the experience to know the importance of discipline and teamwork and landed the plane safely.

The "checklist manifesto" provides guidelines, such as including all "stupid but critical" tasks on the list so they're not overlooked. It also makes it mandatory to let others know when each task is completed and empowers subordinates to question their superiors about the checklist. This does sound like Lean in practice and shows the reach of Lean even on the mass market.

Adapted from: "Make a List. Check It Twice." *Bloomberg Businessweek*, February 22, 2010: 78–79.

---

The second "family" of standards is ISO 14000, which address environmental management. They document what the company is doing to minimize harmful effects on the environment caused by its activities and to achieve continual improvement of its environmental performance. With greater interest in green manufacturing and more awareness of environmental concerns, ISO 14000 standards are becoming an important set of standards for documenting environmental responsibility. To see the latest developments in ISO standards, see www.iso.org.

## Statistical Quality Control (SQC)

**Statistical quality control (SQC)** is the use of statistical tools used to measure product and process quality. These tools provide quantifiable measures that verify quality standards are being met and can be divided into three broad categories:

1. **Descriptive statistics** are statistical tools used to describe quality characteristics. They include the mean, standard deviations, the range, and a measure of the distribution of data. They can also be used to describe relationships, such as whether certain characteristics tend to occur together.

2. **Statistical process control (SPC)** is a statistical process used to verify that the production process is functioning as specified. It involves inspecting a random sample of the output from the process and deciding whether the process is producing products with characteristics that fall within the acceptable range.

3. **Acceptance sampling** is the process of randomly sampling a batch of goods and deciding whether to accept the entire batch based on the results. Acceptance sampling determines whether a batch of goods should be accepted or rejected.

The tools in each category provide different information for evaluating product and process quality. Although descriptions of certain characteristics are helpful, they are not enough to help us evaluate whether there is a problem with quality. Acceptance sampling can help us decide whether to accept or reject the items produced. Although this information is helpful in making the quality acceptance decision after the product has been produced, it does not help us identify and catch a quality problem during the production process. For this we need tools in the SPC category.

## Sources of Variation

All processes have a certain amount of natural variation. This variation can be caused by many factors, some of which we can control and some which are inherent in the process. Variation that is caused by factors that can be clearly identified and managed is called **assignable variation**. An example may be variation in output caused by workers not being equally trained or by improper machine adjustment. Variation that is inherent in the process itself is called **common or random variation**.

Causes of assignable variation can be precisely identified and eliminated. Examples of this type of variation are poor supplier quality, poor worker performance, or a misaligned machine. In each of these examples, the problem can be identified and corrected. In contrast, common causes of variation are based on random causes we cannot identify. If you look at bottles of a soft drink, you will notice that no two bottles are filled to exactly the same level. Similarly, if you look at blueberry muffins in a bakery you will notice that some have more blueberries than others. These types of differences are completely normal. No two products are exactly alike. This is due to slight differences in materials, workers, machines, tools, and other factors. An important task in quality control is to determine the amount of random variation in a process. We can then monitor the process to ensure that the amount of variation does not exceed it.

## Process Capability

**Process capability** is the evaluation of a process on its ability to meet certain quality standards. Quality standards are useless if the production process isn't able to achieve them. It would be akin to expecting every high school athlete to perform at Olympic standards or taking an old family SUV and expecting it to perform in a NASCAR race. They simply aren't capable. The same holds true for business processes. Strict quality standards are useless if the system is not capable of producing products that meet those standards.

### Supply Chain Leader's Box

#### ■ INTEL CORPORATION

Intel Corporation—the world's largest manufacturer of microprocessors—understands the problems with process variation. Process variation leads to quality defects and lack of product consistency. To minimize process variation Intel has implemented a program it calls "copy-exactly" at all its manufacturing facilities. This means that each facility uses the same equipment, the same exact materials, and performs the same tasks in the exact same order. Regardless of whether the chips are made in Arizona, New Mexico, Ireland, or any of its other plants, they are made in exactly the same way. The level of detail to which the "copy-exactly" concept goes is meticulous. For example, when a chip-making machine was found to be a few feet longer at one facility than another, Intel made them match. When water quality was found to be different at one facility, Intel instituted a purification system to eliminate any differences. Even when a worker was found polishing equipment in one direction, he was asked to do it in the approved circular pattern. Such attention to exactness of detail is to minimize all variation possible.

The first question to ask in the development of a quality program is whether the process is capable of achieving the desired product specifications. **Product specifications**, also called tolerances, are set ranges of acceptable quality characteristics. These can be product dimensions, such as length or weight, or customer service standards, such as number of customer complaints. These standards are typically set by design engineers taking into account how the product will be used and customer expectations. For a product to be considered acceptable, its characteristic must fall within the product specification range. For example, the specification width of a machined part may be set as 10 inches ± .5. This specifies that the part should be 10 inches wide but can vary between 9.5 and 10.5 inches. Anything outside this range is unacceptable.

Recall that all production processes have a certain amount of natural variation. For a process to be considered "capable" of producing a product with set specifications, the variation of the process itself cannot exceed this set specification. Therefore, process capability involves evaluating the variation of the process and comparing it to product specifications.

To see how this works, let's look at three cases of process variation relative to product design specifications: (1) Process Variation *equals* Specification Range; (2) Process Variation *exceeds* Specification Range; and (3) Process Variation is *narrower* than Specification Range. Consider Pasta Mania, a company that produces pasta sauces in glass jars specified at 32 ounces ±2 ounces. Therefore, the product specification range is between 30 and 34 ounces. Figure 10.9(a) shows a process (±3 standard deviations) where product volumes fall between 30 and 34 ounces. Assuming a normal distribution, 99.74% of products fall in the range of ±3 standard deviations. In this example we can see that process variation matches product specifications. This means that the process is capable of producing products within the set specifications.

In Figure 10.9(b), however, 99.74% of products (±3 standard deviations) have volumes between 29 and 35 ounces. Here the process variation is outside the product specifications, and a large percentage of products produced fall outside the permissible limits. Here the process is not capable of producing the product within the set specifications.

In Figure 10.9(c), 99.74% of the products produced are with volumes between 31 and 33 ounces. Here, the range of process variation is less than the set specification range, and the process exceeds minimal capability.

Process capability is measured using the process capability index $C_p$. It is computed as the ratio of the product specification range to the process variation range:

$$C_p = \frac{\text{product specification range}}{\text{process variation range}} = \frac{USL - LSL}{6\sigma}$$

The product specification range is the difference between the upper specification limit (USL) and the lower specification limit (LSL) of the process. The process variation range—the denominator—is computed as 6 standard deviations ($6\sigma$) of the process being monitored. We use $6\sigma$ because 99.74% of the products fall within ±3 standard deviations of the distribution—a total of 6 standard deviations. $C_p$ is an easy to interpret:

$C_p = 1$: Process variation just meets specifications, as in Figure 10.9(a). The process is "minimally capable."

$C_p \leq 1$: Process variation *exceeds* the specification range, as in Figure 10.9(b). The process is not capable of producing products within specification.

$C_p \geq 1$: Process variation is *narrower* than specification range, as in Figure 10.9(c). The process exceeds minimal capability.

A $C_p$ value of 1 means that 99.74% of products produced fall within the specification range. This also means that 0.26% (100% − 99.74%) of the products do not fall within the range. This percentage may seem negligibly small. However, 0.26% corresponds to 2,600 parts per

(a) Process variation and product specification range are equal

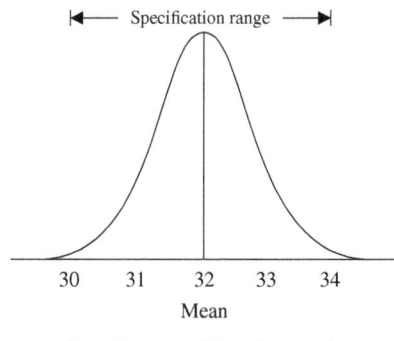

|← Specification range →|

30  31  32  33  34
Mean

|← Process variation ± 3σ →|

(b) Process variation exceeds product specification range

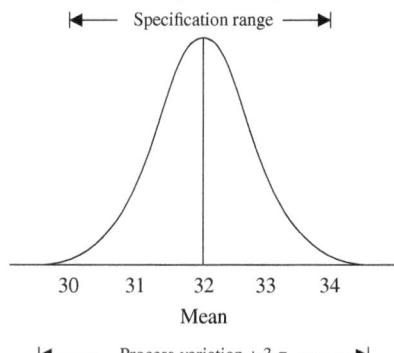

|← Specification range →|

30  31  32  33  34
Mean

|← Process variation ± 3σ →|

(c) Process variation is narrower than process specification range

|← Specification range →|

30  31  32  33  34
Mean

|← Process →|
Variation ± 3σ

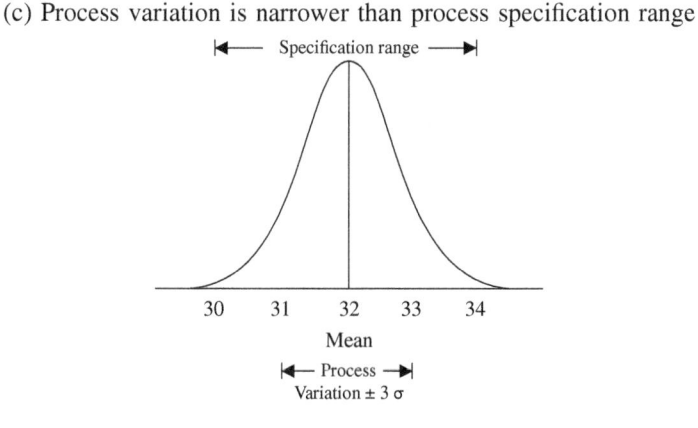

**FIGURE 10.9** Process variation versus product specifications.

million (ppm) defective products (0.0026 × 1,000,000). This translates into 2,600 wrong prescriptions out of a million, 2,600 incorrect medical procedures out of a million, or 2,600 malfunctioning aircraft out of a million. In these terms we can see that this number of defects is high, and the way to reduce it is to increase process capability. This involves studying the process and improving it.

**Example 1    Computing $C_p$**

Pasta Mania is evaluating three different machines for their capability in filling jars with its famous pasta sauce. The product specification range is set between 30 and 34 ounces. Given the standard deviations for each machine provided in the following table, determine which of the machines are capable of producing within specifications.

| Machine | Standard Deviation |
|---------|--------------------|
| A       | 0.6                |
| B       | 0.7                |
| C       | 1.2                |

**SOLUTION:** To determine the capability of each machine, we need to divide the specification width (UCL − LCL = 34 − 30 = 4) by $6\sigma$ for each machine:

| Machine | $\sigma$ | USL − LSL | $6\sigma$ | $C_p = \dfrac{USL - LSL}{6\sigma}$ |
|---------|----------|-----------|-----------|-------------------------------------|
| A       | 0.6      | 4         | 3.6       | 1.11                                |
| B       | 0.7      | 4         | 4.2       | 0.95                                |
| C       | 1.2      | 4         | 7.2       | 0.55                                |

Looking at the $C_p$ values, only machine A is capable of filling bottles within specifications because it is the only machine that has a $C_p$ value at or above 1.

---

Although $C_p$ is a valuable measure of process capability, it has one shortcoming: it assumes that process variability is centered on the specification range. Unfortunately, this is not always the case. Figure 10.10 shows an example from Pasta Mania. Here the process is specified for a mean of 32 ounces, but the variation of the process itself has a mean of 31 ounces, even though both ranges are the same. The process is not centered, and a certain proportion of products will fall outside the specification range.

This problem is common and can lead to mistakes when computing $C_p$. For this reason another measure for process capability is used more frequently:

$$C_p = \min\left(\frac{USL - \mu}{3\sigma}, \frac{\mu - LSL}{3\sigma}\right)$$

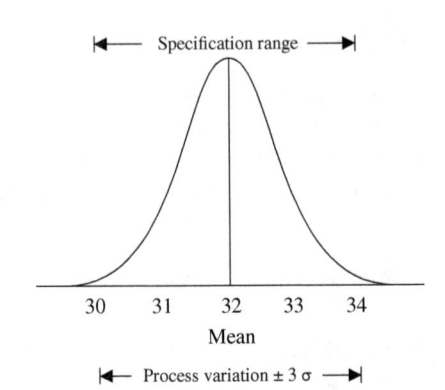

**FIGURE 10.10** Actual process variation is not centered on specification range.

where

$\mu$ = the mean of the process

$\sigma$ = the standard deviation of the process

$C_{pk}$ is a measure of process capability that addresses a possible lack of centering of the process over the specification range. To use this measure, the process capability of each half of the normal distribution is computed, and the minimum of the two is used.

Looking at Figure 10.10, the computed $C_p$ would be 1.00 as both ranges are the same, leading us to conclude that the process is capable. Computing $C_{pk}$, however, leads to a different conclusion. Assuming that the process standard deviation, $\sigma$, is 0.6, we get the following:

$$C_{pk} = \min\left(\frac{USL - \mu}{3\sigma}, \frac{\mu - LSL}{3\sigma}\right)$$

$$C_{pk} = \min\left(\frac{34 - 31}{3(0.6)}, \frac{31 - 30}{3(0.6)}\right)$$

$$C_{pk} = \min(1.66, \ 0.55)$$

$$C_{pk} = 0.55$$

The computed $C_{pk}$ value is less than 1, indicating that the process is not capable.

## Example 2    Computing the $C_{pk}$ Value

Compute and interpret the $C_{pk}$ measure of process capability for the following process. What value would you have obtained with the $C_p$ measure?

$$USL = 22$$
$$LSL = 10$$
$$\text{Process } \sigma = 2$$
$$\text{Process } \mu = 14$$

**SOLUTION:** Compute the $C_{pk}$ measure of process capability:

$$C_{pk} = \min\left(\frac{22 - 14}{3(2)}, \frac{14 - 10}{3(2)}\right)$$
$$= \min(1.33, \ 0.66)$$
$$= 0.66$$

The $C_{pk}$ value is below 1.00, telling us that the process is not capable. The $C_p$ measure, however, provides a different answer in this case:

$$C_p = \frac{USL - LSL}{6\sigma} = \frac{12}{12} = 1.00$$

This measure is misleading in this case. The reason for the difference is that the process is not centered on the specification range.

## Process Control Charts

Once we have ensured that the process is capable of producing products within the set limits, we need to make sure the process continues doing so. This requires regularly monitoring the process to make sure products are produced with characteristics that stay within the set limits. We say that we are ensuring that the process is "in a state of control." The most commonly used tool for doing this is a **process control chart**.

A control chart is a graph that shows whether a sample of data falls within the common or normal range of variation. The chart has upper and lower control limits that separate common from assignable causes of variation. We say that a process is out of control when a plot of data reveals that one or more samples fall outside the control limits. Figure 10.11 shows examples of when the data falls outside the control limits and when we need to investigate causes of variation.

To monitor the process using control charts, samples of the process output are taken at regular intervals and plotted on the control chart. When observed values go outside the control limits, the process is assumed not to be in control. Production is stopped, and employees attempt to identify the cause of the problem and correct it.

Control charts are one of the most commonly used tools in statistical process control and can be used to track the performance of any characteristic of a product, such as the weight of a cereal box, the number of chocolates in a box, or the volume in a bottle of water. Characteristics that can be monitored by control charts can be divided into two groups: **variables** and **attributes**.

Control charts for variables are used to monitor characteristics that can be *measured* and have a continuum of values, such as height, weight, or volume. A soft-drink bottling operation is an example of a variable measure because the amount of liquid in the bottles can be measured and can take on a number of different values. Other examples are the weight of a bag of sugar, the temperature of a baking oven, or the diameter of plastic tubing.

A control chart for attributes, on the other hand, is used to monitor characteristics that have discrete values and can be *counted*. Often they can be evaluated with a simple yes-or-no decision. Examples include color, taste, or smell. An attribute requires only a single decision, such as yes or no, good or bad, acceptable or unacceptable (e.g., the apple is good or rotten, the muffin is fresh or stale, the zipper is or is not broken, the lightbulb works or it does not work) or counting the number of defects (e.g., the number of broken cookies in the box, the number of dents on the car, the number of barnacles on the bottom of a boat). Control charts can be used to monitor both attributes and variables. Here we will look at the control charts for attributes.

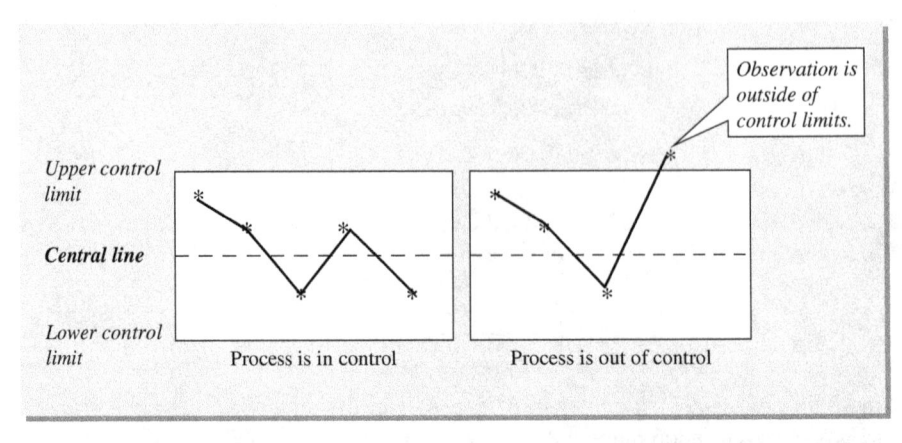

**FIGURE 10.11** Process control charts.

# Control Charts for Attributes

Control charts for attributes, called a **p-chart**, monitor the proportion of defective items in a sample. The center line of the chart is the average proportion defective in the population, or $\bar{p}$. This is obtained by taking a number of sample observations at random and computing the average value of $p$ across all samples. To construct the UCL and LCL for a p-chart we use the following formulas:

$$UCL = \bar{p} + z\, sp$$
$$LCL = \bar{p} - z\, sp$$

where

$z$ = standard normal variable

$\bar{p}$ = the sample proportion defective

$sp$ = the standard deviation of the average proportion defective computed as

$$sp = \sqrt{\frac{\bar{p}(1-\bar{p})}{n}}$$

where $n$ is the sample size.

### Example 3  Designing P-Charts

Mercy Hospital wants to ensure all staff follow a common five-step process when discharging patients. The hospital has put a check sheet in place and is performing random inspection to ensure that the steps are being followed. Conducting random checks of 10 observations per sample the hospital collected the following data to use to develop control chart limits.

| Sample | Number of incorrect procedures | Number inspected | Fraction defective |
|---|---|---|---|
| 1 | 0 | 10 | 0.1 |
| 2 | 1 | 10 | 0.1 |
| 3 | 2 | 10 | 0.2 |
| 4 | 1 | 10 | 0.2 |
| 5 | 1 | 10 | 0.1 |
| Total | 5 | 50 | |

$$\bar{p} = \frac{5}{50} = .10$$

$$sp = \sqrt{\frac{.10(1-.10)}{10}} = .095$$

$$UCL = \bar{p} + z\, sp = .10 + 3(.095) = .385$$

$$LCL = \bar{p} - z\, sp = .10 - 3(.095) = -.185 \rightarrow 0$$

In this example the lower control unit is negative, which sometimes occurs due to approximation of the binomial distribution. When it occurs, LCL is rounded to zero.

## Six Sigma Quality

### What Is Six Sigma?

Six Sigma is a quality management process that uses rigorous measurement to reduce process variation and eliminate defects. It originated at Motorola in the 1970s, and the rigorous standards were later embraced by General Electric, Lockheed Martin, Allied Signal, American Express, Texas Instruments, and other companies. Today, Six Sigma quality standard has become a benchmark in many industries.

Six Sigma defines quality as no more than 3.4 parts per million defective (ppm). Sigma ($\sigma$) stands for the number of standard deviations of the process and measures how far a given process deviates from perfection. A process with $\pm 3$ sigma ($\sigma$) means that 2,600 ppm are defective, whereas with Six Sigma they approximate 3.4 ppm, as shown in Figure 10.12. The process achieves this by eliminating waste through strict improvements in quality and elimination of defects. The idea behind Six Sigma is to systematically identify and eliminate defects and get as close to "zero defects" as possible. The concept of quality is at the core of Lean, and the two go hand in hand eliminating waste and rooting out defects. Six Sigma relies on all the tools we have discussed so far to achieve this.

To achieve the goals of Six Sigma, companies typically institute a quality focus in every aspect of their organization. Before a product is designed, marketing ensures that product characteristics are exactly what customers want. Operations ensures that exact product characteristics can be achieved through product design, the manufacturing process, and the materials used. The Six Sigma concept is an integral part of other functions as well. It is used in the finance and accounting departments to reduce costing errors and the time required to close the books at the end of the month. Six Sigma requires involvement of all parts of the organization as well as the entire supply chain.

### Six Sigma Methodology

There are two aspects to the Six Sigma methodology. First is the use of technical tools to identify and eliminate causes of quality problems. In fact, Six Sigma relies heavily on quantitative and data-driven technical tools. These technical tools include the statistical quality control tools and

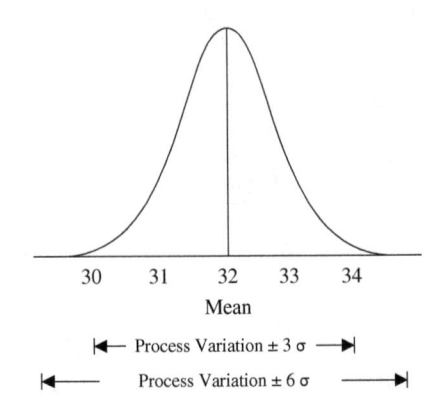

**FIGURE 10.12** Six Sigma versus Three Sigma quality.

the seven tools of quality discussed earlier in this chapter. Company use of these technical tools is integrated throughout the entire organization.

The second aspect of Six Sigma is people involvement, as with all other aspects of Lean. In Six Sigma all employees have the training to use technical tools and are responsible for rooting out quality problems. Employees are given martial arts titles that reflect their skills in the Six Sigma process. Black belts and master black belts are individuals who have extensive training in the use of technical tools and are responsible for carrying out the implementation of Six Sigma. They are experienced individuals who oversee the measuring, analysis, process controlling, and improving. They achieve this by acting as coaches, team leaders, and facilitators of the process of continuous improvement. Green belts are individuals who have sufficient training in technical tools to serve on teams or on small, individual projects.

The Six Sigma approach is organized around a five-step plan known as DMAIC, which stands for the following:

- **DEFINE:** Define the quality problem of the process.
- **MEASURE:** Measure the current performance of the process.
- **ANALYZE:** Analyze the process to identify the root cause of the quality problem.
- **IMPROVE:** Improve the process by eliminating the root causes of the problem.
- **CONTROL:** Control the process to ensure the improvements continue.

The first three steps provide a study of the existing process, whereas the last two steps are involved in process change. All steps extensively utilize quantitative tools, such as measuring the current performance and analyzing the process for root causes of problems. This is a continuous process. Part of Six Sigma is to continuously search for quality problems and improve them. In organizations, this effort is led by the black belts.

Successful Six Sigma implementation requires commitment from top company leaders. These individuals must promote the process, eliminate barriers to implementation, and ensure that proper resources are available. A key individual is the champion of Six Sigma. This is a person who comes from the top ranks of the organization and is responsible for providing direction and overseeing all aspects of the process.

## The Lean Six Sigma Supply Chain

In this chapter we have seen how Lean utilizes all its resources in the most efficient manner possible to create value for the end customer. We have also learned about Six Sigma, as a way to root out quality problems and reduce process variation. The two approaches together result in improved supply chains that can operate at lower relative costs and provide greater customer value than their competitors. They can even perform at levels exceeding customer expectations. As a result, Lean and Six Sigma create a "best-in-class" supply chain that provides a major competitive advantage over competitors. Figure 10.13 shows the tools from each approach that work to create an efficient Lean Six Sigma supply chain.

These practices, however, cannot just be implemented within one stage of the supply chain. They must be implemented across all organizations in the chain to work. Otherwise waste and inefficiencies incurred by even a few members of the chain will be passed down to the final

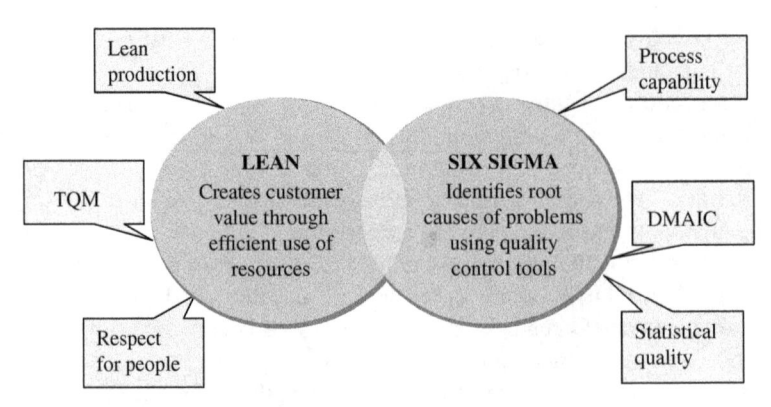

**FIGURE 10.13** Lean Six Sigma.

customer. If a process in the chain does not create value, it should be removed. For this reason the term "value chain" is often used to refer to a Lean supply chain.

A Lean Six Sigma supply chain is a cross-functional team effort comprising individuals across different supply chain processes. In many companies it is the same team as the Sales and Operations Planning (S&OP) we discussed in Chapter 8. S&OP is a process intended to match supply and demand through functional collaboration. The process is designed to coordinate activities between marketing and sales, with those of operations and sourcing, across the supply chain to ensure that supply meets demand requirements. It requires teamwork among sales, distribution and logistics, operations, finance, and product development. This enables supply chains to provide better customer service, lower inventory, reduce customer lead times, and stabilize production schedules. The S&OP is a very good source for Lean Six Sigma, as S&OP must be strategically aligned with executive management objectives. As a result, this team understands the "big picture" and sees major process breakdowns and their impact on the supply chain.

## Developing a Lean Six Sigma Supply Chain

Let's look at the steps in developing a Lean Six Sigma supply chain:

**Step 1—Jointly Define Value.** The cross-functional team jointly defines value as perceived by the final customer. This creates a joint vision of critical attributes of the product and delivery process. This involves identifying the Voice of the Customer (VOC), which we learned about in Chapter 5, and the specific value propositions for each target market.

**Step 2—Conduct Supply Chain Capability Analysis.** This requires establishing how well the current supply chain meets customer requirements. This means conducting a capability analysis. Six Sigma concepts can be used here to characterize the ability of the supply chain to meet customer requirements. The supply chain is viewed as a system and is analyzed for capacity bottlenecks and system constraints.

**Step 3—Develop Key Financial and Operational Metrics.** Key financial and operational metrics for the supply chain are developed. Inventory metrics are an important barometer of supply chain efficiency at this stage. For example, inventory investments and inventory turns ratio are important supply chain metrics that measure the efficiency of supply chain asset utilization. Developing an understanding of the relationships between metrics is important as well. For example, metrics such as lead-time, demand and service levels, impact key process outputs, such as cash flow, profitability, inventory investment and inventory turns.

**Step 4—Identify and Implement System Improvements.** The partners then work together to identify and eliminate waste from the system and to meet target cost. They analyze supply chain work streams using tools such as **Value Stream Mapping (VSM)**. VSM is a flowcharting tool that is used to illustrate product and information flows through various processing steps. It is a valuable tool in identifying all value-adding and non-value-adding processes.

In addition, Lean Six Sigma requires supply chain member transparency to share plans and information, such as forecasts, inventory usage requirements, and production plans. Information technology, as we discussed in Chapter 3, has become a critical tool to enable this degree of information sharing. Often supply chain partners are linked online. They develop joint forecasts, joint production schedules, and joint delivery plans. This permits suppliers to deliver goods when they are needed by their customers in smaller quantities and not carry excess inventories. Also suppliers have adopted stringent quality practices enabling customers to bypass the quality inspection process. All this serves to streamline the supply chain and eliminate steps.

## Impact on Supply Chain Activities

Lean Six Sigma has a transformative impact on the supply chain. However, some activities are more impacted than others. Let's look at some supply chain activities to see how they are impacted by Lean Six Sigma.

### Suppliers

Lean Six Sigma suppliers are a key element of an efficient supply chain. They are better able to respond to changes in customer demand, have lower costs due to efficient systems, and have improved quality that eliminates inbound inspection. They also tend to have shorter and more reliable lead times, which translate into lower safety stock and smoother workflow throughout the chain.

To quickly respond to demand, suppliers often locate their facilities close to their customers. For example, Dell requires its first-tier suppliers to be located within a 15-minute radius of its Austin facility. Also, Lean supply chains tend to rely on networks of small specialized plants that enable efficiency and permit focus. For example, Toyota has 12 separate plants located around Toyota City.

### Operations

Operations is one area where Lean Six Sigma improvements are most evident, from setting uniform work flow to pull production and changes in facility layout. One important aspect of operations is the calculation of the system's takt time, or cycle time, which we discussed in Chapter 5. Proper cycle time calculation ensures that the process will produce according to actual customer demand. Also, cycle time calculations directly tie into inventory calculations, discussed in Chapter 9, and ordering policies. Effective inventory utilization is a critical aspect of the Lean Six Sigma supply chain, as it is one of the most important assets. Metrics such as inventory turnover and utilization, discussed in Chapter 7, are especially important here.

### Logistics

Lean Six Sigma requires substantial changes in logistics, as it is a key function that connects the links in the chain. Location of warehouses and modes of transportation can be selected to optimize movement of materials and meet performance criteria. Optimization models can also be used to select routes and determine shipping quantities. In addition, changes in warehouse design are essential to eliminate waste, create efficiency improvements, and eliminate process variability from order picking to packing. As the logistics function is often outsourced to third-party logistics (3PL) providers, it is important to integrate the service provider into the supply chain planning process.

## CHAPTER HIGHLIGHTS

1. Lean is a management approach for creating value for the end customer through the most efficient utilization of resources possible. The most important tenet of Lean is eliminating waste, where waste is defined as anything that does not add value.

2. Lean consists of three elements that work together: Lean Production, Total Quality Management, and Respect for People.

3. Lean relies on visual signals to pull products through the system. Communication between work centers is made possible by the use of a signaling system called a kanban, which means "signal" or "card" in Japanese.

4. Jidoka is the authority of every worker to stop the production process and fix problems as they occur rather than pushing them down the line.

5. The "seven tools of quality control" are essential in identifying and analyzing quality problems. They include cause-and-effect diagrams, flowcharts, checklists, control charts, scatter diagrams, Pareto analysis, and histograms.

6. ISO 9000 consists of a "family" of standards established by the International Standards Organization that address various aspects of the quality management process. ISO 14000 are standards for environmental management.

7. SQC are statistical tools used to measure quality and identify quality problems in both the product and process. These tools can be divided into three broad categories: descriptive statistics, SPC, and acceptance sampling.

8. All processes have a certain amount of normal variation. Variation that is caused by factors that can be clearly identified and managed is called *assignable variation*. Variation that is inherent in the process itself is called *common or random variation*.

9. Process capability is the evaluation of the production process as to its ability to meet or exceed the set product specifications.

10. Process control charts are statistical quality control tools used to monitor the process to make sure products are being produced with characteristics that are within the set limits. Process control charts ensure that the process is "in a state of control."

11. Six Sigma is a quality management process that uses rigorous measurement to reduce process variation and eliminate defects. Six Sigma defines quality as no more than 3.4 parts per million defective (ppm).

## KEY TERMS

Lean
Six Sigma
Lean Six Sigma
Waste
Kaizen
Kaizen blitz
Lean Production
Total Quality Management (TQM)
Respect for People
just-in-time (JIT)
Pull production
Kanban
Setup time
Jidoka
Quality circle
Voice of the customer (VOC)
Cause-and-effect diagrams
Fishbone diagrams
Flowcharts
Checklists
Control charts
Scatter diagrams
Pareto analysis
Histograms
Statistical quality control
Descriptive statistics
Statistical process control (SPC)
Acceptance sampling
Assignable variation
Common or random variation
Process capability
Product specifications
Process control chart
Variables
Attributes
P-chart
Value Stream Mapping (VSM)

## DISCUSSION QUESTIONS

1. Describe the core beliefs of Lean and how they could be implemented in your own life.

2. Identify the three elements of Lean, and explain how they work together.

3. Find an example of a company that has high respect for people. How does this affect their performance?

4. Find an example of a service organization, and explain how Lean could be implemented in this environment.

5. Describe three recent situations in which you were directly affected by poor product or service quality.

6. Discuss the key differences between common and assignable causes of variation. Give examples.

7. Describe the differences between process capability and process control charts. How should the two be used together?

## PROBLEMS

1. Hawks Soccer is evaluating four different machines for their capability in manufacturing size 5 soccer balls. The specification range for the circumference is set between 68 and 71 cm. Given the standard deviations for each machine in the following table. You need to determine which of the machines are capable of producing within specifications.

| Machine | Standard deviation |
|---|---|
| A | 0.4 |
| B | 0.8 |
| C | 0.7 |
| D | 1.0 |

2. Tommy Suits are evaluating their two tailoring machines for their precision. The specification range is set between 0.2 and 0.5 mm with a mean of 0.3 mm. Given the standard deviation for each machine, determine the $C_{pk}$ values and compare them to $C_p$ values.

| Machine | Standard deviation |
|---|---|
| A | 0.04 |
| B | 0.05 |

3. Hoo-ha Karate Club is evaluating their three members for their strength in kicking. The specification range for the power is set between 300 and 350 KG. Given the standard deviation for each member, determine which of the members are capable of kicking within specification. Is this a reasonable measure here? Why or why not?

| Member | Standard deviation |
|---|---|
| A | 40 |
| B | 50 |
| C | 60 |

4. Compute and interpret the $C_{pk}$ measure of process capability for the following process. And also compute the $C_p$ measure. Explain the differences.

USL = 20
LSL = 12
Process $\sigma = 1$
Process $\mu = 14$

5. Specification range for machine performance is set between 50 and 100, and mean is 80. Given the information in the following table determine the $C_{pk}$ and $C_p$ values. Explain the differences.

| Machine | Standard deviation |
|---|---|
| A | 10 |
| B | 8 |
| C | 12 |

6. New Land Power is conducting random inspections to check the quality of their batteries. Data collected are in the following table. Use the information to develop control chart limits with a 95% confidence interval desired.

| Sample | Number defective | Number inspected | Fraction defective |
|---|---|---|---|
| 1 | 0 | 10 | 0 |
| 2 | 1 | 10 | 0.1 |
| 3 | 0 | 10 | 0 |
| 4 | 1 | 10 | 0.1 |
| 5 | 2 | 10 | 0.2 |

7. Doctor David Miller is conducting random inspections of the accuracy of his new specimen-reading machine. Data collected are shown in the following table. Use the data to develop control chart limits with a 99% confidence interval.

# LEAN SYSTEMS AND SIX-SIGMA QUALITY

| Sample | Number incorrect | Number inspected |
|---|---|---|
| 1 | 0 | 100 |
| 2 | 1 | 100 |
| 3 | 1 | 100 |

| Sample | Number defective | Number inspected |
|---|---|---|
| 1 | 2 | 50 |
| 2 | 1 | 50 |
| 3 | 2 | 50 |
| 4 | 3 | 50 |
| 5 | 1 | 50 |

8. Lucie Tire has conducted random inspections for defects of their new tires. Given the following data, develop control chart limits assuming 95% confidence interval.

## Case Study: Buckeye Technologies

Buckeye Technologies is a manufacturer of semiconductors for mobile consumer electronic devices, such as laptop computers, smart phones, and digital cameras. Ms. Sabina Norton has been working at Buckeye Technologies for about a year as a production manager. The volatile demand of the semiconductor industry has been an obstacle in designing an accurate production schedule. The unstable demand causes the company to carry high amounts of safety stock and incur other types of wastes. Sabina is wondering if the operation can be modified to become more efficient.

Transistors are key components used in the manufacture of a semiconductor. One of the transistors of a cell phone semiconductor is sourced from Xiang, a supplier in China, with a lead time of two months. Buckeye Technologies usually carries enough of these transistors at the plant. When it runs out of them, however, they experience high levels of work-in-process (WIP) inventory and are unable to continue with production. Although this transistor can also be obtained from several suppliers in the United States, the cost is considerable higher compared to the cost of sourcing it from Xiang.

The semiconductors for laptop computers, smart phones, and digital cameras are produced differently, so every time the company needs to produce a different type of semiconductor, the operator is required to change the setting of the production machinery. This can be time consuming, and the company wants to be able to respond quickly to changes in demand. Sabina knows that there must be a way to reduce inventory, but at the same time she wants to keep a flexible production schedule to keep up with the fast-paced environment and the volatility of the demand.

Sabina has also noticed that the current design of the facility is not very efficient. Currently the facility production system is grouped by function, and components move from function to function. There are about 350 steps in producing a semiconductor chip. Some functions of the facility are located at one end of the facility, whereas other functions are at the other end of the facility. This results in long waiting times between procedures. She is thinking about changing the design of the facility to one that will give more flow to the production process.

Sabina recognizes that a number of changes must be made. She has heard of Lean as a method to reduce waste but is not sure where to begin.

### Case Questions

1. What suggestions do you have for Sabina about working with suppliers, and how would you address the sourcing issue from the Chinese supplier based on Lean principles?
2. What should Sabina do about reorganizing the work environment? Should any layout changes be made, and how do you think they should be implemented?
3. How would you address the issue of equipment setup? How would you proceed?
4. What other suggestions would you offer Sabina to improve the operation of this company? In what order should these changes be made?
5. Describe the organizational culture of Lean. How can Sabina promote this at Buckeye?

# REFERENCES

Feigenbaum, A. V. *Total Quality Control.* New York: McGraw-Hill, 1991.

Holweg, Matthias. "The Genealogy of Lean Production." *Journal of Operations Management*, 25(2), 2007: 420–437.

Power, Brad. "How GE Applies Lean Startup Practices." *Harvard Business Review*, April 23, 2014.

Shingo, Shigeo. *Modern Approaches to Manufacturing Improvement.* Cambridge, MA: Productivity Press, 1990.

Womack, James P., and Daniel T. Jones. *Lean Thinking.* Mankato, MN: Free Press, 2003.

Womack, James P., Daniel T. Jones, and Daniel Roos. *The Machine That Changed the World.* New York: Macmillan Publishing Company, 1990.

# 11 Supply Chain Relationship Management

**LEARNING OBJECTIVES**

*After completing this chapter, you should be able to:*

- Explain the importance of relationships to SCM.
- Identify categories of supply chain relationships and their defining dimensions.
- Explain the differences between transactional-based and relational-based relationships.
- Describe the development and management of trust-based relationships.
- Explain different causes of conflict between supply chain members.
- Describe methods of dispute resolution and negotiation.

**CHAPTER OUTLINE**

■ **Supply Chain Relationships**
*Importance of Supply Chain Relationships*
*Relationship Dimensions*
    Scope
    Criticality
*Supply Chain Relationship Matrix*

■ **The Role of Trust**
*Trust-Based versus Power-Based Relationships*
*Developing a Trust-Based Relationship*
    Assessing the Relationship
    Identifying Operational Roles
    Creating Effective Contracts
    Designing Effective Conflict Resolution Mechanisms
*Managing a Trust-Based Relationship*
    Commitment
    Clear Method of Communication
    Performance Visibility
    Fairness

## ■ Managing Conflict and Dispute Resolution
*Sources of Conflict*
*Dispute Resolution Procedures*
*Litigation*
*Arbitration*
*Mediation*
*Negotiation*

## ■ Negotiation Concepts, Styles, and Tactics
*Leverage*
*"Position" versus "Interest"*
*Negotiator's Dilemma*
*Negotiation Styles*
*Adversarial Tactics*
*Problem-Solving Tactics*

## ■ Relationship Management in Practice
*The Keiretsu Supplier-Partnering Model*
*Partnership Agreements*
*Diluting Power*

## ■ Chapter Highlights

## ■ Key Terms

## ■ Discussion Questions

## ■ Case Study: Lucid v. Black Box

---

Verizon Wireless, Inc. is the wireless service provider that owns and operates the largest telecommunications network in the United States. Apple, Inc. is the well-known multinational corporation that creates and markets personal computers and consumer electronics such as the iPhone multifunction cellular phone. Verizon made a name for itself for having a remarkably reliable network. Apple's iPhone revolutionized the cell phone market by including features that allow users to surf the Internet, send and receive photographs and videos, and download content. The two companies are members of the same supply chain.

Today we are accustomed to the partnerships Apple has with wireless giants such as Verizon and AT&T. But how did these partnerships come about? A few years earlier Verizon and Apple almost created their first partnership but it fell through. Verizon, a reputable wireless service provider, would supply the network for Apple's fancy new phone. However, the two companies failed to reach agreement. Verizon feared relinquishing control over maintenance, retail fees, and service fees pursuant to Apple's demands. Apple feared creating a mobile phone device for Verizon's network because it did not operate globally. Despite their telecommunications expertise, Apple and Verizon ceased communicating for two years. As a result, Apple went with a different service provider.

Then Apple began receiving complaints that the wireless service for its iPhone was slow, choppy, and unreliable, given the tremendous amount of data transmitted over the wireless networks by millions of users. As a result of an overloaded service provider, many iPhone users suffered dropped calls. At the same time, Verizon was promising to develop an even faster global network. The CEO of Verizon Wireless reached out to the CEO of Apple to say, "We really ought to talk about how we do business together. We weren't able to [reach an agreement] a couple of years before, but it's probably worth having another discussion to make sure we're not missing something." The CEO of Apple responded, "Yeah, you're probably right. We have missed something."

With excitement swelling on the part of cell phone users around the globe, Verizon and Apple had finally decided to work together. Utilizing Verizon's superb wireless service and Apple's highly-sought-after phone, the two companies decided to collaborate to produce something many have called the "dream phone" with superior service and capabilities.

The partnership between Verizon and Apple illustrates how supply chain companies can enter into a relationship to create value for the final customer. It also illustrates the importance of relationship building, importance of value provided by each party, and the role of negotiation in the process.

Adapted from: Ellison, Sarah "The Dream Phone." *Fortune.* November 15, 2010: 128.

## Supply Chain Relationships

### Importance of Supply Chain Relationships

We have discussed the management and design of the physical network structure of the supply chain, the use of information technology to connect supply chain members, and the management of numerous processes across enterprises. In this chapter we discuss one of the most important aspects of supply chain management (SCM)—the management of relationships between supply chain members. In essence this involves the management of "people." Management of people overlays the physical supply chain structure and the connecting information technology, as shown in Figure 11.1.

Recall that SCM involves coordination of activities, collaboration in planning, and sharing of information among members of the supply chain so that they jointly plan, operate, and execute business decisions. Notice that engaging in these activities relies on relationships between members of the supply chain. In fact, relationship management is probably the most important aspect of SCM. It affects all areas of the supply chain and can have a dramatic impact on performance. Supply chain activities can be highly successful if there is trust and commitment between companies to work together. However, even if all the structural elements of the supply chain are in place—information technology, facilities, distribution centers, transportation management systems, and inventory systems—SCM efforts can fail as a result of sabotage, mistrust, or just poor communication. Information technology only provides the capability for information sharing. It is supply chain relationships that make it happen.

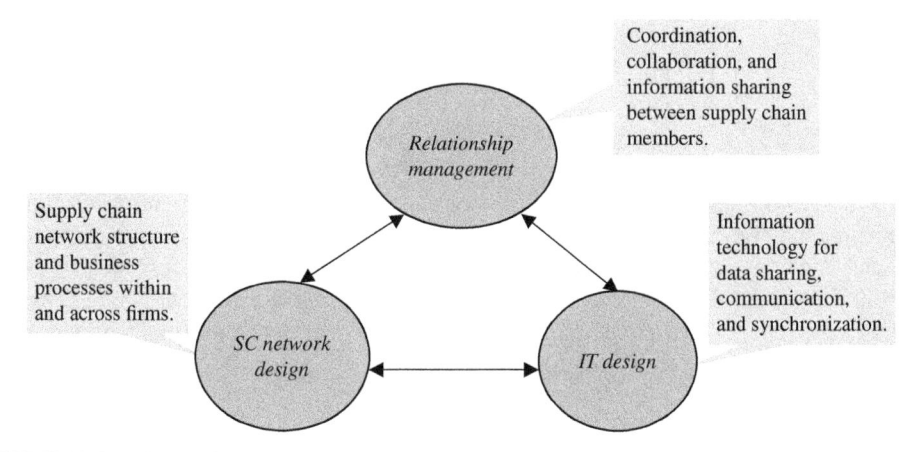

**FIGURE 11.1** Relationship management as an element of SCM.

Managing supply chain relationships involves managing relationships between people. It involves issues that include respect, trust, agreements, negotiation, joint ventures, contracting, and even conflict resolution. Therefore, supply chain management is primarily about the management of relationships across complex networks of companies. As a result, developing and managing relationships between supply chain partners may be the most important element of successful SCM.

## Relationship Dimensions

Not all supply chain relationships need to be, or should be, treated the same. Most companies today have hundreds or even thousands of suppliers. Some provide tangible goods, such as component parts or raw materials, whereas others provide services, such as transportation and logistics. All these relationships are not all of equal importance. Relationship management requires time and effort and should not be wasted on relationships that are transactional in nature. As we will see, supply chain relationships should be carefully segmented based on how much management is needed.

Consider that even a small bakery can have dozens of suppliers—from common items such as sugar and flour, to specialty items such as hazelnut paste or truffle oil. Some suppliers provide commodity items or services where cost is the determining criteria. For example, companies have historically used suppliers for certain routine activities, such as package deliveries, records management, or uniform cleaning. These routine services are transactional in nature and do not require relationship management. On the other hand, some companies use supply chain partners for almost all activities. This may include outsourcing virtually everything, including manufacturing, distribution, R&D, innovation, and even strategic planning. For example, Nike is a company that focuses on marketing and innovation and outsources manufacturing and distribution to other members of its supply chain. Similarly, Apple focuses on product innovation and marketing and outsources all manufacturing to the Chinese manufacturer Foxcon. In these cases, careful and ongoing relationship management is critical.

There are two dimensions that help differentiate supply chain relationships. The first is **scope**, or degree of responsibility, assigned to the supplier. A greater scope means a greater dependence on the supplier. The second dimension is **criticality** of sourced item or task. Criticality is the extent to which the sourced item or task impacts the ability of the organization to perform its core competencies. The greater the criticality of the sourced item, the greater the consequences of poor performance to the company and the greater the requirement for relationship management. Let's look at these dimensions in a bit more detail.

## Scope

At one extreme the relationship can be narrow in scope where a supplier provides a limited amount of items or provides one task from many possible tasks that make up an entire function. For example, this may be a supplier that is responsible for the replenishment of only maintenance, repair, and operating items (MRO) inventories (maintenance, repair, and operating items, discussed in Chapter 9). At another extreme the scope can be broad, where the bulk of items or services are provided by one supplier. An example would be complete manufacturing, as provided by Foxcon for Apple and Sony. Another example would be the comprehensive outsourcing of all aspects of the logistics function to a third-party logistics (3PL) provider, such as provided by UPS.

When the responsibility is relatively small, confined, and specific—such as handling a buyer's returned inventories, arranging for item disposal or restocking, or providing a commodity item such as sugar in the bakery—the risks of such a relationship are small. Such confined relationships are good for standardized products or repeatable tasks that are easily defined and have a limited choice of options.

As the scope of the relationship become more comprehensive, however, the degree of customization provided by the supplier progressively increases, as does the risk to the buyer. For example, this might be using a supplier to manage all inventories, including order management, or the complete management of a company's transportation system. The supplier may now be responsible for all aspects of the function, including equipment, facilities, staffing, software, implementation, management, and ongoing improvement. This is the level of outsourcing often seen with the services provided by 3PL providers.

A large scope of tasks provided by a supply chain partner can bring large benefits, as it allows the company to focus on their core competencies. The risks, however, can also be great as both operational and strategic responsibility is now in the hands of an outside party, requiring close relationship management.

## Criticality

The second differentiating dimension of supply chain relationships is the criticality of the tasks provided by a supplier. At one extreme a supplier can provide commodity items, such as sugar in the bakery example, or a more tactical task, such as records management. At the other extreme, a supplier may provide—and be the only source of—a critical component. Similarly, a firm may just outsource transportation, or it may outsource all aspects of the logistics function, such as the design, implementation, and ongoing management.

The higher the criticality of the outsourced task the greater the business risk to the buyer. As a result, this directly impacts the degree of relationship management required and the nature of the buyer–supplier relationship. When tasks with low criticality are outsourced, the relationship between buyer and supplier is primarily contractual. Relationship management is primarily focused on the transactional nature of the outsourced function. As criticality increases, the relationship moves from being **contractual** to becoming more **relational**. When there is low criticality, the supplier has responsibility over nonstrategic items or tasks. The relationship is contractual, and the buying firm continues to have operational and managerial responsibility over all internal functions and process. As the supplier's role becomes more comprehensive, however, the supplier increasingly becomes responsible for managerial and possibly the strategic aspects of the function. This moves the relationship from more transactional to more relational, as shown in Figure 11.2.

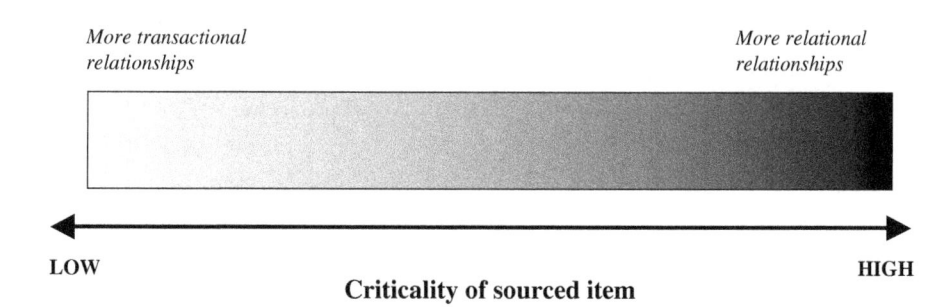

**FIGURE 11.2** Nature of supply chain relationships.

## Big Data Analytics Box—The Network Effect

### ■ AMAZON

Today's companies must rely on connections in addition to producing excellent products. In fact, today's biggest companies rely on connections as much as their industrial products. This is different from the past.

Just consider that four U.S. companies—Apple, Facebook, Google, and Microsoft—can claim billion-customer global businesses. They have well over 1 billion users. These companies operate at breathtaking scale and dominate their categories. This dominance is possible because of a highly linked system of communication and data, coupled with the fact that today's users crave efficiency and speed. As more people engage in these social networks, they attract more people. It is what scientists call "The Network Effect." This is when a system becomes better, faster, and more efficient for everyone as more people use it.

We can see this working in retail. An excellent example is Amazon, a retailer that far outpaces even its closest competitors in e-commerce. This is in large part because Amazon applies "more-is-better network logic" to the back end of its business. The more Amazon sells, the more the algorithms learn about what customers want, and the more customers want to use Amazon. Every company wants this ability to shape its business. Unfortunately, market dynamics mean that those that are using the "network effect" will be even more effective than competitors.

Adapted from: Ramo, Joshua Cooper. "Fueled by 'Network Power." *Fortune,* August 1, 2016, 20.

## Supply Chain Relationship Matrix

To understand categories of supply chain relationships we need to consider both dimensions—scope and criticality. Together these dimensions create four categories of buyer–supplier relationships that differ in the level of relationship management required. For example, a large scope coupled with high criticality leads to more comprehensive buyer–supplier relationships and to different types of managerial requirements than are necessitated by smaller scope and lower criticality. The four categories of relationships are nonstrategic transactions, contractual relationships, partnerships, and alliances, and they are shown in Figure 11.3.

1. **Nonstrategic Transactions.** When both scope and criticality are low, we have relationships that are solely transaction oriented, such as a simple commodity exchange. The product provided by the supplier is typically standardized, and alternative sources of supply or market access are readily available. There is little mutual dependence on which to base a relationship, and there is limited communication between supplier and buyer. Indeed, there is little reason for a relationship to evolve, and an arm's-length approach dominates the communication. From an organizational standpoint, nonstrategic relationships may form simply because there

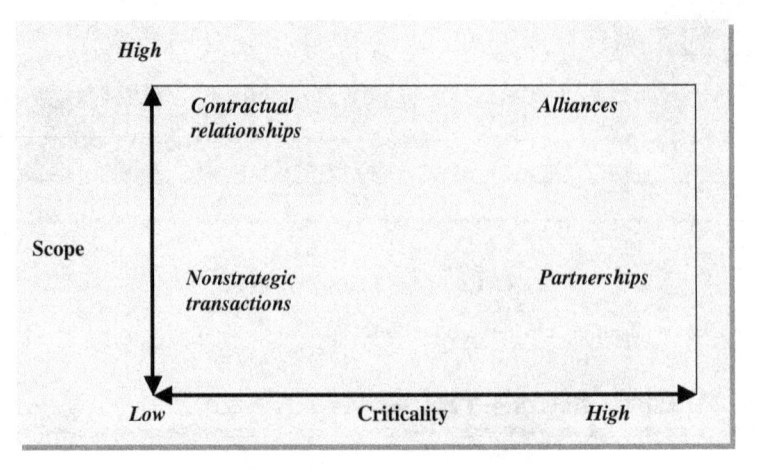

**FIGURE 11.3** Supply chain relationship matrix.

is no need for close interactions. The sourced items are typically standardized, and their low criticality does not necessitate close relationship management. The relationship, however, may evolve into a more encompassing relationship if the scope increases over time and involves multiple transactions. In that case it might become a contractual relationship.

2. **Contractual Relationships.** Contractual relationships occur when the scope is high, although the criticality of purchased items or tasks is low. This relationship is characterized by moderate levels of communication frequency, as there is a greater need for control over supplier activities. From an organizational standpoint, there is an awareness of the need for some management of the relationship due to the sheer size of the arrangement. Also, there is a higher level of trust and greater levels of interaction than in nonstrategic relationships. However, there is no desire to raise the commitment to a more personal relationship due to low criticality. The relationship is strictly based on formal contracts reducing the need for communication between boundary-spanning personnel.

3. **Partnerships.** This relationship type is characterized by the sourcing of critical components or tasks, albeit low in scope. The term "partnership" is used to connote strong and enduring trust between supplier and buyer, as well as a strong commitment to the relationship although the parties may not interact frequently. An example of this relationship could be the sourcing of just-in-time (JIT) replenishments of a critical manufacturing component. Due to the high criticality, the supplier has greater commitment to the relationship. However, given the higher level of trust and relatively small scope, there is limited frequency of interaction. The management of the relationship is not extensive, and the buyer may entrust the supplier with greater control.

4. **Alliances.** The most comprehensive buyer–supplier relationships occur when both criticality and scope are high. These arrangements are defined as alliance relationships, and reflect high interaction frequency and significant trust and commitment between supply chain partners. Alliances presume a high level of confidence in the capabilities and integrity of the other party and require significant resource investment in ongoing relationship management. In alliances, vendor products and services are highly customized and evolve with the business needs of the client. There is also great potential for flexibility given the typically large transaction volumes. In some cases these alliances may even be legalized through incorporation. A case in point is an alliance between Texas Utilities and CapGemini, called CapGemini Energy, for the purpose of outsourcing its entire information management organization.

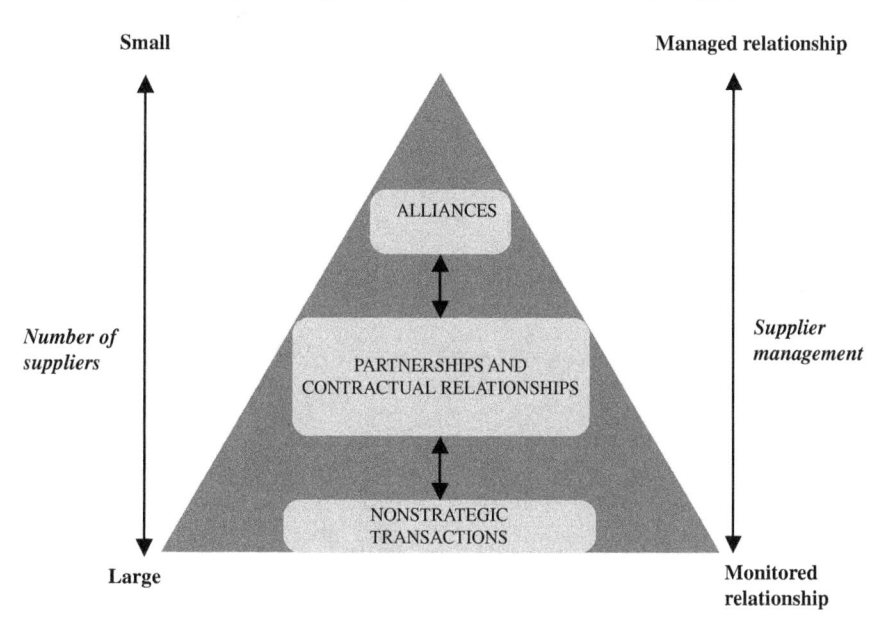

**FIGURE 11.4** Managing supply chain relationships.

These different buyer–supplier relationships have different managerial requirements. More comprehensive relationships, such as alliances, have a greater requirement to manage the relationship. By contrast, less-comprehensive relationships, as exemplified by nonstrategic transactions and contractual, primarily require performance monitoring. This is shown in Figure 11.4. Therefore, the number of comprehensive outsourcing engagements, such as alliance type relationships, must be kept small due to the extensive relationship management requirement. Relationships such as nonstrategic transactions, on the other hand, can be numerous as only monitoring efforts are required.

## Supply Chain Leaders' Box—Open Innovation

### PROCTOR & GAMBLE

Open innovation and strategic licensing are two developments in the business world that show the benefits of supply chain relationships, even with competitors. Open innovation means that, instead of relying exclusively on ideas created by intensive internal R&D efforts, organizations are willing to bring externally generated ideas to market. Strategic licensing means that, instead of guarding internally developed intellectual property jealously, companies are willing to license these innovations to outside companies.

Proctor & Gamble (P&G) is a leading consumer-product developer that created many of its leading brands through costly scientific internal research. That is, until P&G adopted an alternative innovation strategy that seeks to obtain half of its product innovations from external sources. The highly popular SpinBrush marketed by P&G was actually invented by four outside entrepreneurs rather than from P&G's own laboratories. Similar breakthrough products such as Tide Total Care, Olay Smooth Finish, Mr. Clean Magic Eraser, and Tide pods were all developed as part of its open innovation program called Connect+Develop. The program is designed to connect with suppliers, competitors, scientists, entrepreneurs, and others to actively look for proven technologies, packages, and products. P&G can then develop these further and market as either their own or in partnership with other companies. Connect+Develop uses its own web portal, through which innovators can submit their innovations directly to P&G. The company's Development Team then reviews submissions and provides feedback.

Open innovation can save money by reducing reliance on cost-intensive in-house scientific research. P&G is showing that collaboration accelerates innovation. The strategy has proven highly successful. As a result P&G has put forth a strategic effort to systematize innovative and has formalized this strategy through Connect+Develop.

See www.pgconnectdevelop.com.

## The Role of Trust

### Trust-Based versus Power-Based Relationships

An important characteristic of competitive supply chains is the focus on relationship building and the move away from arm's-length adversarial relationships that had been dominant in the past. Underlying this idea is that the buyer–supplier relationship should be based on a partnership of trust, commitment, and fairness. There are numerous advantages to such relationships that can be long-term and mutually beneficial. The competitive advantage of companies such as Toyota and Honda over their competitors in the auto industry comes from the collaborative relationships they have developed with their suppliers. Successful supply chains will be those that are governed by a constant search for win–win relationships based on mutuality and trust.

A trust-based relationship between supply chain partners helps improve performance for the following reasons. First, a cooperative relationship results in the development and sharing of joint objectives. This means that each party is much more likely to consider the other party's objectives when making their decisions. Second, managerial strategies to achieve coordination become easier to implement. Sharing of information is easier between parties that trust each other. Also, it is easier to implement and design operational improvements, as both parties are aiming for a common goal. Third, cooperation and coordination result in the elimination of duplication of efforts between parties. Consequently, supply chain productivity is increased. An example may be that the manufacturing firm does not have to inspect the quality of materials it receives from its supplier. Finally, greater sharing of sales and production information results in enabling members of the supply chain to coordinate production and distribution decisions.

Historically, supply chain relationships have been based on power. In a power-based relationship, the stronger party dictates its view. Although exploiting power may be advantageous in the short term, its negative consequences are felt in the long term for three main reasons. First, exploiting power results in one supply chain partner maximizing its profits, often at the expense of other partners. This decreases total supply chain profits. Second, exploiting power to extract unfair concessions can hurt a company once the balance of power changes. Third, when a member of a supply chain systematically exploits its power advantage, the other members find ways to resist. For example, when retailers tried to exploit their power, manufacturers have sought ways to directly access the consumer. This included selling over the Internet and setting up company stores. The result can be a decrease in supply chain profits because different members are now competing rather than cooperating. Figure 11.5 highlights the differences between trust- and power-based relationships.

Given the negative consequences of power-based relationships, cooperation and trust between supply chain members is highly valuable. However, these qualities are very hard to initiate and sustain. There are two views on how cooperation and trust can be brought into any supply chain relationship:

1. **Contractual-Based View.** This view states that formal contracts should be used to ensure cooperation among supply chain members. With a contract in place, parties are assumed to behave in a trusting manner for reasons of self-interest, although actual trust has not been built.

| TRUST-BASED RELATIONSHIPS | POWER-BASED RELATIONSHIPS |
|---|---|
| • Development of joint objectives | • One partner maximizes its profit at expense of others |
| • Greater sharing of information | • Extracting unfair concessions hurts the company if balance of power shifts |
| • Elimination of duplication of efforts | • Creates competition rather than cooperation |
| • Coordination easier to implement | • Results in decreased supply chain profitability |

**FIGURE 11.5** Characteristics of trust-based versus power-based relationships.

2. **Relationship-Based View.** Trust and cooperation are viewed as a result of a series of interactions between the partners built over time. Positive interactions strengthen the belief in the cooperation of the other party.

In practice, neither view holds exclusively. Initially in the relationship the contractual-based view holds. Over time, however, the relationship evolves toward a relationship-based view, if it is a strong supply chain relationship. A contract is always the basis of a business partnership. Parties that may not trust each other yet have to rely on the building of trust to resolve issues that are not included in the contract. Conversely, parties that trust each other and have a long relationship still rely on contracts. In most effective partnerships, a combination of the two approaches is used. An example of this situation is when suppliers sign an initial contract with manufacturers containing contingencies, yet they never refer to the contract afterward. Their hope is that all contingencies can be resolved through negotiation in a way that is best for all parties.

There are two phases to any long-term supply chain relationship. First is the **design phase** of the relationship, where ground rules are established and the relationship is initiated. Second is the **management phase**, where the interactions based on the ground rules are managed. A manager seeking to build a supply chain relationship must consider how cooperation and trust can be encouraged during both phases of the relationships. Careful consideration is very important because in most supply chains, power tends to be concentrated in relatively few hands. The concentration of power often leads managers to ignore the effort required to build trust and cooperation, hurting supply chain performance in the long term. Next we discuss how supply chain relationships can be designed to encourage cooperation and trust.

## Developing a Trust-Based Relationship

A trust-based relationship between two companies in the supply chain creates a sense that each company can depend on the other and has confidence in joint decisions. Trust creates the belief that each company is interested in the other's welfare and would not take action without considering the impact of those decisions on other companies as well, in addition to themselves. However, building a trust-based relationship can be difficult as it requires changing the nature of traditional relationships between suppliers and customers in the supply chain. Certain key steps can be followed in designing trust-based relationships. We look at these next.

### Assessing the Relationship

The first step in designing a supply chain relationship is to clearly identify the mutual benefit that the relationship provides. In most supply chains, each member of the partnership brings distinct skills, all of which are needed to supply a customer order. For example, a manufacturer produces the product, a carrier transports it between firms, and a retailer makes the product available to the final customer. The contribution of each party to supply chain success and profitability must be made clear.

An important element of the relationship is equity. Fair dealing in the relationship—called equity—should be an important element when developing a relationship. Equity measures the fairness of the division of the total profits between the parties involved. Members of the supply chain are unlikely to participate in true coordination unless they are confident that the resulting increase in profits will be shared equitably. For example, when suppliers make an effort to reduce replenishment lead times, the supply chain benefits because of reduced safety stock inventories at manufacturers and retailers. Suppliers are unlikely to put in the effort if the manufacturers and retailers are not willing to share the increase in profitability with them. Consequently, a supply chain relationship is likely to be sustainable only if it increases profitability, and this increase is shared equitably between the parties.

### Identifying Operational Roles

When identifying operational roles and rights of each party in a supply chain relationship, managers must consider the interdependence between the parties. One source of conflict occurs when the tasks are divided in a way that makes one party more dependent on the other. In fact, dependence of one party on another often leads to frustration among supply chain firms. In many partnerships, an inefficient allocation of tasks results simply because neither party is willing to give the other a perceived upper hand based on the tasks assigned.

Traditionally, supply chain activities have been sequential, with one stage completing all its tasks and then handing them off to the next stage. This was called **sequential interdependence**, where the activities and information of one partner preceded the other. A different relationship is **reciprocal interdependence**, where parties come together and exchange information, with information flowing in both directions. Such a relationship is the one between P&G and Wal-Mart, where the companies have created reciprocal interdependence. An example of this is their use of Collaborative Planning and Forecasting for Replenishment (CPFR), discussed in Chapter 8. The process relies on ongoing work teams with members from both Wal-Mart and P&G. Wal-Mart brings demand information to the process, as it is closest to the customer, and P&G brings information on available capacity. The teams then decide on the production and replenishment policy that is best for the supply chain.

Reciprocal interdependence requires a significant effort to manage and can increase transaction costs if it is not managed properly. However, reciprocal interdependence is more likely to result in supply chain profitability because all decisions take the objectives of both parties into account. Reciprocal interdependence increases the interactions between the two parties, increasing the likelihood of trust and cooperation if positive interactions occur. Reciprocal interdependence also makes it harder for one party to be opportunistic and take self-serving actions that hurt the other party. Therefore, greater reciprocal interdependence in decision making increases the chances of an effective relationship.

### Creating Effective Contracts

Managers can help promote trust by creating contracts that encourage negotiation as unplanned events arise. Contracts are most effective when all future contingencies can be accounted for. Unfortunately, practical realities of the business environment make it impossible to design a contract that includes provisions for all contingencies. Therefore, it is essential that the parties develop a relationship that allows trust to compensate for gaps in the contract. The relationship often develops between appropriate individuals that have been assigned from each side. Over time, the informal understandings and commitments between the individuals tend to be formalized when new contracts are drawn up. When designing the partnership and initial contract, it should be understood that informal understandings will operate side by side, and these will contribute to the development of the formal contract over time. Thus, contracts that evolve over time are likely to be much more effective than contracts that are completely defined at the beginning of the partnership.

Over the long term, contracts can only play a partial role in maintaining supply chain partnerships. What is needed is a combination of a contract, the mutual benefit of the relationship, along with trust that compensates for gaps in the contract.

## Designing Effective Conflict Resolution Mechanisms

Effective conflict resolution mechanisms can strengthen supply chain relationships. Conflicts will inevitably arise. Unsatisfactory resolutions cause the partnership to worsen, whereas satisfactory resolutions strengthen the partnership. A good conflict resolution mechanism should give the parties an opportunity to communicate and work through their differences. An initial formal specification of rules and guidelines for financial procedures and technological transactions can help build trust between partners. The specification of rules and guidelines facilitates the sharing of information among the partners in the supply chain.

Regular and frequent meetings between members of both organizations facilitate communication and are an important part of conflict management. These meetings allow issues to be raised and discussed before they turn into major conflicts. They also provide a basis for resolution at a higher level, should resolution at a lower level not take place. An important goal of these formal conflict resolution mechanisms is to ensure that disputes over financial or technological issues do not turn into interpersonal squabbles.

## Managing a Trust-Based Relationship

Once a trust-based relationship is developed, it must be managed. Effectively managed supply chain relationships promote cooperation and trust, increasing supply chain coordination. In contrast, poorly managed relationships lead to each party being opportunistic, resulting in inefficiency and loss of profitability. One problem, however, is that management of the relationship is often seen by managers as a routine task with little reward. Often top management prefers to be involved in the design of a new partnership that often provides corporate visibility, but is rarely involved in its management. This has led to a mixed record in running successful supply chain alliances and partnerships. The following factors are a part of managing a successful supply relationship.

### Commitment

Commitment of both parties helps a supply chain relationship succeed; in particular, commitment of top management on both sides is crucial for success. The manager directly responsible for the partnership can also facilitate the development of the relationship by clearly identifying the value of the partnership for each party in terms of their own expectations.

### Clear Method of Communication

Having clear organizational arrangements in place significantly increases the chances of relationship success. This is especially important when it comes to information sharing and conflict resolution. Lack of information sharing and the inability to resolve conflicts are the two major factors that lead to the breakdown of supply chain partnerships.

### Performance Visibility

Mechanisms that make the actions of each party and resulting outcomes visible help avoid conflicts and resolve disputes. Such mechanisms make it harder for either party to be opportunistic and help identify defective processes, increasing the value of the relationship for both parties.

### Fairness

The more fairly the stronger partner treats the weaker, vulnerable partner, the stronger the supply chain relationship tends to be. The issue of fairness is extremely important in the supply chain context because most relationships will involve parties with unequal power.

Unanticipated situations that hurt one party more than the other often arise. The more powerful party often has greater control over how the resolution occurs. The fairness of the resolution influences the strength of the relationship in the future. Fairness requires that the benefits and costs of the relationship be shared between the two parties in a way that makes both winners.

## Global Insights Box—Growth Through Partnership

### ■ COCA-COLA IN AFRICA

The Coca-Cola Company is a beverage manufacturer, marketer, and retailer most famous for the sweet, brown, fizzy soda known by almost everyone as "Coke." The red and white Coca-Cola circle may be one of the most recognizable brands the world over. But how about drinks such as Sparletta Stoney Tangawizi? Or maybe a drink such as Krest Bitter Lemon? These are just 2 of 100 drinks that Coca-Cola produces in Africa, and many are tailored to local taste.

Coke's presence in Africa dates back to 1929, but Africa has taken on a new role in the eyes of this major corporation. Growth has slowed down significantly for Coca-Cola products in Western markets such as Europe and the United States. The rate of growth in Africa is considerably higher, and the continent is increasingly becoming a larger part of Coca-Cola's revenue. Many experts predict Africa will grow in the next few decades much as India and China did in the last few decades. Currently, Coke is the African continent's largest employer, with business units in every African country, 145 bottling plants, and 70,000 employees.

Coke's strategy for growth in Africa has been through partnerships. Coke has chosen to partner with small shop owners in alleyways in small villages. The business model needed to partner with these retailers is unique. Coca-Cola provides the refrigerators and even paints the storefronts with the brand logo. Rather than using delivery trucks to restock the retail stores, Coca-Cola ships cases of bottles from bottling plants to one of 3,000 Manual Distribution Centers. Here, young men and women load the cases onto a trolley and deliver drinks by hand. This distribution model is apt for a region with relatively poor transportation infrastructure. Further, given little room for extra inventory, many store owners order just one case per day, which would render truck deliveries an overkill.

In return for helping establish the Coca-Cola brand throughout Africa, Coca-Cola educates its microdistributors in ways that include how to save resources by timing the icing of the bottles for lunch rush and how to purchase real estate with the extra revenue earned by selling Coke. It is an example that win–win partnerships can occur despite differences in power or size.

Adapted from: Nurse, Earl. "The Secret Behind Coca-Cola's Success in Africa." CNN World, January 21, 2016.

# Managing Conflict and Dispute Resolution

As we have seen, there are many types of supply chain relationships that serve many purposes. Even when there is trust and fairness, conflict can arise. In this section we look at sources of conflict and procedures for dispute resolution.

## Sources of Conflict

One of the most problematic issues in relationship management is how to manage conflict. To ward off conflicts before they turn into disputes, we should understand the sources of conflict.

Five potential sources of conflict may arise in supply chain relationships: relationship conflict, data conflict, interest conflict, structural conflict, and values conflicts.[1]

**Relationship conflicts** are a result of strong emotions, misperceptions or stereotypes, poor communication or miscommunication, and repetitive negative behavior. In intercultural communications, stereotypes are especially problematic. We attribute negative features to people or institutions we don't recognize or understand. When different languages are involved—as in multicultural negotiation—the risks of miscommunication increase.

**Data conflicts** are caused by lack of information, misinformation, different views on what is relevant, different interpretation of data, and different data-assessment procedures. Information traveling between multiple supply chain members can be lost just as in the children's game of telephone. Even when all relevant parties have the same spreadsheet before them, with the same data, differences in how the data is interpreted can cause conflicts.

**Interest conflict** can be caused by perceived or actual competition over substantive interest. An example might be the selected criteria used to determine whether a supplier meets a certain quality standard. Interest conflict can also arise from competition over procedural interests, such as a protocol for processing orders. It can also arise over psychological interests, such as how blame or praise is to be allocated. In supply chain management, for example, not equally sharing cost savings between members that result from process improvements can create interest conflict.

**Structural conflicts** are caused by factors such as destructive patterns of behavior or interaction; unequal control, ownership, or distribution of resources; unequal power or authority; geographical, physical, or environmental factors that hinder cooperation; and time constraints. Structural conflicts are among the most prominent sources of conflict in supply chain management relationships.

**Values conflicts** are caused by different criteria for evaluating ideas or behavior; mutually exclusive intrinsically valuable goals; and different ways of life, ideology, or religion. Values conflicts are to be expected in intercultural interactions. For example, Western companies operating in India have found it difficult to engage older workers in a participatory style of management because hierarchical roles are the cultural norm.

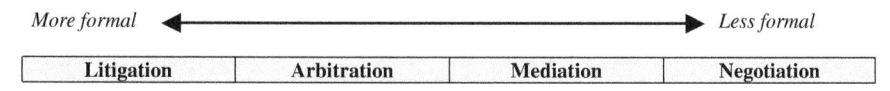

## Dispute Resolution Procedures

Figure 11.6 illustrates the four primary dispute resolution processes. To be sure, there are hybrids that involve combinations of these procedures.

From left to right, the procedures transition from formal and adjudicative (where an independent party determines the outcome of the dispute) to informal and consensual (where the disputants themselves determine the outcome of the dispute). Also, the nature of third-party intervention is different, with litigation involving decisional assistance by a judge, and mediation involving procedural assistance by a mediator. Supply chain partners should decide ahead of time how they will resolve disputes, which will inevitably arise, considering the features unique to each dispute resolution procedure. Figure 11.7 shows differences in dispute resolution procedures.

*More formal* ◄─────────────────────────► *Less formal*

| Litigation | Arbitration | Mediation | Negotiation |

**FIGURE 11.6** Dispute resolution procedures.

---

[1] Christopher W. Moore. *The Mediation Process*, 2nd ed. (Cambridge, MA: Harvard University Press, 1996).

|  | Litigation | Arbitration | Mediation | Negotiation |
|---|---|---|---|---|
| 1. Proceedings type | • Formal proceedings | • Informal Proceedings | • Informal meetings with parties | • Informal meetings with parties |
| 2. Decision maker | • Judge (law) and jury (facts) | • Party-appointed arbitrator | • Disputants | • Disputants |
| 3. Third party role | • Issue judgment based on application of law to facts | • Determines award based on terms of agreement | • Facilitate negotiation between disputants | • Not applicable |
| 4. Basis for decision | • Law, evidence, national policy | • Standards provided by arbitration agreement | • Interests or positions of parties | • Interests or positions of parties |
| 5. Confidentiality | • No | • Yes | • Yes | • Yes |
| 6. Binding | • Yes, by court Decree | • Yes, by court confirmation of arbitration award | • Yes, settlement agreement enforceable as a contract | • Yes, settlement agreement enforced as a contract |
| 7. Appeal | • Yes | • Usually no. | • Not applicable | • Not applicable |

**FIGURE 11.7** Differences in dispute resolution procedures.[2]

## Litigation

When a supply chain member breaches a contract or commits fraud, a legal wrong has been committed. This may be stealing inventory or using lesser grade materials than contracted. Consider the case of Mattel Toys from a few years ago that found its Chinese suppliers were using lead in their materials. The victim may choose to file a lawsuit to be made whole. A legal sanction should deter the wrongdoer from repeating such behavior. However, some companies will factor litigation costs into the overall costs of doing business and will only avoid breaching a contract when the costs exceed the benefits. Litigation costs can be excessive. They involve lawyer fees, court fees, producing sensitive data for evidence, depositions of responsible parties (which can impede productivity), the uncertainty of a jury verdict, and the potential for bad press (because lawsuits are usually public). Time-consuming, uncertain and costly, litigation is viewed by some as the "nuclear option": it should be used only as a last resort. Litigation is viewed by some as a management failure because resolution of the dispute is no longer within the management's control. Rather, factual controversies are resolved by a jury, and questions of rights and obligations are determined by an independent judge. Although trial court opinions can be appealed, the process is usually protracted and costly. Litigated outcomes are usually "all or nothing" for either the plaintiff or the defendant.

## Arbitration

When both parties can agree to procedures and norms for how their disputes should be resolved, they can create an arbitration agreement that stipulates how an arbitrator will be selected and which controversies will be subject to arbitration. This option is especially useful in international

---

[2] Adapted from: Leonard L. Riskin, James E. Westbrook, Chris Guthrie, Richard C. Reuben, Jennifer K. Robbennolt, and Nancy A. Welsh. *Dispute Resolution and Lawyers*, 4th ed. (St. Paul, MN: West Academic Publishers, 2009), p. 14.

commercial contexts, where suing in the courts of another nation may not be desirable to either party. Further, arbitration may be desirable for businesses that specialize in highly technical fields who want to avoid having factual questions decided by a lay jury. Instead, the parties can choose a neutral arbitrator who is an expert in their field to determine the outcome. The parties can also stipulate by agreement that certain issues will be arbitrated, whereas other matters may be litigated. Arbitration allows the parties to customize the dispute resolution procedure. In fact, they may agree that the law is irrelevant and industry norms or customs should govern the outcome. Like litigation, arbitration involves a neutral third party who issues a binding decision. Unlike litigation, however, arbitrators are not obligated to provide a reasoned opinion for their award. The choice to arbitrate a dispute should be made with care because courts usually enforce arbitration agreements, requiring parties to arbitrate disputes when they have agreed to in contract. Further, the choice of arbitrator must be made with care because arbitration awards are almost never subject to review. Instead, they are enforced as mandatory and binding.

## Mediation

Like litigation and arbitration, mediation relies on a neutral third party. Unlike the former two procedures, the mediator does not have power to compel the disputants to accept any particular outcome. Mediators are more like facilitators than decision makers. The mediator acts as a "go-between" or conducts shuttle diplomacy, ferrying information, offers, and counteroffers between the disputants. Although some courts require the parties to attempt mediating their dispute before litigating, mediation is usually voluntary and is the dispute resolution procedure of choice when preserving the relationship between the parties is more important than seeking vindication. In supply chain management, where long-term relationships are important, this is a much preferred method of dispute resolution than litigation and arbitration.

The structure of mediation and the issues that are subject to mediation are determined by the parties. The mediator must be impartial, creative, and patient. Mediators often help the parties devise creative solutions to their problems, but whether to agree to a mediated outcome is up to either party. In other words, mediation is a facilitated negotiation. The effectiveness of mediation depends not only on the attitude of the disputants, but also on the talent and style of the mediator.

## Negotiation

Negotiation is basically the process of gaining concessions from another party. Negotiation is the most informal of dispute resolution procedures and does not involve third-party assistance. The disputants agree to discuss or argue about a problem until they determine a resolution. Sometimes, parties will refuse to negotiate, and the only way to resolve the dispute is through a more formal mechanism. Sometimes, a party will agree to negotiate, but will do so with such aggressive tactics that the initiating party is better off not negotiating. Usually, powerful or sophisticated parties do better in negotiations than weak or unsophisticated parties. Negotiated decisions can be enforced as a contract. Negotiations can be viewed as adversarial, where each party tries to extract as much value from the other as possible. Or, negotiations can be viewed as problem-solving opportunities, where each party helps brainstorm the conflict to determine whether mutually beneficial agreements are possible. In supply chain relationship management, negotiations should consider more collaborative, problem-solving orientations toward dispute resolution. Because negotiation is consensual and does not require third-party intervention, it can be the most inexpensive and swift method for resolving disputes.

## Managerial Insights Box

### ■ COMMODITY SWAPPING

Who says competitors can't be good to one another? One nonobvious way to lower the overall cost of supply chain operations is for competing companies to make a deal with each other to rationalize commodity sourcing. Swapping with a competitor may lead to mutual cost savings where everyone "wins."

Raw materials are traditionally shipped from the point of extraction to the point of processing. This takes place across vast oceans or continents. The innovation of commodity swapping allows some companies in iron, steel, chemicals, paper, oil, electricity, and textile industries to virtually eliminate the cost of transporting commodities. When a shipment of metal bolts makes its way across the ocean, and passes another shipment of nearly identical bolts heading in the opposite direction, the managers receiving these shipments should consider swapping commodities with one another.

Consider the case of the Dow Chemical Company, which makes 100% of its polymers in the United States. Dow Chemical used to ship these polymers to be consumed by its own plants around the world, less than half of which were located in the United States. A competitor company, Arkema, with manufacturing based in France and Italy, made the same polymers and shipped them around the world to be consumed internally, some by plants in North America. Both the European Union and the United States imposed import duties, and the Atlantic Ocean freight cost per metric ton was $40 to $60. The competitors saw an opportunity to engage in a cost-saving collaboration. After each company tested the competitor's product, Dow Chemical and Arkema negotiated a commodity swap to supply one another's polymer plants. This collaborative negotiation between competitors resulted in annual cost savings of tens of millions of dollars.

Swapping allows both parties to eliminate inefficient transport procedures. Commodity swapping is particularly useful when dealing with import taxes, large distances, and bulk quantities. The concept of swapping commodities can be extended to products as well as to manufacturing capacities. Benefits of swapping include reduced transport costs including import and export levies, reduced logistics costs including storage, reduced uncertainty in supply, reduced price volatility, reduced inventory, and reduced environmental impact.

Adapted from: Kosansky, Alan, and Ted Schaefer. "Should You Swap Commodities with Your Competitors?" CSCMP's *Supply Chain Quarterly*, Quarter 2, 2010.

## Negotiation Concepts, Styles, and Tactics

We negotiate, consciously or not, every day. When you decide who will drive in the carpool, when you trade baseball cards, when you and your date decide where to go to dinner, you are negotiating. Negotiations involve give-and-take, a dance of sorts, where positions are exchanged until the two parties can agree to a mutually beneficial settlement—that is, an agreement that satisfies the underlying interest of the parties. In the context of SCM, negotiations are required to determine the terms of the contractual relationship between business units in a supply chain.

Negotiations can take place concerning almost anything. Issues such as cost, quantity, quality, timing, control, options, shared resources, and penalties for noncompliance are usually subject to negotiation. This section introduces you to negotiation concepts, styles, and tactics that are of great use to managing supply chain relationships.

### Leverage

Leverage is one of the most important elements in a negotiation. The party with the most leverage is the one who loses the least from walking away from the negotiation table. The leverage one possesses strongly affects one's relative bargaining power in a negotiation. The party with greater leverage is able to extract the most value from the counterparty. To illustrate, suppose you own the only Model-T Ford that a notorious collector doesn't already possess. You are perfectly happy maintaining ownership of the car because you believe on good evidence that its value will continue to appreciate. However, you do have bills to pay, and the car isn't doing you much financial good sitting in your garage. This collector has an extremely ardent desire to possess this one remaining car so that he may complete his collection. He is, some would say, a fanatic about your Model-T. You have several outstanding offers for the car, though his is the highest bid. Because each of you has something the other wants—you have the product, he has the cash—you are in a position to negotiate. However, because you have less to lose from walking away from the negotiation, you have the most leverage. That is, you can choose not to negotiate with the collector because you have alternative bidders. The collector, however, has no choice but to negotiate with you because you possess the only remaining car. You can use this leverage to request a higher price for the car from the collector, regardless of what the other competing bids are. Before entering into a negotiation, you should reflect on who has the most leverage.

## "Position" versus "Interest"

Suppose you are a widget wholesaler, and you are in a negotiation with a retailer who might purchase your widgets. A **position** is what you signal to the counterparty about your willingness to accept or willingness to pay. When you say, "I won't accept anything less than $10.00 per unit," and the retailer responds with, "I won't pay anything more than $7.00 per unit," you are both stating a position. After this initial exchange of positions, you find yourselves at an impasse. You have both stated mutually exclusive positions, and it looks like there is no way forward unless one of you changes your position.

An **interest** is the underlying reason for your position. Often, negotiators will conceal their underlying interests because they do not trust each other. This is common in arm's-length negotiations. However, if both wholesaler and retailer in this example were to disclose their underlying interests to one another, they could discover possibilities for mutual gains. Perhaps you believe the retailer is only going to purchase a few widgets, and you need to charge a premium for such a small shipment. Your interest is in making a large enough profit from the deal to make processing the order worth your time. The retailer, on the other hand, has an interest in being the only vendor who supplies your brand of widget, but is afraid to mention this because she believes you may use it as leverage against her. If the two of you were to share your underlying interests, several possibilities would emerge. The wholesaler would realize the retailer was not a one-time buyer and would stop treating her as such. The retailer would realize the wholesaler was not fixed at $10.00 per unit, but was offering that price because of a misperception. The retailer may offer to make repeat widget purchases if the wholesaler would offer a lower price per unit. By revealing underlying interests, negotiators are able to find a zone of mutually beneficial agreement.

## Negotiator's Dilemma

When a negotiator shares truthful information, they have a higher chance of achieving mutually beneficial outcomes. **Integrative opportunities** are negotiation opportunities that are non-zero-sum. Here both parties can be made better off without making either party worse off. However, deception confers distributive advantages where one of the parties benefits more than the other. **Distributive opportunities**, on the other hand, are zero-sum negotiation opportunities. This is where what is good for one party is directly adverse to the other party.

Should you share truthful information about your underlying interests? Or should you conceal this information carefully? The negotiator's dilemma is the inevitable paradox at the core of negotiation. The right answer depends on the setting and the nature of the relationship between the negotiators. Usually a negotiation will have integrative and distributive potential. That is, a negotiation will present opportunities for the parties to offer one another things that increase the size of "the pie," and the negotiation will present opportunities for the parties to claim slices of that "pie." A good negotiator looks for integrative and distributive opportunities, making efforts to increase the total value of a deal to both parties, even as the negotiator claims as much value as she can for herself.

## Negotiation Styles

There are two categories of negotiator styles: adversarial and problem solving. **Adversarial negotiators** approach a negotiation as a zero-sum game: every benefit one party receives is a direct loss to the other party, and winners use tough positional bargaining tactics. **Problem-solving negotiators** approach negotiations as a non-zero-sum game, where concessions are made by each party to create value, and trusting, creative discussions address underlying interests. You should be prepared for adversarial tactics to be employed against you in a negotiation. However, you should also be willing to engage in problem-solving tactics in negotiations. To be sure, negotiations may require one to be adversarial as well as problem solving to do what is best for your company, so do not dismiss either kind of tactic out of hand.

## Adversarial Tactics

Extreme opening offers, few and small concessions, withholding information, and manipulating commitments are all adversarial negotiating tactics.[3] Let's look at these briefly.

1. **Extreme Openers—Anchoring.** Extreme opening offers are used to take advantage of what psychologists call the "**anchoring effect**." That is, the initial offer has a powerful effect on the final agreement. An analysis of a large database of negotiation studies found that for every $1.00 increase in opening offer, we can expect the final sale price to increase by $.50.[4] Negotiators can take advantage of the anchoring effect by making an opening offer that is lopsided in their favor. Even when the counterparty forces you to make concessions, you are conceding away from a highly favorable amount toward an amount that is still favorable to you. However, when negotiating with a well-informed counterparty, extreme opening offers can make you look less credible because it suggests you have failed to accurately assess the worth of your good or service.

2. **Few and Small Concessions—Reciprocity.** Concessions are made when the parties realize their stated positions are simply incompatible, and one or more is required to budge. When one party makes a concession, a powerful psychological norm is triggered that encourages the other party to do the same: **the norm of reciprocity**. Adversarial negotiators will make concessions that grow increasingly closer together to signal to the counterparty that they are reaching their bottom line, below which they will not go. For instance, the aggressive negotiator who has a bottom line selling price of $30 will open with $100, then concede to $75, then to $65, then to $60. This suggests to the buyer that the seller's bottom line is somewhere around $60. When the seller makes a concession, the norm of reciprocity encourages the buyer to make a mirror-like concession. Suppose the buyer's original counteroffer

---

[3] Leonard L. Riskin, James E. Westbrook, Chris Guthrie, Richard C. Reuben, Jennifer K. Robbennolt, and Nancy A. Welsh, *Dispute Resolution and Lawyers*, 4th ed. (St. Paul, MN: West Academic Publishers, 2009).
[4] Dan Orr, and Chris Guthrie, "Anchoring, Information, Expectation, and Negotiation: New Insights from Meta-Analysis," *Ohio State Journal on Dispute Resolution*, Vol. 21, 2006: 597.

was $30. To reciprocate the seller's apparently generous concessions, the buyer will end up offering more each time. To be sure, buyers can use this tactic just as well as sellers, by increasing their offer in smaller increments each time to signal to the seller that they are reaching their maximum offer.

Another concessionary tactic is the "**rejection-then-retreat**" trick. This involves making an opening offer that you know will be rejected, only to immediately make your *real* offer that, because of the norm of reciprocity, will more than likely be accepted. Suppose you ask someone to donate $20 to your charity, knowing they will decline, but as soon as they decline, you ask them to purchase a candy bar for $5 instead. This approach is very successful because the counterparty feels obligated to reciprocate your "generous" reduction in the amount of your request by agreeing to the second offer. Like all adversarial tactics, be wary in the use of concessionary tactics, as a savvy counterparty can detect their use, and you may lose credibility or trust as a result.

3. **Withholding Information.** *Information asymmetry* is the term used to describe a situation in which one party has access to information that the other party does not know about. Adversarial negotiators can withhold information to take advantage of information "asymmetries"—that is, the parties' access to information is not equal. For example, imagine you are an oil prospector, and you come to know that a small farm is sitting on a large oil field. The farmer is elderly and relatively uneducated and has no idea that he is sitting on millions of dollars' worth of oil. You approach the farmer and negotiate over the sale of his farm, withholding the information you have about the riches just beneath the surface of his land. The farmer asks for $150,000 for the property, and you counter with $100,000, ultimately agreeing to $125,000 for the property. The farmer walks away believing he secured a good price for his land. By withholding information, you secure an enormous profit for a small expenditure by capitalizing on the information asymmetry with respect to the actual value of the estate. This type of negotiation may be perceived by others as highly unethical, even if it is legal.

One of the risks of withholding information arises when both parties employ the tactic at the same time. This leads to an impasse because neither side knows what the other side's actual position is. Further, this tactic prevents parties from bargaining on the basis of good information about the actual underlying interests of one another. Negotiated outcomes may be less than satisfactory as a result.

4. **Manipulating Commitments.** An adversarial negotiator can use commitments in two ways: binding the counterparty or binding yourself. In the first kind of commitment manipulation, the negotiator can get the counterparty to commit to a principle, then use that commitment against the counterparty later in the negotiation. For example, you could ask, "Now, you agree that no one should do business with a criminal, right?" and the counterparty agrees in principle. Then you say, "Well, my competitor has been convicted of a crime, so you shouldn't do business with him. Therefore, you should do business with me instead." This tactic capitalizes on the need for most people to maintain consistency. By getting the counterparty to commit to a principle, you can manipulate them within a negotiation. However, this type of manipulation can backfire in terms of lost credibility and trust if the counterparty views it as trickery.

The other form of commitment manipulation is to bind yourself. You can say, "I simply cannot agree to anything less than $50,000 or I will be fired by my boss." This sends a clear, forceful message to the counterparty about your bottom line. They will take the $50,000 offer or leave the deal. If you have the most leverage—that is, you have less to lose from walking away from the deal than the counterparty—this can be very effective. However, this type of manipulation of commitments can backfire if you don't have enough leverage.

It ultimately constrains your flexibility within the negotiation and may erode your credibility if the counterparty discovers later that you agreed to something else in a separate negotiation.

## Problem-Solving Tactics

Separating people from the problems (listening), focusing on interests rather than positions (asking), inventing options for mutual gain (inventing), and using objective criteria to evaluate the terms (referencing) are all problem-solving negotiating tactics.[5]

1. **Listening.** Often disagreement can trigger negative emotions, which lead to personal entanglement, and the source of the conflict is mistakenly attributed to the person on the other side of the negotiating table. When egos get involved, conflicts can escalate. Good communication begins with good listening. It is crucial to attack the problem, rather than the people. This requires negotiators to separate the people from the problem. Listening carefully can help identify misperceptions—if they are never identified, opportunities for mutual benefit may be lost. Listening also allows a negotiator to acknowledge an emotional conflict, which goes a long way toward resolving the issue. Listening can transform a conversation from a heated argument into a collaborative dialogue. When people feel they are not being heard, they understandably become angry, and the resolution of the conflict recedes until it is out of our grasp. On the other hand, when your adversary feels you are truly listening to them, they are less likely to attribute callous indifference to you, and hence they are more likely to sympathize with your problems as well. Demonstrating that you understand what your counterparty is saying and how they are feeling can help melt the ice and lead to more amicable relations. The technique used to demonstrate that you are listening is "looping": when the other side responds to your statement, demonstrate that you understand by paraphrasing, and then invite the other side to confirm that you have understood. If the other side confirms that you have understood them, the loop is closed; otherwise, start the loop over. It is crucial for a negotiator to demonstrate listening with authentic, genuine curiosity.

2. **Asking.** Usually, negotiators begin by stating various positions that do not actually reflect their true interests. In other words, positions are usually the means, whereas interests are the ends. Suppose you are selling a stereo to raise money to purchase a new computer. When you say, "I can accept no less than $1,000 for my stereo," you state a position that is a means to your end of purchasing a computer. However, your counterparty has no idea why you need the money. If the counterparty doesn't have $1,000, the deal is dead. However, if the counterparty asked you why you needed the money, and you were to say, "I need $1,000 because I am trying to purchase a computer," the counterparty might very well say, "If you accept $500, I can give you my used computer." Positional statements are used to push back and forth and usually obscure what the parties truly need from one another. Asking questions about underlying interests allows negotiators to focus on interests rather than positions. Asking "why" can uncover hidden interests that can create opportunities for mutual gain. Ask open questions, not closed questions. To continue the example, an open question would be, "Why do you need $1,000?", whereas a closed question would be, "Where did you come up with $1,000?" When you ask "why," clarify that you are not asking for an excuse but rather you are trying to improve your understanding of the counterparty's situation and needs. Be sure to maintain a courteous, genuinely curious tone when you ask questions, otherwise you will come off as interrogating the counterparty, which can erode trust.

3. **Inventing.** Adversarial situations stifle creativity by putting us in a defensive posture. Creative negotiators can find ways out of an impasse by inventing various options that reconcile

---

[5] Leonard L. Riskin, James E. Westbrook, Chris Guthrie, Richard C. Reuben, Jennifer K. Robbennolt, and Nancy A. Welsh, *Dispute Resolution and Lawyers*, 4th ed. (St. Paul, MN: West Academic Publishers, 2009).

competing interests and promote joint gain. Brainstorming can turn a conflict into a constructive endeavor. Differences between the negotiators can actually help lead to mutually beneficial settlements. Differences in resources, relative valuations, forecasts, risk preferences, and time preferences are more helpful in overcoming obstacles than similarities along these dimensions. By highlighting differences between the parties, negotiators create options and increase the likelihood of discovering a mutually attractive outcome. Remain open to thinking creatively, and avoid overcommitting yourself to any particular dispute resolution. Open brainstorming is the opposite of manipulation through self-commitment.

4. **Referencing.** Instead of forcing a settlement with brute strength, negotiators should evaluate the outcome of a dispute using objective criteria to which both sides can agree. This allows the parties to depersonalize the negotiation. Basing outcomes on what one party is willing to do for the other party is likely to fail in an adversarial negotiation, given the mood. However, using objective standards such as industry norms or market value allows negotiators to get past different personal preferences to reach an agreement that is defensible from any perspective. Using objective criteria can also help a negotiator overcome unfair tactics used by the counterparty.

# Relationship Management in Practice

## The Keiretsu Supplier-Partnering Model

An important issue in supply chain relationship management is how to turn arm's-length relationships with suppliers based on power differentials into close partnerships based on trust. The Japanese concept **keiretsu** applied to supplier relationships can provide a model of this. The concept means a close-knit network of suppliers that continuously learn, improve, and prosper along with their parent companies.

Toyota and Honda have established successful keiretsu relationships with suppliers in North America while American automotive companies have struggled to do so. Figure 11.8 illustrates the six strategic and interlocking steps that should be taken in developing these relationships. The process starts with step 1 at the bottom of Figure 11.8, first developing an understanding of how suppliers work. Progressively the steps build to the top and culminate with developing joint improvement programs with suppliers. Consider how these six strategies effectively counteract the various sources of conflict—particularly data and structural conflict—discussed in this chapter.

## Partnership Agreements

Creating a business relationship is usually accompanied by excitement and a sense of opportunity. But like relationships between individuals, success does not come without an honest accounting of one another's expectations and obligations. When disagreement occur, and the contract that created the partnership is either silent or ambiguous with respect to what the parties agreed to, businesses must go to court to litigate the rights and obligations under the contract. Litigation costs are steep enough to persuade reasonable people to expend effort up front to clarify each other's intentions and understandings.

Questions often arise when the parties do not contribute in the same way. For example, if one party contributes ideas, and the other party contributes money or physical effort, how should these contributions stack up? How long will the parties remain involved? What dispute resolution procedures will the parties use in case of disagreement?

## SUPPLY CHAIN RELATIONSHIP MANAGEMENT

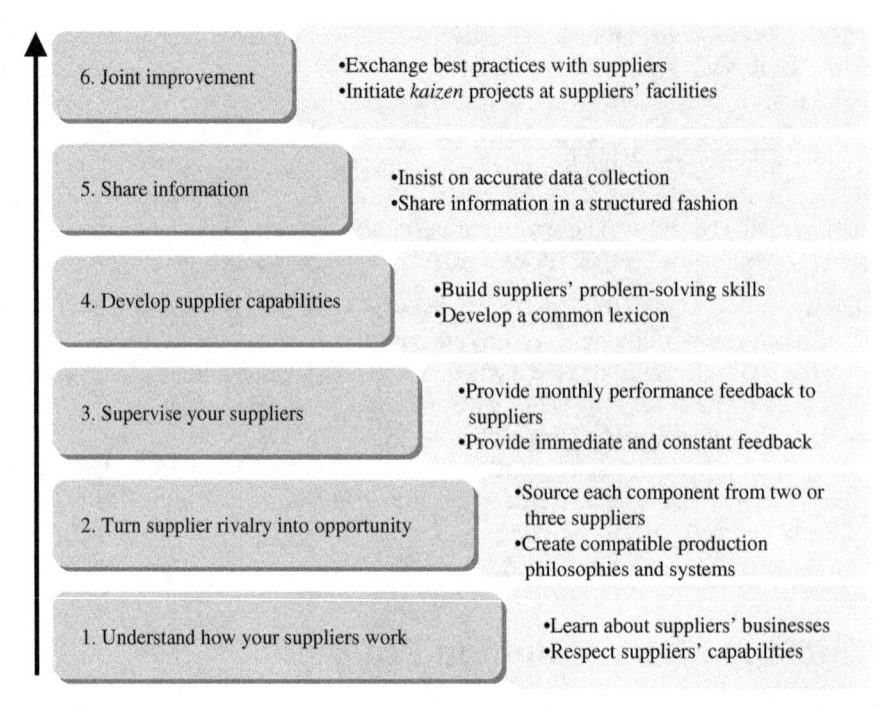

**6. Joint improvement**
- Exchange best practices with suppliers
- Initiate *kaizen* projects at suppliers' facilities

**5. Share information**
- Insist on accurate data collection
- Share information in a structured fashion

**4. Develop supplier capabilities**
- Build suppliers' problem-solving skills
- Develop a common lexicon

**3. Supervise your suppliers**
- Provide monthly performance feedback to suppliers
- Provide immediate and constant feedback

**2. Turn supplier rivalry into opportunity**
- Source each component from two or three suppliers
- Create compatible production philosophies and systems

**1. Understand how your suppliers work**
- Learn about suppliers' businesses
- Respect suppliers' capabilities

**FIGURE 11.8** Steps in developing a keiretsu partnership[6]

A good example of the need for partnership agreements is offered by Steve Hind, a former AP Middle East Correspondent, and Tom Potter, a banker, who both quit their day jobs and cofounded the Brooklyn Brewery in New York in 1987. Today, the Brooklyn Brewery is one of the top 40 breweries in the United States. These two partners explain in their book—called *Beer School*—that it is not sufficient to agree to become partners. "Even a dog can shake hands," they say.[7] In the beginning of their partnership they made sure to "draw up a partnership agreement that defined the agreement financially and also defined a buy–sell agreement, in case one of us wanted out or in case of disputes. Over the years, I saw many partnerships dissolve into chaos. They had shaken hands at the beginning, but there was nothing on paper to define what that meant."

Agreeing to be bound by a formal contract too early in the relationship can create its own set of problems. The businesses must understand one another's capacity to contribute to the success of the supply chain, not simply take one another's word. Like in human relationships, it is important for the parties in a supply chain relationship to know one another before getting too serious.

## Diluting Power

It is not uncommon for companies to seek a partner for additional capital, business connections, or managerial skills or to share expenditures. Obviously, these resources do not come for free. Often they are offered in exchange for a portion of ownership, control, or some type of decision-making power. Power is a limited resource that must be divided carefully. Giving too many people decision-making power can lead to a "tragedy of the commons," an expression

---
[6] Adapted from: Jeffrey K. Liker and Thomas Choi, "Building Deep Supplier Relationships," *Harvard Business Review*, December 2004: 108.

[7] Adapted from: Stacy Perman, "Contemplating a Business Partnership?" *Businessweek*, November 21, 2008. Available at www.businessweek.com.

used to describe situations where resources are not utilized efficiently because too many people exercise control over them simultaneously.

John Mautner founded a successful glazed nut store, Nutty Bavarian, in Florida. Within four years, he was running 20 retail outlets and wanted to expand to 200. However, like many business owners seeking to expand, he lacked sufficient capital to do so on his own. That is when he made a big mistake. He sold half of the ownership rights to his company for $1 million. The mistake was not in the price, but in the percentage. When two people have an equal say, it is difficult to break the tie in case of disagreement. This is true of any supply chain relationship.

For three years, Mautner and his new partner fell into conflict over and over again, from where to locate new storefronts to which strategy to utilize going forward. "With a 50–50 partnership, no one could make a call," he says.[8] Mautner's solution was to sell his interest in the company to his partner and try a different approach. Now, Mautner abides by the principle to never relinquish majority ownership. The lesson for everyone is to avoid 50–50 partnerships unless you are in perfect harmony with your partner, which is an empty set.

## CHAPTER HIGHLIGHTS

1. All supply chain relationships are not of equal importance. Supply chain relationships fall into four categories: nonstrategic transactions, contractual, partnerships, and alliances. Nonstrategic transactions are cost based and do not require relationship management. More comprehensive relationships, such as alliances, require greater attention to relationship management. The keiretsu model is relevant to developing long-term, mutually beneficial outsourcing relationships.

2. Supply chain relationships should be developed and managed on the basis of trust rather than power exploitation. This improves short-term performance and long-term profitability while helping both companies continuously improve. Trust-based relationships are developed by assessing the value of the relationship, identifying operational roles played by each business unit, negotiating effective contracts, and designing effective conflict resolution procedures.

3. Five potential sources of conflict may arise in supply chain relationships: relationship conflicts, data conflicts, interest conflict, structural conflicts, and values conflicts. Turning conflicts into opportunities as they arise between organizations in a supply chain is a highly valuable managerial skill.

4. Prepare for negotiations by studying the business of the counterparty, identify who has the most leverage, and think about underlying interests. Try to create value and improve supply chain performance through enhanced relationships. Although some situations will require distributive tactics, always look for integrative potential.

## KEY TERMS

Scope
Criticality
Contractual
Relational
Design phase
Management phase
Sequential
   interdependence
Reciprocal
   interdependence
Relationship conflicts
Data conflicts
Interest conflict
Structural conflicts
Values conflicts
Position
Interest
Integrative opportunities
Distributive
   opportunities
Adversarial negotiators
Problem-solving
   negotiators
Anchoring effect
The norm of reciprocity
Rejection-then-retreat
Keiretsu

## DISCUSSION QUESTIONS

1. How are supply chain relationships similar to and different from personal relationships?

2. Can you think of a conflict between units in a supply chain in real life? What kind of conflict was it? How was it resolved? Would you have resolved it differently?

3. Identify examples of a supply chain where relationship management is not very important. Identify examples of a supply chain where relationship management is crucial.

4. Do you perceive yourself as a competitive or problem-solving negotiator? Can you think of situations where you may have to adopt a different negotiation style?

---

[8] Adapted from: Anne Field, "Let's Make a Deal," *Businessweek*, June 25, 2007. Available at www.businessweek.com.

## Case Study: Lucid v. Black Box

Lucid is an up-and-coming Chilean distributor of home entertainment technology. Black Box is a well-known television manufacturer headquartered in the United Kingdom. Black Box was interested in reaching out into the South American market and found Lucid to be sufficiently well connected to reach customers throughout the continent. In January of 2008, Lucid signed an exclusive three-year contract to establish a distribution network for Black Box High Res flat screen televisions throughout South American using Black Box's logo. The contract included the following provisions:

1. Lucid has the exclusive right to sell Black Box's High Res televisions and any updates to the High Res product line.
2. Lucid must establish a distribution network within the agreed region.
3. Lucid must order 4,300 High Res televisions or £1,000,000.00 worth of product before January 1, 2011.
4. If Lucid fails to meet these conditions, Black Box has the right to rely on other distributors within South America.
5. If either party is in breach of this contract, the non-breaching party may terminate this agreement after three months' notice.

In August 2008, Lucid placed an order for 1,000 High Res television sets, but the shipment was delayed for several months with no explanation from Black Box. Lucid was frustrated because Black Box's delay in shipment caused Lucid to be late in supplying the televisions to the retailers with whom Lucid had contracted. As a result, some of these retailers terminated their agreement with Lucid before the shipment finally arrived, leaving Lucid with a surplus of High Res televisions and in need of new retailers.

In June 2009, Lucid placed an order for 1,000 High Res television sets, which arrived shortly thereafter. Lucid discovered that a few retailers had High Res televisions with Black Box logos in stock, despite that they were not contracting with Lucid. Lucid believed that Black Box must have contracted directly with these retailers, or perhaps relied on other distributors in violation of the exclusive contract. Either way, Lucid was frustrated that Black Box was competing with them in their agreed-upon distribution region.

In November 2009, Black Box released a new television, the 3-D Flat Screen, and began marketing this in South America. Lucid wrote an angry letter to Black Box because Lucid believed they had the exclusive right to market updates to the High Res product line. Black Box replied that the 3-D Flat Screen was in a distinct product category different from the High Res line, so the contract did not apply.

In June 2010, Lucid was still far from reaching the minimum order requirement in the contract, but felt this was due to the actions of Black Box. Then Black Box sent Lucid a termination letter that stated Lucid had failed to establish a distribution network to their satisfaction. Fed up with Black Box's poor communication and feeling as though they had been treated unfairly, Lucid executives met with their legal advisors and asked what their options were. The attorneys for Lucid say there are four options available: Lucid can litigate, arbitrate, mediate, or negotiate with Black Box to resolve this dispute.

### Case Questions

1. What are the sources of conflict between Lucid and Black Box?
2. Which dispute resolution procedure should Lucid use? Why?
3. If Lucid decides to negotiate with Black Box, what kind of negotiation tactics should be employed?
4. How can Lucid and Black Box improve their supply chain relationship?

## REFERENCES

Cialdini, Robert B. *Influence: Science and Practice*, 4th ed. Needham Heights, MA: Allyn & Bacon, 2001.

Fisher, Roger, William Ury, and Bruce Patton. *Getting to Yes: Negotiating Agreement without Giving In*, 2nd ed. New York: Penguin Books, 1991.

Guthrie, Chris, Leonard L. Riskin, James E. Westbrook, Richard C. Reuben, Jennifer K. Robbennolt, and Nancy A. Welsh. *Dispute Resolution and Lawyers*, 4th ed. St. Paul, MN: West Academic Publishing, 2009.

Kumar, N. "The Power of Trust in Manufacturer-Retailer Relationships." *Harvard Business Review*. November–December 1996: 92–106.

Mnookin, Robert H., Scott R. Peppet, and Andrew S. Tulumello. *Beyond Winning: Negotiating to Create Value in Deals and Disputes*. Eagan, MN: West Thompson, 2000.

Moore, Christopher W. *The Mediation Process*, 2nd ed. Cambridge, MA: Harvard University Press, 1996.

Orr, Dan, and Chris Guthrie, "Anchoring, Information, Expertise, and Negotiation: New Insights from Meta-Analysis." *Ohio State Journal on Dispute Resolution*, 21(3), 2006: 597–628, 2006.

Petros, Paranikas, Grace Puma Whiteford, Bob Tevelson, and Dan Belz. "How to Negotiate with Powerful Suppliers." *Harvard Business Review*, July–August, 2015: 90–96.

Shell, G. Richard. *Bargaining for Advantage: Negotiation Strategies for Reasonable People*, 2nd ed. New York: Penguin Books, 2006.

# 12 Global Supply Chain Management

**LEARNING OBJECTIVES**

*After completing this chapter, you should be able to:*

- Describe the global supply chain environment, and identify key impact factors.
- Explain market and cultural challenges that impact global supply chains.
- Describe global infrastructure challenges and the role of technology.
- Identify key cost and non-cost considerations in managing global supply chains.
- Describe key political factors and non-tariff barriers that impact global supply chain management.

**CHAPTER OUTLINE**

■ **Global Supply Chain Management**
   *The Global Environment*
   *Opportunities and Barriers*
   *Factors Impacting Global Supply Chains*

■ **Global Market Challenges**
   *The Global Consumer*
   *Global versus Local Marketing*
   *Cultural Challenges*

■ **Global Infrastructure Design**
   *Infrastructure Challenges*
      Labor
      Transportation
      Suppliers
   *Role of Technology*

■ **Cost Considerations**
   *Hidden Costs*
   *Non-cost Considerations*

■ **Political and Economic Factors**
   *Impact of Exchange Rate Fluctuations*

*Regional Trade Agreements*
*Impact of Non-Tariff Barriers*

- **Chapter Highlights**
- **Key Terms**
- **Discussion Questions**
- **Case Study: Wú's Brew Works**

---

Today India represents the second-fastest-growing economy in the world. It has an expanding consumer market, a burgeoning middle class, and a growing young and highly educated population. India topped the World Bank's growth outlook for 2015–2016 and an economic growth of 8+% for 2016–2017. In fact, an A. T. Kearney global survey rated India as the greatest consumer market opportunity. For that reason many multinational companies are setting up their supply chains in India. Consider that PepsiCo Chief Executive Officer Indra Nooyi, herself born in India, says she is investing "aggressively" in this emerging market. Retail sales of the company's products in India, including Frito-Lay potato chips, Quaker Oats, and fruit juices, rose by 13% in 2015. Other companies are also positioning themselves for this rapidly growing market hungry for outside products. However, this opportunity also presents numerous challenges typical of managing global supply chains. Let's look at just a few of the issues involved in developing a distribution network in India.

**Warehousing.** Warehousing, needed to store goods, is complicated in India. Most existing warehouses in India are small in size, have dirt rather than cement floors, and have little in the way of technology or material handling. Many distribution facilities are housed in structures that were designed for other purposes. For example, one of the largest pharmaceutical distributors in Mumbai runs a warehouse out of the third floor of an apartment building. There are also land acquisition issues. Even the influential domestic automaker Tata Motors had trouble getting land for a planned factory in West Bengal a few years ago. To obtain the 997 acres required, the company had to work with the state government to consult with 13,000 farmers and pay them either for their land or the rights to use their land. The farmers then protested that their compensation was too low and that some of them were being forced to sell their land. The automaker finally shifted construction to another, less-hostile region of the country. Even big domestic retailers, such as Reliance Retail Ltd. based in Mumbai, have had similar problems. All this means that a company going into India should consider partnering with a third-party logistics (3PL) provider that already has a warehouse or land on which it can build a facility.

**Labor.** Although labor is cheap in India, finding the right skills is much more complicated than expected. The largest market for logistics consulting services in India is not for designing warehouses. Rather, it is for helping teach people how to operate them. The skill gap between educated and uneducated people is much greater in India than it in the West. As a result, U.S. companies doing business in India cannot simply follow the common practice of recruiting warehouse personnel from the less-educated tiers of society to save money. For example, some concepts and equipment considered basic to business, such as computers, are totally alien to the uneducated segment of the Indian population.

For that reason it makes more sense to hire college-educated personnel, even though they may be more costly. Also, the Indian culture has historically emphasized hierarchies, which can be inhibiting to Western companies used to an open decision-making style. Young and educated workers are more willing to adapt to this style.

**Transportation.** Transportation is yet another obstacle in India. When building a distribution network, one must consider slow transit networks and insufficient infrastructure. For example, 70% of India's seaborne trade is handled by just two of the country's 12 major ports. The rail system is also constrained when it comes to freight movements. Historically, the country's rail capacity was restricted to passenger traffic and only recently has the Indian government begun to promote rail shipments. Most commercial shipments in India are made by truck. However, the country has no large national transportation companies, and most are small trucking companies. Transit times are slow and unpredictable compared to those in Western countries. Also, technology that often is used in the West is not yet common in India. Few truck drivers have cell phones that can be used to call in shipment status, and global positioning systems (GPS) are virtually nonexistent.

These are just some of the many supply chain roadblocks companies need to consider if they want to gain a foothold in India and other emerging markets. It can take years to set up a distribution network due to the complexities. However, companies will find ways to overcome them for the opportunity to serve the world's second-fastest-growing economy.

Adapted from: "Now's the Time for an Indian Strategy," *Supply Chain Quarterly*, Quarter 1, 2009: 28–33.

# Global Supply Chain Management

## The Global Environment

All organizations today operate in a global environment and are affected by global trade. Even the smallest of rural farms are affected by the global influx of foreign goods and trade regulations. Many companies serve multiple global markets, with products sourced and produced across many continents. Wal-Mart, the world's largest retailer, operates 11,500 stores in 28 countries. Other multinational companies such as IBM, General Electric, Siemens, and McDonald's have a similar global reach. It is not uncommon for a company to develop a product in the United States, manufacture it in Asia, and sell it in Europe.

The rapid growth of globalization and international trade are a result of advanced transportation and information technology that have connected us across the globe, as well as a rise in personal income creating a heightened ability to buy. These forces have combined to create a global awareness and a demand for goods that translates into opportunities for companies to rapidly expand their markets.

The global trend will only continue in the future. Consider that the International Monetary Fund (IMF) announced that the global economy is growing at a steady pace, with a 3.1% growth rate in 2015, 3.4% growth in 2016, and 3.6% growth expected in 2017. All this is resulting in a changing global landscape and increased competition. For you as a consumer this means greater access to a variety of goods across the globe at competitive prices. However, what does this mean for companies and their supply chains? It means intensified and accelerated competitive pressures at all levels. It also means changes in the nature of competition. Companies that take on a global

| Economic | Cultural |
|---|---|
| • Natural resources | • Social structure and dynamics |
| • Labor | • Work ethics and productivity |
| • Infrastructure | • Gender roles |
| • Technology | • Religion and observances |
| • Capital | • Language |
| **Political** | **Demographic** |
| • Instability | • Population growth |
| • Ideology | • Age structure and health status |
| • Institutions | • Urbanization |
| • International links | • Per capita income |

**FIGURE 12.1** Global environmental factors.

presence focus on challenges of entering markets in other countries, whereas their own markets are being opened to foreign competitors. This creates multiple levels of competition—one strategy for competing in new markets, with another strategy to guard the home turf. Companies need to prepare themselves to compete in this new environment.

In principle conducting global trade is not different from domestic trade, as they both require coordinating supply chain management activities. The primary difference, however, is that global supply chain management involves a company's worldwide focus, including diverse and globally scattered markets, production facilities, and suppliers, rather than a local orientation. It requires a well-planned, designed, and managed supply chain network. This translates into large coordination complexities and risks, which companies need to balance against the opportunities and benefits presented by global markets. Just consider the complexities of global product distribution of a soft-drink beverage. In the United States, beverages are sold by the pallet via warehouse stores. In India and Southeast Asia, this is not an option, and not all cultures use vending machines. In the United States a company would not want a high-end product to be distributed via a "dollar store." By contrast, in France a product promoted as the low-cost option would easily find some success in a pricey boutique.

Managing global supply chains is complicated by the fact that numerous environmental factors must be considered. These factors fall into four categories—**economic**, **cultural**, **political**, and **demographic**—and are shown in Figure 12.1. They present both opportunities and barriers for going global and must be considered carefully. Local operations cannot simply be copied and placed globally, as Wal-Mart found out with their unsuccessful attempt at operating in Germany a few years ago. Local culture must be well understood. We look at these challenges in a bit more detail in the next section.

## Supply Chain Leader's Box—Challenges of Global Culture

### WAL-MART

Even giants like Wal-Mart can underestimate global challenges. Just consider what happened in 1998 when Wal-Mart moved into Germany, hoping to repeat its U.S. success in the Europe's largest economy. Unfortunately things did not turn out as Wal-Mart expected, forcing the company to close operations in Germany in 2006. The biggest mistake Wal-Mart made was to assume it could directly apply its American approach to business to a very different culture and business environment.

The mistakes Wal-Mart made included not understanding the market, the culture, tradition, and even labor laws. For example, Wal-Mart didn't know that American pillowcases are a different size than German ones, resulting in Wal-Mart Germany ending up with a huge pile of pillowcases they couldn't sell to German customers. Also, many German shoppers did not like having their purchases bagged by others. Similar misunderstandings occurred in the work environment as Wal-Mart's American managers pressured German executives to enforce American-style management practices in the workplace. For example, employees were forbidden from dating colleagues in positions of influence, and workers were also told not to flirt with one another. The company even attempted to introduce a telephone hotline for employees to inform on their colleagues, later ruled against by a German court. Other issues included high labor costs, as well as workers who tried to resist management's demands that they felt were unjust. At one point management threatened to close certain stores if staff did not agree to work longer hours than their contracts foresaw and did not permit video surveillance of their work. As a result, Wal-Mart Germany had several run-ins with the trade union that represents retail store workers.

Wal-Mart's retreat from Germany cost the company about $1 billion and is a lesson for all companies that they must tailor their operations to local cultures and tradition when going global. For companies to be successful in a foreign market they have to know their customers and local culture well. They cannot simply force a business model that worked well elsewhere onto another country's market.

Adapted from: Norton, Kate. "Wal-Mart's German Retreat." *Bloomberg Businessweek*, July 28, 2006.

## Opportunities and Barriers

Global reach is critical to a firm's survival. Without going global, companies would be limited to just the goods and services produced within their own borders. Also, multinational firms are typically more profitable and grow faster than their domestic counterparts. Being global provides opportunities to tap into huge and growing markets, capitalize on new economic trends, and utilize technological innovations in other parts of the globe. It also enables utilizing natural resources available in other geographic areas.

Developing a global supply chain network enables companies to achieve economies of scale in production and distribution in specific regions. Being closer to their respective markets, companies can implement good ideas quickly and can target their marketing to local tastes. However, as seen in the chapter opener, numerous barriers must be overcome when going global, listed in Figure 12.2.

Trade on a global, or international, scale is considerably more complicated than domestic. Movement across borders, and even continents, adds numerous additional costs such as tariffs and extends the length and variability of lead time. There are time costs due to border delays, costs of

| Opportunities | Barriers |
|---|---|
| Large market | Longer and more varied lead time |
| Economies of scale in production and distribution | Political risk and instability |
| Lower select costs (e.g., labor, marketing, supply) | Overall cost (e.g., transportation, tariffs, space) |
| Better ability to target markets | Infrastructure access (e.g., facilities, transportation, and labor) |
| Leverage good ideas quickly and efficiently | Exchange rate risks |

**FIGURE 12.2** Global considerations.

transportation, and higher inventory costs due to longer transit times. There are also operational costs involved in conducting business in a different part of the world. This includes differences in labor productivity and access to labor skills, access to transportation and infrastructural support, as well as availability of technology. As seen in the case of Wal-Mart, companies often overlook the cultural impact and traditions, as well as the legal and political differences. There are also significant risks that include political instability, as well as currency fluctuations. All these factors compound across multiple regions adding to the complexity.

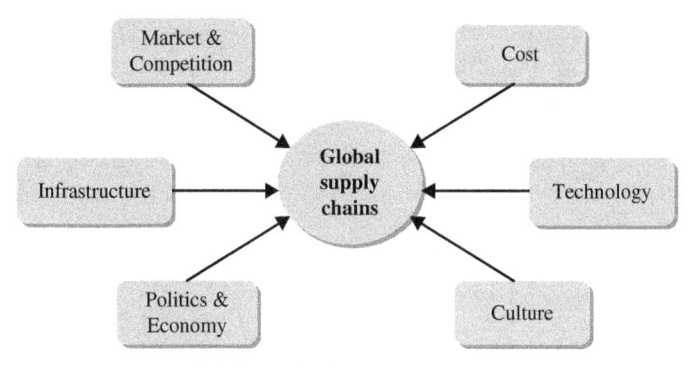

## Factors Impacting Global Supply Chains

The global environment is extremely dynamic. To compete, companies must constantly assess the global landscape. They must continuously identify new markets, anticipate competition and evaluate costs, and adjust their strategies accordingly. There are six significant factors that companies must monitor throughout the process of managing their global supply chains. They are: *market and competition, cost, infrastructure, technology, political and economic environment*, and *culture*, and are shown in Figure 12.3. Although each of these factors will not affect every industry in the same way at the same time, each factor is an important consideration. It is important for companies to always be assessing these factors and proactively reacting to them for competitive positioning. Collectively these factors comprise a conceptual framework for managing global supply chains.

**Market and competition** are all factors involved in marketing and selling to global markets, including considering customer preferences and competition. Customer preferences and expectations are often unique in different global regions. Companies must find ways to compete in these respective markets, whether on price, cost, or innovation. They must then develop global supply chains that enable this type of competition.

**Cost** is often the most cited reason by companies for going global. Often companies only consider individual costs, such as low direct labor cost, marketing cost, or perhaps local supplier cost. However, it is important for companies to consider total supply chain costs when going global. These include costs of quality, differential productivity and design costs, as well as added logistical and transportation costs.

**Infrastructure** availability enables the development and functioning of the supply chain network. This includes access to roads and transportation, equipment and communication networks, distribution systems, and skilled labor. Companies developing global supply chains are often surprised as to the lack of infrastructure in developing countries. This is typically one of the biggest global challenges. The ability to penetrate global markets depends on having global facilities and distribution and supply networks to respond to customer demands.

**FIGURE 12.3** Factors impacting global supply chains.

**Technology** significantly reduces time and distance, enabling global coordination and communication. Without technology global supply chains would not be able to operate. Technology enables manufacturing innovation that allows for more efficient means of changing the product mix and the ability to serve different markets. Information technology, in particular, enables information sharing and collaboration across the globe. Examples of this are availability of bar code technology, GPS, EDI, and RFID, which all enable global product tracking and communication.

**Politics and economy** include government regulation, political stability, formation of trade agreements, and currency fluctuations. Consider the impact on supply chain management when Europe passed environmental regulation making manufacturers responsible for returning product-packaging materials from customers. This regulation resulted in the design of entire networks for managing reverse flows of waste packaging.

**Culture** refers to acceptable behaviors, beliefs, and norms characteristic of a particular global region. This includes social structures and acceptable interactions, work ethic, observances and manners, gender roles, and adherence to formal chains of authority. Recall Wal-Mart's experience in Germany regarding applying the American policy of employee behavior or shoppers not wanting others to bag their purchased items.

## Global Market Challenges

Companies are attracted to global markets due to the potential size of the product market, providing a company with growth and profitability. However, global markets pose a number of challenges. One challenge is identifying customer preferences in globally diverse regions. This is especially difficult, as customers across the globe increasingly want customization. This can result in huge product variety that may be impossible to deliver. Another challenge is deciding how to tailor marketing strategies to fit a variety of environments and customer behaviors. Competing globally requires developing a deep knowledge of global markets and competition, as well as local traditions. Foreign markets differ culturally, and marketing or promotional strategies may have to be modified to meet local needs.

### The Global Consumer

Serving global markets means meeting the needs of the global consumer. The profile of the global consumer has changed over the recent years with a greater emphasis on individualism. Consumers everywhere have higher expectation that companies are going to meet their own individual needs and expectations. This may be customized clothing or unique service expectations. As a result, businesses are redesigning their operations and supply chains to increasingly move from standardization to customization.

This new profile of the global customer has significant implications for business. The reason is that it explodes the number of possible combinations of product features. Coupled with today's expectations of fast delivery, this can wreak havoc on a company. This means that firms must get their products to markets faster to gain a competitive advantage. This also means moving the product quicker through the design stage, through production, and then distribution. This typically requires logistics, operations, and distribution to be organized using lean systems to get the products to customers quickly. At the same time, however, the system must maintain flexibility to be able to produce different types of products with varying quantities. This can be quite an operational challenge.

### Global versus Local Marketing

Two different marketing approaches can be used when developing a global strategy. One is a **global marketing** approach that focuses on bringing standardization to the global market. The other is a **local marketing** approach that stresses microsegmentation and localized differentiation. These approaches are contradictory, but they are best used to complement one another when developing a global strategy. One approach may dominate based on the specific demands of each product and market.

The global marketing approach assumes that there are consumers across the globe with identical needs, resulting in product standardization. The role of marketing here is to identify these consumers and the product characteristics they want. Coca-Cola is a good example of a company that has adopted a global marketing strategy. Although Coca-Cola produces many different beverages for the global market, its primary product remains unchanged. Maintaining product standardization provides many advantages for supply chain management, such as providing uniformity for distribution, sourcing, and packaging. It also makes it easier to balance supply and demand. However, uniformity in product standardization also provides challenges when implemented globally. A consistent and standardized product offered across the globe requires consistency in all global operations. This can be difficult to achieve as there are large variations in logistics, sourcing, and operations capabilities in different geographical locations. To maintain a reputation of product consistency, these capabilities must be uniformly effective, regardless of the location. For example, if a company wants to compete on offering fast and reliable parts distribution service, it must ensure it has the physical capability to provide the same service at all locations.

In contrast to global marketing, the local marketing approach focuses on microsegmentation of customers and products. With the global customer increasingly demanding individuality, local marketing is becoming more important. The important part here is to judiciously segment the market so that it can take on a more national or regional characteristic, and that the regions are relatively homogenous. A localized marketing approach to international business adds significant complexity to a global system. Market segments quickly multiply based on the segmentation. Companies must then ensure that they have the infrastructure to reach and serve the customers in these segments around the world.

The best way, if possible, is to merge global and local marketing approaches. Coca-Cola has done this effectively. The company has 3,300 different products that it sells in over 200 countries and 6 operating regions. One strategy for achieving this is to use product postponement in the product design. Recall that **product postponement** is a strategy where the product is kept in the most generic form as long as possible in the distribution process. The product is differentiated at the last minute, depending on the product and quantities at the location needed. With a beverage it may be differentiating the product by the amount of carbonation, juice, or sweetener, thereby creating different product versions. This differentiation can take place close to the customer.

## Cultural Challenges

Culture is an important element of global supply chain management as it is a critical element of communication. Just consider differences in the amount of acceptable interpersonal distance between individuals of different cultures, or norms of formality in addressing someone. Some cultures tend to value promptness and single-task focus, whereas other cultures do not. In Asia product packaging is much more important than in the West, as it is seen more of a reflection of the product itself. All these differences are attributable to culture and have a significant impact on managing global supply chains. However, culture is especially problematic, as it can often be difficult to understand. This also includes differences in verbal communication and the use of humor, making direct translation of communication between cultures impossible. Further, specific cultural norms can be elusive, and it can be difficult to determine just how pervasive they are.

## Managerial Insights Box

### ■ COCA-COLA'S CHINA BRANDING CHALLENGE

Creating a brand image in a different culture with a different language and word meaning is an enormous challenge for companies competing in global markets. The brand needs to create a direct connection between the product and the market, and the linguistic nuances can affect the brand meaning. This, in turn, can affect consumer perceptions and brand identity.

Coca-Cola encountered this problem when trying to develop its brand name in China. When Coca-Cola first entered the Chinese market in 1928, they had no official representation of their name in Mandarin. The challenge was to find four Chinese characters whose pronunciations approximated the sound of the brand without producing a nonsensical or adverse meaning when strung together.

This was a challenge. Initially shopkeepers created signs that combined characters whose pronunciations formed sounds similar to "coca-cola," but they did so with no regard for the meanings of the written phrases they formed in doing so. In some cases this resulted in unflattering, nonsensical meanings such as "female horse fastened with wax," "wax-flattened mare," or "bite the wax tadpole" when read in Mandarin. The company then chose *ké-kŏu-kĕ-lè*, which meant "Can-Be-Tasty-Can-Be-Happy" opting for the character *lè*, meaning "joy."

The story exemplifies linguistic nuances that can affect brand sound and brand meaning, when creating a brand image in global markets. Companies must realize prior to entry that each market is culturally distinct and that marketing requires some degree of localization.

Adapted from: Alon, I. (Ed.) *Chinese Economic Transition and International Marketing Strategy*. Westport, CT: Praeger Publishers, 2003.

---

There are five important dimensions of culture that can help us understand how to conduct business in different parts of the globe.[1] These dimensions explain differences in culture and help us understand how to do business in different parts of the globe. They are summarized in Figure 12.4. We look at these five dimensions of culture next.

1. POWER DISTANCE
Small: *Democratic* ⟷ Large: *Hierarchical*

2. REWARD & RESPONSIBILITY
Individualism: *Individual* ⟷ Collectivism: *Group*

3. CULTURE
Masculine: *Competitive* ⟷ Feminine: *Cooperative*

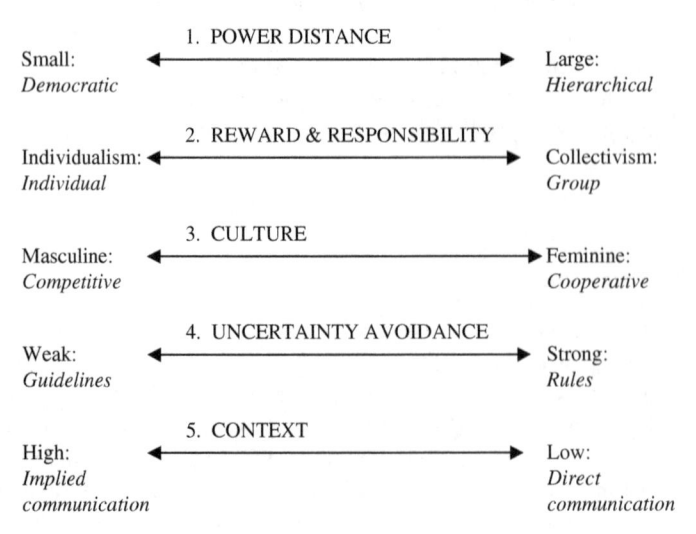

4. UNCERTAINTY AVOIDANCE
Weak: *Guidelines* ⟷ Strong: *Rules*

5. CONTEXT
High: *Implied communication* ⟷ Low: *Direct communication*

**FIGURE 12.4** Dimensional differences of culture.

---

[1] The first four dimensions were identified by Geert Hofstede, a Dutch sociologist, who studied the interactions between national and organizational cultures around the world. The fifth dimension was identified by anthropologist Edward T. Hall.

1. **Small vs. Large Power Distance.** Power distance is the extent to which there is a strong separation of individuals based on rank. Northern Europe and the United States have cultures with small power distance, where people relate to one another more as equals. This means that the organizational setting tends to be more democratic in nature. On the other hand some Latin American, Arab, and Asian countries tend to have a high power distance where relationships are formal and based on hierarchical positions. Understanding power distance has a significant impact on managing the workplace. Recall in the opener that traditionally in India power distance is large and that older workers have a difficult time in a more democratic workplace that is more common in the West.

2. **Individualism vs. Collectivism.** This dimension measures the extent to which people believe in individual responsibility and reward, rather than the reward of the group.

    In individualist cultures, such as the United States, the United Kingdom, and the Netherlands, people are expected to be motivated by individual rewards. However, in collectivist cultures, such as Indonesia and West Africa, people are expected to be motivated by the benefits of the group as a whole. Understanding this dimension helps develop motivational structures for workers in different parts of the globe, as well as managing teams.

3. **Masculinity vs. Femininity.** Masculine cultures are defined as those that value competitiveness, assertiveness, ambition, and the accumulation of wealth. By contrast, feminine cultures are those that value relationships, harmony, the environment, and quality of life. Japan is considered a more masculine culture, whereas the Netherlands a more feminine culture. The United States is close in the middle. Understanding these differences can be important in business negotiations and alliance building, as parties from different cultures may value different aspects of the relationship.

4. **Weak vs. Strong Uncertainty Avoidance.** This dimension refers to the degree of comfort members of a culture have with ambiguity and lack of structure. It measures the extent to which a culture prefers situations with clear rules over ambiguous situations. Cultures with strong uncertainty avoidance prefer explicit rules and are uncomfortable with ambiguity. Cultures with weak uncertainty avoidance prefer guidelines versus formal rules and informal activities. These cultures are also more tolerant of risk, such as Japan and India. The United Kingdom, United States, and Hong Kong tolerate less risk. This has important implications for job design, work structure, and innovation. Cultures that are more comfortable with ambiguity may be more innovative in thinking "outside the box." This dimension also has implications for employee retention rates. Employees in strong uncertainty avoidance cultures tend to stay longer with one employer, whereas in weak uncertainty avoidance employees change employers more frequently.

5. **High vs. Low Context Cultures.** This last dimension of culture refers to the reliance on high context over low context messages when communicating. In high context cultures many things are left unsaid, letting the context explain the meaning. In low context cultures, "what you see is what you get." Here the speaker is expected to precisely make their points with limited ambiguity. This is the case in the United States and Northern Europe. By contrast, in Japan facial expressions and what is not said provide clues to what is actually meant. In the United States and much of Europe, agreements are typically precise and contractual in nature; in Asia, there is a greater tendency to settle issues based on trust and understanding. Also, "saving face"—where no one openly losses or gets embarrassed—is of utmost importance.

These dimensions of culture explain key differences in behaviors and expectations. Their understanding is essential for successful global supply chain initiatives, which are based on communication. It is critical that managers understand these differences and keep them in mind as they conduct negotiations, collaborate, and build rapport with members of their supply chain across the globe.

# Global Infrastructure Design

## Infrastructure Challenges

A successful global presence is dependent on having a physical supply network capable of responding to customer demands. The decisions that are involved in developing and managing the physical aspects of the network are referred to as infrastructure. This includes access to roads and transportation, organizational facilities, availability of skilled labor, systems for operations and distribution planning, quality of materials, and availability of suppliers. One of the biggest challenges for companies setting up global supply chains are the significant differences in infrastructure in developing countries. Companies often overlook the substantial deficiencies in infrastructural resources when they begin doing business in developing countries and often encounter significant challenges.

### Labor

Access to low-cost labor has been a primary draw for companies setting up global operations. A good example of this has been seen when looking for engineering talent. The availability of low-cost, high-quality engineers in some developing countries has been a significant factor contributing to location decision of R&D facilities. Taiwan has been a primary location for firms looking for mechanical and electrical engineers, whereas India has been the primary source of software engineering talent. In contrast, the United States produces only 7% of engineers globally, driving many U.S. firms to locate their facilities offshore, closer to a large supply of this low-cost, high-skill talent.

Having access to affordable and highly trained technical workers provides firms with significant capability. However, there are often many challenges in achieving successful performance. First, there are typically significant productivity differences between laborers in other countries. This includes speed of work, precision, and quality, as well as acceptable work hours. Companies cannot simply translate labor productivity from one region to another. Second, there are often large variation in labor skills and capability. This can make it difficult to place comparable facilities in different parts of the globe. Lack of labor skills may require altering the production processes or the ability to use certain technologies. For example, there has been a growing use of numerically controlled machines in production processes in South American countries due to the difficulty in finding an adequate supply of trained machinists. The result has been an increased reliance on the technology as a substitute for skilled labor.

### Transportation

Access to roadways and transportation can often be poor in developing countries. These weaknesses in transportation infrastructure can increase the length and variability of distribution lead times. Distribution channels in developing countries can be long and unpredictable. Often the product changes hands many times before reaching the final consumer using different modes of transportation. This may result in high variability in shipping times, uncertainty in delivery lead-time, and higher distribution costs. For example, in Russia the primary cause of food shortages is poor distribution. There is ample production, but the difficulty is in distributing the food to all the locations needing it. For this reason when McDonald's went into Russia, it organized its own distribution system with its own trucks.

## Suppliers

Designing a global supply chain requires important decisions regarding the number of suppliers and their geographic locations. In general it is easier to manage fewer suppliers. However, this can create delivery risks due to high dependence on a few suppliers. It also provides less flexibility if sudden excess capacity is needed. Finally, managing numerous and diverse suppliers across the globe can be a daunting task for companies.

Companies are often attracted to foreign suppliers due to substantially lower prices without considering factors such as quality and delivery. It is not uncommon to receive a lower bid without comparable quality from suppliers in developing countries. Lack of availability to high-quality reliable suppliers can be a surprise. This can result in supply shortages and irregular schedules. These then create uncertainty throughout the supply chain and result in everyone keeping higher levels of inventory. In addition, global supply chains sometimes encounter material shortages of certain imported raw materials due to import restrictions. The result may be the unexpected need to redesign production processes to use less of the restricted material.

Companies have become very creative in developing approaches to overcome supply problems. For example, when McDonald's first went into Russia, it faced significant problems as it did not have high-quality reliable Russian suppliers for its restaurant operations. The company finally realized that it would have to control almost all aspects of the supply chain to ensure the quality and reliability it needed. As a result, they utilized a vertical integration strategy by developing their own plant and distribution facility for processing meat patties, producing French fries, preparing dairy products, and baking buns and apple pies. They even grew their own potatoes to have product consistency.

## Big Data Analytics Box—Supplier Risk

### CISCO

Success of supply chains requires a reliable global supply network. However, such a global network has risks. Given the high dependence on suppliers, companies need to evaluate supplier performance and risk on a routine basis. Supplier risk analytics are still underdeveloped compared to other supply chain areas. However, big data analytics can significantly improve supplier risk assessment.

One example of the use of big data analytics is the creation of a **supplier resiliency score**, which can use many variables to identify high-risk areas. These variables can be determined based on managerial expertise and understanding of the problem areas. An example would be high risk of weather events near a supplier's manufacturing location or the availability of alternative production sites. If the variables or the overall resiliency scores suggest a problem, companies can then pursue alternative sourcing or work with existing suppliers to identify contingency plans or alternative locations. Cisco is a case in point of a company effectively using a supplier resiliency scorecard. The company faces significant risks, as most of its manufacturing activities are outsourced. As a result the company relies on a resiliency scorecard that includes four categories—manufacturing resiliency, supplier resiliency, component resiliency, and test equipment resiliency. The scorecard identifies areas with highest risk and helps Cisco take action to remedy the potential problem.

Adapted from: Simchi-Levi, David. *Operations Rules: Delivering Customer Value through Flexible Operations.* Cambridge, MA: MIT Press, 2010.

## Role of Technology

**Information technology** is the tool that has broken down the barrier of distance between companies and geographic regions. Just consider the use of the Internet, bar codes, and RFID technology that enhance the speed and accuracy of information shared. Reliable and uninterrupted communication is essential for the functioning of a global firm. However, it is also something we often take for granted. Some geographic regions do not even have something as simple as reliable phone service. This means that information on supply and demand will not be readily available. This also means that collaboration between members of the supply chain will be difficult. Under these conditions a company will have to make a substantial investment in communication technology and must factor this cost into the location decision.

In addition to information technology, **manufacturing technology** is needed to provide flexibility to manufacturing processes necessary for mass customization. This enables companies to serve many markets. Recall that today's global markets are characterized by product diversity as customers want greater product customization. In addition, product life cycles are short, requiring ever-faster product introductions. Without innovative and flexible manufacturing technology, companies would not be able to produce the large product varieties needed to compete in diverse global markets that change rapidly.

Another important technology is **equipment technology** used to transport and distribute products to different markets. These technologies have sped up the distribution process and made it much more reliable. These technologies coupled with information technology to enhance communication have enabled companies to produce large product varieties delivered efficiently to global markets.

## Cost Considerations

Companies are often attracted to global operations by lower labor costs, especially in underdeveloped or emerging nations. Although local labor costs may be significantly lower, companies must consider overall costs of doing business globally. Often companies find overall operations costs to be significantly higher than expected. This may include higher transportation and distribution costs, cost to upgrade facilities and technology, as well as cost of space, tariffs, taxes, and other expenses related to doing business overseas. We look at these costs next.

### Hidden Costs

The strategy of going after lower labor costs in developing nations became especially popular with U.S. manufacturing firms in the 1980s, in response to their own markets becoming flooded with low-priced imports. To compete, companies began to outsource the manufacture of goods to global sites with low-cost labor. This strategy became especially popular in the assembly of electronic devices, such as computers and cell phones. It has also been popular in the retail industry in the manufacture of clothing.

Seeking low-cost labor has made sense in situations where product life cycles are short, such as the frequent changes in models of cell phones. The alternative to cheap labor would require the building of an expensive assembly plant, and the cost may not be justified for product models that change frequently. However, often the strategy of chasing low labor cost across the globe is a poor one for the following reasons. First, labor cost often constitutes a small percentage of overall cost. Second, locations of cheap labor change and shift over time, often after facilities have been put in place. This can leave companies with facilities and higher labor costs than originally planned. For example, Korea and Taiwan were cheap labor wage countries in the 1970s, Thailand in the early 1980s, then China in the 1990s. China continues to lead in low-cost labor, but preference is increasingly moving into rural China and western China, away from the seaport. Third, companies often find that there are numerous hidden and unexpected costs in going global. Fourth, competitive priorities other than costs are increasingly becoming important, and achieving success on those dimensions may not be optimal at locations with low skilled labor and poor infrastructure. Just being driven by labor cost can be misleading.

There may also be unexpected costs of additional training requirements due to lack of skilled workers. Companies are often surprised to find that workers in developing nations often lack rudimentary education. This can actually result in high costs due to poor quality of work, lower productivity, and a lack of quality culture among workers. Other problems include increased lead-times and associated inventory costs due to poor transportation and communication infrastructure, and unexpected logistics complications due to multilevel and bureaucratic government structures.

Many firms have found that the hidden costs of outsourcing to developing nations can be hard to estimate. Nike learned this lesson in the 1980s with numerous start-up problems at a new production facility in China. In 1981, Nike began shoe production in China, but by 1984, production was well below expectations. The reasons were China's economic structure, a very uneducated labor force, and an unexpectedly poor transportation and communication infrastructure. Also often ignoring cultural incompatibilities between the firm's management and local workers can easily erode cost savings due to turnover and failures in productivity and quality.

## Non-cost Considerations

For many businesses the order-winners in their product markets have shifted beyond just cost toward other considerations, such as quality, delivery speed, product design, and customization. To compete on these dimensions companies need superior quality of labor, productivity, transportation, telecommunications, and a supplier infrastructure. These factors become more important in determining the location of facilities than merely labor cost.

The total quality management (TQM) movement is one development that has contributed to the awareness of non-cost considerations. TQM brought about a focus on the total cost of quality, rather than just direct labor cost, and had shifted from inspection to prevention. Companies began to understand that activities conducted prior to production, such as product design and worker training significantly impacted overall costs. The costs of poor design, poor material quality, defects, scrap, and poor workmanship were all measurable and added to total cost. These realizations placed access to skilled workers and quality suppliers high on the priority list for firms competing on quality. Lack of worker skills, inadequate transportation and communication infrastructure, and low-quality supply are ultimately extremely costly for the implementation of a global supply chain.

### Managerial Insights Box—Beyond Cost

#### BMW

There are many benefits to maintaining geographic proximity to customers, particularly in markets where customers demand high customization and fast delivery. For this reason BMW chose to locate its state-of-the-art plant in Leipzig, Germany, right in the center of its market. The company chose to equip the facility, which opened in 2005, with numerous innovations to give BMW the ability to customize cars very late in the production process. Then in 2014 it rolled out its 1.5 millionth vehicle. Rather than cost, BMW's customers want quick delivery and the possibility of changing their orders *after* they have placed them. What they usually want is to add more optional equipment—a very high margins and lucrative business for BMW. To accommodate its customers, the Leipzig plant is designed to both reduce delivery lead time and increase the possibility of modifying the order after the car is actually put into production. The Leipzig plant is one of the most modern and sustainable in the world. This enables BMW to be responsive to the latest changes in the market and compete on flexibility.

The flexibility of BMW's factories allows for huge variations on basic models that would be virtually impossible for any other automaker. At the Leipzig plant seemingly random parts—ranging from dashboards and seats to axles—snake onto overhead conveyer belts to be lowered into the assembly line in precise sequence according to customers' orders. BMW buyers can select everything from engine type to the color of the gear-shift box to a seemingly limitless number of interior trims. They can then change their mind and order a completely different configuration in as little as five days before production begins. Customers have loved the flexibility with roughly 170,000 changes being placed per month. There are so many variations that line workers assemble exactly the same car only about once every nine months.

That level of individualization would be impossible to achieve at most automakers due to the complexity and cost. However, BMW has emerged as a sort of anti-Toyota. Whereas Toyota excels in simplifying, BMW excels in mastering complexity and tailoring cars to customers' tastes. That's what differentiates BMW from Lexus and the rest of the premium pack. "BMW drivers never change to other brands," says Yoichi Tomihara, president of Toyota Deutschland, who concedes that Toyota lags behind BMW in the sort of customization that creates emotional appeal.

In addition to cutting-edge technology and facilities, this level of innovation comes from a highly inclusive culture. Ideas flow from the bottom up, which helps keep BMW's new models fresh and edgy year after year. Young designers in various company studios, from Munich headquarters to DesignWorks in Los Angeles, are constantly pitted against one another in heated competitions. Unlike many car companies, where a design chief dictates a car's outlines to his staff, BMW designers are given only a rough goal but are otherwise free to come up with their best concepts.

Inclusion in design and production extends to suppliers. The facility has a large building for its major suppliers to set up shop within walking distance of the assembly line. This proximity allows the suppliers to react quickly to changes in the production schedule. A sophisticated IT system connects the factory to its suppliers, distribution channels, and BMW sales offices and dealers to keep everyone abreast of the latest changes. The goal is to reduce the lead time for customers in Germany to 10 days and allow them to modify their orders even within that period.

Adapted from: Bradley, Grant. "Superfactory—Behind the Scenes at BMW's Electric Car Plant." *New Zealand Herald*, July 2, 2015.

## Political and Economic Factors

Decisions to develop and manage a global supply chain network must consider the global political and economic environment. This environment is increasingly complex and turbulent and must be evaluated on a continual basis. Political instability and hostility toward foreign businesses is a serious consideration. Currency rate fluctuations can help or hurt global operations and require careful analysis. **Regional trade agreements**, such as NAFTA, and **trade protection mechanisms**, such as tariffs and trigger price mechanisms, also influence the decision to globalize operations. These factors can either significantly ease global operations or create large barriers and must be carefully considered. Let's look at some of these in a bit more detail.

### Impact of Exchange Rate Fluctuations

Imagine you are visiting Europe and want to purchase a cup of coffee priced at 3.00 euros at the coffee shop. Then you realize that you have to pay 3.60 in U.S. dollars for that coffee, as the exchange rate is 1.20. Suddenly you may find the coffee is a bit more expensive than you thought. This is the same problem supply chain managers encounter with fluctuating currency exchange rates. They can find themselves in a financial situation where their purchasing power is diminished literally overnight.

The exchange rate between two currencies specifies how much one currency is worth in terms of the other. For example, the exchange rate between the European euro and the United States dollar has fluctuated over the past 10 years from one euro being equal to 0.825 dollars (in October 2000) to 1.285 (in February 2004) to 1.40 (in November 2010) to 1.12 (in September 2016). This means that you would need 1.40 dollars to equal one euro. Similarly, the value of the Japanese yen has fluctuated in the range 80 to 140 yen per dollar. These fluctuations occur on a continual basis and can last for months or years. Small fluctuations are expected and do not have a large impact. However, large fluctuations can have huge implications for global operations. It means that the ability to purchase in the currency you possess is suddenly diminished with no fault of your own. Supply chain managers have to include these fluctuations in their management strategies, and there are certain strategies they can use to help minimize their exposure to these risks.

One strategy to minimize risks of exchange rate fluctuations is to maximize operational flexibility. This can be accomplished by diversifying production geographically using global sourcing networks. By diversifying geographically a company can shift more of its production to facilities and suppliers that are located in a lower-cost area when local currencies shift. For example, if the local currency tends to be consistently undervalued—such as in some Eastern European countries—it is better to shift most sourcing to local vendors. However, the firm may still want to source a limited amount of its inputs from less-favorable suppliers in other countries if it feels that maintaining an ongoing relationship may help in the future when strategies need to be reversed.

## Regional Trade Agreements

Trade agreements are pacts between countries that encourage trade in a region by eliminating or lowering tariffs, quotas, and other trade barriers. The purpose is to protect trade in the region, and increase regional growth, by giving preference to members of the pact. Many trading blocks have emerged globally, such as in Europe (Europe 1992) and North America (NAFTA). There are also numerous trade agreements between countries in Asia and the Pacific Rim, such as the Asia-Pacific Economic Cooperation Forum (APEC). APEC has 21 member countries, including the United States, China, and Japan, with the goal of free and open trade in the region by 2020. This has serious implications for the way firms structure their global supply chain network, as they have to be aware of the opportunities, as well as restrictions, such trade agreements provide.

Creation of NAFTA resulted in the elimination of nearly 7,000 individual tariffs, duties, and nontariff barriers to trade. For example, NAFTA changed the role of maquiladoras for American companies. Maquiladoras refers to an operation that involves manufacturing in a foreign country and importing materials and equipment on a tariff-free basis for assembly or manufacturing, then exporting the assembled or manufactured product, often back to the original country. American-owned maquiladoras enabled cheap labor on production, which incurred tariffs only on the low-cost labor portion of the product. NAFTA eliminated the tariff barriers, which changed the role of maquiladoras. NAFTA also resulted in the rise of Mexico's national content requirement from 36% to 62.5%. This resulted in European and Japanese firms now wanting to invest in North American production to qualify for the preferential tariff treatment.

## Impact of Non-Tariff Barriers

Most of us have heard of tariffs—taxes and duties on imported goods—as a barrier to global trade. However, tariffs have become a less-significant form of trade protection due to the General Agreement on Tariffs and Trade (GATT) and more recently the World Trade Organization (WTO), which have dramatically reduced the tariffs for most industrial goods traded among developed countries. GATT and WTO have resulted in a rise of global trade. However, it is the non-tariff barriers—various forms of indirect, non-price trade protection—that have become far more significant as obstacles to global exports and imports. Let's look at some of the most important non-tariff barriers.

**Import quotas**—a quantitative restriction on the volume of imports—is one of the most common forms of non-tariff barriers. An example of this is the use of textile quotas that are imposed by industrialized countries against textile imports from developing countries to keep a viable domestic industry. Another non-tariff barrier is a **trigger price mechanism**, which is the establishment of minimum price for sales by an exporter from a foreign country. Yet another form is the setting of **"local content requirements**," which specify that a certain portion of the value added must be produced inside the country. For example, the European Union has established strict local content rules. This has driven both Texas Instruments and Intel to build semiconductor facilities in Europe to respond to the increase in the amount of semiconductor processing required by the new local content rules.

Other barriers include the use of **technical standards and health regulations**, which relate to matters such as consumer safety, health, the environment, labeling, packaging, and quality standards. For example, for many years Japan refused to import U.S. skis on the grounds that Japanese snow was different from U.S. snow. Similarly, the United States prohibits imports of many types of agricultural products on such grounds.

Countries come with many non-tariff barriers to protect domestic businesses. Despite these efforts, global trade is flourishing. There is an increase in harmonization of regulation and standards across the globe, making managing global supply chains easier.

## CHAPTER HIGHLIGHTS

1. Globalization growth is a result of advances in transportation and information technology and a rise in personal income.

2. Six forces that impact global supply chains are *market and competition, cost, infrastructure, technology, political and economic environment,* and *culture.*

3. Global marketing is an approach that focuses on bringing standardization to the global market. Local marketing stresses microsegmentation and localized differentiation. These approaches are contradictory, but they are best used to complement one another when developing a global strategy.

4. The availability of infrastructure in global supply chains is a significant factor for going global. Infrastructure includes transportation, access to labor, warehousing, and access to suppliers.

5. Technology is a significant factor in enabling the functioning of global supply chains. Three types of technology are important: *information technology, manufacturing technology,* and *equipment technology.*

6. A significant factor in global supply chains is cost. Pursuing apparent cost reductions can be problematic, as there are numerous hidden costs. Also, companies must take into account many non-cost considerations, such as quality and proximity to customers.

7. Global supply chain management is impacted by political and economic factors, such as politics and government regulations, tariffs and various non-tariff barriers that include import quotas, trigger price mechanisms, and labor content regulation.

## KEY TERMS

| | | | | |
|---|---|---|---|---|
| Economic | Infrastructure | Product postponement | Equipment technology | Trigger price mechanism |
| Cultural | Technology | Supplier resiliency score | Regional trade agreements | Local content requirements |
| Political | Politics and economy | Information technology | Trade protection mechanisms | Technical standards and health regulations |
| Demographic | Culture | Manufacturing technology | Import quotas | |
| Market and competition | Global marketing | | | |
| Cost | Local marketing | | | |

## DISCUSSION QUESTIONS

1. Think of a product you are familiar with—the clothes you are wearing or the beverage you just drank or the book you are reading. Identify the challenges that would be involved in distributing this product on a global scale to different markets.

2. Come up with a new product idea. How might you modify this product to sell it to different global markets? How would you market this product globally?

3. You have US$1,500 to spend on a trip abroad. Explain the impact of currency fluctuations on your trip and what you can purchase if you choose to go to Asia versus Australia versus Europe versus Africa.

4. Think of an idea you are passionate about. How would you sell your idea to a high content versus low content culture? How about a low power distance versus high power distance culture?

## Case Study | Wú's Brew Works

One hot afternoon, Kenneth Wú sat on the narrow steps of his apartment complex in Hong Kong, enjoying his latest creation: an alcoholic beverage he made from his own kitchen. The drink tasted so good that he preferred to drink it instead of store-bought beer. When Wú paid a visit to friends in Tai-Koo Sing, they ridiculed him for making his own alcohol, but eventually they tried it out of sheer curiosity. To Wú's surprise, his friends unanimously agreed that his beverage would be worth paying money for. That evening, they developed an entrepreneurial spirit, and by the end of the night, Wú was convinced that his concoction could generate a substantial amount of revenue. Later that week, despite Wú's aversion to taking the risks required of an entrepreneur, he decided to manufacture and sell his beverage.

Wú and his friends began by going to different liquor stores in the Hong Kong region to offer samples. The liquor store owners fell in love with his beverage, and soon Wú had his own drink on shelves around the region. He named the drink "Wú's Brew." After a year of steady sales and considerable profit, Wú decided to expand his sales to other countries in East Asia. Based on the advice and esteem he had received from many of these small liquor store owners, he decided to start a partnership with a few of his close friends to sell the product and market what they believed to be the "next big thing" to hit the bars and shelves around the world. His company was named Wú's Brew Works.

Wú wisely acknowledges that he and his friends will never be able to meet global demand if they continue to manufacture the product from their homes. By relying on the relationships he developed with store owners and their networks, Wú expands his manufacturing operations. Sure enough, Wú's drink becomes the most popular item to hit the market in Hong Kong and countries such as Taiwan and the Philippines. Within a year, the beverage begins receiving global attention throughout East Asia. People and tourists from China, Japan, Vietnam, Malaysia, and other East Asian countries start requesting his beverage when visiting Hong Kong. Eventually, people throughout the world—including Australia, Europe, and even the United States—become interested.

Wú begins to envision his product being sold globally. After securing financial commitments from various Hong Kong investors, Wú and his partners rent out the 65th floor of Central Plaza in Wanchai North of the Hong Kong Island region of Hong Kong to locate company operations and the official Wú's Brew Works headquarters. However, he chooses to locate the manufacturing plant in Yenda, Australia, as it provides more convenient distribution access.

### Wú's Brew Works Manufacturing Plant

Yenda, Australia, is a little town located about 560 km west of Sydney in the New South Wales region of Australia. It is the location where Yellow Tail wine is manufactured and produced. Yenda is a multicultural place where vineyards and rice paddies thrive. It is located at the edge of Cocoparra National Park—a place of spectacular gorges, waterfalls, walking locations in lookouts, and home to more than one hundred species of birds. Wú and Co. decide to have the manufacturing plant in Yenda because of its open land and large capacity for a plant.

Wú decides to target the United States in its business plan to begin global growth; the United States will be the first area outside East Asia to sell Wú's Brew. Wú sought the U.S. market to fulfill his ambition of spreading his product globally because of the large growth potential for alcohol in the United States. However, alcohol is a highly regulated product in the United States, and all alcoholic imports coming into the United States have to follow a three-tier system of alcohol distribution.

### The Three-Tier System

The three-tier system is the system for distributing alcoholic beverages in the United States that was federally mandated after the repeal of the Prohibition in 1933. The three tiers in this system are the producers, distributors, and the retailers. In this system, the delivery of an alcoholic beverage involves the producer to sell to a distributor, who then must sell the product to a retailer, whether it is a liquor store, restaurant, or bar. This system is designed to help ensure the responsible and safe distribution of alcoholic beverages and is a key factor in preventing the distribution of alcohol to minors. It provides a process that guarantees the integrity of products to end consumers.

Different states have various rules and exceptions. In some states, under the brewpub system, a producer (brewers, distillers, wineries, and imports of alcohol) can sell its alcohol directly to retailers and has no obligation to include a distributor in its supply chain. Other states allow a two-tier system, which allows breweries to act as their own distributor so that they can distribute alcohol directly to retailers. In some states such as Oregon, intrastate shipments of alcohol directly from the producers to retailers or customers are permitted. Most of the states, however, including Texas and California, adhere to the three-tier system of alcohol distribution.

## Project Proposal Plan

After becoming fully educated about the risks and regulations of alcohol distribution in the United States, Wú and his company decide that expanding into the United States would be a good growth opportunity. Wú's Brew Works' corporate managers come up with three different project proposals to distribute alcohol to the United States. Each of the three project proposals are plans to market the product to one particular region of the United States and partner with one distributor because Wú's Brew Works and other international importers of alcohol are not allowed to distribute the product while remaining in the country. They are only allowed to sell the product to the distributor (usually located on the West Coast). Their plan is to select only one of the project proposals because of capital constraints. Ultimately, they can afford only to work with one distributor that brings the product to just one region of the United States.

The distributor that Wú's Brew Works chooses would not only sell within their respective area, but would also consolidate Wú's product with other international alcohol products to sell to retailers from inland states. This arrangement allows inland retailers to get around their legal inability to buy alcohol directly from the alcohol producer. Wú's West Coast distributors are therefore also known as distribution consolidators. These consolidators would be able to bring Wú's Brew to distributors in Texas or Kansas.

The first project proposal was a plan to partner with R. F. Michinan, located in the port of Los Angeles, California. The project would require bringing the product to the port of Los Angeles and ultimately marketing it to the southern United States, such as Texas and Louisiana. The second project proposal was with JH Distributors and would allow Wú's Brew to be brought to the northwest region and most of the Midwest regions of the United States. JH Distributors is located in Lake Oswego, Oregon, so the product would have to be brought to the port of Portland, Oregon. The final project proposal was to market the product in the east and northeast regions of the United States by partnering with SJT Distributors, located in San Francisco, California, and accessed through the ports of San Francisco. No project is considerably more profitable than the other.

Each project has its own risks. For the first project proposal, R. F. Michinan said that the risks of distributing alcohol are minimal and that Wú had nothing to worry about. However, based on reports from the city of Los Angeles, there have been many cases of theft of alcohol imports from R. F. Michinan. For the second project proposal, JH Distributors stated the risk of longer lead times and exposure to lost or damaged products due to long transport from Australia to the port of Portland. Delivering from overseas to the port required going through the Columbia River and navigating in Oregon. The last project proposal with SJT Distributors had risk of longer lead times to get the product from California across the United States to the eastern side of the country. This could also make emergency production processes even more complicated.

In order for the plan to be implemented, Wú's Brew would have to be shipped on truck from its manufacturing plant in Yenda, Australia, to the Sydney Harbor in Sydney, Australia. The product would then be loaded onto a ship, which would bring the product to the port of Los Angeles, the port of Portland, or the port of San Francisco, depending on which project Wú chooses. The international transport is DDP, which stands for "delivered duty paid." This is a code that represents the way international shipments are organized. DDP requires the seller (Wú) to bear all costs and risks of bringing the alcohol to the United States. But once Wú's Brew is brought to the port of its destination, the distributor is responsible for the rest.

The statement of operations and balance sheet of the three companies are displayed in Exhibits 12.1 and 12.2, respectively. The projected cash flows of all three projects are displayed in Exhibit 12.3.

|  | For the Year Ending December 31 | | |
| --- | --- | --- | --- |
|  | JH Distributors | SJT | R.F. Michinan |
| Net sales | 8,534,662 | 5,636,884 | 10,534,729 |
| Cost of sales | 7,434,881 | 3,256,774 | 9,783,006 |
| Gross profit | 1,099,781 | 2,380,110 | 751,723 |
| Selling, general and administrative | 528,948 | 598,112 | 201,477 |
| Others | 98,418 | 1,311,001 | 47,551 |
| Total Operating Expenses | 627,366 | 1,909,113 | 249,028 |
| Operating profit (loss) | 472,415 | 470,997 | 502,695 |
| Other income (expense) | 3,407 | 3,589 | 3,287 |
| Earnings before interest and tax | 469,008 | 467,408 | 499,408 |
| Interest Expense | — | — | — |
| Income (loss) before tax | 469,008 | 467,408 | 499,408 |
| Income taxes (benefit) | 175,878 | 175,278 | 187,278 |
| Net income (loss) | 293,130 | 292,130 | 312,130 |

**EXHIBIT 12.1** Consolidated Statement of Operations

## JH Distributors

JH Distributors is a major distributor and consolidator of alcohol located in Lake Oswego, Oregon. They distribute alcohol throughout the northwest region and parts of the Midwest region in the United States. Although they are headquartered in Lake Oswego, a city south of Portland, Oregon, their major warehouse is located in Portland near the port of Portland. They also have several distribution centers located in various parts of Oregon and states that surround Oregon. The owner of this privately held company, Julie Stables, is a long-time friend of Wú's.

After talking and negotiating with each of the companies he is trying to partner with, Wú is convinced that choosing project 2 with JH Distributors would be best for Wú's Brew. This is because of the high net present value this project has over the other two and also because of the trust that he has developed with Julie, his contact at JH Distributors. This personal relationship would help solidify the collaboration between the two companies. Wú's Brew Works and JH Distributors decide to begin the partnership.

## The Challenge

Within two months of agreement between the two companies, Wú's Brew Works reviewed its purchase order from JH Distributors and produced the 2,100 cases ordered. Wú's Brew Works hired a third-party logistics (3PL) provider to deliver the product in full-truck load from Yenda to Sydney, Australia, and then on a ship from Port Jackson in Sydney to the mouth of the Columbia River. From the mouth of the Columbia River in Oregon, the ship sailed to Portland, where it went through customs and other legal screens. Because the international transport was "delivered duty paid," JH Distributors did not have to worry about any of the costs prior to receiving the shipment from the port.

However, when receiving the shipment, JH Distributors claimed that they had only received 1,849 cases of the alcohol. When this was reported to their headquarters in Lake Oswego, Julie thought to herself, "That's strange, we ordered 2,700 cases. How did it get down to 1,849?" Some of the crewmembers aboard the ship claimed that they saw a lot of the alcohol bottles broken from the cases and so they threw what was unusable overboard from the ship. There were some violent storms in the Northern Pacific Ocean that might have caused this. This also caused the shipment to be late by two days. Later, while JH Distributors transported full truckloads of alcohol up north on I-5, they encountered a police chase from a local bank robbery, which delayed the shipment even further. The robbers from California were caught, but had crashed into one of the truckloads of the alcohol delivery JH Distributors was distributing from the port to its main warehouse.

|  | For the Year Ending December 31 | | |
| --- | --- | --- | --- |
|  | JH Distributors | SJT | R.F. Michinan |
| Cash and equivalents | 44,460 | 27,834 | 51,330 |
| Accounts receivable | 374,470 | 417,082 | 435,020 |
| Inventories | 407,776 | 460,684 | 434,442 |
| Prepaid expenses | 26,032 | 28,518 | 30,022 |
| Other | 41,428 | 44,368 | 42,000 |
| **Total current assets** | 894,166 | 978,486 | 992,814 |
| Property, plant, and equipment | 717,682 | 655,206 | 821,976 |
| Less depreciation | 366,972 | 334,828 | 411,060 |
| Net property, plant, and equipment | 350,710 | 320,378 | 410,916 |
| Intangible assets | 4,198 | 18,858 | 3,030 |
| Other assets | 35,376 | 31,446 | 35,938 |
| **Total assets** | **$1,284,450** | **1,349,168** | **1,442,698** |
| Accounts payable | 68,478 | 72,898 | 75,054 |
| Current portion of long-term debt | 1,150 | 1,000 | 3,030 |
| Accruals and other | 465,106 | 326,738 | 515,990 |
| **Total current liabilities** | 534,734 | 400,636 | 594,074 |
| Long-term debt | 17,550 | 18,000 | 60,042 |
| Deferred pension costs | 128,658 | 89,580 | 140,268 |
| Other liabilities | 38,424 | 38,606 | 642,138 |
| **Total liabilities** | 719,366 | 546,822 | 842,448 |
| Common stock | 37,710 | 37,710 | 37,670 |
| Capital in excess of par | 215,814 | 215,748 | 215,778 |
| Retained earnings | 293,130 | 292,130 | 312,130 |
| Treasury stock | −20,988 | −20,988 | −20,928 |
| Other stockholder's equity | 41,418 | 523,600 | 95,600 |
| **Total stockholder's equity** | 565,084 | 802,346 | 600,250 |
| **Total liabilities and equity** | **$1,284,450** | **1,349,168** | **1,442,698** |

**EXHIBIT 12.2** Consolidated Balance Sheet (dollars in thousands)

By the time the shipment had arrived to the warehouse, they realized that there were only 1,507 cases that arrived. When JH Distributors questioned Wú's Brew Works regarding the problem, Wú's Brew Works claimed they had done everything properly. When asked about only producing 2,100 cases, Wú's Brew Works claimed that the purchase order indicated exactly 2,100 cases and not 2,700. After reexamining the PO (purchase order), JH Distributors had realized that the 2,700 on the PO looked like 2,100 and so it was incorrectly inputted in its systems.

### Project 1—R. F. Michinan (to Los Angeles, California)

| | Cash Outflow | Cash Inflow | | | |
|---|---|---|---|---|---|
| | Cost to implement | Year 1 | Year 2 | Year 3 | Year 4 |
| Projected Cash Flows | $100,000 | 31,000 | 31,000 | 31,000 | 31,000 |

Cost of Capital = 10%

Projected life of initial project = 4 years

### Project 2—JH Distributors (to Portland, Oregon)

| | Cash Outflow | Cash Inflow | | | |
|---|---|---|---|---|---|
| | Cost to implement | Year 1 | Year 2 | Year 3 | Year 4 |
| Projected Cash Flows | $95,000 | 30,000 | 30,000 | 30,000 | 30,000 |

Cost of Capital = 10%

Projected life of initial project = 4 years

### Project 3—SJT Distribution (to San Francisco, California)

| | Cash Outflow | Cash Inflow | | | |
|---|---|---|---|---|---|
| | Cost to implement | Year 1 | Year 2 | Year 3 | Year 4 |
| Projected Cash Flows | $93,000 | 30,000 | 30,000 | 30,000 | 30,000 |

Cost of Capital = 12%

Projected life of initial project = 4 years

**EXHIBIT 12.3** Projected Cash Flows for 3 Projects[2]

[2]Note: A project can be evaluated through Net Present Value (NPV) computed as follows:

$$NPV = CF_0 + CF_1/(1+r)^1 + CF_2/(1+r)^2 + \cdots + CF_N/(1+r)^N$$

$$PI = PV \text{ of future cash flows}/\text{initial cost} = (CF_t/(1+r)^t)/CF_0$$

Profitability Index (PI) shows the relative profitability of any project. (PV per dollar of initial cost) A project is acceptable if its PI is greater than 1.0.

After all the troubling events, Wú and Julie wondered if their companies could recover. Although Wú believes that project 2 with JH Distributors is still the project that Wú's Brew Works should pursue, some of his corporate managers beg to differ.

### Case Questions

1. Based on all the setbacks in the alcohol supply chain, whose fault is it for all the events leading to the 1,200 case shortage of Wú's Brew?

2. Was bringing Wú's Brew into the United States a good idea in the first place, given the heavy regulation? Why?

3. Disregarding Wú's Brew first decision to invest in project 2 with JH Distributors, which project should it have invested in based only on the financial information provided? (*Use NPV as noted in the case*)

$$NPV = CF_0 + \frac{CF_1}{(1+i)^1} + \frac{CF_2}{(1+i)^2} + \cdots + \frac{CF_N}{(1+i)^N}$$

4. Kenneth Wú had chosen JH Distributors to partner with in hopes of bringing a very popular product to the United States. Based on all the risks mentioned in the case article, would you have done the same?

5. All the events have left a bad impression on some of Wú's Brew Works managers. Should Wú's Brew Works continue project 2 with JH Distributors? If not, then which project?

# REFERENCES

Ailon, G. "Mirror, Mirror on the Wall: Culture's Consequences in a Value Test of Its Own Design." *Academy of Management Review*, 33(4), 2008: 885–904.

Bird, Mathew. "Merging Two Global Company Cultures." *Harvard Business Review*, August 4, 2015.

Choudhary, Vimal, Akok Kshirsagar, and Ananth Narayanan. "How Multinationals Can Win in India." *McKinsey & Company*, March 1, 2012.

Hofstede, Geert. *Cultures and Organizations: Software of the Mind*, 2nd ed. New York, New York: McGraw-Hill, 2005.

Lee, Hau L., and Chung-Yee Lee. *Building Supply Chain Excellence in Emerging Economies*. New York: Springer Science, 2007.

Samovar, Larry A., and Richard E. Porter. *Communication between Cultures*, 5th ed. Stamford, CT: Thompson and Wadsworth, 2004.

# Sustainable Supply Chain Management

# 13

## LEARNING OBJECTIVES

*After completing this chapter, you should be able to:*

- Define sustainability and explain its role in supply chain management (SCM).
- Identify environmental and social costs inherent in supply chain activities.
- Describe methods of measuring and implementing sustainability.
- Explain the supply chain sustainability model.
- Identify specific changes organizations can make to support a sustainable supply chain.
- Make a business case for sustainable SCM using concepts and examples from this chapter.

## CHAPTER OUTLINE

■ **What Is Sustainability?**
*Defining Sustainability*
*Environmental and Social Sustainability*
    Environmental Sustainability
    Social Sustainability
*Principles of Sustainability*
*Why Sustainability?*
    Legal Compliance
    Community Relations
    Revenue
    Ethical Responsibility

■ **Evaluating Sustainability in SCM**
*The Supply Chain Sustainability Model*
    Model Inputs
    Leadership
    Processes
    Sustainability Performance

Stakeholders' Reaction
  Financial Performance
  Feedback
 *Enforcement, Compliance, and Innovation*
  Enforcement
  Compliance
  Innovation
 *Measures of Sustainability in SCM*
 *Values in Sustainable SCM*
 *Cost Assessment*
  Cost-of-Control
  Damage Costing
  Costing Systems
 *Risk Assessment*
  "Fat Tails"
  Scenario-Based Analysis
  Fuzzy Logic
  Monte Carlo Simulations
  Real Option Analysis

- **Sustainability in Practice**
  *Product Design*
  *Packaging*
  *Sourcing*
  *Process Design*
  *Marketing Sustainability*
  *Unintended Consequences*
- **Chapter Highlights**
- **Key Terms**
- **Discussion Questions**
- **Case Study: Haitian Oil**

On April 20, 2010, a deep-sea oil rig owned by British Petroleum PLC exploded. The explosion immediately killed 11 rig workers and caused the release of almost five million barrels of crude oil into the Gulf of Mexico as the broken pipe on the ocean floor spewed oil until September 19, 2010. The depth of the well, combined with hurricane-season weather within the Gulf of Mexico, made stemming the flow of oil a prolonged, expensive, and technically challenging project. The price of crude oil at the time was averaging over $80 per barrel. That amounted to about $400 million lost in product waste alone, without counting environmental degradation in the form of marine and wildlife habitat destruction, fishing and tourism business losses along the Gulf Coast, cleanup costs, stock price decrease, or the loss of human life.

According to the report of the United States' National Commission on the BP Deepwater Horizon Oil Spill and Offshore Drilling, the oil spill was "an avoidable disaster that resulted from management failures by BP PLC and its (two) contractors," and that "all three companies did a poor job of assessing the risks associated with their decisions and failed to adequately communicate, either with one another or with their own employees." Although some have dismissed the Deepwater Horizon disaster as an irresponsible aberration on the part of the three companies, not to be expected from others in the industry, the report suggests otherwise: "The root causes are systemic and, absent significant reform in both industry practices and government policies," could very well happen again with other companies.

BP suffered an astounding 52% decrease in stock value within 50 days of the explosion as a result of negative shareholder reactions. To avoid litigation over the matter BP created a $20 billion spill response fund to compensate for natural resource damages, government response costs, and individual compensation. To finance the compensation fund, BP plans to significantly reduce capital spending, divest about $10 billion in assets, and reduce payment of dividends to shareholders. These are all potentially ruinous consequences for the company itself, not to mention the environmental and social impact.

To achieve environmentally and socially sustainable performance, companies must be aware of the costs and risks that surround their actions. From resource extraction to product disposal, sustainable supply chain management (SCM) promises to achieve long-term corporate profitability while protecting the environment and human welfare. As demonstrated by the Deepwater Horizon disaster, companies can pay an extremely high price for failing to anticipate low-probability, high-consequence events. Although not all sustainability issues are as dramatic as this example, many have severe consequences for both the organization and the environment. Fortunately, they can be avoided by adequate care and attention to costs and risks; effective leadership and communication; responsiveness to stakeholders such as employees, surrounding communities, and government; and a policy of minimizing environmental and social risks while maximizing long-term corporate profitability.

Adapted from: *The Wall Street Journal*, A2, January 6, 2011, and www.bp.com.

# What Is Sustainability?

## Defining Sustainability

The last few decades have seen increased demand for companies to fully account for the environmental and social impact of their products and services and the associated supply chains. The activities involved in SCM impact these concerns—including biodegradable product packaging, responsible product disposal, control of manufacturing and transportation emissions, and sustainable sourcing practices. As a result, sustainability has become a central theme in SCM.

Supply chains are indispensable to our daily lives, but they can have significant adverse environmental and social consequences. These include environmental costs, health and human safety risks, and the cost of waste. Sustainable SCM is concerned with changing practices to reduce these negative consequences. Sustainability impacts SCM in areas of product design, product manufacturing, packaging, transportation and logistics, sourcing, and product end-of-life. As consumers increasingly demand environmentally and socially sustainable products, businesses are being forced to find ways to achieve sustainable supply chain performance. As a result, the challenge to managers posed by sustainability is to incorporate environmental and social responsibilities into their management practices.

## Global Insights Box

### ■ THE GREAT PACIFIC GARBAGE PATCH

For decades, ocean currents circulating between the coasts of California and Japan have accumulated plastic waste into a gyre of non-biodegradable garbage known as the Great Pacific Garbage Patch. This is a whirling mass of garbage floating in the middle of the ocean. In fact, there may be as many as five garbage patches in the Earth's oceans. The garbage patches are made up of plastic bits from toys, bottles, and packaging that find their way into the ocean from storm sewers, as well as pollution left from marine vessels. Winds drive the surface-level pollution toward the center of the gyre, where the currents are relatively still and the garbage cannot escape. Sunlight breaks down the garbage into microplastics that are loaded with toxins, with the plastics functioning as a sponge, amassing large concentrations of toxins from the surrounding ocean water.

When the plastics degrade into tiny particles, zooplankton and other life forms at the bottom of the marine food chain consume the garbage that is ultimately passed up through the food chain. Marine wildlife, such as sea turtles, albatrosses, and jellyfish, consume the plastic particles, leading to death or hormone disruption. Toxins in the garbage patch can wind up back in the human body, threatening our health.

Estimates of the size of the Great Pacific Garbage Patch range up to twice the size of the continental United States, but it is difficult to measure its actual span and density. The open-sea garbage patches contain plastics that have broken down into smaller polymers, as well as chemical sludge and larger debris such as abandoned fishing nets. They are an indirect consequence of the use of non-biodegradable plastics in consumer products and packaging. Although efforts to clean up the patch are underway, scientists suggest that relying on nontoxic, biodegradable, and recyclable materials is the only way to prevent such phenomena from recurring.

**Sustainability** can be defined as meeting present needs without compromising the ability of future generations to meet their own needs. Sustainability is indispensable when both present and future generations depend on the same set of limited resources. The resources of the Earth used on the input side of supply chains are borrowed from the future and must be stewarded as such. For example, if the present need for timber was consumed at an unsustainable rate, trees would be cut down faster than they could be re-grown, which would compromise the ability of future generations to access timber. The waste output of supply chains must be disposed of responsibly. Otherwise, concentrations of pollution can jeopardize the integrity of ecosystems or human health.

Although typically defined in terms of the relationship between the present and the future, sustainability is not limited to the intergenerational context. Principles of sustainability also apply to balance competing needs. For example, sustainable use of timber for lumber *would not* jeopardize the need to access timber for the purposes of making paper. Sustainable resource consumption or pollution *would not* eliminate resources faster than they could be replenished. Sustainability is not simply for the sake of future populations, but for present purposes as well.

SCM must fulfill consumer demand sustainably. Sustainable SCM requires managers to identify sustainability "issues" when analyzing operations and their effects. To determine whether a supply chain is operating sustainably, managers must focus on both inputs and outputs of each stage of the supply chain, as shown in Figure 13.1. Sustainability analysis of inputs requires all

**FIGURE 13.1** Sustainability considers inputs and outputs of each SC member.

aspects of resource consumption—from raw materials to human resources. A sustainable supply chain avoids consuming so much of a resource that future operations are compromised. Sustainability analysis of outputs involves all aspects of pollutant emissions, so that the health of neighboring ecosystems or populations is not put in jeopardy.

Sustainable SCM is not just an altruistic effort. Four documented types of payoffs come with improving a company's sustainability performance. **Financial payoffs** include reduced operating costs, increased revenue, lower administrative costs, lower capital costs, and stock market premiums. **Customer-related payoffs** include increased customer satisfaction, product innovation, market share increase, improved reputation, and new market opportunities. **Operational payoffs** include process innovation, productivity gains, reduced cycle times, improved resource yields, and waste minimization. **Organizational payoffs** include employee satisfaction, improved stakeholder relationships, reduced regulatory intervention, reduced risk, and increased organizational learning. We will look at all of these throughout this chapter.

## Environmental and Social Sustainability

Stated most generally, sustainability is the capacity of a system to endure. As such, sustainability is a broad concept with numerous applications. There are two types of sustainable practices: environmental sustainability and social sustainability. **Environmental sustainability** is the preservation of diverse biological systems that remain productive over time. **Social sustainability** involves maintaining societies' long-term well-being. Although the criteria for sustainability in ecology are different from the criteria for sustainability in human affairs, the two are mediated by supply chain networks. From the extraction of raw materials to the deposit of final waste products, supply chain networks are the links between human activity and the natural world. Social sustainability depends in part on the benefits of environmental sustainability, such as access to clean water, soil and air, and healthy ecosystems. Some human activities, such as overfishing and excessive pollution, have an adverse impact on environmental integrity. Threats to environmental sustainability, such as oil spills, acidification, or natural resource depletion, have an adverse impact on humanity's welfare. Therefore, environmental and social sustainability are interconnected, as shown in Figure 13.2.

**FIGURE 13.2** Environmental and social sustainability are interconnected.

### Environmental Sustainability

Environmental sustainability is the sustainability practice that deals with either pollution or resource depletion issues. Whether a supply chain network is environmentally sustainable depends on the relationship of the activity in question—say resource procurement or manufacturing—to global warming, acidification, smog, ozone layer depletion, toxin release, habitat destruction, land use issues, and resource depletion.

### Social Sustainability

Social sustainability consists of either economic or population issues. Whether a supply chain network is socially sustainable depends on the relationship of the activity in question to social issues. These include income inequalities, population growth, levels of migration to cities, gender equality and women's rights, poverty, dislocation, and urban or minority unemployment.

## Supply Chain Leaders Box

### ■ FIBRIA CELULOSE

Fibria Celulose is a Brazilian company and the largest producer of eucalyptus pulp in the world. This material is used to manufacture printing and writing paper, tissue paper, and high-value-added specialty papers. Eucalyptus lumber is also used to create high-quality furniture and interior designs. Chances are that you have used paper or furniture from Fibria's lumber. Fibria is an example of a global company that has developed their supply chain while being committed to environmental and social sustainability. They also demonstrate the financial benefits that can come from such practices.

Fibria ensures environmental sustainability by preserving the natural ecosystems surrounding the eucalyptus plantations. The company created a forestry management program to preserve native tree populations and prevent overharvesting. They created a watershed project to preserve the quality of nearby rivers in light of insecticide and fertilizer runoff. They also use strict environmental control technology to protect and monitor the impact of their operations on forests and rivers.

In addition to environmental sustainability, Fibria also focuses on social sustainability by contributing to the communities near their operation sites. The company collaborates with nongovernmental organizations, project experts, and financial advisors to give back to the local communities. In addition, Fibria's employees are encouraged to volunteer in the surrounding communities. Volunteer activities include collecting warm winter clothing, collecting food items to feed the hungry, providing emergency support after catastrophic floods, visiting hospitals, and tutoring local students in economic issues by allowing them to run a "minicompany." Fibria is listed on *Fortune*'s list of companies helping change the world.

From: www.fibria.com.

---

To provide a simple illustration of what a sustainability analysis would include, consider the logistics decision of locating a chemical processing facility. Initially, the choice of location would be determined by considering economic factors, such as real estate cost or transportation, as we discussed in Chapter 7. However, sustainability requires an analysis of environmental and social factors that goes well beyond these basic economic considerations, as shown in Figure 13.3. A chemical factory may affect nearby plant and animal populations as well as local human health by introducing air, water, and noise pollution. Further, the choice of location may implicate job availability and commuter behavior, while requiring decisions about wages for local employees.

| Decision | Environment Impact | Sustainable Decision |
|---|---|---|
| Facility location | • Negative consequences of siting on natural habitats (ecosystems) and habitat destruction.<br>• Negative effect on humans and animals, from increased noise pollution and energy consumption; contamination of air and water. | • Minimize total material and personnel travel distances to and from the facility.<br>• Avoid runoff from construction activity and new pavement.<br>• Abate noise pollution.<br>• Reduce the air pollution effects on the community. |
| Product packaging | • Nonbiodegradable and nonrecyclable packaging leads to landfill clutter and harm to wildlife. | • Eliminate or reduce product packaging.<br>• Rely on biodegradable and recyclable materials. |
| Material flow | • Modes of transportation used to move materials have significant effects on energy consumption, traffic congestion, and pollution. | • Reduce the number of shipments.<br>• Source locally.<br>• Strategically locate warehouses.<br>• Consolidate shipments.<br>• Select transportation modes wisely. |
| Inventory control | • Noise pollution, increased energy use, and increased motor vehicle congestion. | • Minimize total material movement to and from the facility by delivery consolidation and accepting the carrying of larger inventory quantities. |

Adapted from: Beamon, Benita. "Environmental and Sustainability Ethics in Supply Chain Management." *Science and Engineering Ethics*. Vol. 11, No. 2, 2005, 221–234.

**FIGURE 13.3** SCM decisions and related environmental effects.

## Principles of Sustainability

Being able to spot critical sustainability issues, and offer adequate solutions, is a crucial managerial skill in today's business environment. For key "issue spotting" tools, consider the following nine principles of sustainability[1]:

- **Ethics.** Ethics involves promoting a corporate culture that fosters truthful and fair conduct between all stakeholders. Ethics are maintained by monitored and enforced codes of conduct. At the bare minimum, an ethical company prohibits violations of human rights or dignity and adheres to honest and just standards and practices. Positions such as a "corporate ombudsmen" can be used to ensure that external stakeholder voices are heard, as well as an "organizational ombudsmen" to ensure internal stakeholders are respected. This helps create a work environment that encourages the reporting of ethical violations to appropriate authorities by offering a confidential and neutral forum to voice concerns.

- **Governance.** Governance concerns the conscientious execution of duties held by corporate board members and managers. Good governance requires a well-understood mission statement supported by performance metrics, as well as the use of decision tools to support management. Good governance should mandate the evaluation of senior management along multiple dimensions, such as sustainability measures, not merely financial performance.

- **Transparency.** Transparency involves visibility. Companies that care about the information needs of others are transparent with them. Full disclosure of financial performance is important

---

[1] Adapted from: M. Epstein, *Making Sustainability Work* (Sheffield, UK: Greenleaf Publishing, 2008).

with respect to investors or lenders. There are different degrees of transparency—ranging from document disclosure on request to posting information publicly.

- **Business Relationships.** Companies should treat all suppliers, distributors, and partners fairly. They should also deal only with companies that do the same. When forming business partnerships, or seeking sources of supply, they should also consider social, ethical, and environmental factors as selection criteria. Not doing so can put a company's reputation in jeopardy.

- **Financial Return.** To raise capital, companies must provide investors and lenders with a competitive return on investment (ROI). The company should maintain solid financial results and continue to create value, while balancing additional nonmonetary factors. Although positive financial returns are necessary, they should be evaluated in conjunction to other principles of sustainability.

- **Community Involvement and Economic Development.** Investing in community involvement and economic development improves the economic welfare of the community in which the company does business. It serves to enhance the company's long-term profitability by creating additional opportunities in that community. Starbucks invests heavily in the communities of coffee growers. The result is a reliable and consistent source of supply.

- **Value of Products and Services.** Companies typically state a general commitment to customer satisfaction as part of their mission statement. However, they should clarify their obligations and responsibilities to their customers. In addition to products and services being of the highest quality, managers should be aware of the externalities generated by their products or services, and their supply chains.

- **Employment Practices.** A diverse workforce with competitive wages and ample time away from work is bound to be a more loyal, productive workforce than one that is subject to prejudicial abuse, grueling hours, and poor pay. Management practices with respect to employees should go above and beyond minimum requirements of health, safety, and nondiscrimination mandated by labor laws. Employment practices should maximize the productivity and quality of employees by fostering a culture of mutual respect, appreciation, and care in the pursuit of the corporate mission. Investing in employees, in the form of continuing education programs, leave time, child care, and opportunities for advancement, are ultimately investments for the company itself. The result is healthier, happier, more productive employees and an enhanced reputation of the company. An excellent example of these benefits is the SAS Institute in North Carolina, a company consistently on *Fortune* magazine's list of top companies to work for. The company provides a superb work environment—from child care to on-site massages—resulting in high productivity and almost no turnover.

- **Protection of the Environment.** At a bare minimum, all corporations must comply with applicable environmental laws. However, corporations can do much more than this to promote environmental integrity. Innovations that allow corporations to meet demand while simultaneously cutting waste, lowering air and water pollutants, and consuming fewer resources are genuinely praiseworthy. Maximizing the use of recyclable materials, increasing product durability, streamlining product packaging, and encouraging stringent safety standards are all management decisions that can be made internally. Allocating resources to fund research into cleaner, more efficient technology, or to fund land reclamations, or to create wilderness preservations are all means of stewarding corporate capital to offset corporate environmental harms.

These principles are all relevant to a company's sustainability performance. In evaluating the sustainability of a company, analysis should consider these dimensions. Managers should be familiar with them and seek to incorporate them when making decisions.

# Why Sustainability?

The anti-environmental posture prevalent in industry poses an obvious barrier to voluntary sustainability initiatives. This posture stems in part from two paradigms for thinking about environmental management. The "**crisis-oriented**" environmental management paradigm considers the purpose of management to protect and enhance business performance in terms of making more money, which encourages uncooperative behavior toward anyone with a countervailing agenda, including environmental advocates. The "**cost-oriented**" environmental management paradigm considers environmental regulations as simply a cost of doing business. Corporations will pollute as much as necessary to profit from the polluting activity and will count environmental sanctions as one more cost of operations on the balance sheet. Both of these paradigms place priority on business profitability, viewing environmentally sustainable measures as a barrier to that end.

Why implement sustainable measures in SCM? There are at least four reasons:

1. Legal compliance with government regulations
2. Maintaining positive community relations
3. Increasing revenue
4. Satisfying moral obligations

We look at these next.

## Legal Compliance

Environmental regulations typically define two sets of standards that must be adopted by major sources of pollutant emissions. The first is a **design standard**, which specifies the type of technology necessary for the pollution source to be in compliance with the regulation (e.g., a certain type of pollution-scrubbing filter must be installed on a smokestack). The second is a **performance standard**, which specifies the amount of permissible pollution (e.g., effluent pollution must be reduced to $x$ parts of pollutant per million parts water), leaving the choice of pollutant reduction technology to the polluter. Failure to comply with environmental regulation can result in penalties, fines, litigation costs, increased inspections leading to lost productivity, plant closure, and bad press (not to mention potential environmental and human health consequences).

International norms are also relevant to corporate sustainability. Although not a binding law, the United Nations Millennium Development Goals are the product of a gathering of world leaders in 2000 and include goals such as the elimination of extreme poverty, the promotion of gender equality and female empowerment, and the attainment of environmental sustainability. The poverty goal entails reducing the number of people living on less than $1 per day and achieving full and productive employment for all people. The gender equality goal entails increasing the share of women in wage employment in nonagricultural sectors. The environmental goal entails integrating sustainable principles into policies and programs, as well as reversing the loss of biodiversity and environmental resources. Clearly corporate activity can either advance the world toward meeting these goals or undermine our ability to meet these goals.

## Community Relations

Another reason to implement sustainability is to effectively manage community relations. Failure to operate a company sustainably can lead to stigma and lost trust from the community. Consumers will cease purchasing from a company who they feel is not loyal to the interests of the community in which business is done. Negative reputation with stakeholders can negatively impact the financial bottom line of a company. Just consider the community relations issues BP encountered following the Gulf oil spill.

### Revenue

Managers are perennially aware of the need for minimizing costs and maximizing revenue—in other words, creating financial value. Sustainability offers a means to this end. Financial value can be created by lowering operating costs through the adoption of more energy-efficient technology. Further, financial value can be created by process improvements such as lean manufacturing principles, eliminating steps that are unduly burdensome, and eliminating barriers to smooth flowing processes.

### Ethical Responsibility

An additional motive for implementing sustainability principles stems from our sense of moral obligation to preserve life. Hypoxia is the condition of oxygen depletion in aquatic environments that threatens life forms. Caused by pollution and eutrophication from runoff, hypoxia leads to "dead zones" where shark, fish, and invertebrate carcasses can be seen strewn across the ocean floor. Companies concerned that their production processes are causing hypoxia can adopt more effective sewage treatment to prevent pollutants and fertilizers from leaching into bodies of water. Doing so would be motivated by a moral concern for the preservation of living creatures or simply out of self-interest for our access to fish for consumption.

Whether we care for the environment because it is intrinsically valuable or because it ultimately serves our own ends, our moral radars should consider the welfare of living creatures. In addition, morality would prohibit imposing harms on individuals who do not consent to be put at risk. This moral concern would motivate a company to adopt pollution control technology to decrease the amount that surrounding communities are exposed to airborne or waterborne pollutants. If a company knew that emissions from a manufacturing plant were directly responsible for the cancer of many locals, even though the plant was in compliance with environmental laws, managers with sensitivity to moral considerations would protect nearby human lives by taking measures to reduce carcinogenic emissions from their plant. A desire to fulfill our moral obligation to avoid unnecessary harm serves to motivate sustainability.

There are at least three different frameworks for thinking about ethical duties to adopt sustainable practices: minimalism, reasonable care, and good works. A **minimalist ethic** views precautions as worthwhile simply to avoid liability. A **reasonable care ethic** takes available measures to eliminate foreseeable risks either by designing out the risk or providing protection against the risk. A **good works ethic** goes beyond what is legally required to take affirmative steps to discover potential hazards and proactively safeguard society against them. Regardless of which of these moral perspective one adopts, most of us view human welfare as intrinsically valuable, and environmental welfare is worth protecting because of its "instrumental" value for humans. Even under this human-oriented framework, proactive measures to preserve environmental integrity are justified as means of bolstering human welfare.

Governmental regulations, public relations, cost imperatives, and moral obligations are all rationales for sustainability in SCM, and these rationales are interconnected. Failure to adopt sustainable practices can lead to fines for regulatory noncompliance, which negatively impacts the financial bottom line by exacerbating operating costs. Further, noncompliance likely causes some environmental or human health damages, which tarnishes the company's reputation and possibly compromises the moral obligations of managers to avoid imposing uncompensated harms on others. Instead of asking, "Why should we operate sustainably?" the presumptive question should be, "Why *not* operate sustainably?"

## Evaluating Sustainability in SCM

Managers are under the burden of balancing the influences of resource availability, customer demand, consumer activists, employee loyalty, and government regulations. In this section we present a model that integrates social and environmental impacts into a company's supply chain management strategy.

## The Supply Chain Sustainability Model

The Supply Chain Sustainability Model provides the elements of a successful sustainability strategy and shows how they are related. It is illustrated in Figure 13.4. The continuum presented in the model includes inputs that feed into organizational and supply chain processes and lead to outputs.

The model shows that management decisions—in the form of processes and organizational and supply chain structures—create an environmental and social impact. Supply chain sustainability performance, in turn, leads to stakeholder reactions that then impact long-term financial performance. A feedback loop connects processes, outputs, and outcomes, indicating a shift in the inputs as a result of performance. Processes, outputs, and outcomes define the costs and benefits of supply chain activity. Processes also have an immediate effect on long-term financial performance. As shown, financial performance is affected by the stakeholder reaction to sustainability performance. The following expands on each of the elements of this model.

### Model Inputs

The **external context** of SCM pertains to government and market-based influences. In all countries, government regulations impose burdens on industries to follow minimum health and safety standards, although their stringency varies by location. This includes the disposal of hazardous or toxic waste, various emissions pollutants, employee discrimination, safe working conditions, minimum wages, and the minimum age of employees, which are all subject to regulation. Similar to governmental regulations, market influences on the sustainability model depend on where

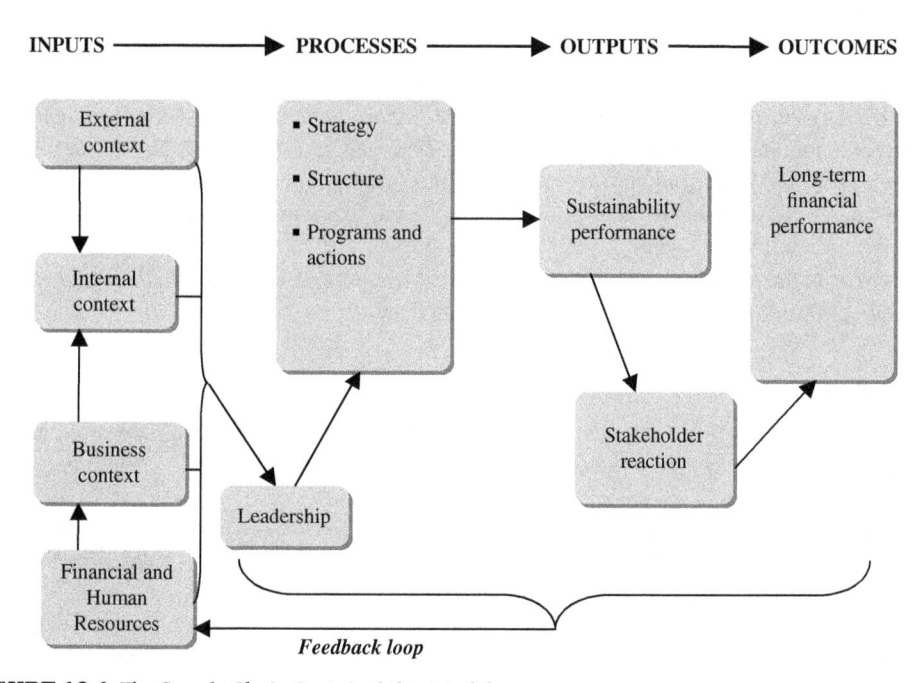

**FIGURE 13.4** The Supply Chain Sustainability Model.
Adapted from: Epstein, Marc J. *Making Sustainability Work: Best Practices in Managing and Measuring Corporate Social, Environmental, and Economic Impacts*. Sheffield, UK: Greenleaf Publishing, 2008, p. 46.

the company does business. The marketplace for products and services will reflect consumer tolerance for pollution, among other things. Other factors such as weather patterns, topography, population wealth, and access to information also sway the market's response to corporate sustainability decisions.

The ability of a supply chain to become sustainable also depends on its **internal context**. Not only the pressure to increase revenue and pay dividends to shareholders, but also the mission statements, dominant strategies, organizational structures, decision-making procedures, and operating systems within each business unit of a corporation form the internal context of sustainability. Each element in this context may have a positive or negative effect on efforts to achieve sustainability and should be critically evaluated in light of its tendency toward efficient, sustainable operations.

Different industry sectors will have to deal with unique issues stemming from different **business contexts**. For example, energy, chemical, and mining industries will create risks to the environment and human health, whereas service industries and product manufacturers may pose social risks in terms of working conditions and consumer relations. Companies with the greatest potential to gain or lose from sustainability initiatives include companies with high-profile brands, companies whose supply chains carry significant environmental impacts, companies who significantly depend on natural resources, and companies that face current or potential regulatory exposure. Uniform labor and inspection standards, as well as industry codes of conduct, are responses to pressures arising from the business context.

Sustainability performance is greatly affected by the **human and financial resources** committed to its achievement. The implementation of sustainability programs requires a significant upfront allocation of company resources. This resource investment should pay for itself in the long run in terms of avoided costs, but upfront capital is needed to adequately educate pertinent employees to detect sustainability issues. Further, these employees must be equipped with sufficient resources to act on revelations of risk.

## Leadership

**Leadership** involves factoring all the "inputs" (external, internal and business contexts, as well as human and financial resources) into management decisions. The most effective leadership comes from a clear commitment to sustainable performance on the part of top management that is effectively communicated through all the layers of the organization. Leaders must be sufficiently knowledgeable and committed to their vision to translate it into actual performance. Creating a vice president position to oversee sustainability, including major business unit managers on a sustainability committee, and joining with suppliers are ways of ensuring sustainability issues are addressed from the top down. Leaders must demonstrate commitment to sustainability, search for risks and opportunities associated with sustainability, and foster a sustainable corporate culture.

## Processes

A sustainability strategy is a plan that guides the company and its supply chain toward long-term profitability that protects consumers, employees, and the environment. This strategy is put into place by a combination of internal structures and programs.

Sustainability can be promoted through changes in organizational design, such as the creation of a sustainable structure. Rather than relegating sustainability concerns to one department within an organization—such as operations or human resources—responsibility for sustainable performance should be diffused within each function of the company. Such a structure enables each operating unit to see the costs and benefits of its environmental and social responsibility. Sustainable structures should be integrated throughout the organization and between supply chain members, capitalize on human resources and provide feedback on sustainability performance from management to top leaders.

Management systems, such as programs and actions, must be aligned to achieve sustainability. Programs to promote sustainability should tie incentives and rewards with effective environmental and social sustainability performance. This requires evaluation of economic, environmental, and social factors in assessing performance, not simply an evaluation of quarterly earnings. Sustainability actions can be either **proactive** or **reactive**, depending on when risks are identified. Further, sustainability actions should be both **internal** (such as training employees or site audits) and **external** (such as supplier audits and public accountability).

## Sustainability Performance

**Sustainability performance** is the overall metric designed to reflect organizational performance along multiple dimensions. This metric incorporates all positive and negative impacts on all of the company's stakeholders. Sustainability performance can be enhanced by reducing negative impacts or increasing positive impacts and preferably both. Regardless of how sustainability performance is measured, it is necessary to evaluate performance, recognize impacts, and look for improvement. One of the most critical variables in evaluating corporate sustainability performance is the definition of stakeholders. A narrowly defined set of stakeholders, such as shareholders in the company, will probably omit a significant array of impacts that accrue to individuals who do not own stock in the company and thus reflect a higher sustainability performance score. A broadly defined set of stakeholders would probably lead to a greater estimate of costs and hence a lower sustainability performance score.

## Stakeholders' Reaction

Given the many potential stakeholders, listening and responding to stakeholder reactions is easier said than done. However, ignoring stakeholder reactions is done at the peril of the supply chain's profitability. At minimum, supply chains should consider impacts of their activities on shareholders, customers, suppliers, employees, and surrounding communities. Stakeholders can react in both positive and negative ways. Customers can remain loyal or boycott. Talented employees can migrate to more sustainable employers. Regulators and surrounding communities can exert pressure on major polluters. Shareholders may use sustainability as a criterion for investment decisions.

## Financial Performance

The monetization of the impact of supply chain activities allows managers to evaluate sustainability initiatives in light of the ultimate goal: improved financial performance. The notion that supply chain sustainability enhances revenue and lowers costs has broad support. Social reputation is a significant success factor in an informed, competitive market. Process improvements can lead to multi-million-dollar energy savings and increase shareholder return on investment. Further, sustainable decisions can lead to decreased incidents of legal fees and penalties as well as lower packaging and distribution costs. Internally, companies that invest in the health and welfare of their employees realize benefits in terms of increased productivity and employee loyalty. The supply chain sustainability model allows us to make a business case for sustainability by relating environmental and social impacts to financial performance.

## Feedback

Effective **feedback loops** enable leaders to take data relating to outputs and outcomes and translate them into improvements in internal processes. To be useful toward the goal of sustainability, feedback mechanisms must not rely solely on monetary information but must include performance criteria relating to environmental, social, and economic matters. Feedback mechanisms are essential for organizational learning and allow each supply chain member to continue to assess their progress toward long-term goals.

## Enforcement, Compliance, and Innovation

Adopting principles of sustainability does not happen accidentally. Owners, directors, and managers must conscientiously and resolutely decide to implement sustainability in their supply chains. There are three drivers of sustainable initiatives. They are enforcement, compliance, and innovation—or a mixture of all three. Let us look at these in a bit more detail.

### Enforcement

Governmental decision makers can require companies to adopt practices that are deemed environmentally safe and socially responsible, using laws and government regulation. With powers of official oversight accompanied by sanctions for noncompliance, these agencies can enforce sustainable initiatives. For example, the U.S. Clean Air Act authorizes the Environmental Protection Agency (EPA) to enact and enforce mandatory regulations that apply to companies that own major pollutant-emitting facilities.

### Compliance

**Compliance** is voluntary participation in sustainable practices. A popular way of encouraging compliance with sustainability has been through industry-initiated certification programs. These programs provide benefits to firms in the form of advertising—such as logos that appeal to the preferences of a growing number of environmentally conscious consumers—and group membership—which provide directory listings and other perks. Rather than imposing sanctions, failure to comply with voluntary programs leads simply to the withdrawal of the firm's membership with the host organization and the revocation of certification for the firm's products or services.

### Innovation

Motivated by internal initiatives, companies may be driven to innovate over current practices to enhance operations. Often an incidental benefit of this is the satisfying of environmental or social priorities. Unlike enforcement, innovation is voluntary. Unlike compliance, innovation is internal. What a company's environmental and social goals are, and whether they have been achieved in measureable ways, are not necessarily disclosed to consumers, or if they are published, the data are used as "bragging rights" by the company.

In practice, these three implementation methods exist in hybrid form. Imagine a large company that emits a great magnitude of pollution in operations that span several countries. This company would be subject to various governmental enforcement measures, would probably voluntarily comply with some industry-sponsored certification programs, and would internally fund research and development to promote sustainable innovation. In this case, all three drivers—enforcement, compliance, and innovation—overlap in realizing sustainable supply chains. These drivers succeed at achieving independent oversight to ensure actual sustainability. Although it appears obvious to everyone that some level of enforcement is necessary, the precise level of enforcement remains an open question.

Implementation of sustainability usually happens incrementally, with companies and their supply chains moving through three stages. This is illustrated in Figure 13.5. *First*, companies begin incorporating common sense measures such as recycling in bulk, shutting down idling electronics, turning off lights when not in use, and using teleconferencing instead of travel for meetings. The goal at this stage is simply to reduce the carbon footprint or other metric of sustainability. *Second*, at more sophisticated levels of sustainable management, sustainable principles become instantiated in operations. Companies begin to conduct internal assessments to reduce the adverse impacts of their operations on surrounding environments. This stage involves implementing lean principles, rationalizing manufacturing, strategic sourcing, changing product design, and optimizing

```
STAGE 1:                    STAGE 2:                    STAGE 3:
Sustainability              Sustainability is           Sustainability
involves "common            instantiated in             treated as
sense" measures             operations                  practical science

Recycling in bulk;          Implementing                Third-party audits
shutting off lights;        lean; changing              document
teleconferencing;           product design;             compliance to all
shutting idle electronics   optimizing distribution     standards
```

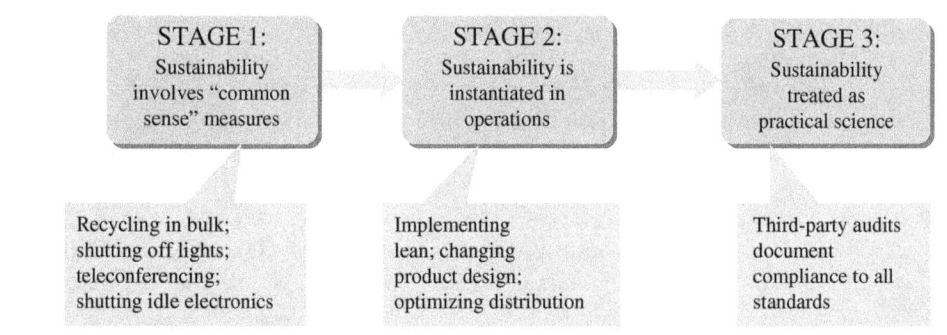

**FIGURE 13.5** Stages of sustainability implementation.

distribution channels. *Third*, the most refined perspective with which to approach sustainability treats sustainability as a practical science. At this stage, third-party audits provide an objective framework against which to evaluate organizations and standards that are set by governmental or industry groups.

## Measures of Sustainability in SCM

Sustainable SCM enables a firm to meet the triple-bottom-line of social responsibility, environmental stewardship, and economic viability. There are several approaches to measuring whether a product or service is sustainable.

**Total cost of ownership (TCO)**, which we discussed in Chapter 7, is a measure that considers economic viability by estimating the sum of all costs of a product, including procurement, manufacture, distribution, usage, and disposal. Consider a frozen pizza or a car battery. Both products involve gathering component parts, combining these parts into a product, shipping these products to retail, using the product, and efforts to dispose of the residual material. Of course, the costs at each step in the supply chain would widely vary and would involve distinct risks. The frozen pizza seems a relatively benign product until one considers the total costs: the product requires the consumption of trees for packaging, consumption of energy in freezing, and consumption of energy in baking. The car battery's most salient risk is in terms of end-of-life: improper disposal of car batteries can pose significant negative effects on the environment. The total cost of ownership approach helps us consider the costs of a product that are not reflected in its individual price tag.

**Life-cycle assessment (LCA)** is an approach that considers environmental stewardship by analyzing the environmental aspects and potential impacts associated with a product, process, or service. For example, certain lines of products require energy intensive manufacturing methods, where energy is predominantly supplied by coal-powered electricity plants. In evaluating the sustainability of this product, the LCA would consider the environmental consequences of coal combustion corresponding to the amount of energy generated by that combustion used to manufacture the product. Therefore, the LCA broadens the scope of costs visible to the manufacturer.

**Ecological footprint** is a metric, similar to LCA, that is sensitive to environmental degradation concerns. However, unlike LCA, it focuses on the consumer rather than the producer. This approach quantifies the land and water area a population requires to produce the resources it consumes and to absorb its wastes. Take for example, hamburgers. In evaluating the sustainability of hamburgers as a food product, the ecological footprint approach asks how much land is necessary to grow the corn that is used to feed the cattle—and how much land is needed for the cattle. Therefore, we can spatially represent the impact of product choices by consumers.

The **carbon footprint** is an ecological footprint metric that measures the amount of carbon released into the atmosphere, which is correlated with adverse effects on climate stability.

It is actually a component of the LCA. Measuring the amount of carbon dioxide emitted by manufacturing processes allows us to roughly gauge how much any individual polluter is contributing to atmospheric degradation and, in turn, climate change.

The **food mile** is a metric that measures the distance between the production source and the retail location, correlating distance traveled with energy consumption and pollution emissions. The longer food travels from its source to the grocery store or restaurant, the more gasoline is combusted, both consuming energy resources and emitting harmful pollutants.

All these measures are effective. Ultimately, it does not matter which analytic criteria is used in measuring the sustainability of a product or service, as long as this framework is employed consistently.

## Values in Sustainable SCM

To accurately gauge the desirability of implementing sustainability, we must understand the full spectrum of costs and values at stake. Sustainable corporations see market benefits such as increased sales from increased demand, increased prices from improvements in quality, reductions in operating costs from efficiencies, improved productivity, and avoided future costs in terms of environmental costs or damaged reputation. Nonmarket benefits are not experienced directly by the company, but also need to be considered. These nonmarket benefits include recreational uses of fishable, swimmable bodies of water, improvements in biodiversity, and greater life span and health on the part of the affected community.

The total value of a natural resource is a combination of three separate values: use value, option value, and existence value. **Use value** is the benefit derived from consumption or utilization of a resource. Option value and existence value are often termed "nonuse" values, as their benefits are not derived from actual use. **Option value** is value placed on the ability to exercise the option in the future. It applies to irreplaceable resources with uncertain benefits: we value the ability to preserve the resource for future potential use. **Existence value** is the benefit people receive from knowing that a resource exists. Unlike the former two concepts of value, existence value is autonomous of human use or utility. For example, people place value on the very existence of a natural resource, such as Yellowstone Park, and seek to preserve it for its own sake. Concepts such as willingness-to-pay (WTP) for an environmental resource, or willingness-to-accept (WTA) compensation in exchange for giving up an environmental resource, are approximate indicators of the value stakeholders place on the environment affected by corporate activity. Managers should attempt to measure these values so as to include them in sustainable organizational behavior.

## Cost Assessment

Measurements of stakeholder preference are inherently uncertain, but approximations give managers at least a sense of the magnitude of the costs at stake. Monetizing external costs translates the impacts of corporate activity into terms that are commensurable with the internal motivators of corporate decisions. Monetization therefore allows firms to "see" the cost of their actions and, perhaps, internalize those costs. The two main models for monetizing environmental and social effects are cost-of-control and damage costing.

### Cost-of-Control

**Cost-of-control** represents the cost of avoiding damages before they actually occur. If avoiding the damage imposes a cost on the corporation, then allowing the damage to occur could be understood as a value to the corporation. This approach effectively places a value on social or environmental damage by calculating the cost to avoid these damages. Consider the decision of whether to upgrade the lining in a waste storage container that holds toxic sludge from coal ash created by electricity generation. The environmental and social costs of such a leaking storage tank could involve (among other things) death of aquatic animal and plant life, loss of agricultural opportunities, and the carcinogenic contamination of drinking water. The monetary value of these items is extremely difficult to determine, especially because each depends on unique circumstances and probabilities and involves distinct forms of measurement. However, the cost of installing an adequate control technology, such as improved synthetic lining inside the storage tank, is easily determined. The cost-of-control method therefore allows simple and accurate calculations of the cost of decisions, without getting into technically challenging determinations of the full consequences of present decisions of future events.

A variation on the cost-of-control model is the **shadow pricing** model. This approach assumes governmental regulations reflect society's willingness to pay for sustainability performance and derives this amount from the cost of compliance with the regulation. This approach depends on the governmental body correctly estimating the level of control society is willing to pay for. It may be true that society would pay much more for improved sustainability performance than what the regulations would suggest, especially when the regulations simply set a minimum safety threshold.

## Damage Costing

**Damage costing** represents the cost of damages as if they had actually occurred. These cost calculations require significant amounts of data, time, and expense to perform accurately. Damage costing approximates the cost of social or environmental damage as an estimate of stakeholders' WTP to avoid the damage. In the coal ash storage tank example discussed earlier, consider how difficult it would be to determine the actual monetary cost of lost amphibious populations, or the slight increase in the probability that a few members of the surrounding community would get cancer. Determining actual costs can be very difficult endeavor and leaves the decision maker with considerable uncertainty. Stakeholders' WTP can be extrapolated from market price or appraisal if the resource is traded on an active market, and even the use of focus groups can help in its determination.

## Costing Systems

Once a company has decided to strive for sustainable performance, it must include adequate costing systems to account for environmental costs. This can be done through activity-based costing, life-cycle costing, or full cost accounting. "**Activity-based costing**" seeks to avoid lumping together environmental costs with overhead or nonenvironmental costs. Disaggregating the amount spent on waste, for example, from the amount paid for buildings, allows managers to discover opportunities to improve sustainability performance. As a result, managers are able to identify the causal relationship between the activities that generate environmental consequences and the company's bottom line. Activity-based costing tries to uncover buried social and environmental costs and attribute them to the activities that cause them.

An alternative to activity-based costing is life-cycle costing, an extension of the life-cycle assessment of environmental impacts. "**Life-cycle costing**" is the amortized annual cost of a product (including capital and disposal costs), discounted over the life cycle of a product. Life-cycle costing requires the monetization of present and future costs and benefits of SCM activities. An alternative to both activity-based and life-cycle costing is full cost accounting, which seeks to incorporate the broadest set of external and future costs.

"**Full cost accounting**" incorporates the result of life-cycle costing into an accounting framework, which allows managers to base decisions such as product design or price on sustainability impacts. This framework incorporates internal, external, present, and future costs and benefits.

Costing systems are important for SCM sustainability because they allow managers to identify areas that need both money savings and environmental performance improvements. Further, clearly articulated cost models allow managers to make optimal pricing decisions.

## Big Data Analytics Box

### ■ COCA-COLA

In the past Coca-Cola had been more focused on its economic bottom line than on global warming. Then in 2004 the company lost a lucrative operating license in India because of a serious water shortage. Global droughts have continued and repeatedly dried up the water needed to produce the company's soda. After a decade of struggles, the company has embraced the idea of climate change as an economically disruptive force to their supply chain. Today the company is using big data analytics for risk assessment.

"Increased droughts, more unpredictable variability, 100-year floods every two years," said Jeffrey Seabright, Coke's vice president for environment and water resources, listing the problems that he said were also disrupting the company's supply of sugar cane and sugar beets, as well as citrus for its fruit juices. "When we look at our most essential ingredients, we see those events as threats."

A report by consulting firm WisdomNet, Inc. identifies a number of factors that are contributing to the vulnerability to organizations and their supply chains. These include globalization resulting in longer supply lines; an increasing trend toward outsourcing, which makes "others" responsible for what goes on in the supply chain; and lean operations that have removed inventory from the system, which make firms more efficient, but more vulnerable when unforeseen events occur. One of the many forces include natural disasters. Coke reflects a growing view among American business leaders and mainstream economists, who see global warming as one force that contributes to lower gross domestic products, higher food and commodity costs, broken supply chains, and increased financial risk. Big data analytics is helping assess risks and optimize sourcing and supply chains to minimize them. Companies like Coke are relying on predictive analytics tools to help them foresee problems and take preemptive actions to prevent supply chain interruptions anywhere in the world.

Adapted from: Davenport, Coral. "Industry Awakens to Threat of Climate Change," *New York Times*, January 23, 2014.

## Risk Assessment

Managers must be able to identify and monetize potential risks and include them in return on investment and net-present-value determinations. An investment decision that fails to consider a risks assessment is unsound. The company may find the costs of mandatory responsibilities, including product take-back and site cleanup, to destroy the expected profits. Risk assessment requires attention to long-time horizons, as well as attention to low-probability events. Sustainability problems pose high costs when they arise, and there is a tendency to omit them as they often take a long time to manifest, and they occur infrequently.

### "Fat Tails"

Environmental crises can be understood statistically as "fat tails," shown in Figure 13.6. If we look at a distribution curve with the probability of an event on the $X$-axis and the magnitude of the harm resulting from the event on the $Y$-axis, these events are called "fat tails" in that they are of low probability (they are many standard deviations away from the mean, at the tail of a distribution curve), yet of high consequence (they are called "fat" relative to the consequences of other issues).

Managers need tools for incorporating risks. These tools include scenario-based analysis, fuzzy logic, Monte Carlo simulations, and real option analysis. We look at these next.

### Scenario-Based Analysis

**Scenario-based analysis** identifies issues and opportunities that may arise in various foreseeable circumstances. Royal Dutch Shell uses descriptive scenarios based on forecasting research to provide decision makers with rough sketches of possible future states of affairs to help them focus

**Distribution curve with a "fat tail"**

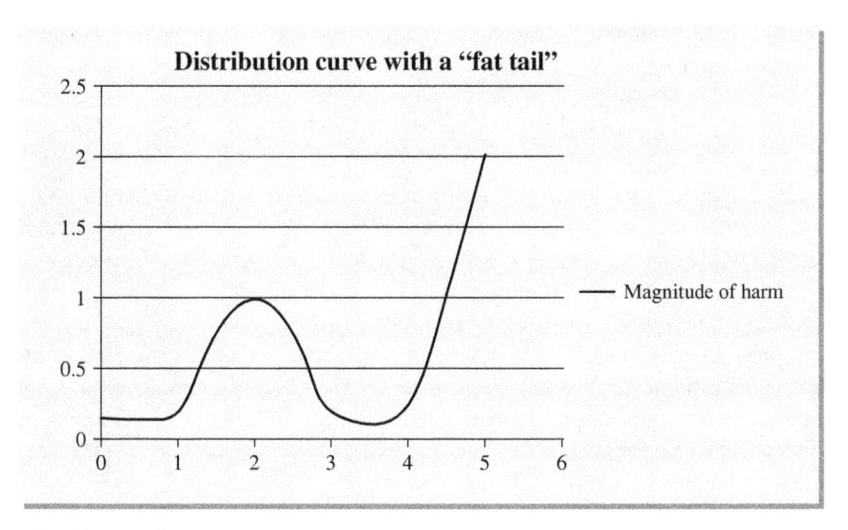

**FIGURE 13.6** "Fat tail" diagram.

on long-term consequences of supply chain impacts. For example, different business scenarios could be envisioned by tweaking variables such as energy source, resource availability, or socioeconomic trends. What would the world look like if we could convert saltwater into energy? What if freshwater ran short? What if the middle class disappeared? How could companies survive in such scenarios? Scenario-based analyses are really thought experiments that bring critical issues into the foreground.

## Fuzzy Logic

**Fuzzy logic** is a tool from mathematics that helps managers deal with sets of information that lack precise boundaries. Using the best estimate of the dollar amount required to cover foreseeable consequences, the best- and worst-case monetary values are estimated. Optimistic and pessimistic magnitudes are assigned a "degree of belief" between 0 and 1 to reflect their likelihood. Fuzzy logic associates the net present value of a decision with its degree of belief, which allows managers to see the range of situations that could give rise to future financial liability.

## Monte Carlo Simulations

When managers must use a complex decision tree, Monte Carlo simulations can help compare the outcomes of one operation against another. The costs associated with environmental remediation depend on numerous contingencies, such as applicable environmental law and the effectiveness of remediation techniques. Monte Carlo simulations draw random samples from the cost-probability distribution for each variable (or option) and algorithmically choose the option of lowest foreseeable cost at each point in the decision tree. The process is performed by computer software that can determine the likelihood that one operation will cost more than another, or simply compare the likely costs of each option. Importantly, cost estimates are associated with confidence levels. The magnitude of a risk standing alone is almost meaningless: it must be associated with a probability of occurrence to be useful to a manager.

## Real Option Analysis

Real option analysis helps to frame risk analysis decisions when static models are insufficient. Sometimes a small investment today that preserves an option can lead to a large return in the future when that option leads to a greater opportunity than was available before. Option assessment and option screenings help visualize reasonable available alternatives courses of conduct, including their relative costs and benefits. The basic concern is to determine whether to leave an option open for future managers to utilize to avoid environmental or social risks that happen to manifest. Option analysis also enables managers to optimize choices that involve numerous objectives, uncertainties, and constraints.

Risks can be social, political, or environmental. "**Social risks**" arise from unmet community expectations and include violence, riots, or economic devastation when monolithic commercial activity dissipates. "**Political risks**" arise when governmental influences compromise the company's economic value. Political risks are company specific when a government targets a single organization for retribution, including the nationalization of an oil company or a state-sponsored terrorist attack on a manufacturing facility. Country-specific political risks include dramatic domestic civil strife, changes in currency value, or changes to the tax code. "**Environmental risks**" arise from unpredictable or uncontrollable risks stemming from geological activity (such as earthquakes or volcanoes) or meteorological activity (such as floods or hurricanes).

To make sustainable SCM decisions, risks must be identified, and their monetary impact should be estimated. This allows managers to make better decisions with respect to the environment, human health and safety, and their company's financial bottom line.

# Sustainability in Practice

SCM has tremendous opportunity to impact sustainability given its cross-functional and cross-enterprise nature. Changes in SCM functions can have a major impact on sustainability. For example, the function of logistics is responsible for the movement and storage activities of the supply chain. These activities are among the most energy intensive. Carbon dioxide emissions from the transportation sector alone account for 33% of the United States' total $CO_2$ emissions. Judicious consideration of modes of transportation and sourcing can dramatically impact sustainability. Just consider the differential between energy consumed to ship a New Zealand lamb chop to a restaurant in New York City, versus procuring a lamb chop from a farm in upstate New York. The same concerns could be raised with respect to sourcing fish from international waters and fruit from foreign producers. The savings in product price or the benefits of product quality may be outweighed by the environmental costs of logistics across large distances.

Many companies are aware of the impact of SCM on sustainability and are making significant changes. For example, to improve environmental performance in logistics, McDonald's has applied the concept of zero waste to delivery processes. In a clever innovation, McDonald's plans to convert the United Kingdom delivery vehicle fleet to run on biodiesel based on the same cooking oil used to make French fries. There are numerous examples such as these of changes that companies are making. We look at some of these changes next.

## Product Design

Innovations in product design can significantly improve environmental and social sustainability performance. Changes in product design affect use of material, sourcing, and disposal. Often companies are not aware that some of their components are harmful to the environment. For example, one of the most distinctive features of Nike shoes, aside from the dramatic swooping check that identifies the brand, is the air bubble in the heel of Nike Air basketball sneakers. However, the company only recently became aware that the pocket contained a gas known as sulphur hexafluoride, or SF6, which is actually a greenhouse gas. As part of Nike's sustainability initiative, Nike replaced SF6 with nitrogen, which breaks up more readily on release and is not a greenhouse gas. A small change such as this can have significant environmental impact.

Some environmentally friendly innovations in product design can actually transform the business model, as happened with Interface Inc., the world's largest carpet manufacturer. Originally, Interface was in the business of selling carpets to clients. When the carpet was worn out, Interface would replace the entire carpet. Now, Interface installs carpets in modular form, giving clients the opportunity to inspect carpet "tiles" for wear on a monthly basis, replacing only the tiles that are worn out. This transformation provides a savings to clients and is better for the environment, as it requires less pollution and energy consumption than the original model of replacing the entire product.

## Managerial Insights Box

### ■ CARBON FIBER AUTO PARTS

Replacing steel with carbon fiber can significantly reduce the weight of automobile vehicles. Unfortunately, carbon fiber costs four times as much as steel by weight. However, an innovative technique for designing the product promises to cut costs of carbon fiber by 25% while reducing vehicle weight by as much as 20%. Carbon molecules are arranged in parallel, forming incredibly strong filaments, which are wound into strands and woven into a fabric, which is mixed with glue and hardened in molds to form car parts. The "knitting-yarn" carbon fiber breakthrough was developed by Oak Ridge National Laboratory in Tennessee, which persuaded a yarn factory in Lisbon, Portugal, to allocate a portion of its plant to produce the new product. BMW AG is getting in on the auto-grade carbon fiber action as well. Because of the energy intensity required to convert the carbon fiber into fabric, BMW produces the product near a cheap hydroelectric power source in Spokane, Washington, then ships it to Germany, where it is formed into car parts by partner SGL Carbon. BMW plans to use the carbon fiber as an interior shell for the MegaCity electric car to drop total weight by over 700 pounds.

Adapted from: Ramsey, Mike. "Technology that Breaks the Car Industry Mold." *The Wall Street Journal*, January 6, 2011.

# Packaging

Packaging offers an excellent opportunity to significantly impact the sustainability of a supply chain. For example, Proctor & Gamble (P&G) reduced the negative environmental consequences of product packaging by designing a toothpaste tube that can be shipped and displayed for retail without any paper packaging. Also, Nestlé Waters North America has created its Eco-Shape bottle that uses 25% less plastic compared to earlier bottles. Similarly, Nestlé decided to use smaller labels on the outside of their water bottles to save paper. In five years, the company saves an estimated 20 million pounds of paper. Product packaging is so important that even Wal-Mart has developed an environmental sustainability scorecard to evaluate product packaging used by its vendors. The criteria include GHG emissions from packaging production, product-to-packaging ratio, recycled packaging content, and emissions from transporting the packaging.

Product packaging can serve multiple purposes. It takes just a little bit of imagination to envision a further use for a package that would otherwise end up in a landfill. Innovations in use of product packaging can lead to considerable environmental and economic savings. For example, Stony-Field Farms, a dairy company famous for its "green" policies, has implemented a zero-waste concept that significantly reduces pollution. The company has a policy of take-back for the yogurt cups it sells. These plastic yogurt cups are then used to manufacture toothbrushes. Other companies use aluminium cans to make office furniture.

Companies can also work together in partnerships to take advantage of each other's talents in creating sustainable packaging. Consider India P&G, which decided to offer Pantene shampoo in single-serve packages for $0.02 each to low-income communities. The goal is to allow individuals at the very bottom of the economic pyramid to access product markets typically only available to consumers in developed countries. However, this creates the problem of disposing of packaging. Companies like Cargill and Dow Chemical are researching to develop biodegradable packages for these mini-products to avoid excess waste. Together, these innovations promote social and environmental sustainability.

## Sourcing

Sourcing practices can dramatically impact sustainability. Selecting suppliers that follow sustainability practices—and finding ways to monitor their compliance—are a large issue for companies. Just consider the reputational problems Home Depot encountered from 1997 to 1999 when environmental groups organized protests against the company, charging it was failing to ensure that its wood didn't come from endangered forests. In response, Home Depot publicly promised that lumber supplies would no longer come from endangered forests and even took affirmative steps to collaborate with environmental groups in Chile to protect such forests.

Improvements in sourcing do not have to be dramatic. Even incremental or piecemeal improvements in sourcing count for something. Instead of overhauling all products, Ben & Jerry's simply released a new product line called For A Change, which procures cocoa, vanilla, and coffee beans from farmers who participate in cooperative farmers' associations that ensure these farmers a fair price for their beans.

Deciding how to evaluate, select, and monitor suppliers is a critical task. A structured screening process can help companies choose suppliers who meet sustainability criteria. For example, Nike developed a New Source Approval Process to determine whether to acquire a new factory. The criteria include inspection results along environmental, safety, and health dimensions, as well as a third-party labor audit. This helps ensure company expansion is consistent with principles of environmental and social sustainability.

Some companies rely on contracting to mandate certain practices from their suppliers. To ensure compliance with labor standards, L'Oréal uses a supplier selection process that begins with contract language requiring compliance from suppliers and supplier subcontractors. L'Oréal enforces these social sustainability initiatives by monitoring compliance through surprise audits involving plant inspections, document review, and interviews with supplier employees. When audit results fail on a rated scale, L'Oréal takes necessary corrective measures.

Other companies rely on third-party audits to monitor sustainability compliance. For example, Unilever—the world's largest tea company—has committed to sustainable sourcing for all tea leaves. In collaboration with Rainforest Alliance, Unilever sees to it that all tea-growing estates are audited ensuring sustainable growth and fair trade of the product. Like Unilever, Wal-Mart has partnered with an oversight organization to ensure sustainable sourcing. Wal-Mart plans to purchase all wild-caught seafood from sustainable fisheries certified by the Marine Stewardship Council. This helps prevent overfishing, as well as keep fish containing unhealthy toxins like mercury off the shelves.

In addition to selecting and monitoring supplier sustainability practices, some companies offer training programs to their suppliers to continue improving. Cadbury Schweppes offers a training program in pest control and labor management techniques to the 4,000 cocoa suppliers in Ghana through the Farmers' Field School. This is a win–win for the suppliers and Cadbury Schweppes: the farmers have improved labor conditions, and Cadbury Schweppes has a more reliable cocoa supply.

## Process Design

Redesign of organizational processes can go a long way toward improving the environmental and social sustainability of a supply chain. Consider Kingfisher—Europe's leading home-improvement retailer and third largest in the world—which uses an evaluation system that provides actions for each operating company to undertake to meet corporate sustainability policy. The program is called Steps to Responsible Growth with formal evaluations taking place two times each year to monitor progress. Similarly, the Swedish hotel chain Scandic Hotels (www.scandichotels.com) created the Resource Hunt program to incentivize employees to improve their use of resources to yield efficiency gains. Hotel employees receive a part of the savings from a reduction in energy and water consumption, as well as a reduction in waste. Through these measures Scandic Hotels was able to save over a million dollars over just a few years.

Process improvements that address disposal of equipment are an important part of sustainability. Technology equipment can contain environmentally damaging materials that are relatively impervious to natural biodegradation. Improper technology equipment disposal can pose serious environmental consequences. In light of this, Hewlett-Packard implemented a product end-of-life or "take back" procedure. This enabled Hewlett-Packard to recycle over 70,000 tons of computer products, which were then refurbished to be resold or donated. In one procedural move, Hewlett-Packard reduced environmentally damaging waste, increased profits by creating a secondary market for used equipment, and promoted social sustainability by donating computers.

## Marketing Sustainability

Products frequently advertise their "green" features, such as their use of recycled materials, or that their packaging is biodegradable, or that they have entered into fair partnerships with international laborers, or the fact that the product does not contain ingredients that are harmful to the environment. Sustainable features are typically displayed through labels on the product itself. Sellers prominently display certifications by independent reviewers as to the genuinely sustainable nature of their product or manufacturing process. As long as consumers place a premium on the sustainability of products and services, advertising will cater to this preference. That is, as long as consumers prefer sustainable products, sellers have an incentive to market their products and services as sustainable, regardless of actual practices. However, without independent and objective evaluation as to the efficacy of the sustainability measures taken, products may be spuriously labeled "sustainable" when in fact they are not. Independent assessment of sustainability practices is important to counteract this "greenwashing" effect and help consumers identify true sustainability measures.

## Unintended Consequences

Before any company goes headlong toward implementing a seemingly beneficial sustainability initiative, a holistic assessment of all foreseeable costs and benefits must be conducted. This should include predictable behavioral changes that a new policy may induce on the part of affected parties. For example, a rule that mandated a company to eliminate a certain type of pollutant from their plant emissions by a certain date, with no other conditions attached, would predictably encourage plant operators to emit as much of this pollutant as possible before the abatement deadline, causing spikes in emissions levels. A rule that prohibited managers from firing elderly employees without good cause could very well have the perverse effect of discouraging employers from hiring elderly employees in the first place. The tendency of good intentions to have unexpected and undesirable consequences requires sustainable SCM decisions to be made only after adequate reflection and analysis.

Consider the hazards to the environment that can occur even with the best of intentions. Suppose a corporation owns manufacturing plants all over the continent. They want to reduce overall pollutant emissions by 20% to protect the health of the environment. They decide to use an auction system to distribute emissions permits, so the permission to continue emitting pollutants goes to the highest bidders. Plants that can reduce emissions cheaply through technology or process innovations do so. Older plants that would require major modifications to comply with the emissions reduction find it more economically feasible to purchase the permits. This leads to an economically efficient allocation of emissions permits. However, suppose the plants that aggregated the most permits were all clustered in the same region. Suppose further that this region was home to many biologically rich ecosystems. The permit allocation auction may have reduced net pollution emissions by 20%, but it lead to a "hot spot" of highly concentrated pollutants in an area where such pollution could lead to devastating environmental costs. In this way an attempt at environmental sustainability could backfire with unintended consequences that end up compromising environmental goods.

The obstacles posed by the environmental and social risks of our world force managers to make decisions where the intuition hesitates and the data is uncertain. Unintended consequences in the context of sustainability initiatives highlight the importance of making well-thought-out and informed decisions even when managers have the best intentions.

## CHAPTER HIGHLIGHTS

1. The environmental and social initiatives that define the current trend toward sustainability can be effectively incorporated into organizational decision making by expanding the concepts of cost, value, and risk to include longer time horizons and the reactions of all stakeholders.

2. The Supply Chain Sustainability Model can be used to enable managers to make effective sustainability decisions by linking *inputs* (external context, internal context, business context, human and financial resources), *processes* (leadership, strategy, structure, and systems), *outputs* (sustainability performance, stakeholder reactions), and *outcomes* (long-term corporate financial performance) in a feedback loop.

3. Nine principles of sustainability performance are ethics, governance, transparency, business relationships, financial return, community involvement and economic development, values of products and services, employment practices, and protection of the environment.

4. Quantifiable data relevant to costs, risks, and stakeholder preferences are needed to accurately measure and predict the impact of sustainability performance.

5. Sustainability implementation requires a concerted effort from top leadership and cuts across all aspects of a supply chain. In other words, sustainability performance is a serious endeavor that requires considerable commitment of corporate assets and attention.

## KEY TERMS

Sustainability
Financial payoffs
Customer-related payoffs
Operational payoffs
Organizational payoffs
Environmental sustainability
Social sustainability
Crisis-oriented
Cost-oriented

Design standard
Performance standard
Minimalist ethic
Reasonable care ethic
Good works ethic
External context
Internal context
Business contexts
Human and financial resources
Leadership

Proactive sustainability actions
Reactive sustainability actions
Internal sustainability actions
External sustainability actions
Sustainability performance
Feedback loops

Compliance
Total cost of ownership (TCO)
Life-cycle assessment (LCA)
Ecological footprint
Carbon footprint
Food mile
Use value
Option value
Existence value

Cost-of-control
Shadow pricing
Damage costing
Activity-based costing
Life-cycle costing
Full cost accounting
Scenario-based analysis
Fuzzy logic
Social risks
Political risks
Environmental risks

## DISCUSSION QUESTIONS

1. What economic arguments can be made for and against environmental sustainability initiatives? What economic arguments can be made for and against social sustainability initiatives? What personal choices have you made as a consumer with respect to environmental or social sustainability?

2. How should a manager handle disagreement over sustainable performance between the various stakeholders to which she is accountable?

3. Identify a sustainability strategy at a company where you are a consumer. Does "green" marketing appeal to you? Does this depend on your assessment of the company's actual versus advertised sustainability performance?

4. Identify a corporate strategy that you believe is unsustainable. Discuss possibilities of changing that strategy within the "Input" constraints of the Supply Chain Sustainability Model (external context, internal context, business context, human and financial resources).

5. Imagine you are a mid-level manager for a manufacturing company driven by the profit motive and only concerned about the financial bottom line. You believe that the operations you oversee could realize great efficiencies by consuming less energy and thereby polluting less, but this would require some additional investment in technology. How do you go about selling your idea to top leadership?

## Case Study: Haitian Oil

Read the following two passages concerning the discovery of petroleum reserves in the nation of Haiti. Try to spot environmental and social sustainability issues, then answer the questions at the end.

**Passage #1**

Adapted from: Polson, Jim. "Haiti Earthquake May Have Exposed Gas, Aiding Economy." January 26, 2010. Available at http://www.bloomberg.com.

In 2010 an earthquake killed more than 150,000 people in Haiti. It may have left clues to petroleum reservoirs that could aid economic recovery in the Western Hemisphere's poorest nation, a geologist said.

"The January 12, 2010, earthquake was on a fault line that passes near potential gas reserves," said Stephen Pierce, a geologist who worked in the region for 30 years. The quake may have cracked rock formations along the fault, allowing gas or oil to temporarily seep toward the surface, he said.

"A geologist, callous as it may seem, tracing that fault zone from Port-au-Prince to the border looking for gas and oil seeps, may find a structure that hasn't been drilled," said Pierce, exploration manager at Zion Oil & Gas Inc., a Dallas-based company that's drilling in Israel. "A discovery could significantly improve the country's economy and stimulate further exploration."

Following the earthquake, the Haitian Prime Minister Jean-Max Bellerive met in Montreal with diplomats, including U.S. Secretary of State Hillary Clinton, to discuss redevelopment initiatives. Canadian Foreign Affairs Minister Lawrence Cannon said wind power may play a role in rebuilding the Caribbean nation, where forests have been denuded for lack of fuel, the Canadian Press reported.

"Haiti, from the standpoint of oil and gas exploration, is a lot less developed than the Dominican Republic," Pierce said. "One could do a lot more work there." More than 600,000 people are without shelter in the Port-au-Prince area, the United Nations said on January 22, 2010. The 7.0 magnitude quake destroyed about one-third of the buildings in Port-au-Prince. It also knocked out the capital's seaport and water and sewage systems. "Relief and recovery for the survivors is the priority now," Mark Fried, a spokesman for British charity Oxfam, said in a statement. "Hundreds of thousands who lost everything but their lives need water, shelter, and toilets to stop the spread of disease," he said.

Haiti will need "massive support" for a "colossal" reconstruction from the earthquake, Bellerive said at the meeting in Montreal. The Greater Antilles, which includes Cuba, Haiti, the Dominican Republic, Puerto Rico, and their offshore waters, probably hold at least 142 million barrels of oil and 159 billion cubic feet of gas, according to a 2000 report by the U.S. Geological Survey. Undiscovered amounts may be as high as 941 million barrels of oil and 1.2 trillion cubic feet of gas, according to the report.

Among nations in the northern Caribbean, Cuba and Jamaica have awarded offshore leases for oil and gas development. Trinidad and Tobago, South American islands off the coast of Venezuela, account for most Caribbean oil production, according to the U.S. Energy Department.

**Passage #2**

Adapted from: Engdahl, F. William. "The Fateful Geological Prize Called Haiti." January 30, 2010. Available at http://www.engdahl.oilgeopolitics.net.

Behind the human tragedy in Haiti, following the 2010 earthquake, a drama is in full play for control of what geophysicists believe may be one of the world's richest zones for hydrocarbons—oil and gas—outside the Middle East.

Haiti, and the larger island of Hispaniola of which it is a part, straddles one of the world's most active geological zones, where the deep-water plates of three huge structures rub against one another: the intersection of the North American, South American, and Caribbean tectonic plates. Below the ocean and the waters of the Caribbean, these plates consist of an oceanic crust some 3 to 6 miles thick, floating atop an adjacent mantle. Haiti also lies at the edge of the region known as the Bermuda Triangle, a vast area in the Caribbean subject to bizarre and unexplained disturbances.

These underwater plates are in constant motion, rubbing against each other along lines analogous to cracks in a broken porcelain vase that has been reglued. The earth's tectonic plates typically move at a rate of 50 to 100 mm annually in relation to one another and are the origin of earthquakes and of volcanoes. The regions of convergence of such plates are also areas where vast volumes of oil and gas can be pushed upward from the Earth's mantle. The geophysics surrounding the convergence of the three plates that run more or less directly beneath Port-au-Prince make the region prone to earthquakes such as the one that struck Haiti with devastating ferocity on January 12, 2010.

Aside from being prone to violent earthquakes, Haiti also happens to lie in a zone that, due to the unusual geographical intersection of its three tectonic plates, might well be straddling one of the world's largest unexplored zones of oil and gas, as well as of valuable rare strategic minerals.

*Case Questions*

1. Imagine you are a mid-level manager for a major international oil company. You have been asked whether an investment in oil exploration in Haiti is a good business decision. What environmental, social, and political risks might arise in supply chain operations in Haiti?

2. What are the foreseeable costs and benefits from supply chain operations in Haiti?

3. How could you ensure that your company's involvement would play a beneficial role in Haiti's economic recovery?

# REFERENCES[2]

Beamon, Benita M. "Environmental and Sustainability Ethics in Supply Chain Management." From Industrial Engineering, University of Washington, USA, *Science and Engineering Ethics*, 11(2), 2005: 221–234.

Epstein, Marc J. *Making Sustainability Work: Best Practices in Managing and Measuring Corporate Social, Environmental, and Economic Impacts.* Sheffield, UK: Greenleaf Publishing, 2008.

Henn, R., and A. Hoffman (Eds.). *Constructing Green: The Social Structures of Sustainability.* Cambridge, MA: MIT Press, 2013.

Hoffman, A. *Finding Purpose: Environmental Stewardship as a Personal Calling.* Leeds, UK: Greenleaf Publishing, 2016.

Lee, Hau. "Embedded Sustainability: Lessons from the Front Line." *International Commerce Review*, 8(1), 2008: 10–20.

Revesz, Richard, and Michael Livermore. *Retaking Rationality: How Cost-Benefit Analysis Can Better Protect the Environment and Human Health.* New York: Oxford University Press, 2008.

Sowell, Thomas. *Basic Economics: A Citizen's Guide to the Economy*, 3rd ed. Cambridge: MA: Perseus Books Group, 2007.

United Nations Environment Programme: "Gender and the Environment." Available at http://www.unep.org/gender_env/About/index.asp.

Winston, Andrew. "Luxury Brands Can No Longer Ignore Sustainability." *Harvard Business Review*, February 8, 2016.

---

[2]For an entertaining but serious learning tool about sustainability in supply chain management, see the online video called "Story of Stuff," available at http://www.youtube.com/watch?v=gLBE5QAYXp8.

# APPENDIX: THE STANDARD NORMAL DISTRIBUTION

This table gives the area under the standardized normal curve from 0 to $z$, as shown by the shaded portion of the following figure.

Examples: If $z$ is the standard normal random variable, then

Prob $(0 \leq z \leq 1.32) = 0.4066$

Prob $(z \geq 1.32) = 0.5000 - 0.4066 = 0.0934$

Prob $(z \leq 1.32) = $ Prob $(z \leq 0) + $ Prob $(0 \leq z \leq 1.32) = 0.5000 + 0.4066 = 0.9066$

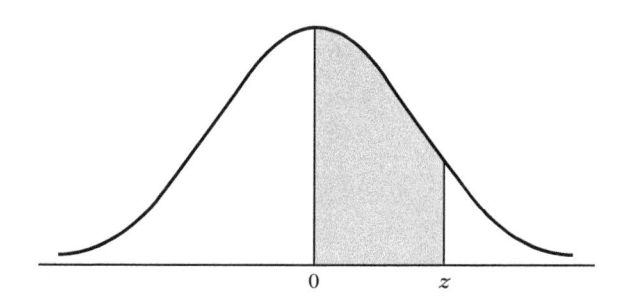

Prob $(z \leq -1.32) = $ Prob $(z \geq 1.32) = 0.0934$ (by symmetry)

# APPENDIX: THE STANDARD NORMAL DISTRIBUTION

| z | 0.00 | 0.01 | 0.02 | 0.03 | 0.04 | 0.05 | 0.06 | 0.07 | 0.08 | 0.09 |
|---|------|------|------|------|------|------|------|------|------|------|
| 0.0 | 0.0000 | 0.0040 | 0.0080 | 0.0120 | 0.0160 | 0.0199 | 0.0239 | 0.0279 | 0.0319 | 0.0359 |
| 0.1 | 0.0398 | 0.0438 | 0.0478 | 0.0517 | 0.0557 | 0.0596 | 0.0636 | 0.0675 | 0.0714 | 0.0753 |
| 0.2 | 0.0793 | 0.0832 | 0.0871 | 0.0910 | 0.0948 | 0.0987 | 0.1026 | 0.1064 | 0.1103 | 0.1141 |
| 0.3 | 0.1179 | 0.1217 | 0.1255 | 0.1293 | 0.1331 | 0.1368 | 0.1406 | 0.1443 | 0.1480 | 0.1517 |
| 0.4 | 0.1554 | 0.1591 | 0.1628 | 0.1664 | 0.1700 | 0.1736 | 0.1772 | 0.1808 | 0.1844 | 0.1879 |
| 0.5 | 0.1915 | 0.1950 | 0.1985 | 0.2019 | 0.2054 | 0.2088 | 0.2123 | 0.2157 | 0.2190 | 0.2224 |
| 0.6 | 0.2257 | 0.2291 | 0.2324 | 0.2357 | 0.2389 | 0.2422 | 0.2454 | 0.2486 | 0.2518 | 0.2549 |
| 0.7 | 0.2580 | 0.2612 | 0.2642 | 0.2673 | 0.2704 | 0.2734 | 0.2764 | 0.2794 | 0.2823 | 0.2852 |
| 0.8 | 0.2881 | 0.2910 | 0.2939 | 0.2967 | 0.2995 | 0.3023 | 0.3051 | 0.3078 | 0.3106 | 0.3133 |
| 0.9 | 0.3159 | 0.3186 | 0.3212 | 0.3238 | 0.3264 | 0.3289 | 0.3315 | 0.3340 | 0.3365 | 0.3389 |
| 1.0 | 0.3413 | 0.3438 | 0.3461 | 0.3485 | 0.3508 | 0.3531 | 0.3554 | 0.3577 | 0.3599 | 0.3621 |
| 1.1 | 0.3643 | 0.3665 | 0.3686 | 0.3708 | 0.3729 | 0.3749 | 0.3770 | 0.3790 | 0.3810 | 0.3830 |
| 1.2 | 0.3849 | 0.3869 | 0.3888 | 0.3907 | 0.3925 | 0.3944 | 0.3962 | 0.3980 | 0.3997 | 0.4015 |
| 1.3 | 0.4032 | 0.4049 | 0.4066 | 0.4082 | 0.4099 | 0.4115 | 0.4131 | 0.4147 | 0.4162 | 0.4177 |
| 1.4 | 0.4192 | 0.4207 | 0.4222 | 0.4236 | 0.4251 | 0.4265 | 0.4279 | 0.4292 | 0.4306 | 0.4319 |
| 1.5 | 0.4332 | 0.4345 | 0.4357 | 0.4370 | 0.4382 | 0.4394 | 0.4406 | 0.4418 | 0.4429 | 0.4441 |
| 1.6 | 0.4452 | 0.4463 | 0.4474 | 0.4484 | 0.4495 | 0.4505 | 0.4515 | 0.4525 | 0.4535 | 0.4545 |
| 1.7 | 0.4554 | 0.4564 | 0.4573 | 0.4582 | 0.4591 | 0.4599 | 0.4608 | 0.4616 | 0.4625 | 0.4633 |
| 1.8 | 0.4641 | 0.4649 | 0.4656 | 0.4664 | 0.4671 | 0.4678 | 0.4686 | 0.4693 | 0.4699 | 0.4706 |
| 1.9 | 0.4713 | 0.4719 | 0.4726 | 0.4732 | 0.4738 | 0.4744 | 0.4750 | 0.4756 | 0.4761 | 0.4767 |
| 2.0 | 0.4772 | 0.4778 | 0.4783 | 0.4788 | 0.4793 | 0.4798 | 0.4803 | 0.4808 | 0.4812 | 0.4817 |
| 2.1 | 0.4821 | 0.4826 | 0.4830 | 0.4834 | 0.4838 | 0.4842 | 0.4846 | 0.4850 | 0.4854 | 0.4857 |
| 2.2 | 0.4861 | 0.4864 | 0.4868 | 0.4871 | 0.4875 | 0.4878 | 0.4881 | 0.4884 | 0.4887 | 0.4890 |
| 2.3 | 0.4893 | 0.4896 | 0.4898 | 0.4901 | 0.4904 | 0.4906 | 0.4909 | 0.4911 | 0.4913 | 0.4916 |
| 2.4 | 0.4918 | 0.4920 | 0.4922 | 0.4925 | 0.4927 | 0.4929 | 0.4931 | 0.4932 | 0.4934 | 0.4936 |
| 2.5 | 0.4938 | 0.4940 | 0.4941 | 0.4943 | 0.4945 | 0.4946 | 0.4948 | 0.4949 | 0.4951 | 0.4952 |
| 2.6 | 0.4953 | 0.4955 | 0.4956 | 0.4957 | 0.4959 | 0.4960 | 0.4961 | 0.4962 | 0.4963 | 0.4964 |
| 2.7 | 0.4965 | 0.4966 | 0.4967 | 0.4968 | 0.4969 | 0.4970 | 0.4971 | 0.4972 | 0.4973 | 0.4974 |
| 2.8 | 0.4974 | 0.4975 | 0.4976 | 0.4977 | 0.4977 | 0.4978 | 0.4979 | 0.4979 | 0.4980 | 0.4981 |
| 2.9 | 0.4981 | 0.4982 | 0.4982 | 0.4983 | 0.4984 | 0.4984 | 0.4985 | 0.4985 | 0.4986 | 0.4986 |
| 3.0 | 0.4986 | 0.4987 | 0.4987 | 0.4988 | 0.4988 | 0.4989 | 0.4989 | 0.4989 | 0.4990 | 0.4990 |
| 3.5 | 0.4998 | | | | | | | | | |

Source: Adapted from Robert Markland, *Topics in Management Science*, 3rd ed. New York: John Wiley & Sons, 1989.

# Glossary

**ABC Analysis**  A tool for classifying inventory based on degree of importance.

**Additive Manufacturing**  Also known as 3-D printing, it is a process that creates a solid object from a software design. The process deposits materials such as plastics and metals in thick layers one on top of the other, gradually building up one layer at a time until the object is produced.

**Alliances**  The most comprehensive of buyer–supplier relationships reflected by high interaction frequency and significant trust and commitment between supply chain partners.

**Anticipation Inventory**  Inventories carried in anticipation of events, such as seasonality or price increases.

**Assemble-to-Order Strategy**  An inventory strategy in which the product is partially completed and kept in a generic form, then finished when an order is received.

**Assignable Variation**  Variation that is caused by factors that can be clearly identified and managed.

**Batch Process**  A process used to produce small quantities of products in groups or batches based on customer orders or product specifications.

**Benchmarking**  A method for comparing and quantifying operational performance to establish internal targets based on best in class results.

**Big Data Analytics**  Applying math and statistics to large data sets referred to as Big Data.

**Bill of Materials (BOM)**  A list that shows all the raw materials, components, and subassemblies that go into a product. It also shows the quantities and relationships of items needed to make a final product.

**Break-Even Analysis**  A tool used to compute the product quantity that needs to be sold for a company to cover their costs—called the "break-even point."

**Bullwhip Effect**  The phenomenon where fluctuation and distortion of information increases as it moves up the supply chain, from retailers, to manufacturers, to suppliers.

**Business Process**  A structured set of activities or steps with specified outcomes.

**Business Strategy**  A plan for the company that defines the company's long-term goals, how it plans to achieve these goals, and the way the company plans to differentiate itself from its competitors.

**Carbon Footprint**  An ecological footprint metric that measures the amount of carbon released into the atmosphere, which is correlated with adverse effects on climate stability.

**Cash-to-Cash Cycle**  The time it takes to convert an order into cash.

**Causal Models**  Forecasting models based on the assumption that the variable being forecast is related to other variables in the environment; a model is developed identifying these relationships, expressing them in mathematical terms, and using that information to forecast the future.

# GLOSSARY

**Cellular Layouts** Sometimes called Group Technology Cell (GT Cells), these are hybrid layout group items based on similar processing characteristics and workstations arranged to form a number of small assembly lines called work cells.

**Channel of Distribution** The way products and services are passed from the manufacturer to the final consumer.

**Collaborative Planning, Forecasting, and Replenishment (CPFR)** A collaborative process of developing joint forecasts and plans with supply chain partners, rather than doing them independently.

**Common (Random) Variation** Variation that is inherent in the process itself.

**Concurrent Engineering** All organizational functions simultaneously working together in product design.

**Continuous Processes** Operations processes that produce a high volume of a standardized product on a continual basis. Examples include oil refineries, water treatment plants, and certain paint facilities.

**Core Competency** The distinctive competency of a company it uses to compete in the marketplace.

**Cross-Docking** An approach used to reconfigure bundles of products where larger shipments are broken down into small shipments for local delivery in an area.

**Cycle Stock** Also called lot size inventories, this is inventory for immediate use and is computed based on expected demand over a certain time period.

**Culture** Acceptable behaviors, beliefs, and norms characteristic of a particular global region.

**Customer Relationship Management (CRM)** Software designed to focus on the interface between the firm and its customers.

**Customer Segmentation** Identification of unique groups of customers with similar needs.

**Customer Service** A process of enhancing the level of customer satisfaction by meeting or exceeding customer expectations.

**Cycle Time** The maximum amount of time each station on the assembly line has to complete its assigned tasks. It is also called **takt time**.

**Demand Management** The process of attempting to modify demand through efforts such as promotional campaigns and advertisements, sales incentives, and cost cutting.

**Dependent Demand** Demand for component parts or subassemblies.

**Design for Manufacture (DFM)** A series of guidelines for producing a product easily and profitably.

**Distribution Strategy** A plan for how a company will get its products and services to customers.

**E-Auctions** The use of Internet technology to conduct auctions as a means of selecting suppliers and determining aspects of the purchase contract.

**Early Supplier Involvement (ESI)** The practice of including suppliers in new product development to tap into their expertise in product, process, and supply chain design.

**Electronic Data Interchange (EDI)** The interorganizational, computer-to-computer communication of business transactions for orders, confirmations, invoices, and shipping notices.

# Glossary

**Enterprise Resource Planning (ERP)** Large software programs used for planning and coordinating all resources throughout the entire enterprise.

**Environmental Sustainability** The preservation of diverse biological systems that remain productive over time.

**Experience Curve** A phenomenon where organizational costs are reduced due to experience and learning effects that result from processing a higher volume.

**Facility Layout** The physical arrangement of all resources within a facility.

**Facility Location** The physical location of all facilities, including warehouses, factories, and retail locations.

**Factor Rating** A tool that can be used to make location decisions.

**Fill Rate** The percent of products ordered that are actually delivered.

**Fixed Position Layout** A layout arrangement used when a product cannot be moved during production, usually due to size.

**Forecasting** The process of predicting future events.

**Functional Products** Products that satisfy basic functions or needs.

**Holding Cost** Holding cost—sometimes called **carrying cost**—includes all the costs that vary with the amount of inventory held in stock. This includes storage facilities, handling, insurance, pilferage, breakage, obsolescence, depreciation, taxes, and the opportunity cost of capital.

**Import Quotas** A quantitative restriction on the volume of imports. It is one of the most common forms of nontariff barriers.

**Independent Demand** Demand for a finished product.

**Information Technology (IT)** Technology that enables communication, storage, and processing of information within and between firms. IT is the backbone of supply chain management that enables managing processes.

**Infrastructure** Availability and access to roads and transportation, equipment and communication networks, distribution systems, and skilled labor.

**Innovative Products** Products that are purchased for reasons other than basic needs, such as innovation or status. These include high-fashion items or technology products, such as those seen in the computer industry.

**Intermittent Processes** A process used to produce a large variety of products with different processing requirements in low volumes.

**Inventory** Quantities of goods in stock.

**Inventory Policy** Inventory decisions that answer the questions of when and how much to order.

**Inventory Turnover** A measure of how quickly inventory moves. It is computed as:

$$Inventory\ Turnover = \frac{Cost\ of\ Goods\ Sold}{Average\ Inventory\ Value}$$

**Jidoka** An element of Lean that allows workers to "stop the line" when discovering production problems.

# GLOSSARY

**Kaizen** An element of quality that means continuous improvement.

**Keiretsu** A close-knit network of suppliers that continuously learn, improve, and prosper along with their parent companies.

**Key Performance Indicators (KPI)** Quantifiable measurements that reflect a company's critical success factors.

**Lean** A management approach for creating value for the end customer through the most efficient utilization of resources possible.

**Lean Six Sigma** A management philosophy that combines the benefits of both Lean and Six Sigma approaches, utilizing the tools from each.

**Leverage** Leverage is the amount of bargaining power in negotiation.

**Life Cycle Assessment (LCA)** An approach that considers environmental stewardship by analyzing the environmental aspects and potential impacts associated with a product, process, or service.

**Line Processes** Processes designed to produce a large volume of a standardized product for mass production. They are also known as flow shops, flow lines, or assembly lines.

**Logistics** The business function responsible for transporting and delivering products to the right place at the right time throughout the supply chain.

**Make-to-Order** A strategy used to produce products to customer specifications after an order has been received.

**Make-to-Stock** A strategy that produces finished products for immediate sale or delivery, in anticipation of demand. Companies using this strategy produce a standardized product in larger volumes.

**Marketing** The business function responsible for linking the organization to its customers and is concerned with the "downstream" part of the supply chain.

**Material Requirements Planning (MRP)** An inventory control system used to compute order quantities for dependent demand inventory items.

**Negotiation** The process of gaining concessions from another party.

**Offshoring** Another name for outsourcing to a different country.

**Omni-Channel** An approach to sales that seeks to provide the customer with a seamless shopping experience across multiple channels.

**Operations Management (OM)** The business function responsible for producing a company's goods and services, in an efficient and cost effective way.

**Operations Strategy** A strategy of a company that involves decisions about how it will produce goods and services.

**Ordering Cost** Costs involved in placing an order and procuring the item.

**Order Qualifiers** Characteristics that qualify the company to be a participant in a particular market.

**Order Winners** Characteristics that win the company orders in the marketplace. A company should excel on their order winners.

**Outsourcing** Outsourcing is hiring a third party to perform a set of tasks for a fee.

**Pareto Principle** A rule that suggests that 80% of an outcome is generated by 20% of an activity.

**Physical Distribution** Outbound logistics.

**Pipeline Inventory** Also called **transportation inventory,** this is inventory that is in transit. It exists because the points of demand and supply are not the same.

**Planning** The process of selecting actions in anticipation of the forecast.

**Power Distance** The extent to which there is a strong separation of individuals based on rank.

**Predictive Analytics** Uses a variety of techniques—such as statistics, modeling, and data mining—to analyze current and historical facts to make predictions about the future.

**Product Design** The process of specifying the exact features and characteristics of a company's product.

**Product Layout** A layout design that arranges resources in sequence to enable efficient production of the product.

**Product Life Cycle (PLC)** A marketing concept that states that products and services evolve through a life cycle, and that the specific management concerns vary with each stage of the life cycle.

**Process Capability** The evaluation of the production process as to its ability to meet or exceed the set product specifications.

**Process Control Charts** A statistical quality control tool used to monitor the process to ensure products are being produced with characteristics that are within the set limits.

**Process Design** The design of a production process that can create the exact product desired.

**Process Layout** A layout design where similar processes are grouped together.

**Product Postponement** A strategy where the product is kept in the most generic form as long as possible in the production and distribution process.

**Product Traceability** The ability to easily trace a product from point of origin in the supply chain, through to the customer, and back down the supply chain in the case of returns.

**Productivity** A measure of how well a company uses its resources. It is computed as a ratio of outputs to inputs.

**Project Processes** A process used to make one-of-a-kind products exactly to customer specifications.

**Purchase Order (PO)** A document that specifies the terms and conditions of the purchase agreement and initiates supplier action.

**Purchasing** A term that defines the process of buying goods and services.

**Qualitative Forecasting Methods** Often called judgmental forecasting methods, these are forecasting methods based on subjective opinions and judgment of individuals, such as managers, sales staff, or customers.

**Quality** A measure of whether or not a product lives up to customer expectations.

**Quality Function Deployment (QFD)** A tool for translating the voice of the customer into specific technical requirements.

**Quantitative Forecasting Methods** Forecasting methods based on mathematical modeling.

**Radio Frequency Identification (RFID)** A wireless technology that uses memory chips equipped with tiny radio antennas that can be attached to objects to transmit streams of data about the object.

**Relationship View** A view of supply chains focused on managing relationships across the supply chain.

**Remanufacturing** A process that uses components of old products in the production of new ones.

**Repetitive Process** A process used to produce one, or a few, standardized products in high volume. Examples include an automobile assembly line, a cafeteria, and an automatic car wash.

**Reverse Logistics** The process of moving products upstream from the customer back toward manufacturers and suppliers.

**Safety Stock** Also called **buffer stock,** is extra inventory carried to serve as a cushion for uncertainties in supply and demand.

**Sales and Operations Planning (S&OP)** An organizational process intended to match supply and demand through functional collaboration between marketing, operations, and finance, in order to ensure that supply can meet demand requirements.

**Setup Cost** Costs involved in preparing a production run when items are made in-house.

**Shortage Costs** Costs that occur when a company runs out of stock.

**Six Sigma** A quality management process that uses rigorous measurement to reduce process variation and eliminate defects. Six Sigma defines quality as no more than 3.4 parts per million defective (ppm).

**Sourcing** The business function responsible for all activities and processes required to purchase goods and services from suppliers.

**Statistical Quality Control (SQC)** Statistical tools used to measure quality and identify quality problems in both the product and process.

**Supply Chain** A network of all entities involved in producing and delivering a finished product to the final customer.

**Supply Chain Management (SCM)** The management of flows of products, information, and funds throughout the supply chain.

**Supply Chain Network Design** The physical structure and business processes included in the system.

**Supply Chain Strategy** A long-range plan for the design and ongoing management of all supply chain decisions that support the business strategy.

**Sustainability** The meeting of present needs without compromising the ability of future generations to meet their own needs.

**Takt Time** Also called **cycle time**, the maximum amount of time each station on the assembly line has to complete its assigned tasks.

**Time Series Models** Models that generate a forecast by identifying and analyzing patterns in a time series of the data.

**Third-Party Logistics (3PL)** An entity that provides some combinations of logistics services to their customers.

**Total Cost of Ownership (TCO)** The purchase price plus *all* other costs associated with acquiring the item.

**Trade Agreements** Pacts between countries that encourage trade in a region by eliminating or lowering tariffs, quotas, and other trade barriers.

**Transactional View** The view of supply chains with a focus on making supply chain processes more efficient and effective based on quantitative metrics.

**Transportation** The primary function of logistics that enables logistics to provide place utility. There are five primary modes of transportation: *truck, water, air, rail*, and *pipeline*.

**Value Stream Mapping** A specific application of process mapping, based on lean manufacturing principles.

**Vendor Managed Inventory (VMI)** An arrangement in which the vendor is responsible for managing the inventory located at a customer's facility.

**Vertical Integration** Ownership of upstream suppliers and downstream customers.

**Voice of the Customer (VOC)** The process of capturing customer needs and preferences.

**Waste** In Lean systems waste is defined as anything that does not add value.

**Weeks-of-Supply** The length of time demand can be met with on-hand inventory.

# INDEX

**A**
ABC inventory classification, 208–209
Accenture, 126
acceptable quality level (AQL), 219
acceptance sampling, 228–229
activity-based costing, 309
adversarial negotiators, 262
adversarial tactics
  anchoring, 262
  concessions, 262–263
  manipulating commitments, 263–264
  withholding information, 263
Amazon, 9, 249
anchoring effect, 262
*anima sana* (ASICS), 50–52, 55, 56
Asia-Pacific Economic Cooperation Forum (APEC), 285
assemble-to-order strategy, 34
assignable variation, 229
auto industry, 123
automated storage and retrieval systems (ASRS), 146

**B**
Barlean's Organic Oils, 42
batch processes, 107
bill of materials (BOM), 207
BMW, 283–284
boundary-spanning nature
  cross-enterprise integration, 11–12
  intraorganizational integration, 10–11
brainware, 169
break-bulk, 151
break-even point, 102
break-even quantity, 102–104
"bricks-and-mortar" bookstores, 89
buffer stock, 201
buffer uncertainty, 192
bullwhip effect, 7
business contexts, 304
business logistics, 141
business process, 51–53
business strategy, 28
business-to-business (B2B), 14, 18
business-to-consumer (B2C), 14, 18

**C**
carbon fiber auto parts, 313
carbon footprint, 307
careers, SCM, 23
carrying cost, 194
causal forecasting models, 168
  linear regression, 175–177
  measuring forecast accuracy, 178–180
  multiple regression, 178
cause-and-effect diagrams, 225
cellular layouts, 110
checklists, 227
Cisco, 281
Coca-cola, 61, 84–85, 256, 310
co-creation, 123
collaborative forecasting
  CPFR, 180–181
  S & OP process, 181–183
Collaborative Planning, Forecasting, and Replenishment (CPFR), 180–181
commercial sourcing, 121–122
commodity swapping, 260
common/random variation, 229
competitive priority, 39
competitive supply chain
  relationshipmanagement, 15
  reliability, 14–15
  responsiveness, 14
component parts, 190
consumer sourcing, 121–122
Container Security Initiative (CSI), 21
continuous processes, 107
continuous review system, 196
contractual, 248
control charts, 227
core competencies, 16
cost-oriented environmental management, 301
crime forecasting, 161
crisis-oriented environmental management, 301
criticality, 129, 247–249
cross-docking, 151
cross-enterprise integration, 11–12
cultural, 273
cultural challenges
  Coca Cola's China branding challenge, 278

cultural challenges (*contd.*)
   high *versus* low context cultures, 279–280
   individualism *versus* collectivism, 279
   masculinity *versus* femininity, 279
   small *versus* large power distance, 279
   weak *versus* strong uncertainty avoidance, 279
customer-driven supply chains
   CRM software, 79–80
   customized strategy, 79
   end consumer, 76
   micro-marketing/one-to-one marketing, 79
   niche strategy, 79
   organizational end user, 77
   standardized strategy, 78
   supplier–customer relationship, 77–78
customer-related payoffs, 297
customer relationship management (CRM), 79–80
customer service, 81–82
customers, SCM, 4
customized strategy, 79
Customs-Trade Partnership Against Terrorism (C-TPAT), 21
cycle time, 111–112

## D

data conflicts, 257
degree of product standardization, 105
Dell Computer Corporation, 6, 13–14, 35, 40, 85, 205
Delphi method, 167
demand management, 160
demand planning
   CPFR, 180–181
   S & OP process, 181–183
demand uncertainty, 126–128
demographic, 273
dependency risk, 37
dependent demand, 207
descriptive statistics, 228
design capacity, 57
design for manufacture (DFM), 104
designing supply chain networks, 51
   segmented structures, 62–63
   supply chain structure and management, 60–62
design phase, 253
design standard, 301
digital supply chain, 19
direct channel, 85
dispute resolution
   arbitration, 258–259
   litigation, 258
   mediation, 259
   negotiation, 259
     adversarial tactics, 262–264
     distributive opportunities, 261
     integrative opportunities, 261
     leverage, 260–261
     "position" *versus* "interest," 261
     problem-solving tactics, 264–265
     styles, 262
distribution strategy, 35–36
distributive opportunities, 261
dollar value, 194

## E

early supplier involvement (ESI), 101
E-Auction Development Program (EDP), 135
ecological footprint, 307
economic environmental factor, 273
economic order quantity (EOQ), 196, 198–200, 210
economics production quantity (EPQ), 202–204
economies of distance, 147, 148
economies of scale, 147
effective capacity, 57
electronic auctions (e-auctions), 130–132
end consumer, 76
enterprise resource planning (ERP), 17, 208
   configuration, 65–66
   implementation, 66–67
   modules, 65
environmental risks, 312
environmental sustainability, 297–299
equipment technology, 282
event logistics, 141
evolving supply process, 126
executive opinion, 166

## F

facility layout
   cellular layouts, 110
   fixed position layout, 109
   planning, 108–109
   process layout, 109–110
   product layout *see* product layout
facility location, 147
factor rating, 152
fair price, 124
FedEx, 40–41, 132
fibria celulose, 298
financial impact, 122
financial payoffs, 297
finished goods, 190
fishbone diagrams, 225
fixed position layout, 109
food mile, 308
Ford Taurus, 101
forecasting
   causal models
     linear regression, 175–177
     measuring forecast accuracy, 178–180
     multiple regression, 178
   CPFR, 180–181
   method selection, factors in, 164
   organization impact, 161–162

Index

*versus* planning, 159–161
principles, 163
qualitative forecasting methods, 166–168
quantitative methods, 168
SCM impact, 162
S & OP, 181–183
steps in, 163
time series forecasting models
    exponential smoothing, 171–172
    mean, 169–170
    moving averages, 170–171
    seasonality adjustment, 174–175
    trend adjusted exponential smoothing, 172–173
forecasting decisions in conflicts, 161
full cost accounting, 309
functional products, 126
fuzzy logic, 311

### G
Gap Inc., 73
General Agreement on Tariffs and Trade (GATT), 285
general electric (GE), 218
global positioning systems (GPS), 17–18, 221
global supply chain management
    culture, 276
    global environment, 272–273
    hidden costs, 282–283
    information technology, 281–282
    infrastructure, 275
    labor, 271–272, 280
    market and competition, 275
    market challenges
        cultural challenges, 277–280
        global consumer, 276
        global *versus* local marketing, 276–277
    non-cost considerations, 283
    opportunities and barriers, 274–275
    political and economic factors
        exchange rate fluctuations, 284–285
        non-tariff barriers, 285
        regional trade agreements, 285
    politics and economy, 276
    suppliers, 281
    technology, 276
    transportation, 272, 280
    Wal-Mart, 273–274
    warehousing, 271
Goldcorp Inc., 22
good works ethic, 302
Great Pacific Garbage Patch, 296

### H
health forecasting, 161
hedge inventory, 193
Hewlett Packard (HP), 7
histograms, 227

holding cost, 194
Honda, 100
human and financial resources, 304

### I
IBM, 127
import quotas, 286
independent demand, 207
indirect channel, 85
information asymmetry, 263
information impact, 122
information sharing, SCM, 6
information technology (IT), 17–18, 51
innovative products, 126
integrative opportunities, 261
Intel Corporation, 208, 229
intelligent assembly robots, 19
intensive distribution, 86
interest conflict, 257
intermittent process, 105–107
internal sustainability actions, 305
International Monetary Fund (IMF), 272
Internet of Things (IoT), 18
intra-organizational integration, 10–11
inventory control, 146–147
inventory management
    anticipation inventory, 193
    cycle stock, 193
    fixed-order quantity system
        EOQ, 198–200
        EPQ, 202–204
        *versus* fixed-time period systems, 197–198
        order quantity (Q), 195–196
        reorder point (ROP), 195–196, 201
        safety stock, 193, 201–202
    fixed-time period system
        computing target inventory, 206–207
        *versus* fixed-order quantity, 197–198
        inventory position (IP), 196, 197
        target inventory $R$, 196, 197
    holding cost, 194
    independent *versus* dependent demand, 207–208
    inventory policy, 191
    managing supply chain inventory
        ABC inventory classification, 208–209
        measuring inventory performance, 210–211
        practical considerations, EOQ, 210
        VMI, 211
    manufacturing and service organizations, 190
    medical tools, 190
    MRO, 193
    ordering cost, 194
    pipeline inventory, 193
    reasons for carrying
        balance supply and demand, 192
        buffer uncertainty, 192

inventory management (*contd.*)
    economic purchase orders, 192–193
    maintain independence of operations, 192
    protect against lead time demand, 191–192
  shortage costs, 194
inventory policy, 191
inventory turnover, 132–133

## J
jidoka, 223
John Deere & Company, 195
just-in-time (JIT), 142, 219

## K
kaizen, 218
Kaizen Blitz, 218
kanban, 221
keiretsu supplier-partnering model, 265, 266
Kozmo.com, 88
KUKA Robotics Corp., 115

## L
labor, 271–272
lean six sigma supply chain
  developing, 238–239
  impact on supply chain activities
    logistics, 239–240
    operations, 239
    suppliers, 239
lean systems
  elements of lean, 219
  Lean Six Sigma, 216
  lean tools in the popular press, 227–228
  philosophy
    broad view, 217
    continuous improvement, 218
    eliminating waste, 217
    flexibility, 218
    simplicity, 217–218
    visibility, 218
  production
    pull system, 220
    small lot production, 222
    uniform plant loading, 222–223
    visual signals, 221–222
  respect for people
    role of management, 223
    role of suppliers, 224
    role of workers, 223
  SQC *see* statistical quality control (SQC)
  TQM *see* total quality management (TQM)
  U.S. Army, 219–220
less-than-truck-load (LTL) shipment, 147
LG Electronics, 54
life-cycle assessment (LCA), 307
life-cycle costing, 309

Li & Fung, 38, 181
linear regression, 175–177
line processes, 107
local content requirements, 286
local marketing, 277
logistics, 10
  evolution of, 141
  function, 139–140
  organization impact
    finance, 143
    marketing, 142
    operations, 141–142
    packaging, 143
  reverse logistics, 144–145
  supply chain impact, 143, 144
  task logistics
    facility location, 147
    inventory control, 146–147
    material handling, 146
    order fulfillment, 147
    packaging, 146
    storage, 146
    transportation *see* transportation
  third-party logistics providers, 153
  warehousing
    cross-docking, 151
    facility location, 151–152
    in supply chain, 150
loss of control, 37
lumpy demand (POQ), 210

## M
maintenance, repair, and operating items (MRO), 193
make-to-order strategy, 34
make-to-stock strategy, 33
management phase, 253
manufacturing technology, 282
marketing, 10
  channel of distribution
    design channel structures, 86
    direct/indirect, 85
    e-commerce impact, 88–89
    *versus* logistics channel, 86–88
    omni-channel, 89–90
  customer-driven supply chains
    CRM software, 79–80
    customized strategy, 79
    end consumer, 76
    micro-marketing/one-to-one marketing, 79
    niche strategy, 79
    organizational end user, 77
    standardized strategy, 78
    supplier–customer relationship, 77–78
  delivering value to customers
    customer service, 81–82

global customer service issues, 84
measuring customer service, 83–84
supply chain impact, 82–83
VOC, 80–81
evolution, 73–74
function, 72–73
organization impact, 74–75
supply chain impact, 76
market research, 167
market segmentation, 73
mass marketing, 73
material handling, 146
material requirements planning (MRP), 207
Mazzi's *versus* Totino's pizza, 110
micro-marketing, 79
military logistics, 141
minimalist ethic, 302
multiple regression, 178

## N

National Oceanic and Atmospheric Administration (NOAA), 168–169
niche strategy, 79
norm of reciprocity, 262
Northeast passage, 149

## O

Oasis, 90
off-shoring, 128
omni-channel, 89–90
one-to-one marketing, 79
open auction, 131
open-source hardware, 19
operational impact, 122
operational payoffs, 297
operations, 10
operations management (OM)
decisions, 96–97
evolution of, 97–98
facility layout
cellular layouts, 110
fixed position layout, 109
planning, 108–109
process layout, 109–110
product layout, 110–114
function, 95–96
manufacturing and service organizations, 97
organization impact, 98
process automation
advantages, 114
disadvantages, 115
in services, 115–116
process design
definition, 105
intermittent process, 105–107
repetitive process, 106, 107

product design
break-even analysis, 102–104
concurrent engineering, 105
definition, 99
design of services, 100
DFM, 104
preliminary design and testing, 101
product life cycle, 104–105
remanufacturing, 105
reverse engineering, 101
screening stage, 101
operations strategy, 33–35
order fulfillment, 147
ordering cost, 194
order qualifiers, 43
order winners, 43
organizational end user, 77
organizational payoffs, 297
outsourcing, 60
outsourcing analytics, 126

## P

packaging, 146
Pareto analysis, 227
Pareto's law, 209
p-chart, 235
PepsiCo, 75
percentage of item cost, 194
performance standard, 301
periodic order quantity (POQ), 210
Periodic Review System, 197
physical distribution, 141
physical element of the service, 100
pipeline transportation, 149
place, marketing decisions, 76
place utility, 147
planning, 108–109, 159
political, environmental factor, 273
political forecasting, 161
political risks, 312
postponement, 127
predictive analytics, 165–166
price, 76
proactive sustainability actions, 305
problem-solving negotiators, 262
process capability, 229–233
process layout, 109–110
Proctor & Gamble (P&G), 7, 8, 77, 251–252
producers, SCM, 4
product, 76
production rate model, 202
product layout
disadvantages, 110
flow through, 110
line balancing, 111
assign tasks to workstations, 113–114

product layout (*contd.*)
    compute efficiency, 114
    cycle time/takt time, 111–112
    precedence diagramof pizza assembly, 112
    precedence relationships for pizza assembly, 111
    theoretical minimum number of stations, 112–113
product life cycle, 104–105
product positioning strategy, 33
product postponement, 277
product specifications, 230
product traceability, 41
product volume, 105
professional organizations, SCM, 23
project processes, 107
promotion, 76
psychological benefits, 100
pull production system, 219
purchasing, 120

## Q
Q-model, 196
qualitative forecasting methods, 166–168
quality circle, 223
quality function deployment (QFD), 80–81
quantitative forecasting methods, 168

## R
radio frequency identification (RFID), 18, 41
rapid manufacturing (RM), 108
raw materials, 190
reactive sustainability actions, 305
reasonable care ethic, 302
reciprocal interdependence, 254
regional trade agreements, 284
rejection-then-retreat, 263
relational criticality, 248
relational marketing, 74
relationship conflicts, 257
relationship view, 53
reorder point (ROP), 195–196, 201
repetitive process, 106, 107
request for proposal (RFP), 123
request for quotation (RFQ), 123
request or invitation for bid (RFB), 123
re-shoring, 128
respect for people, 219
retailers, SCM, 4
Retail Link, 64
return on assets (ROA), 143
return on investment (ROI), 143
reverse auction, 131
reverse engineering, 101
reverse logistics, 6, 144–145
risk mitigation, 122
Roots, 130–131
Ryanair transports, 96, 102

## S
safety stock, 193, 201–202
sales and operations planning (S & OP), 181–183, 238
sawtooth model, 196
scatter diagrams, 227
scope, 129, 247, 248
sealed bid auction, 131
seasonal index, 174
seasonal inventory, 193
selective distribution, 86
sensual elements, 100
sequential interdependence, 254
service inventory, 191
setup cost, 194
setup time, 222
shadow pricing model, 309
shortage costs, 194
signal kanban, 222
simple moving average, 170–171
single sourcing, 128
Six Sigma, 216
Six Sigma quality
    definition, 236
    lean six sigma supply chain
        developing, 238–239
        impact on supply chain activities, 239–240
    methodology, 236–237
Snedeker Global Cruises, 135
social risks, 312
social sustainability, 297, 298
sourcing, 10
    bidding or negotiation, 125
    commercial *versus* consumer sourcing, 121–122
    cost *versus* price, 124–125
    definition, 120
    evolution of, 120–121
    financial impact, 122
    information impact, 122
    measuring sourcing performance, 132–133
    operational impact, 122
    process, 123–124
    risk mitigation, 122
    and SCM
        domestic *versus* global sourcing, 128–129
        e-auctions, 130–132
        functional *versus* innovative products, 125–128
        outsourcing, 129
        single *versus* multiple sourcing, 128
    strategic sourcing, 120
speedy automotive, 185–186
SQC *see* statistical quality control (SQC)
stable supply process, 126
standardized strategy, 78
Starbucks supply chain, 4
statistical process control (SPC), 228
statistical quality control (SQC)

acceptance sampling, 228–229
control charts for attributes, 235
descriptive statistics, 228
process capability, 229–233
process control charts, 234
sources of variation, 229
SPC, 228
Steinway Pianos, 87–88
storage, 146
strategic sourcing, 120
structural conflicts, 257
supplier resiliency score, 281
suppliers, SCM, 4
supply chain management (SCM)
  boundary-spanning nature
    cross-enterprise integration, 11–12
    intraorganizational integration, 10–11
  bullwhip effect, 7
  careers, 23
  collaboration, 6
  competitive supply chain *see* competitive supply chain
  coordination, 5–6
  customer focus, 7–8
  definition, 3
  forecasting, 162
  information sharing, 6
  logistics, 143, 144
  logistics function, 12
  managing flows through, 6–7
  operations management, 99
  professional organizations, 23
  rise of, 12–13
  service supply chain, 8–9
  sourcing
    domestic *versus* global sourcing, 128–129
    e-auctions, 130–132
    functional *versus* innovative products, 125–128
    outsourcing, 129
    single *versus* multiple sourcing, 128
  stages, 4
  sustainability *see* sustainable supply chain management
  trends in
    big data analytics, 18
    3-D printing or additive manufacturing, 19
    financial supply chain, 22–23
    globalization, 16
    information technology, 17–18
    innovation, 21–22
    intelligent assembly robots, 19
    lean supply chain, 20
    managing supply chain disruptions, 20
    open-source hardware, 19
    outsourcing, 16–17
    postponement, 19–20
    supply chain security, 21
    sustainability and the "green" supply chain, 21
supply chain masters, 43
supply chain network, 4–5
supply chain processes
  stages of, 58–60
  vertical integration *versus* coordination, 60
supply chain relationship
  connecting information technology, 246, 247
  diluting power, 266–267
  dimensions, 247–248
  dispute resolution procedures
    arbitration, 258–259
    litigation, 258
    mediation, 259
    negotiation, 259
  keiretsu supplier-partnering model, 265, 266
  management and design, 246
  matrix
    alliances, 250–251
    contractual relationships, 250
    nonstrategic transactions, 249–250
    partnerships, 250
  partnership agreements, 265–266
  physical supply chain structure, 246, 247
  sources of conflict, 256–257
  trust-based relationship
    assessing relationship, 253–254
    effective conflict resolution mechanisms, designing, 255
    effective contracts, creating, 254–255
    identifying operational roles, 254
    managing, 255–256
    *versus* power-based relationships, 252–253
supply chain strategy
  building blocks of
    customer service strategy, 37–39
    distribution strategy, 35–36
    operations strategy, 33–35
    sourcing strategy, 36–37
  *versus* business strategy, 28
  competitive advantage
    cost-productivity advantage, 29–30
    product value advantage, 30–31
    SCM, source of value, 31–32
  competitive priorities
    cost, 40
    dimensions, 42–43
    innovation, 41
    quality, 41–42
    service, 42
    time, 40–41
  definition, 28
  measure of competitiveness
    interpreting productivity, 45–46
    productivity measures, 45
  small *versus* large firms, 43

supply chain strategy (*contd.*)
   strategic alignment, 29
   supply chain adaptability, 43–44
supply chain system
   business process, 51–53
   distribution process, 51
   IT design support, 51, 52
   management process, 51
   managing supply chain processes, 53–54
   supply chain network design, 51, 52
supply uncertainty, 126–128
sustainable supply chain management
   business contexts, 304
   carbon footprint, 307–308
   community relations, 301
   compliance, 306
   costing systems, 309
   cost-of-control, 308–309
   damage costing, 309
   defining sustainability, 295–297
   ecological footprint, 307
   enforcement, 306
   environmental sustainability, 297–299
   ethical responsibility, 302
   existence value, 308
   external context of, 303–304
   feedback loops, 305
   financial performance, 305
   food mile, 308
   Great Pacific Garbage Patch, 296
   Haitian Oil, case study, 317–318
   human and financial resources, 304
   innovation, 306–307
   internal context, 304
   LCA, 307
   leadership, 304
   legal compliance, 301
   option value, 308
   in practice
      marketing sustainability, 315
      packaging, 313–314
      process design, 315
      product design, 311–312
      sourcing, 314
      unintended consequences, 315–316
   principles
      business relationships, 300
      community involvement and economic development, 300
      employment practices, 300
      ethics, 299
      financial return, 300
      governance, 299
      protection of the environment, 300
      transparency, 299–300
      value of products and services, 300
   processes, 304–305
   revenue, 302
   risk assessment
      fat tails, 310
      fuzzy logic, 311
      Monte Carlo simulations, 311
      real option analysis, 311–312
      scenario-based analysis, 310–311
   social sustainability, 297, 298
   stakeholders' reaction, 305
   Supply Chain Sustainability Model, 303
   sustainability performance, 305
   TCO, 307
   use value, 308
Sysco, 148

## T

takt time, 111–112
target marketing, 73, 78
technical standards and health regulations, 286
Tesco, 18–19
Tesla vehicles, 94–95
theory of constraints (TOC)
   capacity implications, 57–58
   system constraints, 54–56
   system variation, 56–57
third-party logistics (3PL) providers, 153
3-D printing/additive manufacturing, 19
time series forecasting models
   exponential smoothing, 171–172
   mean, 169–170
   moving averages, 170–171
   seasonality adjustment, 174–175
   trend adjusted exponential smoothing, 172–173
time series models, 168
total cost of ownership (TCO), 124, 307
total quality management (TQM), 219, 283
   costs of quality, 225
   ISO 9000, 227–228
   quality tools, 225–227
   VOC, 224–225
tourism forecasting, 161
Toyota, 119
Toyota Motor Corporation, 32
trade protection mechanisms, 284
transactional marketing, 74
transactional view, 53
transformation role, 95, 96
transportation, 272
   air, 149
   cost of, 145
   distribution network design, 145
   economies of distance, 147, 148
   economies of scale, 147
   multimode, 149
   Northeast passage, 149

pipeline, 149
place utility, 147
product characteristics, 145
rail, 149
trucks, 148
water, 148–149
transportation inventory, 193
trends in SCM
  big data analytics, 18
  financial supply chain, 22–23
  globalization, 16
  information technology, 17–18
  innovation, 21–22
  intelligent assembly robots, 19
  lean supply chain, 20
  managing supply chain disruptions, 20
  open-source hardware, 19
  outsourcing, 16–17
  postponement, 19–20
  supply chain security, 21
  sustainability and the "green" supply chain, 21
  3-D printing/additive manufacturing, 19
trigger price mechanism, 286
trucks, 148
trust-based relationship
  assessing relationship, 253–254
  effective conflict resolution mechanisms, designing, 255
  effective contracts, creating, 254–255
  identifying operational roles, 254
  managing
    clear method of communication, 255
    commitment, 255
    fairness, 256
    performance visibility, 255
  *versus* power-based relationships, 252–253

**U**
Uber, 145–146
United Parcel Service (UPS), 140–141, 153

**V**
value chain/value network, 4
values conflicts, 257
value segments, 31
Value Stream Mapping (VSM), 239
Vendor Managed Inventory (VMI), 30, 211
vertical integration, 60
virtual teaming, 129
voice of the customer (VOC), 80–81, 224–225
Voluntary Interindustry Commerce Standards (VICS), 180

**W**
Wal-Mart, 8, 13, 16–17, 29, 30, 98–99, 273–274
warehousing, 271
  cross-docking, 151
  facility location, 151–152
  in supply chain, 150
waste, 217
water transportation, 148–149
weeks-of-supply, 133
weighted moving average, 171
wholesalers/distributors, SCM, 4
wireless communication technologies, 17
work-in-process (WIP), 190
World Health Organization (WHO), 162–163
World Trade Organization (WTO), 285

**Z**
Zara, Spanish retailer, 15
Zoots, 191